Saab 9-5
Owners Workshop Manual
Peter T Gill

Models covered
Saloon & Estate
Petrol: 2.0 litre (1985cc) & 2.3 litre (2290cc) turbo
Turbo-Diesel: 1.9 litre (1910cc)

Does NOT cover 'BioPower' models or new range introduced July 2010

(4891 - 336)

© Haynes Publishing 2011

ABCDE
FGHIJ
KLMNO
PQRS

A book in the **Haynes Owners Workshop Manual Series**

All rights reserved. No part of this book may be reproduced or transmitted in any form or by any means, electronic or mechanical, including photocopying, recording or by any information storage or retrieval system, without permission in writing from the copyright holder.

ISBN 978 1 84425 891 8

British Library Cataloguing in Publication Data
A catalogue record for this book is available from the British Library.

Printed in the USA

Haynes Publishing
Sparkford, Yeovil, Somerset BA22 7JJ, England

Haynes North America, Inc
861 Lawrence Drive, Newbury Park, California 91320, USA

Haynes Publishing Nordiska AB
Box 1504, 751 45 UPPSALA, Sverige

Contents

LIVING WITH YOUR SAAB 9-5

Introduction to the Saab 9-5	Page 0•4
Safety first!	Page 0•5

Roadside Repairs

If your car won't start	Page 0•6
Jump starting	Page 0•7
Wheel changing	Page 0•8
Identifying leaks	Page 0•9
Towing	Page 0•9

Weekly Checks

Introduction	Page 0•10
Underbonnet check points	Page 0•10
Engine oil level	Page 0•11
Coolant level	Page 0•11
Brake (and clutch) fluid level	Page 0•12
Screen washer fluid level	Page 0•12
Tyre condition and pressure	Page 0•13
Wiper blades	Page 0•14
Battery	Page 0•14
Electrical systems	Page 0•15

Lubricants and fluids

	Page 0•16

Tyre pressures

	Page 0•16

MAINTENANCE

Routine Maintenance and Servicing

Petrol engine models	Page 1A•1
Servicing specifications	Page 1A•2
Maintenance schedule	Page 1A•3
Maintenance procedures	Page 1A•5
Diesel engine models	Page 1B•1
Servicing specifications	Page 1B•2
Maintenance schedule	Page 1B•3
Maintenance procedures	Page 1B•5

Illegal Copying

It is the policy of Haynes Publishing to actively protect its Copyrights and Trade Marks. Legal action will be taken against anyone who unlawfully copies the cover or contents of this Manual. This includes all forms of unauthorised copying including digital, mechanical, and electronic in any form. Authorisation from Haynes Publishing will only be provided expressly and in writing. Illegal copying will also be reported to the appropriate statutory authorities.

Contents

REPAIRS AND OVERHAUL

Engine and Associated Systems

Petrol engine in-car repair procedures	Page 2A•1
Diesel engine in-car repair procedures	Page 2B•1
Engine removal and overhaul procedures	Page 2C•1
Cooling, heating and ventilation systems	Page 3•1
Fuel and exhaust systems – petrol engines	Page 4A•1
Fuel and exhaust systems – diesel engines	Page 4B•1
Emission control systems	Page 4C•1
Starting and charging systems	Page 5A•1
Ignition system – petrol engines	Page 5B•1

Transmission

Clutch	Page 6•1
Manual transmission	Page 7A•1
Automatic transmission	Page 7B•1
Driveshafts	Page 8•1

Brakes and suspension

Braking system	Page 9•1
Suspension and steering	Page 10•1

Body equipment

Bodywork and fittings	Page 11•1
Body electrical system	Page 12•1

Wiring diagrams

Page 12•27

REFERENCE

Dimensions and weights	Page REF•1
Fuel economy	Page REF•2
Conversion factors	Page REF•6
Buying Spare Parts	Page REF•7
Vehicle Identification	Page REF•7
General repair procedures	Page REF•8
Jacking and vehicle support	Page REF•9
Disconnecting the battery	Page REF•9
Radio/cassette unit anti-theft system – precautions	Page REF•9
Tools and working facilities	Page REF•10
MOT test checks	Page REF•12
Fault finding	Page REF•16

Index

Page REF•24

Introduction

The Saab 9-5 was introduced in the UK in August 1997 as an executive class model. Like the 9-3, which is essentially a rebadged 900, the 9-5 is based on a Vauxhall Vectra chassis, and competes with other models such as the BMW 5-Series, Mercedes E-Class and the Audi A6. It was originally available as a 4-door Saloon with turbocharged 2.0 and 2.3 litre, balancer-shaft, 16-valve engines. The 3.0 litre V6 engine (not covered in this manual) was introduced in February 1998, and was available with automatic transmission and traction control. The Estate version was launched in November 1998. Models may be fitted with a five-speed manual transmission or a four-speed automatic transmission mounted on the left-hand side of the engine. The automatic transmission was changed to five-speed as from September 2001.

Saab 9-5 models from 2005 had a complete facelift, with new body panels from the A-pillar forwards, new rear panels and exterior lighting. The interior trim had a revamp with new facia trim and instrument panel. Suspension and chassis components were also updated.

Standard equipment includes power-assisted steering, ABS brakes, remote deadlock central locking, twin front and side airbags, electric windows and mirrors, and air conditioning. Optional extras include electric sunroof, electric front seats, leather upholstery and CD autochanger.

All models have front-wheel-drive with fully independent front and rear suspension, incorporating struts, gas-filled shock absorbers, and coil springs.

For the home mechanic, the Saab 9-5 is a relatively straightforward vehicle to maintain and repair, since design features have been incorporated to reduce the actual cost of ownership to a minimum, and most of the items requiring frequent attention are easily accessible.

Your Saab 9-5 manual

The aim of this manual is to help you get the best value from your vehicle. It can do so in several ways. It can help you decide what work must be done (even should you choose to get it done by a garage), provide information on routine maintenance and servicing, and give a logical course of action and diagnosis when random faults occur. However, it is hoped that you will use the manual by tackling the work yourself. On simpler jobs, it may even be quicker than booking the car into a garage and going there twice, to leave and collect it. Perhaps most important, a lot of money can be saved by avoiding the costs a garage must charge to cover its labour and overheads.

The manual has drawings and descriptions to show the function of the various components, so that their layout can be understood. Then the tasks are described and photographed in a clear step-by-step sequence.

References to the 'left' or 'right' are in the sense of a person in the driver's seat, facing forward.

Acknowledgements

Thanks are also due to Draper Tools Limited, who provided some of the workshop tools, and to all those people at Sparkford who helped in the production of this manual.

We take great pride in the accuracy of information given in this manual, but vehicle manufacturers make alterations and design changes during the production run of a particular vehicle of which they do not inform us. No liability can be accepted by the authors or publishers for loss, damage or injury caused by any errors in, or omissions from, the information given.

Project vehicle

The main vehicles used in the preparation of this manual, and which appear in many of the photographic sequences, was a 2007 Saab 9-5 Saloon Aero fitted with the 2.3 litre turbocharged petrol engine and automatic transmission.

Safety First! 0•5

Working on your car can be dangerous. This page shows just some of the potential risks and hazards, with the aim of creating a safety-conscious attitude.

General hazards

Scalding
• Don't remove the radiator or expansion tank cap while the engine is hot.
• Engine oil, transmission fluid or power steering fluid may also be dangerously hot if the engine has recently been running.

Burning
• Beware of burns from the exhaust system and from any part of the engine. Brake discs and drums can also be extremely hot immediately after use.

Crushing
• When working under or near a raised vehicle, always supplement the jack with axle stands, or use drive-on ramps. ***Never venture under a car which is only supported by a jack***.

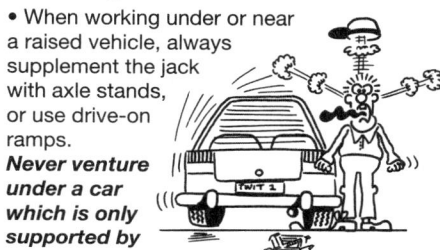

• Take care if loosening or tightening high-torque nuts when the vehicle is on stands. Initial loosening and final tightening should be done with the wheels on the ground.

Fire
• Fuel is highly flammable; fuel vapour is explosive.
• Don't let fuel spill onto a hot engine.
• Do not smoke or allow naked lights (including pilot lights) anywhere near a vehicle being worked on. Also beware of creating sparks (electrically or by use of tools).
• Fuel vapour is heavier than air, so don't work on the fuel system with the vehicle over an inspection pit.
• Another cause of fire is an electrical overload or short-circuit. Take care when repairing or modifying the vehicle wiring.
• Keep a fire extinguisher handy, of a type suitable for use on fuel and electrical fires.

Electric shock
• Ignition HT and Xenon headlight voltages can be dangerous, especially to people with heart problems or a pacemaker. Don't work on or near these systems with the engine running or the ignition switched on.

• Mains voltage is also dangerous. Make sure that any mains-operated equipment is correctly earthed. Mains power points should be protected by a residual current device (RCD) circuit breaker.

Fume or gas intoxication
• Exhaust fumes are poisonous; they can contain carbon monoxide, which is rapidly fatal if inhaled. Never run the engine in a confined space such as a garage with the doors shut.

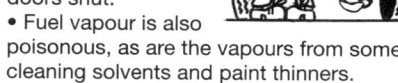

• Fuel vapour is also poisonous, as are the vapours from some cleaning solvents and paint thinners.

Poisonous or irritant substances
• Avoid skin contact with battery acid and with any fuel, fluid or lubricant, especially antifreeze, brake hydraulic fluid and Diesel fuel. Don't syphon them by mouth. If such a substance is swallowed or gets into the eyes, seek medical advice.
• Prolonged contact with used engine oil can cause skin cancer. Wear gloves or use a barrier cream if necessary. Change out of oil-soaked clothes and do not keep oily rags in your pocket.
• Air conditioning refrigerant forms a poisonous gas if exposed to a naked flame (including a cigarette). It can also cause skin burns on contact.

Asbestos
• Asbestos dust can cause cancer if inhaled or swallowed. Asbestos may be found in gaskets and in brake and clutch linings. When dealing with such components it is safest to assume that they contain asbestos.

Special hazards

Hydrofluoric acid
• This extremely corrosive acid is formed when certain types of synthetic rubber, found in some O-rings, oil seals, fuel hoses etc, are exposed to temperatures above 4000C. The rubber changes into a charred or sticky substance containing the acid. *Once formed, the acid remains dangerous for years. If it gets onto the skin, it may be necessary to amputate the limb concerned*.
• When dealing with a vehicle which has suffered a fire, or with components salvaged from such a vehicle, wear protective gloves and discard them after use.

The battery
• Batteries contain sulphuric acid, which attacks clothing, eyes and skin. Take care when topping-up or carrying the battery.
• The hydrogen gas given off by the battery is highly explosive. Never cause a spark or allow a naked light nearby. Be careful when connecting and disconnecting battery chargers or jump leads.

Air bags
• Air bags can cause injury if they go off accidentally. Take care when removing the steering wheel and trim panels. Special storage instructions may apply.

Diesel injection equipment
• Diesel injection pumps supply fuel at very high pressure. Take care when working on the fuel injectors and fuel pipes.

 Warning: Never expose the hands, face or any other part of the body to injector spray; the fuel can penetrate the skin with potentially fatal results.

Remember...

DO
• Do use eye protection when using power tools, and when working under the vehicle.
• Do wear gloves or use barrier cream to protect your hands when necessary.
• Do get someone to check periodically that all is well when working alone on the vehicle.
• Do keep loose clothing and long hair well out of the way of moving mechanical parts.
• Do remove rings, wristwatch etc, before working on the vehicle – especially the electrical system.
• Do ensure that any lifting or jacking equipment has a safe working load rating adequate for the job.

DON'T
• Don't attempt to lift a heavy component which may be beyond your capability – get assistance.
• Don't rush to finish a job, or take unverified short cuts.
• Don't use ill-fitting tools which may slip and cause injury.
• Don't leave tools or parts lying around where someone can trip over them. Mop up oil and fuel spills at once.
• Don't allow children or pets to play in or near a vehicle being worked on.

0•6 Roadside repairs

The following pages are intended to help in dealing with common roadside emergencies and breakdowns. You will find more detailed fault finding information at the back of the manual, and repair information in the main chapters.

If your car won't start and the starter motor doesn't turn

- ☐ If it's a model with automatic transmission, make sure the selector is in the P or N position.
- ☐ Open the bonnet and make sure that the battery terminals are clean and tight.
- ☐ Switch on the headlights and try to start the engine. If the headlights go very dim when you're trying to start, the battery is probably flat. Get out of trouble by jump starting (see next page) using another car.

If your car won't start even though the starter motor turns as normal

- ☐ Is there fuel in the tank?
- ☐ Is there moisture on electrical components under the bonnet? Switch off the ignition, then wipe off any obvious dampness with a dry cloth. Spray a water-repellent aerosol product (WD-40 or equivalent) on ignition and fuel system electrical connectors like those shown in the photos. Pay special attention to the ignition coils wiring connector.

A Check that the battery cables are securely connected.

B Check that the ignition discharge module wiring is securely connected.

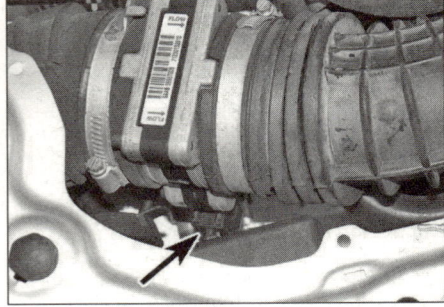

C Check that the mass airflow meter wiring is securely connected.

Check that electrical connections are secure (with the ignition switched off) and spray them with a water-dispersant spray like WD-40 if you suspect a problem due to damp.

D Check the engine wiring loom multi-plugs for security.

E Check that none of the engine compartment fuses have blown.

Roadside repairs 0•7

Jump starting

When jump-starting a car using a booster battery, observe the following precautions:

✔ Before connecting the booster battery, make sure that the ignition is switched off.

Caution: Remove the key in case the central locking engages when the jump leads are connected

✔ Ensure that all electrical equipment (lights, heater, wipers, etc) is switched off.

✔ Take note of any special precautions printed on the battery case.

✔ Make sure that the booster battery is the same voltage as the discharged one in the vehicle.

✔ If the battery is being jump-started from the battery in another vehicle, the two vehicles MUST NOT TOUCH each other.

✔ Make sure that the transmission is in neutral (or PARK, in the case of automatic transmission).

Jump starting will get you out of trouble, but you must correct whatever made the battery go flat in the first place. There are three possibilities:

1 *The battery has been drained by repeated attempts to start, or by leaving the lights on.*

2 *The charging system is not working properly (alternator drivebelt slack or broken, alternator wiring fault or alternator itself faulty).*

3 *The battery itself is at fault (electrolyte low, or battery worn out).*

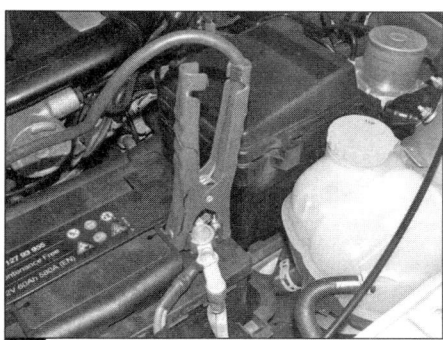

1 Connect one end of the red jump lead to the positive (+) terminal of the flat battery

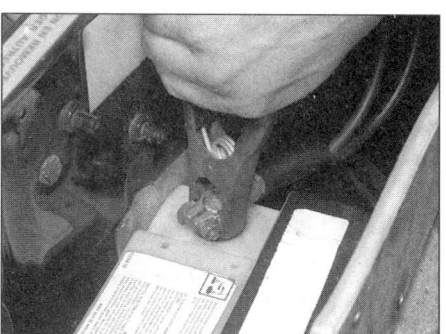

2 Connect the other end of the red lead to the positive (+) terminal of the booster battery.

3 Connect one end of the black jump lead to the negative (-) terminal of the booster battery

4 Connect the other end of the black jump lead to a bolt or bracket on the engine block, well away from the battery, on the vehicle to be started.

5 Make sure that the jump leads will not come into contact with the fan, drive-belts or other moving parts of the engine.

6 Start the engine using the booster battery and run it at idle speed. Switch on the lights, rear window demister and heater blower motor, then disconnect the jump leads in the reverse order of connection. Turn off the lights etc.

0•8 Roadside repairs

Wheel changing

⚠ *Warning: Do not change a wheel in a situation where you risk being hit by other traffic. On busy roads, try to stop in a lay-by or a gateway. Be wary of passing traffic while changing the wheel – it is easy to become distracted by the job in hand.*

Preparation

- ☐ When a puncture occurs, stop as soon as it is safe to do so.
- ☐ Park on firm level ground, if possible, and well out of the way of other traffic.
- ☐ Use hazard warning lights if necessary.
- ☐ If you have one, use a warning triangle to alert other drivers of your presence.
- ☐ Apply the handbrake and engage first or reverse gear.
- ☐ Chock the wheel diagonally opposite the one being removed – a couple of large stones will do for this.
- ☐ If the ground is soft, use a flat piece of wood to spread the load under the jack.

Changing the wheel

1 The spare wheel, jack and wheel removal tools are stored beneath a cover in the luggage compartment.

2 Unscrew the retaining nut and lift out the spare wheel. Place it beneath the sill as a precaution against the jack failing. Note that the spare wheel is a 'space saver' type.

3 Where fitted, pull the wheel trim off the wheel. On models with alloy wheels, use the plastic tool provided to prise the cap from the locking wheel bolt, and then fit the adapter.

4 Before you raise the car, loosen each wheel bolt by half a turn only.

5 Locate the jack head below the jacking points (indicated by the cut-outs in the sill), nearest the wheel to be changed. Turn the handle until the base of the jack touches the ground directly below the sill. Raise the vehicle until the wheel is clear of the ground.

6 Remove the bolts and lift the wheel from the vehicle. Place it beneath the sill in place of the spare as a precaution against the jack failing.

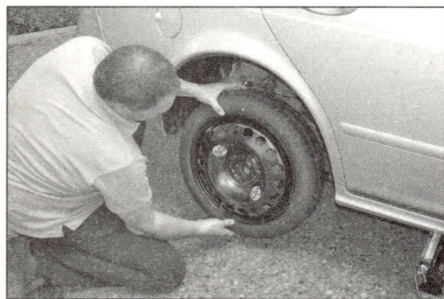

7 Fit the spare wheel, then insert each of the wheel bolts and tighten them moderately using the wheel brace.

8 Lower the vehicle to the ground, and then tighten the wheel bolts in a diagonal sequence. Remove the wheel chocks.

Finally . . .

- ☐ Have the wheel nuts tightened to the specified torque (see Chapter 10) at the earliest possible opportunity.
- ☐ Stow the jack and tools in the correct locations in the car.
- ☐ Check the tyre pressure on the wheel just fitted. If it is low, drive slowly to the nearest garage and inflate the tyre to the right pressure.
- ☐ Have the punctured wheel repaired at the earliest opportunity.
- ☐ Do not exceed 50 mph when driving the vehicle with a 'Space Saver' spare wheel fitted.

Roadside repairs 0•9

Identifying leaks

Puddles on the garage floor or drive, or obvious wetness under the bonnet or underneath the car, suggest a leak that needs investigating. It can sometimes be difficult to decide where the leak is coming from, especially if an engine undershield is fitted. Leaking oil or fluid can also be blown rearwards by the passage of air under the car, giving a false impression of where the problem lies.

 Warning: Most automotive oils and fluids are poisonous. Wash them off skin, and change out of contaminated clothing, without delay.

 HAYNES HINT *The smell of a fluid leaking from the car may provide a clue to what's leaking. Some fluids are distinctively coloured. It may help to remove the engine undershield, clean the car carefully and to park it over some clean paper overnight as an aid to locating the source of the leak. Remember that some leaks may only occur while the engine is running.*

Sump oil

Engine oil may leak from the drain plug...

Oil from filter

...or from the base of the oil filter.

Gearbox oil

Gearbox oil can leak from the seals at the inboard ends of the driveshafts.

Antifreeze

Leaking antifreeze often leaves a crystalline deposit like this.

Brake fluid

A leak occurring at a wheel is almost certainly brake fluid.

Power steering fluid

Power steering fluid may leak from the pipe connectors on the steering rack.

Towing

When all else fails, you may find yourself having to get a tow home – or of course you may be helping somebody else. Long-distance recovery should only be done by a garage or breakdown service. For shorter distances, DIY towing using another car is easy enough, but observe the following points:

☐ Use a proper tow-rope – they are not expensive. The vehicle being towed must display an ON TOW sign in its rear window.
☐ Always turn the ignition key to the 'On' position when the vehicle is being towed, so that the steering lock is released, and the direction indicator and brake lights work.
☐ Only attach the tow-rope to the towing eyes provided. The front towing eye is in the vehicle tool kit, and screws into the hole in the centre of the subframe; use the wheelbrace to tighten it. The rear towing eye is located beneath the centre of the rear bumper and is permanent.
☐ Before being towed, release the handbrake and select neutral on the transmission.
☐ On models with automatic transmission, special precautions apply as follows (if in doubt, do not tow, or transmission damage may result):
 a) Only tow the car in a forward direction.
 b) The gear selector lever must be in the N position.
 c) The vehicle must not be towed at a speed exceeding 30 mph, nor for a distance of more than 30 miles.
☐ Note that greater-than-usual pedal pressure will be required to operate the brakes, since the vacuum servo unit is only operational with the engine running. Similarly, greater-than-usual steering effort will also be required.
☐ The driver of the car being towed must keep the tow-rope taut at all times to avoid snatching.
☐ Make sure that both drivers know the route before setting off.
☐ Only drive at moderate speeds and keep the distance towed to a minimum. Drive smoothly and allow plenty of time for slowing down at junctions.

0•10 Weekly checks

Introduction

There are some very simple checks which need only take a few minutes to carry out, but which could save you a lot of inconvenience and expense.

These *Weekly checks* require no great skill or special tools, and the small amount of time they take to perform could prove to be very well spent, for example:

☐ Keeping an eye on tyre condition and pressures, will not only help to stop them wearing out prematurely, but could also save your life.

☐ Many breakdowns are caused by electrical problems. Battery-related faults are particularly common, and a quick check on a regular basis will often prevent the majority of these.

☐ If your car develops a brake fluid leak, the first time you might know about it is when your brakes don't work properly. Checking the level regularly will give advance warning of this kind of problem.

☐ If the oil or coolant levels run low, the cost of repairing any engine damage will be far greater than fixing the leak, for example.

Underbonnet check points

◀ 2.3 litre petrol engine

A *Engine oil level filler cap and dipstick*
B *Coolant reservoir*
C *Brake fluid reservoir*
D *Washer fluid reservoir*
E *Battery*
F *Power steering fluid reservoir*

◀ 1.9 litre diesel engine

A *Engine oil filler cap*
B *Engine oil level dipstick*
C *Coolant reservoir*
D *Brake fluid reservoir*
E *Washer fluid reservoir*
F *Battery*
G *Power steering fluid reservoir*

Weekly checks

Engine oil level

Before you start

✔ Make sure that the car is on level ground.
✔ Check the oil level before the car is driven, or at least 5 minutes after the engine has been switched off.

 If the oil is checked immediately after driving the vehicle, some of the oil will remain in the upper engine components, resulting in an inaccurate reading on the dipstick.

The correct oil

Modern engines place great demands on their oil. It is very important that the correct oil for your car is used (see *Lubricants and fluids*).

Car care

● If you have to add oil frequently, you should check whether you have any oil leaks. Place some clean paper under the car overnight, and check for stains in the morning. If there are no leaks, then the engine may be burning oil.
● Always maintain the level between the upper and lower dipstick marks (see photo 3). If the level is too low, severe engine damage may occur. Oil seal failure may result if the engine is overfilled by adding too much oil.

1 The dipstick is integral with the oil filler cap, on petrol engines or at the front of the engine on diesel models (see *Underbonnet check points* on page 0•10 for exact location). Withdraw the dipstick

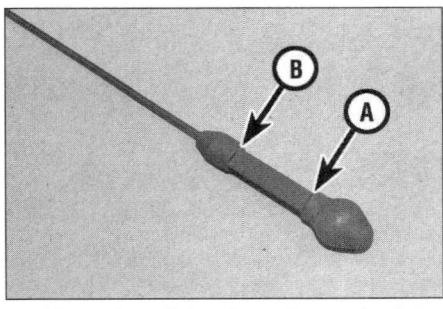

3 Note the oil level on the end of the dipstick, which should be between the upper mark (B) and lower mark (A). Approximately 1.0 litre of oil will raise the level from the lower mark to the upper mark.

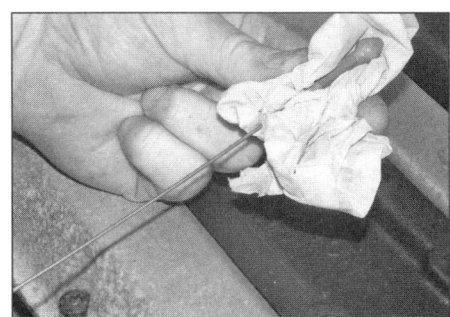

2 Using a clean rag or paper towel remove all oil from the dipstick. Insert the clean dipstick into the tube and tighten the filler cap, then withdraw it again.

4 Oil is added through the filler cap hole. Unscrew the cap and withdraw it. Top-up the level. A funnel may help to reduce spillage. Add the oil slowly, checking the level on the dipstick often. Do not overfill. Refit the cap on completion.

Coolant level

 Warning: Do not attempt to remove the expansion tank pressure cap when the engine is hot, as there is a very great risk of scalding. Do not leave open containers of coolant about, as it is poisonous.

Car care

● With a sealed-type cooling system, adding coolant should not be necessary on a regular basis. If frequent topping-up is required, it is likely there is a leak. Check the radiator, all hoses and joint faces for signs of staining or wetness, and rectify as necessary.

● It is important that antifreeze is used in the cooling system all year round, not just during the winter months. Don't top up with water alone, as the antifreeze will become diluted.

1 The coolant level varies with the temperature of the engine. When the engine is cold, the coolant level should be on or slightly above the KALT/COLD mark on the side of the tank. When the engine is hot, the level will rise.

2 If topping up is necessary, **wait until the engine is cold**. Slowly unscrew the expansion tank cap, to release any pressure present in the cooling system, and remove it.

3 Top up the level by adding a mixture of water and antifreeze to the expansion tank. A funnel may help to reduce spillage. Refit the cap and tighten it securely.

0•12 Weekly checks

Brake (and clutch) fluid level

Warning:
- *Brake fluid can harm your eyes and damage painted surfaces, so use extreme caution when handling and pouring it.*
- *Do not use fluid that has been standing open for some time, as it absorbs moisture from the air, which can cause a dangerous loss of braking effectiveness.*

- *Make sure that your car is on level ground.*
- *The fluid level in the reservoir will drop slightly as the brake pads wear down, but the fluid level must never be allowed to drop below the MIN mark.*

Safety first!
● If the reservoir requires repeated topping-up this is an indication of a fluid leak somewhere in the system, which should be investigated immediately.
● If a leak is suspected, the car should not be driven until the braking system has been checked. Never take any risks where brakes are concerned

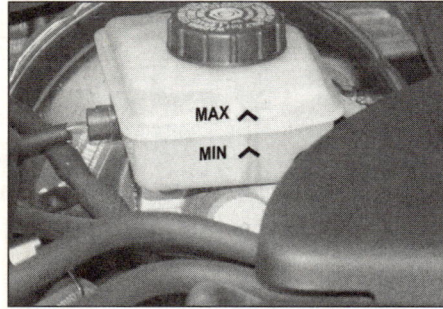

1 The MAX and MIN marks are indicated on the front of the reservoir located in the right-hand rear corner of the engine compartment. The fluid level must always be kept between the marks.

2 If topping-up is necessary, first wipe clean the area around the filler cap to prevent dirt entering the hydraulic system. Unscrew the cap and place it on an absorbent rag.

3 Carefully add fluid, taking care not to spill it onto the surrounding components. Use only the specified fluid; mixing different types can cause damage to the system. After topping-up to the correct level, securely refit the cap and wipe off any spilt fluid.

Screen washer fluid level

● Screenwash additives not only keep the windscreen clean during bad weather, they also prevent the washer system freezing in cold weather – which is when you are likely to need it most. Don't top-up using plain water, as the screenwash will become diluted, and will freeze in cold weather.

Warning: On no account use engine coolant antifreeze in the screen washer system – this may damage the paintwork.

1 The reservoir for the windscreen, headlight and rear window (where applicable) washer systems is located on the front left-hand side of the engine compartment. If topping-up is necessary, open the cap.

2 When topping-up the reservoir a screenwash additive should be added in the quantities recommended on the bottle.

Weekly checks

Tyre condition and pressure

It is very important that tyres are in good condition, and at the correct pressure - having a tyre failure at any speed is highly dangerous. Tyre wear is influenced by driving style - harsh braking and acceleration, or fast cornering, will all produce more rapid tyre wear. As a general rule, the front tyres wear out faster than the rears. Interchanging the tyres from front to rear ("rotating" the tyres) may result in more even wear. However, if this is completely effective, you may have the expense of replacing all four tyres at once!

Remove any nails or stones embedded in the tread before they penetrate the tyre to cause deflation. If removal of a nail does reveal that the tyre has been punctured, refit the nail so that its point of penetration is marked. Then immediately change the wheel, and have the tyre repaired by a tyre dealer.

Regularly check the tyres for damage in the form of cuts or bulges, especially in the sidewalls. Periodically remove the wheels, and clean any dirt or mud from the inside and outside surfaces. Examine the wheel rims for signs of rusting, corrosion or other damage. Light alloy wheels are easily damaged by "kerbing" whilst parking; steel wheels may also become dented or buckled. A new wheel is very often the only way to overcome severe damage.

New tyres should be balanced when they are fitted, but it may become necessary to re-balance them as they wear, or if the balance weights fitted to the wheel rim should fall off. Unbalanced tyres will wear more quickly, as will the steering and suspension components. Wheel imbalance is normally signified by vibration, particularly at a certain speed (typically around 50 mph). If this vibration is felt only through the steering, then it is likely that just the front wheels need balancing. If, however, the vibration is felt through the whole car, the rear wheels could be out of balance. Wheel balancing should be carried out by a tyre dealer or garage.

1 Tread Depth - visual check
The original tyres have tread wear safety bands (B), which will appear when the tread depth reaches approximately 1.6 mm. The band positions are indicated by a triangular mark on the tyre sidewall (A).

2 Tread Depth - manual check
Alternatively, tread wear can be monitored with a simple, inexpensive device known as a tread depth indicator gauge.

3 Tyre Pressure Check
Check the tyre pressures regularly with the tyres cold. Do not adjust the tyre pressures immediately after the vehicle has been used, or an inaccurate setting will result.

Tyre tread wear patterns

Shoulder Wear

Underinflation (wear on both sides)
Under-inflation will cause overheating of the tyre, because the tyre will flex too much, and the tread will not sit correctly on the road surface. This will cause a loss of grip and excessive wear, not to mention the danger of sudden tyre failure due to heat build-up.
Check and adjust pressures
Incorrect wheel camber (wear on one side)
Repair or renew suspension parts
Hard cornering
Reduce speed!

Centre Wear

Overinflation
Over-inflation will cause rapid wear of the centre part of the tyre tread, coupled with reduced grip, harsher ride, and the danger of shock damage occurring in the tyre casing.
Check and adjust pressures

If you sometimes have to inflate your car's tyres to the higher pressures specified for maximum load or sustained high speed, don't forget to reduce the pressures to normal afterwards.

Uneven Wear

Front tyres may wear unevenly as a result of wheel misalignment. Most tyre dealers and garages can check and adjust the wheel alignment (or "tracking") for a modest charge.
Incorrect camber or castor
Repair or renew suspension parts
Malfunctioning suspension
Repair or renew suspension parts
Unbalanced wheel
Balance tyres
Incorrect toe setting
Adjust front wheel alignment
Note: *The feathered edge of the tread which typifies toe wear is best checked by feel.*

0•14 Weekly checks

Wiper blades

1 Check the condition of the wiper blades; if they are cracked or show any signs of deterioration, or if the glass swept area is smeared, renew them. For maximum clarity of vision, wiper blades should be renewed annually.

2 To remove a windscreen wiper blade, pull the arm fully away from the glass until it locks. Swivel the blade through 90°, then squeeze the locking clip, and detach the blade from the arm. When fitting the new blade, make sure that the blade locks securely into the arm, and that the blade is orientated correctly.

3 Don't forget to check the tailgate wiper blade as well on Estate models. The blade is clipped onto the arm.

Battery

Caution: Before carrying out any work on the vehicle battery, read the precautions given in 'Safety first!' at the start of this manual.

✔ Make sure that the battery tray is in good condition, and that the clamp is tight. Corrosion on the tray, retaining clamp and the battery itself can be removed with a solution of water and baking soda, after removing the affected components from the car (see Chapter 5A). Thoroughly rinse all cleaned areas with water. Any metal parts damaged by corrosion should be covered with a zinc-based primer, then painted.

✔ Periodically (approximately every three months), check the charge condition of the battery as described in Chapter 5A.

✔ If the battery is flat, and you need to jump start your vehicle, see *Roadside Repairs*.

1 The battery is located at the front, left-hand side of the engine compartment, and is covered with a plastic protective cover. The exterior of the battery should be inspected periodically for damage such as a cracked casing or cover.

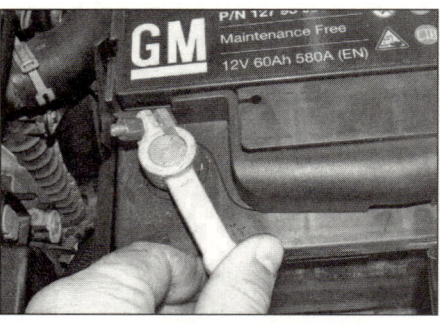

2 Check the tightness of battery clamps to ensure good electrical connections. You should not be able to move them. Also check each cable for cracks and frayed conductors.

HAYNES HiNT

Battery corrosion can be kept to a minimum by applying a layer of petroleum jelly to the clamps and terminals after they are reconnected.

3 If corrosion (white, fluffy deposits) is evident, remove the cables from the battery terminals, clean them with a small wire brush, then refit them. Automotive stores sell a tool for cleaning the battery post . . .

4 . . . as well as the battery cable clamps.

Weekly checks 0•15

Electrical systems

✔ Check all external lights and the horn. Refer to the appropriate Sections of Chapter 12 for details if any of the circuits are found to be inoperative.

✔ Visually check all accessible wiring connectors, harnesses and retaining clips for security, and for signs of chafing or damage.

HAYNES HiNT *If you need to check your brake lights and indicators unaided, back up to a wall or garage door and operate the lights. The reflected light should show if they are working properly.*

1 If a single indicator light, stop-light or headlight has failed, it is likely that a bulb has blown and will need to be renewed. Refer to Chapter 12 for details. If both stop-lights have failed, it is possible that the switch has failed (see Chapter 9).

2 If more than one indicator light or headlight has failed, it is likely that either a fuse has blown or that there is a fault in the circuit (see Chapter 12). The main fuses are accessed by removing a cover on the driver's end of the facia. Additional fuses and relays are located in the left-hand side of the engine compartment.

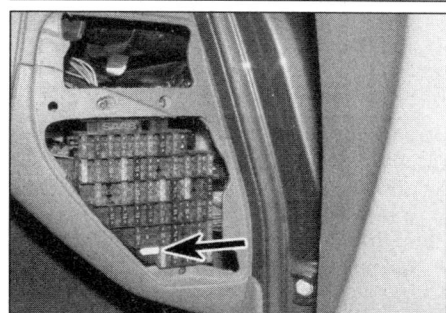

3 To renew a blown fuse, remove it using the plastic tool provided. Fit a new fuse of the same rating, available from car accessory shops. If the fuse blows repeatedly, refer to Chapter 12 to locate the fault.

Lubricants, fluids and tyre pressures

Lubricants and fluids

Engine:
   Petrol.. Saab Long Life Turbo Engine Oil or any fully synthetic oil with viscosity 0W-30 or 0W-40 to specification GM-LL-A025
   Diesel.. Saab Long Life Turbo Engine Oil or any synthetic engine oil with viscosity 5W-40 to specification GM-LL-B025
Cooling system.. Saab original coolant/antifreeze only
Manual gearbox...................................... Saab synthetic manual gearbox oil MTF 0063, part No 93 165 290
Automatic transmission........................... Saab automatic transmission fluid 3309
Power steering reservoir......................... Saab Power Steering Fluid CHF 11S or CHF 202
Brake fluid reservoir................................ Hydraulic fluid to DOT 4

Tyre pressures (cold)

Note: *Pressures apply to original-equipment tyres, and may vary if any other make or type of tyre is fitted; check with the tyre manufacturer or supplier for correct pressures if necessary. Pressures are also given on the passenger side B-pillar.*

Tyre size	Front	Rear
195/65 R15:		
1 to 3 persons, up to 100 mph	35 psi (2.4 bar)	35 psi (2.4 bar)
4 to 5 persons, up to 100 mph	38 psi (2.6 bar)	38 psi (2.6 bar)
205/65 R15:		
1 to 3 persons, up to 100 mph	33 psi (2.3 bar)	30 psi (2.1 bar)
4 to 5 persons, up to 100 mph	33 psi (2.3 bar)	30 psi (2.1 bar)
1 to 5 persons, up to 100 mph	41 psi (2.8 bar)	38 psi (2.6 bar)
215/55 R16:		
1 to 3 persons, up to 100 mph	35 psi (2.4 bar)	32 psi (2.2 bar)
4 to 5 persons, up to 100 mph	35 psi (2.4 bar)	32 psi (2.2 bar)
1 to 5 persons, up to 100 mph	42 psi (2.9 bar)	39 psi (2.7 bar)
225/45 R17:		
1 to 3 persons, up to 100 mph	36 psi (2.5 bar)	35 psi (2.4 bar)
4 to 5 persons, up to 100 mph	36 psi (2.5 bar)	35 psi (2.4 bar)
1 to 5 persons, up to 100 mph	44 psi (3.0 bar)	42 psi (2.9 bar)
235/45 R17:		
1 to 3 persons, up to 100 mph	35 psi (2.4 bar)	35 psi (2.4 bar)
4 to 5 persons, up to 100 mph	35 psi (2.4 bar)	35 psi (2.4 bar)
1 to 5 persons, up to 100 mph	41 psi (2.8 bar)	41 psi (2.8 bar)
T115/70 R16 (space saver spare)	61 psi (4.2 bar)	

Chapter 1 Part A:
Routine maintenance and servicing – petrol engines

Contents

	Section number
Air conditioning drain hoses – check	19
Air filter element – renewal	24
Airbag system – check	9
Automatic transmission fluid – renewal	28
Automatic transmission fluid level – check	14
Auxiliary drivebelt – renewal	27
Auxiliary drivebelt condition – check	21
Brake fluid – renewal	29
Brake pad wear – check	17
Coolant – renewal	25
Coolant antifreeze concentration – check	13
Driveshaft joints and gaiters – check	15
Engine oil and filter – renewal	3
Exhaust system – check	16
Fuel filter – renewal	26

	Section number
General information	1
Handbrake – check and adjustment	7
Headlight beam alignment – check	10
Hinges and locks – lubrication	18
Hoses and fluids – leak check	5
Manual transmission oil level – check	23
Pollen filter – renew	20
Power steering fluid level – check	11
Regular maintenance	2
Road test	12
Seat belt condition – check	8
Service indicator – resetting	4
Spark plugs – renewal	22
Steering and suspension components – check	6

Degrees of difficulty

| Easy, suitable for novice with little experience | Fairly easy, suitable for beginner with some experience | Fairly difficult, suitable for competent DIY mechanic | Difficult, suitable for experienced DIY mechanic | Very difficult, suitable for expert DIY or professional |

1A•2 Servicing specifications – petrol engines

Lubricants and fluids
See end of *Weekly checks* on page 0•16

Capacities

Engine oil
All engines (drain and refill, with filter change)	4.0 litres
Total from dry, including engine oil cooler	5.4 litres
Between dipstick MAX and MIN markings	1.0 litres

Cooling system ... 7.4 litres

Transmission
Manual:
- Drain and refill ... 1.5 litres
- Total from dry ... 1.9 litres

Automatic:
- Drain and refill ... 3.5 litres
- Total from dry (including torque converter and cooler) ... 7.0 litres

Braking system
System capacity ... 0.9 litres

Power-assisted steering
System capacity ... 1.3 litres

Fuel tank ... 75.0 litres (16.5 gallons)

Cooling system
Antifreeze mixture:*
- 50% antifreeze ... Protection down to -37°C
- 55% antifreeze ... Protection down to -45°C

* Note: Coolant from Saab dealers is premixed with water at the correct ratio.

Ignition system

Firing order	1 – 3 – 4 – 2	
Spark plugs:	**Type**	**Electrode gap**
2.0 litre engines	NGK BCPR6ES-11	1.0 mm
2.3 litre engines	NGK PFR 6H-10	1.0 mm

Brakes
Brake pad friction material minimum thickness ... 4.0 mm at time of service (acoustic warning at 3.0 mm)

Tyre pressures
Refer to the end of *Weekly checks* on page 0•16

Torque wrench settings

	Nm	lbf ft
Automatic transmission drain plug	40	30
Engine oil sump drain plug	25	18
Manual transmission drain, level and filler plugs	50	37
Spark plugs	28	21
Wheel bolts	110	81

Maintenance schedule – petrol engines

The maintenance intervals in this manual are provided with the assumption that you will be carrying out the work yourself. These are the minimum maintenance intervals recommended by the manufacturer for vehicles driven daily. If you wish to keep your vehicle in peak condition at all times, you may wish to perform some of these procedures more often. We encourage frequent maintenance, because it enhances the efficiency, performance and resale value of your vehicle.

If the vehicle is driven in dusty areas, used to tow a trailer, or driven frequently at slow speeds (idling in traffic) or on short journeys, more frequent maintenance intervals are recommended.

When the vehicle is new, it should be serviced by a dealer service department (or other workshop recognised by the vehicle manufacturer as providing the same standard of service) in order to preserve the warranty. The vehicle manufacturer may reject warranty claims if you are unable to prove that servicing has been carried out as and when specified, using only original equipment parts or parts certified to be of equivalent quality.

All Saab models are equipped with a service interval display (or Saab Information Display – SID) on the facia, which will indicate TIME FOR SERVICE when a service is due. However, Saab point out that, 'due to the relationship between time and mileage, some operating conditions will make annual service more suitable'.

Every 250 miles or weekly
- [ ] Refer to *Weekly checks*

Every 9000 miles
- [ ] Engine oil and filter – renewal (Section 3)

Note: *Frequent oil and filter changes are good for the engine. We recommend changing the oil at the mileage specified here, or at least annually if the mileage covered is less.*

Every 18 000 miles
- [ ] Service indicator – resetting (Section 4)
- [ ] Hoses and fluids – leak check (Section 5)
- [ ] Steering and suspension components – check (Section 6)
- [ ] Handbrake – check and adjustment (Section 7)
- [ ] Seat belt condition – check (Section 8)
- [ ] Airbag system – check (Section 9)
- [ ] Headlight beam alignment – check (Section 10)
- [ ] Power steering fluid level – check (Section 11)
- [ ] Road test (Section 12)
- [ ] Coolant antifreeze concentration – check (Section 13)
- [ ] Automatic transmission fluid level – check (Section 14)
- [ ] Driveshaft joints and gaiters – check (Section 15)
- [ ] Exhaust system – check (Section 16)
- [ ] Brake pad wear – check (Section 17)
- [ ] Hinges and locks – lubrication (Section 18)
- [ ] Air conditioning drain hoses – check (Section 19)
- [ ] Pollen filter – renew (Section 20)
- [ ] Auxiliary drivebelt condition – check (Section 21)

Every 36 000 miles
- [ ] Spark plugs – renewal (Section 22)
- [ ] Manual transmission oil level – check (Section 23)
- [ ] Air filter element – renewal (Section 24)

Every 3 years
- [ ] Coolant – renewal (Section 25)

Note: *This work is not included in the Saab schedule, and should not be required if the recommended Saab antifreeze/inhibitor is used.*

Every 72 000 miles
- [ ] Fuel filter – renewal (Section 26)
- [ ] Auxiliary drivebelt – renewal (Section 27)
- [ ] Automatic transmission fluid – renewal (Section 28)

Every 4 years
- [ ] Brake fluid – renewal (Section 29)

1A•4 Component locations – petrol engines

Underbonnet view of a 2.3 litre turbocharged petrol engine

1. Engine oil filler cap and dipstick
2. Hydraulic brake fluid reservoir
3. Spark plugs (hidden)
4. Ignition coil module
5. Turbocharger-to-engine air intake pipe
6. Engine compartment fusebox
7. Front suspension strut top mountings
8. Power steering fluid reservoir
9. Coolant expansion tank
10. Battery
11. Turbocharger control by-pass valve
12. ABS unit
13. Radiator top hose
14. Fuel injection system air-mass meter
15. Windscreen washer fluid reservoir filler cap

Front underbody view

1. Engine oil drain plug
2. Automatic transmission fluid drain plug
3. Engine oil filter
4. Exhaust front pipe
5. Front suspension/engine subframe
6. Steering gear
7. Exhaust mounting rubbers
8. Front suspension lower arms
9. Steering track rod ends
10. Front brake calipers
11. Air filter housing
12. Windscreen washer fluid reservoir
13. Front foglights
14. Front towing eye position

Component locations – petrol engines

Rear underbody view

1 Rear suspension crossmember
2 Rear anti-roll bar
3 Rear suspension lower transverse link
4 Brake hydraulic flexible hoses
5 Handbrake cables
6 Fuel tank
7 Rear suspension trailing arms
8 Rear suspension strut/shock absorbers
9 Exhaust rear silencer and tailpipe

Maintenance procedures

1 General information

1 This Chapter is designed to help the home mechanic maintain his/her vehicle for safety, economy, long life and peak performance.
2 The Chapter contains a master maintenance schedule, followed by Sections dealing specifically with each task in the schedule. Visual checks, adjustments, component renewal and other helpful items are included. Refer to the accompanying illustrations of the engine compartment and the underside of the vehicle for the locations of the various components.
3 Servicing your vehicle in accordance with the mileage/time maintenance schedule and the following Sections will provide a planned maintenance programme, which should result in a long and reliable service life. This is a comprehensive plan, so maintaining some items but not others at the specified service intervals will not produce the same results.
4 As you service your vehicle, you will discover that many of the procedures can – and should – be grouped together, because of the particular procedure being performed, or because of the close proximity of two otherwise-unrelated components to one another. For example, if the vehicle is raised for any reason, the exhaust system could be inspected at the same time as the suspension and steering components.
5 The first step in this maintenance programme is to prepare yourself before the actual work begins. Read through all the Sections relevant to the work to be carried out, then make a list and gather together all the parts and tools required. If a problem is encountered, seek advice from a parts specialist, or a dealer service department.

2 Regular maintenance

1 If, from the time the vehicle is new, the routine maintenance schedule is followed closely, and frequent checks are made of fluid levels and high-wear items, as suggested throughout this manual, the engine will be kept in relatively good running condition, and the need for additional work will be minimised.
2 It is possible that there will be times when the engine is running poorly due to the lack of regular maintenance. This is even more likely if a used vehicle, which has not received regular and frequent maintenance checks, is purchased. In such cases, additional work may need to be carried out, outside of the regular maintenance intervals.
3 If engine wear is suspected, a compression test (refer to Chapter 2A) will provide valuable information regarding the overall performance of the main internal components. Such a test can be used as a basis to decide on the extent of the work to be carried out. If, for example, a compression test indicates serious internal engine wear, conventional maintenance as described in this Chapter will not greatly improve the performance of the engine, and may prove a waste of time and money, unless extensive overhaul work (Chapter 2C) is carried out first.
4 The following series of operations are those most often required to improve the performance of a generally poor-running engine:

Primary operations

a) Clean, inspect and test the battery ('Weekly checks' and Chapter 5A)
b) Check all the engine-related fluids ('Weekly checks').
c) Check the condition and tension of the auxiliary drivebelt (Section 21).
d) Renew the spark plugs (Section 22).
e) Check the condition of the air filter element, and renew if necessary (Section 2).
f) Renew the fuel filter (Section 26).
g) Check the condition of all hoses, and check for fluid leaks (Section 5).

Secondary operations

5 If the above operations do not prove fully effective, carry out the following secondary operations:

a) Check the charging system (Chapter 5A).
b) Check the ignition system (Chapter 5B).
c) Check the fuel system (Chapter 4A).

1A•6 Maintenance procedures – petrol engines

3.4 Engine oil drain plug

3.6 Renew the oil sump drain plug washer if necessary

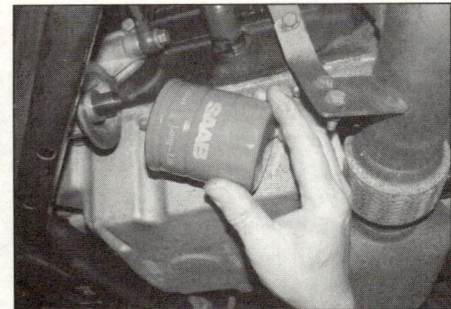

3.8 Removing the oil filter

Every 9000 miles

3 Engine oil and filter – renewal

1 Frequent oil changes are the most important preventative maintenance the DIY home mechanic can give the engine, because ageing oil becomes diluted and contaminated, which leads to premature engine wear.
2 Before starting this procedure, gather together all the necessary tools and materials. Also make sure that you have plenty of clean rags and newspapers handy, to mop-up any spills. Ideally, the engine oil should be warm, as it will drain better, and more built-up sludge will be removed with it. Take care, however, not to touch the exhaust or any other hot parts of the engine when working under the vehicle. To avoid any possibility of scalding, and to protect yourself from possible skin irritants and other harmful contaminants in used engine oils, it is advisable to wear gloves when carrying out this work.
3 Apply the handbrake, and then jack up the front of the vehicle and support it on axle stands (see *Jacking and vehicle support*).
4 The engine oil drain plug is located on the rear of the sump; slacken the plug about half a turn. Position the draining container under the drain plug, then remove the plug completely – recover the sealing washer **(see illustration)**.
5 Allow some time for the old oil to drain, noting that it may be necessary to reposition the container as the oil flow slows to a trickle.
6 After all the oil has drained; wipe off the drain plug with a clean rag. Check the sealing washer for condition, and renew it if necessary **(see illustration)**. Clean the area around the drain plug opening, and refit the plug. Tighten the plug to the specified torque.
7 Move the container into position under the oil filter, which is located at the front of the cylinder block and accessed from under the vehicle.
8 Using an oil filter removal tool or strap, slacken the filter initially, then unscrew it by hand the rest of the way **(see illustration)**. Empty the oil from the old filter into the container, and discard the filter.
9 Use a clean rag to remove all oil, dirt and sludge from the filter sealing area on the mounting bracket.
10 Apply a light coating of clean engine oil to the sealing ring on the new filter, and then screw it into position on the engine. Tighten the filter firmly by hand only – **do not** use any tools. Wipe clean the filter and sump drain plug.
11 Remove the old oil and all tools, and then lower the vehicle to the ground.
12 Remove the oil filler cap and withdraw the dipstick from the top of the filler tube. Fill the engine, using the correct grade and type of oil (see *Lubricants and fluids*). An oil can spout or funnel may help to reduce spillage. Pour in half the specified quantity of oil first, and then wait a few minutes for the oil to run to the sump. Continue adding oil a small quantity at a time until the level is up to the lower mark on the dipstick. Adding a further 1.0 litre will bring the level up to the upper mark on the dipstick. Insert the dipstick, and refit the filler cap.
13 Start the engine and run it for a few minutes; check for leaks around the oil filter seal and the sump drain plug. Note that there may be a delay of a few seconds before the oil pressure warning light goes out when the engine is first started, as the oil circulates through the engine oil galleries and the new oil filter, before the pressure builds-up.
14 Switch off the engine, and wait a few minutes for the oil to settle in the sump once more. With the new oil circulated and the filter completely full, recheck the level on the dipstick, and add more oil as necessary.
15 Dispose of the used engine oil safely, in accordance with the guidance given in the Reference Section.

Every 18 000 miles

4 Service indicator – resetting

1 The facia-mounted SID (Saab Information Display) system incorporates a service interval indicator. When the distance covered between services approaches the next service, a visual message is displayed: 'Time for service. Contact service'. The service indicator is then manually reset to zero by the technician, after the vehicle has been serviced. **Note:** *The indicator is automatically reset after the message has been displayed 20 times.*
2 To manually reset the service indicator, press and hold the CLEAR button on the SID panel for 8 seconds, you will hear two beeps in quick succession, and then release it. The SERVICE message will start to flash, this means the service interval is reset.
3 The indicator can be reset at any time by a technician, using the Saab diagnostic tool.

5 Hoses and fluids – leak check

Cooling system

 Warning: Refer to the safety information given in 'Safety First!' and Chapter 3 before disturbing any of the cooling system components.

1 Carefully check the radiator and heater coolant

hoses along their entire length. Renew any hose which is cracked, swollen or which shows signs of deterioration. Cracks will show up better if the hose is squeezed. Pay close attention to the clips that secure the hoses to the cooling system components. Hose clips that have been overtightened can pinch and puncture hoses, resulting in cooling system leaks.

2 Inspect all the cooling system components (hoses, joint faces, etc) for leaks. Where any problems of this nature are found on system components, renew the component or gasket with reference to Chapter 3 **(see Haynes Hint)**.

Fuel system

 Warning: Refer to the safety information given in 'Safety First!' and Chapter 4A before disturbing any of the fuel system components.

3 Petrol leaks can be difficult to pinpoint, unless the leakage is significant and hence easily visible. Fuel tends to evaporate quickly once it comes into contact with air, especially in a hot engine bay. Small drips can disappear before you get a chance to identify the point of leakage. If you suspect that there is a fuel leak from the area of the engine bay, leave the vehicle overnight then start the engine from cold, with the bonnet open. Metal components tend to shrink when they are cold, and rubber seals and hoses tend to harden, so any leaks will be more apparent whilst the engine is warming-up from a cold start.

4 Check all fuel lines at their connections to the fuel rail, fuel pressure regulator and fuel filter. Examine each rubber fuel hose along its length for splits or cracks. Check for leakage from the crimped joints between rubber and metal fuel lines. Examine the unions between the metal fuel lines and the fuel filter housing. Also check the area around the fuel injectors for signs of O-ring leakage.

5 To identify fuel leaks between the fuel tank and the engine bay, the vehicle should be raised and securely supported on axle stands (see *Jacking and vehicle support*). Inspect the petrol tank and filler neck for punctures, cracks and other damage. The connection between the filler neck and tank is especially critical. Sometimes a rubber filler neck or connecting hose will leak due to loose retaining clamps or deteriorated rubber.

6 Carefully check all rubber hoses and metal fuel lines leading away from the petrol tank. Check for loose connections, deteriorated hoses, kinked lines, and other damage. Pay particular attention to the vent pipes and hoses, which often loop up around the filler neck and can become blocked or kinked, making tank filling difficult. Follow the fuel supply and return lines to the front of the vehicle, carefully inspecting them all the way for signs of damage or corrosion. Renew damaged sections as necessary.

Engine oil

7 Inspect the area around the camshaft cover, cylinder head, oil filter and sump joint faces. Bear in mind that, over a period of time, some very slight seepage from these areas is to be expected – what you are really looking for is any indication of a serious leak caused by gasket failure. Engine oil seeping from the base of the timing chain cover or the transmission bellhousing may be an indication of crankshaft or transmission input shaft oil seal failure. Should a leak be found, renew the failed gasket or oil seal by referring to the appropriate Chapters in this manual.

Automatic transmission fluid

8 Where applicable, check the hoses leading to the transmission fluid cooler which is integral with the radiator. Look for deterioration caused by corrosion and damage from grounding, or debris thrown up from the road surface. Automatic transmission fluid is thin oil and is usually red in colour.

Power-assisted steering fluid

9 Examine the hose running between the fluid reservoir and the power steering pump, and the return hose running from the steering rack to the fluid reservoir. Also examine the high-pressure supply hose between the pump and the steering rack.

10 Check the condition of each hose carefully. Look for deterioration caused by corrosion and damage from grounding, or debris thrown up from the road surface.

11 Pay particular attention to crimped unions, and the area surrounding the hoses that are secured with adjustable worm drive clips. Like automatic transmission fluid, PAS fluid is thin oil, and is usually red in colour.

Air conditioning refrigerant

 Warning: Refer to the safety information given in 'Safety First!' and Chapter 3, regarding the dangers of disturbing any of the air conditioning system components.

12 The air conditioning system is filled with a liquid refrigerant, which is retained under high pressure. If the air conditioning system is opened and depressurised without the aid of specialised equipment, the refrigerant will immediately turn into gas and escape into the atmosphere. If the liquid comes into contact with your skin, it can cause severe frostbite. In addition, the refrigerant contains substances which are environmentally damaging; for this reason, it should not be allowed to escape into the atmosphere in an uncontrolled fashion.

13 Any suspected air conditioning system leaks should be immediately referred to a Saab dealer or air conditioning specialist. Leakage will be shown up as a steady drop in the level of refrigerant in the system.

14 Note that water may drip from the condenser drain pipe, underneath the car, immediately after the air conditioning system has been in use. This is normal, and should not be cause for concern.

A leak in the cooling system will usually show up as white- or antifreeze-coloured, crusty deposits around the area of the leak.

Brake (and clutch) fluid

 Warning: Refer to the safety information given in 'Safety First!' and Chapter 9, regarding the dangers of handling brake fluid.

15 With reference to Chapter 9, examine the area surrounding the brake pipe unions at the master cylinder for signs of leakage. Check the area around the base of fluid reservoir, for signs of leakage caused by seal failure. Also examine the brake pipe unions at the ABS hydraulic unit.

16 If fluid loss is evident, but the leak cannot be pinpointed in the engine bay, the brake calipers and underbody brake lines should be carefully checked with the vehicle raised and supported on axle stands (see *Jacking and vehicle support*). Leakage of fluid from the braking system is a serious fault that must be rectified immediately.

17 Brake/clutch hydraulic fluid is a toxic substance with a watery consistency. New fluid is almost colourless, but it becomes darker with age and use.

Unidentified fluid leaks

18 If there are signs that a fluid of some description is leaking from the vehicle, but you cannot identify the type of fluid or its exact origin, park the vehicle overnight and slide a large piece of card underneath it. Providing that the card is positioned in roughly the right location, even the smallest leak will show up on the card. Not only will this help you to pinpoint the exact location of the leak, it should be easier to identify the fluid from its colour. Bear in mind, though, that the leak may only be occurring when the engine is running!

Vacuum hoses

19 Although the braking system is hydraulically operated, the brake servo unit amplifies the effort applied at the brake pedal by making use of the vacuum in the intake manifold, generated by the engine and supplemented by the vacuum pump on automatic transmission models or an 'ejector' device on manual transmission models (refer to Chapter 9 for more information). Vacuum is ported to the

1A•8 Every 18 000 miles – petrol engines

servo by means of a large-bore hose. Any leaks that develop in this hose will reduce the effectiveness of the braking system, and may affect the running of the engine.
20 In addition, a number of the underbonnet components, particularly the emission control components, are driven by vacuum supplied from the intake manifold via narrow-bore hoses. A leak in a vacuum hose means that air is being drawn into the hose (rather than escaping from it) and this makes leakage very difficult to detect. One method is to use an old length of vacuum hose as a kind of stethoscope – hold one end close to your ear and use the other end to probe the area around the suspected leak. When the end of the hose is directly over a vacuum leak, a hissing sound will be heard clearly through the hose. Care must be taken to avoid contacting hot or moving components, as the engine must be running when testing in this manner. Renew any vacuum hoses that are found to be defective.

6 Steering and suspension components – check

Front suspension and steering

1 Raise the front of the vehicle, and securely support it on axle stands (see *Jacking and vehicle support*).
2 Visually inspect the balljoint dust covers and the steering rack-and-pinion gaiters for splits, chafing or deterioration. Any wear of these components will cause loss of lubricant, together with dirt and water entry, resulting in rapid deterioration of the balljoints or steering gear.
3 Check the power steering fluid hoses for chafing or deterioration, and the pipe and hose unions for fluid leaks. Also check for signs of fluid leakage under pressure from the steering gear rubber gaiters, which would indicate failed fluid seals within the steering gear.
4 Grasp the roadwheel at the 12 o'clock and 6 o'clock positions, and try to rock it **(see illustration)**. Very slight free play may be felt, but if the movement is appreciable, further investigation is necessary to determine the source. Continue rocking the wheel while an assistant depresses the footbrake. If the movement is now eliminated or significantly reduced, it is likely that the hub bearings are at fault. If the free play is still evident with the footbrake depressed, then there is wear in the suspension joints or mountings.
5 Now grasp the wheel at the 9 o'clock and 3 o'clock positions, and try to rock it as before. Any movement felt now may again be caused by wear in the hub bearings or the steering track rod balljoints. If the outer balljoint is worn, the visual movement will be obvious. If the inner joint is suspect, it can be felt by placing a hand over the rack-and-pinion rubber gaiter and gripping the track rod. If the wheel is now rocked, movement will be felt at the inner joint if wear has taken place.
6 Using a large screwdriver or flat bar, check for wear in the suspension mounting bushes by levering between the relevant suspension component and its attachment point. Some movement is to be expected, as the mountings are made of rubber, but excessive wear should be obvious. Also check the condition of any visible rubber bushes, looking for splits, cracks or contamination of the rubber.
7 With the car standing on its wheels, have an assistant turn the steering wheel back-and-forth, about an eighth of a turn each way. There should be very little, if any, lost movement between the steering wheel and roadwheels. If this is not the case, closely observe the joints and mountings previously described. In addition, check the steering column universal joints for wear, and also check the rack-and-pinion steering gear itself.
8 The front suspension mountings should be checked for tightness.

Rear suspension

9 Chock the front wheels, then jack up the rear of the vehicle and support securely on axle stands (see *Jacking and vehicle support*).
10 Working as described previously for the front suspension, check the rear hub bearings, the suspension bushes and the strut or shock absorber mountings (as applicable) for wear.
11 The rear suspension mountings should be checked for tightness.

Shock absorber

12 Check for any signs of fluid leakage around the shock absorber bodies, or from the rubber gaiters around the piston rods. Should any fluid be noticed, the shock absorber is defective internally, and should be renewed.
Note: *Shock absorbers should always be renewed in pairs on the same axle.*
13 The efficiency of the shock absorber may be checked by bouncing the vehicle at each corner. Generally speaking, the body will return to its normal position and stop after being depressed. If it rises and returns on a rebound, the shock absorber is probably suspect. Also examine the shock absorber upper and lower mountings for any signs of wear.

Removable towbar attachment

14 Where applicable, clean the coupling pin then apply a little grease to the socket. Make sure that the removable towbar attachment fits easily to its mounting and locks correctly in position.

7 Handbrake – check and adjustment

1 Chock the front wheels, then jack up the rear of the vehicle and support on axle stands (see *Jacking and vehicle support*).
2 Fully release the handbrake lever.
3 Apply the lever to the 4th notch position, and check that both rear wheels are locked when attempting to turn them by hand.
4 If adjustment is necessary, refer to Chapter 9.
5 Lower the vehicle to the ground.

8 Seat belt condition – check

1 Working on each seat belt in turn, carefully examine the seat belt webbing for cuts, or for any signs of serious fraying or deterioration. Pull the belt all the way out, and examine the full extent of the webbing.
2 Fasten and unfasten the belt, ensuring that the locking mechanism holds securely, and releases properly when intended. Check also that the retracting mechanism operates correctly when the belt is released.
3 Check the security of all seat belt mountings and attachments which are accessible, without removing any trim or other components, from inside the vehicle.
4 Check the function of the seat belt reminder lamp.

9 Airbag system – check

1 The following work can be carried out by the home mechanic, however if an electronic fault is apparent, it will be necessary to take the car to a Saab dealer, who will have the necessary diagnostic equipment to extract fault codes from the system.
2 Turn the ignition switch to the drive position (ignition warning lights on), and check that the SRS (Supplementary Restraint System) warning light is illuminated for 3 to 4 seconds. After this period the light should go out, indicating that the system has been checked and is functioning correctly.
3 If the warning light remains on or refuses to light, have the system checked by a Saab dealer.
4 Visually examine the steering wheel centre pad and the passenger airbag module for external damage. Also check the exterior of the front seats around the side airbag locations. If damage is evident, consult a Saab dealer.
5 In the interests of safety, make sure that

6.4 Check for wear in the hub bearings by grasping the wheel and trying to rock it

Every 18 000 miles – petrol engines

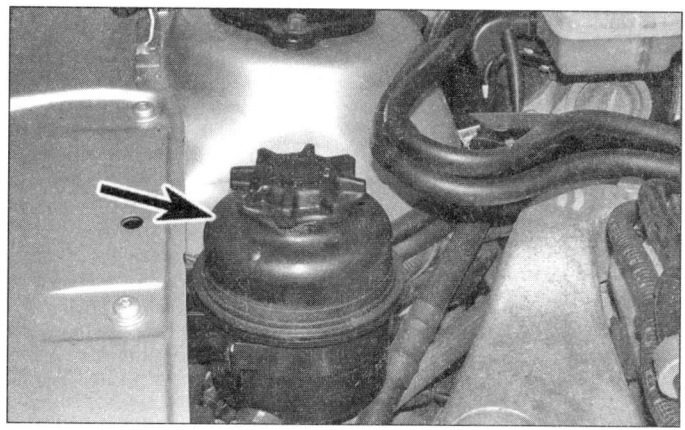

11.1 Power steering fluid reservoir

11.3 Fluid level marks on the dipstick

there are no loose items inside the car that could be thrown onto the airbag modules in the event of an accident.

10 Headlight beam alignment – check

Refer to Chapter 12 for details

11 Power steering fluid level – check

1 The power steering fluid reservoir is located on the right-hand side of the engine compartment, in front of the suspension turret (see illustration). The fluid level should be checked with the engine stopped and the front wheels pointing straight-ahead.
2 First wipe the filler cap and surrounding area of the reservoir. Unscrew the cap from the top of the reservoir, and wipe all fluid from the cap dipstick with a clean rag.
3 Screw on the cap completely again, then remove it and check the fluid level on the dipstick. When the engine is cold at an ambient temperature of 20°C, the fluid level should be between the upper (MAX) and lower (MIN) marks on the dipstick, preferably near the MAX mark (see illustration). If the engine is warm, the level can be slightly higher, but the level must never be allowed to be lower than the MIN mark.
4 Top-up the fluid level using the specified type of fluid (do not overfill the reservoir) (see illustration), then refit and tighten the filler cap.

12 Road test

Instruments and electrical equipment

1 Check the operation of all instruments and electrical equipment.

2 Make sure that all instruments read correctly, and switch on all electrical equipment in turn to check that it functions properly. Check the function of the heating, air conditioning and automatic climate control systems.

Steering and suspension

3 Check for any abnormalities in the steering, suspension, handling or road 'feel'.
4 Drive the vehicle, and check that there are no unusual vibrations or noises.
5 Check that the steering feels positive, with no excessive 'sloppiness', or roughness, and check for any suspension noises when cornering, or when driving over bumps. Check that the power steering system operates correctly.

Drivetrain

6 Check the performance of the engine, clutch (manual transmission), transmission and driveshafts. Check that the turbo boost pressure needle moves up to the upper limit during sharp acceleration. The needle may occasionally enter the red zone for an instant, but if this happens frequently, or for extended periods, a problem may exist within the turbo boost control mechanism.
7 Listen for any unusual noises from the engine, clutch (manual transmission) and transmission.
8 Make sure that the engine runs smoothly when idling, and that there is no hesitation when accelerating.
9 On manual transmission models, check that the clutch action is smooth and progressive, that the drive is taken up smoothly, and that the pedal travel is correct. Also listen for any noises when the clutch pedal is depressed. Check that all gears can be engaged smoothly, without noise, and that the gear lever action is smooth and not abnormally vague or 'notchy'.
10 On automatic transmission models, make sure that all gearchanges occur smoothly without snatching, and without an increase in engine speed between changes. Check that all the gear positions can be selected with the vehicle at rest. If any problems are found, they should be referred to a Saab dealer.

11 Listen for a metallic clicking sound from the front of the vehicle, as the vehicle is driven slowly in a circle with the steering on full lock. Carry out this check in both directions. If a clicking noise is heard, this indicates wear in a driveshaft joint, in which case, refer to Chapter 8.

Braking system

12 Make sure that the vehicle does not pull to one side when braking, and that the wheels do not lock when braking hard.
13 Check that there is no vibration through the steering when braking.
14 Check that the handbrake operates correctly, without excessive movement of the lever, and that it holds the vehicle stationary on a slope.
15 Test the operation of the brake servo unit as follows. With the engine off, depress the footbrake four or five times to exhaust the vacuum, and then start the engine while holding the brake pedal depressed. As the engine starts, there should be a noticeable 'give' in the brake pedal as vacuum builds-up. Allow the engine to run for at least two minutes, and then switch it off. If the brake pedal is now depressed again, it should be possible to detect a 'hiss' from the servo as the pedal is depressed. After about four or five applications, no further sound should be heard, and the pedal should feel considerably harder.

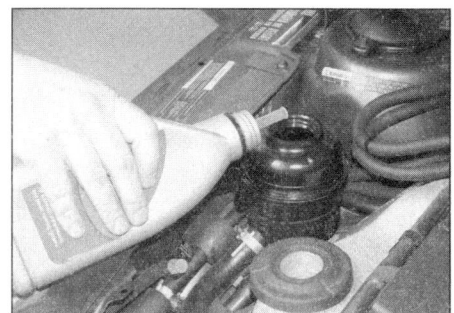

11.4 Topping-up the power steering fluid level

1A•10 Every 18 000 miles – petrol engines

14.3a Withdrawing the automatic transmission fluid level dipstick

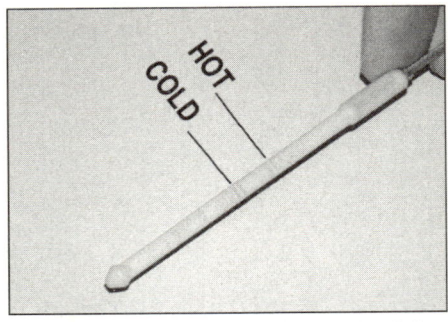

14.3b Fluid level marks on the dipstick

15.2 Checking the condition of the driveshaft gaiters

13 Coolant antifreeze concentration – check

1 The cooling system should be filled with the recommended antifreeze and corrosion protection fluid. Over a period of time, the concentration of fluid may be reduced due to topping-up (this can be avoided by topping-up with the correct antifreeze mixture) or fluid loss. If loss of coolant has been evident, it is important to make the necessary repair before adding fresh fluid. The exact mixture of antifreeze-to-water which you should use depends on the weather conditions. The mixture should contain at least 40% antifreeze, but not more than 70%. Consult the mixture ratio chart on the antifreeze container before adding coolant. Use antifreeze that meets the vehicle manufacturer's specifications. Note that antifreeze coolant available from Saab dealers is premixed with water at the correct ratio.
2 With the engine **cold**, carefully remove the cap from the expansion tank. If the engine is not completely cold, place a cloth rag over the cap before removing it, and remove it slowly to allow any pressure to escape.
3 Antifreeze checkers are available from car accessory shops. Draw some coolant from the expansion tank and observe how many plastic balls are floating in the checker. Usually, 2 or 3 balls must be floating for the correct concentration of antifreeze, but follow the manufacturer's instructions.
4 If the concentration is incorrect, it will be necessary to either withdraw some coolant and add antifreeze, or alternatively drain the old coolant and add fresh coolant of the correct concentration.

14 Automatic transmission fluid level – check

1 The fluid level is checked using the dipstick located on the front of the transmission, on the left-hand side of the engine compartment, beneath the battery location.
2 With the engine idling, select D for approximately 15 seconds, then engage R and wait a further 15 seconds. Do this again in position P, and leave the engine idling.
3 Withdraw the dipstick from the tube, and wipe all the fluid from its end with a clean rag or paper towel. Insert the clean dipstick back into the tube as far as it will go, then withdraw it once more. Note the fluid level on the end of the dipstick – there are level marks for cold and hot fluid conditions **(see illustrations)**. Use the hot marks if the engine has reached normal operating temperature.
4 If topping-up is necessary, add fluid as necessary through the dipstick tube. **Note:** *Never overfill the transmission so that the fluid level is above the upper mark. Use a funnel with a fine mesh gauze, to avoid spillage and to ensure that no foreign matter enters the transmission.* Note that the quantity of oil between the MIN and MAX marks is 0.4 litres.
5 After topping-up, take the car on a short run to distribute the fresh fluid, and then recheck the level again, topping-up if necessary.
6 Always maintain the fluid at the correct level. If the level is allowed to fall below the lower mark, fluid starvation may result, which could lead to severe transmission damage.

15 Driveshaft joints and gaiters – check

1 The driveshaft rubber gaiters are very important, because they prevent dirt, water and foreign material from entering and damaging the constant velocity (CV) joints. External contamination can cause the gaiter material to deteriorate prematurely, so it's a good idea to wash the gaiters with soap and water occasionally.
2 With the vehicle raised and securely supported on axle stands, turn the steering onto full-lock, and then slowly rotate each front wheel in turn. Inspect the condition of the outer constant velocity (CV) joint rubber gaiters, squeezing the gaiters to open out the folds **(see illustration)**. Check for signs of cracking, splits, or deterioration of the rubber, which may allow the escape of grease, and lead to the ingress of water and grit into the joint. Also check the security and condition of the retaining clips. Repeat these checks on the inner CV joints. If any damage or deterioration is found, the gaiters should be renewed as described in Chapter 8.
3 At the same time, check the general condition of the outer CV joints themselves, by first holding the driveshaft and attempting to rotate the wheels. Repeat this check on the inner joints, by holding the inner joint yoke and attempting to rotate the driveshaft.
4 Any appreciable movement in the CV joint indicates wear in the joint, wear in the driveshaft splines, or a loose driveshaft retaining nut.

16 Exhaust system – check

1 With the engine cold, check the complete exhaust system from its starting point at the engine to the end of the tailpipe. If necessary, raise the front and rear of the vehicle and support it on axle stands (see *Jacking and vehicle support*). Remove any engine undershields as necessary for full access to the exhaust system.
2 Check the exhaust pipes and connections for evidence of leaks, severe corrosion, and damage. Make sure that all brackets and mountings are in good condition and that all relevant nuts and bolts are tight. Leakage at any of the joints or in other parts of the system will usually show up as a black sooty stain in the vicinity of the leak.
3 Rattles and other noises can often be traced to the exhaust system, especially the brackets and rubber mountings. Try to move the pipes and silencers. If the components are able to come into contact with the body or suspension parts, secure the system with new mountings. Otherwise separate the joints (if possible) and twist the pipes as necessary to provide additional clearance.

Every 18 000 miles – petrol engines 1A•11

17 Brake pad wear – check

Note: *An acoustic wear warning device is fitted to the outer pad, consisting of a metal strip, which contacts the brake disc when the thickness of the friction material is less than 3.0 mm. This device causes a scraping noise that warns the driver that the pads are worn excessively (see illustration).*

1 To check the brake pads, firmly apply the handbrake, and then jack up the front or rear of the vehicle (depending on brakes to be checked) and support it securely on axle stands (see *Jacking and vehicle support*).
2 For a quick check, the pad thickness can be checked through the gaps in the alloy wheels **(see illustration)**. Measure the thickness of the pad lining excluding the backing plate. This must not be less than that indicated in the Specifications.
3 The view through the wheel gives an indication of the **outer** brake pad wear only. For a comprehensive check, remove the wheels, and then the brake pads should be removed and cleaned. The operation of the caliper can then also be checked, and the condition of the brake disc itself can be fully examined on both sides.
4 If any pad's friction material is worn to the specified thickness or less; *all four pads must be renewed as a set*. Refer to Chapter 9 for details.
5 On completion, refit the roadwheels and lower the vehicle to the ground.

18 Hinges and locks – lubrication

1 Work around the vehicle and lubricate the hinges of the bonnet, doors and boot lid or tailgate with a light machine oil.
2 Lightly lubricate the two bonnet release locks with a smear of grease.
3 Check carefully the security and operation of all hinges, latches and locks. Check that the central locking system operates correctly.

17.0 Acoustic wear warning device fitted to the outer front brake pad

4 Check the condition and operation of the bonnet and boot lid/tailgate struts, renewing them if either is leaking or no longer able to support the bonnet/boot lid/tailgate.

19 Air conditioning drain hoses – check

1 Working beneath the glovebox, remove the side trim from the filter housing.
2 Remove the sound insulation from both sides of the heater unit.
3 Fold down the carpet from both sides of the centre console, and remove the insulation from the passenger's side.
4 Loosen the clips and remove both drain hoses from the side of the heater unit.
5 Ideally, blow compressed air through the drain hoses to clear them, alternatively use a cloth rag. Also clear the spigots on the heater unit.
6 Refit the hoses using a reversal of the removal procedure.

20 Pollen filter – renew

1 Remove the glovebox as described in Chapter 11.
2 Remove the side trim/carpet from the centre console with reference to Chapter 11. At the same time, cut the plastic ties holding

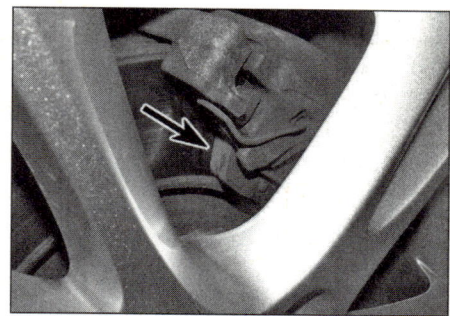

17.2 The outer brake pad wear can be checked through the aperture in the wheel

the wiring harness to the cover, and the cooler hose to the glovebox.
3 Undo the screws and remove the cover from over the pollen filter **(see illustrations)**.
4 Slide the pollen filter from the housing **(see illustration)**. Note the arrows indicating the direction of airflow through the filter.
5 Check that a seal is fitted to the top of the filter; if not, obtain and fit one. On models which have had air conditioning fitted after original manufacture, break off the plastic lugs from the top of the filter.
6 Loosen the clips and disconnect the two drain hoses from each side of the heater unit. Ideally, blow compressed air through the hoses to clear any accumulated debris, alternatively, clear the hoses with a suitable brush. Also, clear the spigots on the heater unit.
7 Refit the drain hoses and tighten the clips, then fit the new pollen filter using a reversal of the removal procedure.

21 Auxiliary drivebelt condition – check

1 A single, multi-grooved auxiliary drivebelt is used to transmit drive from the crankshaft pulley to the coolant pump, alternator, power steering pump and the air conditioning compressor **(see illustration 28.6)**. The drivebelt is guided by two idler pulleys and is tensioned automatically by a spring-loaded tensioner pulley.

20.3a Undo the screws . . .

20.3b . . . and remove the cover . . .

20.4 . . . then slide the pollen filter from the housing

1A•12 Every 18 000 miles – petrol engines

2 For better access to the drivebelt, apply the handbrake then jack up the front of the car and support it on axle stands (see *Jacking and vehicle support*). Remove the right-hand front roadwheel, and then remove the lower section of the plastic liner from under the right-hand wheel arch to expose the crankshaft pulley and drivebelt.

3 Check that the mark on top of the tensioner arm (right-hand rear of engine) is positioned within the two marks on the fixed tensioner mounting bracket. If it is outside the rearmost mark, the belt has stretched excessively and should be renewed.

4 Depress the front section of drivebelt between the power steering pump and compressor pulleys, then release the belt and check that it returns to its tensioned position again, proving that the tensioner is operating correctly. If the tensioner does not operate freely, it should be removed for examination and renewed if necessary.

5 Using a suitable socket and extension bar fitted to the crankshaft pulley bolt, rotate the crankshaft so that the entire length of the drivebelt can be examined. Examine the drivebelt for cracks, splitting, fraying, or other damage. Check also for signs of glazing (shiny patches) and for separation of the belt plies. Renew the belt if worn or damaged.

Every 36 000 miles

22 Spark plugs – renewal

Note: *The spark plugs should be renewed at 12 000 mile intervals on models with the 2.0 litre engine. On 2.3 litre engines, they should be renewed at 24 000 mile intervals.*

1 The correct functioning of the spark plugs is vital for the correct running and efficiency of the engine. It is essential that the plugs fitted are appropriate for the engine. If this type is used and the engine is in good condition, the spark plugs should not need attention between scheduled renewal intervals.

2 Remove the ignition discharge module as described in Chapter 5A.

⚠ **Warning:** *When the ignition discharge module is removed, it must be kept in the upright position. If the module has been turned upside down for a length of time, leave it in the fitted position for a couple of hours before starting.*

3 It is advisable to remove the dirt from the spark plug recesses using a clean brush, vacuum cleaner or compressed air before removing the plugs, to prevent dirt dropping into the cylinders.

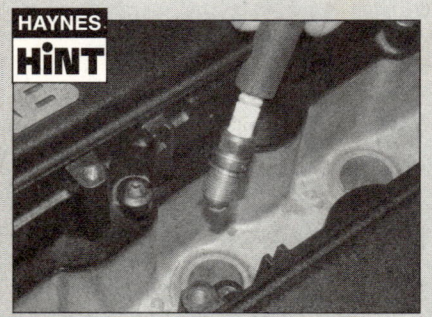

It is very often difficult to insert spark plugs into their holes without cross-threading them. To avoid this possibility, fit a short length of hose over the end of the spark plug.

4 Unscrew the plugs using a spark plug spanner or a deep socket and extension bar. Keep the socket aligned with the spark plug – if it is forcibly moved to one side, the ceramic insulator may be broken off.

5 Examination of the spark plugs will give a good indication of the condition of the engine. If the insulator nose of the spark plug is clean and white, with no deposits, this is indicative of a weak mixture or too hot a plug (a hot plug transfers heat away from the electrode slowly, a cold plug transfers heat away quickly).

6 If the tip and insulator nose are covered with hard black-looking deposits, then this is indicative that the mixture is too rich. Should the plug be black and oily, and then it is likely that the engine is fairly worn, as well as the mixture being too rich.

7 If the insulator nose is covered with light tan to greyish-brown deposits, then the mixture is correct, and it is likely that the engine is in good condition.

8 The electrode gap is of considerable importance as, if it is too large or too small, the size of the spark and its efficiency will be seriously impaired. The gap should be set to the value given in the Specifications.

9 To set the gap, measure it with a feeler blade or wire gauge and then bend open, or closed, the outer plug electrode until the correct gap is achieved. The centre electrode should never be bent, as this will crack the insulator and cause plug failure, if nothing worse. If using feeler blades, the gap is correct when the appropriate-size blade is a firm sliding fit. Note that some models may be fitted with multi-electrode spark plugs – no attempt to adjust the electrode gap should be made on this type of spark plug.

10 Special spark plug electrode gap adjusting tools are available from most motor accessory shops, or from some spark plug manufacturers.

11 Before fitting the spark plugs, check that the threaded connector sleeves are tight, and that the plug exterior surfaces and threads are clean. It is very often difficult to insert spark plugs into their holes without cross-threading them. To avoid this possibility, fit a short length of hose over the end of the spark plug **(see Haynes Hint)**.

12 Remove the rubber hose (if used), and tighten the plug to the specified torque (see Specifications) using the spark plug socket and a torque wrench. Refit the remaining plugs in the same way.

13 Refit the ignition discharge module with reference to Chapter 5A.

23 Manual transmission oil level – check

Note: *A suitable Allen key will be required to unscrew the manual transmission filler and level plugs. This can be obtained from most motor factors, or from your Saab dealer.*

1 Make sure that the car is parked on a level surface. Wipe clean the area around the level plug, which is located on the left hand side of the differential casing at the rear of the transmission, behind the left-hand driveshaft. Access to the plug can be gained from the engine compartment, or alternatively, apply the handbrake, then jack up the vehicle and support it on axle stands (see *Jacking and vehicle support*), but note that the vehicle must be level.

2 Unscrew the plug, using a suitable Allen key and wipe it clean **(see illustration)**. The oil level should reach the lower edge of the level hole. A certain amount of oil will have gathered behind the level plug, and will trickle out when it is removed; this does **not** necessarily indicate that the level is correct.

23.2 Unscrew the transmission oil level plug, using an Allen key

Every 36 000 miles – petrol engines 1A•13

23.3a The transmission oil filler plug is located at the top of the transmission casing

23.3b Unscrew the plug using an Allen key

23.4 Topping-up the transmission

To ensure that a true level is established, wait until the initial trickle has stopped, then use a length of clean wire, bent into a right angle, as a dipstick.

3 If the oil level requires topping-up, wipe clean the area around the filler plug, which is located on top of the transmission. Unscrew the plug, and wipe it clean **(see illustrations)**.

4 Add oil as necessary until a steady trickle of oil can be seen emerging from the level hole **(see illustration)**. Use **only** the specified grade of oil. A funnel will be helpful when adding oil to the transmission through the filler plug aperture.

5 When the level is correct, refit and tighten the filler plug (and where necessary, the level plug) to the specified torque wrench setting. Wipe off any spilt oil.

24 Air filter element – renewal

1 The air cleaner is located beneath the front right-hand wing, behind the front bumper, and the air inlet is taken from the front of the car behind the radiator grille area. For improved access to the filter, apply the handbrake, then jack up the front of the vehicle and support it on axle stands (see *Jacking and vehicle support*), then undo the single screw and pull aside the front bumper/spoiler.

2 Undo the screws and remove the cover together with filter element from the bottom

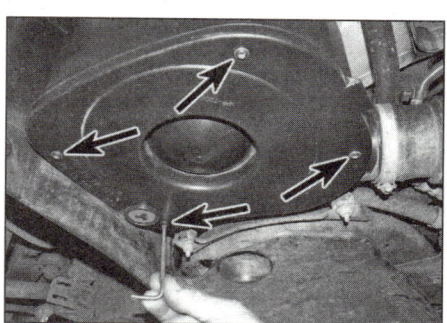
24.2a Undo the screws (arrowed) . . .

24.2b . . . then remove the cover and air filter element

of the air filter housing **(see illustrations)**. Recover the O-ring seal.

3 Note how the element is fitted, then remove it from the cover.

4 Wipe clean the inner surfaces of the cover and main housing.

5 Locate the new element on the cover, and then fit the cover complete with O-ring seal to the bottom of the housing. Insert and tighten the screws.

6 Lower the vehicle to the ground.

Every 3 years

25 Coolant – renewal

Note: *This work is not included in the Saab schedule, and should not be required if the recommended Saab antifreeze/inhibitor is used.*

⚠ **Warning: Do not allow antifreeze to come in contact with your skin or painted surfaces of the vehicle. Flush contaminated areas immediately with plenty of water. Don't store new coolant, or leave old coolant lying around, where it's accessible to children or pets – they're** attracted by its sweet smell. Ingestion of even a small amount of coolant can be fatal. Wipe up garage-floor and drip-pan spills immediately. Keep antifreeze containers covered, and repair cooling system leaks as soon as they're noticed.

⚠ **Warning: Never remove the expansion tank filler cap when the engine is running, or has just been switched off, as the cooling system will be hot, and the consequent escaping steam and scalding coolant could cause serious injury.**

⚠ **Warning: Wait until the engine is cold before starting these procedures.**

Cooling system draining

1 With the engine completely cold, remove the expansion tank filler cap. Turn the cap anti-clockwise, wait until any pressure remaining in the system is released, then unscrew it and lift it off.

2 Where applicable, remove the engine undershield, and then position a suitable container beneath the left-hand side of the radiator.

3 Loosen the drain plug located on the left-hand lower mounting stub **(see illustration)**, and allow the coolant to drain into the container. If necessary, attach a hose to the drain plug to direct the coolant into the container.

1A•14 Every 3 years – petrol engines

25.3 Radiator drain plug – arrowed

4 When the flow of coolant stops, tighten the drain plug and where necessary refit the undershield.
5 If the coolant has been drained for a reason other than renewal, then provided it is clean and less than two years old, it can be re-used, though this is not recommended.

Cooling system flushing

6 If coolant renewal has been neglected, or if the antifreeze mixture has become diluted, then in time the cooling system may gradually lose efficiency, as the coolant passages become restricted due to rust, scale deposits and other sediment. The cooling system efficiency can be restored by flushing the system clean.
7 The radiator should be flushed independently of the engine, to avoid unnecessary contamination.

Radiator flushing

8 Disconnect the top and bottom hoses and any other relevant hoses from the radiator, with reference to Chapter 3.
9 Insert a garden hose into the radiator top inlet. Direct a flow of clean water through the radiator, and continue flushing until clean water emerges from the radiator bottom outlet.
10 If after a reasonable period, the water still does not run clear, the radiator can be flushed with a good proprietary cleaning agent. It is important that the manufacturer's instructions are followed carefully. If the contamination is particularly bad, remove the radiator and insert the hose in the bottom outlet, and reverse-flush the radiator, then refit it.

Engine flushing

11 Remove the thermostat as described in Chapter 3, then temporarily refit the thermostat cover. If the radiator top hose has been disconnected, temporarily reconnect the hose.
12 With the top and bottom hoses disconnected from the radiator, insert a garden hose into the radiator top hose. Direct a clean flow of water through the engine, and continue flushing until clean water emerges from the radiator bottom hose.
13 On completion of flushing, refit the thermostat and reconnect the hoses with reference to Chapter 3.

Cooling system filling

14 Before attempting to fill the cooling system, make sure that all hoses and clips are in good condition, and that the clips are tight. Note that an antifreeze mixture must be used all year round, to prevent corrosion of the engine components.
15 Make sure that the air conditioning (A/C) or automatic climate control (ACC) is switched off. This is to prevent the air conditioning system starting the radiator cooling fan before the engine is at normal temperature when refilling the system.
16 Remove the expansion tank filler cap and slowly fill the system until the coolant level reaches the MAX mark on the side of the expansion tank.
17 Refit and tighten the expansion tank filler cap.
18 Start the engine and set the heater to hot, then run the engine until it reaches normal operating temperature (until the cooling fan cuts in and out). Running the engine at varying speeds will allow the engine to warm-up quickly.
19 Stop the engine, and allow it to cool, and then recheck the coolant level with reference to *Weekly checks*. Top-up the level if necessary and refit the expansion tank filler cap. Refit the splash cover beneath the radiator.

Antifreeze mixture

20 The antifreeze should always be renewed at the specified intervals. This is necessary not only to maintain the antifreeze properties, but also to prevent corrosion that would otherwise occur as the corrosion inhibitors become progressively less effective.
21 Always use an ethylene glycol based antifreeze, which is suitable for use in mixed-metal cooling systems. The quantity of antifreeze and levels of protection are given in the Specifications.
22 Before adding antifreeze, the cooling system should be completely drained, preferably flushed, and all hoses checked for condition and security.
23 After filling with antifreeze, a label should be attached to the expansion tank, stating the type and concentration of antifreeze used, and the date installed. Any subsequent topping-up should be made with the same type and concentration of antifreeze.
Caution: Do not use engine antifreeze in the windscreen/tailgate washer system, as it will cause damage to the vehicle paintwork. A screenwash additive should be added to the washer system in the quantities stated on the bottle.

Every 72 000 miles

26 Fuel filter – renewal

26.4 Removing the fuel filter plastic guard

⚠ *Warning: Before carrying out the following operation, refer to the precautions given in 'Safety first!' at the beginning of this manual, and follow them implicitly. Petrol is a highly dangerous and volatile liquid, and the precautions necessary when handling it cannot be overstressed.*

1 On all models, the fuel filter is mounted adjacent to the fuel tank underneath the rear of the car.
2 Depressurise the fuel system with reference to Chapter 4A.
3 Chock the front wheels, then jack up the rear of the car and support on axle stands (see *Jacking and vehicle support*).
4 Pull off the plastic guard where fitted, and then clean the areas around the fuel filter inlet and outlet unions **(see illustration)**.
5 Position a small container or cloth rags beneath the filter to catch spilt fuel.
6 On filters with banjo coupling bolts, unscrew the bolts from each end of the filter, while holding the coupling with a further spanner. Recover the sealing washers **(see illustrations)**.

26.6a Use two spanners to unscrew the banjo coupling bolts from each end of the fuel filter . . .

Every 72 000 miles – petrol engines   1A•15

26.6b ... and recover the sealing washers

26.7a Fit special tool around filter outlet pipe ...

26.7b ... pull the tool into the fuel hose connection ...

26.7c ... and release the hose

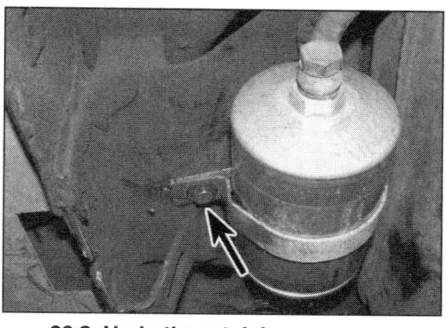
26.8 Undo the retaining screw ...

26.9 ... and remove the fuel filter

7 On filters with push-on connections, a special tool will be required to release the locking clips inside the hose connections. Fit tool around the fuel filter outlet pipe and slide it along to release the locking clips inside the hose **(see illustrations)**. Repeat the procedure at the other side of the filter.
8 Undo the mounting clamp securing screw **(see illustration)**.
9 Remove the filter from its mounting bracket, noting the direction of the arrow marked on the filter body, loosen the retaining clip and withdraw the filter from under the car **(see illustration)**.
10 Locate the new filter in the retaining clip, and then fit and tighten the securing screw. Make sure that the direction of flow arrow on the filter body is pointing towards the outlet, which leads to the engine compartment **(see illustration)**.
11 On filters with banjo coupling bolts,

check the condition of the sealing washers, and renew them if necessary. Refit the banjo couplings and hoses to each end of the filter, together with the sealing washers. Tighten the bolts securely, while holding the couplings with a second spanner.
12 On filters with push-on connections, refit the couplings/hoses to each end of the filter, press the hoses firmly onto the filter outlet and inlet pipes, making sure the retaining clips have secured correctly.
13 Wipe away any excess fuel, refit the plastic cover where fitted, then lower the car to the ground.
14 Start the engine, and check the filter hose connections for leaks.
15 The old filter should be disposed of safely, bearing in mind that it will be highly inflammable.

27 Auxiliary drivebelt – renewal

1 Apply the handbrake. Open the bonnet and unclip the engine upper cover panel (where fitted) from above the intake manifold, then slacken its two retaining clips and withdraw the mass airflow sensor's rubber intake hose; cover the sensor's intake to prevent the entry of dirt or other foreign matter into the intake tract **(see illustration)**. Jack up the front of the car and support it on axle stands (see *Jacking and vehicle support*). Remove the right-hand front roadwheel, then

undo the retaining screws and withdraw the lower section of the plastic liner from under the right-hand wheel arch and the wheel arch liner itself as necessary to expose the crankshaft pulley and drivebelt. Unbolt the clip securing the power steering pipe to the subframe, immediately beneath the crankshaft pulley.
2 Position a trolley jack underneath the engine and raise the jack head until it is just taking the weight of the engine. Ensure that the jack head does not bear on the underside of the sump; place a block of wood between the sump and the jack head. Alternatively, position a lifting beam across the engine bay and support the engine by the lifting eyelet located at the rear right-hand side of the cylinder head. Unbolt the engine right-hand mounting bracket from the engine and remove the retaining nut on top of the engine mounting **(see illustration)**. Withdraw the engine mounting bracket,

26.10 Make sure that the direction of flow arrow on the filter body is pointing towards the engine compartment

27.1 Slacken the retaining screws (arrows) and withdraw the rubber intake hose ...

1A•16 Every 72 000 miles – petrol engines

27.2 ... remove engine mounting bracket (nut and bolts arrowed) to reach auxiliary drivebelt and tensioner

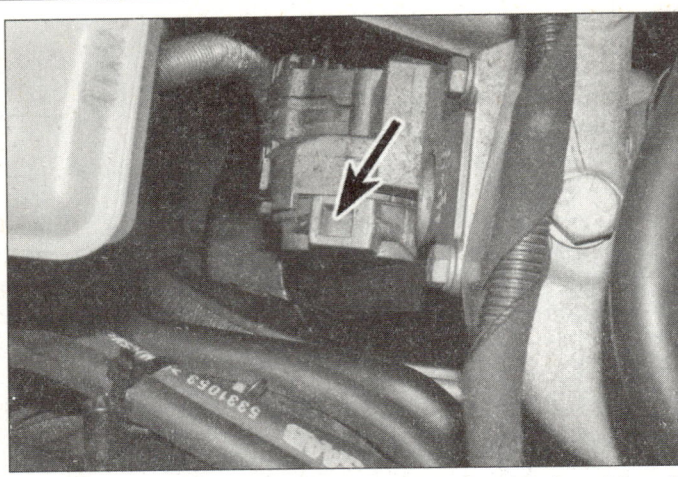

27.3a Insert a 1/2 in drive straight extension bar into lug at top of outboard (moving) part of tensioner ...

27.3b ... and rotate tensioner against spring tension until hole in stop lug aligns with hole in inboard (fixed) part of tensioner

27.4 Insert 3 mm drill bit (or similar) to lock tensioner assembly in position

releasing the power steering hose from its retaining clip underneath.

3 The tensioner pulley spring must now be compressed and locked in position. Insert a 1/2 in drive straight extension bar or similar into the square hole in the lug at the top of the outboard (moving) part of the tensioner assembly. Rotate the tensioner clockwise, against the spring tension, until the hole in the stop lug lines up with the corresponding hole in the inboard (fixed) part of the tensioner assembly. Note that the tensioner spring is very strong, and considerable pressure is required to compress it, but do not try to force it beyond the limit of its travel, or allow it to snap back against spring pressure; it will break **(see illustrations)**.

4 Hold the tensioner in that position and slide a 3 mm Allen key (or drill bit) through the holes in the stop lug and in the inboard (fixed) part of the tensioner assembly **(see illustration)**. Release slowly the effort on the straight extension bar, checking that the tensioner remains locked in position.

5 Slip the drivebelt from the pulleys and remove it **(see illustration)**. Carefully check the pulleys (particularly the tensioner and idlers) and renew any that are damaged or that show signs of roughness or jerkiness when rotated **(see illustrations)**.

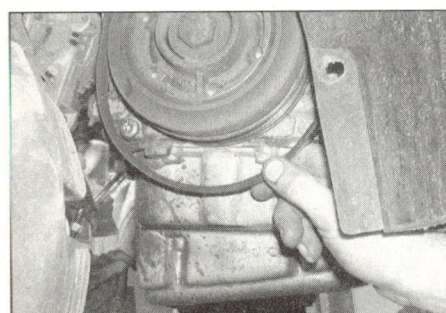

27.5a Removing the auxiliary drivebelt from the crankshaft pulley

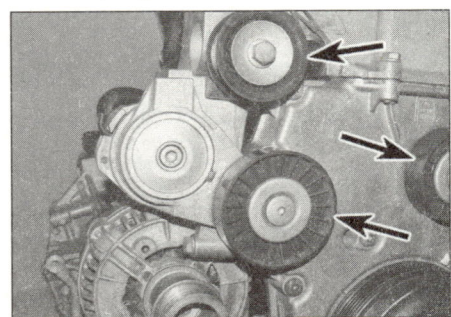

27.5b Check carefully tensioner and idler pulleys ...

27.5c ... and renew any that are damaged or that rotate roughly or jerkily

Every 72 000 miles – petrol engines

27.6 Auxiliary drivebelt correctly routed

28.2 Automatic transmission drain plug

Note: *A shorter drivebelt is found on later vehicles, running straight from the upper idler (item 3) to the power steering pump pulley (item 5) – the lower, or centre, idler pulley (item 4) having been deleted.*

1 Alternator
2 Tensioner
3 Upper idler pulley
4 Lower/centre idler pulley (where fitted)
5 Power steering pump
6 Coolant pump
7 Air conditioning compressor
8 Crankshaft pulley

6 On refitting, route the drivebelt over all the pulleys as shown, making sure that, where applicable, the multi-grooved side is correctly engaged with the pulley grooves **(see illustration)**. **Note:** *A shorter drivebelt is found on later vehicles.*

7 Compress the tensioner spring as described for the removal procedure. Remove the locking tool and then slowly release the tensioner, allowing it to apply pressure to the drivebelt.

8 Ensure that the belt is correctly seated on all the pulleys, and then refit the engine right-hand mounting bracket, clipping the power steering hose on its underside and tightening its nut and bolts to the torque wrench settings specified (see Chapter 2A). Tighten securely the bolt securing the power steering hose clip to the subframe, and then refit the plastic wheel arch liner and its lower section. Refit the roadwheel and lower the car to the ground. Uncover the mass airflow sensor and refit its rubber intake hose, then refit the engine upper cover panel to the intake manifold.

9 On completion, start the engine and allow it to idle for a few minutes. This will allow the tensioner to settle in position and distribute the tension evenly throughout the belt. Stop the engine and check once again that the belt is correctly seated on all the pulleys.

28 Automatic transmission fluid – renewal

1 Take the car on a short journey to warm the transmission up to normal operating temperature. Position the car over an inspection pit, or alternatively jack up the front and rear of the car and support on axle stands (see *Jacking and vehicle support*). Whichever method is used, make sure that the car is level for checking the fluid level later. Where fitted, undo the fasteners and remove the engine under shield.

2 Position a suitable container beneath the transmission, then unscrew the drain plug and allow the fluid to drain **(see illustration)**. Note that a special adapter key will be required to unscrew the plug.

⚠ **Warning:** *The fluid will be very hot, so take necessary precautions to prevent scalding. The use of thick waterproof gloves is recommended.*

3 With all the fluid drained, wipe clean the plug and refit it to the automatic transmission housing. Where applicable, fit a new sealing washer to the drain plug. Tighten the plug to the specified torque.

4 Fill the automatic transmission with the specified grade and quantity of fluid. Referring to Section 14, top it up to the correct level. Use the low temperature set of dipstick markings first, then take the car for a run. With the fluid at operating temperature, recheck the fluid level using the high temperature set of dipstick markings.

Every 4 years

29 Brake fluid – renewal

⚠ **Warning:** *Brake hydraulic fluid can harm your eyes and damage painted surfaces, so use extreme caution when handling and pouring it. Do not use fluid that has been standing open for some time, as it absorbs moisture from the air. Excess moisture can cause a dangerous loss of braking effectiveness.*

1 The procedure is similar to that for the bleeding of the hydraulic system as described in Chapter 9.

2 Working as described in Chapter 9, open the first bleed screw in the sequence, and pump the brake pedal gently until nearly all the old fluid has been emptied from the master cylinder reservoir. Top-up to the MAX level with new fluid, and continue pumping until only the new fluid remains in the reservoir, and new fluid can be seen emerging from the

bleed screw. Tighten the screw, and top the reservoir level up to the MAX level line.
3 Work through all the remaining bleed screws in the sequence until new fluid can be seen at all of them. Be careful to keep the master cylinder reservoir topped-up to above the MIN level at all times, or air may enter the system and greatly increase the length of the task.
4 When the operation is complete, check that all bleed screws are securely tightened, and that their dust caps are refitted. Wash off all traces of spilt fluid, and recheck the master cylinder reservoir fluid level.
5 Check the operation of the brakes before taking the car on the road.

Chapter 1 Part B:
Routine maintenance and servicing – diesel models

Contents

	Section number
Air conditioning drain hoses – check	20
Air filter element – renewal	23
Airbag system – check	9
Automatic transmission fluid – renewal	26
Automatic transmission fluid level – check	14
Auxiliary drivebelt – renewal	27
Auxiliary drivebelt condition – check	21
Brake fluid – renewal	29
Brake pad wear – check	17
Coolant – renewal	28
Coolant antifreeze concentration – check	13
Driveshaft joints and gaiters – check	15
Engine oil and filter – renewal	3
Exhaust system – check	16
Fuel filter – renewal	22

	Section number
General information	1
Handbrake – check and adjustment	7
Headlight beam alignment – check	10
Hinges and locks – lubrication	18
Hoses and fluids – leak check	5
Manual transmission fluid level – check	24
Pollen filter – renewal	19
Power steering fluid level – check	11
Regular maintenance	2
Road test	12
Seat belt condition – check	8
Service indicator – resetting	4
Steering and suspension components – check	6
Timing belt renewal	25

Degrees of difficulty

| Easy, suitable for novice with little experience | Fairly easy, suitable for beginner with some experience | Fairly difficult, suitable for competent DIY mechanic | Difficult, suitable for experienced DIY mechanic | Very difficult, suitable for expert DIY or professional |

Servicing specifications – diesel engines

Lubricants and fluids
See end of Weekly checks on page 0•16

Capacities

Engine oil
Drain and refill, with filter change............................ 4.3 litres
Between dipstick MAX and MIN markings..................... 1.0 litres

Cooling system.. 8.0 litres

Transmission
Manual:
    Drain and refill.. 1.5 litres
    Total from dry... 1.9 litres
Automatic:
    Drain and refill.. 3.5 litres
    Total from dry (including torque converter and cooler)........ 7.0 litres

Braking system
System capacity... 0.9 litres

Power-assisted steering
System capacity... 1.3 litres

Fuel tank... 72.0 litres (15.8 gallons)

Cooling system
Antifreeze mixture:*
  50% antifreeze.. Protection down to -37°C
  55% antifreeze.. Protection down to -45°C
* Note: Coolant from Saab dealers is premixed with water at the correct ratio.

Brakes
Brake pad friction material minimum thickness................... 4.0 mm at time of service (acoustic warning at 3.0 mm)

Tyre pressures
Refer to the end of Weekly checks on page 0•16

Torque wrench settings

	Nm	lbf ft
Automatic transmission drain plug	40	30
Engine oil filter cover	25	18
Engine oil sump drain plug	25	18
Fuel filter	20	15
Manual transmission level/filler plug	50	37
Wheel bolts	110	81

Maintenance schedule – diesel engines 1B•3

The maintenance intervals in this manual are provided with the assumption that you will be carrying out the work yourself. These are the minimum maintenance intervals recommended by the manufacturer for vehicles driven daily. If you wish to keep your vehicle in peak condition at all times, you may wish to perform some of these procedures more often. We encourage frequent maintenance, because it enhances the efficiency, performance and resale value of your vehicle.

If the vehicle is driven in dusty areas, used to tow a trailer, or driven frequently at slow speeds (idling in traffic) or on short journeys, more frequent maintenance intervals are recommended.

When the vehicle is new, it should be serviced by a dealer service department (or other workshop recognised by the vehicle manufacturer as providing the same standard of service) in order to preserve the warranty. The vehicle manufacturer may reject warranty claims if you are unable to prove that servicing has been carried out as and when specified, using only original equipment parts or parts certified to be of equivalent quality.

All Saab models are equipped with a service interval display (or Saab Information Display – SID) on the facia, which will indicate TIME FOR SERVICE when a service is due. However, Saab point out that, 'due to the relationship between time and mileage, some operating conditions will make annual service more suitable'.

Every 250 miles or weekly
☐ Refer to Weekly checks

Every 9000 miles
☐ Engine oil and filter – renewal (Section 3)

Note: *Frequent oil and filter changes are good for the engine. We recommend changing the oil at the mileage specified here, or at least annually if the mileage covered is less.*

Every 18 000 miles
☐ Service indicator – resetting (Section 4)
☐ Hoses and fluids – leak check (Section 5)
☐ Steering and suspension components – check (Section 6)
☐ Handbrake – check and adjustment (Section 7)
☐ Seat belt condition – check (Section 8)
☐ Airbag system – check (Section 9)
☐ Headlight beam alignment – check (Section 10)
☐ Power steering fluid level – check (Section 11)
☐ Road test (Section 12)
☐ Coolant antifreeze concentration – check (Section 13)
☐ Automatic transmission fluid level – check (Section 14)
☐ Driveshaft joints and gaiters – check (Section 15)
☐ Exhaust system – check (Section 16)
☐ Brake pad wear – check (Section 17)
☐ Hinges and locks – lubrication (Section 18)
☐ Pollen air filter – renewal (Section 19)
☐ Air conditioning drain hoses – check (Section 20)
☐ Auxiliary drivebelt condition – check (Section 21)
☐ Fuel filter – renewal (Section 22)

Every 36 000 miles
☐ Air filter element – renewal (Section 23)
☐ Manual transmission fluid level – check (Section 24)

Every 72 000 miles
☐ Timing belt – renewal (Section 25)

Note: *Saab recommend that the interval for timing belt renewal is 72 000 miles or 6 years. However, if the vehicle is used mainly for short journeys or a lot of stop-start driving it is recommended that the renewal interval is shortened. The actual belt renewal interval is very much up to the individual owner but, bearing in mind that severe engine damage will result if the belt breaks in use, we recommend you err on the side of caution.*

☐ Automatic transmission fluid – renewal (Section 26)
☐ Auxiliary drivebelt – renewal (Section 27)

Every 3 years
☐ Coolant – renewal (Section 28)

Note: *This work is not included in the Saab schedule, and should not be required if the recommended Saab antifreeze/inhibitor is used.*

Every 4 years
☐ Brake fluid – renewal (Section 29)

1B•4 Component locations – diesel engines

Underbonnet view

1. Engine oil level dipstick
2. Engine oil filler cap
3. Coolant expansion tank
4. Air cleaner assembly
5. Brake (and clutch) fluid reservoir
6. Mass airflow meter
7. Battery
8. Power steering fluid
9. Fusebox
10. Common (fuel) rail
11. Windscreen washer fluid
12. ABS unit

Front underbody view

1. Engine oil sump drain plug
2. Engine oil filter
3. Exhaust front pipe
4. Front suspension/engine subframe
5. Exhaust mounting rubbers
6. Front lower arm
7. Steering track rod ends
8. Front brake caliper
9. Air filter housing
10. Windscreen washer fluid reservoir
11. Air conditioning compressor
12. Intermediate driveshaft

Component locations – diesel engines 1B•5

Rear underbody view

1. Rear suspension crossmember
2. Rear anti-roll bar
3. Rear suspension lower transverse link
4. Brake hydraulic flexible hoses
5. Handbrake cables
6. Fuel tank
7. Rear suspension trailing arms
8. Rear suspension strut/shock absorbers
9. Exhaust rear silencer and tailpipe

Maintenance procedures

1 General information

1 This Chapter is designed to help the home mechanic maintain his/her vehicle for safety, economy, long life and peak performance.
2 The Chapter contains a master maintenance schedule, followed by Sections dealing specifically with each task in the schedule. Visual checks, adjustments, component renewal and other helpful items are included. Refer to the accompanying illustrations of the engine compartment and the underside of the vehicle for the locations of the various components.
3 Servicing your vehicle in accordance with the mileage/time maintenance schedule and the following Sections will provide a planned maintenance programme, which should result in a long and reliable service life. This is a comprehensive plan, so maintaining some items, but not others, at the specified service intervals will not produce the same results.
4 As you service your vehicle, you will discover that many of the procedures can – and should – be grouped together, because of the particular procedure being performed, or because of the close proximity of two otherwise-unrelated components to one another. For example, if the vehicle is raised for any reason, the exhaust system could be inspected at the same time as the suspension and steering components.
5 The first step in this maintenance programme is to prepare yourself before the actual work begins. Read through all the Sections relevant to the work to be carried out, then make a list and gather together all the parts and tools required. If a problem is encountered, seek advice from a parts specialist, or a dealer service department.

2 Regular maintenance

1 If, from the time the vehicle is new, the routine maintenance schedule is followed closely, and frequent checks are made of fluid levels and high-wear items, as suggested throughout this manual, the engine will be kept in relatively good running condition, and the need for additional work will be minimised.
2 It is possible that there will be times when the engine is running poorly due to the lack of regular maintenance. This is even more likely if a used vehicle, which has not received regular and frequent maintenance checks, is purchased. In such cases, additional work may need to be carried out, outside of the regular maintenance intervals.
3 If engine wear is suspected, a compression test (refer to Chapter 2B) will provide valuable information regarding the overall performance of the main internal components. Such a test can be used as a basis to decide on the extent of the work to be carried out. If, for example, a compression test indicates serious internal engine wear, conventional maintenance as described in this Chapter will not greatly improve the performance of the engine, and may prove a waste of time and money, unless extensive overhaul work (Chapter 2C) is carried out first.
4 The following series of operations are those most often required to improve the performance of a generally poor-running engine:

Primary operations

a) Clean, inspect and test the battery ('Weekly checks' and Chapter 5A)
b) Check all the engine-related fluids ('Weekly checks').
c) Check the condition and tension of the auxiliary drivebelt (Section 21).
d) Check the condition of the air filter element, and renew if necessary (Section 23).
e) Renew the fuel filter (Section 22).
f) Check the condition of all hoses, and check for fluid leaks (Section 5).

Secondary operations

5 If the above operations do not prove fully effective, carry out the following secondary operations:

a) Check the charging system (Chapter 5A).
b) Check the fuel system (Chapter 4B).

1B•6 Maintenance procedures – diesel engines

3.5a The engine oil drain plug is located at the rear of the sump (arrowed)

3.5b Unscrew the plug and allow the oil to drain

3.7 Refit the drain plug with a new sealing washer

Every 9000 miles

3 Engine oil and filter – renewal

1 Frequent oil changes are the most important preventative maintenance the DIY home mechanic can give the engine, because ageing oil becomes diluted and contaminated, which leads to premature engine wear.
2 Before starting this procedure, gather together all the necessary tools and materials. Also make sure that you have plenty of clean rags and newspapers handy, to mop-up any spills. Ideally, the engine oil should be warm, as it will drain better, and more built-up sludge will be removed with it. Take care, however, not to touch the exhaust or any other hot parts of the engine when working under the vehicle. To avoid any possibility of scalding, and to protect yourself from possible skin irritants and other harmful contaminants in used engine oils, it is advisable to wear gloves when carrying out this work.
3 Apply the handbrake, then jack up the front of the vehicle and support it on axle stands (see *Jacking and vehicle support*).
4 Where applicable, undo the fasteners and remove the engine undershield.
5 The engine oil drain plug is located on the rear of the sump; slacken the plug about half a turn. Position the draining container under the drain plug, then remove the plug completely – recover the sealing washer **(see illustrations)**.
6 Allow some time for the old oil to drain, noting that it may be necessary to reposition the container as the oil flow slows to a trickle.
7 After all the oil has drained, wipe off the drain plug with a clean rag. Clean the area around the drain plug opening, and refit the plug with a new O-ring seal. Tighten the plug to the specified torque **(see illustration)**.
8 Position the container under the oil filter housing, then slacken the filter housing cover a few turns, using a 32 mm socket, and allow the oil to drain into the container. On some models, to prevent the oil contacting the exhaust system, the filter housing has a drain tube on the side. Attach a length of hose to the drain tube on the filter housing **(see illustrations)**.
9 When the oil has finished draining, completely unscrew and remove the oil filter cover along with the filter element. Discard the cover O-ring seals, new ones must be fitted.
10 Use a clean rag to remove all oil, dirt and sludge from the filter housing and cover.
11 Fit the new filter element to the filter housing, and the O-ring seals to the filter cover **(see illustrations)**.
12 Apply a light coating of clean engine oil to the O-ring seal on the filter cover, then fit the element and cover into the housing, and tighten it to the specified torque **(see illustration)**. Lower the vehicle to the ground.
13 Remove the oil filler cap and withdraw the level dipstick from the tube. Fill the engine, using the correct oil (see *Lubricants and fluids*). An oil can spout or funnel may help to reduce

3.8a Unscrew the housing cap (arrowed) a few turns with a 32 mm socket . . .

3.8b . . . and allow the oil to drain through the hose before removing the cap

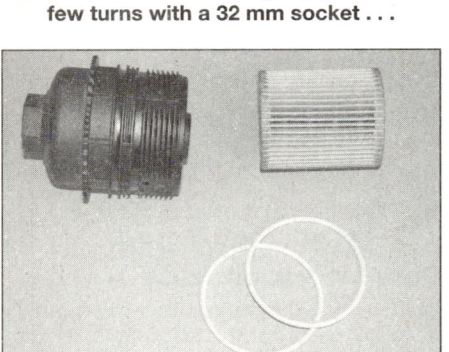

3.11a The new oil filter should be supplied with new O-ring seals

3.11b Fit the new filter into the housing . . .

3.11c . . . and the new O-rings seals to the housing cap

Every 9000 miles – diesel engines 1B•7

spillage. Pour in half the specified quantity of oil first, and then wait a few minutes for the oil to run to the sump. Continue adding oil a small quantity at a time until the level is up to the lower mark on the dipstick. Adding a further 1.0 litre will bring the level up to the upper mark on the dipstick. Insert the dipstick, and refit the filler cap **(see illustration)**.

14 Start the engine and run it for a few minutes; check for leaks around the oil filter seal and the sump drain plug. Note that there may be a delay of a few seconds before the oil pressure warning light goes out when the engine is first started, as the oil circulates through the engine oil galleries and the new oil filter, before the pressure builds-up.

15 Switch off the engine, and wait a few minutes for the oil to settle in the sump once more. With the new oil circulated and the

3.12 Fit the cap with the O-rings to the housing

filter completely full, recheck the level on the dipstick, and add more oil as necessary.
16 If removed, refit the engine undershield.

3.13 The difference between the upper and lower marks on the dipstick is approximately 1.0 litre

17 Dispose of the used engine oil safely, in accordance with the guidance given in *General repair procedures*.

Every 18 000 miles

4 Service indicator – resetting

1 The facia-mounted SID (Saab Information Display) system incorporates a service interval indicator. When the distance covered between services approaches the next service, a visual message is displayed, 'Time for service. Contact service'. The service indicator is then manually reset to zero by the technician, after the vehicle has been serviced. **Note:** *The indicator is automatically reset after the message has been displayed 20 times.*

2 To manually reset the service indicator, press and hold the CLEAR button on the SID panel for 8 seconds, you will hear two beeps in quick succession, and then release it. The SERVICE message will start to flash, this means the service interval is reset.

3 The indicator can be reset at any time by a technician, using the Saab diagnostic tool.

5 Hoses and fluids – leak check

Cooling system

⚠ *Warning: Refer to the safety information given in 'Safety first!' and Chapter 3 before disturbing any of the cooling system components.*

1 Carefully check the radiator and heater coolant hoses along their entire length. Renew any hose which is cracked, swollen or which shows signs of deterioration. Cracks will show up better if the hose is squeezed. Pay close attention to the clips that secure the hoses to the cooling system components. Hose clips that have been overtightened can pinch and puncture hoses, resulting in cooling system leaks.

2 Inspect all the cooling system components (hoses, joint faces, etc) for leaks. Where any problems of this nature are found on system components, renew the component or gasket with reference to Chapter 3 **(see Haynes Hint)**.

Fuel system

⚠ *Warning: Refer to the safety information given in 'Safety first!' and Chapter 4B before disturbing any of the fuel system components.*

3 Diesel leaks can be difficult to pinpoint, unless the leakage is significant and hence easily visible. Fuel tends to evaporate once it comes into contact with air, especially in a hot engine bay. Small drips can disappear before you get a chance to identify the point of leakage. If you suspect that there is a fuel leak from the area of the engine bay, leave the vehicle overnight then start the engine from cold, with the bonnet open. Metal components tend to shrink when they are cold, and rubber seals and hoses tend to harden, so any leaks will be more apparent whilst the engine is warming-up from a cold start.

4 Check all fuel lines at their connections to the fuel pump, common rail and fuel filter. Examine each rubber fuel hose along its length for splits or cracks. Check for leakage from the crimped joints between rubber and metal fuel lines. Examine the unions between the metal fuel lines and the fuel filter housing. Also check the area around the fuel injectors for signs of O-ring leakage.

5 To identify fuel leaks between the fuel tank and the engine bay, the vehicle should be raised and securely supported on axle stands (see *Jacking and vehicle support*). Inspect the petrol tank and filler neck for punctures, cracks and other damage. The connection between the filler neck and tank is especially critical. Sometimes a rubber filler neck or connecting hose will leak due to loose retaining clamps or deteriorated rubber.

6 Carefully check all rubber hoses and metal fuel lines leading away from the petrol tank. Check for loose connections, deteriorated hoses, kinked lines, and other damage. Pay particular attention to the vent pipes and hoses, which often loop up around the filler neck and can become blocked or kinked, making tank filling difficult. Follow the fuel supply and return lines to the front of the vehicle, carefully inspecting them all the way for signs of damage or corrosion. Renew damaged sections as necessary.

Engine oil

7 Inspect the area around the camshaft cover, cylinder head, oil filter and sump joint faces. Bear in mind that, over a period of time, some very slight seepage from these areas is to be expected – what you are really looking for is any indication of a serious leak

A leak in the cooling system will usually show up as white- or antifreeze-coloured deposits on the area adjoining the leak.

1B•8 Every 18 000 miles – diesel engines

caused by gasket failure. Engine oil seeping from the base of the timing belt cover or the transmission bellhousing may be an indication of crankshaft or transmission input shaft oil seal failure. Should a leak be found, renew the failed gasket or oil seal by referring to the appropriate Chapters in this manual.

Automatic transmission fluid

8 Where applicable, check the hoses leading to the transmission fluid cooler at the front of the engine bay for leakage. Look for deterioration caused by corrosion and damage from grounding, or debris thrown up from the road surface. Automatic transmission fluid is thin oil and is usually red in colour.

Power-assisted steering fluid

9 Examine the hose running between the fluid reservoir and the power steering pump, and the return hose running from the steering rack to the fluid reservoir. Also examine the high-pressure supply hose between the pump and the steering rack.
10 Check the condition of each hose carefully. Look for deterioration caused by corrosion and damage from grounding, or debris thrown up from the road surface.
11 Pay particular attention to crimped unions, and the area surrounding the hoses that are secured with adjustable worm-drive clips. Like automatic transmission fluid, PAS fluid is thin oil, and is usually red in colour.

Air conditioning refrigerant

 Warning: Refer to the safety information given in 'Safety first!' and Chapter 3 regarding the dangers of disturbing any of the air conditioning system components.

12 The air conditioning system is filled with a liquid refrigerant, which is retained under high pressure. If the air conditioning system is opened and depressurised without the aid of specialised equipment, the refrigerant will immediately turn into gas and escape into the atmosphere. If the liquid comes into contact with your skin, it can cause severe frostbite. In addition, the refrigerant contains substances that are environmentally damaging; for this reason, it should not be allowed to escape into the atmosphere in an uncontrolled fashion.

6.4 Check for wear in the hub bearings by grasping the wheel and trying to rock it

13 Any suspected air conditioning system leaks should be immediately referred to a Saab dealer or air conditioning specialist. Leakage will be shown up as a steady drop in the level of refrigerant in the system.
14 Note that water may drip from the condenser drain pipe, underneath the car, immediately after the air conditioning system has been in use. This is normal, and should not be cause for concern.

Brake (and clutch) fluid

Warning: Refer to the safety information given in 'Safety first!' and Chapter 9 regarding the dangers of handling brake fluid.

15 With reference to Chapter 9, examine the area surrounding the brake pipe unions at the master cylinder for signs of leakage. Check the area around the base of fluid reservoir, for signs of leakage caused by seal failure. Also examine the brake pipe unions at the ABS hydraulic unit.
16 If fluid loss is evident, but the leak cannot be pinpointed in the engine bay, the brake calipers and underbody brake lines should be carefully checked with the vehicle raised and supported on axle stands (see *Jacking and vehicle support*). Leakage of fluid from the braking system is a serious fault that must be rectified immediately.
17 Brake/clutch hydraulic fluid is a toxic substance with a watery consistency. New fluid is almost colourless, but it becomes darker with age and use.

Unidentified fluid leaks

18 If there are signs that a fluid of some description is leaking from the vehicle, but you cannot identify the type of fluid or its exact origin, park the vehicle overnight and slide a large piece of card underneath it. Providing that the card is positioned in roughly the right location, even the smallest leak will show up on the card. Not only will this help you to pinpoint the exact location of the leak, it should be easier to identify the fluid from its colour. Bear in mind, though, that the leak may only be occurring when the engine is running!

Vacuum hoses

19 Although the braking system is hydraulically-operated, the brake servo unit amplifies the effort applied at the brake pedal by making use of the vacuum in the intake manifold generated by the engine and supplemented by the vacuum pump driven by the exhaust camshaft. Vacuum is ported to the servo by means of a large-bore hose. Any leaks that develop in this hose will reduce the effectiveness of the braking system, and may affect the running of the engine.
20 In addition, a number of the underbonnet components, particularly the emission control components, are driven by vacuum supplied from the intake manifold via narrow-bore hoses. A leak in a vacuum hose means that

air is being drawn into the hose (rather than escaping from it) and this makes leakage very difficult to detect. One method is to use an old length of vacuum hose as a kind of stethoscope – hold one end close to (but not in) your ear and use the other end to probe the area around the suspected leak. When the end of the hose is directly over a vacuum leak, a hissing sound will be heard clearly through the hose. Care must be taken to avoid contacting hot or moving components when testing in this manner, as the engine must be running. Renew any vacuum hoses that are found to be defective.

6 Steering and suspension components – check

Front suspension and steering

1 Raise the front of the vehicle, and securely support it on axle stands (see *Jacking and vehicle support*).
2 Visually inspect the balljoint dust covers and the steering rack-and-pinion gaiters for splits, chafing or deterioration. Any wear of these components will cause loss of lubricant, together with dirt and water entry, resulting in rapid deterioration of the balljoints or steering gear.
3 Check the power steering fluid hoses for chafing or deterioration, and the pipe and hose unions for fluid leaks. Also check for signs of fluid leakage under pressure from the steering gear rubber gaiters, which would indicate failed fluid seals within the steering gear.
4 Grasp the roadwheel at the 12 o'clock and 6 o'clock positions, and try to rock it **(see illustration)**. Very slight free play may be felt, but if the movement is appreciable, further investigation is necessary to determine the source. Continue rocking the wheel while an assistant depresses the footbrake. If the movement is now eliminated or significantly reduced, it is likely that the hub bearings are at fault. If the free play is still evident with the footbrake depressed, then there is wear in the suspension joints or mountings.
5 Now grasp the wheel at the 9 o'clock and 3 o'clock positions, and try to rock it as before. Any movement felt now may again be caused by wear in the hub bearings or the steering track rod balljoints. If the outer balljoint is worn, the visual movement will be obvious. If the inner joint is suspect, it can be felt by placing a hand over the rack-and-pinion rubber gaiter and gripping the track rod. If the wheel is now rocked, movement will be felt at the inner joint if wear has taken place.
6 Using a large screwdriver or flat bar, check for wear in the suspension mounting bushes by levering between the relevant suspension component and its attachment point. Some movement is to be expected, as the mountings are made of rubber, but excessive

Every 18 000 miles – diesel engines

wear should be obvious. Also check the condition of any visible rubber bushes, looking for splits, cracks or contamination of the rubber.

7 With the car standing on its wheels, have an assistant turn the steering wheel back-and-forth, about an eighth of a turn each way. There should be very little, if any, lost movement between the steering wheel and roadwheels. If this is not the case, closely observe the joints and mountings previously described. In addition, check the steering column universal joints for wear, and also check the rack-and-pinion steering gear itself.

8 The front suspension mountings should be checked for tightness.

Rear suspension

9 Chock the front wheels, then jack up the rear of the vehicle and support securely on axle stands (see *Jacking and vehicle support*).
10 Working as described previously for the front suspension, check the rear hub bearings, the suspension bushes and the strut or shock absorber mountings (as applicable) for wear.
11 The rear suspension mountings should be checked for tightness.

Shock absorber

12 Check for any signs of fluid leakage around the shock absorber bodies, or from the rubber gaiters around the piston rods. Should any fluid be noticed, the shock absorber is defective internally, and should be renewed.
Note: *Shock absorbers should always be renewed in pairs on the same axle.*
13 The efficiency of the shock absorber may be checked by bouncing the vehicle at each corner. Generally speaking, the body will return to its normal position and stop after being depressed. If it rises and returns on a rebound, the shock absorber is probably suspect. Also examine the shock absorber upper and lower mountings for any signs of wear.

Removable towbar attachment

14 Where applicable, clean the coupling pin then apply a little grease to the socket. Make sure that the removable towbar attachment fits easily to its mounting and locks correctly in position.

7 Handbrake – check and adjustment

1 Chock the front wheels, then jack up the rear of the vehicle and support on axle stands (see *Jacking and vehicle support*).
2 Fully release the handbrake lever.
3 Apply the lever to the 4th notch position, and check that both rear wheels are locked when attempting to turn them by hand.
4 If adjustment is necessary, refer to Chapter 9.
5 Lower the vehicle to the ground.

11.1 Power steering fluid reservoir

8 Seat belt condition – check

1 Working on each seat belt in turn, carefully examine the seat belt webbing for cuts, or for any signs of serious fraying or deterioration. Pull the belt all the way out, and examine the full extent of the webbing.
2 Fasten and unfasten the belt, ensuring that the locking mechanism holds securely, and releases properly when intended. Check also that the retracting mechanism operates correctly when the belt is released.
3 Check the security of all seat belt mountings and attachments which are accessible, without removing any trim or other components, from inside the vehicle.
4 Check the function of the seat belt reminder lamp.

9 Airbag system – check

1 The following work can be carried out by the home mechanic, however, if an electronic fault is apparent, it will be necessary to take the car to a Saab dealer or specialist, who will have the necessary diagnostic equipment to extract fault codes from the system.
2 Turn the ignition switch to the drive position (ignition warning lights on), and check that the SRS (Supplementary Restraint System) warning light is illuminated for 3 to 4 seconds. After this period the light should go out, indicating that the system has been checked and is functioning correctly.
3 If the warning light remains on or refuses to light, have the system checked by a Saab dealer or specialist.
4 Visually examine the steering wheel centre pad and the passenger airbag module for external damage. Also check the exterior of the front seats around the side airbag locations. If damage is evident, consult a Saab dealer or specialist.
5 In the interests of safety, make sure that there are no loose items inside the car that could be thrown onto the airbag modules in the event of an accident.

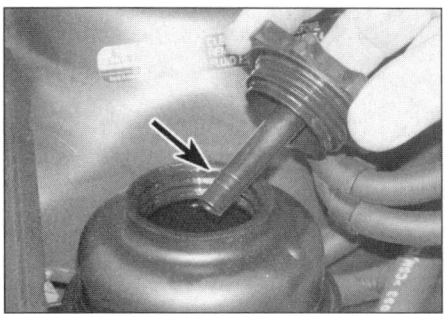
11.3 Fluid level marks on the dipstick

10 Headlight beam alignment – check

Refer to Chapter 12 for details.

11 Power steering fluid level – check

1 The power steering fluid reservoir is located on the right-hand side of the engine compartment, in front of the suspension turret **(see illustration)**. The fluid level should be checked with the engine stopped and the front wheels pointing straight-ahead.
2 First wipe the filler cap and surrounding area of the reservoir. Unscrew the cap from the top of the reservoir, and wipe all fluid from the cap dipstick with a clean rag.
3 Screw on the cap completely again, then remove it and check the fluid level on the dipstick. When the engine is cold at an ambient temperature of 20°C, the fluid level should be between the upper (MAX) and lower (MIN) marks on the dipstick, preferably near the MAX mark **(see illustration)**. If the engine is warm, the level can be slightly higher, but the level must never be allowed to be lower than the MIN mark.
4 Top-up the fluid level using the specified type of fluid (do not overfill the reservoir) **(see illustration)**, then refit and tighten the filler cap.

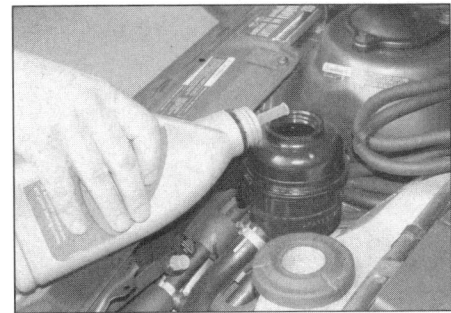
11.4 Topping-up the power steering fluid level

12 Road test

Instruments and electrical equipment

1 Check the operation of all instruments and electrical equipment.
2 Make sure that all instruments read correctly, and switch on all electrical equipment in turn to check that it functions properly. Check the function of the heating, air conditioning and automatic climate control systems.

Steering and suspension

3 Check for any abnormalities in the steering, suspension, handling or road 'feel'.
4 Drive the vehicle, and check that there are no unusual vibrations or noises.
5 Check that the steering feels positive, with no excessive 'sloppiness', or roughness, and check for any suspension noises when cornering, or when driving over bumps. Check that the power steering system operates correctly.

Drivetrain

6 Check the performance of the engine, clutch (manual transmission), transmission and driveshafts. Check that the turbo boost pressure needle moves up to the upper limit during sharp acceleration. The needle may occasionally enter the red zone for an instant, but if this happens frequently, or for extended periods, a problem may exist within the turbo boost control mechanism (see Chapter 4B).
7 Listen for any unusual noises from the engine, clutch (manual transmission) and transmission.
8 Make sure that the engine runs smoothly when idling, and that there is no hesitation when accelerating.
9 On manual transmission models, check that the clutch action is smooth and progressive, that the drive is taken up smoothly, and that the pedal travel is correct. Also listen for any noises when the clutch pedal is depressed. Check that all gears can be engaged smoothly, without noise, and that the gear lever action is smooth and not abnormally vague or 'notchy'.
10 On automatic transmission models, make sure that all gearchanges occur smoothly without snatching, and without an increase in engine speed between changes. Check that all the gear positions can be selected with the vehicle at rest. If any problems are found, they should be referred to a Saab dealer.
11 Listen for a metallic clicking sound from the front of the vehicle, as the vehicle is driven slowly in a circle with the steering on full lock. Carry out this check in both directions. If a clicking noise is heard, this indicates wear in a driveshaft joint, in which case, refer to Chapter 8.

Braking system

12 Make sure that the vehicle does not pull to one side when braking, and that the wheels do not lock when braking hard.
13 Check that there is no vibration through the steering when braking.
14 Check that the handbrake operates correctly, without excessive movement of the lever, and that it holds the vehicle stationary on a slope.
15 Test the operation of the brake servo unit as follows. With the engine off, depress the footbrake four or five times to exhaust the vacuum, and then start the engine while holding the brake pedal depressed. As the engine starts, there should be a noticeable 'give' in the brake pedal as vacuum builds-up. Allow the engine to run for at least two minutes, and then switch it off. If the brake pedal is now depressed again, it should be possible to detect a 'hiss' from the servo as the pedal is depressed. After about four or five applications, no further sound should be heard, and the pedal should feel considerably harder.

13 Coolant antifreeze concentration – check

1 The cooling system should be filled with the recommended antifreeze and corrosion protection fluid. Over a period of time, the concentration of fluid may be reduced due to topping-up (this can be avoided by topping-up with the correct antifreeze mixture) or fluid loss. If loss of coolant has been evident, it is important to make the necessary repair before adding fresh fluid. The exact mixture of antifreeze-to-water which you should use depends on the relative weather conditions. The mixture should contain at least 40% antifreeze, but not more than 70%. Consult the mixture ratio chart on the antifreeze container before adding coolant. Use antifreeze that meets the vehicle manufacturer's specifications. Note that antifreeze coolant available from Saab dealers is premixed with water at the correct ratio.
2 With the engine **cold**, carefully remove the cap from the expansion tank. If the engine is not completely cold, place a cloth rag over the cap before removing it, and remove it slowly to allow any pressure to escape.
3 Antifreeze checkers are available from car accessory shops. Draw some coolant from the expansion tank and observe how many plastic balls are floating in the checker. Usually, 2 or 3 balls must be floating for the correct concentration of antifreeze, but follow the manufacturer's instructions.
4 If the concentration is incorrect, it will be necessary to either withdraw some coolant and add antifreeze, or alternatively drain the old coolant and add fresh coolant of the correct concentration.

14 Automatic transmission fluid level – check

1 The fluid level is checked using the dipstick located on the front of the transmission, on the left-hand side of the engine compartment, beneath the battery location.
2 With the engine idling, select D for approximately 15 seconds, then engage R and wait a further 15 seconds. Do this again in position P, and leave the engine idling.
3 Withdraw the dipstick from the tube, and wipe all the fluid from its end with a clean rag or paper towel. Insert the clean dipstick back into the tube as far as it will go, then withdraw it once more. Note the fluid level on the end of the dipstick – there are level marks for cold and hot fluid conditions **(see illustrations)**. Use the hot marks if the engine has reached normal operating temperature.
4 If topping-up is necessary, add fluid as necessary through the dipstick tube. **Note:** *Never overfill the transmission so that the fluid level is above the upper mark. Use a funnel with a fine mesh gauze, to avoid spillage and to ensure that no foreign matter enters the transmission.* Note that the quantity of oil between the MIN and MAX marks is 0.4 litres.
5 After topping-up, take the car on a short run to distribute the fresh fluid, and then recheck the level again, topping-up if necessary.
6 Always maintain the fluid at the correct level. If the level is allowed to fall below the lower mark, fluid starvation may result, which could lead to severe transmission damage.

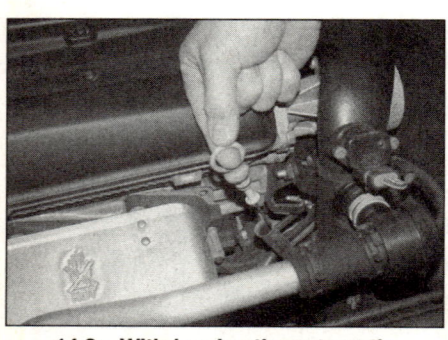

14.3a Withdrawing the automatic transmission fluid level dipstick

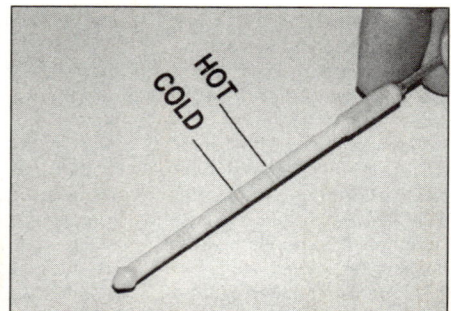

14.3b Fluid level marks on the dipstick

Every 18 000 miles – diesel engines 1B•11

15.2 Check the condition of the driveshaft gaiters (1) and the retaining clips (2)

17.0 Acoustic wear warning device fitted to the outer front brake pad

17.2 The outer brake pad wear can be checked through the aperture in the wheel

15 Driveshaft joints and gaiters – check

1 The driveshaft rubber gaiters are very important, because they prevent dirt, water and foreign material from entering and damaging the constant velocity (CV) joints. External contamination can cause the gaiter material to deteriorate prematurely, so it's a good idea to wash the gaiters with soap and water occasionally.
2 With the front of the vehicle raised and securely supported on stands, turn the steering onto full lock then slowly rotate the roadwheel. Inspect the condition of the outer constant velocity (CV) joint rubber gaiters while squeezing the gaiters to open out the folds **(see illustration)**. Check for signs of cracking, splits or deterioration of the rubber, which may allow the grease to escape and lead to water and grit entry into the joint. Also check the security and condition of the retaining clips. Repeat these checks on the inner CV joints. If any damage or deterioration is found, the gaiters should be renewed as described in Chapter 8.
3 At the same time check the general condition of the CV joints themselves by first holding the driveshaft and attempting to rotate the wheel. Repeat this check by holding the inner joint and attempting to rotate the driveshaft.
4 Any appreciable movement in the CV joint indicates wear in the joint, wear in the driveshaft splines, or a loose driveshaft retaining nut.

16 Exhaust system – check

1 With the engine cold, check the complete exhaust system from its starting point at the engine to the end of the tailpipe. If necessary, raise the front and rear of the vehicle and support it on axle stands (see *Jacking and vehicle support*). Remove any engine undershields as necessary for full access to the exhaust system.
2 Check the exhaust pipes and connections for evidence of leaks, severe corrosion, and damage. Make sure that all brackets and mountings are in good condition and that all relevant nuts and bolts are tight. Leakage at any of the joints or in other parts of the system will usually show up as a black sooty stain in the vicinity of the leak.
3 Rattles and other noises can often be traced to the exhaust system, especially the brackets and rubber mountings. Try to move the pipes and silencers. If the components are able to come into contact with the body or suspension parts, secure the system with new mountings. Otherwise separate the joints (if possible) and twist the pipes as necessary to provide additional clearance.

17 Brake pad wear – check

Note: *An acoustic wear warning device is fitted to the outer pad, consisting of a metal strip, which contacts the brake disc when the thickness of the friction material is less than 3.0 mm. This device causes a scraping noise that warns the driver that the pads are worn excessively* **(see illustration)**.
1 To check the brake pads, firmly apply the handbrake, and then jack up the front or rear of the vehicle (depending on brakes to be checked) and support it securely on axle stands (see *Jacking and vehicle support*).
2 For a quick check, the pad thickness can be checked through the gaps in the alloy wheels **(see illustration)**. Measure the thickness of the pad lining excluding the backing plate. This must not be less than that indicated in the Specifications.
3 The view through the wheel gives an indication of the **outer** brake pad wear only. For a comprehensive check, remove the wheels, and then the brake pads should be removed and cleaned. The operation of the caliper can then also be checked, and the condition of the brake disc itself can be fully examined on both sides.
4 If any pad's friction material is worn to the specified thickness or less; *all four pads must be renewed as a set*. Refer to Chapter 9 for details.

5 On completion, refit the roadwheels and lower the vehicle to the ground.

18 Hinges and locks – lubrication

1 Work around the vehicle and lubricate the hinges of the bonnet, doors and boot lid or tailgate with a light machine oil.
2 Lightly lubricate the two bonnet release locks with a smear of grease.
3 Check carefully the security and operation of all hinges, latches and locks. Check that the central locking system operates correctly.
4 Check the condition and operation of the bonnet and boot lid/tailgate struts, renewing them if either is leaking or no longer able to support the bonnet/boot lid/tailgate.

19 Pollen filter – renewal

1 Remove the glovebox as described in Chapter 11.
2 Remove the side trim/carpet from the centre console with reference to Chapter 11. At the same time, cut the plastic ties holding the wiring harness to the cover, and the cooler hose to the glovebox.
3 Undo the screws and remove the cover from over the pollen filter **(see illustrations)**.
4 Slide the pollen filter from the housing (see

19.3a Undo the screws . . .

1B•12 Every 18 000 miles – diesel engines

19.3b . . . and remove the cover . . .

illustration). Note the arrows indicating the direction of airflow through the filter.
5 Check that a seal is fitted to the top of the filter; if not, obtain and fit one. On models which have had air conditioning fitted after original manufacture, break off the plastic lugs from the top of the filter.
6 Loosen the clips and disconnect the two drain hoses from each side of the heater unit. Ideally, blow compressed air through the hoses to clear any accumulated debris, alternatively, clear the hoses with a suitable brush. Also, clear the spigots on the heater unit.
7 Refit the drain hoses and tighten the clips, then fit the new pollen filter using a reversal of the removal procedure.

20 Air conditioning drain hoses – check

1 Working beneath the glovebox, remove the side trim from the filter housing.
2 Remove the sound insulation from both sides of the heater unit.
3 Fold down the carpet from both sides of the centre console, and remove the insulation from the passenger's side.
4 Loosen the clips and remove both drain hoses from the side of the heater unit.
5 Ideally, blow compressed air through the drain hoses to clear them, alternatively use a cloth rag. Also clear the spigots on the heater unit.
6 Refit the hoses using a reversal of the removal procedure.

21 Auxiliary drivebelt condition – check

1 On all engines, a single, multi-grooved auxiliary drivebelt is used to transmit drive from the crankshaft pulley to the alternator, power steering pump and the refrigerant compressor **(see illustration)**. The drivebelt is tensioned automatically by a spring-loaded tensioner pulley.

2 For better access to the drivebelt, apply the handbrake then jack up the front of the car and support it on axle stands (see *Jacking and vehicle support*). Remove the right-hand front roadwheel, and then remove the plastic liner from under the right-hand wheel arch to expose the crankshaft pulley **(see illustration)**.
3 Using a suitable socket and extension bar fitted to the crankshaft pulley bolt; rotate the crankshaft so that the entire length of the drivebelt can be examined. Examine the drivebelt for cracks, splitting, fraying, or other damage. Check also for signs of glazing (shiny patches) and for separation of the belt plies. Renew the belt if worn or damaged.

22 Fuel filter – renewal

⚠️ **Warning:** *Absolute cleanliness must be observed during this procedure. Even the smallest particle of dirt could cause extensive damage to the fuel system.*

1 The fuel filter is attached to the side of the fuel tank under the vehicle.
2 Undo the Torx screw and pull down the protective cover on the base of the filter **(see illustration)**.

19.4 . . . then slide the pollen filter from the housing

21.1 Auxiliary drivebelt correctly routed

21.2 Remove the wheel arch liner to expose the crankshaft pulley and auxiliary belt

22.2 Undo the Torx screw (arrowed) and lower the plastic cover

22.3a Disconnect the sensor wiring plug (arrowed) . . .

Every 18 000 miles – diesel engines

3 Disconnect the water sensor wiring plug then unscrew the sensor from the base of the filter **(see illustrations)**. Be prepared for fuel spillage – position a container under the filter to catch the fuel.
4 Unscrew the filter cartridge from the housing, using a strap wrench or filter removal tool **(see illustration)**.
5 Lubricate the new filter seal with a little clean diesel fuel, and then screw the new filter into position **(see illustrations)**. Tighten the filter to the specified torque.
6 Screw the water sensor into the base of the new filter, ensuring the rubber seal is fitted.
7 Reconnect the water sensor wiring plug, refit the cover and tighten the retaining screw.
8 Start the engine, and check the filter for leaks.
9 The old filter should be disposed of safely.

22.3b . . . then unscrew the sensor and allow the filter to drain

22.4 Using a filter removal tool to unscrew the filter

22.5a Lubricate the filter seal with clean fuel . . .

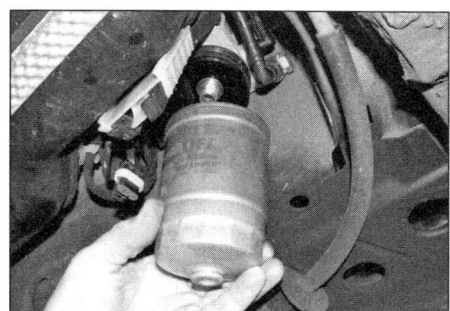

22.5b . . . and screw it into position

Every 36 000 miles

23 Air filter element – renewal

1 The air cleaner is located beneath the front right-hand wing, behind the front bumper, and the air inlet is taken from the front of the car behind the radiator grille area. For improved access to the filter, apply the handbrake, then jack up the front of the vehicle and support it on axle stands (see *Jacking and vehicle support*), then undo the single screw and pull aside the front bumper/spoiler.
2 Undo the screws and remove the cover together with filter element from the bottom of the air filter housing **(see illustrations)**. Recover the O-ring seal.
3 Note how the element is fitted, then remove it from the cover.
4 Wipe clean the inner surfaces of the cover and main housing.
5 Locate the new element on the cover, and then fit the cover complete with O-ring seal to the bottom of the housing. Insert and tighten the screws.
6 Lower the vehicle to the ground.

23.2a Remove the cover . . .

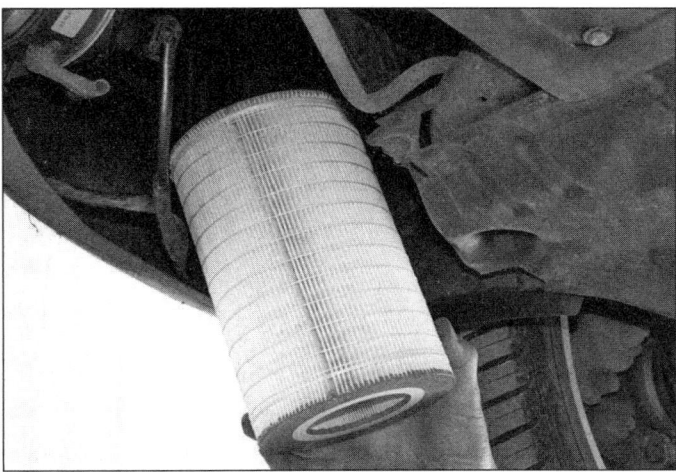

23.2b . . . and remove the filter element

1B•14 Every 36 000 miles – diesel engines

24 Manual transmission fluid level – check

Note: *A suitable Allen key will be required to unscrew the manual transmission filler and level plugs. This can be obtained from most motor factors, or from your Saab dealer.*

1 Make sure that the car is parked on a level surface. Wipe clean the area around the level plug, which is located on the left hand side of the differential casing at the rear of the transmission, behind the left-hand driveshaft. Access to the plug can be gained from the engine compartment, or alternatively, apply the handbrake, then jack up the vehicle and support it on axle stands (see *Jacking and vehicle support*), but note that the vehicle must be level.

2 Unscrew the plug, using a suitable Allen key and wipe it clean **(see illustration)**. The oil level should reach the lower edge of the level hole. A certain amount of oil will have gathered behind the level plug, and will trickle out when it is removed; this does **not** necessarily indicate that the level is correct. To ensure that a true level is established, wait until the initial trickle has stopped, then use a length of clean wire, bent into a right angle, as a dipstick.

3 If the oil level requires topping-up, wipe clean the area around the filler plug, which is located on top of the transmission. Unscrew the plug, and wipe it clean **(see illustrations)**.

4 Add oil as necessary until a steady trickle

24.2 Unscrew the transmission oil level plug, using an Allen key

24.3b Unscrew the plug using an Allen key

24.3a The transmission oil filler plug is located at the top of the transmission casing

24.4 Topping-up the transmission

of oil can be seen emerging from the level hole **(see illustration)**. Use **only** the specified grade of oil. A funnel will be helpful when adding oil to the transmission through the filler plug aperture.

5 When the level is correct, refit and tighten the filler plug (and where necessary, the level plug) to the specified torque wrench setting. Wipe off any spilt oil.

Every 72 000 miles

25 Timing belt renewal

Refer to Chapter 2B.

26.2 Transmission fluid drain plug (1)

26 Automatic transmission fluid – renewal

1 Take the car on a short journey to warm the transmission up to normal operating temperature. Position the car over an inspection pit, or alternatively jack up the front and rear of the car and support on axle stands (see *Jacking and vehicle support*). Whichever method is used, make sure that the car is level for checking the fluid level later. Where fitted, undo the fasteners and remove the engine undershield.

2 Position a suitable container beneath the transmission, then unscrew the drain plug and allow the fluid to drain **(see illustration)**. Note that a special adapter key will be required to unscrew the plug.

 Warning: *The fluid will be very hot, so take necessary precautions to prevent scalding. The use of thick waterproof gloves is recommended.*

3 With all the fluid drained, wipe clean the plug and refit it to the automatic transmission

housing. Where applicable, fit a new sealing washer to the drain plug. Tighten the plug to the specified torque.

4 Fill the automatic transmission with the specified grade and quantity of fluid. Referring to Section 14, top it up to the correct level. Use the low temperature set of dipstick markings first, then take the car for a run. With the fluid at operating temperature, recheck the fluid level using the high temperature set of dipstick markings.

27 Auxiliary drivebelt – renewal

1 On all engines, a single, multi-grooved auxiliary drivebelt is used to transmit drive from the crankshaft pulley to the alternator and the refrigerant compressor. The drivebelt is tensioned automatically by a spring-loaded tensioner pulley.

2 For better access to the drivebelt, apply the handbrake then jack up the front of the car and support it on axle stands (see *Jacking*

Every 72 000 miles – diesel engines 1B•15

27.3a Turn the drivebelt tensioner clockwise using a spanner on the pulley centre bolt (arrowed) ...

27.3b ... then lock the tensioner by inserting a locking pin or drill bit (arrowed) through the special hole

and vehicle support). Remove the right-hand front roadwheel, and then remove the plastic liner from under the right-hand wheel arch to expose the crankshaft pulley.

3 The tensioner pulley spring must now be compressed and locked in position. Using a spanner or socket and bar, rotate the tensioner clockwise, then insert a locking pin/5 mm drill bit once the holes in the arm and body align, to lock the tensioner in place **(see illustrations)**.

4 Slip the drivebelt from the pulleys, then remove it from the engine compartment from the right-hand wheel arch. If the belt is to be re-used, mark its direction of rotation.

5 Locate the drivebelt over all the pulleys, making sure that the multi-grooved side is correctly engaged with the grooves on the pulleys **(see illustration 21.1)**.

6 Compress the tensioner spring and withdrawn the locking pin/drill bit. Slowly release the tensioner, allowing it to apply pressure to the rear surface of drivebelt.

7 Ensure that the belt is correctly seated on all the pulleys, then start the engine and allow it to idle for a few minutes. This will allow the tensioner to settle in position and distribute the tension evenly throughout the belt. Stop the engine and check once again that the belt is correctly seated on all the pulleys.

8 On completion, refit the plastic wheel arch liner and roadwheel, and then lower the car to the ground.

Every 3 years

28 Coolant – renewal

Note: *This work is not included in the Saab schedule, and should not be required if the recommended Saab antifreeze/inhibitor is used.*

> **Warning:** *Do not allow antifreeze to come in contact with your skin or painted surfaces of the vehicle. Flush contaminated areas immediately with plenty of water. Don't store new coolant, or leave old coolant lying around, where it's accessible to children or pets – they're attracted by its sweet smell. Ingestion of even a small amount of coolant can be fatal. Wipe up garage-floor and drip-pan spills immediately. Keep antifreeze containers covered, and repair cooling system leaks as soon as they're noticed.*

> **Warning:** *Never remove the expansion tank filler cap when the engine is running, or has just been switched off, as the cooling system will be hot, and the consequent escaping steam and scalding coolant could cause serious injury.*

> **Warning:** *Wait until the engine is cold before starting these procedures.*

Cooling system draining

1 With the engine completely cold, remove the expansion tank filler cap. Turn the cap anti-clockwise, wait until any pressure remaining in the system is released, then unscrew it and lift it off.

2 Raise the front of the vehicle and support it on axle stands (see *Jacking and vehicle support*).

3 Where applicable, remove the engine undershield, and then position a suitable container beneath the left-hand side of the radiator.

4 Loosen the drain plug located on the left-hand lower mounting stub **(see illustration)**, and allow the coolant to drain into the container. If necessary, attach a hose to the drain plug to direct the coolant into the container.

5 When the flow of coolant stops, tighten the drain plug and where necessary refit the undershield.

6 If the coolant has been drained for a reason other than renewal, then provided it is clean and less than two years old, it can be re-used, though this is not recommended.

Cooling system flushing

7 If coolant renewal has been neglected, or if the antifreeze mixture has become diluted, then in time the cooling system may gradually lose efficiency, as the coolant passages become restricted due to rust, scale deposits and other sediment. The cooling system efficiency can be restored by flushing the system clean.

8 The radiator should be flushed independently of the engine, to avoid unnecessary contamination.

Radiator flushing

9 Disconnect the top and bottom hoses and any other relevant hoses from the radiator, with reference to Chapter 3.

10 Insert a garden hose into the radiator top inlet. Direct a flow of clean water through the radiator, and continue flushing until clean

28.4 Drain plug (arrowed) is located on the left-hand end of the radiator

1B•16 Every 3 years – diesel engines

28.18 The bleed screw (arrowed) is located in the metal coolant pipe at the front of the engine

water emerges from the radiator bottom outlet.
11 If after a reasonable period, the water still does not run clear, the radiator can be flushed with a good proprietary cleaning agent. It is important that the manufacturer's instructions are followed carefully. If the contamination is particularly bad, remove the radiator and insert the hose in the bottom outlet, and reverse-flush the radiator, then refit it.

Engine flushing

12 Remove the thermostat housing as described in Chapter 3. If the radiator top hose has been disconnected, temporarily reconnect the hose.
13 With the top and bottom hoses disconnected from the radiator, insert a garden hose into the radiator top hose. Direct a clean flow of water through the engine, and continue flushing until clean water emerges from the radiator bottom hose.
14 On completion of flushing, refit the thermostat and reconnect the hoses with reference to Chapter 3.

Cooling system filling

15 Before attempting to fill the cooling system, make sure that all hoses and clips are in good condition, and that the clips are tight. Note that an antifreeze mixture must be used all year round, to prevent corrosion of the engine components.
16 Make sure that the air conditioning (A/C) or automatic climate control (ACC) is switched off. This is to prevent the air conditioning system starting the radiator cooling fan before the engine is at normal temperature when refilling the system.
17 Remove the expansion tank filler cap and slowly fill the system until the coolant level reaches 30 mm above the MAX mark on the side of the expansion tank.
18 Undo the bleed screw in the coolant pipe at the front of the engine **(see illustration)**. Allow any trapped air to escape, and close the bleed screw once bubble-free coolant emerges from the pipe.
19 Check the coolant level, top-up if necessary, then refit and tighten the expansion tank filler cap.
20 Start the engine and set the heater to hot, and then run the engine until it reaches normal operating temperature (until the cooling fan cuts in and out). Running the engine at varying speeds will allow the engine to warm-up quickly.
21 Stop the engine, and allow it to cool, and then recheck the coolant level with reference to *Weekly checks*. Top-up the level if necessary and refit the expansion tank filler cap.

Antifreeze mixture

22 The antifreeze should always be renewed at the specified intervals. This is necessary not only to maintain the antifreeze properties, but also to prevent corrosion that would otherwise occur as the corrosion inhibitors become progressively less effective.
23 Always use an ethylene glycol based antifreeze, which is suitable for use in mixed-metal cooling systems. The quantity of antifreeze and levels of protection are given in the Specifications.
24 Before adding antifreeze, the cooling system should be completely drained, preferably flushed, and all hoses checked for condition and security.
25 After filling with antifreeze, a label should be attached to the expansion tank, stating the type and concentration of antifreeze used, and the date installed. Any subsequent topping-up should be made with the same type and concentration of antifreeze.
Caution: Do not use engine antifreeze in the windscreen/tailgate washer system, as it will cause damage to the vehicle paintwork. A screenwash additive should be added to the washer system in the quantities stated on the bottle.

Every 4 years

29 Brake fluid – renewal

⚠ **Warning: Brake hydraulic fluid can harm your eyes and damage painted surfaces, so use extreme caution when handling and pouring it. Do not use fluid that has been standing open for some time, as it absorbs moisture from the air. Excess moisture can cause a dangerous loss of braking effectiveness.**

1 The procedure is similar to that for the bleeding of the hydraulic system as described in Chapter 9.
2 Working as described in Chapter 9, open the first bleed screw in the sequence, and pump the brake pedal gently until nearly all the old fluid has been emptied from the master cylinder reservoir. Top-up to the MAX level with new fluid, and continue pumping until only the new fluid remains in the reservoir, and new fluid can be seen emerging from the bleed screw. Tighten the screw, and top the reservoir level up to the MAX level line.
3 Work through all the remaining bleed screws in the sequence until new fluid can be seen at all of them. Be careful to keep the master cylinder reservoir topped-up to above the MIN level at all times, or air may enter the system and greatly increase the length of the task.
4 When the operation is complete, check that all bleed screws are securely tightened, and that their dust caps are refitted. Wash off all traces of spilt fluid, and recheck the master cylinder reservoir fluid level.
5 Check the operation of the brakes before taking the car on the road.

Chapter 2 Part A:
Petrol engine in-car repair procedures

Contents

	Section number		Section number
Camshafts and hydraulic cam followers – removal, inspection and refitting	5	Flywheel/driveplate – removal, inspection and refitting	12
Compression test – description and interpretation	2	General information	1
Crankshaft oil seals – renewal	11	Oil cooler and thermostat – removal and refitting	9
Cylinder head – removal and refitting	6	Oil pressure warning light switch – removal and refitting	10
Cylinder head cover – removal and refitting	4	Oil pump – removal, inspection and refitting	8
Engine/transmission mountings – inspection and renewal	13	Sump – removal and refitting	7
		Top dead centre (TDC) for No 1 piston – locating	3

Degrees of difficulty

Easy, suitable for novice with little experience	**Fairly easy,** suitable for beginner with some experience	**Fairly difficult,** suitable for competent DIY mechanic	**Difficult,** suitable for experienced DIY mechanic	**Very difficult,** suitable for expert DIY or professional

Specifications

General
Designation:
- 1985 cc engine: B205
- 2290 cc engine: B235

Bore: 90.00 mm

Stroke:
- 1985 cc engine: 78.00 mm
- 2290 cc engine: 90.00 mm

Direction of crankshaft rotation: Clockwise (viewed from right-hand side of vehicle)
No 1 cylinder location: At timing chain end of engine

Compression ratio:
- B205: 8.8 : 1
- B235: 9.3 : 1

Maximum power/torque:
- B205E: 110 kW @ 5500 rpm/240 Nm @ 1800 rpm
- B205E (with accessory kit fitted): 136 kW @ 5500 rpm/280 Nm @ 1800 rpm
- B235E: 136 kW @ 5500 rpm/280 Nm @ 1800 rpm
- B235R (HOT Aero models): 184 kW @ 5300 rpm/350 Nm @ 1900 rpm

Camshafts
Drive: Chain from crankshaft
Number of bearings: 5 per camshaft
Camshaft bearing journal diameter (outside diameter): 28.922 to 28.935 mm
Cam lift: 8.31 mm
Endfloat: 0.08 to 0.35 mm

Lubrication system
Oil pump type: Bi-rotor type, driven off the crankshaft
Minimum oil pressure at 80°C: 2.5 bars at 2000 rpm, using 10W/30 engine oil
Oil pressure warning switch operating pressure: 0.3 to 0.5 bar
Clearance between pump outer rotor and timing cover housing: 0.03 to 0.08 mm
Pressure release valve opens at: 3.8 bars
Oil cooler thermostat opens at: 105°C approx.

Torque wrench settings

	Nm	lbf ft
Balance shaft chain idler sprocket	25	18
Balance shaft sprockets	22	16
Big-end bearing cap nuts:		
Stage 1	20	15
Stage 2	Angle-tighten a further 70°	
Camshaft bearing cap	15	11
Camshaft sprockets	63	46
Crankshaft pulley bolt	175	129
Cylinder head bolts:		
Stage 1	40	30
Stage 2	60	44
Stage 3	Angle-tighten a further 90°	
Cylinder head cover	15	11
Driveplate	95	70
Engine oil drain plug	25	18
Engine-to-transmission bolts	70	52
Flywheel	80	59
Front engine mounting:		
Bracket to engine	47	35
Torque arm to body	121	89
Torque arm to bracket	47	35
Left-hand transmission mounting:		
Mounting nut	85	63
Mounting to body	60	44
Bracket to transmission:		
Manual	40	30
Automatic	84	62
Main bearing cap bolts:		
Stage 1	20	15
Stage 2	Angle-tighten a further 70°	
Oil cooler hose unions	8	6
Piston cooling jet	18	13
Plug for camshaft chain tensioner	22	16
Plug for oil cooler thermostat	60	44
Plug for oil pressure reducing valve	30	22
Rear engine mounting:		
Bracket to transmission	84	62
Mounting to subframe	26	19
Mounting nut	26	19
Right-hand engine mounting:		
Mounting-to-inner wing bolts	47	35
Mounting-to-bracket-to=engine bolts	47	35
Mounting-to-bracket nut	105	77
Sump bolts	22	16
Timing chain tensioner body	63	46
Timing chain tensioner spring plug	22	16
Timing cover bolts	22	16

1 General information

How to use this Chapter

This Part of Chapter 2 describes those repair procedures that can reasonably be carried out on the engine while it remains in the car. If the engine has been removed from the car, and is being dismantled as described in Part C, any preliminary dismantling procedures can be ignored.

Note that, while it may be possible physically to overhaul items such as the piston/connecting rod assemblies while the engine is in the car, such tasks are not normally carried out as separate operations. Usually, several additional procedures (not to mention the cleaning of components and oilways) have to be carried out. For this reason, all such tasks are classed as major overhaul procedures, and are described in Part C of this Chapter.

Part C describes the removal of the engine/transmission from the vehicle, and the full overhaul procedures that can then be carried out.

Engine description

The engine is of in-line four-cylinder, double-overhead camshaft (DOHC), 16-valve type, mounted transversely at the front of the car with the transmission attached to its left-hand end. The Saab 9-5 is fitted with 1985 cc or 2290 cc engine versions, which have balance shafts that are situated in the cylinder block to smooth out vibrations. All engines are fuel-injected using a Saab-manufactured 'Trionic' engine management system.

The crankshaft runs in five main bearings. Thrustwashers are fitted to the centre main bearing (upper half only) to control crankshaft endfloat.

The connecting rods rotate on horizontally split bearing shells at their big ends. The pistons are attached to the connecting rods by fully-loating gudgeon pins, which are retained in the pistons by circlips. The aluminium-alloy pistons are fitted with three piston rings – two compression rings and an oil control ring.

The cylinder block is of cast-iron, and the cylinder bores are an integral part of the cylinder block. The intake and exhaust valves are closed by coil springs, and operate in guides pressed into the cylinder head; the valve seat inserts are also pressed into the cylinder head, and can be renewed separately if worn. There are four valves per cylinder.

The camshafts are driven by a single-row timing chain, and they operate the 16 valves via hydraulic cam followers. The hydraulic cam followers maintain a predetermined clearance between the cam lobe and the end of the valve stem, using hydraulic chambers and a tension spring. The followers are fed with oil from the main engine lubrication circuit.

The balance shafts are driven in counter-rotation by a small single-row chain from a sprocket on the front of the crankshaft. The run of the balance shaft chain is controlled by two fixed guide rails and an idler sprocket. The chain is located on the outside of the main camshaft timing chain, with its tension being controlled by a dedicated oil pressure-driven tensioner.

Lubrication is by means of a bi-rotor oil pump, driven from the front of the crankshaft and located in the timing cover. A relief valve in the timing cover limits the oil pressure at high engine speeds by returning excess oil to the sump. Oil is drawn from the sump through a strainer and, after passing through the oil pump, is forced through an externally-mounted filter and oil cooler into galleries in the cylinder block/crankcase. From there, the oil is distributed to the crankshaft (main bearings), balance shafts, camshaft bearings and hydraulic cam followers. It also lubricates the water-cooled turbocharger and the crankcase-mounted piston cooling jets. The big-end bearings are supplied with oil via internal drillings in the crankshaft, while the camshaft lobes and valves are lubricated by splash, as are all other engine components.

Repairs with engine in car

The following work can be carried out with the engine in the car:
a) Compression pressure – testing.
b) Cylinder head cover – removal and refitting.
c) Camshaft oil seals – renewal.
d) Camshafts – removal, inspection and refitting.
e) Cylinder head – removal and refitting.
f) Cylinder head and pistons – decarbonising (refer to Part C of this Chapter).
g) Sump – removal and refitting.
h) Oil pump – removal, overhaul and refitting.
i) Crankshaft oil seals – renewal.
j) Flywheel/driveplate – removal, inspection and refitting.
k) Engine/transmission mountings – inspection and renewal.

2 Compression test – description and interpretation

1 When engine performance is down, or if misfiring occurs which cannot be attributed to the ignition or fuel systems, a compression test can provide diagnostic clues as to the engine's condition. If the test is performed regularly, it can give warning of trouble before any other symptoms become apparent.
2 The engine must be fully warmed-up to normal operating temperature, the battery must be fully-charged, and all the spark plugs must be removed (Chapter 1A). The aid of an assistant will also be required.
3 Disable the ignition system by disconnecting the wiring plug from the Direct Ignition cartridge.
4 To prevent unburnt fuel from being supplied to the catalytic converter, the fuel pump must also be disabled by removing the relevant fuse and/or relay; see Chapter 4A as applicable for further details.
5 Fit a compression tester to the No 1 cylinder spark plug hole – the type of tester which screws into the plug thread must be used to obtain accurate readings.
6 Have the assistant depress the accelerator pedal fully, and crank the engine on the starter motor; after one or two revolutions, the compression pressure should build-up to a maximum figure, and then stabilise. Record the highest reading obtained.
7 Repeat the test on the remaining cylinders, recording the pressure in each.
8 All cylinders should produce very similar pressures; a difference of more than 2 bars between any two cylinders indicates a fault. Note that the compression should build-up quickly in a healthy engine; low compression on the first stroke, followed by gradually increasing pressure on successive strokes, indicates worn piston rings. A low compression reading on the first stroke, which does not build-up during successive strokes, indicates leaking valves or a blown head gasket (a cracked cylinder head could also be the cause). Deposits on the undersides of the valve heads can also cause low compression.
9 Saab specify that the expected compression pressures required are 12 bars for the B205 (1985 cc) engine and 14 bars for the B235 (2290 cc) engine. Any cylinder pressure of below 10 bars for the B205 engine or 12 bars for the B235 engine can be considered as less than healthy. Refer to a Saab dealer or other specialist if in doubt as to whether a particular pressure reading is acceptable.
10 If the pressure in any cylinder is low, carry out the following test to isolate the cause. Introduce a teaspoonful of clean oil into that cylinder through its spark plug hole, and repeat the test.
11 If the addition of oil temporarily improves the compression pressure, this indicates that bore or piston wear is responsible for the pressure loss. No improvement suggests that leaking or burnt valves, or a blown head gasket, may be to blame.
12 A low reading only from two adjacent cylinders is almost certainly due to the head gasket having blown between them; the presence of coolant in the engine oil will confirm this.

3.1 TDC timing marks (arrowed) on the flywheel and engine backplate

13 If one cylinder is about 20 percent lower than the others and the engine has a slightly rough idle; a worn camshaft lobe could be the cause.
14 On completion of the test, refit the spark plugs and reconnect the ignition system and fuel pump as necessary.

3 Top dead centre (TDC) for No 1 piston – locating

1 TDC timing marks are provided in the form of a slot machined into the crankshaft pulley and a corresponding bar cast into the timing chain cover. In addition, TDC marks are provided on the flywheel and oil seal housing – these are useful if the engine is being dismantled on the bench (see illustration). Note: *With the timing marks correctly aligned, piston Nos 1 (at the timing chain end of the engine) and 4 (at the flywheel end of the engine) will be at top dead centre (TDC), with piston No 1 on its compression stroke.*
2 For access to the crankshaft pulley bolt, jack up the front of the car and support on axle stands (see *Jacking and vehicle support*). Remove the right-hand front wheel, then remove the screws and detach the inspection cover from the right-hand wheel arch liner.
3 Using a socket on the crankshaft pulley, turn the engine until the TDC slot in the crankshaft pulley is aligned with the slot on the timing cover (see illustration). No 1 piston (at the timing chain end of the engine) will be at the top of its compression stroke.

3.3 TDC timing marks (arrowed) on the timing chain cover and crankshaft pulley

2A•4 Petrol engine in-car repair procedures

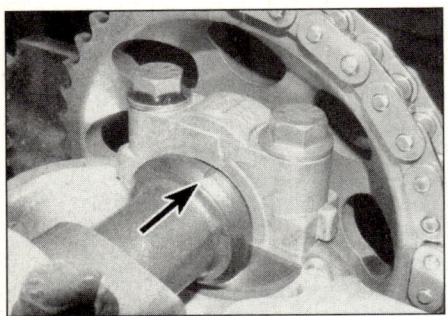

3.5 TDC timing marks (arrowed) on the camshaft and bearing cap

4.1 Unclip the plastic cover

4.2 Unclip the wiring and hose from the securing clips (arrowed)

4.3 Disconnect the breather hose from the cover

4.4a Disconnecting the wiring connector from the ignition cartridge . . .

The compression stroke can be confirmed by removing the No 1 spark plug, and checking for compression with a finger over the plug hole as the piston approaches the top of its stroke. No compression indicates that the cylinder is on its exhaust stroke and is therefore one crankshaft revolution out of alignment.

4 Remove the cylinder head cover with reference to Section 4.

5 Check that the TDC marks at the sprocket ends of the camshafts are aligned with the corresponding TDC marks on the camshaft bearing caps **(see illustration)**. If necessary, turn the crankshaft to bring the marks into alignment.

4 Cylinder head cover – removal and refitting

Removal

1 Open the bonnet and unclip the plastic cover away from the intake manifold **(see illustration)**.
2 Unclip the wiring and crankcase breather pipe from the right-hand end of the cylinder head cover **(see illustration)**.
3 Disconnect the crankcase breather hose from the cover, by releasing the securing clip (and where applicable, the vacuum hose), and then position them to one side **(see illustration)**.
4 Disconnect the wiring connector, then undo the screws and remove the ignition cartridge from the centre of the cylinder head cover; refer to Chapter 5B, Section 3, if necessary **(see illustrations)**.
5 Unbolt and remove the cylinder head cover, and remove the gasket. If the cover is stuck, tap it gently with the palm of your hand to free it.

Refitting

6 Clean the contact surfaces of the cylinder head cover and cylinder head. Locate the gasket securely in the groove in the cylinder head cover. **Note:** *The gasket is in two parts: inner and outer gaskets* **(see illustrations)**.
7 Refit the cylinder head cover, and insert the securing bolts. Tighten the bolts progressively and in sequence **(see illustration)** until all the bolts are tightened to the specified torque.
8 Reconnect the crankcase breather hose (and where applicable, the vacuum hose) to the cylinder head cover.

4.4b . . . then remove the cylinder head cover retaining screws (arrowed)

4.6a Refitting the cylinder head cover inner gasket . . .

Petrol engine in-car repair procedures 2A•5

4.6b ... and outer gasket, securely in the groove

4.7 Tightening sequence for the cylinder head cover bolts

9 Refit the direct ignition cartridge to the centre of the cylinder head cover, and tighten the screws, refer to Chapter 5B if necessary.
10 Refit the engine upper cover.

5 Camshafts and hydraulic cam followers – removal, inspection and refitting

Note: *The following procedure describes removal and refitting of the camshafts and hydraulic cam followers with the cylinder head in position in the car. If necessary, the work can be carried out on the bench, with the cylinder head removed from the engine. In this case, start the procedure at paragraph 8, after removing the cylinder head.*

Removal

1 Open the bonnet, and clean the engine around the cylinder head.
2 Apply the handbrake, then jack up the front of the car and support on axle stands (see *Jacking and vehicle support*). Remove the right-hand front wheel.
3 Remove the screws, and withdraw the front wing moulding and wheel arch liner from under the right-hand front wing.
4 Remove the battery cover then disconnect the battery negative lead, and position the lead away from the battery terminal.
5 Unbolt and remove the cylinder head cover as described in Section 4.
6 Using a socket on the crankshaft pulley, turn the engine until the TDC slot in the crankshaft pulley is aligned with the timing bar on the timing cover. If necessary, refer to Section 3 for more information. Check also that the TDC marks on the sprocket ends of the camshafts are aligned with the corresponding TDC marks on the camshaft bearing caps.
7 Unscrew the bolt on the idler sprocket and remove the timing chain tensioner, use a 27 mm socket after removing the plug with spring and pushrod.
8 While holding each camshaft stationary with a spanner on the special flats at the transmission end of the camshaft, unscrew the bolts, then withdraw the sprockets and allow them to rest on the timing chain guides. Note that the sprockets have projections which engage with cutouts in the ends of the camshafts. The timing chain cannot come off the crankshaft sprocket, since there is a guide located below the sprocket.
9 Check that the camshaft bearing caps and the camshafts are identified for position. They have stamped markings on the caps – do not mix up these when refitting, 1 to 5 for the intake side and 6 to 10 for the exhaust side **(see illustration)**.
10 Progressively unscrew the bearing cap bolts, so that the caps are not stressed unduly by the valve springs. Ensure that the bearing caps closest to the open valves are removed last, to avoid stressing the camshaft unduly. Fully remove the bolts and lift off the caps, then lift the camshafts from the cylinder head. Note that the bearing cap inner bolts (except at the timing chain end) have black heads, and incorporate drillings for the oil supply to the hydraulic cam followers; always make sure that the correct bolts are fitted **(see illustrations)**. Keep the camshafts carefully identified for location.
11 Obtain sixteen small, clean plastic containers, and number them 1i to 8i (intake)

5.9 The camshaft bearing caps are marked for position (arrowed – No 10 bearing cap)

5.10a The camshaft bearing cap inner bolts (arrowed) are hollow for the oil supply to the hydraulic cam followers

5.10b Locations (arrowed) of the black-headed inner bearing cap bolts incorporating oil drillings

2A•6 Petrol engine in-car repair procedures

5.11a Removing a hydraulic cam follower

5.11b Hydraulic cam follower removed from the cylinder head. Store cam followers in an oil bath while removed

and 1e to 8e (exhaust). Alternatively, divide a larger container into sixteen compartments, similarly marked for the intake and exhaust camshafts. Using a rubber sucker or a magnet, withdraw each hydraulic cam follower in turn, and place it in its respective container **(see illustrations)**. **Do not** interchange the cam followers. To prevent the oil draining from the hydraulic cam followers, pour fresh oil into the containers until it covers them.

Caution: *Take great care to avoid scratching the cylinder head bores as the followers are withdrawn.*

Inspection

12 Examine the camshaft bearing surfaces and cam lobes for signs of wear ridges and scoring. Renew the camshaft if any of these conditions are apparent. Examine the condition of the bearing surfaces on the camshaft journals, in the camshaft bearing caps, and in the cylinder head. If the head or cap bearing surfaces are worn excessively, the cylinder head will need to be renewed. If the necessary measuring equipment is available, camshaft bearing journal wear can be checked by direct measurement and comparison with the specifications given.

13 Camshaft endfloat can be measured by locating each camshaft in the cylinder head, refitting the sprockets, and using feeler blades between the shoulder on the front of the camshaft and the front bearing surface on the cylinder head.

14 Check the hydraulic cam followers where

they contact the bores in the cylinder head for wear, scoring and pitting. Occasionally, a hydraulic cam follower may be noisy and require renewal, and this will have been noticed when the engine was running. It is not easy to check a cam follower for internal damage or wear once it has been removed; if there is any doubt, the complete set of cam followers should be renewed.

15 Clean the internal drillings of the hollow camshaft bearing cap bolts, to ensure oil supply to the hydraulic cam followers.

Refitting

16 Lubricate the bores for the hydraulic cam followers in the cylinder head, and the followers themselves, then insert them in their original positions **(see illustration)**.

17 Lubricate the bearing surfaces of the camshafts in the cylinder head.

18 Locate the camshafts in their correct positions in the cylinder head, so that the valves of No 1 cylinder (timing chain end) are closed, and the valves of No 4 cylinder are 'rocking'.

19 The timing marks on the sprocket ends of the camshafts should be aligned **(see illustration 3.5)**.

20 Lubricate the bearing surfaces in the bearing caps, then locate them in their correct positions and insert the retaining bolts. Progressively tighten the bolts to the specified torque. **Note:** *Ensure that the black-coloured oil supply bolts are in their correct positions* **(see illustration 5.10b)**.

21 Check that each camshaft is at its TDC position – the timing marks are located on the front of the camshafts, and must be aligned with the mark on the bearing caps – see Section 3.

22 Check that the TDC slot in the crankshaft pulley is aligned with the timing bar on the timing cover **(see illustration 3.3)**.

23 Locate the sprockets on the camshafts, fitting the exhaust one first, followed by the intake one. Do not fully tighten the bolts at this stage. Check that the timing chain is correctly located on the guides and sprockets.

24 Refit the timing chain tensioner, with reference to Chapter 2C.

25 Using a socket on the crankshaft pulley, rotate the engine two complete turns clockwise, then check that the TDC timing marks are still correctly aligned.

26 Fully tighten the camshaft sprocket retaining bolts to the specified torque, while holding them stationary with a spanner on the special flats provided **(see illustration)**.

27 Clean the contact surfaces of the cylinder head cover and cylinder head. Refit the cylinder head cover with reference to Section 4.

28 Refit the inspection cover or DI ignition cartridge to the centre of the cylinder head cover, and tighten the securing screws.

29 Reconnect the crankcase breather hose.

30 Refit the front wing moulding and wheel arch liner under the right-hand front wing, and tighten the screws.

31 Refit the right-hand front wheel, and lower the car to the ground.

32 Reconnect the battery negative lead and refit the covers to the battery and the engine.

6 Cylinder head – removal and refitting

Removal

1 Open the bonnet, and clean the engine around the cylinder head. Run the engine at idling speed and remove the fuel pump fuse (passenger compartment – fuse number 15); check in Chapter 12 for exact location of fuse for your model. Turn the ignition off after the engine has stopped, there will then be no fuel pressure in the fuel lines. Refit the fuse.

2 Apply the handbrake, then jack up the front of the car and support on axle stands (see *Jacking and vehicle support*). Remove the right-hand front wheel and remove the lower engine cover.

3 Remove the battery cover and disconnect the battery negative lead, and position the lead away from the battery terminal.

4 Remove the retaining screws, and withdraw the wheel arch liner from under the right-hand front wing.

5 Drain the cooling system, with reference to Chapter 1A.

6 Remove the oil filler cap/dipstick and unclip the intake manifold cover away from the intake manifold.

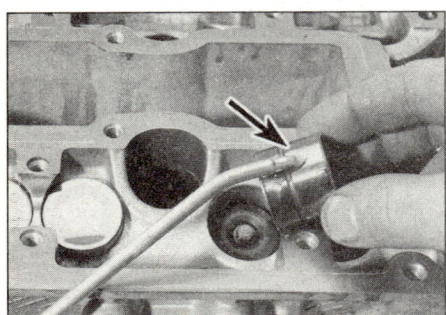

5.16 Oiling a hydraulic cam follower prior to fitting

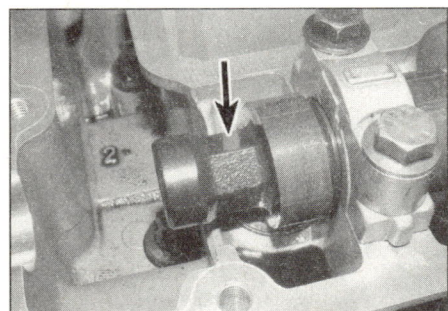

5.26 Tighten the camshaft sprocket retaining bolts, using a spanner on the camshaft flats (arrowed) to hold it stationary

Petrol engine in-car repair procedures 2A•7

7 Support the engine under the right-hand side, then undo the retaining bolts and remove the right-hand upper engine mounting assembly from the vehicle. For further information see Section 13.

8 With reference to Chapter 4A, Section 14, remove the mass airflow sensor and rubber gaiter from the engine compartment. Pull back the rubber cover and disconnect the wiring plug from the charge air control valve **(see illustration)**. Release the hose clips and remove the turbocharger-to-intercooler and intercooler-to-throttle body intake air ducts. Cover the turbocharger port with a cloth to prevent the ingress of debris.

9 Press down on the red securing clip to release the crankcase breather pipe from the air intake hose **(see illustrations)**.

10 Unbolt and remove the engine lifting eye from the front right-hand side of the cylinder head **(see illustration)**.

11 Release the securing clips and remove the charge air pipe from across the left-hand end of the cylinder head. Undo the retaining bolt from the end of the cylinder head. Disconnect the bypass valve and pressure/temperature sensor connectors. Disconnect the bypass valve vacuum hose. Plug the throttle body and the hose by the charge air cooler **(see illustrations)**.

12 Refer to Chapter 1A and remove the auxiliary drivebelt.

13 Remove the alternator to one side (referring to Chapter 5A), and then unbolt the alternator bracket from the cylinder head **(see illustration)**.

14 Disconnect the wiring connector from the temperature sensor in the left-hand end of the cylinder head.

15 Slacken the hose clips and disconnect the coolant hoses from the cylinder head.

16 Unbolt the cover from the throttle body lever, and disconnect the throttle cable from the throttle body **(see illustration)**.

17 Unbolt the support bracket and release the engine oil dipstick tube and dipstick from the cylinder head.

6.8 Disconnect the wiring plug (arrowed) from the charge air control valve

6.9a Release the red locking ring . . .

6.9b . . . and remove the crankcase breather pipe

6.10 Undo the retaining bolts (arrowed) to remove the engine lifting eye

6.11a Slacken the retaining clip (arrowed) . . .

6.11b . . . remove the retaining clips (arrowed) . . .

6.11c . . . undo the mounting bolt (arrowed) . . .

6.11d . . . then disconnect the sensor wiring connector (arrowed) and vacuum pipe (arrowed)

6.13 Undo the alternator bracket upper mounting bolts (arrowed)

6.16 Remove the cover to access the throttle linkage/cable

2A•8 Petrol engine in-car repair procedures

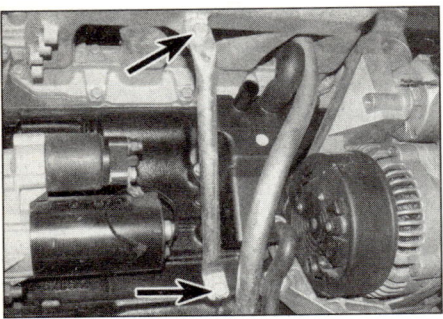

6.19 Undo the two bracing bracket retaining bolts (arrowed)

6.21 Remove the lower retaining bolt (arrowed) from the power steering pump bracket

6.26 Remove the idler roller, then slacken and remove the timing chain tensioner (arrowed)

18 Slacken the hose clips and disconnect the hoses from the throttle body.
19 From under the vehicle, unbolt and remove the intake manifold bracing bracket from the rear of the engine **(see illustration)**.
20 Refer to Chapter 4A and remove the exhaust heat shield, then unbolt the exhaust system front pipe from the turbocharger.
21 Unbolt the power steering pump from its mountings, with reference to Chapter 10, and secure to one side using nylon cable ties or similar. Note that there is no need to disconnect the hydraulic fluid hoses from the pump. Slacken and remove the lower retaining bolt in the power steering pump bracket **(see illustration)**.
22 Unbolt and remove the rear engine lifting eye from the intake manifold and move the wiring harness bracket to one side. Refer to Chapter 4A and remove the intake manifold from the cylinder head.
23 Unbolt and remove the cylinder head cover, and remove the gasket with reference to Section 4. If the cover is stuck, tap it gently with the palm of your hand to free it. If necessary, remove all four spark plugs, as described in Chapter 1A.
24 Using a socket on the crankshaft pulley, turn the engine until the TDC mark on the crankshaft pulley is aligned with the timing mark on the timing cover, and No 1 piston (at the timing chain end of the engine) is at the top of its compression stroke. If necessary, refer to Section 3 for more information. Check also that the TDC marks on the sprocket ends of the camshafts are aligned with the corresponding TDC marks on the camshaft bearing caps.
25 While holding each camshaft stationary with a spanner on the special flats at the flywheel/driveplate end of the camshaft, slacken the bolts **(see illustration 5.26)**. Do not remove them at this stage.
26 Unscrew the bolt on the idler roller and remove the timing chain tensioner **(see illustration)**, use a 27 mm socket after removing the plug with spring and pushrod.
27 Unscrew the camshaft sprocket retaining bolts, then disengage the sprockets from the chain and remove from the engine. Fit a rubber band/cable-tie around the chain guides to prevent the chain from dropping down.
28 Unscrew and remove the two bolts securing the timing cover to the cylinder head **(see illustration)**.
29 Working in the **reverse** sequence **(see illustration 6.44)**, progressively slacken the ten cylinder head bolts by half a turn at a time, until all bolts can be unscrewed by hand. The bolts require the use of a Torx socket to unscrew them, as they have six external splines.
30 With all the cylinder head bolts removed, check that the timing chain is positioned so that the pivoting chain guide will not obstruct removal of the head. Lift the cylinder head directly from the top of the cylinder block and place it on a clean workbench, without damaging the mating surface. If necessary, enlist the help of an assistant, since the cylinder head is quite heavy. If the cylinder head is stuck, try rocking it slightly to free it from the gasket – **do not** insert a screwdriver or similar tool between the gasket joint, otherwise the gasket mating faces will be damaged. The head is located on dowels; so do not try to free it by tapping it sideways.
31 Remove the gasket from the top of the block, noting the two locating dowels. If the locating dowels are a loose fit, remove them and store them with the head for safe-keeping **(see illustration)**. Do not discard the gasket – it may be needed for identification purposes.
32 If the cylinder head is to be dismantled for overhaul, remove the camshafts as described in Section 5.

Preparation for refitting

33 The mating faces of the cylinder head and cylinder block must be perfectly clean before refitting the head. Use a hard plastic or wood scraper to remove all traces of gasket and carbon; also clean the piston crowns. Take particular care during the cleaning operations, as the soft aluminium alloy is damaged easily. Also, make sure that the carbon is not allowed to enter the oil and water passages – this is particularly important for the lubrication system, as carbon could block the oil supply to the engine's components. Using adhesive tape and paper, seal the water, oil and bolt holes in the cylinder block. After cleaning each piston, use a small brush to remove all traces of grease and carbon from the gap, and then wipe away the remainder with a clean rag. Clean all the pistons in the same way.
34 Check the mating surfaces of the cylinder block and the cylinder head for nicks, deep scratches and other damage. If slight, they may be removed carefully with a file, but if excessive, machining may be the only alternative to renewal.
35 If warpage of the cylinder head gasket surface is suspected, use a straight-edge to check it for distortion. Refer to Part C of this Chapter if necessary.
36 Check the condition of the cylinder head bolts, and particularly their threads, whenever they are removed. Wash the bolts in suitable solvent, and wipe them dry. Check each for any sign of visible wear or damage, renewing any bolt if necessary. Measure the length of each bolt, and compare with the length of a new bolt.

6.28 Slacken and remove the two bolts (arrowed) securing the timing cover to the cylinder head

6.31 Removing a cylinder head locating dowel

Although Saab does not specify that the bolts must be renewed, it is strongly recommended that the bolts be renewed as a complete set if the engine has completed a high mileage.

Refitting

37 Where removed, refit the camshafts with reference to Section 5.
38 Wipe clean the mating surfaces of the cylinder head and cylinder block/crankcase. Check that the two locating dowels are in position on the cylinder block.
39 Position a new gasket on the cylinder block surface; making sure that it is fitted the correct way round.
40 Check that each camshaft is at its TDC position – the timing marks are located on the front of the camshaft, and must be aligned with the marks on the bearing caps – see Section 3.
41 Rotate the crankshaft one quarter of a turn away from TDC; this will position all four pistons part-way along their bores, keeping them out of the way during cylinder head refitting.
42 Check that the timing chain is located correctly on the chain guides, and then carefully lower the cylinder head onto the block, aligning it with the locating dowels.
43 Apply a smear of grease to the threads, and to the underside of the heads, of the cylinder head bolts. Insert the bolts, and screw them in finger-tight.
44 Working progressively and in sequence, tighten the cylinder head bolts to their Stage 1 torque setting, using a torque wrench (see illustration).
45 Using the same sequence, tighten the cylinder head bolts to their Stage 2 torque setting.
46 With all the cylinder head bolts tightened to their Stage 2 setting, working again in the given sequence, angle-tighten the bolts further through the specified Stage 3 angle, using a socket and extension bar. It is recommended that an angle-measuring gauge be used during this stage of the tightening, to ensure accuracy (see illustration).
47 Rotate the crankshaft through one quarter of a turn back to its TDC position (see Section 3).
48 Insert and tighten the two bolts securing the timing cover to the cylinder head.
49 With reference to Section 3, check that the camshafts are both aligned at their respective TDC positions. Engage the camshaft sprockets with the timing chain (with reference to Chapter 2C, Section 10, if necessary) and then locate the sprockets on the camshafts, fitting the intake one first, followed by the exhaust one. Do not fully tighten the bolts at this stage. Check that the timing chain is correctly located on the guides and sprockets.
50 Refit the timing chain tensioner with reference to Chapter 2C, Section 11, if necessary.
51 Using a socket on the crankshaft pulley, rotate the engine two complete turns clockwise, then check that the TDC timing marks are still correctly aligned.
52 Fully tighten the camshaft sprocket

6.44 Cylinder head bolt tightening sequence

retaining bolts to the specified torque, while holding each camshaft stationary, using a spanner on the special flats machined into the transmission end of each shaft.
53 Refit the cylinder head cover as described in Section 4, then refit the spark plugs with reference to Chapter 1A.
54 Refit the intake manifold with reference to Chapter 4A. Bolt the engine lifting eyelets and the wiring harness support bracket in position.
55 Reconnect the coolant hoses for the throttle body, thermostat housing and cabin heater to their respective ports on the cylinder head, tightening the hose clips securely.
56 Position the engine oil dipstick tube against the cylinder head and secure it with the retaining bolt.
57 Reconnect the vacuum and crankcase breather hoses to the cylinder head cover.
58 With reference to Chapter 4A, refit the exhaust system front pipe to the turbocharger and tighten the bolts to the specified torque.
59 Refit the power steering pump with reference to Chapter 10.
60 Refit the alternator with reference to Chapter 5A, then refit the auxiliary drivebelt with reference to Chapter 1A.
61 Refit the intake air ducting and mass airflow meter with reference to Chapter 4A.
62 Refit the turbocharger crankcase breather pipe, then refit the intercooler-to-throttle body intake air ducts.
63 Refit the cover panel to the top of the intake manifold and insert the oil filler cap/dipstick.

7.4 Oxygen sensor wiring connectors (arrowed) – model with two oxygen sensors fitted

6.46 Using an angle-measuring gauge to tighten the cylinder head bolts through their Stage 3 angle

64 Reconnect the battery negative lead and refit the battery cover.
65 Refit the central panel under the radiator, followed by the right-hand front wing wheel arch liner and moulding.
66 Refit the right-hand front wheel, and lower the car to the ground.
67 Refill the cooling system (see Chapter 1A).
68 Start the engine, observing the precautions given in Chapter 2C, Section 23.

7 Sump – removal and refitting

Removal

1 Firmly apply the handbrake, and then jack up the front of the car and support it on axle stands (see *Jacking and vehicle support*). Remove the battery cover and disconnect the negative lead.
2 Remove both front roadwheels, and undo the securing screws and lower the undershield from under the vehicle.
3 Remove the engine upper cover then drain the engine oil, clean and refit the engine oil drain plug, tightening it to the specified torque. Remove the dipstick from its tube and place clean rag over the engine oil filler neck to prevent the ingress of debris. If the engine is nearing its service interval when the oil and filter are due for renewal, it is recommended that the filter is also removed, and a new one fitted. After reassembly, the engine can then be refilled with fresh oil. Refer to Chapter 1A for further information.
4 Unplug the oxygen sensor wiring connectors, located on a bracket at the left-hand end of the cylinder head (see illustration).
5 With reference to Chapter 4A, unbolt the exhaust system front pipe from the turbocharger. Unbolt the front pipe from its support bracket and withdraw it from the underside of the engine compartment. **Note:** *the flexible section of the exhaust pipe MUST NOT be put under excessive strain, as it may cause it to leak and eventually break.*
6 Undo the retaining bolts and remove the flywheel cover plate from the transmission end of the sump (see illustration).

2A•10 Petrol engine in-car repair procedures

7.6 Remove the retaining bolts (arrowed) and remove the cover plate

7.11 Remove the retaining bolts (arrowed) to remove the oil pump pick-up and strainer

7.13 Apply a bead of sealant to the sump flange

7 Where applicable, disconnect the crankcase breather hose from the rear of the sump.
8 Progressively unscrew and remove the bolts securing the sump to the cylinder block, leaving one or two bolts in position to prevent the sump falling.
9 Remove the remaining bolts, and lower the sump to the ground. Break the joint between the sump and crankcase by striking the sump with the palm of your hand.
10 It may be necessary to use a lever between the inner wing panel and the crankshaft pulley to move the engine to the left for the sump to be removed.
11 While the sump is removed, take the opportunity to check the oil pump pick-up/strainer for signs of clogging or damage **(see illustration)**.

Refitting

12 Clean all traces of sealant from the mating surfaces of the cylinder block/crankcase and sump, then use a clean rag to wipe out the sump and the engine's interior.
13 Ensure that the sump and cylinder block/crankcase mating surfaces are clean and dry, then apply a bead of suitable sealant approximately 1mm thick to the sump flange **(see illustration)**.
14 Offer up the sump and refit its retaining bolts, tightening them progressively to the specified torque.
15 Refer to Chapter 4A and refit the exhaust system front pipe. Apply a suitable anti-seize agent to the front pipe-to-turbocharger securing nut studs, and tighten the nuts to the specified torque. Fit the front pipe-to-support bracket securing bolt and tighten it securely.
16 Refit the flywheel cover plate to the transmission end of the sump.
17 Refit the undershield(s) to the front of the vehicle and tighten the securing screws.
18 Refit both front roadwheels and lower the vehicle to the ground.

19 Reconnect the oxygen sensor wiring block connectors.
20 Refill the engine with the correct quantity and grade of oil as described in Chapter 1A, then clean and refit the dipstick/filler cap.
21 Start the engine and allow it to warm-up. Check around the sump mating surface for signs of leakage.

8 Oil pump – removal, inspection and refitting

Removal

1 Apply the handbrake, then jack up the front of the car and support on axle stands (see *Jacking and vehicle support*). Remove the right-hand front wheel.
2 Undo the securing screws and withdraw the wheel arch liner from under the wing, then unclip the power steering pipe from the subframe.
3 Support the engine under the right-hand side, then undo the retaining bolts and remove the right-hand upper engine mounting assembly from the vehicle.
4 Remove the auxiliary drivebelt with reference to Chapter 1A.
5 Slacken the centre bolt from the crankshaft pulley. To do this, the crankshaft must be held stationary using one of the following methods. On manual transmission models, have an assistant depress the brake pedal and engage 4th gear. Alternatively, remove the flywheel cover or starter motor as described in Chapter 5A, then insert a stout flat-bladed screwdriver through the transmission bellhousing and engage it with the starter ring gear to prevent the crankshaft turning. On automatic transmission models, use the latter method only.
6 Remove the crankshaft pulley bolt, and then withdraw the crankshaft pulley and hub from the end of the crankshaft. If it is tight, careful use of two levers may be required **(see illustration)**.
7 Extract the large circlip, and then withdraw the oil pump cover from the timing cover. Note that the circlip has a high tension, and a large pair of circlip pliers will be required to compress it. Also note the alignment arrows on the cover and timing cover **(see illustrations)**.

8.6 Remove the crankshaft pulley bolt and withdraw the crankshaft pulley

8.7a Using circlip pliers to remove the oil pump cover circlip

8.7b Withdrawing the oil pump cover from the timing cover

8.7c Alignment arrows on the oil pump cover

Petrol engine in-car repair procedures 2A•11

8.8 Removing the O-ring seal from the groove in the oil pump cover

8.9a Using a vernier gauge to check the depth of the oil seal in the cover . . .

8.9b . . . then prise out the crankshaft oil seal from the oil pump cover

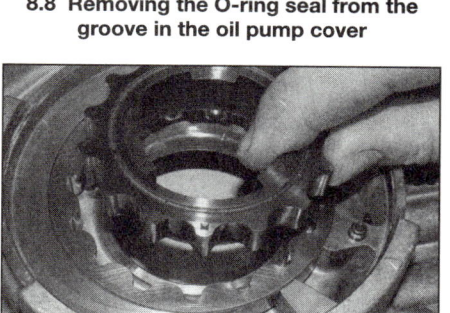

8.11a Removing the inner rotor . . .

8.11b . . . and outer rotor from the timing cover. Note that the position mark (arrowed) is facing outwards

8.12 Unscrew the plug and remove the relief valve spring (A) and plunger (B)

8 Remove the O-ring seal from the groove in the cover (see illustration).
9 Note the position of the crankshaft oil seal in the oil pump cover, then prise it out with a screwdriver (see illustrations).

Inspection

10 Wipe clean the inner faces of the pump rotors, and identify them for position with a marker pen. It is important that the rotors remain in their correct original positions on reassembly. Note that the outer rotor position is identified by the punch hole facing outwards.
11 Remove the rotors from the timing cover (oil pump body), keeping them identified for position (see illustrations).
12 Unscrew the plug, and remove the relief valve spring and plunger, noting which way round they are fitted (see illustration). Recover the plug washer.
13 Clean all components, and examine them for wear and damage. Examine the pump rotors and body for signs of wear ridges and scoring. Using a feeler blade check the clearance between the outer rotor and the timing cover, with reference to the Specifications (see illustration). If worn excessively, the complete pump assembly must be renewed.
14 Examine the relief valve plunger for signs of wear or damage, and renew if necessary. The condition of the relief valve spring can only be measured by comparing it with a new one; if there is any doubt about its condition, it should also be renewed.
15 If there are any signs of dirt or sediment in the oil pump, it will be necessary to remove the sump (see Section 7), and clean the pick-up/strainer.
16 Insert the relief valve plunger and spring, then refit the plug together with a new washer, and tighten the plug.
17 Lubricate the rotors with fresh engine oil, then insert them in the oil pump body in their original positions. The rotors must be positioned with the identification mark facing outwards, see paragraph 11.

Refitting

18 Wipe clean the oil seal seating in the oil pump casing, then drive a new oil seal into the casing (see illustration), making sure that it enters squarely and is fitted in the previously-noted position.
19 Fit a new O-ring seal, then insert the oil pump in the timing cover, making sure that the alignment arrows point to each other. Refit the large circlip in the groove with its chamfer

8.13 Checking the clearance between the oil pump outer rotor and the timing cover

facing outwards, and the opening facing downwards.
20 Locate the crankshaft pulley and hub on the end of the crankshaft. Insert the centre bolt and tighten it to the specified torque, holding the crankshaft stationary using one of the methods described in paragraph 5.
21 Refit the auxiliary drivebelt with reference to Chapter 1A.
22 Refit the wing liner and moulding, and tighten the screws.
23 Refit the right-hand front wheel, and lower the car to the ground.
24 Before running the engine, disconnect the ignition wiring harness to the DI ignition cartridge to disable the ignition system (see Chapter 5B), then remove the fuel pump fuse (see Chapter 12). Crank the engine on the starter motor until oil pressure is restored and the oil pressure warning light is extinguished. Restore the ignition and fuel systems, and run the engine to check for oil leaks.

8.18 Fitting a new oil seal to the oil pump cover

9.4a Undo the oil pipe retaining bolt (arrowed) . . .

9.4b . . . and the oil pipe retaining bracket and nut (arrowed) from the oil cooler

9.5 Slacken and remove the mounting bolts (arrowed) to remove the oil cooler

9.9 Slacken and remove plug to access thermostat

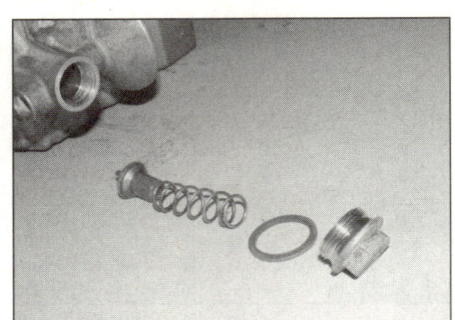

9.10 Thermostat, spring, sealing washer and securing bolt/plug

9 Oil cooler and thermostat – removal and refitting

Oil cooler/adapter

Removal

1 An oil cooler/adapter is fitted between the oil filter and cylinder block. If the engine is nearing its service interval when the oil and filter are due for renewal, it is recommended that the filter is removed, and a new one fitted. After reassembly, the engine can then be refilled with fresh oil. Refer to Chapter 1A for further information.
2 Drain the engine oil as described in Chapter 1A, then refit and tighten the drain plug.
3 Jack up the front of the car and support it securely on axle stands (see *Jacking and vehicle support*). Slacken and withdraw the securing screws, and remove the front lower cover/spoiler.
4 Position a suitable container beneath the oil cooler on the right-hand side front of the engine compartment. Unscrew the unions from the top and bottom of the oil cooler **(see illustrations)**. Allow any oil to drain into the container.
5 Unscrew the mounting bolts and remove the oil cooler from the engine compartment **(see illustration)**.

Refitting

6 Refitting is a reversal of removal, but tighten the unions to the specified torque. Fill the engine with oil with reference to Chapter 1A. On completion, start the engine and run it at a fast idle speed for several minutes, to allow the oil to fill the oil cooler. Check and if necessary top-up the engine oil level with reference to *Weekly checks*.

Thermostat

Removal

7 The oil temperature thermostat is mounted on the right-hand side front of the oil filter cooler/adapter.
8 Drain the engine oil as described in Chapter 1A, then refit and tighten the drain plug.
9 Position a suitable container beneath the thermostat, then unscrew the plug, recover the seal/washer and allow the surplus oil to run into the container **(see illustration)**.
10 Withdraw the thermostat and spring from the filter adapter **(see illustration)**.

Refitting

11 Fit the new thermostat into the filter adapter, ensuring that the flange rests on the machined recess in the housing.
12 Slide the spring into position, then fit the seal/washer to the plug and screw the plug into the filter housing, tightening it to the correct torque.
13 Fill the engine with oil with reference to Chapter 1A. On completion, start the engine and run it at a fast idle speed for several minutes, then check around the thermostat plug for signs of leakage. Check the engine oil level and top-up if necessary (see *Weekly checks*).

10 Oil pressure warning light switch – removal and refitting

Removal

1 The oil pressure switch is screwed into the rear of the cylinder block, beneath the intake manifold and behind the starter motor **(see illustration)**. First jack up the front of the car, and support on axle stands (see *Jacking and vehicle support*).
2 Trace the wiring back from the switch and disconnect the wiring block connector **(see illustration)**.
3 Unscrew the switch from the cylinder block; be prepared for slight loss of oil **(see illustration)**. If the switch is to be left removed for any length of time, plug the hole, to prevent the entry of debris.

10.1 The oil pressure switch (arrowed) is screwed into the rear of the cylinder block

10.2 Disconnecting the wiring from the oil pressure switch

Petrol engine in-car repair procedures 2A•13

Refitting

4 Wipe clean the threads of the switch and the location aperture. Do not insert tools or wire into the hole at the tip of the switch, in an attempt to clean it out; as this may damage the internal components.
5 Insert the switch into the cylinder block and tighten it securely.
6 Reconnect the switch wiring block connector.
7 Start the engine and check for leakage, then lower the car to the ground. Check the engine oil level and top-up if necessary (see *Weekly checks*).

11 Crankshaft oil seals – renewal

Right-hand oil seal

Note: *This procedure explains the fitting of the seal in situ. See Section 8 for the removal of the oil pump cover and renewing the seal off the engine.*

1 Apply the handbrake, then jack up the front of the car and support on axle stands (see *Jacking and vehicle support*). Remove the right-hand front wheel, undo the securing screws and withdraw the wheel arch liner. Where applicable, unclip the power steering pipe from the subframe.
2 Support the engine under the right-hand side, then undo the retaining bolts and remove the right-hand upper engine mounting assembly from the vehicle (with reference to Section 13).
3 Remove the auxiliary drivebelt with reference to Chapter 1A.
4 Unscrew and remove the centre bolt from the crankshaft pulley. To do this, the crankshaft must be held stationary using one of the following methods. On manual transmission models, have an assistant depress the brake pedal and engage 4th gear. Alternatively, remove the flywheel cover plate or starter motor as described in Chapter 5A, then insert a flat-bladed screwdriver through the bellhousing and jam the starter ring gear to prevent the crankshaft turning. On automatic transmission models, use the latter method only.
5 Pull the crankshaft pulley and hub from the end of the crankshaft. If it is tight, careful use of two levers may be required.
6 Note the fitted depth of the oil seal in its housing, then using a screwdriver, carefully prise the oil seal from the oil pump casing. Alternatively, punch or drill two small holes opposite each other in the seal. Thread a self-tapping screw into each hole, and pull on the screw heads with pliers to extract the seal. Another method is to remove the oil pump cover as described in Section 8, and remove the oil seal on the bench (see illustrations in Section 8).
7 Clean the seating in the oil pump casing, then lubricate the lips of the new oil seal with clean engine oil, and locate it squarely on the oil pump casing. Make sure that the closed side is facing outwards. Using a suitable tubular drift (such as a socket), which bears only on the hard outer edge of the seal, tap the seal into position, to the same depth in the casing as the original was prior to removal.
8 Locate the crankshaft pulley and hub on the end of the crankshaft. Insert the centre bolt and tighten it to the specified torque, holding the crankshaft stationary using one of the methods described in paragraph 4.
9 Refit the auxiliary drivebelt with reference to Chapter 1A, then refit the engine mounting assembly.
10 Refit the wheel arch liner front section and moulding, and tighten the screws.
11 Refit the right-hand front wheel, and lower the car to the ground.

Left-hand oil seal

12 Remove the flywheel/driveplate as described in Section 12.
13 Make a note of the fitted depth of the seal in its housing. Punch or drill two small holes opposite each other in the seal. Thread a self-tapping screw into each hole, and pull on the screw heads with pliers to extract the seal. Alternatively, use a screwdriver to prise out the oil seal.
14 Clean the seal housing, then lubricate the lips of the new seal with clean engine oil, and carefully locate the seal on the end of the crankshaft.
15 Using a suitable tubular drift, which bears only on the hard outer edge of the seal, drive the seal into position, to the same depth in the housing as the original was prior to removal.
16 Wipe clean the oil seal, then refit the flywheel/driveplate as described in Section 12.

12 Flywheel/driveplate – removal, inspection and refitting

Removal

1 Remove the transmission as described in Chapter 7A or 7B.
2 On manual transmission models, remove the clutch assembly as described in Chapter 6.
3 Prevent the flywheel/driveplate from turning by jamming the ring gear teeth with a wide-bladed screwdriver or similar tool. Alternatively, bolt a metal link between the flywheel/driveplate (using the clutch or torque converter bolt holes) and the cylinder block/crankcase.
4 Unscrew and remove the retaining bolts, remove the locking tool, then remove the flywheel/driveplate from the crankshaft flange. Note that the unit is located by a dowel pin, and must be fitted correctly.

10.3 Using a ring spanner to remove the oil pressure switch

Inspection

5 On manual transmission models, if the flywheel's clutch mating surface is deeply scored, cracked or otherwise damaged, the flywheel must be renewed. However, it may be possible to have it surface-ground; seek the advice of a Saab dealer or engine reconditioning specialist.
6 Similarly check the condition of the driveplate on automatic transmission models.
7 If the ring gear is badly worn or has missing teeth, it may be possible to renew it. This job is best left to a Saab dealer or engine reconditioning specialist. The temperature to which the new ring gear must be heated for installation is critical and, if not done accurately, the hardness of the teeth will be destroyed.

Refitting

8 Clean the mating surfaces of the flywheel/driveplate and crankshaft. Clean the threads of the retaining bolts and the crankshaft holes.
9 Ensure that the locating dowel is in position, then offer up the flywheel and locate it on the dowel.
10 Apply locking fluid to the threads of the retaining bolts. Insert and tighten them to the specified torque, holding the flywheel/driveplate stationary using one of the methods described in paragraph 3 **(see illustration)**.
11 On manual transmission models, refit the clutch assembly as described in Chapter 6.
12 Refit the transmission with reference to Chapter 7A or 7B.

12.10 Apply locking fluid to the bolt threads, and tighten to the specified torque

2A•14 Petrol engine in-car repair procedures

13.10 Slacken and remove the bolts and nut (arrowed) to remove the engine mounting bracket

13.11 Unclip the hose from the retaining clip (arrowed) under the engine mounting

13 Engine/transmission mountings – inspection and renewal

Inspection

1 For improved access, raise the front of the car and support it securely on axle stands (see *Jacking and vehicle support*).
2 The engine mountings are located at the front right-hand side, the left-hand side of the transmission under the battery tray, at the rear of the engine and, on some models, a torque arm mounting at the front.
3 Check the mounting rubbers to see if they are cracked, hardened or separated from the metal at any point; renew the mounting if any such damage or deterioration is evident.
4 Check that all the mounting's fasteners are securely tightened.
5 Using a large screwdriver or a crowbar, check for wear in the mounting by carefully levering against it to check for freeplay. Where this is not possible, enlist the aid of an assistant to move the engine/transmission back-and-forth, or from side-to-side, while you watch the mounting. While some freeplay is to be expected even from new components, excessive wear should be obvious. If excessive freeplay is found, check first that the fasteners are securely tightened, then if necessary renew any worn components as described below.

Renewal

Right-hand mounting

6 Apply the handbrake, then jack up the front of the car and support on axle stands (see *Jacking and vehicle support*). Remove the right-hand front wheel.
7 Remove the screws, and withdraw the right-hand front wing plastic moulding and front wheel arch liner.
8 Remove the securing screws and detach the plastic undershield from under the engine.
9 Position a trolley jack underneath the engine and raise the jack head until it is just taking the weight of the engine. Ensure that the jack head does not bear on the underside of the sump, use a block of wood between the sump and the jack head. Alternatively, position a lifting beam across the engine bay and support the engine by the lifting eyelet located at the rear right-hand side of the cylinder head.
10 Undo the bolts securing the engine mounting bracket to the engine and the retaining nut on the top of the engine mounting **(see illustration)**. Take care to avoid straining the other engine mountings as you do this.
11 Withdraw the engine mounting bracket from the vehicle, unclipping the power steering hose from its retaining clip **(see illustration)**. Undo the three retaining bolts and remove the engine mounting from the inner wing panel.
12 Fit the new mountings using a reversal of the removal procedure, making sure that the bolts/nuts are tightened to the correct torque.

Left-hand mounting

13 Apply the handbrake, then jack up the front of the car and support on axle stands (see *Jacking and vehicle support*).
14 Remove the battery cover and disconnect the battery leads (negative first), and position the leads away from the battery terminals.
15 Remove the securing screws and detach the plastic undershield from under the engine.
16 Position a trolley jack underneath the transmission and raise the jack head until it is just taking the combined weight of the engine and transmission. On models with automatic transmission, ensure that the jack head does not bear on the underside of the transmission sump; use a block of wood between the sump and the jack head. Alternatively, position a lifting beam across the engine bay and support the engine by the lifting eyelet located at the rear left-hand side of the cylinder head.
17 Undo the securing nut and remove the battery from the vehicle (disconnect the vent hose, where applicable), slacken and remove the retaining bolts and withdraw the battery tray from the vehicle **(see illustration)**.
18 Unscrew the bolts securing the engine/transmission mounting bracket to the bodywork and the centre nut from the mounting **(see illustration)**. Make sure the transmission is supported, taking care to avoid straining the other engine mountings as you do this.
19 Withdraw the mounting from the inner wing panel and transmission. Where applicable, disconnect the clutch hydraulic hose from the mounting bracket.
20 If required the transmission mounting

13.17 Undo the mounting bolts (arrowed) to remove the battery tray

13.18 Slacken and remove the bolts, nut and retaining screw (arrowed) to remove the engine mounting bracket

Petrol engine in-car repair procedures 2A•15

bracket can then be withdrawn from the transmission by removing the retaining bolts from the transmission casing.

21 Fit the new mounting using a reversal of the removal procedure, making sure that the nuts are tightened to the correct torque.

Rear mounting

22 Mount a lifting beam across the engine compartment, in-line with the front suspension turrets. Attach the jib to the engine lifting eyelet at the left hand end of the cylinder head. Raise the jib until the beam just starts to take the weight of the engine.

23 Remove the battery cover and disconnect the battery leads (negative first), and position the leads away from the battery terminals. Remove the engine upper cover.

24 On manual models, release the stay for the gearchange linkage from the rear engine mounting bracket.

25 Undo the upper nut and bolts securing the rear engine mounting to the subframe.

26 Disengage the bypass pipe and valve from the turbo intake pipe, then undo the retaining bolts and remove the exhaust manifold heat shield.

27 Unplug the oxygen sensor wiring at the connector, located on a bracket at the left hand end of the cylinder head and release it from any cable ties.

28 Ensure that the lifting beam is supporting the engine and transmission adequately, then slacken and withdraw the rear engine mounting centre bolts.

13.31 Undo the bolts (arrowed – two upper bolts inside housing) to remove the rear engine mounting bracket

29 Raise the front of the vehicle and support it securely on axle stands (see *Jacking and vehicle support*). Remove both front roadwheels.

30 With reference to Chapter 4A, unbolt the exhaust system front pipe from the turbocharger. Unbolt the front pipe from its support bracket and withdraw it from the underside of the engine compartment. **Note:** *the flexible section of the exhaust pipe MUST NOT be put under excessive strain, as it may cause it to leak and eventually break.*

31 Unbolt the engine mounting bracket from the rear of the transmission casing and remove it from the engine compartment complete with engine mounting **(see illustration)**.

32 Fit the new mounting using a reversal of the removal procedure, making sure that the nuts are tightened to the correct torque.

13.35 Slacken and remove the bolts (arrowed) on the front engine mounting/ torque arm

Front mounting

33 Raise the front of the vehicle and support it securely on axle stands (see *Jacking and vehicle support*).

34 Remove the securing screws and detach the plastic undershield from under the engine.

35 Slacken and remove the two nuts and bolts securing the torque arm mounting to the transmission and subframe **(see illustration)**. It can then be withdrawn from the vehicle.

36 If required the transmission mounting bracket can then be withdrawn from the transmission by removing the retaining bolts from the transmission casing.

37 Fit the new mounting using a reversal of the removal procedure, making sure that the nuts are tightened to the correct torque.

Notes

Chapter 2 Part B:
Diesel engine in-car repair procedures

Contents

	Section number		Section number
Camshaft followers and hydraulic tappets – removal, inspection and refitting	11	Flywheel/driveplate – removal, inspection and refitting	17
Camshaft housing – removal and refitting	9	General information	1
Camshaft oil seal – renewal	8	Oil filter housing – removal and refitting	15
Camshafts – removal, inspection and refitting	10	Oil pump – removal, overhaul and refitting	14
Compression and leakdown tests – description and interpretation	2	Sump – removal and refitting	13
Crankshaft oil seals – renewal	16	Timing belt – removal and refitting	6
Crankshaft pulley/vibration damper – removal and refitting	5	Timing belt sprockets, tensioner and idler pulley – removal and refitting	7
Cylinder head – removal and refitting	12	Top dead centre (TDC) for No 1 piston – locating	3
Engine/transmission mountings – inspection and renewal	18	Valve timing – checking and adjustment	4

Degrees of difficulty

Easy, suitable for novice with little experience	Fairly easy, suitable for beginner with some experience	Fairly difficult, suitable for competent DIY mechanic	Difficult, suitable for experienced DIY mechanic	Very difficult, suitable for expert DIY or professional

Specifications

General
Engine type	Four-cylinder, in-line, water-cooled. Double overhead camshaft, belt-driven
Manufacturer's engine code*	Z19DTH
Bore	82.0 mm
Stroke	90.4 mm
Capacity	1910 cc
Compression ratio	17.5:1
Output:	
Torque	320 Nm @ 2000-2700 rpm
Power	110 kW @ 4000 rpm
Firing order	1-3-4-2 (No 1 cylinder at timing belt end of engine)
Direction of crankshaft rotation	Clockwise (viewed from timing belt end of engine)

*For details of engine code location, see 'Vehicle identification' in the Reference Chapter.

Compression pressures
Maximum difference between any two cylinders	1.5 bar

Lubrication system
Minimum oil pressure at 80°C:	
At idle speed	1.0 bar
At 4000 rpm	4.0 bar
Oil pump type	Rotor-type, driven by crankshaft pulley/vibration damper from crankshaft

Torque wrench settings

	Nm	lbf ft
Air conditioning compressor mounting bracket to cylinder block/sump	50	37
Auxiliary drivebelt idler pulley bolt	25	18
Auxiliary drivebelt tensioner assembly bolts	50	37
Camshaft drivegear bolts*	120	89
Camshaft housing bolts	25	18
Camshaft housing closure bolt	16	12
Camshaft sprocket bolt*	120	89
Connecting rod big-end bearing cap bolt:*		
Stage 1	25	18
Stage 2	Angle-tighten a further 60°	
Crankshaft oil seal housing	9	7
Crankshaft pulley/vibration damper bolts	25	18
Crankshaft sprocket bolt*†	360	266
Cylinder head bolts:*		
Stage 1	20	15
Stage 2	65	48
Stage 3	Angle-tighten a further 90°	
Stage 4	Angle-tighten a further 90°	
Stage 5	Angle-tighten a further 90°	
Driveplate bolts*	160	118
Engine mountings:		
Front mounting/torque link bracket to transmission	80	59
Front mounting/torque link to subframe	80	59
Left-hand:		
Mounting-to-body bolts	20	15
Mounting bracket to transmission bracket	55	41
Transmission bracket to transmission	55	41
Rear mounting/torque link bracket to transmission	80	59
Rear mounting/torque link to subframe	60	44
Rear mounting/torque link to transmission bracket	80	59
Right-hand:		
Engine bracket-to-engine bolts	55	41
Lower bolts (M8)	25	18
Upper bolts (M10)	50	37
Mounting-to-body bolts/nut	55	41
Mounting-to-engine bracket bolts	55	41
Engine-to-transmission unit bolts:		
M10 bolts	40	30
M12 bolts	60	44
Flywheel bolts*	160	118
High-pressure fuel pump sprocket nut*	50	37
Intermediate shaft bearing housing support bracket bolts	55	41
Main bearing cap bolts:*		
Stage 1	25	18
Stage 2	Angle-tighten a further 100°	
Oil filler housing bolts	9	7
Oil filter housing to cylinder block	50	37
Oil pump housing to cylinder block	9	7
Oil pump pick-up/strainer bolts	9	7
Roadwheel bolts	110	81
Sump bolts:		
M6 bolts	9	7
M8 bolts	25	18
M10 bolts	40	30
Sump drain plug	20	15
Timing belt idler pulley bolt	50	37
Timing belt tensioner bolt	25	18
Timing belt upper cover bolts:		
M6 bolts	9	7
M8 bolts	25	18

* Do not re-use
† Left-hand thread

1 General information

How to use this Chapter

This Part of Chapter 2 describes the repair procedures which can reasonably be carried out, on the engine while it remains in the vehicle. If the engine has been removed from the vehicle and is being dismantled as described in Chapter 2C, any preliminary dismantling procedures can be ignored.

Note that, while it may be possible physically to overhaul items such as the piston/connecting rod assemblies while the engine is in the vehicle, such tasks are not usually carried out as separate operations, and usually require the execution of several additional procedures (not to mention the cleaning of components and of oilways); for this reason, all such tasks are classed as major overhaul procedures, and are described in Chapter 2C.

Chapter 2C describes the removal of the engine/transmission unit from the vehicle, and the full overhaul procedures which can then be carried out.

Engine description

The 1.9 litre DOHC diesel engine is of the sixteen-valve, in-line four-cylinder, double overhead camshaft type, mounted transversely at the front of the car, with the transmission on its left-hand end.

The crankshaft is supported within the cylinder block on five shell-type main bearings. Thrustwashers are fitted to number 3 main bearing, to control crankshaft endfloat.

The connecting rods rotate on horizontally split bearing shells at their big ends. The pistons are attached to the connecting rods by gudgeon pins, which are retained by circlips. The aluminium-alloy pistons are fitted with three piston rings – two compression rings and scraper-type oil control ring.

The camshafts are situated in a separate housing bolted to the top of the cylinder head. The exhaust camshaft is driven by the crankshaft via a toothed composite rubber timing belt (which also drives the high-pressure fuel pump and the coolant pump). The exhaust camshaft drives the intake camshaft via a spur gear. Each cylinder has four valves (two intake and two exhaust), operated via followers, which are supported at their pivot ends by hydraulic self-adjusting tappets. One camshaft operates the intake valves, and the other operates the exhaust valves.

The intake and exhaust valves are each closed by a single valve spring, and operate in guides pressed into the cylinder head.

Lubrication is by pressure-feed from a rotor-type oil pump, which is mounted on the right-hand end of the crankshaft. The pump draws oil through a strainer located in the sump, and then forces it through an externally mounted full-flow cartridge-type filter. The oil flows into galleries in the cylinder block/crankcase, from where it is distributed to the crankshaft (main bearings) and camshafts. The big-end bearings are supplied with oil via internal drillings in the crankshaft, while the camshaft bearings also receive a pressurised supply. The camshaft lobes and valves are lubricated by splash, as are all other engine components.

A semi-closed crankcase ventilation system is employed; crankcase fumes are drawn from the oil separator attached to the cylinder block via a hose to the camshaft housing. The fumes are then passed via a hose to the intake manifold.

Operations with engine in car

The following operations can be carried out without having to remove the engine from the car.

a) Removal and refitting of the cylinder head.
b) Removal and refitting of the timing belt, tensioner, idler pulleys and sprockets.
c) Renewal of the camshaft oil seal.
d) Removal and refitting of the camshaft housing.
e) Removal and refitting of the camshafts and followers.
f) Removal and refitting of the sump.
g) Removal and refitting of the connecting rods and pistons.*
h) Removal and refitting of the oil pump.
i) Removal and refitting of the oil filter housing.
j) Renewal of the crankshaft oil seals.
k) Renewal of the engine mountings.
l) Removal and refitting of the flywheel/driveplate.

* Although the operation marked with an asterisk can be carried out with the engine in the car (after removal of the sump), it is preferable for the engine to be removed, in the interests of cleanliness and improved access. For this reason, the procedure is described in Chapter 2C.

2 Compression and leakdown tests – description and interpretation

Compression test

Note 1: *A compression tester specifically designed for diesel engines must be used for this test because of the higher pressures involved.*

Note 2: *The battery must be in a good state of charge, the air filter must be clean, and the engine should be at normal operating temperature.*

1 When engine performance is down, or if misfiring occurs which cannot be attributed to the fuel system, a compression test can provide diagnostic clues as to the engine's condition. If the test is performed regularly, it can give warning of trouble before any other symptoms become apparent.
2 The tester is connected to an adapter, which screws into the glow plug holes. It is unlikely to be worthwhile buying such a tester for occasional use, but it may be possible to borrow or hire one – if not, have the test performed by a Saab dealer, or suitably-equipped garage. If the necessary equipment is available, proceed as follows.
3 Remove the glow plugs as described in Chapter 5A.
4 Screw the compression tester adapter in to the glow plug hole of No 1 cylinder.
5 With the help of an assistant, crank the engine on the starter motor; after one or two revolutions, the compression pressure should build-up to a maximum figure, and then stabilise. Record the highest reading obtained.
6 Repeat the test on the remaining cylinders, recording the pressure in each.
7 All cylinders should produce very similar pressures; any difference greater than the maximum figure given in the Specifications indicates the existence of a fault. Note that the compression should build-up quickly in a healthy engine; low compression on the first stroke, followed by gradually increasing pressure on successive strokes, indicates worn piston rings. A low compression reading on the first stroke, which does not build-up during successive strokes, indicates leaking valves or a blown head gasket (a cracked head could also be the cause). **Note:** *The cause of poor compression is less easy to establish on a diesel engine than on a petrol engine. The effect of introducing oil into the cylinders ('wet' testing) is not conclusive, because there is a risk that the oil will sit in the recess on the piston crown instead of passing to the rings.*
8 On completion of the test refit the glow plugs as described in Chapter 5A.

Leakdown test

9 A leakdown test measures the rate at which compressed air fed into the cylinder is lost. It is an alternative to a compression test, and in many ways it is better, since the escaping air provides easy identification of where pressure loss is occurring (piston rings, valves or head gasket).
10 The equipment needed for leakdown testing is unlikely to be available to the home mechanic. If poor compression is suspected, have the test performed by a Saab dealer, or suitably-equipped garage.

3 Top dead centre (TDC) for No 1 piston – locating

Note: *To accurately determine the TDC position for No 1 piston, it will be necessary to use Saab special tool 32 025 009 (or suitable equivalent) to set the crankshaft at the TDC position, together with the camshaft*

2B•4 Diesel engine in-car repair procedures

3.0a Saab special tool (or equivalent) is required to set the TDC position for No 1 piston . . .

3.0b . . . together with tools to set the camshaft position

3.5 Undo the central mounting bolt (arrowed), and remove the auxiliary drivebelt tensioner assembly

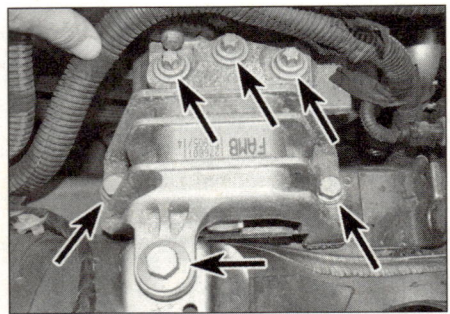

3.8 Undo the 6 bolts (arrowed) securing the engine mounting to the body and engine bracket

positioning tool, Saab special tool 32 025 008 (or suitable equivalent) **(see illustrations)**.

3.9 Engine breather pipe retaining bolts (arrowed)

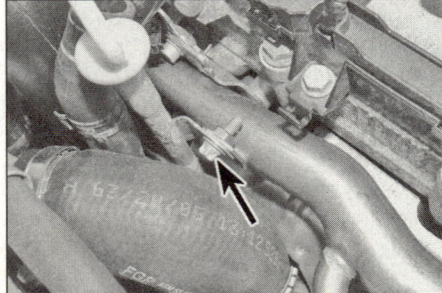

3.10 Undo the bolt (arrowed) and release the engine oil dipstick guide tube from the coolant pipe

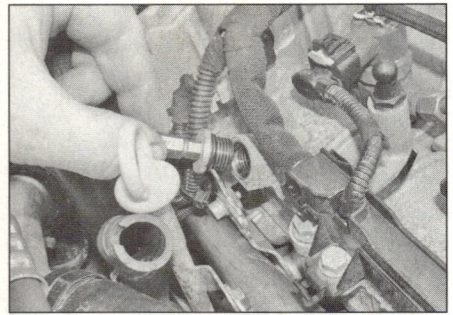

3.11 Unscrew the closure bolt from the valve timing checking hole in the camshaft housing

3.14 Screw the fastening stud of special tool 32 025 009 into the oil pump housing

1 In its travel up-and-down its cylinder bore, Top Dead Centre (TDC) is the highest point that each piston reaches as the crankshaft rotates. While each piston reaches TDC both at the top of the compression stroke and again at the top of the exhaust stroke, for the purpose of timing the engine, TDC refers to the piston position of No 1 cylinder at the top of its compression stroke.

2 Number 1 piston (and cylinder) is at the right-hand (timing belt) end of the engine, and its TDC position is located as follows. Note that the crankshaft rotates clockwise when viewed from the right-hand side of the car.

3 Disconnect the battery negative terminal as described in Chapter 5A, then lift off the plastic cover over the top of the engine.

4 Remove the crankshaft pulley/vibration damper as described in Section 5.

5 Undo the central mounting bolt, and remove the auxiliary drivebelt tensioner assembly from the engine **(see illustration)**.

6 Remove the air cleaner assembly and air intake duct as described in Chapter 4B.

7 Remove the engine undershield, then place a trolley jack beneath the right-hand end of the engine with a block of wood on the jack head. Raise the jack until it is supporting the weight of the engine.

8 Mark the bolt positions for correct refitting, then undo the three bolts securing the right-hand engine mounting to the engine bracket, and the three bolts securing the mounting to the body. Remove the mounting **(see illustration)**.

9 Release the retaining clip securing the engine breather hose to the breather pipe adjacent to the engine oil dipstick. Undo the two bolts securing the breather pipe to the cylinder head, and disconnect the pipe from the hose **(see illustration)**.

10 Undo the bolt and release the engine oil dipstick guide tube from the coolant pipe **(see illustration)**.

11 Unscrew the closure bolt from the valve timing checking hole in the camshaft housing **(see illustration)**.

12 Screw the camshaft positioning tool (Saab special tool 32 025 008) into the valve timing checking hole.

13 Using a socket and extension bar on the crankshaft sprocket bolt, rotate the crankshaft in the normal direction of rotation until the spring-loaded plunger of the positioning tool slides into engagement with the slot in the camshaft. There will be an audible click from the tool when this happens.

14 Unscrew the bolt from the lower left-hand side of the oil pump housing and screw in the fastening stud of Saab special tool 32 025 009 **(see illustration)**.

15 Fit the positioning ring of tool 32 025 009 over the fastening stud and engage it with the crankshaft sprocket. Ensure that the hole in the positioning ring engages with the lug on the sprocket. Secure the tool in position with the retaining bolt and nut **(see illustration)**.

16 With the crankshaft positioning ring in place and the camshaft positioning tool engaged with the slot in the camshaft, the engine is positioned with No 1 piston at TDC on compression.

4 Valve timing – checking and adjustment

Note: *To check and adjust the valve timing, it will be necessary to use Saab special tools (or suitable equivalents) to set the crankshaft and camshafts in the TDC position (see Section 3).*

Checking

1 Disconnect the battery negative terminal (refer Chapter 5A), then lift off the plastic cover over the top of the engine.
2 Release the retaining clip securing the engine breather hose to the breather pipe adjacent to the engine oil dipstick. Undo the two bolts securing the breather pipe to the cylinder head, and disconnect the pipe from the hose **(see illustration 3.9)**.
3 Undo the bolt and release the engine oil dipstick guide tube from the coolant pipe **(see illustration 3.10)**.
4 Unscrew the closure bolt from the valve timing checking hole in the exhaust side of camshaft housing **(see illustration 3.11)**.
5 Screw the exhaust camshaft positioning tool (Saab special tool 32 025 008) into the valve timing checking hole.
6 Unscrew the closure bolt from the valve timing checking hole in the intake side of the camshaft housing. The closure bolt is located below the fuel pressure regulating valve on the fuel rail.
7 Screw the intake camshaft positioning tool (Saab special tool 32 025 008) into the valve timing checking hole.
8 Using a socket and extension bar on the crankshaft sprocket bolt, rotate the crankshaft in the normal direction of rotation until the spring-loaded plungers of the positioning tools slide into engagement with the slots in the camshafts. There will be an audible click from the tools when this happens.
9 Remove the crankshaft pulley/vibration damper as described in Section 5.
10 Unscrew the bolt from the lower left-hand side of the oil pump housing and screw in the fastening stud of Saab special tool 32 025 009 **(see illustration 3.14)**.
11 Fit the positioning ring of tool 32 025 009 over the fastening stud and engage it with the crankshaft sprocket. Ensure that the hole in the positioning ring engages with the lug on the sprocket. Secure the tool in position with the retaining bolt and nut **(see illustration 3.15)**.
12 If it is not possible to fit the positioning ring of tool 32 025 009 as described, or if the camshaft positioning tools did not engage with the camshaft slots, adjust the valve timing as follows.

Adjustment

13 Remove the timing belt as described in Section 6.
14 Using a socket and extension bar on the crankshaft sprocket bolt, rotate the crankshaft anti-clockwise by 90°. This will position all the pistons halfway down their bores, and prevent any chance of the valves touching the piston crowns during the following procedure.
15 Remove the intake and exhaust camshaft positioning tools from the valve timing checking holes.
16 Using a suitable tool engaged with the timing belt sprocket on the exhaust camshaft, rotate the sprocket approximately 90° clockwise **(see Tool Tip in Section 7)**. Take care not to damage the camshaft sensor with the tool as the sprocket is rotated.
17 Screw the intake camshaft positioning tool (Saab special tool 32 025 008) into the valve timing checking hole.
18 Rotate the camshaft sprocket clockwise until the spring-loaded plunger of the positioning tool slides into engagement with the slot in the intake camshaft. There will be an audible click from the tool when this happens.
19 Release the two retaining clips and disconnect the charge air hose from the throttle body/housing, and intercooler charge air pipe.
20 Release the clip and disconnect the crankcase ventilation hose from the engine oil filler housing.
21 Disconnect the wiring connector from the coolant temperature sensor, then undo the three retaining bolts and remove the oil filler housing.
22 Remove the braking system vacuum pump as described in Chapter 9.
23 Working through the oil filler housing aperture, and using the holding tool to prevent rotation of the camshaft, slacken the intake camshaft drivegear retaining bolt. Working through the vacuum pump aperture, slacken the exhaust camshaft drivegear retaining bolt in the same way.
24 Screw the exhaust camshaft positioning tool (Saab special tool 32 025 008) into the valve timing checking hole.
25 Rotate the camshaft sprocket clockwise until the spring-loaded plunger of the positioning tool slides into engagement with the slot in the exhaust camshaft. There will be an audible click from the tool when this happens.
26 Hold the camshaft sprocket with the tool and tighten both drivegear retaining bolts to the specified torque.
27 Remove the positioning tool from the intake camshaft and refit the closure bolt. Tighten the bolt to the specified torque.
28 Refit the oil filler housing to the camshaft housing using a new gasket, refit the retaining bolts and tighten the bolts to the specified torque. Reconnect the coolant temperature sensor wiring connector, and reconnect the crankcase ventilation hose.
29 Refit the braking system vacuum pump as described in Chapter 9.
30 Refit the charge air hose to the throttle body/housing, and intercooler charge air pipe and secure with the retaining clips.

3.15 Positioning ring of tool 32 025 009 (arrowed) attached to the fastening stud and crankshaft sprocket

31 Refit the timing belt as described in Section 6.

5 Crankshaft pulley/ vibration damper – removal and refitting

Removal

1 Apply the handbrake, then jack up the front of the vehicle and support it on axle stands (see *Jacking and vehicle support*). Remove the right-hand front roadwheel, then undo the bolts and remove the engine undershield for access to the crankshaft pulley.
2 Remove the auxiliary drivebelt as described in Chapter 1B. Prior to removal, mark the direction of rotation on the belt to ensure the belt is refitted the same way around.
3 Undo the four bolts securing the pulley to the crankshaft sprocket and remove the pulley from the sprocket **(see illustration)**.

Refitting

4 Locate the crankshaft pulley on the sprocket, ensuring that the hole on the rear face of the pulley engages with the lug on the sprocket.
5 Refit the four retaining bolts and tighten them progressively to the specified torque.
6 Refit the auxiliary drivebelt as described in Chapter 1B using the mark made prior to removal to ensure the belt is fitted the correct way around.
7 Refit the roadwheel and engine undershield, then lower the car to the ground and tighten the wheel bolts to the specified torque.

5.3 Crankshaft pulley/vibration damper retaining bolts (arrowed)

2B•6 Diesel engine in-car repair procedures

6.2 Upper timing belt cover retaining bolts (arrowed)

6.3 Undo the bolt (arrowed) and remove the auxiliary drivebelt idler pulley from the engine bracket

6 Timing belt – removal and refitting

Note: *The timing belt must be removed and refitted with the engine cold.*

Removal

1 Position No 1 cylinder at TDC on its compression stroke as described in Section 3.
2 Unclip the wiring harness from the side of the upper timing belt cover. Unscrew the seven retaining bolts and lift off the upper timing belt cover **(see illustration)**.
3 Undo the retaining bolt and remove the auxiliary drivebelt idler pulley from the engine bracket **(see illustration)**.
4 Undo the two lower bolts, and the three upper bolts, and remove the engine bracket from the engine **(see illustrations)**.
5 Undo the nut and bolt and remove the crankshaft positioning tool (32 025 009) from the crankshaft sprocket.
6 Slacken the timing belt tensioner retaining bolt and allow the tensioner to retract, relieving the tension on the timing belt.
7 Slide the timing belt from its sprockets and remove it from the engine. If the belt is to be re-used, use white paint or similar to mark the direction of rotation on the belt. Do not rotate the crankshaft or camshafts until the timing belt has been refitted.
8 Check the timing belt carefully for any signs of uneven wear, splitting or oil contamination, and renew it if there is the slightest doubt about its condition. If the engine is undergoing an overhaul and is approaching the specified interval for belt renewal (see Chapter 1B) renew the belt as a matter of course, regardless of its apparent condition. If signs of oil contamination are found, trace the source of the oil leak and rectify it, then wash down the engine timing belt area and all related components to remove all traces of oil.

Refitting

9 On reassembly, thoroughly clean the timing belt sprockets and tensioner/idler pulleys.
10 Place the timing belt in position over the crankshaft sprocket. If the original belt is being refitted, ensure that the arrow mark made on removal points in the normal direction of rotation, as before.
11 Check that the camshaft and crankshaft are still positioned with No 1 piston at TDC on compression as described in Section 3, and with the camshaft positioning tool still in place. Now refit the crankshaft positioning tool.
12 Fit the timing belt over the crankshaft, camshaft and fuel pump sprockets, and around the idler pulleys, ensuring that the belt front run is taut (ie, all slack is on the tensioner side of the belt), then fit the belt over the coolant pump sprocket and tensioner pulley. Do not twist the belt sharply while refitting it. Ensure that the belt teeth are correctly seated centrally in the sprockets. Note that the marks on the new belt correspond to the marks on the crankshaft and camshaft sprockets.
13 Screw in a suitable bolt, approximately 50 mm in length, into the threaded hole directly below the timing belt tensioner. Using a screwdriver resting on the bolt as a pivot, move the adjusting lever on the tensioner until the tensioner pointer is aligned with the mark on the backplate. Hold the tensioner in this position and tighten the tensioner retaining bolt **(see illustrations)**.
14 Remove the crankshaft and camshaft positioning tools.
15 Using a socket on the crankshaft sprocket bolt, rotate the crankshaft smoothly through two complete turns (720°) in the normal direction of rotation to settle the timing belt in position. Stop rotating the crankshaft just before completing the second turn.
16 Refit the camshaft positioning tool and continue turning the crankshaft until the camshaft positioning tool engages.

6.4a Undo the two lower bolts (arrowed) . . .

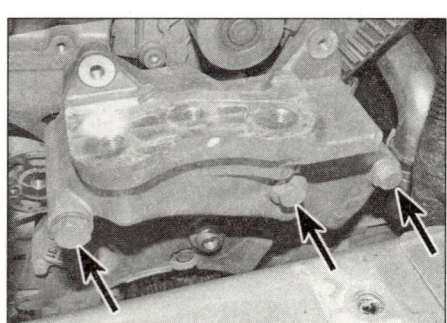

6.4b . . . and the three upper bolts (arrowed) . . .

6.4c . . . and remove the bracket from the engine

17 Refit the positioning ring of tool 32 025 009 over the fastening stud and engage it with the crankshaft sprocket. Ensure that the hole in the positioning ring engages with the lug on the sprocket. Secure the tool in position with the retaining bolt and nut.

18 Slacken the timing belt tensioner retaining bolt and, using a screwdriver resting on the pivot bolt as before, move the adjusting lever on the tensioner until the tensioner pointer is once again aligned with the mark on the backplate. Hold the tensioner in this position and tighten the tensioner retaining bolt to the specified torque.

19 Remove all the positioning tools and again rotate the crankshaft smoothly through two complete turns (720°) in the normal direction of rotation. Check that the timing belt tensioner pointer is still aligned with the mark on the backplate. If not, repeat the procedure described in paragraph 18.

20 When all is correct, remove the tensioner position pivot bolt. Refit the bolt removed from the oil pump housing and tighten it to the specified torque. Refit the closure plug to the camshaft housing and tighten to the specified torque.

21 Place the engine bracket in position and refit the two lower bolts, and the three upper bolts. Tighten the bolts to the specified torque. Refit the auxiliary drivebelt idler pulley to the engine bracket and tighten the retaining bolt to the specified torque.

22 Refit the upper timing belt cover and tighten the retaining bolts to the specified torque. Clip the wiring harness back into position.

23 Place the right-hand engine mounting assembly in position and refit the three bolts securing the mounting to the body. Tighten the bolts/nut to the specified torque. Align the mounting in its original position, and then tighten the three mounting bracket bolts to the specified torque. Remove the jack from under the engine.

24 Refit the air cleaner assembly and air intake duct as described in Chapter 4B.

25 Place the auxiliary drivebelt tensioner assembly in position ensuring that the locating peg on the tensioner mounting surface engages correctly with the corresponding hole in the mounting bracket. Tighten the tensioner central mounting bolt to the specified torque.

26 Refit the crankshaft pulley/vibration damper as described in Section 5, then refit the auxiliary drivebelt as described in Chapter 1B.

27 Move the engine oil dipstick guide tube back into position. Refit the bolt securing the guide tube to the coolant pipe and tighten the bolt securely.

28 Attach the engine breather hose to the breather pipe and secure with the retaining clip. Secure the breather pipe to the cylinder head with the two bolts securely tightened.

29 Refit the plastic cover to the top of the engine.

30 Refit the roadwheel and engine under shield, then lower the car to the ground and tighten the wheel bolts to the specified torque.

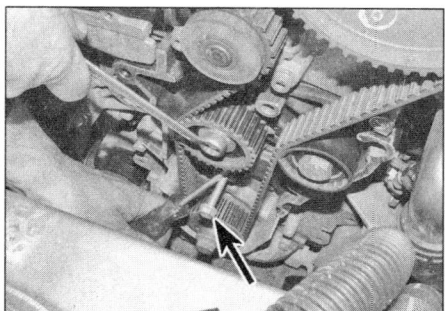

6.13a Use a screwdriver resting on a pivot bolt (arrowed), to move the adjusting lever on the tensioner . . .

7 Timing belt sprockets, tensioner and idler pulley – removal and refitting

Note: Certain special tools will be required for the removal and refitting of the sprockets. Read through the entire procedure to familiarise yourself with the work involved, then either obtain the manufacturer's special tools, or use the alternatives described.

Camshaft sprocket

Note: A new sprocket retaining bolt will be required for refitting.

Removal

1 Remove the timing belt as described in Section 6, then remove camshaft positioning tool from the valve timing checking hole.

2 It will now be necessary to hold the camshaft sprocket to enable the retaining bolt to be removed. Saab special tool 32 025 035 is available for this purpose, however, a home-made tool can easily be fabricated **(see Tool Tip)**.

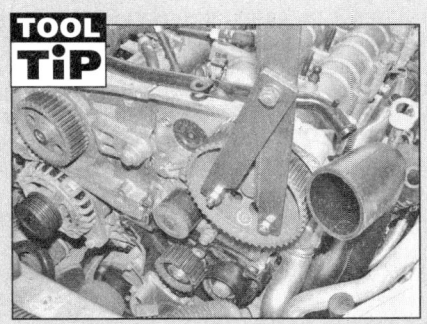

To make a sprocket holding tool, obtain two lengths of steel strip about 6 mm thick by about 30 mm wide or similar, one 600 mm long, the other 200 mm long (all dimensions are approximate). Bolt the two strips together to form a forked end, leaving the bolt slack so the shorter strip can pivot freely. At the other end of each 'prong' of the fork, fit a nut and bolt to allow the tool to engage with the spokes in the sprocket.

6.13b . . . until the tensioner pointer (arrowed) is aligned with the mark on the backplate

3 Engage the tool with the holes in the camshaft sprocket, taking care not to damage the camshaft sensor located behind the sprocket.

4 Unscrew the retaining bolt and remove the sprocket from the end of the camshaft.

Refitting

5 Prior to refitting check the oil seal for signs of damage or leakage. If necessary, renew as described in Section 8.

6 Refit the sprocket to the camshaft end, aligning its cutout with the locating peg, and fit the new retaining bolt finger-tight only at this stage. Final tightening is carried out after the timing belt has been fitted and tensioned.

7 Refit the camshaft positioning tool to the valve timing checking hole. If necessary, rotate the camshaft slightly, by means of the sprocket, until the tool audibly engages.

8 Proceed with the timing belt refitting procedure as described in Section 6, paragraphs 9 to 14.

9 Retain the camshaft sprocket using the holding tool, and tighten the retaining bolt to the specified torque.

10 Continue with the timing belt refitting procedure as described in Section 6, paragraphs 15 to 30.

Crankshaft sprocket

Note 1: The crankshaft sprocket retaining bolt is extremely tight. Ensure that the holding tool used to prevent rotation as the bolt is slackened is of sturdy construction and securely attached.

Note 2: A new sprocket retaining bolt will be required for refitting.

Removal

11 Remove the timing belt as described in Section 6.

12 It will now be necessary to hold the crankshaft sprocket to enable the retaining bolt to be removed. Saab special tools 32 025 006 and 83 95 360 are available for this purpose, however, a home-made tool similar to that described in paragraph 2, can easily be fabricated.

13 Using the crankshaft pulley retaining bolts, securely attach the tool to the crankshaft sprocket. With the help of an assistant, hold

7.14a Remove the bolt and washer . . .

7.14b . . . and slide the sprocket off the end of the crankshaft

7.20 Engage the holding tool with the holes in the fuel pump sprocket and undo the retaining nut

7.21 Use a suitable puller to release the fuel pump sprocket taper

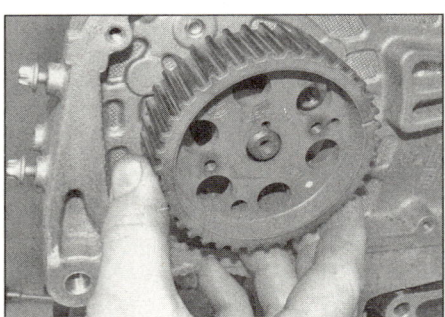

7.22a Once the taper releases, withdraw the sprocket . . .

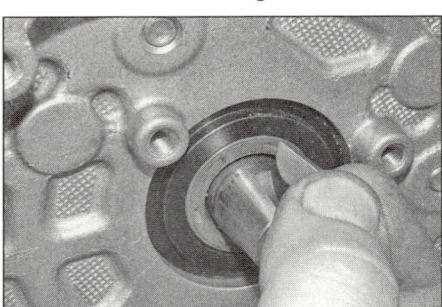

7.22b . . . and collect the Woodruff key from the pump shaft

the sprocket stationary and unscrew the retaining bolt. **Note:** *The sprocket retaining bolt has a **left-hand thread** and is unscrewed by turning it clockwise.*

14 Remove the bolt and washer and slide the sprocket off the end of the crankshaft **(see illustrations)**. Note that a new bolt will be required for refitting.

Refitting

15 Align the sprocket location key with the crankshaft groove and slide the sprocket into position. Fit the new retaining bolt and washer.

16 Hold the sprocket stationary using the holding tool and tighten the retaining bolt to the specified torque, remembering it has a **left-hand thread**. Remove the holding tool.

17 Refit the timing belt as described in Section 6.

High-pressure pump sprocket

Note: *A new sprocket retaining nut will be required for refitting.*

Removal

18 Remove the timing belt as described in Section 6.

19 It will now be necessary to hold the fuel pump sprocket to enable the retaining nut to be removed. Saab special tools 32 025 019 and 83 95 360 are available for this purpose, however, a home-made tool similar to that described in paragraph 2, can easily be fabricated.

20 Engage the tool with the holes in the fuel pump sprocket and undo the sprocket retaining nut **(see illustration)**. Note that a new nut will be required for refitting.

21 Attach a suitable puller to the threaded holes in the fuel pump sprocket using bolts and washers similar to the arrangement shown **(see illustration)**.

22 Tighten the puller centre bolt to release the sprocket from the taper on the pump shaft. Once the taper releases, remove the puller and withdraw the sprocket. Collect the Woodruff key from the pump shaft **(see illustrations)**.

Refitting

23 Clean the fuel pump shaft and the sprocket hub ensuring that all traces of oil or grease are removed.

24 Refit the Woodruff key to the pump shaft, and then locate the sprocket in position. Fit the new retaining nut.

25 Hold the sprocket stationary using the holding tool and tighten the retaining nut to the specified torque. Remove the holding tool.

26 Refit the timing belt as described in Section 6.

Tensioner assembly

Removal

27 Remove the timing belt as described in Section 6.

28 Slacken and remove the retaining bolt and remove the tensioner assembly from the engine **(see illustrations)**.

Refitting

29 Fit the tensioner to the engine, making sure that the slot on the tensioner backplate is correctly located over the peg on the engine bracket **(see illustration)**.

30 Clean the threads of the retaining bolt and

7.28a Slacken and remove the retaining bolt . . .

7.28b . . . and remove the timing belt tensioner assembly

Diesel engine in-car repair procedures 2B•9

apply thread-locking compound to the bolt threads. Screw in the retaining bolt, set the tensioner in the retracted position and tighten the retaining bolt.
31 Refit the timing belt as described in Section 6.

Idler pulley

Removal
32 Remove the timing belt as described in Section 6.
33 Slacken and remove the retaining bolt and remove the idler pulley from the engine (see illustration).

Refitting
34 Refit the idler pulley and tighten the retaining bolt to the specified torque.
35 Refit the timing belt as described in Section 6.

8 Camshaft oil seal – renewal

1 Remove the camshaft sprocket as described in Section 7.
2 Carefully punch or drill a small hole in the oil seal. Screw in a self-tapping screw, and pull on the screw with pliers to extract the seal.
3 Clean the seal housing, and polish off any burrs or raised edges, which may have caused the seal to fail in the first place.
4 Lubricate the lips of the new seal with clean engine oil, and press it into position using a suitable tubular drift (such as a socket) which bears only on the hard outer edge of the seal. Take care not to damage the seal lips during fitting; note that the seal lips should face inwards.
5 Refit the camshaft sprocket as described in Section 7.

9 Camshaft housing – removal and refitting

Removal
1 Remove the timing belt as described in Section 6.

9.2e . . . and air conditioning compressor (arrowed)

7.29 The slot on the tensioner backplate must locate over the peg (arrowed) on the engine bracket

2 Disconnect the wiring harness connectors from the following components (see illustrations):
a) Fuel injectors.
b) Fuel pressure regulating valve.
c) Fuel pressure sensor.
d) Camshaft sensor.

9.2a Disconnect the wiring plugs at the fuel injectors . . .

9.2c . . . fuel pressure sensor . . .

9.3a Undo the two bolts (arrowed) securing the wiring harness guide to the camshaft housing . . .

7.33 Slacken and remove the retaining bolt and remove the idler pulley from the engine

e) Air conditioning compressor.
3 Release the air conditioning compressor wiring harness from the clip on the oil dipstick guide tube. Undo the two bolts securing the plastic wiring harness guide to the camshaft housing and move the disconnected wiring harness to one side (see illustrations).

9.2b . . . fuel pressure regulating valve . . .

9.2d . . . camshaft sensor . . .

9.3b . . . and move the harness to one side

2B•10 Diesel engine in-car repair procedures

9.4a Disconnect the two vacuum hoses (arrowed) from the pipe assembly . . .

9.4b . . . then undo the two retaining bolts (arrowed) and move the pipe assembly to one side

9.6 Release the retaining clips and remove the charge air hose (arrowed)

4 Disconnect the two vacuum hoses from the vacuum pipe assembly on top of the camshaft housing. Undo the two retaining bolts and move the pipe assembly to one side **(see illustrations)**.
5 Remove the fuel injectors and the fuel rail as described in Chapter 4B.
6 Release the two retaining clips and disconnect the charge air hose from the throttle body/housing, and intercooler charge air pipe **(see illustration)**.
7 Disconnect the vacuum hose quick-release fitting from the braking system vacuum pump **(see illustration)**.
8 Release the clip and disconnect the crankcase ventilation hose from the engine oil filler housing **(see illustration)**.
9 Undo the retaining bolts and remove the two engine lifting brackets from the left-hand end of the camshaft housing. Undo the bolt securing the turbocharger charge air pipe to the right-hand end of the camshaft housing.
10 Working in a spiral pattern from the outside inwards, progressively slacken, then remove, the sixteen bolts securing the camshaft housing to the cylinder head. Ensure that the housing releases evenly from the cylinder block.
11 Lift the camshaft housing off the cylinder head and recover the gasket **(see illustration)**.
12 Thoroughly clean the mating faces of the cylinder head, camshaft housing and vacuum pump and obtain a new gasket for refitting.

Refitting

13 Check that all the hydraulic tappets and rocker arms are correctly positioned in the cylinder head and none have been disturbed.
14 Commence refitting by turning the crankshaft anti-clockwise by 90°. This will position all the pistons half-way down their bores, and prevent any chance of the valves touching the piston crowns as the camshaft housing is being fitted.
15 Place a new gasket on the cylinder head, then locate the camshaft housing in position aligning it with the locating dowels.
16 Refit the sixteen camshaft housing retaining bolts. Progressively screw in the bolts to gradually draw the housing down and into contact with the cylinder head.
17 Working in a spiral pattern from the inside outwards, progressively tighten the sixteen bolts to the specified torque.
18 Refit the two engine lifting brackets to the left-hand end of the camshaft housing and tighten the retaining bolts securely. Refit and tighten the charge air pipe retaining bolt.
19 Reconnect the crankcase ventilation hose to the engine oil filler housing.
20 Reconnect the vacuum hose quick-release fitting to the braking system vacuum pump ensuring that the fitting engages audibly.
21 Refit the charge air hose to the throttle body/housing, and intercooler charge air pipe and secure with the retaining clips.
22 Refit the fuel rail and fuel injectors as described in Chapter 4B.

23 Place the vacuum pipe assembly in position on the top of the camshaft housing and refit the two retaining bolts. Tighten the bolts securely, and then reconnect the two vacuum hoses.
24 Lay the plastic wiring harness guide in position on the camshaft housing, then refit and tighten the two retaining bolts.
25 Reconnect the wiring harness connectors to the components listed in paragraph 2, ensuring that the harness is secured by all the relevant retaining clips.
26 Turn the crankshaft clockwise by 90° to bring No 1 and 4 pistons to approximately the TDC position.
27 Refit the timing belt as described in Section 6.

10 Camshafts – removal, inspection and refitting

Note: *Additional camshaft positioning tools will be required for this operation – two in total (see Section 3).*

Removal

1 Carry out the operations described in Section 9, paragraphs 1 to 8.
2 Remove the braking system vacuum pump as described in Chapter 9.
3 Disconnect the wiring connector from the coolant temperature sensor, then undo the three retaining bolts and remove the oil filler housing **(see illustration)**.

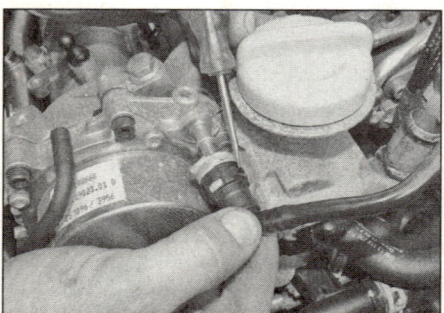

9.7 Depress the clip and disconnect the vacuum hose quick-release fitting from the braking system vacuum pump

9.8 Disconnect the crankshaft ventilation hose from the engine oil filler housing

9.11 Lift the camshaft housing off the cylinder head and recover the gasket

Diesel engine in-car repair procedures 2B•11

10.3 Undo the 3 bolts and remove the oil filler housing

10.8a Slacken the intake camshaft drivegear retaining bolt . . .

10.8b . . . and the exhaust camshaft drivegear retaining bolt

10.12a Unscrew and remove the two previously-slackened retaining bolts . . .

10.12b . . . then lift out the exhaust camshaft drivegear . . .

10.12c . . . and the intake camshaft drivegear

4 Undo the retaining bolt and remove the camshaft sensor from the right-hand end of the camshaft housing.
5 Before removing the camshaft housing completely, the retaining bolts for the camshaft drivegears and sprocket should be slackened as follows.
6 Remove the exhaust camshaft positioning tool from the valve timing checking hole.
7 It will be necessary to hold the camshaft sprocket to enable the drivegear and sprocket retaining bolts to be slackened. A home-made tool can easily be fabricated (see Tool Tip in Section 7).
8 Working through the oil filler housing aperture, and using the holding tool to prevent rotation of the camshaft, slacken the intake camshaft drivegear retaining bolt. Working through the vacuum pump aperture, slacken the exhaust camshaft drivegear retaining bolt in the same way (see illustrations).
9 Again, using the holding tool, slacken the camshaft sprocket retaining bolt.
10 Continue with the camshaft housing removal procedure as described in Section 9, paragraphs 9 to 11.
11 With the camshaft housing placed upside-down on the bench, unscrew and remove the previously-slackened retaining bolt, and remove the timing belt sprocket from the exhaust camshaft.
12 At the other end of the housing, unscrew and remove the two previously-slackened retaining bolts, and lift off the drivegears from the intake and exhaust camshafts (see illustrations).
13 Carefully prise out the exhaust camshaft oil seal with a screwdriver or similar hooked tool. Carefully withdraw the exhaust camshaft out from the timing belt end of the camshaft housing (see illustration).
14 Using a wooden dowel or similar, carefully tap the end of the intake camshaft toward the timing belt end of the housing, to release the blanking cap. Remove the cap, and then carefully withdraw the intake camshaft from the housing (see illustration).

Inspection
15 Examine the camshaft bearing surfaces and cam lobes for signs of wear ridges and scoring. Renew the camshaft(s) if any of these conditions are apparent. Examine the condition of the bearing surfaces in the camshaft housing. If the any wear or scoring is evident, the camshaft housing will need to be renewed.
16 If either camshaft is being renewed, it will be necessary to renew all the rocker arms and tappets for that particular camshaft also (see Section 11).
17 Check the condition of the camshaft drivegears and sprocket for chipped or damaged teeth, wear ridges and scoring. Renew any components as necessary.

Refitting
18 Prior to refitting, thoroughly clean all components and dry with a lint-free cloth. Ensure that all traces of oil and grease are removed from the contact faces of the drivegears, sprocket and camshafts.
19 Lubricate the camshaft bearing journals in the camshaft housing and carefully insert the intake and exhaust camshafts.
20 Ensuring that the contact faces are clean and dry, refit the drivegear to each camshaft. Note that the gear with the vacuum pump drive dogs is fitted to the exhaust camshaft, and the plain gear is fitted to the intake camshaft.

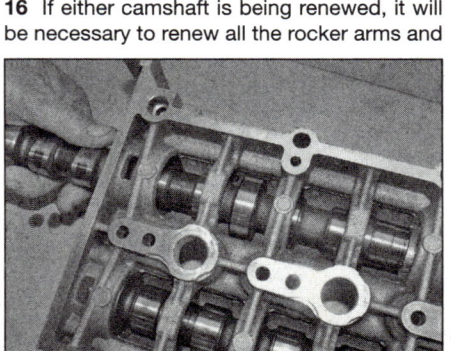

10.13 Withdraw the exhaust camshaft . . .

10.14 . . . and intake camshaft from the housing

10.22 Refit the camshaft positioning tool to the valve timing checking hole of the exhaust camshaft

10.23a Unscrew the closure bolt from the intake camshaft side of the housing ...

10.23b ... and fit a camshaft positioning tool for the intake camshaft

21 Screw in a new drivegear retaining bolt for each camshaft and tighten both bolts finger-tight only at this stage.
22 Refit the camshaft positioning tool to the valve timing checking hole of the exhaust camshaft. If necessary, rotate the exhaust camshaft slightly, until the tool engages audibly **(see illustration)**.
23 Unscrew and remove the closure bolt from the intake camshaft side of the camshaft housing and fit a second camshaft positioning tool **(see illustrations)**. If necessary, rotate the camshaft slightly, until the tool engages audibly.
24 With both camshafts locked by means of the positioning tools, tighten both drivegear retaining bolts to the specified torque **(see illustration)**. It may be beneficial to have an assistant securely support the camshaft housing as the bolts are tightened.

25 Remove the positioning tool from the intake camshaft and refit the closure bolt. Tighten the bolt to the specified torque.
26 Fit a new intake camshaft blanking cap to the timing belt end of the camshaft housing and tap it into position until it is flush with the outer face of the housing, using a suitable socket or tube, or a wooden block **(see illustrations)**.
27 Similarly, fit a new exhaust camshaft oil seal to the timing belt end of the camshaft housing and tap it into position until it is flush with the outer face of the housing, using a suitable socket or tube, or a wooden block **(see illustration)**.
28 Refit the timing belt sprocket to the exhaust camshaft, aligning its cut-out with the locating peg, and fit the new retaining bolt finger-tight only at this stage. Final tightening

is carried out after the timing belt has been fitted and tensioned.
29 Refit the camshaft sensor to the camshaft housing and tighten the retaining bolt securely.
30 Refit the oil filler housing to the camshaft housing using a new gasket, refit the retaining bolts and tighten the bolts to the specified torque. Reconnect the coolant temperature sensor wiring connector.
31 Refit the braking system vacuum pump as described in Chapter 9.
32 Thoroughly clean the mating faces of the cylinder head and camshaft housing.
33 Refit the camshaft housing to the cylinder head as described in Section 9, paragraphs 13 to 26.
34 Commence refitting of the timing belt as described in Section 6, paragraphs 9 to 14.
35 Retain the camshaft sprocket using the holding tool, and tighten the retaining bolt to the specified torque.
36 Continue refitting of the timing belt as described in Section 6, paragraphs 15 to 30.

11 Camshaft followers and hydraulic tappets – removal, inspection and refitting

Removal

1 Remove the camshaft housing as described in Section 9.
2 Obtain sixteen small, oil-tight clean plastic containers, and number them intake 1 to 8 and exhaust 1 to 8; alternatively, divide a larger container into sixteen compartments and number each compartment accordingly.
3 Withdraw each camshaft follower and hydraulic tappet in turn, unclip the follower from the tappet, and place them in their respective container **(see illustrations)**. Do not interchange the followers and tappets, or the rate of wear will be much increased. Fill each container with clean engine oil and ensure that the tappet is submerged.

Inspection

4 Examine the followers and hydraulic tappet bearing surfaces for wear ridges and scoring.

10.24 With both camshafts locked, tighten both drivegear retaining bolts to the specified torque

10.26a Fit a new intake camshaft blanking cap to the camshaft housing ...

10.26b ... and tap it into position until it is flush with the outer face of the housing

10.27 Similarly, fit a new exhaust camshaft oil seal to the camshaft housing

Diesel engine in-car repair procedures 2B•13

Renew any follower or tappet on which these conditions are apparent.

5 If any new hydraulic tappets are obtained, they should be immersed in a container of clean engine oil prior to refitting.

Refitting

6 Liberally oil the cylinder head hydraulic tappet bores and the tappets. Working on one assembly at a time, clip the follower back onto the tappet, then refit the tappet to the cylinder head, ensuring that it is refitted to its original bore. Lay the follower over its respective valve **(see illustrations)**.

7 Refit the remaining tappets and followers in the same way.

8 With all the tappets and followers in place, refit the camshaft housing as described in Section 9.

12 Cylinder head – removal and refitting

Note: *New cylinder head bolts will be required for refitting.*

Removal

1 Disconnect the battery negative terminal as described in Chapter 5A.
2 Drain the cooling system as described in Chapter 1B.
3 Remove the camshaft housing as described in Section 9.
4 Remove the camshaft followers and hydraulic tappets as described in Section 11.
5 Remove the intake and exhaust manifolds as described in Chapter 4B.
6 Release the clips and disconnect the remaining two coolant hoses at the thermostat housing, and the coolant hose at the EGR valve heat exchanger **(see illustration)**.
7 Release the coolant pipe from the stud at the base of the thermostat housing **(see illustration)**.

11.3a Withdraw each camshaft follower . . .

11.6a Clip the follower back onto the tappet . . .

11.3b . . . and hydraulic tappet in turn, then place them in their respective container

11.6b . . . then refit the tappet to its original bore, and lay the follower over its respective valve

8 Undo the bolt securing the high-pressure fuel pump mounting bracket to the cylinder head **(see illustration)**.
9 Make a final check to ensure that all relevant hoses, pipes and wires have been disconnected.
10 Working in the **reverse** of the tightening sequence **(see illustration 12.27)**, progressively slacken the cylinder head bolts by half a turn at a time, until all bolts can be unscrewed by hand. Note that an M14 RIBE socket bit will be required to unscrew the bolts. Remove the cylinder head bolts and recover the washers.

11 Engage the help of an assistant, if necessary, and lift the cylinder head from the cylinder block **(see illustration)**.
Caution: Do not lay the head on its lower mating surface; support the head on wooden blocks, ensuring each block only contacts the head mating surface.
12 Remove the gasket and keep it for identification purposes (see paragraph 19).
13 If the cylinder head is to be dismantled for overhaul, then refer to Part C of this Chapter.

Preparation for refitting

14 The mating faces of the cylinder head and

12.6 Disconnect the coolant hoses at the thermostat housing (A), and at the EGR valve heat exchanger (B)

12.7 Release the coolant pipe from the stud (arrowed) at the base of the thermostat housing

12.8 Undo the bolt (arrowed) securing the high-pressure fuel pump mounting bracket to the cylinder head

12.11 Lift the cylinder head from the cylinder block

12.19 Cylinder head gasket thickness identification holes (arrowed)

cylinder block/crankcase must be perfectly clean before refitting the head. Use a hard plastic or wood scraper to remove all traces of gasket and carbon; also clean the piston crowns. Take particular care, as the surfaces are damaged easily. Also, make sure that the carbon is not allowed to enter the oil and water passages – this is particularly important for the lubrication system, as carbon could block the oil supply to any of the engine's components. Using adhesive tape and paper, seal the water, oil and bolt holes in the cylinder block/crankcase. To prevent carbon entering the gap between the pistons and bores, smear a little grease in the gap. After cleaning each piston, use a small brush to remove all traces of grease and carbon from the gap, and then wipe away the remainder with a clean rag. Clean all the pistons in the same way.

15 Check the mating surfaces of the cylinder block/crankcase and the cylinder head for nicks, deep scratches and other damage. If slight, they may be removed carefully with a file, but if excessive, machining may be the only alternative to renewal.

16 Ensure that the cylinder head bolt holes in the crankcase are clean and free of oil. Syringe or soak up any oil left in the bolt holes. This is most important in order that the correct bolt tightening torque can be applied and to prevent the possibility of the block being cracked by hydraulic pressure when the bolts are tightened.

17 The cylinder head bolts must be discarded and renewed, regardless of their apparent condition.

18 If warpage of the cylinder head gasket surface is suspected, use a straight-edge to check it for distortion. Refer to Part C of this Chapter if necessary.

19 On this engine, the cylinder head-to-piston clearance is controlled by fitting different thickness head gaskets. The gasket thickness can be determined by looking at the holes stamped on the edge of the gasket **(see illustration)**.

Number of holes	Gasket thickness
No holes	0.77 to 0.87 mm
One hole	0.87 to 0.97 mm
Two holes	0.97 to 1.07 mm

The correct thickness of gasket required is selected by measuring the piston protrusions as follows.

20 Mount a dial test indicator securely on the block so that its pointer can be easily pivoted between the piston crown and block mating surface. Turn the crankshaft to bring No 1 piston roughly to the TDC position. Move the dial test indicator probe over and in contact with No 1 piston. Turn the crankshaft back-and-forth slightly until the highest reading is shown on the gauge, indicating that the piston is at TDC.

21 Zero the dial test indicator on the gasket surface of the cylinder block then carefully move the indicator over No 1 piston. Measure its protrusion at the highest point between the valve cut-outs, and then again at its highest point between the valve cut-outs at 90° to the first measurement **(see illustration)**. Repeat this procedure with No 4 piston.

22 Rotate the crankshaft half a turn (180°) to bring No 2 and 3 pistons to TDC. Ensure the crankshaft is accurately positioned then measure the protrusions of No 2 and 3 pistons at the specified points. Once all pistons have been measured, rotate the crankshaft to position all the pistons at their mid-stroke.

23 Select the correct thickness of head gasket required by determining the largest amount of piston protrusion, and using the following table.

Piston protrusion measurement	Gasket thickness required
0.020 to 0.100 mm	0.77 to 0.87 mm (no holes)
0.101 to 0.200 mm	0.87 to 0.97 mm (one hole)
0.201 to 0.295 mm	0.97 to 1.07 mm (two holes)

Refitting

24 Wipe clean the mating surfaces of the cylinder head and cylinder block/crankcase. Place the new gasket in position with the words ALTO/TOP uppermost **(see illustration)**.

25 Carefully refit the cylinder head assembly to the block, aligning it with the locating dowels.

26 Apply a thin film of engine oil to the bolt threads and the underside of the bolt heads. Carefully enter each new cylinder head bolt into its relevant hole (do not drop them in). Screw all bolts in, by hand only, until finger-tight.

27 Working progressively in sequence, tighten the cylinder head bolts to their Stage 1 torque setting, using a torque wrench and suitable socket **(see illustration)**. Working again in the same sequence, go around and tighten all bolts through the specified Stage 2 torque setting.

28 Once all bolts have been tightened to the Stage 2 torque, working again in the same sequence, go around and tighten all bolts

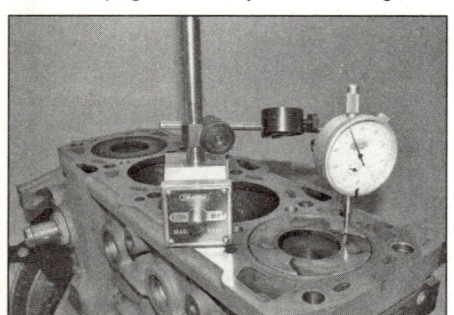

12.21 Use a dial test indicator to measure piston protrusion

12.24 Place the new gasket in position with the words ALTO/TOP uppermost (arrowed)

12.27 Cylinder head bolt tightening sequence

Diesel engine in-car repair procedures 2B•15

through the specified Stage 3 angle, then through the specified Stage 4 angle, and finally through the specified Stage 5 angle using an angle-measuring gauge.
29 Refit the bolt securing the high-pressure fuel pump mounting bracket to the cylinder head and tighten the bolt securely.
30 Engage the coolant pipe with the stud on the thermostat housing, then reconnect the coolant hoses to the thermostat housing and EGR valve heat exchanger.
31 Refit the intake and exhaust manifolds as described in Chapter 4B.
32 Refit the camshaft followers and hydraulic tappets as described in Section 11.
33 Refit the camshaft housing as described in Section 9.
34 On completion, reconnect the battery negative terminal, then refill the cooling system as described in Chapter 1B.

13 Sump – removal and refitting

Removal

1 Disconnect the battery negative terminal as described in Chapter 5A.
2 Apply the handbrake, then jack up the front of the vehicle and support it on axle stands (see *Jacking and vehicle support*). Remove the right-hand front roadwheel, then undo the bolts and remove the engine undershield.
3 Remove the right-hand driveshaft and the intermediate shaft as described in Chapter 8.
4 Undo the three bolts securing the intermediate shaft bearing housing support bracket to the cylinder block and remove the support bracket (see illustration).
5 Remove the exhaust system as described in Chapter 4B.
6 Undo the three bolts and remove the support bracket from the catalytic converter and sump.
7 Remove the crankshaft pulley/vibration damper as described in Section 5.
8 Disconnect the wiring connector from the air conditioning compressor. Undo the three bolts securing the air conditioning compressor to the mounting bracket and suitably support the compressor on the front subframe.

13.4 Intermediate shaft bearing housing support bracket retaining bolts (arrowed)

9 Undo the four bolts securing the compressor mounting bracket to the cylinder block and sump (see illustration). Unclip the wiring harness and remove the mounting bracket.
10 Drain the engine oil as described in Chapter 1B. When the oil has completely drained, refit the drain plug with new sealing washer, and tighten to the specified torque.
11 Undo the upper bolt securing the oil dipstick guide tube to the coolant pipe. Undo the lower bolt securing the guide tube to the sump flange, then unclip the wiring harness and withdraw the tube from the sump flange sealing grommet.
12 Disconnect the wiring connector from the oil level sensor, then release the retaining clip and disconnect the oil return hose.
13 Undo the two bolts securing the sump flange to the transmission bellhousing.
14 Using a socket and extension on the crankshaft pulley bolt, rotate the crankshaft in the normal direction of rotation (clockwise when viewed from the right-hand end of the engine) until the opening in the flywheel is positioned to allow access to one of the rear sump retaining bolts. Undo and remove the bolt, then rotate the crankshaft again until the flywheel allows access to the second rear retaining bolt. Undo and remove the bolt.
15 Progressively slacken and remove the remaining twelve bolts securing the sump to the base of the cylinder block and oil pump housing. Using a wide-bladed scraper or similar tool inserted between the sump and cylinder block, carefully break the joint to release the sump.
16 Manoeuvre the sump out from under the

13.9 Air conditioning compressor mounting bracket retaining bolts (arrowed)

car. Clearance is extremely limited between the sump and subframe, and it may be necessary to release the oil pump pick-up/strainer, by undoing its two retaining bolts, to enable the sump to be removed.
17 If required, undo the retaining bolts and remove the oil baffle plate from inside the sump (see illustration).
18 While the sump is removed, take the opportunity to check the oil pump pick-up/strainer for signs of clogging or splitting. If not already done, unbolt the oil pump pick-up/strainer and remove it from the engine along with its sealing ring. The strainer can then be cleaned easily in solvent or renewed. Renew the pick-up/strainer sealing ring prior to refitting (see illustration).

Refitting

19 Thoroughly clean the sump and remove all traces of silicone sealer and oil from the mating surfaces of the sump and cylinder block. If removed, refit the oil baffle plate and tighten its retaining bolts securely.
20 If clearance allows, refit the oil pump pick-up/strainer using a new sealing ring, and tighten its two retaining bolts securely. If it was necessary to unbolt the pick-up/strainer to allow the sump to be removed, place the unit in position and loosely screw in the bolt securing it to the main bearing cap. It must still be possible for the forward end of the pipe to be moved to the rear as the sump is refitted.
21 Apply a continuous bead of silicone sealing compound (90 543 772 – available from your Saab dealer) at approximately 1.0 mm from the inner edge of the sump (see illustration). The

13.17 Remove the oil baffle plate from inside the sump

13.18 Renew the pick-up/strainer sealing ring prior to refitting

13.21 Apply a continuous bead of silicone sealing compound to the sump flange

2B•16 Diesel engine in-car repair procedures

14.4 Oil pump housing retaining bolts (arrowed)

14.5 Undo the retaining screws and lift off the oil pump cover

bead of sealant should be between 2.0 and 2.5 mm in diameter.

22 Locate the sump over the pick-up/strainer then, where applicable, fit the forward end of the pick-up/strainer to the oil pump housing and fit the retaining bolt. Tighten both retaining bolts securely.

23 Engage the sump with the cylinder block and loosely refit all the retaining bolts.

24 Working out from the centre in a diagonal sequence, progressively tighten the bolts securing the sump to the cylinder block and oil pump housing. Tighten all the bolts to their specified torque setting.

25 Tighten the two bolts securing the sump flange to the transmission bellhousing to their specified torque settings.

26 Reconnect the wiring connector to the oil level sensor, then refit the oil return hose and secure with the retaining clip.

27 Refit the oil dipstick guide tube and secure with the two bolts tightened securely.

28 Locate the air conditioning compressor mounting bracket in position and refit the four retaining bolts. Tighten the bolts to the specified torque. Clip the wiring harness back into position on the bracket.

29 Position the air conditioning compressor on the mounting bracket. Fit and tighten the three retaining bolts to the specified torque (see Chapter 3), then reconnect the compressor wiring connector.

30 Refit the crankshaft pulley/vibration damper as described in Section 5.

31 Refit the catalytic converter support bracket and securely tighten the three bolts.

32 Refit the exhaust system as described in Chapter 4B.

33 Position the intermediate shaft bearing housing support bracket on the cylinder block and secure with the three retaining bolts tightened to the specified torque.

34 Refit the intermediate shaft and right-hand driveshaft as described in Chapter 8.

35 Refit the roadwheel and engine undershield, then lower the car to the ground and tighten the wheel bolts to the specified torque.

36 Fill the engine with fresh engine oil as described in Chapter 1B.

37 On completion, reconnect the battery negative terminal as described in Chapter 5A.

14 Oil pump – removal, overhaul and refitting

Removal

1 Remove the timing belt as described in Section 6.

2 Remove the crankshaft sprocket as described in Section 7.

3 Remove the sump and oil pump pick-up/strainer as described in Section 13.

4 Slacken and remove the seven retaining bolts then slide the oil pump housing assembly off of the end of the crankshaft (see illustration). Remove the housing gasket and discard it.

Overhaul

5 Undo the retaining screws and lift off the pump cover from the rear of the housing (see illustration).

6 Check the inner and outer rotors for identification dots indicating which way round they are fitted (see illustration). If no marks are visible, use a suitable marker pen to mark the surface of both the pump inner and outer rotors.

7 Lift out the inner and outer rotors from the pump housing.

8 Unscrew the oil pressure relief valve bolt from the base of the housing and withdraw the spring and plunger, noting which way around the plunger is fitted (see illustrations).

14.6 Oil pump inner and outer rotor identification dots (arrowed)

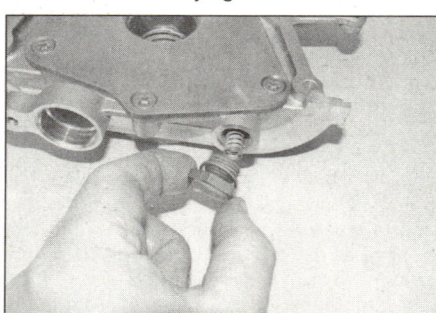

14.8a Unscrew the oil pressure relief valve bolt . . .

14.8b . . . then withdraw the spring . . .

14.8c . . . and plunger

Diesel engine in-car repair procedures 2B•17

Remove the sealing washer from the valve bolt.
9 Clean the components, and carefully examine the rotors, pump body and relief valve plunger for any signs of scoring or wear. If any damage or wear is noticed, it will be necessary to renew the complete pump assembly.
10 If the pump is satisfactory, reassemble the components in the reverse order of removal, noting the following.
 a) Ensure both rotors are fitted the correct way around.
 b) Fit a new sealing ring to the pressure relief valve bolt and securely tighten the bolt.
 c) Apply a little locking compound to the threads, and securely tighten the pump cover screws.
 d) On completion prime the oil pump by filling it with clean engine oil whilst rotating the inner rotor (see illustration).

Refitting

11 Prior to refitting, carefully lever out the crankshaft oil seal using a flat-bladed screwdriver. Fit the new oil seal, ensuring its sealing lip is facing inwards, and press it squarely into the housing using a tubular drift which bears only on the hard outer edge of the seal. Press the seal into position so that it is flush with the housing and lubricate the oil seal lip with clean engine oil.
12 Ensure the mating surfaces of the oil pump and cylinder block are clean and dry.
13 Fit a new gasket to the oil pump housing and bend down the tabs on the edge of the gasket to retain it on the pump housing (see illustration).
14 Locate the pump housing over the end of the crankshaft and into position on the cylinder block.
15 Refit the pump housing retaining bolts and tighten them to the specified torque.
16 Refit the oil pump pick-up/strainer and sump as described in Section 13.
17 Refit the crankshaft sprocket as described in Section 7.
18 Refit the timing belt as described in Section 6.
19 On completion, fit a new oil filter and fill the engine with clean oil as described in Chapter 1B.

14.10 Prime the oil pump by filling it with clean engine oil whilst rotating the inner rotor

15 Oil filter housing – removal and refitting

Removal

1 The oil filter housing with integral oil cooler is located at the rear of the cylinder block, above the right-hand driveshaft.
2 Disconnect the battery negative terminal as described in Chapter 5A.
3 Apply the handbrake, then jack up the front of the vehicle and support it on axle stands (see Jacking and vehicle support). Remove the right-hand front roadwheel, then undo the bolts and remove the engine undershield.
4 Drain the cooling system as described in Chapter 1B.
5 Remove the engine oil filter element as described in Chapter 1B.
6 Remove the right-hand driveshaft and the intermediate shaft as described in Chapter 8.
7 Undo the three bolts securing the intermediate shaft bearing housing support bracket to the cylinder block and remove the support bracket (see illustration 13.4).
8 Disconnect the wiring connector from the oil pressure switch.
9 Release the retaining clips and disconnect the two coolant hoses from the oil cooler on the oil filter housing.
10 Undo the three retaining bolts and remove the oil filter housing from the cylinder block (see illustration). Recover the two rubber seals from the rear of the housing. Note that new seals will be required for refitting.

14.13 Bend down the tabs on the edge of the gasket to retain it on the oil pump housing

Refitting

11 Thoroughly clean the oil filter housing, then fit the two new sealing rings (see illustrations).
12 Position the oil filter housing on the cylinder block and refit the retaining bolts. Tighten the bolts to the specified torque.
13 Refit the two coolant hoses and secure with their retaining clips. Reconnect the oil pressure switch wiring connector.
14 Position the intermediate shaft bearing housing support bracket on the cylinder block and secure with the three retaining bolts tightened to the specified torque.
15 Refit the intermediate shaft and right-hand driveshaft as described in Chapter 8.
16 Fit a new oil filter element as described in Chapter 1B.
17 Refit the roadwheel and engine undershield, then lower the car to the ground and tighten the wheel bolts to the specified torque.
18 Refill the cooling system as described in Chapter 1B.
19 Top-up the engine oil as described in Weekly checks.
20 On completion, reconnect the battery negative terminal as described in Chapter 5A.

16 Crankshaft oil seals – renewal

Right-hand oil seal

1 Remove the crankshaft sprocket as described in Section 7.

15.10 Oil filter housing retaining bolts (arrowed)

15.11a Fit a new sealing ring to the oil filter housing supply channel . . .

15.11b . . . and to the return channel

2B•18 Diesel engine in-car repair procedures

16.2 Screw in a self-tapping screw and pull on the screw with pliers to extract the oil seal

16.4 Use a socket as a tubular drift to fit the new oil seal

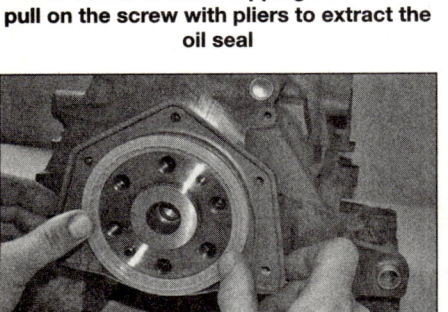

16.10 Fit the new housing with integral oil seal over the crankshaft

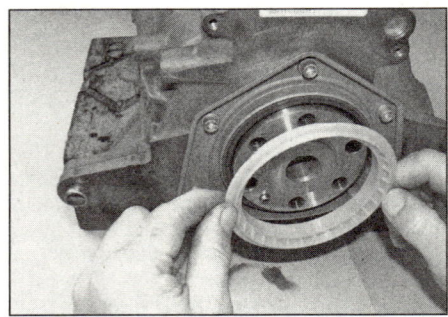

16.12 After fitting, remove the protector sleeve from the housing

2 Carefully punch or drill a small hole in the oil seal. Screw in a self-tapping screw and pull on the screw with pliers to extract the seal **(see illustration)**.
3 Clean the seal housing and polish off any burrs or raised edges which may have caused the seal to fail in the first place.
4 Lubricate the lips of the new seal with clean engine oil and ease it into position on the end of the shaft. Press the seal squarely into position until it is flush with the housing. If necessary, a suitable tubular drift, which bears only on the hard outer edge of the seal, can be used to tap the seal into position **(see illustration)**. Take great care not to damage the seal lips during fitting and ensure that the seal lips face inwards.
5 Wash off any traces of oil, then refit the crankshaft sprocket as described in Section 7.

Left-hand oil seal

6 Remove the flywheel/driveplate as described in Section 17.
7 Remove the sump as described in Section 13.
8 Undo the five bolts and remove the oil seal housing. Note that the oil seal and the housing are a single assembly.
9 Clean the crankshaft and polish off any burrs or raised edges which may have caused the seal to fail in the first place.
10 Position the new oil seal housing, complete with seal, over the crankshaft and into position on the cylinder block **(see illustration)**. Note that the new oil seal housing is supplied with a protector sleeve over the oil seal. Leave the sleeve in position as the housing is fitted.
11 Refit the five retaining bolts and tighten to the specified torque.

12 Remove the protector sleeve from the housing **(see illustration)**.
13 Refit the sump as described in Section 13.
14 Refit the flywheel/drive plate as described in Section 17.

17 Flywheel/driveplate – removal, inspection and refitting

Note: *New flywheel/driveplate retaining bolts will be required on refitting.*

Removal

Manual transmission models

1 Remove the transmission as described in Chapter 7A, then remove the clutch assembly as described in Chapter 6.
2 Prevent the flywheel from turning by locking the ring gear teeth with a similar arrangement to that shown **(see illustration)**.
3 Slacken and remove the retaining bolts and remove the flywheel **(see illustration)**. Do not drop it, as it is very heavy.

Automatic transmission models

4 Remove the transmission as described in Chapter 7B then remove the driveplate as described in paragraphs 2 and 3.

Inspection

5 If there is any doubt about the condition of the flywheel/driveplate, seek the advice of a Saab dealer or engine reconditioning specialist. They will be able to advise if it is possible to recondition it or whether renewal is necessary.

Refitting

Manual transmission models

6 Clean the mating surfaces of the flywheel and crankshaft.
7 Offer up the flywheel and engage it over the positioning dowel on the crankshaft. Apply a drop of locking compound to the threads of each new flywheel retaining bolt (unless they are pre-coated) and install the new bolts.
8 Lock the flywheel by the method used on removal then, working in a diagonal sequence, evenly and progressively tighten the retaining bolts to the specified torque.
9 Refit the clutch as described in Chapter 6, then remove the locking tool, and refit the transmission as described in Chapter 7A.

Automatic transmission models

10 Refit the driveplate as described in paragraphs 6 to 8.
11 Remove the locking tool, and refit the transmission as described in Chapter 7B.

18 Engine/transmission mountings – inspection and renewal

Refer to Chapter 2A, Section 13.

17.2 Prevent the flywheel from turning by locking the ring gear teeth

17.3 Flywheel retaining bolts (arrowed)

Chapter 2 Part C:
Engine removal and overhaul procedures

Contents

	Section number
Balance shafts (petrol engines) – removal, inspection and refitting	12
Crankshaft – inspection	17
Crankshaft – refitting	21
Crankshaft – removal	14
Cylinder block/crankcase – cleaning and inspection	15
Cylinder head – dismantling	6
Cylinder head – reassembly	8
Cylinder head and valves – cleaning and inspection	7
Engine – initial start-up after overhaul	23
Engine and transmission – removal, separation and refitting	4
Engine overhaul – dismantling sequence	5
Engine overhaul – general information	2
Engine overhaul – reassembly sequence	19
Engine removal – methods and precautions	3
General information	1
Main and big-end bearings – inspection	18
Piston rings – refitting	20
Piston/connecting rod assembly – inspection	16
Piston/connecting rod assembly – refitting and big-end bearing clearance check	22
Piston/connecting rod assembly – removal	13
Timing chain and sprockets (petrol engines) – removal, inspection and refitting	10
Timing chain guides and tensioner (petrol engines) – removal, inspection and refitting	11
Timing cover (petrol engines) – removal and refitting	9

Degrees of difficulty

Easy, suitable for novice with little experience	Fairly easy, suitable for beginner with some experience	Fairly difficult, suitable for competent DIY mechanic	Difficult, suitable for experienced DIY mechanic	Very difficult, suitable for expert DIY or professional

Specifications

Note: *Where specifications are given as N/A, no information was available at the time of writing. Refer to your Saab dealer for the latest information available.*

Petrol engines

Cylinder head

Height (new)	139.4 to 139.6 mm
Height (minimum)	139.0 mm
Valve guide-to-valve stem clearance (max):	
Intake	0.17 mm
Exhaust	0.22 mm

Valves

	Intake	Exhaust
Valve head diameter	33.0 mm	29.0 mm
Valve length	107.30 mm	107.84 mm
Valve stem diameter	4.970 to 4.985 mm	4.950 to 4.965 mm
Valve spring:		
Free length	57.1 to 60.1 mm	57.1 to 60.1 mm
Fitted length	37.5 mm	37.5 mm

Cylinder block

Cylinder bore diameter:	
Standard (A)	90.000 to 90.020 mm
Standard (B)	90.020 to 90.040 mm
First oversize	90.500 to 90.520 mm
Second oversize	91.000 to 91.020 mm

Balance shafts

Endfloat	0.060 to 0.460 mm
Diameter of journal:	
Larger, inner	39.892 to 39.908 mm
Smaller, outer	19.947 to 19.960 mm
Diameter of bearing:	
Larger, inner	39.988 to 40.043 mm
Smaller, outer	20.000 to 20.021 mm
Bearing running clearance	0.080 to 0.151 mm

Petrol engines (continued)

Pistons
Note: *Piston diameter is measured at right angles to the gudgeon pin holes, 11mm from the bottom of the piston skirt. The piston classification is stamped on the crown.*

Piston diameter:
AB	89.964 to 89.975 mm
B	89.975 to 89.982 mm
First oversize (+0.5 mm)	90.457 to 90.475 mm
Second oversize (+1.0 mm)	90.957 to 90.975 mm
Nominal piston clearance (new)	0.025 to 0.056 mm

Connecting rods
Length (centre to centre):
2.0 litre engine	159 mm
2.3 litre engine	153 mm

Crankshaft
Endfloat	0.08 to 0.34 mm
Maximum bearing journal out-of-round	0.005 mm

Main bearing journal diameter:
Standard	57.981 to 58.000 mm
First undersize	57.731 to 57.750 mm
Second undersize	57.481 to 57.500 mm
Main bearing running clearance	0.014 to 0.062 mm

Big-end bearing journal diameter:
Standard	51.981 to 52.000 mm
First undersize	51.731 to 51.750 mm
Second undersize	51.481 to 51.500 mm
Big-end bearing running clearance	0.020 to 0.068 mm

Piston rings
End gaps in cylinder:
Upper compression ring	0.30 to 0.50 mm
Lower compression ring	0.30 to 0.50 mm
Scraper ring	0.75 to 1.00 mm

Side clearance in groove:
Top compression ring	0.035 to 0.080 mm
Second compression ring	0.040 to 0.075 mm
Oil control ring	N/A

Torque wrench settings
Refer to Chapter 2A Specifications

Diesel engines

Cylinder head
Maximum gasket face distortion	0.10 mm
Cylinder head height	105.95 to 107.05 mm

Valves and guides
Valve stem diameter:
Intake valve	5.982 to 6.000 mm
Exhaust valve	5.972 to 5.990 mm

Valve head diameter:
Intake	29.489 mm
Exhaust	27.491 mm

Valve length:
Intake	107.95 mm
Exhaust	107.95 mm
Maximum permissible valve stem play in guide	N/A
Valve spring free length (intake and exhaust)	43.1 mm

Cylinder block
Maximum gasket face distortion	0.15 mm
Cylinder bore diameter	82.000 to 82.030 mm
Maximum cylinder bore ovality	0.050 mm
Maximum cylinder bore taper	0.005 mm

Diesel engines (continued)

Crankshaft and bearings

Number of main bearings	5
Main bearing journal diameter	59.855 to 60.000 mm
Big-end bearing journal diameter	50.660 to 50.805 mm
Big-end bearing running clearance	N/A
Crankshaft endfloat	0.049 to 0.211 mm

Pistons

Piston diameter	81.920 to 81.950 mm

Piston rings

Number of rings (per piston)	2 compression, 1 oil control
Ring end gap:	
Top compression	0.20 to 0.35 mm
Second compression	0.60 to 0.80 mm
Oil control	0.25 to 0.50 mm

Torque wrench settings
Refer to Chapter 2B Specifications

1 General information

Included in this Part of Chapter 2 are details of removing the engine from the vehicle, and general overhaul procedures for the cylinder head, cylinder block/crankcase, and all engine internal components.

The information given ranges from advice concerning preparation for an overhaul and the purchase of new parts, to detailed step-by-step procedures covering removal, inspection, renovation and refitting of engine internal components.

After Section 8, all instructions are based on the assumption that the engine has been removed from the vehicle. For information concerning in-car engine repair, as well as the removal and refitting of those external components necessary for full overhaul, refer to Part A or B of this Chapter. Ignore any preliminary dismantling operations described in Part A or B that are no longer relevant once the engine has been removed from the vehicle.

2 Engine overhaul – general information

It is not always easy to determine when, or if, an engine should be completely overhauled, as a number of factors must be considered.

High mileage is not necessarily an indication that an overhaul is needed, while low mileage does not preclude the need for an overhaul. Frequency of servicing is probably the most important consideration. An engine which has had regular and frequent oil and filter changes, as well as other required maintenance, should give many thousands of miles of reliable service. Conversely, a neglected engine may require an overhaul very early in its life.

Excessive oil consumption is an indication that piston rings, valve seals and/or valve guides are in need of attention. Make sure that oil leaks are not responsible before deciding that the rings and/or guides are worn. Have a compression test performed (refer to Part A of this Chapter for petrol engines and to Part B for diesel engines), to determine the likely cause of the problem.

Check the oil pressure with a gauge fitted in place of the oil pressure switch, and compare it with that specified. If it is extremely low, the main and big-end bearings, and/or the oil pump, are probably worn out.

Loss of power, rough running, knocking or metallic engine noises, excessive valve gear noise, and high fuel consumption may also point to the need for an overhaul, especially if they are all present at the same time. If a complete service does not remedy the situation, major mechanical work is the only solution.

A full engine overhaul involves restoring all internal parts to the specification of a new engine. During a complete overhaul, the pistons and the piston rings are renewed, and the cylinder bores are reconditioned. New main and big-end bearings are generally fitted; if necessary, the crankshaft may be reground, to compensate for wear in the journals. The valves are also serviced as well, since they are usually in less-than-perfect condition at this point. Always pay careful attention to the condition of the oil pump when overhauling the engine, and renew it if there is any doubt as to its serviceability. The end result should be an as-new engine that will give many trouble-free miles.

Critical cooling system components such as the hoses, thermostat and coolant pump should be renewed when an engine is overhauled. The radiator should also be checked carefully, to ensure that it is not clogged or leaking.

Before beginning the engine overhaul, read through the entire procedure, to familiarise yourself with the scope and requirements of the job. Check on the availability of parts and make sure that any necessary special tools and equipment are obtained in advance. Most work can be done with typical hand tools, although a number of precision measuring tools are required for inspecting parts to determine if they must be renewed.

The services provided by an engineering machine shop or engine reconditioning specialist will almost certainly be required, particularly if major repairs such as crankshaft regrinding or cylinder reboring are necessary. Apart from carrying out machining operations, these establishments will normally handle the inspection of parts; offer advice concerning reconditioning or renewal and supply new components such as pistons, piston rings and bearing shells. It is recommended that the establishment used is a member of the Federation of Engine Re-Manufacturers, or a similar society.

Always wait until the engine has been completely dismantled, and until all components (especially the cylinder block/crankcase and the crankshaft) have been inspected, before deciding what service and repair operations must be performed by an engineering works. The condition of these components will be the major factor to consider when determining whether to overhaul the original engine, or to buy a reconditioned unit. Do not, therefore, purchase parts or have overhaul work done on other components until they have been thoroughly inspected. As a general rule, time is the primary cost of an overhaul, so it does not pay to fit worn or sub-standard parts.

As a final note, to ensure maximum life and minimum trouble from a reconditioned engine, everything must be assembled with care, in a spotlessly clean environment.

3 Engine removal – methods and precautions

If you have decided that the engine must be removed for overhaul or major repair work, several preliminary steps should be taken.

Locating a suitable place to work is extremely important. Adequate workspace,

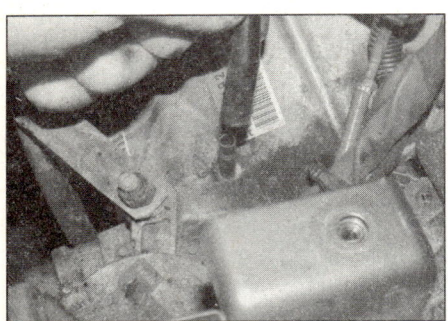

4.9 Disconnecting the breather hose from the top of the automatic transmission

4.12 Disconnect the vacuum hose (arrowed) from the rear of the intake manifold

4 Engine and transmission – removal, separation and refitting

Note: *The engine is removed from the car as a unit complete with the transmission; the engine and transmission can then be separated for overhaul. The engine/transmission is lowered and removed from the underside of the engine compartment. Note that it is possible to remove the transmission, leaving the engine in position – refer to Chapter 7A or 7B (as applicable) for details.*

Removal

1 Park the vehicle on firm, level ground. Chock the rear wheels, then firmly apply the handbrake. It may be useful at this point to slacken the front wheel bolts. Jack up the front of the vehicle, and securely support it on axle stands (see *Jacking and vehicle support*).
2 Remove both front wheels, and then unbolt both wing mouldings and front wheel arch liners, for access to either side of the engine bay.
3 Unbolt and remove the lower covers from under the engine and radiator.
4 Drain the coolant with reference to Chapter 1A or 1B. Save the coolant in a clean container if it is fit for re-use.

⚠️ **Warning: The engine should be cold before draining the coolant.**

5 With the coolant drained, tighten the drain plug on the left-hand bottom of the radiator.
6 If required, remove the bonnet as described in Chapter 11. Alternatively, disconnect the support struts from the bonnet, and support it in the fully open position.
7 Remove the covers from the top of the engine, intake manifold and battery, then remove the battery with reference to Chapter 5A.
8 Unbolt the battery tray from the side of the engine bay, and disconnect the earth cable(s) between the transmission and the vehicle body.
9 On models with automatic transmission, disconnect the breather hose from the top of the transmission **(see illustration)**; plug the open port to prevent the ingress of foreign material.
10 On manual models, unplug the wiring from the reversing lamp switch at the connector on the top of the transmission casing.
11 Detach the throttle cable (where applicable) from the throttle body, with reference to Chapter 4A or 4B.
12 On petrol models, release the retaining clip and disconnect the EVAP canister purge valve's vacuum hose from the intake manifold **(see illustration)**.
13 Press the red sleeve inwards and pull the braking system vacuum hose to disconnect it from the vacuum pump and intake manifold **(see illustrations)**; see Chapter 9 for further details.

along with storage space for the vehicle, will be needed. If a workshop or garage is not available, at the very least, a flat, level, clean work surface is required.

Cleaning the engine compartment and engine/transmission before beginning the removal procedure will help keep tools clean and organised.

An engine hoist or A-frame will also be necessary. Make sure the equipment is rated in excess of the combined weight of the engine and transmission. Safety is of primary importance, considering the potential hazards involved in lifting the engine/transmission out of the vehicle.

If this is the first time you have removed an engine, an assistant should ideally be available. Advice and aid from someone more experienced would also be helpful. There are many instances when one person cannot simultaneously perform all of the operations required when lifting the engine out of the vehicle.

Plan the operation ahead of time. Before starting work, arrange for the hire of, or obtain, all of the tools and equipment you will need. Some of the equipment necessary to perform engine/transmission removal and installation safely and with relative ease (in addition to an engine hoist) is as follows: a heavy-duty trolley jack, complete sets of spanners and sockets as described in the back of this manual, wooden blocks, and plenty of rags and cleaning solvent for mopping-up spilled oil, coolant and fuel. If the hoist must be hired, make sure that you arrange for it in advance, and perform all of the operations possible without it beforehand. This will save you money and time.

Plan for the vehicle to be out of use for quite a while. An engineering works will be required to perform some of the work, which the do-it-yourselfer cannot accomplish without special equipment. These places often have a busy schedule, so it would be a good idea to consult them before removing the engine, in order to accurately estimate the amount of time required to rebuild or repair components that may need work.

During the engine/transmission removal procedure, it is advisable to make notes of the locations of all brackets, cable-ties, earthing points, etc, as well as how the wiring harnesses, hoses and electrical connections are attached and routed around the engine and engine compartment. An effective way of doing this is to take a series of photographs of the various components before they are disconnected or removed; the resulting photographs will prove invaluable when the engine/transmission is refitted.

Always be extremely careful when removing and refitting the engine/transmission. Serious injury can result from careless actions. Plan ahead and take your time, and a job of this nature, although major, can be accomplished successfully.

On all 9-5 models, the engine must be removed complete with the transmission as an assembly. There is insufficient clearance in the engine compartment to remove the engine leaving the transmission in the vehicle. The engine/transmission unit is removed by raising the front of the vehicle, and lowering the complete assembly from the engine compartment.

4.13a Press the red sleeve in and pull the vacuum hose (arrowed) from the pump . . .

4.13b . . . then press the red sleeve down and pull the vacuum hose from the intake manifold

Engine removal and overhaul procedures 2C•5

14 Disconnect the fuel supply and return hoses at the quick-release unions as described in Chapter 4A or 4B. Plug both sides of the open fuel lines to minimise leakage and to prevent the ingress of foreign material.

15 On manual models, release the securing clip and disconnect the connection for the clutch fluid delivery at the top of the transmission. Refit the securing clip to the connector after it has been disconnected for safekeeping. Plug both sides of the open clutch fluid lines to minimise leakage and to prevent the ingress of foreign material.

16 Disconnect the gear selector cable (automatic models) or shaft (manual models) at the rear of the transmission casing; refer to Chapter 7A or 7B for details. On automatic models, also unplug the transmission control system wiring harness, at the two multiway connectors located to the front of the battery tray **(see illustration)**.

17 Slacken the hose clip and disconnect the cooling system top hose from the thermostat housing and the expansion tank hose on the end of the cylinder head. Also disconnect the heater hoses from the rear of the engine; refer to Chapter 3 for further information.

18 Disconnect the vacuum hose from the bypass valve, and then disconnect the wiring connector from the pressure/temperature sensor **(see illustration)**.

19 Undo the retaining clips and securing bolt, then remove the air intake pipe to the throttle body. Undo the securing bolt from the air bypass pipe and withdraw from the vehicle **(see illustrations)**.

20 On petrol models, remove the mass airflow sensor and air intake hose from the vehicle as described in Chapter 4A, Section 14.

21 Slacken the hose clip and disconnect the radiator bottom hose from the coolant pump; refer to Chapter 3 for further information.

22 Remove the wiper arms and windscreen lower trim panel which covers the wiper motor, as described in Chapter 12.

23 Undo the four retaining nuts and withdraw the rubber cover, then disconnect the wiring connector from the electronic control module. Pull the rubber grommet from the bulkhead and rest the wiring harness on the top of the engine. Remove the wiring connection cover on the rear of the bulkhead and release any retaining clips/cable-ties as required **(see illustrations)**.

24 Release the tension on the auxiliary belt and remove it from the pulleys. Refer to Chapter 1A or 1B for further information.

25 Disconnect the power steering pump from the engine mounting bracket, then using suitable straps/cable-ties suspend it from the radiator upper crossmember.

26 Slacken and remove the air conditioning compressor retaining bolts, then using suitable straps/cable-ties suspend the compressor, condenser cooler and charge air cooler from the radiator upper crossmember. Note that the engine oil cooler will be removed with the engine.

4.16 Unplug the automatic transmission control system wiring harness

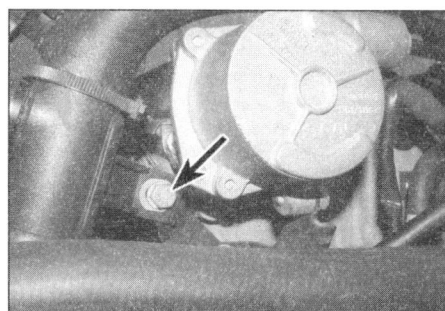

4.19a Slacken and remove the air intake pipe retaining bolt (arrowed) . . .

27 Disconnect the wiring connector to the air conditioning compressor and release the coupling on the vacuum hose connected to the wastegate.

28 Undo the retaining nut and disconnect

4.23a Remove the four retaining nuts (arrowed) . . .

4.23c Withdraw the rubber wiring grommet from the bulkhead panel

4.18 Disconnect the vacuum hose and the wiring connector (arrowed)

4.19b . . . and the air bypass pipe retaining bolt (arrowed)

the oil cooler pipes from the oil filter housing, then undo the retaining bolts and remove the engine oil cooler, complete with cooler pipes from the vehicle **(see illustrations)**.

29 On models with automatic transmission,

4.23b . . . and release the multiplug wiring connector from the control module

4.23d Unclip the cover from the wiring block connector on the bulkhead

2C•6 Engine removal and overhaul procedures

4.28a Undo the retaining nut (arrowed) . . .

4.28b . . . and the retaining bolts (arrowed)

4.42 Undo the bolts (one shown) securing the torque converter to the flywheel

disconnect the quick-release connectors to the transmission oil cooler. Plug ends of the open fluid lines to minimise leakage and to prevent the ingress of foreign material.

30 Position an engine-lifting hoist over the engine compartment. Attach the lifting jib to the eyelets at either end of the cylinder head. It may be necessary to attach an extra lifting eye to the transmission to allow the engine/transmission to be kept level for removal. Raise the hoist until it is just taking the weight of the engine/transmission.

31 Referring to Chapter 8, unbolt and remove the both driveshafts.

32 Referring to Chapter 10, unbolt and remove the front subframe.

33 Unbolt and remove the right- and left-hand engine/transmission mountings, with reference to Chapter 2A, Section 13.

34 Make a final check that any components, which would prevent the removal of the engine/transmission from the car, have been removed or disconnected. Ensure that components such as the gearchange selector rod, clutch cable and accelerator cable are secured so that they cannot be damaged on removal.

35 Slowly lower the engine/transmission assembly from the engine compartment, making sure that it clears the components on the surrounding panels. In particular, make sure that it clears the ABS unit and the radiator. Enlist the help of an assistant during this procedure, as it may be necessary to tilt and twist the assembly slightly to clear the body panels. Lower the assembly to the ground and remove it from the underside of the engine compartment.

Separation from transmission

36 If the engine is to be dismantled, working as described in Chapter 1A or 1B, drain the oil and if required remove the oil filter. Clean and refit the drain plug, tightening it securely.

37 Support the engine/transmission assembly on suitable blocks of wood, on a workbench (or failing that, on a clean area of the workshop floor).

38 Remove the starter motor with reference to Chapter 5A.

Manual transmission models

39 Unscrew the bolt securing the turbo oil pipe bracket to the transmission.

40 Unbolt and remove the flywheel protection plate from the underside of the transmission bellhousing.

41 Ensure that both engine and transmission are adequately supported, then with reference to Chapter 7A, unscrew the bolts securing the transmission housing to the engine. Note the correct fitted positions of each bolt as they are removed, to use as a reference on refitting. Withdraw the transmission directly from the engine. Take care not to allow the weight of the transmission to bear on the input shaft and clutch friction plate.

Automatic transmission models

42 Working through the aperture exposed by the removal of the starter motor, unscrew the bolts securing the flywheel to the torque converter **(see illustration)**. To bring each bolt into view, turn the engine using a socket on the crankshaft pulley bolt.

43 Saab technicians use a special tool to hold the torque converter inside the transmission while the transmission is separated from the engine. The tool is quite basic, and consists of a plate which engages the torque converter through the timing hole in the top of the transmission.

44 Support the weight of the transmission, preferably using a hoist.

45 Ensure that both engine and transmission are adequately supported, then unscrew the bolts securing the transmission housing to the engine. Note the correct fitted positions of each bolt as they are removed, to use as a reference on refitting. Withdraw the transmission directly from the engine (see Chapter 7B for details). Make sure that the torque converter stays inside the transmission bellhousing, otherwise it may fall out and be damaged.

Reconnection to transmission

Automatic transmission models

46 Carefully offer the transmission to the engine. Make sure that the torque converter is held fully engaged with the transmission, using the special tool described earlier in this procedure (refer to Chapter 7B for settings and further details).

47 Insert and tighten the bolts securing the transmission to the engine to the specified torque.

48 Remove the special tool, then insert and tighten the bolts securing the driveplate to the torque converter to the specified torque. Turn the engine by means of a socket on the crankshaft pulley.

Manual transmission models

Caution: If a new clutch slave cylinder has been fitted, or if any hydraulic fluid has been allowed to drain from the existing slave cylinder, the cylinder must be primed and bled BEFORE the transmission is refitted; see Chapter 6 for details.

49 Apply a smear of high melting-point grease to the splines of the transmission input shaft. Do not apply too much; otherwise there is a possibility of the grease contaminating the clutch friction plate.

50 Carefully offer the transmission to the engine. Ensure that the weight of the transmission is not allowed to hang on the input shaft as it is engaged with the clutch friction plate. Insert and tighten the bolts securing the transmission to the engine to the specified torque.

51 Where applicable, insert and tighten the bolts securing the turbo oil pipe bracket to the transmission.

All models

52 Refit the lower cover plate to the transmission bellhousing, and tighten the bolts.

53 Refit the starter motor with reference to Chapter 5A.

Refitting

54 Refit the engine and transmission by following the removal procedure in reverse, noting the following points:
a) Hoist the engine and transmission into position in the engine compartment, then refit the right- and left-hand engine mountings as described in Chapter 2A or 2B.
b) Refit the front subframe with reference to Chapter 10, refit the driveshafts with reference to Chapter 8.
c) Tighten all nuts and bolts to the specified torque.
d) Renew all copper sealing washers on unions, as applicable.
e) Where applicable, reconnect the accelerator cable with reference to Chapter 4A or 4B.
f) With reference to Chapter 6, reconnect

the fluid supply pipe to the slave cylinder, and then bleed the clutch hydraulic system.
g) Ensure that all wiring has been securely reconnected, and all nuts and bolts have been tightened.
h) Refill the engine and transmission with the correct quantity and grade of oil/fluid, with reference to Chapter 1A or 1B.
i) Refill the cooling system with reference to Chapter 1A or 1B.
j) Check and if necessary top-up the power steering fluid, with reference to Chapter 1A or 1B.

5 Engine overhaul – dismantling sequence

1 It is much easier to dismantle and work on the engine if it is mounted on a portable engine stand. These stands can often be hired from a tool hire shop. Before the engine is mounted on a stand, the flywheel/driveplate should be removed, so that the stand bolts can be tightened into the end of the cylinder block/crankcase.

2 If a stand is not available, it is possible to dismantle the engine with it blocked up on a sturdy workbench, or on the floor. Be extra careful not to tip or drop the engine when working without a stand.

3 If you are going to obtain a reconditioned engine, all the external components must be removed from the old engine first, to be transferred to the new engine (just as they will if you are doing a complete engine overhaul yourself). These components normally include the following, but check with your engine supplier first:
a) Engine wiring harness and supports.
b) Alternator and air conditioning compressor mounting brackets (as applicable).
c) Coolant pump (where applicable) and inlet/outlet housings.
d) Dipstick tube.
e) Fuel system components.
f) All electrical switches and sensors.
g) Intake and exhaust manifolds, and the turbocharger.
h) Oil filter and oil cooler/heat exchanger.
i) Flywheel/driveplate.
j) The Direct Ignition cartridge and spark plugs – petrol engines.
k) Engine mounting brackets.

4 If you are obtaining a 'short' engine (which consists of the engine cylinder block/crankcase, crankshaft, pistons and connecting rods all assembled), then the cylinder head and sump will have to be removed also.

5 If you are planning a complete overhaul, the engine can be dismantled, and the internal components removed, in the order given below:

Petrol engines

a) Intake and exhaust manifolds (Chapter 4A).
b) Cylinder head (Chapter 2A).
c) Timing chain and balance shaft chain, sprockets and tensioner (Sections 10 and 11).
d) Flywheel/driveplate (Chapter 2A).
e) Balance shafts (Section 12).
f) Sump (Chapter 2A).
g) Piston/connecting rod assemblies (Section 13).
h) Crankshaft (Section 14).

Diesel engines

a) Intake and exhaust manifolds (see Chapter 4B).
b) Timing belt, sprockets, tensioner and idler pulleys (see Chapter 2B).
c) Coolant pump (see Chapter 3).
d) Cylinder head (see Chapter 2B).
e) Flywheel/driveplate (see Chapter 2B).
f) Sump (see Chapter 2B).
g) Oil pump (see Chapter 2B).
h) Piston/connecting rod assemblies (see Section 13).
i) Crankshaft (see Section 14).

6 Before beginning the dismantling and overhaul procedures, make sure that you have all of the correct tools necessary. Refer to *Tools and working facilities* for further information.

6 Cylinder head – dismantling

Note: *New/reconditioned cylinder heads are obtainable from Saab, or from engine overhaul specialists. Be aware that some specialist tools are required for the dismantling and inspection procedures, and new components may not be readily available. It may therefore be more practical and economical for the home mechanic to purchase a reconditioned head, rather than dismantle, inspect and recondition the original head. A valve spring compressor tool will be required for this operation.*

1 With the cylinder head removed as described in the relevant Part of this Chapter, clean away all external dirt, and remove the following components as applicable, if not already done:
a) Manifolds (see Chapter 4A or 4B).
b) Spark plugs (petrol engines – see Chapter 1A).
c) Glow plugs (diesel engines – see Chapter 5A).
d) Camshafts and associated valve train components (see Chapter 2A or 2B).
e) Fuel injectors (diesel engines – see Chapter 4B).
f) Engine lifting brackets.

2 Remove the camshafts and hydraulic cam followers, with reference to Chapter 2A or 2B.

3 Before removing the valves, consider obtaining plastic protectors for the hydraulic cam follower bores. When using certain valve spring compressors, the bores can easily be damaged should the compressor slip off the end of the valve.

4 Position the protector in the cam follower bore then; using a valve spring compressor, compress the valve spring until the split collets can be removed. Release the compressor, and lift off the spring retainer, spring and seat.

6.4a Use a compressor to compress the valve springs and remove the split collets

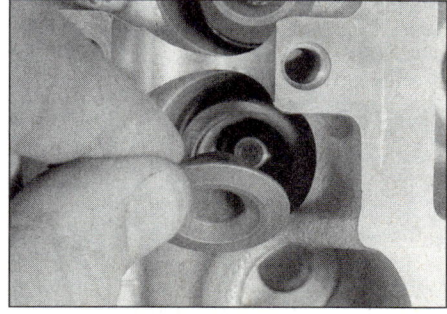

6.4b Removing the spring retainer . . .

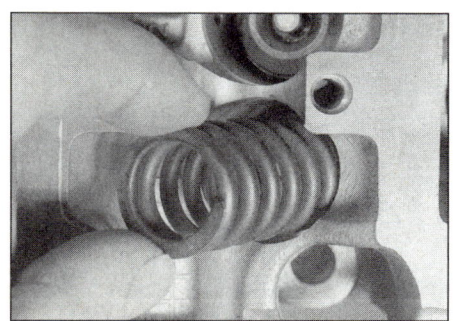

6.4c . . . valve spring . . .

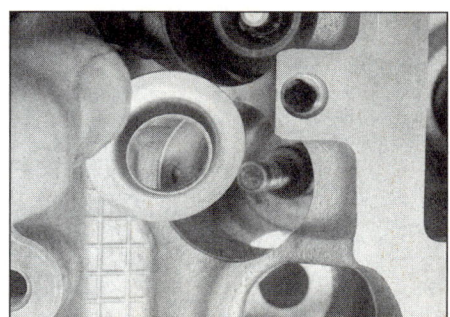

6.4d . . . and seat

2C•8 Engine removal and overhaul procedures

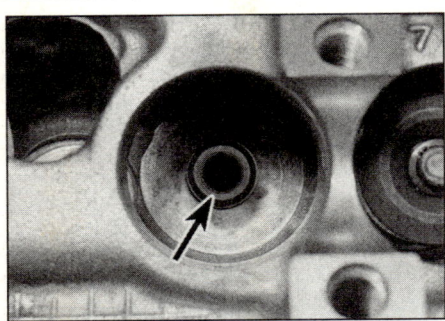

6.4e Valve stem seal location

6.4f Removing a valve stem seal

6.7a The valve spring components

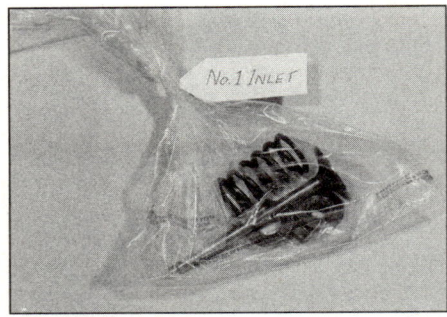

6.7b Place each valve and its associated components in a labelled polythene bag

Using a pair of pliers, carefully extract the valve stem seal from the top of the guide **(see illustrations)**.

5 If, when the valve spring compressor is screwed down, the spring retainer refuses to free and expose the split collets, gently tap the top of the tool, directly over the retainer, with a light hammer. This will free the retainer.

6 Withdraw the valve through the combustion chamber.

7 It is essential that each valve is stored together with its collets, retainer, spring, and spring seat. The valves should also be kept in their correct sequence, unless they are so badly worn that they are to be renewed. If they are going to be kept and used again, place each valve assembly in a labelled polythene bag or similar small container **(see illustrations)**. Note that No 1 cylinder is nearest to the timing chain/belt end of the engine.

7.6 Checking the cylinder head gasket face for distortion

7 Cylinder head and valves – cleaning and inspection

1 Thorough cleaning of the cylinder head and valve components, followed by a detailed inspection, will enable you to decide how much valve service work must be carried out during the engine overhaul. **Note:** *If the engine has been severely overheated, it is best to assume that the cylinder head is warped – check carefully for signs of this.*

Cleaning

2 Scrape away all traces of old gasket material from the cylinder head.

3 Scrape away the carbon from the combustion chambers and ports, then wash the cylinder head thoroughly with paraffin or a suitable solvent.

7.10 Measuring a valve stem diameter

4 Scrape off any heavy carbon deposits that may have formed on the valves, then use a power-operated wire brush to remove deposits from the valve heads and stems.

Inspection

Note: *Be sure to perform all the following inspection procedures before concluding that the services of a machine shop or engine overhaul specialist are required. Make a list of all items that require attention.*

Cylinder head

5 Inspect the head very carefully for cracks, evidence of coolant leakage, and other damage. If cracks are found, a new cylinder head should be obtained.

6 Use a straight-edge and feeler blade to check that the cylinder head surface is not distorted **(see illustration)**. If it is, it may be possible to have it machined, provided that the cylinder head is not reduced to less than the specified height.

7 Examine the valve seats in each of the combustion chambers. If they are severely pitted, cracked, or burned, they will need to be renewed or recut by an engine overhaul specialist. If they are only slightly pitted, this can be removed by grinding-in the valve heads and seats with fine valve-grinding compound, as described below. Note that the exhaust valves have a hardened coating and, although they may be ground-in with paste, they must not be machined.

8 Check the valve guides for wear by inserting the relevant valve, and checking for side-to-side motion of the valve. A very small amount of movement is acceptable. If the movement seems excessive, remove the valve. Measure the valve stem diameter (see below), and renew the valve if it is worn. If the valve stem is not worn, the wear must be in the valve guide, and the guide must be renewed. The renewal of valve guides is best carried out by a Saab dealer or engine overhaul specialist, who will have the necessary tools available.

Valves

9 Examine the head of each valve for pitting, burning, cracks, and general wear. Check the valve stem for scoring and wear ridges. Rotate the valve, and check for any obvious indication that it is bent. Look for pits and excessive wear on the tip of each valve stem. Renew any valve that shows any such signs of wear or damage.

10 If the valve appears satisfactory at this stage, measure the valve stem diameter at several points using a micrometer **(see illustration)**. Any significant difference in the readings obtained indicates wear of the valve stem. Should any of these conditions be apparent, the valve(s) must be renewed.

11 If the valves are in satisfactory condition, they should be ground (lapped) into their respective seats, to ensure a smooth, gas-tight seal. If the seat is only lightly pitted, or if it has been recut, fine grinding compound should be used to produce the required finish. Coarse

Engine removal and overhaul procedures 2C•9

7.16 Check the depth of the valve stems below the camshaft bearing surface

7.18 Checking the valve spring free length

7.19 Checking the valve springs for squareness

valve-grinding compound should *not* be used, unless a seat is badly burned or deeply pitted. If this is the case, the cylinder head and valves should be inspected by an expert, to decide whether seat recutting, or even the renewal of the valve or seat insert (where possible) is required.

12 Valve grinding is carried out as follows. Place the cylinder head upside-down on a bench.

13 Smear a trace of (the appropriate grade of) valve-grinding compound on the seat face, and press a suction grinding tool onto the valve head. With a semi-rotary action, grind the valve head to its seat, lifting the valve occasionally to redistribute the grinding compound. A light spring placed under the valve head will greatly ease this operation.

14 If coarse grinding compound is being used, work only until a dull, matt even surface is produced on both the valve seat and the valve, then wipe off the used compound, and repeat the process with fine compound. When a smooth unbroken ring of light grey matt finish is produced on both the valve and seat, the grinding operation is complete. *Do not* grind-in the valves any further than absolutely necessary, or the seat will be prematurely sunk into the cylinder head.

15 When all the valves have been ground-in, carefully wash off *all* traces of grinding compound using paraffin or a suitable solvent, before reassembling the cylinder head.

16 To ensure that the hydraulic cam followers operate correctly, the depth of the valve stems below the camshaft bearing surface must be within certain limits. It may be possible to obtain a Saab checking tool from a dealer, but if not, the check may be made using a steel rule and straight-edge. Check that the dimension is within the limits given in the illustration by inserting each valve it its guide in turn, and measuring the dimension between the end of the valve stem and the camshaft bearing surface **(see illustration)**.

17 If the dimension is not within the specified limits, adjustment must be made either to the end of the valve stem or to the valve seat height. If lower than the minimum amount, the length of the valve stem must be reduced, and if more than the maximum amount, the valve seat must be milled. Seek the advice of a Saab dealer or engine reconditioning specialist.

Valve components

18 Examine the valve springs for signs of damage and discoloration, and measure their free length **(see illustration)**.

19 Stand each spring on a flat surface, and check it for squareness **(see illustration)**. If any of the springs are less than the minimum free length, or are damaged, distorted or have lost their tension, obtain a complete new set of springs.

20 Obtain new valve stem oil seals, regardless of their apparent condition.

8 Cylinder head – reassembly

1 Lubricate the stems of the valves, and insert the valves into their original locations **(see illustration)**. If new valves are being fitted, insert them into the locations to which they have been ground.

2 Working on the first valve, dip the new valve stem seal in fresh engine oil. Carefully locate it over the valve and onto the guide. Take care not to damage the seal as it is passed over the valve stem. Use a suitable socket or metal tube to press the seal firmly onto the guide **(see illustration)**.

8.1 Inserting a valve in the cylinder head

3 Refit the valve spring followed by the spring retainer, then locate the plastic protector in the hydraulic cam follower bore.

4 Compress the valve spring, and locate the split collets in the recess in the valve stem. Release the compressor and remove the protector, then repeat the procedure on the remaining valves.

5 With all the valves installed, place the cylinder head flat on the bench and, using a hammer and interposed block of wood, tap the end of each valve stem to settle the components.

6 Refit the hydraulic cam followers and camshafts with reference to Chapter 2A or 2B.

7 Refit the external components removed in Section 6.

8 The cylinder head may now be refitted as described in Chapter 2A or 2B.

9 Timing cover (petrol engines) – removal and refitting

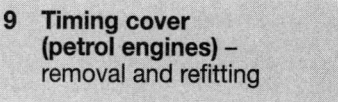

Note: *This procedure describes removal of the timing cover, leaving the cylinder head in position. The alternative method (which is less likely to damage the cylinder head gasket) is to remove the cylinder head first, as described in Chapter 2A.*

Removal

1 Unbolt and remove the auxiliary drivebelt tensioner unit and idler pulley **(see illustrations)**.

2 Remove the alternator as described in

8.2 Using a socket to fit the valve stem seals

2C•10 Engine removal and overhaul procedures

9.1a Unscrewing the tensioner retaining bolt . . .

9.1b . . . and idler pulley retaining bolt

9.2 Unscrew the mounting bracket retaining bolts (arrowed) . . .

9.6a Remove the crankshaft pulley bolt . . .

9.6b . . . and slide the pulley off the crankshaft

flywheel by inserting a flat-bladed screwdriver through the bellhousing and locking the starter ring gear to prevent the crankshaft turning. Loosen the crankshaft pulley bolt using a long socket bar. Note that the bolt is tightened to a very high torque.

6 Fully unscrew the crankshaft pulley bolt, and slide the pulley off the end of the crankshaft **(see illustrations)**.

7 Remove the sump as described in Chapter 2A, Section 7.

8 Remove the two locating dowels (one in the left-hand bottom corner and one in the top right-hand corner) in the timing cover by cutting an internal thread in them using a 3/8 in UNC thread tap and withdraw them with sliding hammer. A bolt can be threaded into the locating dowels, and then attached to the end of the slide hammer **(see illustrations)**.

9 Unscrew and remove the bolts securing the timing cover to the cylinder block and cylinder head. Note the fitted position of the bolts; the two upper bolts on the cylinder head and the two lower bolts in the sump are different **(see illustrations)**.

10 Taking care not to damage the cylinder head gasket, withdraw the timing cover, complete with the oil pump, from the end of the crankshaft. Carefully move the timing cover down and outwards, away from the cylinder block.

11 Thoroughly clean all traces of sealant from the contact faces of the timing cover, sump, cylinder head and block. **Note:** *Check the condition of the cylinder head gasket; if there is any damage to the gasket, then the cylinder*

Chapter 5A, then undo the retaining bolts and remove the mounting bracket from the rear of the cylinder block **(see illustration)**.

3 Undo the retaining bolts and remove the power steering pump mounting bracket, including the lifting eye, from the front of the cylinder head.

4 Remove the water pump as described in Chapter 3.

5 Have an assistant hold the crankshaft/

9.8a Cutting an internal thread in the dowel using a thread tap

9.8b A bolt fitted to the end of a slide hammer

9.8c Using the slide hammer to withdraw the dowels from the timing cover

9.9a Note two upper bolts securing the timing cover to the cylinder head

9.9b Removing the timing cover from the engine

Engine removal and overhaul procedures

head will need to be removed to renew the gasket.

12 If required, remove the oil pump from the timing cover, with reference to Chapter 2A, Section 8.

Refitting

13 Where applicable, refit the oil pump with reference to Chapter 2A, Section 8.

14 Apply a bead of sealant (Loctite 518 or similar) about 1 mm thick to the timing cover flanges, then carefully locate the timing cover on the cylinder block **(see illustration)**.

15 Insert the timing cover retaining bolts including the two upper cylinder head bolts but do not tighten them at this stage. Tap the locating dowels back into place **(see illustration)**, and then tighten the cover retaining bolts to the specified torque, including the two upper cylinder head bolts.

16 Refit the sump as described in Chapter 2A, Section 7.

17 Slide the crankshaft pulley onto the crankshaft, then insert the pulley bolt. Tighten the bolt to the specified torque, while an assistant holds the crankshaft stationary using a wide-bladed screwdriver inserted in the starter ring gear.

18 Refit the water pump, with reference to Chapter 3.

19 Refit the alternator and power steering pump mounting brackets, and tighten the retaining bolts.

20 Refit the alternator with reference to Chapter 5A.

21 Refit the drivebelt tensioner assembly and idler pulley, and tighten the bolts.

9.14 Applying sealant (arrowed) on the timing cover flanges

10 Timing chain and sprockets (petrol engines) – removal, inspection and refitting

Removal

1 Position the crankshaft at TDC compression for No 1 piston (timing chain end of the engine) as described in Chapter 2A, Section 3.

2 Remove the timing cover as described in Section 9. Also remove the oil pump drive dog from the crankshaft **(see illustration)**.

3 The balance shafts are 'timed' at TDC, but since they rotate at twice the speed of the crankshaft, they may also be correctly 'timed' at BDC. Check that the timing marks on the shafts are correctly aligned with the marks on the front of the cylinder block/bearing housing. Note that the balance shaft sprockets are marked 'intake' and 'exhaust'

9.15 Using the slide hammer to tap the dowels back into the timing cover

for their positions, but both front bearings are marked identically. However, as the bearings are located with single bolts, the 'intake' and 'exhaust' marks will always be correctly located at the top of the bearings **(see illustrations)**.

4 Unbolt the balance shaft chain upper guide, then remove the tensioner and side guide **(see illustrations)**.

5 Unbolt the idler from the block, then release the chain from the balance shaft sprockets and crankshaft sprocket. Note that the idler is in two parts **(see illustrations)**.

6 Slide the balance shaft chain sprocket from the front of the crankshaft **(see illustration)**. Note that the word 'Saab' is facing outwards.

7 Unscrew the retaining bolts, and remove the sprockets from the ends of the balance shafts. To do this, hold the sprockets stationary with a chain-type oil filter removal tool or similar. Keep the sprockets identified for position.

10.2 Removing the oil pump drive dog from the crankshaft

10.3a INL mark on the intake (inlet) balance shaft front bearing

10.3b EXH mark on the exhaust balance shaft front bearing

10.4a Unscrew the bolts (arrowed) and remove the balance shaft chain upper guide

10.4b Note how the upper guide locates on the dowel

10.4c Removing the balance shaft chain tensioner . . .

2C•12 Engine removal and overhaul procedures

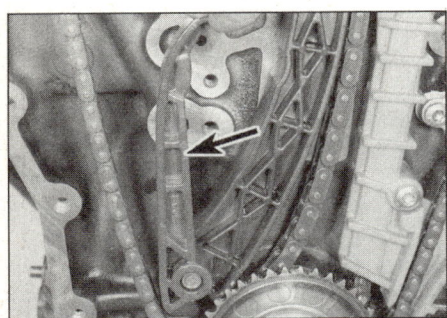

10.4d ... and side guide

10.5a Loosen ...

10.5b ... and remove the idler retaining bolt (note alignment marks between idler and chain) ...

10.5c ... then withdraw the idler and remove the balance shaft chain

10.5d The idler is in two parts

10.6 Removing the balance shaft chain sprocket from the front of the crankshaft

8 Remove the cylinder head cover as described in Chapter 2A.
9 Unscrew and remove the timing chain tensioner from the rear of the cylinder head. To do this, first unscrew the centre bolt and remove the spring, then unscrew and remove the tensioner from the cylinder head **(see illustrations)**.
10 While holding each camshaft stationary with a spanner on the flats at the flywheel/driveplate end of the camshaft, loosen (but do not remove) the camshaft sprocket securing bolts.

11 Unscrew and remove the bolt, and withdraw the sprocket from the end of the intake camshaft **(see illustration)**. Hold the timing chain with one hand, and release the sprocket from it with the other hand.
12 Identify each sprocket for position. Note

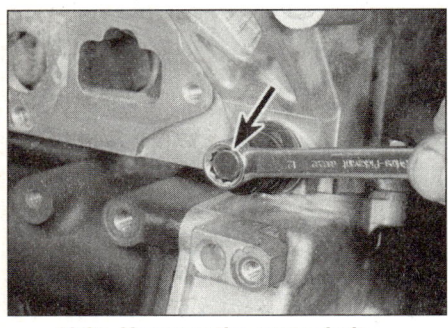

10.9a Unscrew the centre bolt ...

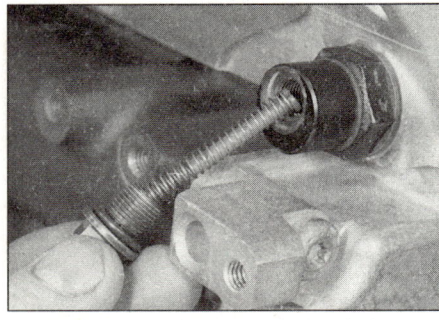

10.9b ... and remove the spring ...

10.9c ... then unscrew the tensioner ...

10.9d ... and remove it from the cylinder head

10.9e The timing chain tensioner components

10.11 Removing the sprocket from the end of the intake camshaft

Engine removal and overhaul procedures 2C•13

10.13a Remove the retaining bolt . . .

10.13b . . . then disengage the sprocket from the chain

10.14a Unscrew the bolts . . .

10.14b . . . and remove the timing chain fixed guide

10.15a Removing the timing chain retainer (arrowed) from the cylinder block

10.15b Removing the crankshaft sprocket from the end of the crankshaft

that each sprocket has a projection, which engages with a cut-out in the end of the camshaft.

13 Unscrew the bolt and withdraw the sprocket from the end of the exhaust camshaft, then disengage it from the chain **(see illustrations)**.

14 Unscrew the bolts, and remove the timing chain fixed guide from the cylinder block **(see illustrations)**.

15 Unbolt the chain retainer from the cylinder block, then disengage the timing chain and remove the sprocket from the end of the crankshaft **(see illustrations)**. If necessary, remove the Woodruff key from the groove in the crankshaft using a screwdriver.

Inspection

16 The timing chain **(see illustration)** and the balance shaft chain should be renewed if the sprockets are worn, or if the chain is loose and noisy in operation. It's a good idea to renew the chains as a matter of course if the engine is stripped down for overhaul. The rollers on a very badly worn chain may be slightly grooved. To avoid future problems, if there's any doubt at all about the chain's condition, renew it. The chain tensioner and guides should be examined and if necessary renewed at the same time (refer to Section 11).

17 Examine the teeth on the crankshaft sprocket, camshaft sprockets and the balance shaft sprockets for wear. Each tooth forms an inverted V. If worn, the side of each tooth under tension will be slightly concave (hooked) in shape, when compared with the other side of the tooth (ie, one side of the inverted V will be concave when compared with the other). If the teeth appear to be worn, the sprockets must be renewed.

Refitting

18 Locate the Woodruff key in the groove in the crankshaft. Tap it fully into the groove, making sure that its plane surface is parallel to the crankshaft.

19 Engage the timing chain with the crankshaft sprocket, then locate the crankshaft sprocket on the end of the crankshaft, making sure that it locates correctly on the Woodruff key. Where the timing chain has bright links, locate the single bright link at the bottom of the sprocket, aligned with the slot in the sprocket. Refit the chain retainer and tighten the bolts **(see illustrations)**.

20 Locate the timing chain in the fixed guide, then refit the guide and tighten the bolts.

21 Refit the sprocket to the end of the exhaust camshaft, insert the bolt and finger-tighten it at this stage. **Do not** apply thread-locking fluid to the threads of the bolt.

10.16 Timing chain removed from the engine

10.19a Where timing chain has bright links, these must be aligned with the slot in the sprocket (arrowed)

10.19b Tightening the timing chain retainer bolts

2C•14 Engine removal and overhaul procedures

10.25 Setting the timing chain tensioner

Before refitting the tensioner, hold its plunger depressed by fitting a plastic cable-tie around it. Cut the tie after refitting.

22 Check that the crankshaft and camshafts are still aligned at their TDC positions.
23 Feed the timing chain up through the cylinder head aperture, and locate it on the exhaust camshaft sprocket, making sure that it is taut between the two sprockets. Check that it is correctly located on the guides. Where the chain has a bright link, make sure that it is aligned with the timing mark.
24 Engage the intake sprocket with the timing chain so that the engagement cut-out and projection are in alignment, then locate the sprocket on the intake camshaft, and insert the bolt. Finger-tighten the bolt at this stage. **Do not** apply thread-locking fluid to the threads of the bolt. Where the chain has a bright link, make sure that it is aligned with the timing mark.
25 Set the timing chain tensioner by pressing

11.2 Removing the pivoting guide from the pin on the cylinder block

10.33 The balance shaft timing marks must be correctly aligned before refitting the chain

down on the ratchet with a screwdriver, then push the plunger fully into the tensioner, and release the ratchet **(see illustration)**. Check the tensioner washer for condition and renew it if necessary.
26 Insert the tensioner body in the cylinder head, and tighten to the specified torque.
27 Insert the spring and plastic guide pin in the tensioner, then fit the plug together with a new O-ring, and tighten it to the specified torque. **Note:** *New tensioners are supplied with the tensioner spring held pretensioned with a pin.* **Do not** *remove this pin until after the tensioner has been tightened into the cylinder head.* When the engine is started, hydraulic pressure will take up any remaining slack.
28 Temporarily refit the crankshaft pulley bolt, and rotate the engine two complete turns clockwise. Check that the timing marks still align correctly. Remove the pulley bolt. Where the chain has bright links, note that these will not now be aligned with the timing marks.
29 Fully tighten the camshaft sprocket bolts to the specified torque, while holding the camshafts with a spanner on the flats.
30 Refit the cylinder head cover with reference to Chapter 2A.
31 Refit the sprockets to the ends of the balance shafts, and tighten the retaining bolts.
32 Locate the balance shaft chain sprocket on the front of the crankshaft, with the word 'Saab' facing outwards.
33 Fit the chain to the sprockets, making sure that the timing marks are aligned correctly **(see illustration)**.

11.4 Cross-section of the timing chain tensioner

10.35 Depress the balance shaft chain tensioner plunger (arrowed) and retain with a plastic cable-tie

34 Refit the idler to the front of the block, and tighten the retaining bolt.
35 Refit the side guide, tensioner and upper guide to the balance shaft chain **(see illustration and Tool Tip)**.
36 Rotate the crankshaft one turn, and check that the balance shaft timing marks are still correctly aligned.
37 Refit the timing cover with reference to Section 5.

11 Timing chain guides and tensioner (petrol engines) – removal, inspection and refitting

Removal

1 Remove the timing chain as described in Section 10; note that this procedure includes removal of the fixed guide and balance shaft chain guides. The timing chain need not be removed from the crankshaft sprocket.
2 Unbolt and remove the fixed timing chain guide and release the pivoting guide from the pin on the cylinder block **(see illustration)**.

Inspection

3 Inspect the chain guides for damage and excessive wear, and renew them if necessary.
4 Clean the tensioner plunger and body, and examine them for damage and wear **(see illustration)**. The plunger may be removed by depressing the ratchet against the spring. If the plunger or body is excessively scored, the complete tensioner should be renewed.

Refitting

5 Locate the pivoting guide on the pin on the cylinder block, then refit the fixed guide and tighten the retaining bolts.
6 Refit the timing chain (see Section 10).

12 Balance shafts (petrol engines) – removal, inspection and refitting

Removal

1 Position the crankshaft at TDC compression for No 1 piston (timing chain end of the engine) as described in Chapter 2A, Section 3.

Engine removal and overhaul procedures 2C•15

2 Remove the timing cover as described in Section 9.

3 The balance shafts are 'timed' at TDC, but since they rotate at twice the speed of the crankshaft, they may also be correctly 'timed' at BDC. Check that the timing marks on the shafts are correctly aligned with the marks on the bearing brackets. As an extra precaution, apply dabs of paint to the chain and sprockets, to ensure correct refitting. Note that the balance shaft sprockets are marked 'intake' and 'exhaust' for position, but the front bearings are marked identically. However, as the bearings are located with single bolts, the 'intake' and 'exhaust' marks will always be correctly located at the top of the bearings – refer to Section 10 for further information.

4 Unbolt the balance shaft chain upper guide, then remove the tensioner and side guide **(see illustrations in Section 10)**.

5 Unscrew the retaining bolt and remove the idler from the block.

6 Release the chain from the balance shaft sprockets and crankshaft sprocket.

7 Unscrew the bearing retaining bolts, and withdraw the balance shafts from the cylinder block **(see illustrations)**. Keep the shafts identified for position.

8 Unscrew the retaining bolts, and remove the sprockets from the ends of the balance shafts, while holding each shaft in a soft-jawed vice.

Inspection

9 Clean the balance shafts and examine the bearing journals for wear and damage. The bearings inside the cylinder block should also be examined. If these are excessively worn or damaged, get advice from a Saab dealer or engine reconditioner.

Refitting

10 Fit the sprockets to the ends of the balance shafts, and tighten the retaining bolts.

11 Lubricate the bearing journals with clean engine oil, then insert the balance shafts in the cylinder block in their correct positions.

12 Locate the balance shaft chain sprocket on the front of the crankshaft, with the word 'Saab' facing outwards.

13 Fit the chain to the sprockets, and refit the idler to the front of the block, making sure that the timing marks remain aligned correctly.

14 Refit the side guide, tensioner and upper guide to the balance shaft chain.

15 Rotate the crankshaft one turn, and check that the balance shaft sprockets are still correctly aligned.

16 Refit the timing cover with reference to Section 9.

13 Piston/connecting rod assembly – removal
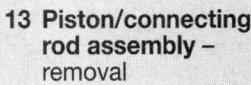

Note: *New connecting rod big-end cap bolts will be needed on refitting.*

1 Remove the cylinder head, sump and oil pump pick-up/strainer as described in Part A or Part B of this Chapter.

2 If there is a pronounced wear ridge at the top of any bore, it may be necessary to remove it with a scraper or ridge reamer, to avoid piston damage during removal. Such a ridge indicates excessive wear of the cylinder bore.

3 Using a hammer and centre-punch, paint or similar, mark each connecting rod big-end bearing cap with its respective cylinder number on the flat machined surface provided; if the engine has been dismantled before, note carefully any identifying marks made previously.

4 Turn the crankshaft to bring pistons 1 and 4 to BDC (bottom dead centre).

5 Unscrew the nuts/bolts from No 1 piston big-end bearing cap. Take off the cap, and recover the bottom half bearing shell. If the bearing shells are to be re-used, tape the cap and the shell together **(see illustrations)**.

12.7a Unscrew the bearing retaining bolts . . .

12.7c Removing the intake balance shaft from the cylinder block

13.5a Removing a big-end bearing cap

12.7b . . . and withdraw the exhaust balance shaft from the cylinder block

12.7d The two balance shafts removed from the engine

***Caution:** On some engines, the connecting rod/bearing cap mating surfaces are not machined flat; the big-end bearing caps are 'cracked' off from the rod during production and left untouched to ensure the cap and rod mate perfectly. Where this type of connecting rod is fitted, great care must be taken to ensure the mating surfaces of the cap and rod are not marked or damaged in anyway. Any damage to the mating surfaces will adversely affect the strength of the connecting rod and could lead to premature failure.*

6 To prevent the possibility of damage to the crankshaft bearing journals, tape over the connecting rod stud threads.

7 Using a hammer handle, push the piston up through the bore, and remove it from the top of the cylinder block. Recover the bearing shell, and tape it to the connecting rod for safekeeping.

13.5b Removing a bearing shell from a big-end bearing cap

14.5 The main bearing caps are numbered from the timing chain end of the engine

14.6a Unscrew and remove the main bearing cap bolts . . .

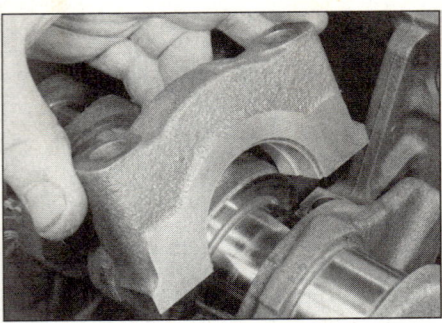

14.6b . . . and remove the main bearing caps

8 Loosely refit the big-end cap to the connecting rod, and secure with the nuts/bolts – this will help to keep the components in their correct order.
9 Remove No 4 piston assembly in the same way.
10 Turn the crankshaft through 180° to bring pistons 2 and 3 to BDC (bottom dead centre), and remove them in the same way.

14 Crankshaft – removal

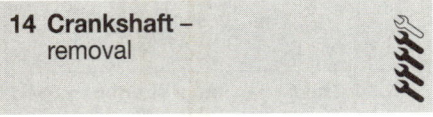

Note: *New main bearing bolts will be required on refitting.*
1 Remove the timing chain and sprocket (petrol engines), the sump and oil pump pick-up/strainer/transfer tube, and the flywheel/driveplate.

14.7 Removing a main bearing shell from its cap

14.9a Removing the thrustwashers (arrowed) . . .

2 Remove the pistons and connecting rods, as described in Section 13. **Note:** *If no work is to be done on the pistons and connecting rods, there is no need to remove the cylinder head, or to push the pistons out of the cylinder bores. The pistons should just be pushed far enough up the bores that they are positioned clear of the crankshaft journals.*
3 Check the crankshaft endfloat with reference to Section 17, then proceed as follows.
4 Unbolt and remove the crankshaft oil seal housing from the end of the cylinder block, noting the correct fitted locations of the locating dowels. If the locating dowels are a loose fit, remove them and store them with the housing for safe-keeping. Remove the gasket.
5 Identification numbers should already be cast onto the base of each main bearing cap **(see illustration)**. If not, number the cap and crankcase using a centre-punch, as was done for the connecting rods and caps.

14.8 Lifting the crankshaft from the crankcase

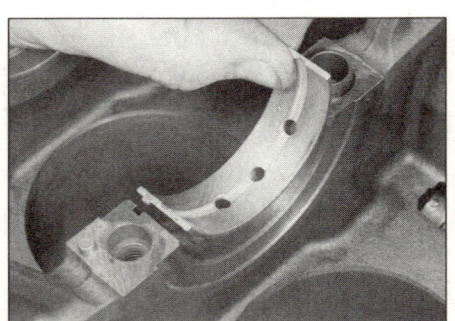

14.9b . . . and main bearing shells

6 Working in a diagonal sequence, evenly and progressively slacken the ten main bearing cap retaining bolts by half a turn at a time until all bolts are loose. Remove all the bolts and withdraw the caps, complete with bearing shells **(see illustrations)**. Tap the caps with a wooden or copper mallet if they are stuck.
7 Remove the bearing shells from the caps, but keep them with their relevant caps and identified for position to ensure correct refitting **(see illustration)**.
8 Carefully lift out the crankshaft, taking care not to displace the upper main bearing shells **(see illustration)**.
9 Remove the upper bearing shells from the crankcase, keeping them identified for position. Also remove the thrustwashers at each side of the centre main bearing, and store them with the bearing cap **(see illustrations)**.
10 With the crankshaft removed, the crankshaft position sensor reluctor (where applicable) may be removed if necessary, by unscrewing the screws and withdrawing the reluctor over the end of the crankshaft **(see illustration)**. Note that the screws are arranged so that it is only possible to refit the reluctor in one position.

15 Cylinder block/crankcase – cleaning and inspection

Cleaning

1 Remove all external components and electrical switches/sensors from the block.

14.10 Location of the screws securing the crankshaft position sensor reluctor

Engine removal and overhaul procedures 2C•17

15.1 Removing an oil jet from the crankcase

For complete cleaning, the core plugs should ideally be removed, as follows. Drill a small hole in the plugs, and then insert a self-tapping screw into the hole. Pull out the plugs by pulling on the screw with a pair of grips, or by using a slide hammer. Also unbolt the four oil jets (where fitted) from the lower part of the crankcase **(see illustration)**.

2 Scrape all traces of sealant from the cylinder block/crankcase, taking care not to damage the gasket/sealing surfaces.

3 Remove all oil gallery plugs (where fitted). The plugs are usually very tight – they may have to be drilled out, and the holes retapped. Use new plugs when the engine is reassembled.

4 If the cylinder block/crankcase is extremely dirty, it should be steam-cleaned.

5 Clean all oil holes and oil galleries, and flush all internal passages with warm water until the water runs clear. Dry thoroughly, and apply a light film of oil to all mating surfaces, to prevent rusting. Also oil the cylinder bores. If you have access to compressed air, use it to speed up the drying process, and to blow out all the oil holes and galleries.

 Warning: Wear eye protection when using compressed air.

6 If the cylinder block is not very dirty, you can do an adequate cleaning job with hot (as hot as you can stand!), soapy water and a stiff brush. Take plenty of time, and do a thorough job. Regardless of the cleaning method used, be sure to clean all oil holes and galleries very thoroughly, and to dry all components well. On completion, protect the cylinder bores as described above, to prevent rusting.

7 All threaded holes must be clean, to ensure accurate torque readings during reassembly. To clean the threads, run the correct-size tap into each of the holes to remove rust, corrosion, thread sealant or sludge, and to restore damaged threads **(see illustration)**. If possible, use compressed air to clear the holes of debris produced by this operation.

8 Apply suitable sealant to the new oil gallery plugs, and insert them into the holes in the block. Tighten them securely. Apply suitable sealant to new core plugs and tap them into place with a socket or tube. Refit and tighten the oil jets to the bottom of the crankcase where applicable.

15.7 Cleaning a cylinder head bolt hole in the cylinder block using a tap

15.12b Cylinder bore classification on the front of the block

9 If the engine is not going to be reassembled right away, cover it with a large plastic bag to keep it clean; protect all mating surfaces and the cylinder bores as described above, to prevent rusting.

Inspection

10 Visually check the cylinder block for cracks and corrosion. Look for stripped threads in the threaded holes. If there has been any history of internal water leakage, it may be worthwhile having an engine overhaul specialist check the cylinder block/crankcase with special equipment. If defects are found, have them repaired if possible; otherwise, a new block will be needed.

11 Check each cylinder bore for scuffing and scoring. Check for signs of a wear ridge at the top of the cylinder, indicating that the bore is excessively worn.

12 On petrol engines, the cylinder bores and

16.1 Piston/connecting rod assembly components

15.12a Piston and cylinder bore classification code locations

15.12c Piston classification on the piston crown

pistons are matched and classified according to four codes – AB, B, 1 (0.5 mm oversize), and 2 (1.0 mm oversize). The code is stamped on the piston crowns, and on the front of the cylinder block **(see illustrations)**. **Note:** *At the time of writing, no figures where given for the diesel engine. Refer to manufacturer or engine reconditioning specialist.*

13 If in any doubt as to the condition of the cylinder block, have it inspected and measured by an engine-reconditioning specialist. If the bores are worn or damaged, they will be able to carry out any necessary reboring (where possible), and supply appropriate oversized pistons, etc.

16 Piston/connecting rod assembly – inspection

1 Before the inspection process can begin, the piston/connecting rod assemblies must be cleaned, and the original piston rings removed from the pistons **(see illustration)**. **Note:** *Always use new piston rings when the engine is reassembled.*

2 Carefully expand the old rings over the top of the pistons. The use of two or three old feeler blades will be helpful in preventing the rings dropping into empty grooves **(see illustrations)**. Be careful not to scratch the piston with the ends of the ring. The rings are brittle, and will snap if they are spread too far. They're also very sharp – protect your hands and fingers. Note that the third ring incorporates an expander. Always remove the

2C•18 Engine removal and overhaul procedures

16.2a Removing a piston compression ring with the aid of a feeler blade

16.2b Removing the oil control ring

16.13a Prise out the gudgeon pin circlip . . .

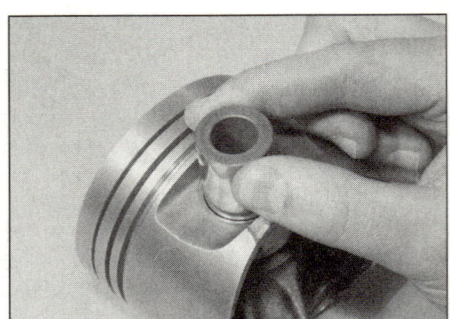

16.13b . . . then withdraw the gudgeon pin, and separate the piston from the connecting rod

rings from the top of the piston. Keep each set of rings with its piston, if the old rings are to be re-used.

3 Scrape away all traces of carbon from the top of the piston. A hand-held wire brush (or a piece of fine emery cloth) can be used, once the majority of the deposits have been scraped away.

4 Remove the carbon from the ring grooves in the piston, using an old ring. Break the ring in half to do this (be careful not to cut your fingers – piston rings are sharp). Be careful to remove only the carbon deposits – do not remove any metal, and do not nick or scratch the sides of the ring grooves.

5 Once the deposits have been removed, clean the piston/connecting rod assembly with paraffin or a suitable solvent, and dry thoroughly. Make sure that the oil return holes in the ring grooves are clear.

16.17 Relationship of the piston and connecting rod

6 If the pistons and cylinder bores are not damaged or worn excessively, and if the cylinder block does not need to be rebored, the original pistons can be refitted. Normal piston wear shows up as even vertical wear on the piston thrust surfaces, and slight looseness of the top ring in its groove.

7 Carefully inspect each piston for cracks around the skirt, around the gudgeon pin holes, and at the piston ring 'lands' (between the ring grooves).

8 Look for scoring and scuffing on the piston skirt, holes in the piston crown, and burned areas at the edge of the crown. If the skirt is scored or scuffed, the engine may have been suffering from overheating, and/or abnormal combustion, which caused excessively high operating temperatures. The cooling and lubrication systems should be checked thoroughly. Scorch marks on the sides of the pistons show that blow-by has occurred. A hole in the piston crown, or burned areas at the edge of the piston crown, indicates that abnormal combustion (pre-ignition, knocking, or detonation) has been occurring. If any of the above problems exist, the causes must be investigated and corrected, or the damage will occur again. The causes may include incorrect ignition timing and/or fuel/air mixture.

9 Corrosion of the piston, in the form of pitting, indicates that coolant has been leaking into the combustion chamber and/or the crankcase. Again, the cause must be corrected, or the problem may persist in the rebuilt engine.

10 Where needed, pistons can be purchased from a Saab dealer.

11 Examine each connecting rod carefully for signs of damage, such as cracks around the big-end and small-end bearings. Check that the rod is not bent or distorted. Damage is highly unlikely, unless the engine has been seized or badly overheated. Detailed checking of the connecting rod assembly can only be carried out by a Saab dealer or engine repair specialist with the necessary equipment.

12 The gudgeon pins are of the floating type, secured in position by two circlips, and the pistons and connecting rods can be separated and reassembled as follows.

13 Using a small flat-bladed screwdriver, prise out the circlips, and push out the gudgeon pin **(see illustrations)**. Hand pressure should be sufficient to remove the pin. Identify the piston, gudgeon pin and rod to ensure correct reassembly.

14 Examine the gudgeon pin and connecting rod small-end bearing for signs of wear or damage. Wear can be cured by renewing both the pin and bush. Bush renewal, however, is a specialist job – press facilities are required, and the new bush must be reamed accurately.

15 The connecting rods themselves should not be in need of renewal, unless seizure or some other major mechanical failure has occurred. Check the alignment of the connecting rods visually, and if the rods are not straight, take them to an engine overhaul specialist for a more detailed check.

16 Examine all components, and obtain any new parts from your Saab dealer. If new pistons are purchased, they will be supplied complete with gudgeon pins and circlips. Circlips can also be purchased individually.

17 Position the piston so that the notch on the edge of the crown faces the timing end of the engine, and the numbers on the connecting rod and big-end cap face the exhaust side of the cylinder block. With the piston held in your hand and the notch facing the left, the connecting rod numbering should face towards you **(see illustration)**. Apply a smear of clean engine oil to the gudgeon pin. Slide it into the piston and through the connecting rod small-end. Check that the piston pivots freely on the rod, then secure the gudgeon pin in position with the circlips. Ensure that each circlip is correctly located in its groove in the piston.

18 Measure the piston diameters, and check that they are within limits for the corresponding bore diameters. If the piston-to-bore clearance is excessive, the block will have to be rebored, and new pistons and rings fitted.

19 Examine the mating surfaces of the big-end caps and connecting rods, to see if they have ever been filed in a mistaken attempt to take up bearing wear. This is extremely unlikely, but if evident, the offending connecting rods and caps must be renewed.

Engine removal and overhaul procedures 2C•19

17.2 Using a dial gauge to check the crankshaft endfloat

17.3 Using feeler blades to check the crankshaft endfloat

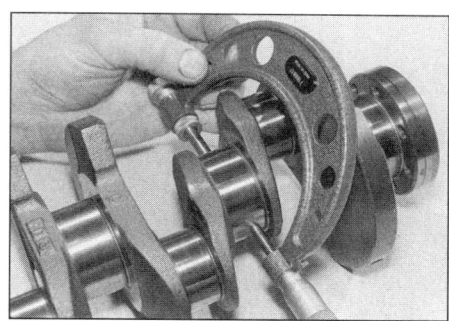

17.10 Measuring a crankshaft big-end bearing journal diameter

17 Crankshaft – inspection

Checking endfloat

1 If the crankshaft endfloat is to be checked, this must be done when the crankshaft is still installed in the cylinder block/crankcase, but is free to move (see Section 14).
2 Check the endfloat using a dial gauge in contact with the end of the crankshaft. Push the crankshaft fully one way, and then zero the gauge. Push the crankshaft fully the other way, and check the endfloat (see illustration). The result can be compared with the specified amount, and will give an indication as to whether new thrustwashers are required.
3 If a dial gauge is not available, feeler blades can be used. First push the crankshaft fully towards the flywheel end of the engine, then use feeler blades to measure the gap between the No 3 crankpin web and the centre main bearing thrustwasher (see illustration).

Inspection

4 Clean the crankshaft using paraffin or a suitable solvent, and dry it, preferably with compressed air if available. Be sure to clean the oil holes with a pipe cleaner or similar probe, to ensure that they are not obstructed.

 Warning: Wear eye protection when using compressed air.

5 Check the main and big-end bearing journals for uneven wear, scoring, pitting and cracking.
6 Big-end bearing wear is accompanied by distinct metallic knocking when the engine is running (particularly noticeable when the engine is pulling from low speed), and some loss of oil pressure.
7 Main bearing wear is accompanied by severe engine vibration and rumble – getting progressively worse as engine speed increases – and again by loss of oil pressure.
8 If there are any signs of wear, take the crankshaft to your local engine reconditioning specialist, where they will check the bearing journals. Any roughness (which will be accompanied by obvious bearing wear) indicates that the crankshaft requires regrinding (where possible) or renewal.

9 If the crankshaft has been reground, check for burrs around the crankshaft oil holes (the holes are usually chamfered, so burrs should not be a problem, unless regrinding has been carried out carelessly). Remove any burrs with a fine file or scraper, and thoroughly clean the oil holes as described previously.
10 Using a micrometer, measure the diameter of the main and big-end bearing journals, and compare the results with the Specifications (see illustration). By measuring the diameter at a number of points around each journal's circumference, you will be able to determine whether or not the journal is out-of-round. Take the measurement at each end of the journal, near the webs, to determine if the journal is tapered. Compare the results obtained with those given in the Specifications.
11 Check the oil seal contact surfaces at each end of the crankshaft for wear and damage. If the seal has worn a deep groove in the surface of the crankshaft, consult an engine overhaul specialist; repair may be possible, but otherwise a new crankshaft will be required.

18 Main and big-end bearings – inspection

1 Even though the main and big-end bearings are renewed during the engine overhaul, the old bearings should be retained for close examination, as they may reveal valuable information about the condition of the engine. On petrol engines, the bearing shells are

18.1 STD marking on the backing of a big-end bearing shell

graded by thickness, the grade of each shell being indicated by the colour code marked on it – they may also have markings on their backing faces (see illustration).
- The thinnest shells are red – 0.005mm thinner than yellow.
- The standard shells are yellow (only size stocked as spare part).
- The first undersize shells are blue – 0.005mm thicker than yellow.

Note: *At the time of writing, no figures where given for the diesel engine. Refer to manufacturer or engine reconditioning specialist for more information.*

2 Bearing failure can occur due to lack of lubrication, the presence of dirt or other foreign particles, overloading the engine, or corrosion (see illustration). Regardless of the cause of bearing failure, the cause must be corrected (where applicable) before the engine is reassembled, to prevent it from happening again.
3 When examining the bearing shells, remove them from the cylinder block/crankcase, the main bearing caps, the connecting rods and the connecting rod big-end bearing caps.

18.2 Typical bearing failures

20.3 Using the top of a piston to push a piston ring into the bore

20.4 Measuring a piston ring end gap

Lay them out on a clean surface in the same general position as their location in the engine. This will enable you to match any bearing problems with the corresponding crankshaft journal. *Do not* touch any shell's bearing surface with your fingers while checking it, or the delicate surface may be scratched.

4 Dirt and other foreign matter could get into the engine in a variety of ways. It may be left in the engine during assembly, or it may pass through filters or the crankcase ventilation system. It may get into the oil, and from there into the bearings. Metal chips from machining operations and normal engine wear are often present. Abrasives are sometimes left in engine components after reconditioning, especially when parts are not thoroughly cleaned using the proper cleaning methods. Whatever the source, these foreign objects often end up embedded in the soft bearing material, and are easily recognised. Large particles will not embed in the bearing, and will score or gouge the bearing and journal. The best prevention for this cause of bearing failure is to clean all parts thoroughly, and keep everything spotlessly clean during engine assembly. Frequent and regular engine oil and filter changes are also recommended.

5 Lack of lubrication (or lubrication breakdown) has a number of interrelated causes. Excessive heat (which thins the oil), overloading (which squeezes the oil from the bearing face) and oil leakage (from excessive bearing clearances, worn oil pump or high engine speeds) all contribute to lubrication breakdown. Blocked oil passages, which usually are the result of misaligned oil holes in a bearing shell, will also oil-starve a bearing, and destroy it. When lack of lubrication is the cause of bearing failure, the bearing material is wiped or extruded from the steel backing of the bearing. Temperatures may increase to the point where the steel backing turns blue from overheating.

6 Driving habits can have a definite effect on bearing life. Full-throttle, low-speed operation (labouring the engine) puts very high loads on bearings, tending to squeeze out the oil film. These loads cause the bearings to flex, which produces fine cracks in the bearing face (fatigue failure). Eventually, the bearing material will loosen in pieces, and tear away from the steel backing.

7 Short-distance driving leads to corrosion of bearings, because insufficient engine heat is produced to drive off the condensed water and corrosive gases. These products collect in the engine oil, forming acid and sludge. As the oil is carried to the engine bearings, the acid attacks and corrodes the bearing material.

8 Incorrect bearing installation during engine assembly will lead to bearing failure as well. Tight-fitting bearings leave insufficient bearing running clearance, and will result in oil starvation. Dirt or foreign particles trapped behind a bearing shell result in high spots on the bearing, which lead to failure.

9 *Do not* touch any shell's bearing surface with your fingers during reassembly; there is a risk of scratching the delicate surface, or of depositing particles of dirt on it.

10 As mentioned at the beginning of this Section, the bearing shells should be renewed as a matter of course during engine overhaul; to do otherwise is false economy.

19 Engine overhaul – reassembly sequence

1 Before reassembly begins, ensure that all new parts have been obtained, and that all necessary tools are available. Read through the entire procedure, to familiarise yourself with the work involved, and to ensure that all items necessary for reassembly of the engine are at hand. In addition to all normal tools and materials, thread-locking compound will be needed. A suitable tube of sealant will also be required for the joint faces that are fitted without gaskets.

2 At this stage, all engine components should be absolutely clean and dry, with all faults repaired. The components should be laid out (or in individual containers) on a completely clean work surface.

3 In order to save time and avoid problems, engine reassembly can be carried out in the following order:

Petrol engines

a) *Piston rings (see Section 20).*
b) *Crankshaft (Section 21).*
c) *Piston/connecting rod assemblies (Section 22).*

d) *Sump (Chapter 2A).*
e) *Balance shafts (Section 12).*
f) *Flywheel/driveplate (Chapter 2A).*
g) *Timing chain and balance shaft chain, sprockets and tensioner (Section 10 and 11).*
h) *Cylinder head (Chapter 2A).*
i) *Intake and exhaust manifolds (Chapter 4A).*
j) *Engine external components.*

Diesel engines

a) *Piston rings (see Section 20).*
b) *Crankshaft (see Section 21).*
c) *Pistons/connecting rod assemblies (see Section 22).*
d) *Cylinder head (see Chapter 2B).*
e) *Oil pump (see Chapter 2B).*
f) *Sump (see Chapter 2B).*
g) *Flywheel/driveplate (see Chapter 2B).*
h) *Coolant pump (see Chapter 3).*
i) *Timing belt, sprockets, tensioner and idler pulleys (see Chapter 2B).*
j) *Intake and exhaust manifolds (see Chapter 4B).*

20 Piston rings – refitting

1 Before fitting new piston rings, the ring end gaps must be checked as follows.
2 Lay out the piston/connecting rod assemblies and the new piston ring sets, so that the ring sets will be matched with the same piston and cylinder during the end gap measurement and subsequent engine reassembly.
3 Insert the top ring into the first cylinder, and push it down the bore using the top of the piston **(see illustration)**. This will ensure that the ring remains square with the cylinder walls. Position the ring near the bottom of the cylinder bore, at the lower limit of ring travel. Note that the top and second compression rings are different.
4 Measure the end gap using feeler blades, and compare the measurements with the figures given in the Specifications **(see illustration)**.
5 If the gap is too small (unlikely if genuine Saab parts are used), it must be enlarged, or the ring ends may contact each other during engine operation, causing serious damage. Ideally, new piston rings providing the correct end gap should be fitted. As a last resort, the end gap can be increased by filing the ring ends very carefully with a fine file. Mount the file in a vice with soft jaws, slip the ring over the file with the ends contacting the file face, and slowly move the ring to remove material from the ends. Take care, as piston rings are sharp, and are easily broken.
6 With new piston rings, it is unlikely that the end gap will be too large. If the gaps are too large, check that you have the correct rings for your particular engine.
7 Repeat the checking procedure for each ring in the first cylinder, and then for the rings in the remaining cylinders. Remember to keep rings, pistons and cylinders matched up.

Engine removal and overhaul procedures

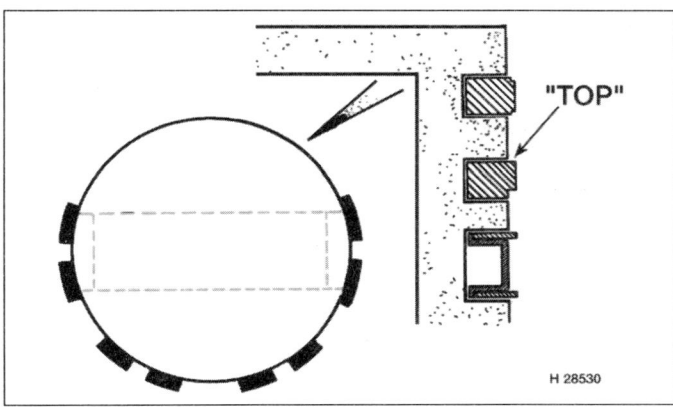

20.9 Piston ring cross-section and gap positioning

21.3 Lubricating the main bearing shells

8 Once the ring end gaps have been checked and if necessary corrected, the rings can be fitted to the pistons.

9 Fit the piston rings using the same technique as for removal. Fit the bottom (oil control) ring first, and work up. When fitting the oil control ring, first insert the expander, and then fit the lower and upper rings with the ring gaps both on the non-thrust side of the piston, with approximately 60° between them. Ensure that the second compression ring is fitted the correct way up, with the word TOP uppermost. Arrange the gaps of the top and second compression rings on opposite sides of the piston, above the ends of the gudgeon pin (see illustration). Note: *Always follow any instructions supplied with the new piston ring sets – different manufacturers may specify different procedures. Do not mix up the top and second compression rings, as they have different cross-sections.*

21 Crankshaft – refitting

Note: *It is recommended that new main bearing shells be fitted regardless of the condition of the original ones.*

1 Refit the crankshaft position sensor reluctor (where applicable) if removed and tighten the screws, with reference to Section 14.

2 Using a little grease, stick the upper thrustwashers to each side of the centre main bearing upper location; ensure that the oilway grooves on each thrustwasher face outwards (away from the cylinder block).

3 Place the bearing shells in their locations in the caps, ensuring that the tab on each shell engages with the notch in the cylinder block or main bearing cap location. Take care not to touch any shell's bearing surface with your fingers. If new shells are being fitted, ensure that all traces of protective grease are cleaned off, using paraffin. Wipe dry the shells and connecting rods with a lint-free cloth. Liberally lubricate each bearing shell in the cylinder block/crankcase with clean engine oil (see illustration).

4 Lower the crankshaft into position so that Nos 2 and 3 cylinder crankpins are at TDC. In this position, Nos 1 and 4 cylinder crankpins will be at BDC, ready for fitting No 1 piston. Check the crankshaft endfloat as described in Section 17.

5 Lubricate the lower bearing shells in the main bearing caps with clean engine oil. Make sure that the locating lugs on the shells engage with the corresponding recesses in the caps.

6 Fit the main bearing caps to their correct locations, ensuring that they are fitted the correct way round (the bearing shell lug recesses in the block and caps must be on the same side). Insert the bolts loosely.

7 Progressively tighten the main bearing cap bolts to the specified torque wrench setting.

8 Check that the crankshaft rotates freely.

9 Refit the piston/connecting rod assemblies to the crankshaft, as described in Section 22.

10 Before refitting the crankshaft oil seal housing, fit a new oil seal in the housing, with reference to Chapter 2A or 2B. Use a mallet and block of wood to drive it into the housing, or alternatively, use the block of wood in a vice (see illustrations).

11 Apply suitable sealant to the contact faces of the oil seal housing, then smear a little oil on the oil seal lips, and refit the locating dowels where necessary. Locate the housing on the cylinder block. To prevent damage to the oil seal as it locates over the crankshaft, make up a guide out of a plastic container, or alternatively use adhesive tape. Once the housing is in position, remove the guide or tape, then insert the bolts and tighten them securely (see illustrations).

21.10a Driving the crankshaft oil seal into the housing

21.10b Fitting the crankshaft oil seal using a block of wood in a vice

21.11a Adhesive tape over the end of the crankshaft will prevent damage to the oil seal when refitting

21.11b Applying sealant to the oil seal housing

2C•22 Engine removal and overhaul procedures

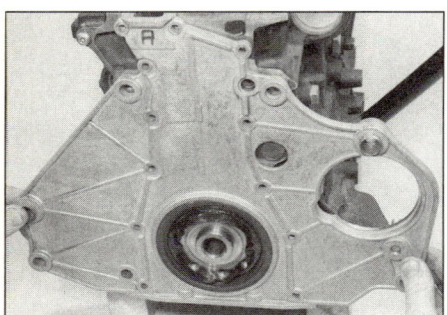

21.11c Refitting the oil seal housing (engine backplate)

22.5 Piston ring compressor fitted over the piston rings

22.6a The arrow on the piston crown must point towards the timing chain/belt end of the engine

22.6b Using a hammer handle to tap the piston down the cylinder bore

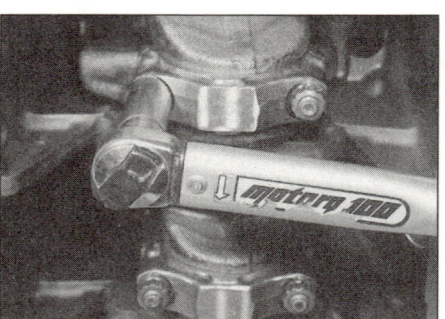

22.8 Tightening the big-end bearing cap nuts

12 Refit the flywheel/driveplate, oil pick-up/strainer/transfer tube and sump, with reference to Chapter 2A or 2B.
13 Where removed, refit the cylinder head as described in Chapter 2A or 2B.
14 Refit the timing chain and sprocket (petrol engines).

22 Piston/connecting rod assembly – refitting and big-end bearing clearance check

Note: *It is recommended that new bearing shells be fitted regardless of the condition of the original ones.*

Running clearance check

1 One method of checking the clearance is to refit the big-end bearing cap to the connecting rod before refitting the pistons to the cylinder block, ensuring that they are fitted the correct way round, with the bearing shells in place. With the cap retaining nuts correctly tightened, use an internal micrometer or vernier caliper to measure the internal diameter of each assembled pair of bearing shells. If the diameter of each corresponding crankshaft journal is measured and then subtracted from the bearing internal diameter, the result will be the big-end bearing running clearance.
2 The second, and more accurate, method is to take the components to your local engine reconditioning specialist, where they will be able to do a more comprehensive check.

Refitting

3 Lubricate the cylinder bores, pistons, piston rings and bearing shells with clean engine oil, then lay out each piston/connecting rod assembly in its respective position on a clean dust free surface.
4 Press the bearing shells into their locations, ensuring that the tab on each shell engages in the notch in the connecting rod and cap. Take care not to touch any shell's bearing surface with your fingers. If the original bearing shells are being used for the check, ensure that they are refitted in their original locations.
5 Start with assembly No 1. Position No 1 crankpin at the bottom of its stroke. Make sure that the piston rings are still spaced as described in Section 20, and then clamp them in position with a piston ring compressor **(see illustration)**.
6 Insert the piston/connecting rod assembly into the top of cylinder No 1; taking care not to mark the cylinder bores. Ensure that the notch or arrow on the piston crown is pointing towards the timing chain/belt end of the engine. Using a block of wood or hammer handle against the piston crown, tap the assembly into the cylinder bore until the piston crown is flush with the top of the cylinder **(see illustrations)**.
7 With the No 1 crankpin at the bottom of its stroke, guide the connecting rod onto it while tapping the top of the piston with the hammer handle.
8 Refit the big-end bearing cap, using the marks made or noted on removal to ensure that they are fitted the correct way round. Tighten the bearing cap nuts/bolts to the specified torque **(see illustration)**.
9 Rotate the crankshaft. Check that it turns freely; some stiffness is to be expected if new components have been fitted, but there should be no signs of binding or tight spots.
10 Refit the remaining piston/connecting rod assemblies to their crankpins in the same way.
11 Refit the oil pump pick-up/strainer, sump and cylinder head with reference to Chapter 2A or 2B.

23 Engine – initial start-up after overhaul

1 With the engine refitted in the vehicle, double-check the engine oil and coolant levels. Make a final check that everything has been reconnected, and that there are no tools or rags left in the engine compartment.
2 Start the engine, noting that this may take a little longer than usual. Make sure that the oil pressure warning light goes out.
3 While the engine is idling, check for fuel, water and oil leaks. Don't be alarmed if there are some odd smells and smoke from parts getting hot and burning off oil deposits.
4 Assuming all is well, run the engine until it reaches normal operating temperature, then switch off the engine.
5 After a few minutes, recheck the oil and coolant levels as described in *Weekly checks*, and top-up as necessary.
6 Note that there is no need to retighten the cylinder head bolts once the engine has first run after reassembly.
7 If new pistons, rings or crankshaft bearings have been fitted, the engine must be treated as new, and run-in for the first 600 miles. Do not operate the engine at full-throttle, or allow it to labour at low engine speeds in any gear. It is recommended that the oil and filter be changed at the end of this period.

Chapter 3
Cooling, heating and ventilation systems

Contents

	Section number
Air conditioning system – general information and precautions	10
Air conditioning system components – removal and refitting	11
Climate control system components – removal and refitting	9
Climate control systems – general information	8
Coolant temperature sensor – testing, removal and refitting	6
Cooling system hoses – disconnection and renewal	2
Electric cooling fan – testing, removal and refitting	5
General information and precautions	1
Radiator – removal, inspection and refitting	3
Thermostat – removal, testing and refitting	4
Water pump – removal and refitting	7

Degrees of difficulty

Easy, suitable for novice with little experience	Fairly easy, suitable for beginner with some experience	Fairly difficult, suitable for competent DIY mechanic	Difficult, suitable for experienced DIY mechanic	Very difficult, suitable for expert DIY or professional

Specifications

General
Expansion tank cap opening pressure .... 1.4 to 1.5 bars

Thermostat
Opening temperature .... 89°C ± 2°C

Electric cooling fan
Cut-in temperature:
  Stage 1 .... 100° ± 2°C
  Stage 2 .... 113° ± 2°C
Cut-out temperature:
  Stage 1 .... 96° ± 1°C
  Stage 2 .... 109° ± 1°C

Coolant temperature sensor

	Resistance (kOhm)	Voltage
At -30°C	20 to 30	Approx. 4.8
At -10°C	7.0 to 11.4	Approx. 4.5
At 20°C	2.1 to 2.9	Approx. 3.6
At 40°C	1.0 to 1.3	Approx. 2.7
At 60°C	0.565 to 0.670	Approx. 1.9
At 80°C	0.295 to 0.365	Approx. 1.2
At 90°C	0.24 to 0.26	Approx. 1.0
At 110°C	0.14 to 0.16	Approx. 0.65

3•2 Cooling, heating and ventilation systems

Torque wrench settings	Nm	lbf ft
Air conditioning:		
Compressor mounting:		
M8 bolts	24	18
M10 bolts	40	30
Compressor refrigerant pipe connections	18	13
Condenser refrigerant pipe connections	18	13
Hose-to-compressor retaining bolts	20	15
Refrigerant pipe connection at bulkhead	15	11
Coolant temperature sensor:		
Petrol engines	13	10
Diesel engines	22	16
Electric cooling fan unit	8	6
Rigid heater pipe:		
To turbocharger	25	18
To water pump	20	15
To cylinder block	10	7
Thermostat housing:		
Petrol engines	22	16
Diesel engines	25	18
Water pump:		
Petrol engines	22	16
Diesel engines	25	18

1 General information and precautions

The cooling system is of pressurised type, comprising a water pump driven by the auxiliary drivebelt, (petrol engines) or timing belt (diesel engines), a crossflow radiator, electric cooling fan, a thermostat, heater matrix and all associated hoses. The expansion tank is located on the left-hand side of the engine compartment. The water pump is bolted to the cylinder block.

The system functions as follows. Cold coolant in the bottom of the radiator passes through the bottom hose to the water pump, where it is pumped around the cylinder block and head passages. After cooling the cylinder bores, combustion surfaces and valve seats, the coolant reaches the underside of the thermostat, which is initially closed. The coolant passes through the heater, and is returned to the water pump. On petrol models, a small proportion of coolant is channeled from the cylinder head through the throttle body. A further amount of coolant is then channeled through the turbocharger.

When the engine is cold, the coolant circulates only through the cylinder block, cylinder head, throttle body, heater and turbocharger. When the coolant reaches a predetermined temperature, the thermostat opens, and the coolant passes through the top hose to the radiator. As the coolant circulates through the radiator, it is cooled by the inrush of air when the car is in forward motion, and also by the action of the electric cooling fan when necessary. Upon reaching the bottom of the radiator, the coolant has now cooled, and the cycle is repeated.

When the engine is at normal operating temperature, the coolant expands, and some of it is displaced into the expansion tank. Coolant collects in the tank, and is returned to the radiator when the system cools.

A double-speed electric cooling fan is mounted on the rear of the radiator, and is controlled by a thermostatic switch. At a predetermined coolant temperature, the switch/sensor actuates the fan. On models with air conditioning, two double-speed fans are fitted.

⚠ **Warning: Do not attempt to remove the expansion tank filler cap, or to disturb any part of the cooling system, while the engine is hot, as there is a high risk of scalding. If the expansion tank filler cap must be removed before the engine and radiator have fully cooled (even though this is not recommended), the pressure in the cooling system must first be relieved. Cover the cap with a thick layer of cloth, to avoid scalding, and slowly unscrew the filler cap until a hissing sound is heard. When the hissing has stopped, indicating that the pressure has reduced, slowly unscrew the filler cap until it can be removed; if more hissing sounds are heard, wait until they have stopped before unscrewing the cap completely. At all times, keep well away from the filler cap opening, and protect your hands.**

• **Do not allow antifreeze to come into contact with your skin, or with the painted surfaces of the vehicle. Rinse off spills immediately, with plenty of water. Never leave antifreeze lying around in an open container, or in a puddle in the driveway or on the garage floor. Children and pets are attracted by its sweet smell, but antifreeze can be fatal if ingested.**

• **If the engine is hot, the electric cooling fan may start rotating even if the engine is not running. Be careful to keep your hands, hair and any loose clothing well clear when working in the engine compartment.**

• **Refer to Section 10 for precautions to be observed when working on models with air conditioning.**

2 Cooling system hoses – disconnection and renewal

1 The number, routing and pattern of the hoses will vary according to the model, but the same basic procedure applies. Before commencing work, make sure that the new hoses are to hand, along with new hose clips if needed. It is good practice to renew the hose clips at the same time as the hoses.
2 Drain the cooling system, as described in Chapter 1A or 1B, saving the coolant if it is fit for re-use. Squirt a little penetrating oil onto the hose clips if they are corroded.
3 Loosen and release the hose clips from the hose concerned.
4 Unclip any wires, cables or other hoses, which may be attached to the hose being removed. Make notes for reference when reassembling if necessary. The hoses can be removed with relative ease when new, however on an older vehicle they may be stuck to the outlet.
5 If a hose proves stubborn, try to release it by rotating it before attempting to work it off. Take care not to damage the pipe stubs or hoses. Note in particular that the radiator hose stubs are fragile; do not use excessive force when attempting to remove the hoses.
6 Before fitting the new hose, smear the stubs with washing-up liquid or a suitable rubber lubricant to aid fitting. Do not use oil or grease, which may attack the rubber.
7 Fit the hose clips over the ends of the hose, and then fit the hose to the stub. Work the hose into position. When satisfied, locate and tighten the hose clips.
8 Refill the cooling system as described in

Cooling, heating and ventilation systems 3•3

Chapter 1A or 1B. Run the engine, and check that there are no leaks.
9 Top-up the coolant level if necessary (see *Weekly checks*).

3 Radiator – removal, inspection and refitting

Note: *If the reason for removing the radiator is to cure a leak, bear in mind that minor leaks can often be cured using a radiator sealant added to the coolant.*

Removal

1 Drain the cooling system as described in Chapter 1A or 1B. This procedure includes removing the splash cover from under the radiator. If the coolant is relatively new or in good condition, drain it into a clean container and re-use it.
2 Remove the front bumper as described in Chapter 11.
3 Loosen the clip and disconnect the top hose from the upper left-hand side of the radiator **(see illustration)**.
4 Remove the electric cooling fan as described in Section 5.
5 On automatic transmission models the fluid oil cooler is incorporated in the radiator. Position suitable containers beneath the radiator and transmission, then disconnect the oil cooler-to-transmission pipes and allow the hydraulic fluid to drain **(see illustration)**. Tape over or plug the ends of the pipes, and discard the seals, as new ones will be required for refitting.
6 Loosen the securing clip and disconnect the coolant reservoir hose from the top of the radiator **(see illustration)**.
7 Disconnect the wiring from the air conditioning compressor.
8 Loosen the clip and disconnect the bottom hose from the lower right-hand side of the radiator. Alternatively, if the radiator clip is not accessible, disconnect the hose from the coolant pump on the right-hand end of the engine **(see illustration)**.
9 Secure the air conditioning condenser, power steering fluid oil cooler and intercooler (depending on model), to the front crossmember.
10 Undo the two retaining bolts and remove the engine oil cooler from along the bottom of the radiator **(see illustration)**. Move the oil cooler to one side with the pipes still connected, taking care not to damage them.
11 Undo the retaining nuts/bolts and remove the two mounting brackets from beneath the radiator **(see illustration)**. Check the lower mounting rubbers when the brackets are removed.
12 With the condenser, power steering fluid oil cooler and intercooler (depending on model) secure, withdraw the radiator downwards and out from under the front of the vehicle, taking care not to damage any of the cooling fins.

3.3 Release the top hose retaining clip

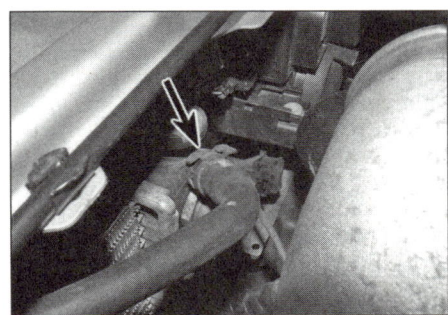

3.6 Release the hose retaining clip

Inspection

13 If the radiator has been removed due to suspected blockage, reverse-flush it as described in Chapter 1A or 1B. Clean dirt and debris from the radiator fins, using an airline or a soft brush.
14 If necessary, a radiator specialist can perform a 'flow test' on the radiator, to establish whether an internal blockage exists. A leaking radiator must be referred to a specialist for permanent repair. Do not attempt to weld or solder a leaking radiator. If the radiator is to be sent for repair, or is to be renewed, remove the cooling fan thermostatic switch.
15 Inspect the condition of the upper and lower radiator mounting rubbers, and renew them if necessary.

Refitting

16 Before refitting the radiator, make sure the bottom hose is in position, making sure that

3.10 Engine oil cooler

3.5 Automatic transmission oil cooler pipe connection

3.8 Release the bottom hose retaining clip

the retaining clip will be accessible when in the car.
17 Refit the radiator into position and fit the lower mounting brackets in place on the front crossmember. Check the mounting rubbers are located correctly on the lower pegs of the radiator and intercooler.
18 Refit the engine oil cooler to the bottom of the radiator.
19 With the lower mounting brackets in position, release the secure ties from holding the air conditioning condenser, power steering fluid oil cooler and intercooler (depending on model), to the front crossmember.
20 Refit the bottom hose to the lower right-hand side of the radiator or coolant pump, depending on where it was removed.
21 Reconnect the wiring to the air conditioning compressor.
22 Reconnect the coolant reservoir hose to the top of the radiator and tighten the clip.

3.11 Radiator lower mounting bracket – one side shown

4.3 Earth cable bolted to the thermostat housing

4.5 Thermostat housing bolts

23 On automatic transmission models, reconnect the oil cooler pipes (together with new sealing washers) and tighten the banjo bolts.
24 Refit the electric cooling fan with reference to Section 5.
25 Reconnect the top hose to the top of the radiator and tighten the clip.
26 Refit the front bumper as described in Chapter 11.
27 Refill and bleed the cooling system as described in Chapter 1A or 1B. Check and if necessary top-up the fluid level in the automatic transmission with reference to Chapter 1A or 1B.
28 Finally, check the cooling system for leaks.

4 Thermostat – removal, testing and refitting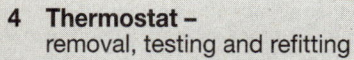

Removal

1 Drain the cooling system as described in Chapter 1A or 1B. This procedure includes removing the splash cover from under the radiator. If the coolant is relatively new or in good condition, drain it into a clean container and re-use it.

Petrol models

2 At the left-hand end of the cylinder head, loosen the clip and disconnect the top hose from the thermostat housing. Move the hose to one side.
3 Unscrew the bolt securing the earth cable to the thermostat housing and move the cable to one side (see illustration).
4 Unbolt the hose support bracket from the thermostat housing.
5 Unscrew and remove the upper and lower mounting bolts, and withdraw the thermostat housing and thermostat from the cylinder head (see illustration). Recover the sealing ring.

Diesel models

6 The thermostat is located on the left-hand end of the cylinder head, and is integral with the housing.
7 Slacken the securing clips, and remove the charge air pipe from the left-hand end of the cylinder head (see illustration).
8 Release the securing clips and disconnect the hoses from the thermostat housing (see illustration).
9 Disconnect the coolant temperature sensor wiring plug.
10 Undo the two retaining bolts and remove the thermostat housing.

Testing

Note: *If there is any question about the operation of the thermostat, it's best to renew it – they are not usually expensive items. Testing involves heating in, or over, an open pan of boiling water, which carries with it the risk of scalding. A thermostat which has seen more than five years' service may well be past its best already.*

11 A rough test of the thermostat may be made by suspending it with a piece of string in a container full of water. Heat the water to boiling point and check that the thermostat opens. If not, renew it.
12 If a thermometer is available, the precise opening temperature of the thermostat may be determined and compared with the figures given in the Specifications. The opening temperature is normally marked on the thermostat.
13 A thermostat which fails to close as the water cools down must also be renewed.

Refitting

14 Clean the surfaces of the thermostat housing and cylinder head.
15 On petrol models, locate the thermostat and sealing ring in the cylinder head, making sure that the vent hole is located at the top. The hole is to allow air to purge from the system.
16 Refit the thermostat housing and tighten the bolts to the specified torque.
17 The remainder of the refitting procedure is the reversal of the removal procedure, on completion refill and bleed the cooling system with reference to Chapter 1A or 1B.

5 Electric cooling fan – testing, removal and refitting

Testing

1 Current supply to the cooling fan is controlled by the DICE Control Module (see Chapter 12, Section 23). The module is supplied with information from the coolant temperature sensor, air conditioning pressure, vehicle speed and outside temperature. Models with air conditioning are fitted with two cooling fans controlled by the DICE Control Module.
2 If the fan does not appear to work, first check that the wiring plug located near the cooling fan is intact. Note that Saab technicians use an electronic tester to check the DICE Control Module for fault codes, and if necessary a Saab dealer should carry out a diagnostic check to locate the fault.
3 If the wiring is in good condition, use a voltmeter to check that 12 volts is reaching the motor when the engine temperature dictates. The motor itself can be checked by disconnecting it from the wiring loom, and connecting a 12 volt supply directly to it.

Removal

4 Remove the bypass pipe and valve from the left-hand end of the cylinder head (see illustration), noting that an O-ring is fitted on the turbo intake pipe.
5 Disconnect the wiring for the cooling fan(s) from the top of the radiator (see illustration).
6 Drain the cooling system as described in Chapter 1A or 1B. Note this only needs to be drained until the level in the cooling system is lower than the outlet for the top hose.
7 Loosen the clip and disconnect the top hose from the upper left-hand side of the radiator.

4.7 Remove the charge air pipe

4.8 Release the three hose retaining clips

Cooling, heating and ventilation systems 3•5

5.4 Remove the by-pass valve

5.5 Disconnect the wiring connector

5.6 Unclip the expansion tank hose

8 Release the clips holding the expansion tank vent hose to the top of the fan cowling **(see illustration)**.
9 On automatic transmission models, release the cooler pipes and wiring (where applicable) from along the bottom of the fan cowling.
10 Unscrew the bolts securing the electric cooling fan shroud to the radiator side tanks; a single bolt is located on each side of the unit **(see illustration)**.
11 Lift the electric cooling fan unit slightly and release it from the lower mounting hooks, then move the unit to one side and withdraw it from the engine compartment **(see illustration)**.
12 To remove a motor and fan blade unit, unclip the plastic cowl and wiring, and then undo the retaining screws **(see illustrations)**.

Refitting

13 Refitting is a reversal of removal but tighten the mounting bolts to the specified torque. On completion refill and bleed the cooling system with reference to Chapter 1A or 1B.

6 Coolant temperature sensor – testing, removal and refitting

Testing

1 The engine coolant temperature sensor is located on the thermostat housing, on the left-hand end of the cylinder head. The resistance of the sensor varies according to the temperature of the coolant.

5.10 Undo the cooling fan shroud retaining bolt – one side shown

2 To test the sensor, disconnect the wiring at the plug then connect an ohmmeter to the sensor **(see illustration)**.
3 Determine the temperature of the coolant,

5.12a Undo the screws and remove the fan blades

5.11 Withdraw the assembly out from the engine compartment

then compare the resistance with the information given in the Specifications. If the reading is incorrect, the sender must be renewed.

512b Unclip the plastic cover . . .

5.12c . . . then undo the screws and remove the fan motor

6.2a Disconnect the wiring from the sensor (petrol engine)

6.2b Disconnect the wiring from the sensor (diesel engine)

3•6 Cooling, heating and ventilation systems

7.15 Water pump removed from the engine

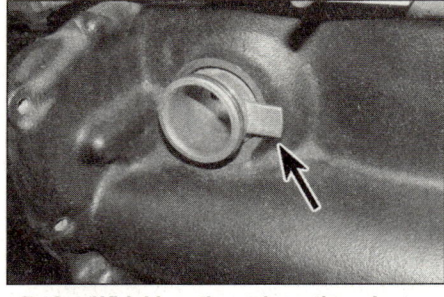

7.16a 'Wide' location tab on the adapter which locates in the 'wide' cut-out on the water pump

7.16b The adapter locates in cut-outs in the water pump body

7.16c Removing the O-ring seals from the adapter

Removal

4 Drain the cooling system as described in Chapter 1A or 1B. To make access easier, remove the hose(s) from the thermostat housing.
5 Alternatively, if you do not want to drain the cooling system, the new sensor may be fitted immediately after removing the old one, or a suitable plug may be fitted in the aperture while the sensor is removed. If the latter option is used, make sure the cooling system has cooled down and then carefully loosen the expansion tank filler cap, to release any pressure in the cooling system, and then retighten the cap.
6 With the wiring disconnected, unscrew the sensor and remove it from the thermostat housing. Where applicable, remove the sealing washer.

Refitting

7 Apply some copper grease to its threads,

7.17a Unscrew the bolts . . .

then insert the sensor, together with a new sealing washer where applicable, and tighten it to the specified torque.
8 Reconnect the wiring.
9 Refill the cooling system as described in Chapter 1A or 1B. If the system was not completely drained, top it up (*Weekly checks*).

7 Water pump – removal and refitting

Petrol models

Removal

1 Drain the cooling system as described in Chapter 1A. This procedure includes removing the splash cover from under the radiator. If the coolant is relatively new or in good condition, drain it into a clean container and re-use it.

7.17b . . . and separate the halves of the water pump

2 Disconnect the wiring from the mass airflow sensor in the front right-hand corner of the engine compartment, then loosen the clips and remove the air hose complete with airflow sensor.
3 Remove the auxiliary drivebelt as described in Chapter 1A.
4 Disconnect the crankcase ventilation hose and release it from the turbocharger intake pipe and camshaft cover.
5 Disconnect the wiring from the turbocharger boost pressure control valve.
6 Unbolt the engine lifting eye from the cylinder head.
7 Disconnect the hoses from the turbocharger wastegate valve.
8 Disconnect the turbocharger bypass pipe and valve, noting that there is an O-ring at the connection to the turbo intake pipe.
9 Unscrew the nut and unclip the heat shield from the exhaust manifold.
10 Disconnect the crankcase ventilation hose at the quick-release coupling.
11 Remove the turbocharger intake pipe, and cover the intake aperture with tape or a plastic bag to prevent entry of dust and dirt.
12 Refer to Chapter 10 and remove the power steering pump, however, do not disconnect the fluid hoses.
13 Loosen the clip and disconnect the inlet hose from the water pump.
14 Unscrew the two bolts from the left-hand end of the cylinder block, and remove the rigid heater return pipe from the water pump. Recover the O-ring from the water pump. Also, unscrew the bolt and remove the rigid heater supply pipe support from the turbocharger.
15 Unscrew the three coolant pump mounting bolts and carefully ease the pump from the bracket and connecting adapter on the cylinder block **(see illustration)**.
16 Remove the adapter from the cylinder block, and examine the O-ring seals for deterioration. It is recommended that new seals be fitted. Note that on later models, the adapter has two location tabs of different widths which locate in the water pump; the adapter can only be fitted one way round; this ensures the correct direction of the internal channel **(see illustrations)**.
17 The water pump may be obtained as a complete unit, or alternatively just the impeller/pulley section may be obtained. To separate the two sections, first mark them in relation to each other. Unscrew the bolts and separate the halves **(see illustrations)**.

Refitting

18 If separated, clean the mating faces and assemble the halves together with a new gasket. Insert the bolts and tighten securely.
19 Refit the adapter to the cylinder block together with new O-rings. Apply a little petroleum jelly to the O-rings to help them enter the cylinder block. On later models, make sure the adapter is positioned correctly.
20 Locate the water pump on the adapter

then insert the bolts and tighten to the specified torque.
21 Refit the rigid heater pipes together with a new O-ring on the return pipe, and also refit the pipe support. Tighten the retaining bolts to the specified torque.
22 Reconnect the inlet hose to the water pump and tighten the clip.
23 Refit the power steering pump with reference to Chapter 10.
24 Refit the turbocharger intake pipe.
25 Reconnect the crankcase ventilation hose at the quick-release coupling.
26 Refit the heat shield to the exhaust manifold.
27 Reconnect the turbocharger bypass pipe and valve together with a new O-ring at the connection to the turbo intake pipe.
28 Reconnect the hoses to the turbocharger wastegate valve.
29 Refit the engine lifting eye to the cylinder head and tighten the bolt.
30 Reconnect the wiring to the turbocharger boost pressure control valve.
31 Reconnect the crankcase ventilation hose to the turbocharger intake pipe and camshaft cover.
32 Refit the auxiliary drivebelt as described in Chapter 1A.
33 Refit the air hose and airflow sensor, and reconnect the wiring.
34 Refit the splash cover beneath the radiator.
35 Refill and bleed the cooling system with reference to Chapter 1A.

Diesel models

Removal

36 On diesel engines, the water pump is driven by the timing belt. Remove the timing belt as described in Chapter 2B.
37 Undo the Allen screws and remove the water pump from the engine (see illustration).

Refitting

38 Refitting is a reversal of removal, but note the following additional points:
a) Clean the pump and block contact faces.
b) Fit new O-rings (where applicable), and apply a little petroleum jelly to them to aid seating.
c) Apply a little thread-locking compound to the water pump retaining bolts.
d) Tighten all nuts/bolts to the specified torque where given.
e) Refill and bleed the cooling system with reference to Chapter 1B.

7.37 Water pump retaining bolts

8 Climate control systems – general information

1 Two types of climate control systems are fitted – the Manual Climate Control (MCC) system and the Automatic Climate Control (ACC) system, which maintains the temperature inside the car at a selected temperature, regardless of the temperature outside the car (see illustration). The basic heating/ventilation unit is common to all versions, and consists of air ducting from the centrally-located heater assembly to a central vent and two side vents, with an extension leading from the bottom of the heater through the centre console to the rear passenger footwell areas.
2 The heating and ventilation controls are mounted in the centre of the facia. Electrically controlled flap valves are contained in the air distribution housing, to divert the air to the various ducts and vents.
3 Cold air enters the system through the grille at the bottom of the windscreen. If required, the airflow is boosted by the blower, and then flows through the various ducts, according to the settings of the controls. Stale air is expelled through ducts at the rear of the vehicle behind the rear bumper. If warm air is required, the cold air is passed over the heater matrix, which is heated by the engine coolant.
4 On all models, a recirculation switch enables the outside air supply to be closed off, while the air inside the vehicle is recirculated. This can be useful to prevent unpleasant odours entering from outside the vehicle, but should only be used briefly, as the recirculated air inside the vehicle will soon become stale.
5 A solar sensor located on top of the facia panel detects increased solar radiation, and increases the speed of the blower motor. This is necessary in order to increase the throughput of air in the vehicle.

8.1 Standard heating/ventilation system

1 Right-hand mixed air stepping motor
2 Control module
3 Left-hand mixed air stepping motor
4 Ventilation fan control
5 Circulation pump (certain versions only)
6 Heat exchanger shut-off valve
7 Air recirculation motor
8 Air distribution stepping motor

3•8 Cooling, heating and ventilation systems

9.3a Unscrew the nuts . . .

9.3b . . . then unclip the frame from around the blower motor

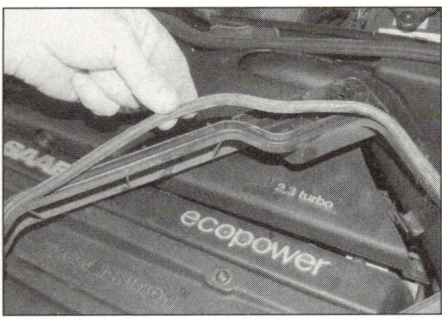

9.3c Removing the weatherstrip from the groove

Air conditioning

6 Air conditioning enables the temperature of air inside the car to be lowered, and also dehumidifies the air, which makes for rapid demisting and increased comfort.

7 The cooling side of the system works in the same way as a domestic refrigerator. Refrigerant gas is drawn into a belt-driven compressor, and passes into a condenser mounted in front of the radiator, where it loses heat and becomes liquid. The liquid passes through a receiver and expansion valve to an evaporator, where it changes from liquid under high pressure to gas under low pressure. This change is accompanied by a drop in temperature, which then cools the evaporator. The refrigerant returns to the compressor, and the cycle begins again.

8 Air drawn through the evaporator passes to the air distribution unit. The air conditioning system is switched on with the switch located on the heater panel.

9 The compressor operation is controlled by an electromagnetic clutch on the drive pulley. Any problems with the system should be referred to a Saab dealer or specialist.

10 The air conditioning refrigerant circuit service ports are located in front of the power steering reservoir on the right-hand side of the engine compartment on the inner wing panel and at the front left-hand corner in the front cross-panel (see illustrations 10.5a and 10.5b).

11 When working on the air conditioning system, it is necessary to observe special precautions (see section 10). If for any reason the system must be evacuated, entrust this task to a Saab dealer or a suitably-equipped specialist.

 Warning: The refrigeration circuit contains a liquid refrigerant under pressure, and it is therefore dangerous to disconnect any part of the system without specialised knowledge and equipment. The refrigerant is potentially dangerous, and should only be handled by qualified persons. If it is splashed onto the skin, it can cause frostbite. It is not itself poisonous, but in the presence of a naked flame (including a cigarette) it forms a poisonous gas. Uncontrolled discharging of the refrigerant is dangerous, and potentially damaging to the environment. Do not operate the air conditioning system if it is known to be short of refrigerant, as this may damage the compressor.

9 Climate control system components – removal and refitting

Heater blower motor

1 Set the air recirculation control to OFF.

2 Remove the wiper motor and linkage as described in Chapter 12.

3 Unscrew the nuts then unclip the frame from around the blower motor. If necessary, remove the weatherstrip from the groove (see illustrations).

4 Unbolt and remove the wiper arm bracket (see illustration).

5 Release the wiring harness from the blower motor cover (see illustration).

6 Undo the screws and remove the blower motor cover by lifting it to one side, at the same time releasing the wiring (see illustrations).

7 Lift out the blower motor sufficiently to

9.4 Remove the wiper arm bracket . . .

9.5 . . . release the wiring harness from the blower motor cover . . .

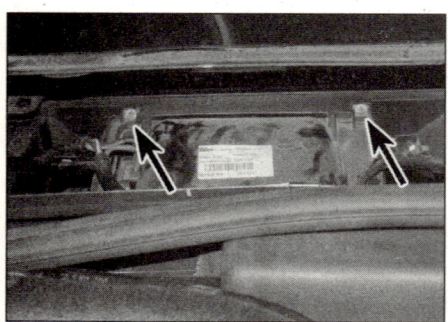

9.6a . . . undo the upper screws . . .

9.6b . . . and lower screws . . .

9.6c . . . and remove the blower motor cover . . .

Cooling, heating and ventilation systems 3•9

9.6d . . . at the same time releasing the wiring

9.8 Using a ratchet strap to pull back the panel when removing the heater blower motor

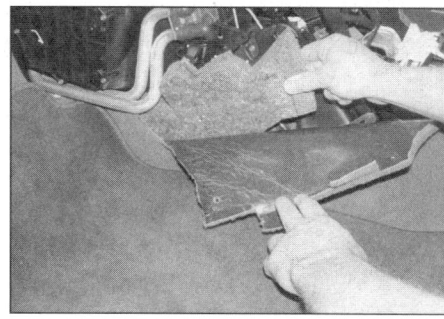

9.12 Removing the console side trim and packing

disconnect the wiring. Also cut the plastic cable-tie and release the wiring.

8 Withdraw the blower motor from the bulkhead. On right-hand drive models, there may be insufficient clearance between the windscreen and engine compartment rear panel, in which case the panel must be temporarily pulled back using a ratchet strap between the panel and front crossmember **(see illustration)**.

9 Refitting is a reversal of removal, but make sure that the wiring is clear of the fan before refitting the cover.

Heater matrix

10 Drain the cooling system as described in Chapter 1A or 1B. This procedure includes removing the splash cover from under the radiator. If the coolant is relatively new or in good condition, drain it into a clean container and re-use it.

11 At the rear of the engine compartment, identify the two heater hoses for position, and then disconnect them from the heater pipes. Place a container beneath the pipes to catch spilt coolant. To remove most of the coolant from the matrix, blow through one of the pipes, and the coolant will escape from the other.

12 Remove the glovebox and centre console side trim and packing with reference to Chapter 11 **(see illustration)**.

13 On right-hand drive models, undo the screws and remove the plastic bracket from the side of the heater **(see illustrations)**. On left-hand drive models, remove the air vent from the air duct on the right-hand side of the heater unit, however, do not remove the seal.

14 Undo the centre screw and remove the clamp plate, then withdraw the two pipes from the matrix. Recover the O-ring seals and check them for deterioration, renewing them as necessary **(see illustrations)**.

15 Undo the four screws and carefully slide the heater matrix from the housing **(see illustration)**.

16 Refitting is a reversal of removal, but renew the O-rings and finally refill the cooling system with reference to Chapter 1A or 1B.

Heater unit

17 On models with air conditioning, the refrigerant must be evacuated by a qualified engineer.

 Warning: Do not attempt to carry out this work yourself, as it is potentially dangerous.

18 Drain the cooling system as described in

9.13a Undo the screws . . .

9.14a Undo the centre screw . . .

9.14c . . . and remove the O-ring seals

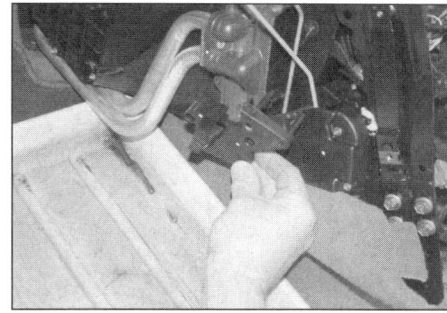

9.13b . . . and remove the plastic bracket from the side of the heater

Chapter 1A or 1B. This procedure includes removing the splash cover from under the radiator. If the coolant is relatively new or in good condition, drain it into a clean container and re-use it.

19 At the rear of the engine compartment,

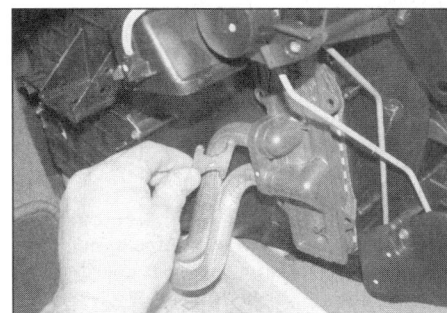

9.14b . . . remove the clamp plate . . .

9.15 Removing the matrix from the heater housing

3•10 Cooling, heating and ventilation systems

9.23 Nuts securing the wiring loom support to the crossmember

9.29 Facia mounting crossmember side retaining bolts

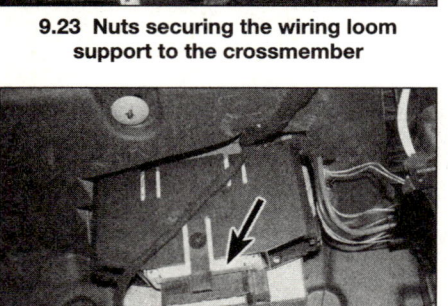

9.30a Disconnect the wiring from the automatic transmission control module, located next to the Trionic engine management ECU mounting box

9.30b Disconnect the wiring from the side of the heater unit

identify the two heater hoses for position, and then disconnect them from the heater pipes. Place a container beneath the pipes to catch spilt coolant. To remove most of the coolant from the matrix, blow through one of the pipes, and the coolant will escape from the other.

20 Remove the centre console and front seats as described in Chapter 11.
21 Fold up the carpet and remove the air ducts located under the front seat positions.
22 Remove the facia panel as described in Chapter 11.
23 Unscrew the nuts and remove the heater earth cables from the facia mounting crossmember. Also unscrew the nuts and detach the wiring loom support from the crossmember **(see illustration)**. Cut the plastic cable-ties securing the wiring harness as required.

24 Unscrew the nuts and remove the central wiring conduit.
25 Unscrew the nuts and remove the driver's knee shield.
26 Unbolt the relay holder and place to one side.
27 Remove the steering column as described in Chapter 10.
28 Unbolt and remove the pedal bracket, the two braces supporting the facia mounting crossmember, and the centre mounting from the crossmember.
29 Unbolt the facia mounting crossmember and withdraw it through one of the front door apertures **(see illustration)**.
30 On automatic transmission models remove the automatic transmission control module from its mounting box, and disconnect the upper wiring, then disconnect the wiring

from the side of the heater unit and place the module to one side **(see illustrations)**.
31 In the engine compartment, remove the air pipe leading from the intercooler to the throttle body.
32 Remove the turbocharger bypass valve solenoid valve holder from the bulkhead as follows. Remove the cover, disconnect the wiring and unbolt the holder.
33 Either remove the heater matrix as described earlier, or disconnect the two pipes from the matrix leaving it fitted to the heater unit.
34 Unbolt and remove the expansion valve.
35 Disconnect the drain hoses from the heater unit.
36 Working in the engine compartment, undo the heater unit mounting bolts from the bulkhead.
37 Inside the vehicle, place cloth rags on the floor to soak up spilled coolant, then raise the rear of the heater unit and withdraw it past the gear selector housing. Remove it through one of the front door apertures.
38 Refitting is a reversal of removal, but refill the cooling system as described in Chapter 1A or 1B. Have the air conditioning system recharged by a qualified engineer.

Climate Control Module

Note: *If a new control module is to be fitted, access to Saab's TECH2 diagnostic equipment is necessary to save various stored values, which will need to be transferred to the new unit. If necessary, entrust this task to a Saab dealer or suitably-equipped specialist.*

39 Remove the audio unit as described in Chapter 12.
40 Reach in through the radio aperture and push out the climate control unit **(see illustration)**. It is secured in position by securing clips at the top and bottom of the unit and also at each side.
41 Disconnect the wiring connectors, as the unit is withdrawn from the facia **(see illustration)**.
42 On Manual Climate Control modules (MCC), if necessary, remove the control knobs by carefully pulling them from their spindles. The bulbholders may also be twisted from the rear of the unit.
43 Refitting is a reversal of removal, noting the following point:
   a) On Automatic Climate Control Modules (ACC), the system will require calibrating, by pressing the AUTO and OFF buttons simultaneously.

Solar sensor

44 At the centre top of the facia panel, slide the solar sensor cover forwards to release it from the facia **(see illustration)**.
45 Disconnect the wiring and remove the anti-theft LED **(see illustration)**.
46 With the cover on the bench, depress and twist the solar sensor anti-clockwise to remove it from the cover **(see illustration)**.
47 Refitting is a reversal of removal, but on completion the ACC system will require

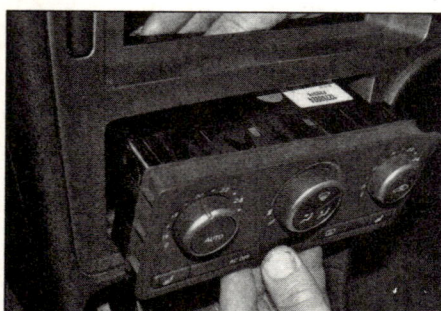

9.40 Remove the climate control unit...

9.41 ...and disconnect the wiring

Cooling, heating and ventilation systems

9.44 Slide the solar sensor cover forwards and lift from the facia

9.45 Disconnect the LED and sensor wiring

9.46 Depress and twist the solar sensor to remove it from the cover

calibrating, by pressing the AUTO and OFF buttons simultaneously.

Interior temperature sensor

48 Carefully prise out the roof console lens with a screwdriver.
49 Undo the screw and remove the sensor from the clips.
50 Disconnect the wiring.
51 Refitting is a reversal of removal, but on completion the ACC system will require calibrating, by pressing the AUTO and OFF buttons simultaneously.

Mixed air sensor

Driver's side

52 Remove the facia lower trim panel, then undo the screws and remove the datalink connector and disconnect the floor lighting wiring.
53 Pull out the sensor from the air duct leading to the lower panel.
54 Remove the audio unit and control panel as described in Chapter 12 and this Section.
55 Disconnect the black upper wiring plug, then note the locations of the sensor pins and remove them from the connector. **Note:** *It may be necessary to cut the wires and fit new ones on refitting.*
56 Refitting is a reversal of removal, but on completion the ACC system will require calibrating, by pressing the AUTO and OFF buttons simultaneously.

Passenger's side

57 Remove the glovebox and the centre console side trims as described in Chapter 11.
58 Pull out the sensor from the air duct leading to the lower panel.
59 Remove the audio unit and control panel as described in Chapter 12 and this Section.
60 Disconnect the grey lower wiring plug, then note the locations of the sensor pins and remove them from the connector. **Note:** *It may be necessary to cut the wires and fit new ones on refitting.*
61 Refitting is a reversal of removal, but on completion the ACC system will require calibrating, by pressing the AUTO and OFF buttons simultaneously.

Air distribution stepping motor

62 Remove the glovebox and the centre console side trims as described in Chapter 11.

63 Undo the screws and remove the stepping motor.
64 Disconnect the wiring.
65 Refitting is a reversal of removal, but on completion the ACC system will require calibrating, by pressing the AUTO and OFF buttons simultaneously.

Air blending stepping motor

Driver's side

66 Set the air blending control to MAX HEAT or MAX COLD before commencing work.
67 Remove the facia lower trim panel, then undo the screws and remove the datalink connector and disconnect the floor lighting wiring.
68 Disconnect the wiring.
69 Undo the screws and withdraw the air blending stepping motor.
70 Refitting is a reversal of removal, but when fitting the stepping motor, hold the flap by the floor air duct to prevent the flap coming out of its mounting. On completion calibrate the ACC system by pressing the AUTO and OFF buttons simultaneously.

Passenger's side

71 Set the air blending control to MAX HEAT or MAX COLD before commencing work.
72 Remove the glovebox and the centre console side trims as described in Chapter 11.
73 Disconnect the wiring.
74 Undo the screws and withdraw the air blending stepping motor.
75 Refitting is a reversal of removal, but on completion the ACC system will require calibrating, by pressing the AUTO and OFF buttons simultaneously.

Heater blower motor control unit

Note: *The following sub-section describes removal of the control unit on a left-hand drive model. The procedure is similar for a right-hand drive model.*

76 The control unit is located on the right-hand side of the heater assembly. First, remove the facia lower trim panel from the driver's side, then undo the screws and remove the diagnostic/datalink connector and disconnect the floor lighting wiring.
77 Remove the accelerator pedal assembly (see Chapter 4A).

78 Remove the glovebox as described in Chapter 11.
79 Disconnect the two front wiring plugs located above the pollen filter. Detach the plugs from the plate and cut the plastic cable-tie.
80 Temporarily switch on the ignition and set the air recirculation flap to OFF, then switch off the ignition.
81 Remove the windscreen wiper arms (see Chapter 12), and remove the rubber seals from the spindles.
82 Pull off the weatherstrip located at the rear of the engine compartment, then undo the screws and remove the scuttle cover by lifting its front edge and pulling it from the rear retaining clips.
83 Remove the wiper motor and linkage as described in Chapter 12.
84 Unscrew the nuts then unclip the frame from around the blower motor.
85 Unbolt and remove the wiper arm bracket.
86 Release the wiring harness from the blower motor cover.
87 Unbolt and remove the blower motor cover by lifting it to one side.
88 Lift out the blower motor sufficient to disconnect the wiring. Also cut the plastic cable-tie and release the wiring.
89 Note the location of the wiring harness on the blower motor control unit, then pull it up together with the rubber seal and cut the plastic cable-tie.
90 Unbolt and remove the control unit.
91 Refitting is a reversal of removal.

10 Air conditioning system – general information and precautions

1 Air conditioning is available as an option on all models. It enables the temperature of air inside the car to be lowered, and also dehumidifies the air, which makes for rapid demisting and increased comfort.
2 The cooling side of the system works in the same way as a domestic refrigerator. Refrigerant gas is drawn into a belt-driven compressor, and passes into a condenser mounted in front of the radiator, where it loses heat and becomes liquid. The liquid passes through a receiver

3•12 Cooling, heating and ventilation systems

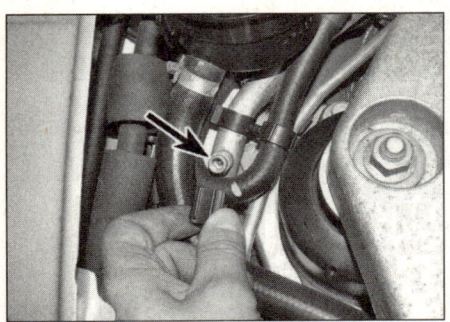

10.5a Low-pressure service port . . .

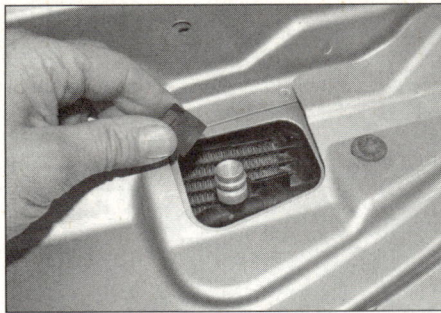

10.5b . . . and high-pressure service port

and expansion valve to an evaporator, where it changes from liquid under high pressure to gas under low pressure. This change is accompanied by a drop in temperature, which then cools the evaporator. The refrigerant returns to the compressor, and the cycle begins again.
3 Air drawn through the evaporator passes to the air distribution unit. The air conditioning system is switched on with the switch located on the heater panel.
4 The compressor operation is controlled by an electromagnetic clutch on the drive pulley. Any problems with the system should be referred to a Saab dealer.
5 The air conditioning refrigerant circuit service ports are located in front of the power steering reservoir on the right-hand side of the engine compartment on the inner wing panel and at the front left-hand corner in the front cross-panel **(see illustrations)**.
6 When working on the air conditioning system, it is necessary to observe special precautions. If for any reason the system must be disconnected, entrust this task to your Saab dealer or a refrigeration engineer.

⚠ **Warning: The refrigeration circuit contains a liquid refrigerant under pressure, and it is therefore dangerous to disconnect any part of the system without specialised knowledge and equipment. The refrigerant is potentially dangerous, and should only be handled by qualified persons. If it is splashed onto the skin, it can cause frostbite. It is not itself poisonous, but in the presence of a naked flame (including a cigarette) it forms a poisonous gas. Uncontrolled discharging of the refrigerant is dangerous, and potentially damaging to the environment. Do not operate the air conditioning system if it is known to be short of refrigerant, as this may damage the compressor.**

11 Air conditioning system components – removal and refitting

Warning: Do not attempt to open the refrigerant circuit. Refer to the precautions given in Section 10.
1 These following operations can only be carried out after discharging the refrigerant. This will need to be carried out by a Saab dealer or suitably-equipped specialist.
2 If necessary for access to any other engine components, the compressor can be unbolted and moved aside, **without** disconnecting its flexible hoses, after removing the drivebelt (see Chapter 1A or 1B).

Condenser

Removal

3 Have the refrigerant circuit evacuated by a suitably-equipped specialist.
4 Raise the front of the vehicle and support it securely on axle stands (see *Jacking and vehicle support*).
5 Remove the front bumper as described in Chapter 11.
6 Slacken the securing clip and disconnect the air intake hose from the air filter housing. Then undo the retaining bolt and remove the air intake hose from the front of the condenser **(see illustrations)**.
7 Undo the power steering fluid cooler mounting bracket bolts and move it to one side, taking care not to damage the pipe **(see illustrations)**.
8 Disconnect the wiring connector from the switch on the right-hand side of the condenser **(see illustration)**.
9 Undo the bolts and disconnect the refrigerant pipes from the receiver/drier **(see illustration)**. Plug the openings to prevent contamination.
10 Undo the bolts securing the condenser to the intercooler, and then undo the lower rubber mounting retaining nuts and withdraw the condenser out from under the front of the car **(see illustrations)**.

Refitting

11 Refitting is a reversal of removal, noting the following points:

11.6a Slacken the retaining clip . . .

11.6b . . . and undo the retaining bolt

11.7a Undo the right-hand mounting bolt . . .

11.7b . . . and left-hand bolt from the power steering fluid cooler pipe

11.8 Disconnect the wiring connector from the switch

Cooling, heating and ventilation systems 3•13

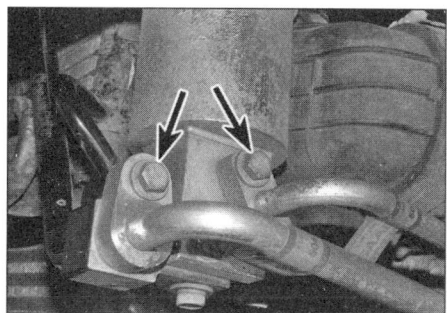

11.9 Undo the refrigerant pipe retaining bolts

11.10a Condenser mounting bolt – one side shown

11.10b Condenser lower rubber mounting – one side shown

a) Renew the pipe connection's O-ring seals.
b) Tighten the fasteners to the specified torque where given.
c) Have the refrigerant recharged by a suitably-equipped specialist.

Compressor

Removal

12 Have the refrigerant circuit evacuated by a suitably-equipped specialist.
13 Raise the front of the vehicle and support it securely on axle stands (see *Jacking and vehicle support*). Undo the fasteners and remove the undershield beneath the radiator, and the one below the engine.
14 Remove the auxiliary drivebelt as described in Chapter 1A or 1B.
15 Where applicable, undo the screws/clamps and remove the charge air pipe attached to the engine sump.

11.17 Refrigerant pipe securing bolts to compressor

16 Disconnect the wiring connector from the compressor.
17 Undo the fastener and disconnect the refrigerant pipes from the compressor (see illustration). Plug the openings to prevent contamination.

11.18 Compressor mounting bolts

18 Undo the retaining bolts and remove the compressor (see illustration).
19 If required, undo the nut and pull the drive pulley and clutch from the compressor (see illustrations). When refitting the pulley/cover, measure the clearance between the cover and

11.19a Home-made tool used to hold the cover whilst slackening the nut (arrowed)

11.19b Remove the cover . . .

11.19c . . . and recover the shims behind it

11.19d Remove the circlip, and pull off the friction disc/pulley and bearing

11.19e The bearing is crimped into the pulley

11.19f Remove the circlip and pull away the electromagnetic clutch

3•14 Cooling, heating and ventilation systems

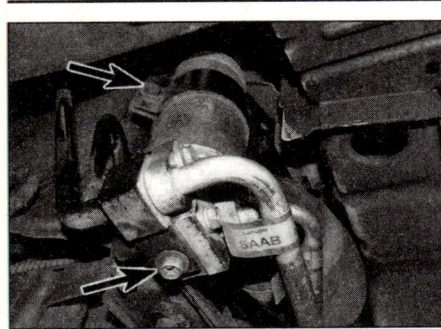

11.25 Receiver/drier mounting bolts

the pulley – the correct specification is 0.5 ± 0.15 mm. If necessary, adjust the clearance by adding or removing shims behind the cover.

Refitting

20 Refitting is a reversal of removal, noting the following points:
 a) *Renew the refrigerant pipe connection seals.*
 b) *Tighten all fasteners to the specified torque where given.*
 c) *Have the refrigerant circuit recharged by a suitably-equipped specialist.*

Receiver/drier

Removal

21 Have the refrigerant circuit evacuated by a suitably-equipped specialist.
22 The receiver/drier located at the left-hand side front of the condenser.
23 Remove the front bumper as described in Chapter 11.
24 Undo the bolts and disconnect the refrigerant pipes from the receiver/drier **(see illustration 11.9)**. Plug the openings to prevent contamination.
25 Undo the two mounting bracket bolts and remove the receiver/drier **(see illustration)**.

Refitting

26 Refitting is a reversal of removal, noting the following points:
 a) *Renew the refrigerant pipe connection O-ring seal.*
 b) *Tighten all fasteners to the specified torque where given.*
 c) *Have the refrigerant circuit recharged by a suitably-equipped specialist.*

Chapter 4 Part A:
Fuel and exhaust systems – petrol engines

Contents

	Section number		Section number
Accelerator cable – removal and refitting	3	Fuel pump – removal and refitting	9
Accelerator pedal – removal and refitting	4	Fuel pump relay – removal and refitting	10
Air cleaner assembly – removal and refitting	2	Fuel supply system – precautions and depressurisation	8
Cruise control system – description and component renewal	5	Fuel tank – removal, repair and refitting	12
Engine management system – general information	13	General information and precautions	1
Engine management system – general information	7	Intake manifold – removal and refitting	18
Engine management system components – removal and refitting	14	Intercooler – removal and refitting	17
Exhaust manifold – removal and refitting	19	Turbocharger – description and precautions	15
Exhaust system – general information and component removal	20	Turbocharger – removal and refitting	16
Fuel gauge sender unit – removal and refitting	11	Unleaded petrol – general information and usage	6

Degrees of difficulty

Easy, suitable for novice with little experience	Fairly easy, suitable for beginner with some experience	Fairly difficult, suitable for competent DIY mechanic	Difficult, suitable for experienced DIY mechanic	Very difficult, suitable for expert DIY or professional

Specifications

System type
All models .... Saab Trionic SFi engine management system

Manifold absolute pressure (MAP) sensor

Pressure: | Voltage (approx.)
- -0.75 bar 0.9
- -0.50 bar 1.3
- 0 bar 2.1
- 0.25 bar 2.5
- 0.50 bar 2.9
- 0.75 bar 3.3

Manifold absolute pressure (MAP) sensor – supply voltage .... 5 volts

Intake air temperature (IAC) sensor

Temperature (°C): | Voltage (approx.)
- -30 .... 4.5
- -10 .... 3.9
- 20 .... 2.4
- 40 .... 1.5
- 60 .... 0.9
- 80 .... 0.54
- 90 .... 0.41

Intake air temperature (IAC) sensor – supply voltage .... 5 volts

Throttle body

Throttle motor – pins 10 and 5 at 20°C .... 1.13 ± 0.5 ohms
Throttle position sensor 1:
  Closed – pins 6 and 9 .... 0.065 to 1.090 volts
  Fully open – pins 6 and 9 .... 3.930 to 4.775 volts
Throttle position sensor 2:
  Closed – pins 8 and 9 .... 3.910 to 4.935 volts
  Fully open – pins 8 and 9 .... 0.025 to 1.070 volts

Pedal switch

Pedal position sensor 1:
  Released – pins 1 and 9 .... 3.990 to 4.645 volts
  Fully depressed – pins 1 and 9 .... 0.400 to 1.055 volts
Pedal position sensor 2:
  Released – pins 3 and 9 .... 0.355 to 1.010 volts
  Fully depressed – pins 3 and 9 .... 3.945 to 4.600 volts

Fuel and exhaust systems – petrol engines

Crankshaft position sensor
Resistance (pins 1 and 2) at 20°C .... 860 ± 90 ohms

Fuel pressure regulator
Pressure .... 3.0 ± 0.1 bars

Injectors
Type .... Bosch EV6 E
Version .... 4 hole nozzle
Nozzle colour code .... brown
Resistance at 20°C .... 15.95 ± 0.8 ohms
Flow rating (at 3 bar fuel pressure) .... 176 ± 7 ml/30 seconds
Maximum flow difference between injectors .... 20 ml

Idle air control valve
Resistance at 20°C .... 8.0 ± 1 ohms
Fuel filter capacity .... 0.6 litres

Fuel pump
Type .... Electric immersed in fuel tank
Capacity at 3.0 bars .... 700 ml/30 seconds (minimum)
Resistance (ohms):
    Fuel level sensor in full position .... 425 ± 6.5
    Fuel level sensor in empty position .... 50 ± 1.5

Turbocharger
Type:
    2.0t engine .... Garrett GT17
        Pressure .... 0.40 ± 0.03 bars
    2.3t engine .... Garrett GT17
        Pressure .... 0.40 ± 0.03 bars
    2.3HOT Aero engine .... Mitsubushi TD04HL-15T-5
        Pressure .... 0.45 ± 0.03 bars
Wastegate preload (all types) .... 2.0 mm
Turbo shaft play (axial) .... 0.036 to 0.091 mm

Fuel system
System pressure .... 3.0 bars
Residual pressure (after 20 mins) .... 2.3 bars (min)

Recommended fuel
2.0t and 2.3t engines .... 95 RON unleaded
2.3HOT Aero engine .... 98 RON unleaded

Idle speed
All models .... Controlled by ECM (not adjustable)

Exhaust gas CO content
All models .... Controlled by ECM (not adjustable)

Torque wrench settings	Nm	lbf ft
Coolant temperature sensor	13	10
Exhaust heat shield	20	15
Exhaust manifold to cylinder head	25	18
Exhaust manifold-to-turbocharger nuts	24	18
Exhaust pipe to turbocharger	24	18
Exhaust system joint nuts and bolts	22	16
Fuel filter banjo fittings	21	15
Fuel pump screw ring	75	55
Intake manifold	24	18
Oxygen sensor	55	41
Throttle body to intake manifold	8	6
Turbocharger to exhaust manifold	24	18

Fuel and exhaust systems – petrol engines 4A•3

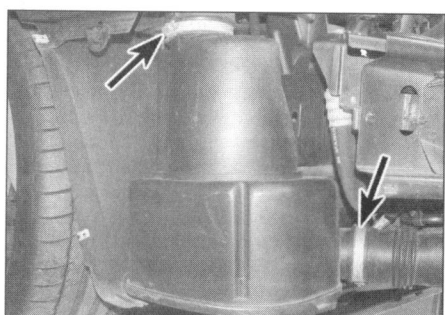

2.5 Slacken the retaining clips (arrowed) and disconnect the intake pipes

2.6 Remove the lower mounting nuts (arrowed) and withdraw the air cleaner housing

2.7 Undo the retaining bolt (arrowed) from the air intake pipe

1 General information and precautions

The fuel supply system consists of a fuel tank mounted under the rear of the car (with an electric fuel pump immersed in it), a fuel filter, and the fuel feed and return lines. The fuel pump supplies fuel to the fuel rail, which acts as a reservoir for the four fuel injectors, which inject fuel into the intake tracts. A fuel filter is incorporated in the feed line from the pump to the fuel rail to ensure that the fuel supplied to the injectors is clean. The filter is mounted adjacent to the fuel tank.

The engine management system is of Saab Trionic type; refer to the relevant Sections for further information on the operation of the system.

A cruise control system is fitted as standard equipment on most of the later Saab models, and is available as an option on earlier models.

The turbocharger fitted is of a water-cooled type. Boost pressure is controlled by the Saab Trionic engine management.

Precautions

• Many of the procedures in this Chapter require the disconnection of fuel lines, which may result in some fuel spillage. Before carrying out any operation on the fuel system, refer to Section 8.

• See the precautions given in 'Safety first!' at the front of this manual and follow them implicitly. Petrol is a highly dangerous and volatile liquid, and the precautions necessary when handling it cannot be overstressed.

2 Air cleaner assembly – removal and refitting

Removal

1 Remove the front grille as described in Chapter 11.
2 Remove the right-hand headlight unit as described in Chapter 12.
3 Slacken the retaining clip, and disconnect the intake pipe from the top of the air cleaner assembly **(see illustration 2.5)**.
4 Apply the handbrake, then jack up the front of the car and support on axle stands (see *Jacking and vehicle support*). Remove the right-hand front wheel, undo the retaining screws and remove the wheel arch liner.
5 From under the vehicle, slacken the retaining clip, and disconnect the intake pipe from the bottom of the air cleaner assembly **(see illustration)**.
6 Unscrew the lower mounting nuts **(see illustration)**, and lower the air cleaner assembly from under the inner wing. **Note:** *It may be necessary to remove a couple of retaining screws from the right-hand side of the front bumper to allow removal of the air cleaner assembly.*
7 If required, undo the retaining bolt(s) and remove the bracket for the air intake pipe **(see illustration)**, then withdraw the air intake pipe from across the front of the radiator.

> **Warning:** Do not run the engine with the air cleaner housing and/or ducting removed – the depression at the turbocharger intake may increase very suddenly if the engine speed is raised above idle.

Refitting

8 Refitting is a reversal of the removal procedure. **Note:** *Make sure the peg at the top of the air cleaner assembly, locates in the hole in the inner wing panel.*

3 Accelerator cable – removal and refitting

Removal

1 From inside the vehicle, undo the retaining screws and withdraw the facia lower panel from the driver's footwell as described in Chapter 11.
2 While holding the accelerator pedal, slide the bush backwards and disconnect the cable from the top of the pedal **(see illustration)**.
3 Working under the bonnet, remove the engine oil filler cap/dipstick then unclip and remove the cover from the top of the engine. Undo the retaining bolts and remove the cover from the throttle linkage **(see illustrations)**.
4 Attach a piece of string (or wire) to the end of the accelerator cable inside the vehicle, and then pull the cable (with string or wire connected) into the engine compartment. Disconnect the string or wire and leave it through the bulkhead for refitting.

3.2 Disconnect the inner cable (arrowed) from the top of the accelerator pedal

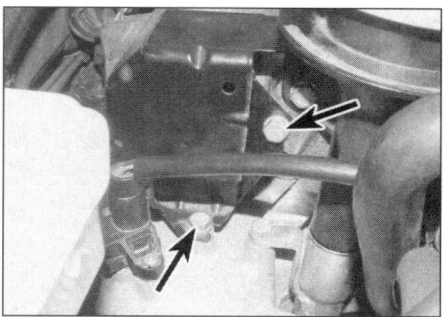

3.3a Undo the two bolts (arrowed) . . .

3.3b . . . and remove the throttle linkage cover

5 Rotate the throttle housing sector and disconnect the inner cable.
6 Pull out the locking clip (noting its position in the grooves on the sleeve), and disconnect the accelerator outer cable from the bracket on the throttle housing **(see illustration)**.

Refitting

7 Apply a little petroleum jelly to the rubber bush (grommet) in the bulkhead, connect the string or wire to the accelerator cable, and draw it back through the bulkhead.
8 Untie the string, and reconnect the cable and bushing to the accelerator pedal inside the car.
9 Refit the accelerator outer cable to the bracket on the throttle housing, and secure with the locking clip in the position noted on removal.
10 Reconnect the inner cable to the throttle housing sector. If there is too much slack in the inner cable, move the locking clip further along the grooves in the outer cable sleeve.
11 Refit the inner facia lower trim panel, this is a reversal of the removal procedure; see Chapter 11.
12 Refit the engine upper cover and throttle valve cover; this is a reversal of the removal procedure.

4 Accelerator pedal – removal and refitting

Removal

1 From inside the vehicle, undo the retaining screws and withdraw the facia lower panel from the driver's footwell as described in Chapter 11.
2 While holding the accelerator pedal, slide the bush backwards and disconnect the cable from the top of the accelerator pedal. On models without an accelerator cable, disconnect the wiring connector from the pedal position sensor assembly.
3 Unscrew the bolts on the pedal bracket, and remove the pedal **(see illustrations)**.

Refitting

4 Refitting is a reversal of removal, but make sure that the mounting bolts are tightened

4.3a Undo the two retaining bolts (arrowed) . . .

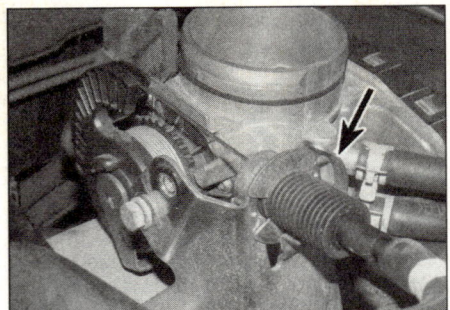

3.6 Remove the outer cable clip (arrowed) securing the accelerator cable to the bracket

securely. If necessary, adjust the accelerator cable as described in Section 3, paragraph 10.

5 Cruise control system – description and component renewal

Description

1 The cruise control system allows the driver to pre-select the speed of the car and then release the accelerator pedal. The cruise control system then adjusts the throttle automatically to maintain a constant roadspeed. The system is deactivated when either the clutch or brake pedals are depressed, when neutral gear is selected (models with automatic transmission) or when the main cruise control switch is switched off. The system has a memory function, which allows a pre-selected cruising speed to be resumed if the operation of the cruise control has been interrupted by depressing the brake or clutch pedals.
2 When the cruise control system is active, the pre-selected roadspeed may be increased or decreased in small increments, by means of the multifunction cruise control system switch.
3 In the event of a fault in the cruise control system, first check all relevant wiring for security. Further testing is best left to a Saab dealer, who will have the necessary diagnostic equipment to find the fault quickly.
4 The main components of the system are as follows:

4.3b . . . then remove the three pedal securing nuts (arrowed)

a) **Electronic Control Module (ECM):** The module is supplied with the speed of the car by signals sent from the speedometer in the instrument panel. The system is not operative at speeds below 25 mph. When the cruise control system is active, the engine management system ECM is informed of this fact by a signal to ensure smoother control of the car's speed. The ECM determines the vehicle's roadspeed from a signal supplied by the Anti-lock Braking System (ABS) ECM.

b) **Switches:** the main multifunction control switch for the cruise control system is integral with the steering column left-hand stalk switch. Switches mounted behind the facia and operated by the brake and clutch pedals deactivate the system when either pedal is depressed. As a fail-safe, the brake pedal cruise control switch is earthed through the brake stop-light bulbs, via the main stop-light switch – if this circuit develops a fault, the cruise control system will not operate.

c) **Indicator light:** the CRUISE indicator light on the instrument panel is illuminated whenever the cruise control system is operating.

Component renewal

Electronic Control Module

5 The cruise control uses the same electronic control module as the engine management system. Refer to the information given in Section 14 of this Chapter for the removal and refitting procedure.

Multifunction control switch

6 Refer to the information given in Chapter 12, Section 4, for the removal of the steering column switch.

Stop-light switch

7 Refer to the information given in Chapter 9.

Pedal switches

8 From inside the vehicle, undo the retaining screws and withdraw the facia lower panel from the driver's foot well as described in Chapter 11.
9 Reach behind the facia and unplug the wiring from the relevant switch.
10 Carefully prise the switch from its mounting bracket.
11 To refit the switch, carefully pull the switch plunger out, and then depress the brake/clutch pedal (as applicable). Insert the switch into its mounting bracket, and slowly release the pedal until it contacts the switch plunger. Reconnect the wiring securely.

6 Unleaded petrol – general information and usage

Note: *The information given in this Chapter is correct at the time of writing, and applies only to fuels currently available in the UK. If*

Fuel and exhaust systems – petrol engines

updated information is thought to be required, check with a Saab dealer. If travelling abroad, consult one of the motoring organisations (or a similar authority) for advice on the petrol available, and their suitability for your vehicle.

1 The fuel recommended by Saab is given in the Specifications at the start of this Chapter.

2 RON and MON are different testing standards; RON stands for Research Octane Number (also written as RM), while MON stands for Motor Octane Number (also written as MM).

3 All Saab 9-5 models covered in this manual are designed to run on unleaded fuel with a minimum octane rating of 91 RON; 95 RON and 98 RON unleaded fuel is recommended. All models are equipped with a catalytic converter, and must be run on unleaded fuel only. Under no circumstances should leaded fuel/LRP be used, as this will damage the catalytic converter.

7 Engine management system – general information

The Saab Trionic engine management system controls three functions of the engine from a single electronic control module (ECM). The three functions comprise the fuel injection system, ignition system, and the turbocharger boost control system. Details of the components related to the ignition function are given in Chapter 5B.

The system is microprocessor-controlled, and the fuel system provides the correct amount of fuel necessary for complete combustion under all engine conditions. Data from various sensors is processed in the ECM, in order to determine the opening period of the fuel injectors for the exact amount of fuel to be injected into the intake manifold.

The system is of sequential type, where fuel is injected in sequence with the engine's firing order. Conventional sequential fuel injection systems require a camshaft sensor, which works in conjunction with the crankshaft position sensor to indicate which cylinder at TDC is on its compression stroke and which is on its exhaust stroke. The Trionic system has no camshaft sensor; it determines each cylinder's stroke by applying a small direct current voltage across each spark plug. When a cylinder on its combustion stroke approaches TDC, this voltage causes an ionisation current to flow across the terminals of the spark plug, thus indicating which cylinder requires fuel injection and ignition next. Sequential control of the ignition timing to control combustion knock is achieved in the same manner (see Chapter 5B).

When the ignition is initially switched on and after the fuel pump is operating, all the injectors operate simultaneously for a short period; this helps to minimise cold start cranking times.

The main components of the system are as follows:

a) **ECM:** the electronic control module controls the entire operation of the fuel injection system, ignition system, cruise control and turbocharger boost control system.

b) **Crankshaft position sensor:** the crankshaft position sensor provides a datum for the ECM to calculate the position of the crankshaft in relation to TDC. The sensor is triggered by a reluctor disc that rotates inside the crankcase.

c) **Manifold absolute pressure (MAP) sensor:** the MAP sensor provides a voltage to the ECM, proportional to the pressure in the intake manifold.

d) **Charge air (boost) pressure/ temperature sensor:** the air pressure/ temperature sensor is integrated into one component and informs the ECM of the pressure and temperature of the air in the hose between the intercooler and the throttle body.

e) **Engine coolant temperature sensor:** the engine coolant temperature sensor informs the ECM of the engine temperature.

f) **Mass airflow sensor:** is located behind the right-hand headlamp. The engine load is measured by means of a hot-film type air mass flow meter, rather than by measuring intake manifold depression. The meter houses a heated metal filament, which is mounted in the flow of the air intake. The temperature reduction in the wire caused by the flow of air over it causes a change in electrical resistance, which is converted to a variable voltage output signal. Measuring air mass flow, rather than volume flow compensates for the changes in air density encountered when driving on roads at different altitudes. Note that this method of measurement also precludes the need for a measurement of intake air temperature.

g) **Throttle position sensor:** the throttle position sensor informs the ECM of the throttle valve position.

h) **Charge air (boost) control valve:** the boost pressure control valve (also referred to as the solenoid valve) is located on a bracket at the front of the cylinder head. It controls the operation of the turbocharger. Under certain conditions (ie, in 1st gear), boost pressure is reduced.

i) **Charge air (boost) bypass valve:** the bypass valve is located on the engine wiring harness connector bracket at the rear of the engine compartment on the bulkhead. It is a safety device to prevent any damage to the turbocharger. Under certain conditions, when there is a build-up of pressure the valve is opened by the vacuum from the intake manifold.

j) **Fuel pressure regulator:** is connected to the end of the fuel rail on the intake manifold and regulates the fuel pressure to approximately 3.0 bars.

k) **Fuel pump:** the fuel pump is housed in the fuel tank. The pump housing incorporates a separate feed pump, which supplies the main fuel pump with pressurised fuel, free of air bubbles.

l) **Injectors:** each fuel injector consists of a solenoid-operated needle valve, which opens under the commands from the ECM. Fuel from the fuel rail is then delivered through the injector nozzle into the intake manifold.

m) **Oxygen sensor:** the oxygen sensor provides the ECM with constant feedback on the oxygen content of the exhaust gases (see Chapter 4C).

n) **EVAP canister-purge valve:** the EVAP canister-purge valve is operated when the engine is started, to purge fuel accumulated in the canister. In order to allow the oxygen sensor to compensate for the additional fuel, the system is operated in short phases (see Chapter 4C).

o) **Ignition discharge module and spark plugs:** the ignition discharge module (or cartridge) contains four HT coils connected directly to the spark plugs (see Chapter 5B).

p) **Limp-home solenoid:** the limp-home solenoid is located on the rear of the throttle body. If a safety related fault occurs in the throttle control, it will go into the limp-home mode. The Check Engine lamp will go on immediately and the diagnostic trouble code will have to be cleared with the diagnostic tool.

Check Engine indicator lamp

If the Check Engine warning light comes on, the car should be taken to a Saab dealer at the earliest opportunity. A complete test of the engine management system can then be carried out, using dedicated Saab electronic diagnostic test equipment.

8 Fuel supply system – precautions and depressurisation

Note: *Refer to the Precautions at the end of Section 1 before proceeding.*

⚠ **Warning:** *Residual fuel pressure may remain for some time after the ignition has been switched off, and must be relieved before any of these components are disturbed for servicing work.*

1 The fuel system referred to in this Section is defined as the tank-mounted fuel pump, the fuel filter, the fuel injectors, the fuel rail and the pressure regulator, and the metal pipes and flexible hoses connected between these components. All these contain fuel, which will be under pressure while the engine is running and/or while the ignition is switched on.

⚠ **Warning:** *The following procedure will merely relieve the pressure in the fuel system – remember that fuel will still be present in the system components, and to take precautions*

4A•6 Fuel and exhaust systems – petrol engines

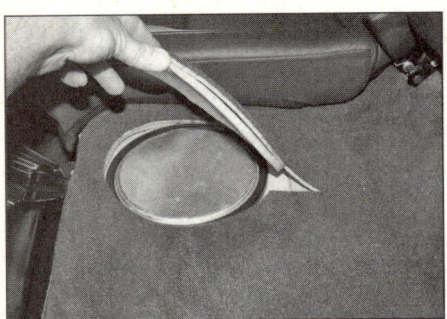

9.2a Lift up the carpet under the rear seat ...

9.2b ... and prise out the fuel pump cover

9.3 Disconnect the wiring plug

9.4 Undo the retaining screw to release the fuel pipes from the pump

Note: *On all models, the fuel pump also incorporates the fuel gauge sender unit.*

Removal

1 Release the pressure in the fuel system as described in Section 8, then disconnect the battery negative cable and position it away from the terminal.
2 Lift up the rear seat cushion as described in Chapter 11. Fold the carpet out of the way and unclip the fuel pump cover from the floor panel **(see illustrations)**.
3 Disconnect the upper wiring plug connector. DO NOT disconnect the connector directly on the top of the fuel pump sender **(see illustration)**.
4 Remove the two fuel lines/check valves from the fuel pump/sender unit. Use a screwdriver to undo the retaining screw from the securing bracket **(see illustration)**, position a rag around the connection to catch any fuel spray, which may be expelled. Note the fitted position of the fuel lines, the white one is the pressure feed line and the black one is the return (which may also be marked on the top of the fuel pump/sender unit).
5 The unit is secured by a screwed ring. Saab technicians use a special tool to unscrew the ring, but a large pair of grips (water pump pliers) inserted between the serrations on the inside edge of the ring will achieve the same result. Unscrew and remove the ring **(see illustration)**. Note the location arrows on the top of the pump and tank.
6 Carefully lift the pump flange away from the surface of the fuel tank. Allow the excess fuel to drain back into the tank, then rotate the pump clockwise through about one quarter of a turn and withdraw it from the fuel tank **(see illustration)**, have a large rag ready to soak up any escaping fuel not drained out of the unit. Recover the O-ring seal from the tank aperture.

accordingly before disconnecting any of them.
2 Open the fusebox cover, on the right-hand side of the facia panel (see *Weekly checks*) and remove the fuel pump fuse (should be fuse number 15 – check in Chapter 12 for exact location for your model).
3 Turn the ignition key and crank the engine. If it starts and runs, allow it to idle until it stops through fuel starvation; this should not take more than a few seconds. Try to start it two more times, to ensure that all pressure has been relieved.
4 Disconnect the battery negative terminal, then refit the fuel pump fuse.
5 Place a suitable container beneath the relevant connection/union to be disconnected, and have a large rag ready to soak up any escaping fuel not being caught by the container.
6 Slowly loosen the connection or union nut (as applicable) to avoid a sudden release of pressure, and position the rag around the connection to catch any fuel spray which may be expelled. Once the pressure is released, disconnect the fuel line.

9 Fuel pump – removal and refitting

⚠ **Warning:** *Refer to the precautions given in Section 8 and the information detailed in the 'Safety First!' Section of this manual, before disturbing any component in the fuel supply system.*

9.5 Unscrew and remove the locking ring from the top of the fuel pump

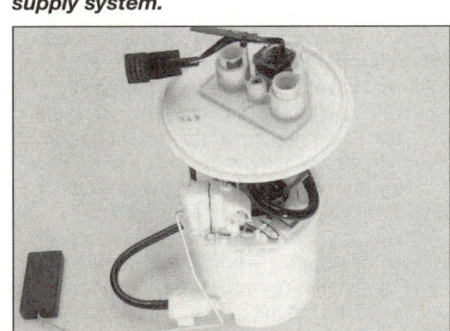

9.6 Fuel pump removed from the fuel tank

9.8 When refitting the fuel pump, ensure that the markings on the fuel pump and tank are aligned

Fuel and exhaust systems – petrol engines 4A•7

Refitting

7 Fit a new O-ring seal to the fuel tank aperture, pressing it firmly into its recess.
8 Lower the fuel pump into the fuel tank, rotating it to ensure that the alignment markings on the fuel pump and tank line up **(see illustration)**.
9 Screw the large plastic locking ring into position and tighten it using the method described for its removal. Apply acid-free petroleum jelly to the screw threads.
10 Refit the fuel lines and wiring connectors to the fuel pump/sender unit, noting the correct fitted position (see paragraph 4). The refitting is a reversal of removal procedure.
11 Refit the rear seat cushion, then reconnect the battery negative cable.

10 Fuel pump relay – removal and refitting

Removal

1 The fuel pump relay is located on the main relay board, behind the facia (see Chapter 12 for further information).
2 Remove the battery cover, then disconnect the battery negative cable and position it away from the terminal.
3 Release the fasteners and detach the lower cover panel from the driver's side of the facia.
4 Remove the securing screw and lower the fuseboard away from the facia.
5 The fuel pump relay is the one that is labelled G; 1st column from the left, 3rd row from the top **(see illustration)**.
6 Grasp the relay and pull it squarely from the relay board.

Refitting

7 Refitting is a reversal of removal. Ensure that the relay is pushed firmly into its base.

11 Fuel gauge sender unit – removal and refitting

On all models, the fuel gauge sender unit is integral with the fuel pump and can only be

10.5 Fuel pump relay (arrowed)

purchased as a complete assembly; refer to Section 9 for fuel pump removal and refitting.

12 Fuel tank – removal, repair and refitting

⚠️ **Warning:** Refer to the precautions given in Section 8, and the information detailed in the 'Safety First!' Section of this manual, before disturbing any component in the fuel supply system.

1 Before removing the fuel tank, it is preferable that all the fuel is first removed from the tank. Since a fuel tank drain plug is not provided, carry out the removal operation when the tank is almost empty.

Removal

2 Release the pressure in the fuel system as described in Section 8, then disconnect the battery negative cable and position it away from the terminal.
3 Select first gear (manual transmission) or Park (automatic transmission) and chock the front wheels securely. Raise the rear of the car and support it securely on axle stands (see *Jacking and vehicle support*).
4 With reference to Section 9 (fuel pump removal), carry out the procedures from paragraphs 2 to 4, disconnecting the fuel pipes and wiring connectors from the fuel pump.
5 Remove the rear section of the exhaust system as described in Section 20.

6 Release the locking clip and disconnect the purge pipe.
7 Undo the retaining bolt and detach the filler neck hose from the tank **(see illustration)**.
8 With reference to Chapter 9, disconnect the both handbrake cables from the rear brakes.
9 Position a trolley jack centrally underneath the fuel tank, with a plank of wood placed on the jack head. Raise the jack until it just starts to take the weight of the fuel tank.
10 Progressively undo the bolts securing the fuel tank support straps to their respective mounting brackets **(see illustrations)**. Unhook the ends of each support strap from their brackets, as they become slack.
11 Disconnect any remaining breather hoses or cables that may prevent the removal of the tank.
12 With the help of an assistant, lower the fuel tank to the ground and remove it from under the car.

Repair

13 If the tank is contaminated with sediment or water, remove the fuel pump and wash the tank out with clean fuel. In certain cases, it may be possible to have small leaks or minor damage repaired. Seek the advice of a suitable specialist before attempting to repair the fuel tank.

Refitting

14 Refitting is a reversal of removal, noting the following points:
 a) Inspect the O-rings at the fuel supply and return quick-release unions, on the top of the fuel pump.
 b) Ensure that all fuel lines and breather hoses are correctly routed and are not kinked or twisted.
 c) Tighten the fuel tank support straps securely.

13 Engine management system – general information

1 The engine idle speed and air-to-fuel mixture (and hence the exhaust gas CO content) are automatically controlled by the ECM. The *checking* of idle speed and

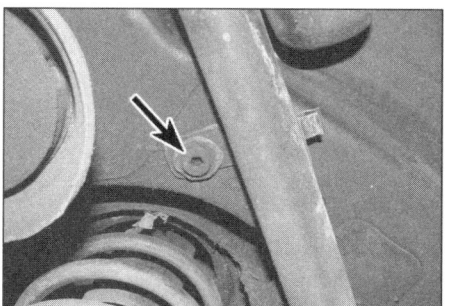

12.7 Undo the fuel filler pipe retaining bolt (arrowed)

12.10a Progressively undo one fuel tank support strap bolt (arrowed) . . .

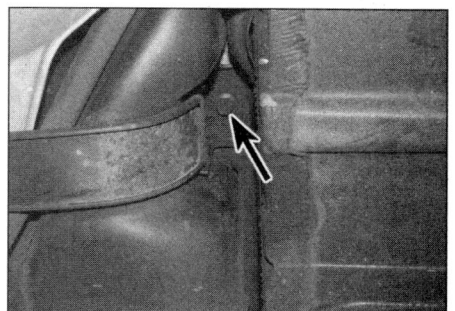

12.10b . . . and then the other strap bolt (arrowed) to release the fuel tank

4A•8 Fuel and exhaust systems – petrol engines

13.3 Diagnostic connector (arrowed) under driver's side facia panel

mixture is possible on all models by using a tachometer and exhaust gas analyser, note some difficulty may be experienced connecting a conventional tachometer to the engine because of the Direct Ignition system. In addition, as all models are fitted with catalytic converters, the levels of CO, HC and NOx produced may be difficult to measure accurately with anything other than professional test equipment if the system is operating normally. However, it may be possible to at least confirm the existence of a fuelling or ignition fault, by detecting high levels of one or more of these exhaust gas pollutants, using a commercially-available exhaust gas analyser.

2 If a fault appears to be present in the engine management system, first ensure that all the system wiring connectors are securely connected and free of corrosion. Then ensure that the fault is not due to poor maintenance – ie, check that the air cleaner filter element is clean, that the fuel filter has been renewed at the specified interval, and that the spark plugs and associated HT components are in good condition. Also check that the engine breather hoses are clear and undamaged. Finally, check that the cylinder compression pressures are correct, referring to Chapters 1A, 2A and 5B for further information.

3 If these checks fail to reveal the cause of the problem, the car should be taken to a Saab dealer for testing. A diagnostic connector is incorporated in the engine management system wiring harness, into which a special Saab electronic diagnostic tester can be plugged. The tester will identify any faults detected by the engine management system ECM by interpreting fault codes stored in the ECM's memory. It also allows system sensors and actuators to be tested remotely without disconnecting them or removing them from the vehicle. This alleviates the need to test all the system components individually, using conventional test equipment. The diagnostic connector is located on the underside of the facia, on the driver's side of the vehicle **(see illustration)**.

4 If the Check Engine warning light comes on, the car should be taken to a Saab dealer at the earliest opportunity. A complete test of the engine management system can then be carried out, using dedicated Saab electronic diagnostic test equipment.

14 Engine management system components – removal and refitting

Warning: Refer to the precautions given in Section 8, and the information detailed in the 'Safety First!' Section of this manual, before disturbing any component in the fuel supply system.

Electronic Control Module (ECM)

Removal

1 Ensure that the ignition is switched off. Disconnect the battery negative cable and position it away from the terminal.
2 Remove the windscreen wipers and windscreen lower scuttle panel as described in Chapter 12.
3 Undo the retaining nuts from the control module cover inside the scuttle panel **(see illustration)**.
4 Carefully lift the cover, release the locking lever and disconnect the multiconnector from the control module **(see illustration)**.
5 Undo the two retaining nuts (a magnetic socket will be useful for this) and withdraw the ECM straight up from the vehicle **(see illustration)**.

Refitting

6 Refitting is a reversal of removal. Ensure that the wiring harness multiway connector is secured with the locking lever. Note that if a new ECM has been fitted, it will gradually 'learn' the engine's characteristics as the vehicle is driven. Driveability, performance and fuel economy may be slightly reduced during this period.

Charge air (boost) pressure/ temperature sensor

Removal

7 The pressure/temperature sensor is located in the main air intake duct to the throttle housing.
8 Disconnect the wiring connector from the sensor, unscrew the sensor from the air intake duct, and recover the sealing washer **(see illustration)**.

Refitting

9 Refitting is a reversal of removal, but check and if necessary renew any sealing washers.

Manifold absolute pressure sensor

Removal

10 Unclip the engine upper cover panel from above the intake manifold **(see illustration)**.
11 Disconnect the wiring plug, then remove the securing screws and withdraw the sensor from the intake manifold **(see illustrations)**.

Refitting

12 Refitting is a reversal of removal, but check and if necessary renew any sealing washers.

14.3 Undo the four retaining nuts (arrowed)

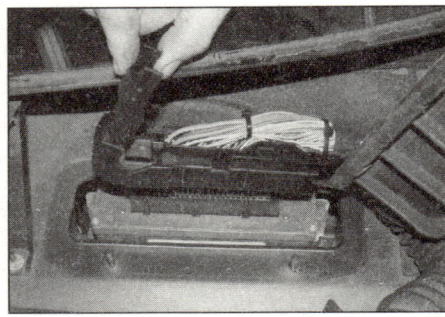

14.4 Unclip the multiplug wiring connector from the control module

14.5 Undo the two retaining nuts (arrowed) to withdraw the ECM

14.8 Disconnect the wiring plug, then undo the two retaining screws (arrowed)

Fuel and exhaust systems – petrol engines 4A•9

14.10 Removing the engine upper plastic cover

14.11a Disconnect the wiring connector...

14.11b ...then undo the two retaining screws (arrowed)

14.13 Slacken the two retaining clips (arrowed)

14.14a Slacken the hose clip, and withdraw the airflow sensor...

14.14b ...note the direction of the arrow

Mass airflow sensor

Removal

13 The mass airflow sensor is located in the right-hand front corner of the engine bay behind the right-hand headlamp unit. Slacken the two retaining clips and withdraw the rubber intake hose from the vehicle **(see illustration)**.

14 Slacken the hose clip on the intake hose and withdraw the airflow sensor. Note the direction of the arrow on the sensor; this is for the correct direction of the airflow **(see illustrations)**.

15 Disconnect the wiring connector from the bottom of the sensor as it is removed **(see illustration)**.

Refitting

16 Refitting is a reversal of removal, but check that the arrows on the sensor are pointing in the direction of flow and the wiring connector is secure.

Coolant temperature sensor

Removal

17 The sensor is threaded into the left-hand side of the cylinder head. Ensure that the engine is completely cold, and then release the pressure in the cooling system by removing and then refitting the expansion tank filler cap (see Weekly checks).

18 To make access easier, it may be necessary to slacken the hose clips and remove the air intake assembly from the top of the throttle body.

19 Unplug the wiring connector from the sensor **(see illustration)**.

20 Unscrew the sensor from the coolant housing on the left-hand end of the cylinder head. Be prepared for some coolant loss **(see illustration)**.

Refitting

21 Clean the threads, then insert the sensor into the intake manifold, and tighten securely. Fit new sealing washer if necessary.

22 Ensure that the wiring connector is securely refitted.

23 Top-up the cooling system with reference to Weekly checks.

Crankshaft position sensor

Removal

24 The crankshaft position sensor is located on the front surface of the cylinder block, at the transmission end **(see illustration)**.

25 Undo the retaining nut and unclip the heat

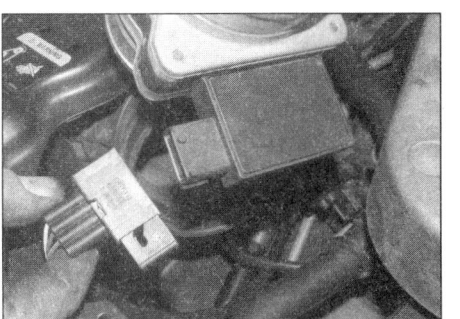

14.15 Disconnecting the wiring connector as the sensor is withdrawn

14.19 Disconnect the wiring connector (arrowed)...

14.20 ...then remove the sensor (arrowed) from the coolant housing

4A•10 Fuel and exhaust systems – petrol engines

14.24 Crankshaft sensor is located behind a shield on the front of the cylinder block

14.25a Undo the retaining nut (arrowed) and remove the heat shield

14.25b Undo the retaining screw and remove the sensor shield

14.26 Withdraw the sensor and recover the O-ring

14.27a Wiring plug connector location (arrowed)

14.27b Pull out locking clip (arrowed) to disconnect the wiring plug connector

shield from the exhaust manifold, then undo the securing bolt and remove the shield/cover from the sensor **(see illustrations)**.

⚠ **Warning:** *The exhaust system and turbocharger may be hot.*

26 Withdraw the sensor from its location on the front left-hand side of the cylinder block **(see illustration)**. Recover the O-ring, noting how it is fitted. Clean the seating in the cylinder block.

27 Note the routing of the wiring around the left-hand end of the cylinder head, and then disconnect the wiring at the connector **(see illustrations)**. Release the wiring from any retaining clips along its length.

Refitting

28 Refitting is a reversal of removal, ensuring that the O-ring is properly seated. Tighten the sensor retaining screw securely. Ensure that the wiring is retained with the clips/cable-ties, following its original routing, and that the multiway connector is securely reconnected.

Throttle body

Removal

29 Ensure that the ignition switch is turned to the OFF position. Making sure the engine is completely cold; release the pressure in the cooling system by removing and then refitting the expansion tank filler cap (see *Weekly checks*).

30 Unclip the engine upper cover panel from the top of the throttle body, then undo the retaining bolts and remove the cover from the throttle linkage **(see illustration)**.

31 Remove the lower vacuum hose from the throttle body **(see illustration)**.

32 Clamp the two coolant hoses that are connected to the throttle body, and then release the retaining clips and disconnect the hoses **(see illustrations)**.

33 Remove the air bypass hose from the front lower part of the throttle body. Slacken the securing clip and disconnect the hose at the rear of the throttle body, below the limp-home solenoid **(see illustration)**.

14.30 Undo the retaining bolts (arrowed) and remove the cover

14.31 Disconnect the vacuum hose (arrowed)

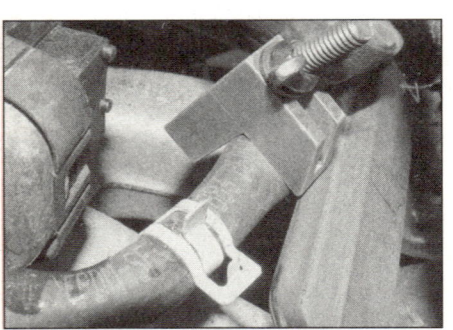

14.32a Clamp the coolant hoses . . .

14.32b . . . then release the securing clips (arrowed) and disconnect the coolant hoses

Fuel and exhaust systems – petrol engines 4A•11

14.33 Disconnect the hose (arrowed) from the rear of the throttle body

14.34a Undo the retaining bolt (arrowed) . . .

14.34b . . . then slacken the retaining clip on the air intake pipe

14.35 Disconnecting the wiring plug from the limp-home solenoid

14.36 Pull out locking clip (arrowed) to disconnect the wiring plug connector from the throttle body

14.37 Undo the three throttle body retaining bolts (arrowed)

34 Undo the retaining bolt on the front of the cylinder head for the turbocharger delivery pipe. Slacken the retaining clip and carefully lift the delivery pipe from the top of the throttle body **(see illustrations)**.
35 Unclip the accelerator inner cable from the throttle linkage, then remove the rubber cover and disconnect the wiring connector from the limp-home solenoid on the back of the throttle body **(see illustration)**.
36 Disconnect the 10-pin multiplug connector from the side of the throttle body **(see illustration)**.
37 Undo the three retaining bolts and remove the throttle body from the intake manifold **(see illustration)**.

Refitting

38 Refitting is a reversal of removal. Renew the seal if necessary and ensure that all connections are secure.

Fuel supply rail, injectors and pressure regulator

Removal

39 Depressurise the fuel system as described in Section 8. Ensure that the ignition switch is then turned to the OFF position.
40 Unclip the engine upper cover panel from the top of the throttle body.
41 Release the securing clip and disconnect the crankcase breather hose from the cylinder head cover **(see illustration)**.
42 Unbolt the dipstick/filler tube from the rear of the cylinder head and remove **(see illustrations)**. Plug the pipe to prevent dirt entering the engine.

43 Refer to Section 3 and disconnect the accelerator cable from the throttle body. Disconnect the quick-release fuel lines from the fuel rail, fit caps to the open fuel lines to prevent ingress of dirt **(see illustration)**.
44 Undo the retaining bolt on the front of cylinder head for the turbocharger delivery pipe. Slacken the retaining clip and carefully lift the delivery pipe from the top of the throttle body **(see illustrations 14.34a and 14.34b)**.

14.41 Disconnect the breather hose from the cylinder head cover

14.42a Undo the retaining bolt (arrowed) . . .

14.42b . . . and withdraw the oil filler tube

14.43 Using a plastic sleeve to release the securing clips on the fuel lines

4A•12 Fuel and exhaust systems – petrol engines

14.45a Undo the two lower retaining bolts (arrowed) . . .

14.45b . . . and the upper retaining bolt (arrowed) from the wiring harness guide

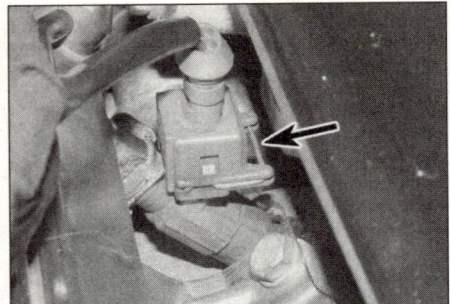

14.46a Press in the securing clip (arrowed) . . .

14.46b . . . and disconnect the wiring connector from the injector

14.47 Fuel rail securing bolts (arrowed)

45 Slacken and withdraw the bolts securing the cable guide bracket to the left-hand end of the cylinder head/intake manifold (see illustrations). For better access, release the cable-ties and detach the wiring harness from the cable guide, then move the cable guide to one side.

46 Release the locking clips and then unplug the wiring from all four injectors (see illustrations), release any cable-ties and move wiring loom to one side.

47 Remove the two bolts securing the fuel rail to the cylinder head (see illustration). Place a cloth beneath the fuel rail, to soak up fuel, which will escape as the fuel rail is removed.

48 Disconnect the vacuum hose from the fuel pressure regulator, then lift the fuel rail from the intake manifold complete with the fuel injectors (see illustrations). Recover the O-ring seals and discard; new ones should be used on refitting. Plug up the holes in the cylinder head to prevent dirt entering the engine.

49 If required, release the metal clamp and remove the fuel pressure regulator from the end of the fuel rail (see illustration).

50 To remove the injectors from the fuel rail, release the retaining clips and pull the injectors from the fuel rail. Recover the rubber O-ring seals and discard; new ones should be used on refitting (see illustrations).

Refitting

51 Refitting is a reversal of the removal procedure. Fit the injectors to the fuel rail (using new O-rings), then press the fuel rail and injectors into the intake manifold as an assembly. Before locating the new rubber O-rings in the intake manifold, apply a little petroleum jelly to them, to facilitate entry of the injectors. Make sure that all the wiring plugs are connected securely. When refitting the turbocharger air intake to the throttle body, ensure that the O-ring seals are properly seated.

14.48a Disconnect the vacuum hose from the regulator . . .

14.48b . . . then withdraw the fuel rail from the intake manifold

14.49 Undo the retaining screw (arrowed) to release the regulator from the fuel rail

14.50a Prise out the retaining clips . . .

14.50b . . . and pull the injectors from the fuel rail

Fuel and exhaust systems – petrol engines 4A•13

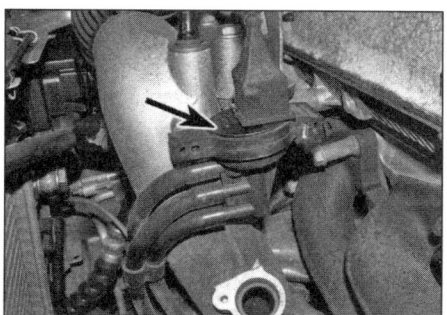

14.52 Charge air (boost) control valve

14.53 Pull back rubber cover and disconnect the wiring connector

14.54 Note the markings on the valve for the hoses

Charge air (boost) control valve

Removal

52 The valve is located at the front right-hand corner of the engine, mounted on a bracket on the air intake pipe (see illustration).
53 Ensure that the ignition is switched off, and then unplug the wiring connector from the valve (see illustration).
54 Mark each of the hoses leading to the valve to identify their fitted positions, then release the clips and detach the hoses from the valve ports (see illustration).
55 Slide the control valve off the two locating pegs and remove from the engine compartment.

Refitting

56 Refitting is a reversal of removal. It is vitally important that the hoses are refitted to the correct ports on the boost control valve.

Charge air (boost) bypass valve

Removal

57 Unclip the engine upper cover panel from the top of the throttle body, then unclip the cover from the engine harness bracket on the bulkhead (see illustration).
58 Undo the two retaining nuts from the mounting bracket (see illustration), then lift the control valve mounting plate and unhook it from the bulkhead.
59 As the unit is withdrawn, disconnect the lower multiplug connector from the bypass valve (see illustration).
60 Mark each of the vacuum hoses leading to the valve to identify their fitted positions, and then detach the hoses from the valve body.
61 Drill out the two rivets and remove the control valve (see illustration).

Refitting

62 Refitting is a reversal of removal. Using new pop rivets, fasten the control valve to the mounting plate.

Limp-home solenoid

Removal

63 Unclip the engine upper cover panel from above the intake manifold (see illustration 14.10).
64 Pull back the rubber cover then disconnect the wiring plug from the limp-home solenoid. Remove the securing screws and withdraw the sensor from the throttle body (see illustrations).

Refitting

65 Refitting is a reversal of removal, but check and if necessary renew any sealing washers.

Oxygen sensor

66 Refer to the information given in Chapter 4C.

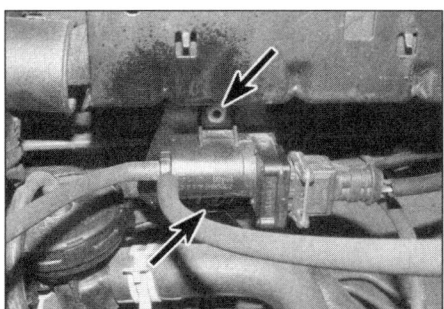

14.57 Unclip the cover from the engine harness on the bulkhead

14.58 Undo the two retaining nuts (arrowed)

14.59 Disconnect the wiring connector from the valve

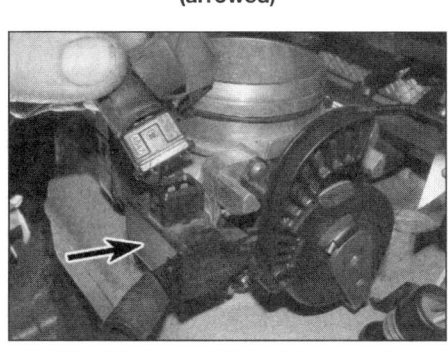

14.61 Drill out the two rivets (arrowed)

14.64a Disconnect the wiring plug from the limp-home solenoid (arrowed) . . .

14.64b . . . then undo the two retaining screws (arrowed)

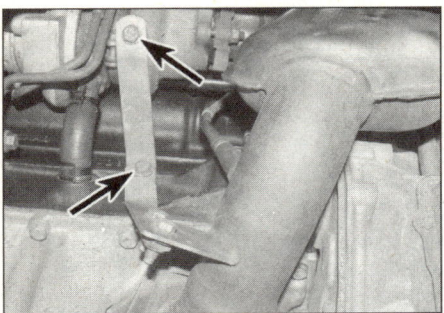

16.3 Undo the two retaining bolts (arrowed) from the exhaust stay bracket

16.4a Disconnect the oil supply pipe (A) and oil return pipe (B)

16.4b On some models the return pipe (arrowed) is a metal corrugated pipe

15 Turbocharger – description and precautions

1 The turbocharger increases engine efficiency and performance by raising the pressure in the intake manifold above atmospheric pressure. Instead of the intake air being sucked into the combustion chambers, it is forced in under pressure. This leads to a greater charge pressure increase during combustion and improved fuel burning, which raises the thermal efficiency of the engine. Under these conditions, additional fuel is supplied by the fuel injection system, in proportion to the increased airflow.

2 Energy for the operation of the turbocharger comes from the exhaust gas. The gas flows through a specially shaped housing (the turbine housing) and in so doing spins the turbine wheel. The turbine wheel is attached to a shaft, at the end of which is another vaned wheel known as the compressor wheel. The compressor wheel spins in its own housing, and compresses the intake air on the way to the intake manifold.

3 Between the turbocharger and the intake manifold, the compressed air passes through an intercooler. This is an air-to-air heat exchanger, mounted in front of the radiator and supplied with cooling air from the front grille and electric cooling fans. The temperature of the intake air rises due to the compression action of the turbocharger – the purpose of the intercooler is to cool the intake air again, before it enters the engine. Because cool air is denser than hot air, this allows a greater mass of air (occupying the same volume) to be forced into the combustion chambers, resulting in a further increase in the engine's thermal efficiency.

4 Boost pressure (the pressure in the intake manifold) is limited by a wastegate, which diverts the exhaust gas away from the turbine wheel in response to a pressure-sensitive actuator. The wastegate valve is controlled by the engine management system ECM, via an electronic boost control valve. The ECM opens and closes (modulates) the boost valve several times a second, which results in manifold vacuum being applied to the wastegate valve in a series of rapid pulses – the duty ratio of the pulses depends primarily on engine speed and load. The ECM monitors boost pressure via the manifold pressure sensor, and uses the boost control valve to maintain pressure at an optimum level throughout the engine speed range. If the ECM detects that combustion pre-ignition ('pinking' or 'knocking') is taking place, the boost pressure is reduced accordingly to prevent engine damage; see Chapter 5B for greater detail.

5 A boost bypass valve fitted in the airflow between the low-pressure supply and high-pressure delivery sides of the turbocharger compressor allows excess boost to be dumped into the intake air ducting when the throttle is closed at high engine speed (ie, during overrun or deceleration). This improves driveability by preventing compressor stall (and therefore reducing turbo 'lag'), and also by eliminating the surging that would otherwise occur when the throttle is reopened.

6 The turbo shaft is pressure-lubricated by an oil feed pipe from the main oil gallery. The shaft 'floats' on a cushion of oil and has no moving bearings. A drain pipe returns the oil to the sump. The turbine housing is water-cooled and has a dedicated system of coolant supply and return pipes.

7 The turbocharger operates at extremely high speeds and temperatures. Certain precautions must be observed during servicing activities, to avoid injury to the operator, or premature failure of the turbo.

• Do not operate the turbo with any of its parts exposed, or with any of its hoses removed. Foreign objects falling onto the rotating vanes could cause excessive damage, and (if ejected) personal injury.

• Do not race the engine immediately after start-up, especially if it is cold. Give the oil a few seconds to circulate.

• Always allow the engine to return to idle speed before switching it off – do not blip the throttle and switch off, as this will leave the turbo spinning without lubrication.

• Allow the engine to idle for a few minutes before switching off after a high-speed run. This will allow the turbine housing to cool before the coolant stops circulating under pressure.

• Observe the recommended intervals for oil and filter changing, and use a reputable oil of the specified quality. Infrequent oil changes, or use of inferior oil, can cause carbon formation on the turbo shaft, leading to subsequent failure.

16 Turbocharger – removal and refitting

Note 1: *The exhaust system and turbocharger may still be hot, make sure the vehicle has cooled down before working on the engine.*
Note 2: *Saab recommends that the oil and filter should be changed (as described in Chapter 1A), when removing the turbocharger.*

Removal

1 Apply the handbrake, then jack up the front of the car and support on axle stands (see *Jacking and vehicle support*).
2 Remove the shield from beneath the radiator, then drain the cooling system as described in Chapter 1A.
3 Undo the retaining bolts and remove the turbocharger stay bracket **(see illustration)**.
4 Slacken the unions and disconnect the oil supply and return pipes from the turbocharger **(see illustrations)**. Plug the open ports to prevent contamination.
5 Working at the top of the engine, undo the retaining nut and unclip the heat shield from the exhaust manifold.
6 Undo the retaining bolt/clips and remove the air bypass hose **(see illustrations)**. Note that there is an O-ring seal at the connection to the intake pipe.

16.6a Undo the retaining bolt (arrowed) . . .

Fuel and exhaust systems – petrol engines 4A•15

16.6b ... and release the securing clip (arrowed)

16.7 Remove the rubber cover (arrowed) and disconnect the wiring connector

16.8a Remove the intake pipe ...

16.8b ... and release the breather pipe

16.10 Undo the three retaining bolts (arrowed)

16.11 Disconnect the coupling on the EVAP hose

7 Disconnect the wiring connectors from the charge air control valve **(see illustration)**.
8 Slacken the retaining clip on the hose to the intake pipe/turbo unit and disconnect the breather pipe (banjo bolt or quick-release coupling) from the intake pipe **(see illustrations)**.
9 Undo the retaining bolt (or unclip) the breather pipe and wiring loom from the right-hand end of the camshaft cover and move them to one side.
10 Undo the retaining bolt(s) and remove the lifting eye from the front of the cylinder head **(see illustration)**.
11 Disconnect the quick-release coupling on the EVAP hose **(see illustration)**.
12 Undo the retaining bolt and withdraw the intake pipe V-clamp from the turbo, then withdraw the intake pipe **(see illustrations)**. Disconnect the vacuum hose as the intake pipe is removed.
13 From under the vehicle, slacken the securing clip on the hose from the charge air cooler to the turbo and disconnect **(see illustration)**. Plug the open ports to prevent contamination or damage to the turbo.
14 Unbolt and remove the exhaust system front pipe from the turbo, carefully lower the front pipe onto an axle stand (or similar) taking care not to damage it (see Section 20 of this Chapter).

> ⚠ **Warning:** The flexible section of the exhaust should not be bent out of alignment by anymore than 5° as this can cause damage to the exhaust causing leakage and noise.

15 Undo the unions and detach the coolant supply pipe from the coolant pump and the turbo housing **(see illustrations)**, retrieve the copper sealing washers. Plug the open ports to prevent contamination.

16.12a Slacken the clamp securing bolt (arrowed)

16.13 Slacken the retaining clip (arrowed) from the hose

16 Undo the unions and detach the coolant return pipe from the turbo housing **(see illustration)**. Retrieve the copper sealing washers, and then plug the open ports to prevent contamination.

16.12b Disconnect the vacuum pipe as the intake pipe is removed

16.15a Undo the coolant pipe (arrowed) from the coolant pump ...

4A•16 Fuel and exhaust systems – petrol engines

16.15b ... and the coolant pipe (arrowed) from the front of the turbocharger

16.16 Undo the coolant pipe (arrowed) from the rear of the turbocharger

16.17 Slacken the four turbocharger securing bolts (arrowed)

17 Apply some easing oil to the exhaust manifold studs, then slacken the turbocharger securing nuts and remove the turbocharger from the vehicle **(see illustration)**. Check around the turbocharger for any pipes that may still be connected.

Refitting

18 Refitting is a reversal of removal, noting the following points:
 a) Fill the turbocharger interchamber with clean engine oil, through the oil supply union on the turbocharger. This is important, as the turbocharger must have oil in it when the engine is started.
 b) Thoroughly clean the exhaust manifold mating surface, before refitting the turbocharger.
 c) Renew all copper union sealing washers, O-ring seals and gaskets, where applicable.
 d) Tighten all nuts, bolts and oil and coolant unions to the correct torque settings, where specified.
 e) Apply a suitable high-temperature, anti-seize compound to the threads of the exhaust system-to-turbocharger and exhaust manifold-to-turbocharger studs and nuts.
 f) Ensure that the charge air (boost) control valve hoses are refitted correctly to the turbocharger, wastegate actuator and air hose **(see illustration 14.54)**.

19 On completion, check that the radiator drain plug is tight, and then refit the shield panel.

20 Lower the car to the ground, then check and if necessary top-up the engine oil level (see Weekly checks). If not already done, it is strongly recommended that the engine oil be changed before starting the engine if a new turbocharger has been fitted, as this will protect the turbo bearings during the 'running-in' period.

21 Refill the cooling system as described in Chapter 1A.

22 It is recommended that the boost pressure is checked by a Saab dealer at the earliest opportunity.

17 Intercooler – removal and refitting

Removal

1 Raise the front of the vehicle and support it securely on axle stands (see Jacking and vehicle support).

2 Remove the front bumper as described in Chapter 11.

3 The intercooler is sandwiched between the radiator and the air conditioning condenser. Remove the radiator as described in Chapter 3.

4 Undo the retaining bolts and remove the oil cooler from below the front of the vehicle **(see illustration)**. Suspend the oil cooler from the subframe by using cable-ties or similar, taking care not to damage the cooler pipes.

5 Using cable-ties secure the condenser to the front crossmember and then undo the two bolts (one each side) securing the condenser to the intercooler **(see illustrations)**.

6 Release the hose clips and disconnect the air hoses from the left-hand end and the right-hand end of the intercooler.

7 Move the intercooler out from the front panel, lift it from its mountings, and withdraw it from the engine compartment.

Refitting

8 Refitting is a reversal of removal, using the relevant Chapters for reference. Ensure that the air hose clips are securely tightened.

18 Intake manifold – removal and refitting

⚠ **Warning:** Refer to the precautions given in Section 1, and the information detailed in the 'Safety First!' Section of this manual, before disturbing any component in the fuel supply system.

Removal

1 Disconnect the battery negative lead.

2 Refer to Section 14, and remove the throttle body from the intake manifold.

3 Remove the fuel rail and fuel injectors from the intake manifold as described in Section 14.

4 Disconnect the brake servo vacuum hose from the intake manifold **(see illustration)**.

17.4 Engine oil cooler

17.5a Condenser mounting bolt – left-hand side ...

17.5b ... and right-hand side

Fuel and exhaust systems – petrol engines 4A•17

5 Unplug the wiring from the coolant temperature sensor **(see illustration)**.
6 Unscrew the mounting bolts securing the intake manifold to the cylinder head. Also unscrew the lower bolt from the steady bar **(see illustration)**.
7 Withdraw the intake manifold from the cylinder head **(see illustration)**. Where applicable, carefully withdraw the intake air heating plate, unplugging the wiring at the multiway connector. Recover the gasket from the cylinder head.

Refitting

8 Refitting is a reversal of removal. Fit a new gasket and, where applicable, reconnect the intake air heating plate wiring. Ensure that the manifold retaining bolts are tightened to the specified torque.

19 Exhaust manifold – removal and refitting

Removal

1 Apply the handbrake, then jack up the front of the car and support on axle stands (see *Jacking and vehicle support*).
2 Disconnect the oxygen sensor wiring with reference to Chapter 4C, Section 2.
3 Remove the exhaust system front pipe and catalytic converter with reference to Section 20.
4 Remove the auxiliary drivebelt as described in Chapter 1A. To gain access to the right-hand exhaust manifold nuts, the power steering fluid pump must be unbolted and moved aside; see Chapter 10 for details. Note that there is no need to disconnect the hydraulic fluid pipes.
5 Unscrew and remove the exhaust manifold mounting nuts, and then lift the manifold from the cylinder head. Note the position of the sleeves fitted beneath some of the stud nuts **(see illustration)**.
6 Remove the gasket from the studs on the cylinder head **(see illustration)**.

Refitting

7 Clean the contact surfaces of the cylinder head and exhaust manifold.
8 Refit the exhaust manifold to the studs on the cylinder head together with a new gasket, then tighten the mounting nuts to the specified torque. Make sure that the sleeves are correctly located, as previously noted.
9 Refit the power steering pump with reference to Chapter 10.
10 Refit the auxiliary drivebelt as described in Chapter 1A.
11 Refit the exhaust front pipe with reference to Section 20.
12 Reconnect the oxygen sensor wiring with reference to Chapter 4C, Section 2.
13 Lower the car to the ground.

18.4 Press the collar down and release the vacuum pipe

18.6 Remove the upper and lower retaining bolts (arrowed)

20 Exhaust system – general information and component removal

General information

1 The exhaust system consists of two sections:
1) The front section (incorporating one catalytic converter on 2.0 litre models, and two catalytic converters on 2.3 litre models).
2) The rear section (incorporating two silencers, which are a combination of resonance and absorption types).

2 If one of the silencers in the rear section of exhaust is leaking or damaged, it can be renewed by cutting the exhaust pipe approximately 95 mm ahead of the rear silencer. A new silencer can then be fitted (making the system into three sections). Check with your local exhaust dealer for availability of parts.
3 The exhaust system sections are joined by flanges with no gaskets, this is for the ease of removing the exhaust and ensuring a good fit. The outer exhaust casing is aluminised to protect against corrosion and the silencers are made of stainless 12% chrome steel.
4 On 2.0 litre models, there is one oxygen sensor located in the front pipe. On 2.3 litre models, there are two oxygen sensors located in the front pipe.
5 The front pipe incorporates a support bracket, which is also connected to the turbocharger.
6 On all models, the system is suspended throughout its entire length by rubber mountings.

19.5 Note the position of the sleeves fitted beneath some of the stud nuts (two shown)

18.5 Disconnecting the wiring connector from the temperature sensor (arrowed)

18.7 Removing the intake manifold and gasket

19.6 Renew the manifold gasket

4A•18 Fuel and exhaust systems – petrol engines

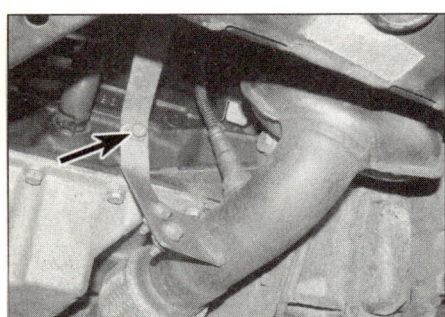

20.12 Undo the exhaust bracket bolt (arrowed)

20.19 Heat shield retaining nuts (arrowed) – two shown

Removal

7 Each exhaust section can be removed individually as described in the following paragraphs. Alternatively, it is possible to remove the complete exhaust system in one piece, but without disconnecting the flange between the front and rear sections.

8 To remove a section of the system, first jack up the front or rear of the car and support it on axle stands (see *Jacking and vehicle support*). Alternatively, position the car over an inspection pit, or on car ramps.

Front section

Note: *Do not drop the catalytic converter, as it contains a fragile ceramic element.*

9 Remove the front oxygen sensor as described in Chapter 4C, Section 2.

10 Undo the retaining nut and unclip the heat shield from the exhaust manifold. Slacken the three nuts securing the front pipe to the turbocharger; do not fully remove at this point.

11 Where applicable, remove the lower engine cover from under the vehicle.

12 Remove the bolts securing the front pipe to its support bracket under the front of the engine **(see illustration)**.

13 Unscrew the nuts and separate the flange joint between the front pipe and the rear exhaust section.

14 Support the exhaust front section and remove the three retaining nuts which where slackened in paragraph 10.

15 Remove the clips from the rubber mountings, then unhook the mounting rubbers from the underbody and lower the pipe between the engine and the subframe crossmember.

⚠ **Warning: The flexible section of the exhaust should not be bent out of alignment by anymore than 5° as this can cause damage to the exhaust causing leakage and noise.**

Rear section

16 Unscrew the nuts and separate the flange joint between the front pipe and the rear exhaust section.

17 Remove the clips from the rubber mountings, then support the exhaust and unhook the mounting rubbers from the underbody of the vehicle. Lower the exhaust rear section to the ground.

18 If either one of the silencers in the rear section of exhaust is leaking or damaged, then it can be renewed individually by cutting the exhaust pipe as described above.

Heat shields

19 The heat shields are secured to the underbody by securing nuts **(see illustration)**. Each shield can be removed once the relevant exhaust section has been removed.

Refitting

20 Each section is refitted by a reversal of the removal sequence, noting the following points:
a) Ensure that all traces of corrosion have been removed from the flared tube ends in the flanges, and where applicable, renew the front pipe-to-exhaust manifold/turbocharger gasket(s).
b) When tightening the nuts on the front section of exhaust to the turbo, tighten them alternately to avoid distortion of the flange.
c) Inspect the rubber mountings for signs of damage or deterioration, and renew as necessary.
d) Refit the oxygen sensor with reference to Chapter 4C, Section 2.
e) Make sure that all rubber mountings are correctly located with their retaining clips, and that there is adequate clearance between the exhaust system and underbody.
f) Make sure the rear of the exhaust is aligned centrally with the cut-out in the rear bumper and matches the bumper profile.

Chapter 4 Part B:
Fuel and exhaust systems – diesel engines

Contents

	Section number
Accelerator pedal/position sensor – removal and refitting	4
Air cleaner assembly – removal and refitting	3
Exhaust manifold and turbocharger – removal and refitting	17
Exhaust system – general information, removal and refitting	18
Fuel gauge sender unit – removal and refitting	6
Fuel injectors – removal and refitting	12
Fuel rail – removal and refitting	11
Fuel supply pump – removal and refitting	7
Fuel system – priming and bleeding	5
Fuel tank – removal and refitting	8

	Section number
General information and precautions	1
High-pressure diesel injection system – special information	2
High-pressure fuel pump – removal and refitting	10
Injection system electrical components – removal and refitting	9
Intake manifold – removal and refitting	13
Intake manifold changeover flap actuator drive – removal and refitting	14
Intercooler – removal and refitting	15
Turbocharger – description and precautions	16

Degrees of difficulty

Easy, suitable for novice with little experience	Fairly easy, suitable for beginner with some experience	Fairly difficult, suitable for competent DIY mechanic	Difficult, suitable for experienced DIY mechanic	Very difficult, suitable for expert DIY or professional

Specifications

System type
All engines .... Bosch EDC 16C9 high-pressure direct injection 'common-rail' system, electronically controlled

Fuel system data
Firing order .... 1–3–4–2 (No 1 at timing belt end of engine)
Fuel system operating pressure .... 1600 bar at 2200 rpm
Idle speed .... Controlled by ECM
Maximum speed .... Controlled by ECM
High-pressure fuel pump:
  Type .... Bosch CP1H
Fuel supply pump:
  Type .... Electric, mounted in fuel tank
  Delivery pressure .... 3.3 bar (maximum)
Injectors:
  Type .... Bosch CRIP 1-MI
  Injection holes (per injector) 6
  Resistance .... 0.255 ± 0.04 ohms

4B•2 Fuel and exhaust systems – diesel engines

Torque wrench settings	Nm	lbf ft
Alternator and high-pressure fuel pump bracket bolts	25	18
Camshaft sensor retaining bolt(s)	9	7
Catalytic converter clamp bolt	20	15
Crankshaft sensor retaining bolt	9	7
EGR valve pipe to exhaust manifold	25	18
Exhaust manifold nuts*	20	15
Exhaust front pipe-to-catalytic converter nuts*	20	15
Fuel injector clamp bracket nuts	25	18
Fuel pressure regulator to fuel rail	60	44
Fuel pressure sensor to fuel rail	70	52
Fuel rail retaining nuts/bolts	25	18
High-pressure fuel pipe unions:		
M12 union nuts	25	18
M14 union nuts	30	22
High-pressure fuel pump mounting bolts	25	18
Intake air sensor retaining bolt	9	7
Intake manifold nuts	25	18
Injector clamp bracket nut	32	24
Throttle body/housing bolts	9	7
Turbocharger oil return pipe bolts:		
M6 bolts	9	7
M8 bolts	25	18
Turbocharger oil supply pipe banjo union bolt	15	11

Do not re-use

1 General information and precautions

1 These engines are fitted with a high-pressure direct injection system that incorporates the very latest in diesel injection technology. On this system, a high-pressure fuel pump is used purely to provide the pressure required for the injection system and has no control over the injection timing (unlike conventional diesel injection systems). The injection timing is controlled by the electronic control module (ECM), via the electrically-operated injectors. The system operates as follows.

2 The fuel system consists of a fuel tank (which is mounted under the rear of the car, with an electric fuel supply pump immersed in it), a fuel filter with integral water separator, a high-pressure fuel pump, injectors and associated components.

3 Fuel is supplied to the fuel filter housing which is located in the engine compartment. The fuel filter removes all foreign matter and water, and ensures that the fuel supplied to the pump is clean. Excess fuel is returned from the outlet on the filter housing lid to the tank via the fuel cooler. The fuel cooler is fitted to the underside of the vehicle and is cooled by the passing airflow to ensure the fuel is cool before it enters the fuel tank.

4 The fuel is heated to ensure no problems occur when the ambient temperature is very low. This is achieved by an electrically-operated fuel heater incorporated in the filter housing; the heater is controlled by the ECM.

5 The high-pressure fuel pump is driven at half crankshaft speed by the timing belt. The high pressure required in the system (up to 1600 bar) is produced by the three pistons in the pump. The high-pressure pump supplies high-pressure fuel to the fuel rail, which acts as a reservoir for the four injectors. Since the pump has no control over the injection timing (unlike conventional diesel injection systems), this means that there is no need to time the pump when installing the timing belt.

6 The electrical control system consists of the ECM, along with the following sensors:

a) **Accelerator pedal position sensor** – informs the ECM of the accelerator pedal position, and the rate of throttle opening/closing.
b) **Coolant temperature sensor** – informs the ECM of engine temperature.
c) **Airflow meter** – informs the ECM of the amount of air passing through the intake duct.
d) **Crankshaft sensor** – informs the ECM of the crankshaft position and speed of rotation.
e) **Camshaft sensor** – informs the ECM of the positions of the pistons.
f) **Intake air sensor** – informs ECM of the intake air temperature and (boost) pressure in the intake manifold.
g) **Fuel pressure sensor** – informs the ECM of the fuel pressure present in the fuel rail.
h) **ABS control unit** – informs the ECM of the vehicle speed.
i) **Particle trap sensor** – measures the differential pressure across the particulate filter, and informs the ECM when the filter is full.
j) **Exhaust temperature sensor** – informs the ECM of the exhaust gas temperature before and after the catalytic converters.

7 All the above signals are analysed by the ECM, which selects the fuelling response appropriate to those values. The ECM controls the fuel injectors (varying the pulse width – the length of time the injectors are held open – to provide a richer or weaker mixture, as appropriate). The mixture is constantly varied by the ECM, to provide the best setting for cranking, starting (with either a hot or cold engine), warm-up, idle, cruising and acceleration.

8 The ECM also has full control over the fuel pressure present in the fuel rail via the high-pressure fuel regulator and third piston deactivator solenoid valve, which are fitted to the high-pressure fuel pump. To reduce the pressure, the ECM opens the high-pressure fuel regulator, which allows the excess fuel to return direct to the tank from the pump. The third piston deactivator is used mainly to reduce the load on the engine, but can also be used to lower the fuel pressure. The deactivator solenoid valve relieves the fuel pressure from the third piston of the pump, which results in only two of the pistons pressurising the fuel system.

9 The ECM also controls the exhaust gas recirculation (EGR) system, described in detail in Part C of this Chapter, the pre/post-heating system (see Chapter 5A), and the engine cooling fan.

10 The intake manifold is fitted with a butterfly valve arrangement to improve efficiency at low engine speeds. Each cylinder has two intake tracts in the manifold, one of which is fitted with a valve; the operation of the valve is controlled by the ECM via an electric motor actuator drive arrangement. At low engine speeds (below approximately 1500 rpm) the valves remain closed, meaning that air entering each cylinder is passing through only one of the two manifold tracts. At higher engine speeds, the ECM opens up each of the four valves allowing the air passing through the manifold to pass through both intake tracts.

11 A variable-vane turbocharger is fitted to increase engine efficiency. It does this by raising the pressure in the intake manifold above atmospheric pressure. Instead of the air simply being sucked into the cylinders,

Fuel and exhaust systems – diesel engines 4B•3

it is forced in. Note that the turbocharger is integral with the exhaust manifold.

12 Between the turbocharger and the intake manifold, the compressed air passes through an intercooler. This is an air-to-air heat exchanger is mounted next to the radiator, and supplied with cooling air from the front of the vehicle. The purpose of the intercooler is to remove some of the heat gained in being compressed from the intake air. Because cooler air is denser, removal of this heat further increases engine efficiency.

13 Energy for the operation of the turbocharger comes from the exhaust gas. The gas flows through a specially-shaped housing (the turbine housing) and in so doing, spins the turbine wheel. The turbine wheel is attached to a shaft, at the end of which is another vaned wheel known as the compressor wheel. The compressor wheel spins in its own housing, and compresses the intake air on the way to the intake manifold. The turbo shaft is pressure-lubricated by an oil feed pipe from the main oil gallery. The shaft 'floats' on a cushion of oil. A drain pipe returns the oil to the sump. Boost pressure (the pressure in the intake manifold) is limited by a wastegate, which diverts the exhaust gas away from the turbine wheel in response to a pressure-sensitive actuator.

14 If certain sensors fail, and send abnormal signals to the ECM, the ECM has a back-up programme. In this event, the abnormal signals are ignored, and a pre-programmed value is substituted for the sensor signal, allowing the engine to continue running, albeit at reduced efficiency. If the ECM enters its back-up mode, a warning light on the instrument panel will illuminate, and a fault code will be stored in the ECM memory. This fault code can be read using suitable specialist test equipment plugged into the system's diagnostic socket. The diagnostic socket is located beneath the driver's side of the facia, above the pedals **(see illustration)**.

⚠ **Warning: It is necessary to take certain precautions when working on the fuel system components, particularly the high-pressure side of the system. Before carrying out any operations on the fuel system, refer to the precautions given in 'Safety first!' at the beginning of this manual, and to any additional warning notes at the start of the relevant Sections. Also refer to the additional information contained in Section 2.**

- **Do not operate the engine if any of air intake ducts are disconnected or the filter element is removed. Any debris entering the engine will cause severe damage to the turbocharger.**
- **To prevent damage to the turbocharger, do not race the engine immediately after start-up, especially if it is cold. Allow it to idle smoothly to give the oil a few seconds to circulate around the turbocharger bearings. Always allow the engine to return to idle speed before switching it off – do not blip the throttle and switch off, as this will leave the turbo spinning without lubrication.**

1.14 Diagnostic socket (arrowed)

- **Observe the recommended intervals for oil and filter changing, and use a reputable oil of the specified quality. Neglect of oil changing, or use of inferior oil, can cause carbon formation on the turbo shaft, leading to subsequent failure.**

2 High-pressure diesel injection system – special information

Warnings and precautions

1 It is essential to observe strict precautions when working on the fuel system components, particularly the high pressure side of the system. Before carrying out any operations on the fuel system, refer to the precautions given in *Safety first!* at the beginning of this manual, and to the following additional information.

- Do not carry out any repair work on the high-pressure fuel system unless you are competent to do so, have all the necessary tools and equipment required, and are aware of the safety implications involved.
- Before starting any repair work on the fuel system, wait at least 30 seconds after switching off the engine to allow the fuel circuit to return to atmospheric pressure.
- Never work on the high-pressure fuel system with the engine running.
- Keep well clear of any possible source of fuel leakage, particularly when starting the engine after carrying out repair work. A leak in the system could cause an extremely high-pressure jet of fuel to escape, which could result in severe personal injury.
- Never place your hands or any part of your body near to a leak in the high-pressure fuel system.
- Do not use steam cleaning equipment or compressed air to clean the engine or any of the fuel system components.

Repair procedures and general information

2 Strict cleanliness must be observed at all times when working on any part of the fuel system. This applies to the working area in general, the person doing the work, and the components being worked on.

3 Before working on the fuel system components, they must be thoroughly cleaned with a suitable degreasing fluid. Cleanliness is particularly important when working on the fuel system connections at the following components:
 a) *Fuel filter.*
 b) *High-pressure fuel pump.*
 c) *Fuel rail.*
 d) *Fuel injectors.*
 e) *High-pressure fuel pipes.*

4 After disconnecting any fuel pipes or components, the open union or orifice must be immediately sealed to prevent the entry of dirt or foreign material. Plastic plugs and caps in various sizes are available in packs from motor factors and accessory outlets, and are particularly suitable for this application **(see illustration)**. Fingers cut from disposable rubber gloves should be used to protect components such as fuel pipes, fuel injectors and wiring connectors, and can be secured in place using elastic bands. Suitable gloves of this type are available at no cost from most petrol station forecourts.

5 Whenever any of the high-pressure fuel pipes are disconnected or removed, a new pipe(s) must be obtained for refitting.

6 The torque wrench settings given in the Specifications must be strictly observed when tightening component mountings and connections. This is particularly important when tightening the high-pressure fuel pipe unions. To enable a torque wrench to be used on the fuel pipe unions, two crow-foot adapters are required. Suitable types are available from motor factors and accessory outlets **(see illustration)**.

2.4 Typical plastic plug and cap set for sealing disconnected fuel pipes and components

2.6 Two crow-foot adapters will be necessary for tightening the fuel pipe unions

4B•4 Fuel and exhaust systems – diesel engines

3.5 Slacken the retaining clips (arrowed) and disconnect the intake pipes

3.6 Remove the lower mounting nuts (arrowed) and withdraw the air cleaner housing

3.7 Undo the retaining bolt (arrowed) from the air intake pipe

3 Air cleaner assembly – removal and refitting

Removal

1 Remove the front grille (see Chapter 11).
2 Remove the right-hand headlight unit as described in Chapter 12.
3 Slacken the retaining clip, and disconnect the intake pipe from the top of the air cleaner assembly **(see illustration 3.5)**.
4 Apply the handbrake, then jack up the front of the car and support on axle stands (see *Jacking and vehicle support*). Remove the right-hand front wheel, undo the retaining screws and remove the wheel arch liner.
5 From under the vehicle, slacken the retaining clip, and disconnect the intake pipe from the bottom of the air cleaner assembly **(see illustration)**.
6 Unscrew the lower mounting nuts **(see illustration)**, and lower the air cleaner assembly from under the inner wing. **Note:** *It may be necessary to remove a couple of retaining screws from the right-hand side of the front bumper to allow removal of the air cleaner assembly.*
7 If required, undo the retaining bolt(s) and remove the bracket for the air intake pipe **(see illustration)**, then withdraw the air intake pipe from across the front of the radiator.

 Warning: Do not run the engine with the air cleaner housing and/or ducting removed – the depression at the turbocharger

intake may increase very suddenly if the engine speed is raised above idle.

Refitting

8 Refitting is a reversal of the removal procedure. **Note:** *Make sure the peg at the top of the air cleaner assembly, locates in the hole in the inner wing panel.*

4 Accelerator pedal/ position sensor – removal and refitting

Refer to Chapter 4A, Section 4.

5 Fuel system – priming and bleeding

1 After disconnecting the fuel supply system or running out of fuel, it is necessary to prime the fuel system and bleed off any air, which may have entered the system components, as follows.
2 Operate the fuel supply pump by switching on the ignition three times for approximately 15 seconds. The engine should now start. If it doesn't, wait a few minutes and repeat the procedure.

6 Fuel gauge sender unit – removal and refitting

On all models, the fuel gauge sender unit is integral with the fuel pump and can only be

purchased as a complete assembly. Refer to Chapter 4A, Section 9, for fuel pump removal and refitting.

7 Fuel pump – removal and refitting

The diesel fuel supply pump is located in the same position as the fuel pump on petrol engine models, and the removal and refitting procedures are virtually identical **(see illustrations)**. Refer to Chapter 4A, Section 9. On completion, bleed the fuel system as described in Section 5.

8 Fuel tank – removal and refitting

Refer to Chapter 4A, Section 12. On completion, bleed the fuel system as described in Section 5.

9 Injection system electrical components – removal and refitting

Airflow meter

1 Slacken the retaining clip securing the air intake duct to the airflow meter and disconnect the duct.
2 Disconnect the airflow meter wiring connector **(see illustration)**.

7.1a Disconnect the wiring connector . . .

7.1b . . . and release the fuel pipes

9.2 Disconnect the airflow meter wiring connector

Fuel and exhaust systems – diesel engines 4B•5

9.6 Disconnect the charge air hose from the throttle body/housing, and intercooler charge air pipe

9.10 The crankshaft sensor (arrowed) is located beneath the starter motor

9.15 Camshaft sensor location (arrowed)

9.19 The coolant temperature sensor (arrowed) is located at the left-hand end of the cylinder head

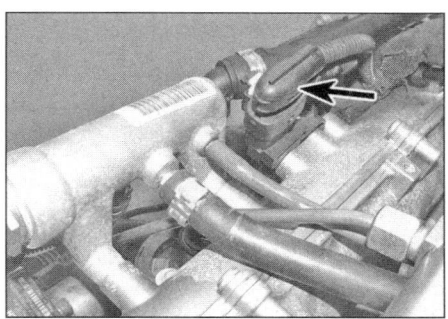

9.21 Disconnect the charge air pressure sensor wiring plug (arrowed)

3 Slacken the retaining clip and remove the airflow meter from the air cleaner housing lid.
4 Refitting is a reversal of removal, but ensure that the arrow on the airflow meter points toward the throttle body/housing when fitted.

Throttle body/housing

5 Remove the plastic cover from the top of the engine.
6 Release the retaining clip and disconnect the charge air hose from the throttle body/housing (see illustration).
7 Disconnect the throttle body wiring plug.
8 Undo the three retaining bolts and remove the throttle body/housing from the intake manifold. Note the location of any wiring harness support brackets also secured by the retaining bolts.
9 Refitting is a reversal of removal, but thoroughly clean the mating faces and use a new gasket/seal. Tighten the retaining bolts to the specified torque.

Crankshaft sensor

10 The sensor is located at the rear of the cylinder block, below the starter motor (see illustration). To gain access, firmly apply the handbrake, and then jack up the front of the car and support it securely on axle stands (see *Jacking and vehicle support*).
11 Undo the retaining bolts and remove the undershield from beneath the engine/transmission unit.
12 Wipe clean the area around the crankshaft sensor then disconnect the wiring connector.
13 Slacken and remove the retaining bolt and remove the sensor from the cylinder block. Recover the sealing ring.
14 Refitting is the reverse of removal, using a new sealing ring. Tighten the sensor retaining bolt to the specified torque.

Camshaft sensor

15 The camshaft sensor is located at the right-hand end of the camshaft housing (see illustration). To gain access, remove the plastic cover from the top of the engine.
16 Wipe the area clean around the camshaft sensor, and then disconnect the wiring connector.

17 Slacken and remove the retaining bolt and remove the sensor from the camshaft cover. Recover the sealing ring.
18 Refitting is the reverse of removal, using a new sealing ring. Tighten the sensor retaining bolt to the specified torque.

Coolant temperature sensor

19 The coolant temperature sensor is located on the thermostat housing on the left-hand end of the cylinder head. Partially drain the cooling system, disconnect the wiring plug and unscrew the sensor (see illustration).
20 Refitting is a reversal of removal. Top-up the cooling system as described in Chapter 1B.

Intake air pressure/temperature sensor

21 Remove the plastic cover from the top of the engine, then disconnect the wiring connector from the charge pressure sensor located in the centre of the intake manifold (see illustration).
22 Slacken and remove the retaining bolt and remove the sensor from the manifold. Recover the sealing ring.
23 Refitting is the reverse of removal, using a new sealing ring. Tighten the sensor retaining bolt to the specified torque.

Fuel pressure regulator

24 Disconnect the battery negative terminal as described in Chapter 5A.
25 Remove the plastic cover over the top of the engine.

26 Disconnect the wiring connector from the fuel pressure regulator (see illustration).
27 Remove the regulator from the fuel rail by unscrewing the inner nut (nearest the fuel rail) while counter-holding the regulator body with a second spanner. Be prepared for some loss of fuel.
28 Refitting is the reverse of removal, tightening the regulator to the specified torque.

Fuel pressure sensor

29 Disconnect the battery negative terminal as described in Chapter 5A.
30 Remove the plastic cover over the top of the engine.
31 Disconnect the wiring connector at the fuel pressure sensor (see illustration).
32 Unscrew the sensor and remove it from the fuel rail. Be prepared for some loss of fuel.

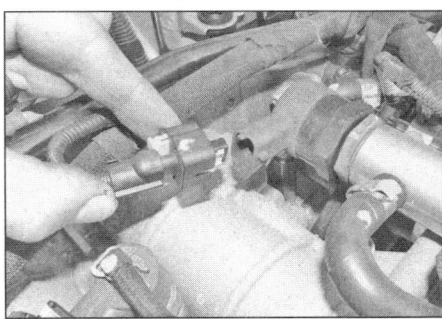

9.26 Slide out the yellow locking catch, depress the clip and disconnect the fuel pressure regulator wiring plug

4B•6 Fuel and exhaust systems – diesel engines

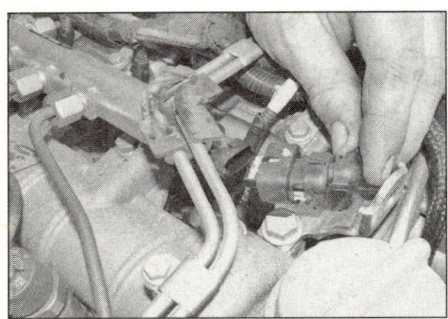

9.31 Disconnect the fuel pressure sensor wiring plug

33 Refitting is the reverse of removal, tightening the sensor to the specified torque.

Electronic control module (ECM)

Note: *If a new ECM is to be fitted, this work must be entrusted to a Saab dealer or suitably-equipped specialist, as it is necessary to programme the new ECM after installation. This work requires the use of dedicated Saab diagnostic equipment or a compatible alternative.*

34 On all models, the electronic control module (ECM) is located in the same position. Refer to Chapter 4A, Section 14, for the electronic control module removal and refitting.

Turbocharger wastegate solenoid

35 The wastegate (charge pressure) solenoid valve is located at the front of the engine compartment **(see illustration)**.
36 Disconnect the wiring connector and the

9.35 The turbocharger wastegate solenoid is located at the front of the engine compartment

two vacuum hoses from the valve then undo the retaining nuts and remove the valve from its mounting bracket.
37 Refitting is the reverse of removal.

10 High-pressure fuel pump – removal and refitting

Warning: *Refer to the information contained in Section 2 before proceeding.*
Note: *A new fuel pump-to-fuel rail high-pressure fuel pipe will be required for refitting.*

Removal

1 Disconnect the battery negative terminal as described in Chapter 5A.
2 Remove the plastic cover over the top of the engine.
3 Remove the timing belt and the high-

pressure fuel pump sprocket as described in Chapter 2B.
4 Release the retaining clips and disconnect the two fuel return hoses at the fuel return damping chamber **(see illustrations)**. Suitably plug or cover the open unions to prevent dirt entry.
5 Disconnect the injector leak-off pipe and the fuel return quick-release fitting, then undo the two bolts and remove the damping chamber. Suitably plug or cover the open unions to prevent dirt entry.
6 Disconnect the fuel supply hose quick-release fitting to the high-pressure fuel pump. Suitably plug or cover the open unions to prevent dirt entry **(see illustration)**.
7 Disconnect the wiring connector from the high-pressure fuel pump.
8 Thoroughly clean the fuel pipe unions on the fuel pump and fuel rail. Using an open-ended spanner, unscrew the union nuts securing the high-pressure fuel pipe to the fuel pump and fuel rail. Counter-hold the union on the pump with a second spanner, while unscrewing the union nut **(see illustration)**. Withdraw the high-pressure fuel pipe and plug or cover the open unions to prevent dirt entry.
9 Unscrew the three retaining nuts and remove the pump from the engine bracket **(see illustrations)**.
Caution: *The high-pressure fuel pump is manufactured to extremely close tolerances and must not be dismantled in any way. No parts for the pump are available separately and if the unit is in any way suspect, it must be renewed.*

10.4a Release the clips and disconnect the upper (arrowed) . . .

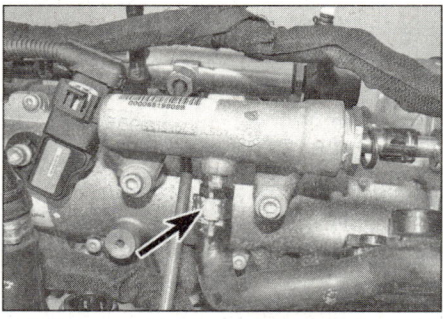

10.4b . . . and lower (arrowed) fuel return hoses at the damping chamber

10.6 Insert a generic release tool around the fuel pipe, and push it into the coupling to release the clips and disconnect the pipe

10.8 Unscrew the union nuts securing the high-pressure fuel pipe to the fuel pump and fuel rail

10.9a Unscrew the three retaining nuts (arrowed) . . .

10.9b . . . and remove the high-pressure fuel pump from the engine bracket

Fuel and exhaust systems – diesel engines 4B•7

Refitting

10 Refit the pump to the engine bracket and tighten the retaining bolts to the specified torque.
11 Remove the blanking plugs from the fuel pipe unions on the pump and fuel rail. Locate a new high-pressure fuel pipe over the unions and screw on the union nuts finger-tight at this stage.
12 Using a torque wrench and crow-foot adapter, tighten the fuel pipe union nuts to the specified torque. Counter-hold the unions on the pump with an open-ended spanner, while tightening the union nuts.
13 Reconnect the pump wiring connector and the fuel return hose quick-release fitting.
14 Refit the damping chamber and tighten the retaining bolts securely. Reconnect the injector leak-off pipe, and the two remaining fuel return hoses.
15 Refit the high-pressure fuel pump sprocket and the timing belt as described in Chapter 2B.
16 Reconnect the battery negative terminal as described in Chapter 5A.
17 Observing the precautions listed in Section 2, prime the fuel system as described in Section 5, then start the engine and allow it to idle. Check for leaks at the high-pressure fuel pipe unions with the engine idling. If satisfactory, increase the engine speed to 4000 rpm and check again for leaks. Take the car for a short road test and check for leaks once again on return. If any leaks are detected, obtain and fit a new high-pressure fuel pipe.
18 Refit the engine cover on completion.

11 Fuel rail – removal and refitting

⚠ **Warning:** *Refer to the information contained in Section 2 before proceeding.*

Note: *A complete new set of high-pressure fuel pipes will be required for refitting.*

Removal

1 Disconnect the battery negative terminal as described in Chapter 5A.
2 Remove the plastic cover over the top of the engine.
3 Thoroughly clean all the high-pressure fuel pipe unions on the fuel rail, fuel pump and injectors. Using two spanners, hold the unions and unscrew the union nuts securing the high-pressure fuel pipes to the fuel injectors. Unscrew the union nuts securing the high-pressure fuel pipes to the fuel rail, withdraw the pipes and plug or cover the open unions to prevent dirt entry **(see illustration)**.
4 Using an open-ended spanner, unscrew the union nuts securing the high-pressure fuel pipe to the fuel pump and fuel rail **(see illustration)**. Counter-hold the unions on the pump with a second spanner, while unscrewing the union nuts. Withdraw the high-pressure fuel pipe

11.3 Unscrew the union nuts securing the high-pressure fuel pipes to the fuel rail and injectors

and plug or cover the open unions to prevent dirt entry.
5 Disconnect the wiring connectors at the fuel pressure regulator and fuel pressure sensor, then release the clip and disconnect the fuel return hose. Undo the two bolts and remove the fuel rail **(see illustrations)**.

Refitting

6 Refit the fuel rail and tighten the retaining bolts to the specified torque. Reconnect the fuel pressure regulator and fuel pressure sensor wiring connectors, and reconnect the fuel return hose.
7 Working on one fuel injector at a time, remove the blanking plugs from the fuel pipe unions on the fuel rail and the relevant injector. Locate the new high-pressure fuel pipe over the unions and screw on the union nuts finger-tight. Tighten the union nuts to the specified torque using a torque wrench and crow-foot adapter. Counter-hold the union on the injector with an open-ended spanner, while tightening the union nut. Repeat this operation for the remaining three injectors.
8 Similarly, fit the new high-pressure fuel pipe to the fuel pump and fuel rail, and tighten the union nuts to the specified torque. Counter-hold the union on the pump with an open-ended spanner, while tightening the union nut.
9 Reconnect the battery negative terminal as described in Chapter 5A.
10 Observing the precautions listed in Section 2, prime the fuel system as described in Section 5, then start the engine and allow

11.5a Disconnect the fuel return hose . . .

11.4 Unscrew the union nuts securing the high-pressure fuel pipe to the pump and fuel rail

it to idle. Check for leaks at the high-pressure fuel pipe unions with the engine idling. If satisfactory, increase the engine speed to 4000 rpm and check again for leaks. Take the car for a short road test and check for leaks once again on return. If any leaks are detected, obtain and fit a new high-pressure fuel pipe.
11 Refit the engine cover on completion.

12 Fuel injectors – removal and refitting

⚠ **Warning:** *Refer to the information contained in Section 2 before proceeding.*

Note 1: *A new copper washer, retaining nut and high-pressure fuel pipe will be required for each injector when refitting.*
Note 2: *The injector is an extremely tight fit in the cylinder head, and it is likely that the special Saab puller (32 025 013) and adapter (32 025 012) or suitable alternatives, will be needed.*

Removal

1 Disconnect the battery negative terminal as described in Chapter 5A.
2 Remove the plastic cover over the top of the engine.
3 Release the retaining clip securing the engine breather hose to the breather pipe adjacent to the engine oil dipstick. Undo the two bolts securing the breather pipe to the

11.5b . . . then undo the two bolts (arrowed) and remove the fuel rail

4B•8 Fuel and exhaust systems – diesel engines

12.3 Undo the two bolts (arrowed) and remove the breather pipe from the cylinder head

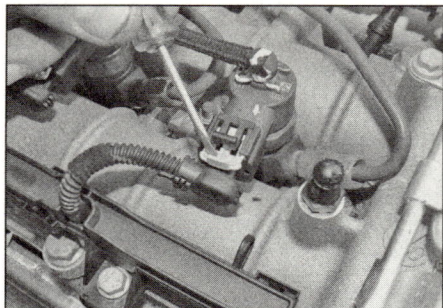

12.4a Slide out the locking catch . . .

12.4b . . . depress the clip and disconnect the injector wiring plugs

12.5a Disconnect the fuel leak-off hose connection at each injector . . .

12.5b . . . then plug or cap the leak-off hose union on each injector

12.6 Counter-hold the injector union when unscrewing the high-pressure fuel pipe unions

cylinder head, and disconnect the pipe from the hose **(see illustration)**.

4 Release the locking catches securing the wiring connectors to the four injectors, then disconnect the injector wiring **(see illustrations)**.

5 Disconnect the fuel leak-off hose connection at each injector by pushing in the locking clip and lifting out the hose fitting. Suitably plug or cap the leak-off hose union on each injector, and slip a plastic bag over the disconnected leak-off hose to prevent dirt entry **(see illustrations)**.

6 Thoroughly clean the fuel pipe unions on the fuel rail and injector. Using two spanners, hold the unions and unscrew the union nut securing the high-pressure fuel pipe to the fuel injector **(see illustration)**. Unscrew the union nut securing the high-pressure fuel pipe to the fuel rail, withdraw the pipe and plug or cover the open unions to prevent dirt entry.

7 Starting with injector No 1, unscrew the retaining nut then remove the washer from the injector clamp bracket **(see illustration)**.

8 Withdraw the injector together with the clamp bracket from the cylinder head. If difficulty is experienced removing the injector, liberally apply penetrating oil to the base of the injector and allow time for the oil to penetrate. If the injector is still reluctant to free, it will be necessary to use a small slide hammer engaged under the flange of the injector body casting, and gently tap it free **(see illustration)**. If available, use Saab special tools 32 025 013, 32 025 012 and 83 90 270 for this purpose. Note that it is not possible to twist the injector from side-to-side to free them due to the design of the clamp bracket.

9 Once the injector has been removed, separate it from the clamp bracket and remove the copper washer from the injector base **(see illustrations)**. The copper washer may have remained in place at the base of the injector orifice in the cylinder head. If so, hook it out with a length of wire.

10 Remove the remaining injectors in the same way.

11 Examine the injector visually for any signs of obvious damage or deterioration. If any defects are apparent, renew the injector.

Caution: The injectors are manufactured to

12.7 Unscrew the injector clamp bracket retaining nut then remove the washer

12.8 Use a small slide hammer to free the injector body from the cylinder head

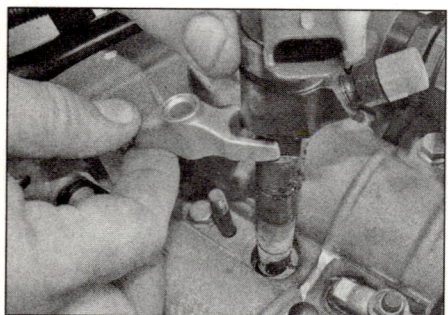

12.9a Once the injector has been removed, separate it from the clamp bracket

12.9b Remove the copper washer from the injector base

Fuel and exhaust systems – diesel engines 4B•9

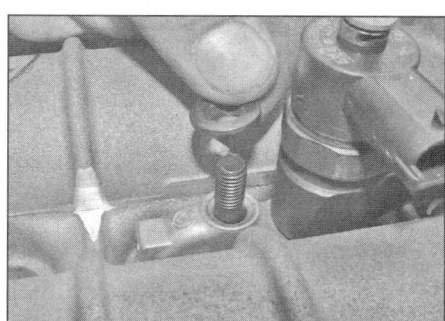

12.17a Fit the washer . . .

12.17b . . . and the injector clamp bracket retaining nut

12.19 Tighten the fuel pipe union nuts to the specified torque using a torque wrench and crow-foot adapter

extremely close tolerances and must not be dismantled in any way. Do not unscrew the fuel pipe union on the side of the injector, or separate any parts of the injector body. Do not attempt to clean carbon deposits from the injector nozzle or carry out any form of ultrasonic or pressure testing.

12 If the injectors are in a satisfactory condition, plug the fuel pipe union (if not already done) and suitably cover the electrical element and the injector nozzle.
13 Prior to refitting, obtain a new set of copper washers, retaining nuts and high-pressure fuel pipes.

Refitting

14 Thoroughly clean the injector seat in the cylinder head, ensuring all traces of carbon and other deposits are removed.
15 Starting with injector No 4, locate a new copper washer on the base of the injector.
16 Place the injector clamp bracket in the slot on the injector body and refit the injector to the cylinder head.
17 Fit the washer and the injector clamp bracket retaining nut and tighten the nut to the specified torque **(see illustrations)**.
18 Remove the blanking plug from the fuel pipe union on the fuel rail and the injector. Locate the new high-pressure fuel pipe over the unions and screw on the union nuts. Take care not to cross-thread the nuts or strain the fuel pipe as it is fitted.
19 Tighten the fuel pipe union nuts to the specified torque using a torque wrench and crow-foot adapter **(see illustration)**. Counter-hold the union on the injector with an open-ended spanner, while tightening the union nut.
20 Repeat this procedure for the remaining injectors.
21 Reconnect the leak-off hose fittings to the injectors by pushing in the locking clip, attaching the fitting, then releasing the locking clip. Ensure that each fitting is securely connected and retained by the clip.
22 Reconnect the wiring connectors to the fuel injectors.
23 Attach the engine breather hose to the breather pipe and secure with the retaining clip. Secure the breather pipe to the cylinder head with the two bolts securely tightened.
24 Reconnect the battery negative terminal as described in Chapter 5A.

25 Observing the precautions listed in Section 2, prime the fuel system as described in Section 5, then start the engine and allow it to idle. Check for leaks at the high-pressure fuel pipe unions with the engine idling. If satisfactory, increase the engine speed to 4000 rpm and check again for leaks. Take the car for a short road test and check for leaks once again on return. If any leaks are detected, obtain and fit a new high-pressure fuel pipe.
26 Refit the engine cover on completion.

13 Intake manifold – removal and refitting

Removal

1 Disconnect the battery negative terminal as described in Chapter 5A.

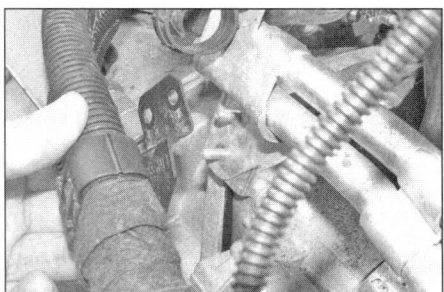

13.9 Unscrew the nuts and free the wiring harness and coolant pipe from the starter motor bracket

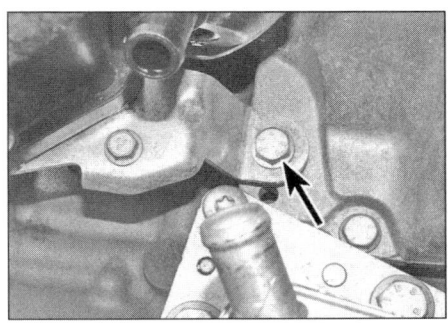

13.10b . . . the bolt (arrowed) at the base of the vacuum reservoir . . .

2 Remove the plastic cover over the top of the engine.
3 Remove the high-pressure fuel pump as described in Section 10.
4 Remove the exhaust gas recirculation (EGR) valve as described in Chapter 4C.
5 Drain the cooling system as described in Chapter 1B.
6 Release the clips and remove the turbocharger delivery hose from the throttle body.
7 Disconnect the coolant pipe, disconnect the level sensor wiring plug, then remove the coolant reservoir.
8 Disconnect the hose from the thermostat housing.
9 Undo the nuts securing the coolant pipe to the starter motor bracket, and bend the pipe away slightly **(see illustration)**.
10 Remove the oil separator and vacuum reservoir mounting bracket by undoing the two nuts above the vacuum reservoir, the bolt at the

13.10a Undo the two nuts (arrowed) above the vacuum reservoir . . .

13.10c . . . and the bolts (arrowed) on the right-hand side of the oil separator . . .

4B•10 Fuel and exhaust systems – diesel engines

13.10d ... then remove the mounting bracket complete with oil separator and vacuum reservoir

13.12 Lock two nuts together and unscrew the fuel pump stud from the engine bracket

13.14 Intake manifold retaining nuts (arrowed)

base of the vacuum reservoir, and the bolt at the right-hand side of the oil separator. Remove the mounting bracket complete with oil separator and vacuum reservoir **(see illustrations)**.

11 Undo the three bolts, release the hose clip, free the wiring harness and detach the coolant pipe from the intake manifold.

12 Screw two nuts onto the inner high-pressure fuel pump mounting stud. Lock the two nuts together and unscrew the stud from the engine bracket **(see illustration)**.

13 Disconnect the wiring connectors at the throttle body/housing, coolant temperature sensor, intake air sensor, fuel pressure sensor, and fuel pressure control valve.

14 Undo the nine retaining nuts and remove the intake manifold from the cylinder head studs **(see illustration)**. Recover the gasket.

15 With the manifold removed, if required, remove the throttle body/housing with reference to Section 9.

16 The changeover flap actuator drive can be removed by disconnecting the drive motor actuating rod ball socket, and undoing the two stud bolts.

Refitting

17 If removed, refit the throttle body/housing with reference to Section 9, then refit the changeover flap actuator drive.

18 Thoroughly clean the intake manifold and cylinder head mating faces, and then locate a new gasket on the intake manifold flange.

19 Locate the manifold in position and refit the retaining nuts. Diagonally and progressively, tighten the nuts to the specified torque.

14.11 Disconnect the actuating rod ball socket (A), undo the two stud bolts (B) and remove the actuator drive

20 Reconnect the wiring connectors at the throttle body/housing and charge (boost) pressure sensor.

21 Refit the high-pressure fuel pump mounting stud, then remove the two nuts used to remove/refit the stud.

22 Refit the coolant pipe to the manifold, and secure with the three bolts tightened securely. Reconnect the coolant pipe and attach the wiring harness.

23 Refit the oil separator and vacuum reservoir mounting bracket. Refit and tighten the two bolts and two nuts, then reconnect the crankcase breather hoses.

24 Refit the coolant pipe and wiring harness to the starter motor bracket, then refit and tighten the two nuts.

25 Refit the exhaust gas recirculation (EGR) valve as described in Chapter 4C.

26 Refit the high-pressure fuel pump as described in Section 10.

27 Reconnect the battery negative terminal as described in Chapter 5A.

28 Observing the precautions listed in Section 2, prime the fuel system as described in Section 5, then start the engine and allow it to idle. Check for leaks at the high-pressure fuel pipe unions with the engine idling. If satisfactory, increase the engine speed to 4000 rpm and check again for leaks. Take the car for a short road test and check for leaks once again on return. If any leaks are detected, obtain and fit a new high-pressure fuel pipe.

29 Refit the engine cover on completion.

14 Intake manifold changeover flap actuator drive – removal and refitting

Removal

1 Disconnect the battery negative terminal as described in Chapter 5A.

2 Remove the plastic cover over the top of the engine.

3 Remove the high-pressure fuel pump as described in Section 10.

4 Remove the exhaust gas recirculation (EGR) valve as described in Chapter 4C.

5 Drain the cooling system as described in Chapter 1B.

6 Release the clips and remove the turbocharger delivery hose from the throttle body.

7 Disconnect the coolant pipe, disconnect the level sensor wiring plug, then remove the coolant reservoir.

8 Disconnect the hose from the thermostat housing.

9 Undo the nuts securing the coolant pipe to the starter motor bracket, and bend the pipe away slightly **(see illustration 13.9)**.

10 Remove the oil separator and vacuum reservoir mounting bracket by undoing the two nuts above the vacuum reservoir, the bolt at the base of the vacuum reservoir, and the bolt at the right-hand side of the oil separator. Remove the mounting bracket complete with oil separator and vacuum reservoir **(see illustrations 13.10a to 13.10d)**.

11 Disconnect the drive motor actuating rod ball socket, and undo the 2 stud bolts **(see illustration)**.

12 Withdraw the assembly from the intake manifold and disconnect the wiring plug.

Refitting

13 Refitting is the reverse of removal.

15 Intercooler – removal and refitting

Refer to Chapter 4A, Section 17.

16 Turbocharger – description and precautions

Description

1 The turbocharger increases engine efficiency by raising the pressure in the intake manifold above atmospheric pressure. Instead of the air simply being sucked into the cylinders, it is forced in.

2 Energy for the operation of the turbocharger comes from the exhaust gas. The gas flows through a specially-shaped housing (the turbine housing) and, in so doing, spins the turbine wheel. The turbine wheel is attached to a shaft, at the end of which is another vaned

Fuel and exhaust systems – diesel engines 4B•11

wheel known as the compressor wheel. The compressor wheel spins in its own housing, and compresses the intake air on the way to the intake manifold.

3 The turbocharger operates on the principle of variable vane geometry. At low engine speed the vanes close to give less flow cross-section, then as the speed increases the vanes open to give an increased flow cross-section. This helps improve the efficiency of the turbocharger.

4 Boost pressure (the pressure in the intake manifold) is limited by a wastegate, which diverts the exhaust gas away from the turbine wheel in response to a pressure-sensitive actuator.

5 The turbo shaft is pressure-lubricated by an oil feed pipe from the main oil gallery. The shaft 'floats' on a cushion of oil. A drain pipe returns the oil to the sump.

Precautions

6 The turbocharger operates at extremely high speeds and temperatures. Certain precautions must be observed, to avoid premature failure of the turbo, or injury to the operator.

- Do not operate the turbo with any of its parts exposed, or with any of its hoses removed. Foreign objects falling onto the rotating vanes could cause excessive damage, and (if ejected) personal injury.
- Do not race the engine immediately after start-up, especially if it is cold. Give the oil a few seconds to circulate.
- Always allow the engine to return to idle speed before switching it off – do not blip the throttle and switch off, as this will leave the turbo spinning without lubrication.
- Allow the engine to idle for several minutes before switching off after a high-speed run.
- Observe the recommended intervals for oil and filter changing, and use a reputable oil of the specified quality. Neglect of oil changing, or use of inferior oil, can cause carbon formation on the turbo shaft, leading to subsequent failure.

17 Exhaust manifold and turbocharger – removal and refitting

Note: *New manifold retaining nuts, new*

17.7 Undo the oil level dipstick tube bolt (arrowed)

gaskets for all disturbed joints, and new copper washers for the turbocharger oil supply pipe banjo union will be required for refitting.

Removal

1 Disconnect the battery negative terminal as described in Chapter 5A.
2 Remove the plastic cover from the top of the engine.
3 Firmly apply the handbrake, and then jack up the front of the car and support it securely on axle stands (see *Jacking and vehicle support*). Undo the bolts and remove the engine undershield.
4 Drain the cooling system as described in Chapter 1B.
5 Undo the fasteners and remove the front section of the exhaust pipe.
6 Undo the 2 nuts and remove the heat shield over the catalytic converter.
7 Undo the bolt securing the oil level dipstick tube (see illustration).
8 Release the retaining clip securing the engine breather hose to the breather pipe adjacent to the engine oil dipstick. Undo the two bolts securing the breather pipe to the cylinder head, and disconnect the pipe from the hose.
9 Remove the air cleaner assembly and air intake duct as described in Section 3.
10 Remove the turbocharger intake hose.
11 Remove the turbocharger delivery pipe from the throttle body, and turbocharger.
12 Release the clip and disconnect the radiator top hose from the thermostat housing.
13 Disconnect the coolant hose between the

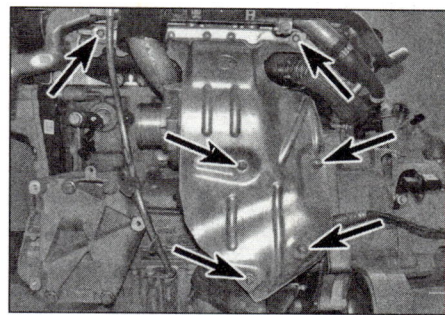

17.17 Heat shield retaining nuts and bolts (arrowed)

reservoir and the manifold. Undo the mounting and remove the hose.
14 Disconnect the coolant hoses from the coolant pipe at the left-hand end of the engine, then remove the lower coolant hose from the coolant pipe.
15 Undo the 3 front bolts and wedge the upper timing cover away from the engine slightly.
16 Undo the 3 fasteners and remove the coolant pipe from the front of the engine.
17 Remove the heat shield at the front of the turbocharger (see illustration).
18 Working underneath the vehicle, unscrew the temperature sensor from the catalytic converter (where fitted) (see illustration).
19 Undo the catalytic converter lower mounting bolts, and then bend the lower bracket down a little.
20 Undo the upper clamp securing the catalytic converter to the turbocharger, and lower the catalytic converter from place (see illustrations).
21 Disconnect the vacuum hose from the turbocharger wastegate actuator.
22 Unscrew the four bolts securing the oil return pipe to the turbocharger and cylinder block (see illustration). Remove the pipe and recover the gaskets.
23 Unscrew the turbocharger oil supply pipe banjo union from the cylinder block and collect the two copper washers (see illustration).
24 Undo the retaining nut and bolt and release the metal EGR pipe clamp from the EGR valve heat exchanger. Separate the pipe from the heat exchanger and recover

17.18 Unscrew the sensor from the catalytic converter

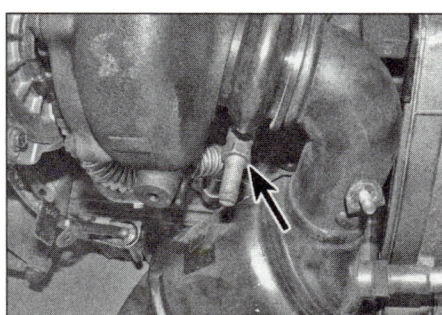

17.20a Unscrew the clamp bolt (arrowed) . . .

17.20b . . . and remove the catalytic converter

4B•12 Fuel and exhaust systems – diesel engines

17.22 Unscrew the bolts (arrowed) securing the oil return pipe to the turbocharger and cylinder block

17.23 Unscrew the turbocharger oil supply banjo union (arrowed) and collect the two copper washers

17.24 Release the EGR pipe clamp from the heat exchanger, separate the pipe and recover the gasket

17.25 Exhaust manifold retaining nuts (arrowed)

the gasket from the pipe connection **(see illustration)**.

25 Unscrew the eight nuts securing the exhaust manifold to the cylinder head **(see illustration)**. Note that new nuts will be required for refitting. Withdraw the manifold and turbocharger assembly from the mounting studs, manipulate it sideways, and remove from under the car. Recover the gasket.

Refitting

26 Refitting is the reverse of removal, noting the following points.
 a) *Ensure all mating surfaces are clean and dry and renew all gaskets, seals and copper washers.*
 b) *Fit the new manifold nuts and tighten them evenly and progressively to the specified torque, working in a diagonal sequence.*
 c) *Tighten all other retaining nuts and bolts to the specified torque (where given).*
 d) *Refit the exhaust system as described in Section 18.*
 e) *On completion refill the cooling system as described in Chapter 1B and, if necessary, top-up the oil level as described in 'Weekly checks'.*
 f) *On starting the engine for the first time, allow the engine to idle for a few minutes before increasing the engine speed; this will allow oil to be circulated around the turbocharger bearings.*

18.5 Spray penetrating oil over the exhaust rubber mounting blocks in the area arrowed

18.7 Undo the 3 nuts (arrowed) and detach the front exhaust pipe from the catalytic converter

18 Exhaust system – general information, removal and refitting

General information

1 Two different exhaust systems may be fitted dependent on model, market, etc. On some models a four-piece system is fitted, comprising a front catalytic converter, front pipe, particulate filter, and a rear pipe with silencer. On others, a second catalytic converter/silencer is fitted in place of the particulate filter.
2 The front pipe is attached to the exhaust manifold/catalytic converter by a flange joint secured by nuts. The other exhaust sections are joined by overlap joints, which are secured by clamps, or flange joints secured by nuts. The system is suspended throughout its entire length by rubber mountings.
3 The manufacturers specify that if any of the exhaust sections are separated, the clamps must be renewed. As the clamps are attached to the exhaust sections by means of a spot weld at manufacture, it will be necessary to use a suitable grinder to remove the spot weld.

Removal

Complete system

4 To remove the system, first jack up the front and rear of the car and support it securely on axle stands. Alternatively, position the car over an inspection pit or on car ramps. The help of an assistant will be needed. Undo the fasteners and remove the engine undershield.
5 Spray some penetrating oil over the exhaust rubber mounting blocks so that the mounting blocks will slide easily on the exhaust and underbody hangers **(see illustration)**.
6 Undo the two bolts securing the front pipe support bracket to the transmission bracket/sump.
7 Undo the three retaining nuts and separate the exhaust front pipe from the exhaust manifold/catalytic converter, taking care to support the flexible section. **Note:** *Angular movement in excess of 10° can cause permanent damage to the flexible section.* Recover the gasket **(see illustration)**. Note that new nuts will be required for refitting.
8 Slide the front pipe rubber mounting blocks as far forward as possible. Move the exhaust system to the rear and disengage the front pipe hangers from the mounting blocks.
9 Move the exhaust system forward and disengage the intermediate pipe and tailpipe hangers from the rubber mounting blocks. Lower the system to the ground and slide it out from under the car.

Individual section

10 Individual sections of the exhaust system can be removed by slackening the relevant clamp and releasing the exhaust from the rubber mountings.

Fuel and exhaust systems – diesel engines 4B•13

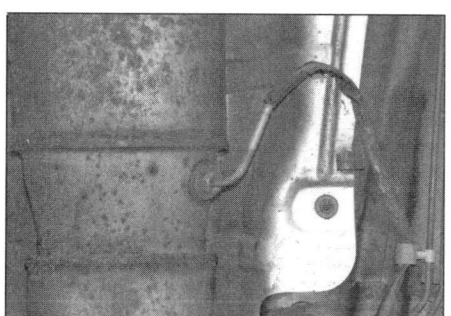

18.17 Pipe to particulate filter in exhaust

18.19 Undo the three retaining nuts – arrowed

18.20 Remove the rear mounting bracket

11 Slacken and remove the nut from the relevant exhaust clamp retaining bolt. Apply liberal amounts of penetrating oil to the joint and tap around the joint and clamp with a hammer to free it. Twist the pipe to be removed in both directions while holding the adjacent pipe. Once the joint is free, pull the pipes apart.
12 Mark the position of the clamp on the pipe, so the new clamp can be fitted in the same position, then grind off the clamp retaining spot weld. Remove the clamp.

Catalytic converter

13 There maybe one or two catalytic converters, dependent on model, market, etc – one fitted between the exhaust manifold and the exhaust front pipe, and a second unit, integral with the exhaust front pipe. Refer to Section 17 for removal and refitting details for the converter fitted between the front pipe and manifold.
14 Where no second catalytic converter in fitted, a particulate filter is installed.

Heat shield(s)

15 The heat shields are secured to the underside of the body by various nuts and threaded caps. Each shield can be removed once the relevant exhaust section has been removed. If a shield is being removed to gain access to a component located behind it, it may prove sufficient in some cases to remove the retaining nuts/caps, and simply lower the shield, without disturbing the exhaust system. If any of the threaded caps are damaged during removal, a suitable nut and washer can be used when refitting.

Particulate filter

16 Raise the vehicle and support it securely on axle stands (see *Jacking and vehicle support*).
17 Note their fitted positions, and disconnect the exhaust gas temperature sensor pipe(s) from the particulate filter **(see illustration)**.
18 If required, unscrew the temperature sensor from the filter.
19 Undo the 3 nuts securing the filter to the front pipe **(see illustration)**. Note that new nuts will be required for refitting.
20 Undo the bolts securing the filter rear mounting bracket to the vehicle body **(see illustration)**.
21 Slacken the clamp and separate the rear exhaust pipe from the filter.
22 Release the filter from the rubber mountings and withdrawn it from under the vehicle.
23 Upon refitting, apply a little high-temperature anti-seize grease to the temperature sensor threads. Note that if a new particle filter has been fitted, Saab diagnostic equipment must be connected to the vehicle's diagnostic plug to reset adaptation values in the engine management ECM. Entrust this task to a Saab dealer or suitably-equipped specialist.

Refitting

24 Refitting is a reversal of the removal sequence, noting the following points:
 a) *Ensure that all traces of corrosion have been removed from the system joints and renew all disturbed clamps.*
 b) *Inspect the rubber mountings for signs of damage or deterioration, and renew as necessary.*
 c) *When refitting the front pipe to the manifold/catalytic converter, use a new gasket and new retaining nuts, and tighten the nuts to the specified torque.*
 d) *Prior to tightening the exhaust system clamps, ensure that all rubber mountings are correctly located, and that there is adequate clearance between the exhaust system and vehicle underbody. Tighten the clamp bolt retaining nuts securely.*

Notes

Chapter 4 Part C:
Emission control systems

Contents

	Section number		Section number
Catalytic converter – general information and precautions	4	General information	1
Diesel engine emission control systems – testing and component renewal	3	Petrol engine emissions control systems – component renewal	2

Degrees of difficulty

Easy, suitable for novice with little experience	**Fairly easy,** suitable for beginner with some experience	**Fairly difficult,** suitable for competent DIY mechanic	**Difficult,** suitable for experienced DIY mechanic	**Very difficult,** suitable for expert DIY or professional

Specifications

EVAP canister purge valve
Resistance at 20°C... 45 ± 5 ohms

EVAP pressure sensor
Pressure:	Voltage (approx)
-0.038 bar	0.1
0 bar	2.5
0.012 bar	2.0

EVAP shut-off control valve
Resistance at 20°C... 24.5 ±1.5 ohms

Heated oxygen sensors
Type... Bosch LSF 4.7 (with preheating)
Resistance at 20°C (pins 1 and 2).............................. 9.0 ohms (approx)

Torque wrench settings
	Nm	lbf ft
Petrol engines		
Oxygen sensor	40	30
Diesel engines		
Exhaust gas recirculation (EGR) pipe bolts	25	18
Exhaust gas recirculation (EGR) valve bolts/nuts	25	18
Exhaust gas temperature sensors	45	33

1 General information

1 All petrol engine models use unleaded petrol and also have various other features built into the fuel system to help minimise harmful emissions. These include a crankcase emission control system, a catalytic converter, and an evaporative emission control system to keep fuel vapour/exhaust gas emissions down to a minimum.

2 All diesel engine models are also designed to meet strict emission requirements. All models are fitted with a crankcase emission control system, one or two catalytic converters, and a particulate filter (model and market dependent) to keep exhaust emissions down to a minimum. All models are also fitted with an exhaust gas recirculation (EGR) system to further decrease exhaust emissions.

3 In certain non-UK territories, having strict emissions laws, a secondary air injection system is fitted.

Petrol engines

Evaporative emissions control

4 To minimise the escape into the atmosphere of unburned hydrocarbons, an evaporative emissions control system is fitted. The system is sometimes referred to as the 'evaporative-loss control device' (ELCD). The fuel tank filler cap is sealed, and a charcoal canister collects the petrol vapours generated in the tank when the car is parked. The vapours are stored until they can be cleared from the canister (under the control of the fuel system ECM via the purge valve) into the intake tract, to be burned by the engine during normal combustion.

5 To ensure that the engine runs correctly when it is cold and/or idling, and to protect the catalytic converter from the effects of an over-rich mixture, the purge control valve is not opened by the ECM until the engine has warmed-up, and the engine is under load; the valve solenoid is then modulated on and off, to allow the stored vapour to pass into the intake tract.

Crankcase emissions control

6 To reduce emissions of unburned hydrocarbons from the crankcase into the atmosphere, the engine is sealed. The blow-by gases and oil vapour are drawn from inside the crankcase, through an external oil trap, which is connected to the crankcase via the camshaft cover and breather hose. The gases are then

evacuated to the throttle housing and also via the turbocharger to the intake manifold.

7 Under conditions of high manifold depression (idling, deceleration) the gases will be sucked positively out of the crankcase to the throttle housing. Under conditions of low manifold depression (acceleration, full-throttle running) the gases are forced out of the crankcase by the (relatively) higher crankcase pressure; if the engine is worn, the raised crankcase pressure (due to increased blow-by) will cause some of the flow to return under all manifold conditions.

Exhaust emissions control

8 To minimise the amount of pollutants, which escape into the atmosphere, all models are fitted with a catalytic converter in the exhaust system. The catalytic converter system is of the 'closed-loop' type, in which an oxygen sensor (two on some models) in the exhaust system provides the fuel-injection/ignition system ECM with constant feedback on the oxygen content of the exhaust gases. This enables the ECM to adjust the mixture to provide the best possible conditions for the converter to operate.

9 The oxygen sensors have a built-in heating element, controlled by the ECM through the sensor relay, to quickly bring the sensor's tip to an efficient operating temperature. The sensor's tip is sensitive to oxygen, and sends the ECM a varying voltage depending on the amount of oxygen in the exhaust gases; if the intake air/fuel mixture is too rich, the sensor sends a high-voltage signal. The voltage falls as the mixture weakens. Peak conversion efficiency of all major pollutants occurs if the intake air/fuel mixture is maintained at the chemically correct ratio for the complete combustion of petrol – 14.7 parts (by weight) of air to 1 part of fuel (the 'stoichiometric' ratio). The sensor output voltage alters in a large step at this point, the ECM using the signal change as a reference point, and correcting the intake air/fuel mixture accordingly by altering the fuel injector pulse width (injector opening time).

Diesel engines

Crankcase emission control

10 Refer to paragraphs 6 and 7.

Exhaust emission control

11 To minimise the level of exhaust pollutants released into the atmosphere, a catalytic converter is fitted in the exhaust system. On some models, a second catalytic converter is fitted instead of the particulate filter.

12 The catalytic converter consists of a canister containing a fine mesh impregnated with a catalyst material, over which the hot exhaust gases pass. The catalyst speeds up the oxidation of harmful carbon monoxide, unburned hydrocarbons and soot, effectively reducing the quantity of harmful products released into the atmosphere via the exhaust gases.

13 The particulate filter is designed to trap

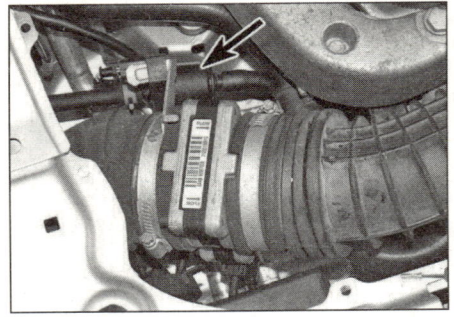

2.16 Purge valve (arrowed) mounted on the airflow sensor retaining clip

soot particles. A pressure sensor measures the pressure drop across the filter, to inform the engine management ECM when the filter is full. The ECM then initiates filter regeneration. This process involves injecting extra fuel into the cylinders during the exhaust stroke. This fuel greatly raises the temperature of the exhaust gases, and burns off the soot trapped into the filter. This process is completely automatic, and takes approximately 15 minutes.

Exhaust gas recirculation system

14 This system is designed to recirculate small quantities of exhaust gas into the intake tract, and therefore into the combustion process. This process reduces the level of unburnt hydrocarbons present in the exhaust gas before it reaches the catalytic converter. The system is controlled by the injection system ECM, using the information from its various sensors, via the electrically-operated EGR valve.

2 Petrol engine emissions control systems – component renewal

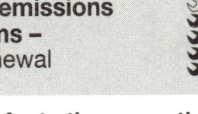

Warning: *Refer to the precautions given in Chapter 4A, Section 8, and the information detailed in the 'Safety First!' Section of this manual, before disturbing any component in the fuel supply system.*

Evaporative emission control

Pressure sensor

1 The pressure sensor is located on top of the

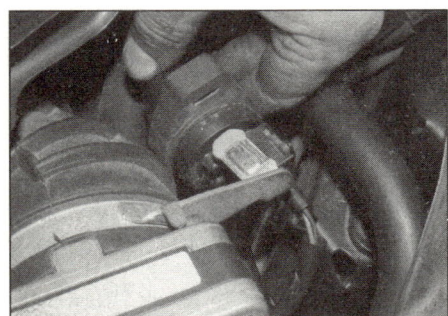

2.18 Pull the valve rubber mounting from the mounting bracket

fuel tank, remove the fuel tank as described in Chapter 4A, Section 12.

2 Clean around the pressure sensor, to make sure no dirt enters the fuel tank when the sensor is removed.

3 Undo the retaining screw and withdraw the sensor and O-ring seal from the fuel tank.

4 Refitting is a reversal of removal procedure. **Note:** *Renew the sensor O-ring seal and lubricate with acid-free petroleum jelly or similar.*

Charcoal canister (early models)

5 The charcoal canister is mounted on the front right-hand side of the car beneath the right-hand wing with the purge valve.

6 Apply the handbrake, then jack up the front of the car and support on axle stands (see *Jacking and vehicle support*). Remove the right-hand front wheel.

7 Remove the right-hand front wing plastic moulding, followed by the front section of the wheel arch liner.

8 Note the positions of the hoses on the canister (A is connected to the tank and B is connected to the purge valve) then disconnect them from the canister.

9 Unhook the canister from its mounting bracket and remove it from under the wing.

10 Refitting is a reversal of the removal procedure. **Note:** *Make sure the retaining clips for the hoses are not damaged and the hoses are securely fitted in the position noted on removal.*

Charcoal canister (later models)

11 The charcoal canister is located on top of the fuel tank, remove the fuel tank as described in Chapter 4A, Section 12.

12 Clean around the charcoal canister, to make sure no dirt enters the fuel tank when the canister is removed.

13 Release the retaining clips on the hoses to the canister and disconnect them, noting their fitted position.

14 Undo the retaining screw and withdraw the canister, unhooking it from its holder in the top of the fuel tank.

15 Refitting is a reversal of removal procedure. **Note:** *Make sure the retaining clips for the hoses are not damaged and the hoses are securely fitted in the position noted on removal.*

Purge valve

16 The purge valve is mounted on the front right-hand side inner wing panel **(see illustration)**. Check that the hoses from the purge control valve are clear by removing them and blowing through them. If the purge control valve is thought to be faulty, it must be renewed.

17 Release the retaining clip(s) on the hose(s) to the valve and disconnect them, noting their fitted position.

18 Remove purge valve from the mounting bracket, noting its fitted position **(see illustration)**.

19 Twist the valve and unplug the connector,

Emission control systems 4C•3

then withdraw the purge valve from the vehicle.
20 Refitting is a reversal of the removal procedure, but make sure that the purge valve is fitted in the correct position as noted on removal.

Shut-off control valve

21 The shut-off valve (where fitted) is clipped to the side of the fuel filler pipe at the rear of the vehicle (see illustration). Park the vehicle on a firm level surface, and then select first gear (manual transmission) or Park (automatic transmission) and chock the front wheels securely. Raise the rear of the car and support it securely on axle stands (see *Jacking and vehicle support*).
22 Cut the cable-tie and disconnect the wiring connector to the shut-off valve.
23 Using a screwdriver carefully prise the control valve, to unclip it from the fuel filler pipe.
24 Clean off any dirt from around the control valve, then unclip the cover from the top of the valve. Disconnect the wiring connector from the top of the valve and withdraw the washer.
25 Unclip the cover from the bottom of the valve, then release the securing clip and disconnect the hose from the bottom of the valve. If required, the filter can now be renewed.
26 Refitting is a reversal of the removal procedure, but make sure that the wiring at the top of the valve locates correctly in the recess in the washer.

Crankcase emissions control

27 The components of this system require no attention other than to check at regular intervals that the hose(s) and the external oil trap on the cylinder block are clear and undamaged (see illustrations).

Oxygen sensors

 Warning: *When renewing the sensors, check the type fitted and refit with the same type.*

Note: *On some models there are two oxygen sensors fitted, one before the catalytic converter and one after. On other models there is one oxygen sensor fitted to the front of the catalytic converter. The oxygen sensor is DELICATE. It will not work if it is dropped or knocked, if its power supply is disrupted, or if any cleaning materials are used on it.*

Front oxygen sensor

28 Open the bonnet and remove the upper cover from the intake manifold (see illustration).
29 Release the securing clip and disconnect the wiring plug connectors, then press lugs together to release from the mounting bracket at the left-hand side rear of the cylinder head (see illustration).
30 Remove the heat shield from above the exhaust manifold; disconnect the bypass pipe from across the top of the heat shield if required.
31 Release the cable-tie from the wiring to

2.21 Shut-off valve (arrowed) mounted on the fuel filler pipe

2.27b On later models the hoses (arrowed) have quick-release connections on the oil trap

the oxygen sensor, and withdraw the wiring harness.
32 Unscrew the sensor from the exhaust system downpipe (see illustration), and remove it. The sensor may be tight, in which case it will help if it is turned back-and-forth on its threads as it is being removed. Note that it is possible to obtain a special slotted socket, which locates on the sensor without causing any damage to the wiring.
33 Refitting is a reverse of the removal procedure. Prior to installing the sensor, apply a smear of high-temperature grease to the sensor threads. Tighten the sensor to the specified torque. The wiring must be correctly routed, and in no danger of contacting the exhaust system.

Rear oxygen sensor

34 Open the bonnet and remove the upper cover from the intake manifold (see illustration 2.28).

2.29 Disconnect the two wiring connectors (arrowed) for the oxygen sensors

2.27a Oil trap (arrowed) mounted on the rear of the cylinder block

2.28 Removing the upper cover from the intake manifold

35 Release the securing clip and disconnect the wiring plug connectors then press the lugs together and release the wiring plug from the mounting bracket at the rear left-hand side of the cylinder head (see illustration 2.29).
36 Release the cable-tie from the wiring to the oxygen sensor, and withdraw the wiring harness.
37 Apply the handbrake, then jack up the front of the car and support on axle stands (see *Jacking and vehicle support*).
38 Pull the wiring harness down, then unscrew the sensor from the exhaust system front pipe (see illustration), and remove it. The sensor may be tight, in which case it will help if it is turned back-and-forth on its threads as it is being removed. Note that it is possible to obtain a special slotted socket which locates on the sensor without causing any damage to the wiring.
39 Refitting is a reverse of the removal

2.32 Slacken and remove the oxygen sensor (arrowed)

2.38 Slacken and remove the oxygen sensor (arrowed)

procedure. Prior to installing the sensor, apply a smear of high-temperature grease to the sensor threads. Tighten the sensor to the specified torque. The wiring must be correctly routed, and in no danger of contacting the exhaust system.

Testing

40 The oxygen sensors may be tested with a multimeter by disconnecting the wiring at the connector, trace the wiring back from the sensor and disconnect the wiring plug.
41 Connect an ohmmeter between terminals 1 and 2 on the sensor wiring plug. **Do not** connect the ohmmeter to the ECM wiring. The resistance should be approximately 9 ohms, when the temperature of the sensor is 20°C.
42 Reconnect the wiring after making the test.

Catalytic converter

43 Removal and refitting of the catalytic converter is described in Chapter 4A, Section 20, as part of the exhaust system procedures.

3.8 Particulate filter pressure sensor

1. Delivery hoses 3. Wiring plug
2. Retaining bolt

Testing

44 The performance of the catalytic converter can only be checked by measuring the exhaust gases using a good quality, carefully calibrated exhaust gas analyser.
45 If the CO level at the tailpipe is too high, the vehicle should be taken to a Saab dealer so that the fuel injection and ignition systems, including the oxygen sensor, can be thoroughly checked using special diagnostic equipment. Once these have been checked and are known to be free from faults, the fault must be in the catalytic converter, which must be renewed as described in Chapter 4A.

| 3 | Diesel engine emission control systems – testing and component renewal | |

Crankcase emission control

1 The components of this system require no attention other than to check that the hose(s) are clear and undamaged at regular intervals.

Exhaust emission control

Testing

2 The performance of the catalytic converter(s) can only be checked by measuring the exhaust gases using a good quality, carefully calibrated exhaust gas analyser.
3 If the catalytic converter(s) is thought to be faulty, before assuming a fault, it is worth checking the problem is not due to a faulty injector(s). Refer to your Saab dealer or specialist for further information.

Catalytic converter renewal

4 Catalytic converter renewal is described in Chapter 4B, Section 18.

Particulate filter renewal

5 Particulate filter renewal is described in Chapter 4B, Section 18.

Particulate filter pressure sensor renewal

6 Remove the plastic cover from the top of the engine.
7 The sensor is located on the bulkhead at the left-hand side of the engine compartment. Disconnect the sensor wiring plug.

3.14a Front exhaust gas temperature sensor

8 Note their fitted positions, then release the clips and disconnect the hoses from the sensor **(see illustration)**.
9 Undo the screw and remove the sensor.
10 Refitting is a reversal of removal. Note that if a new sensor has been fitted, the engine management ECM adaptation values must be reset using Saab diagnostic equipment. Entrust this task to a Saab dealer or suitably-equipped specialist.

Exhaust gas temperature sensors

11 Two temperature sensors are fitted to the exhaust system. The front sensor is fitted in the intake to the front catalytic converter, and the rear sensor is fitted into the front edge of the rear catalytic converter. To remove the sensor, raise the vehicle and support it securely on axle stands (see *Jacking and vehicle support*).
12 Remove the front right-hand roadwheel, and wheel arch liner.
13 Disconnect the sensor wiring plug.
14 Working underneath the vehicle, unscrew the sensor from the catalytic converter, and release the wiring from any retaining clips **(see illustrations)**.
15 Upon refitting the sensor, apply a little high-temperature anti-seize grease to the sensor threads, and tighten it to the specified torque.

Exhaust gas recirculation system

Testing

16 Comprehensive testing of the system can only be carried out using specialist electronic equipment which is connected to the injection system diagnostic wiring connector.

EGR valve renewal

17 Remove the plastic cover over the top of the engine.
18 Disconnect the EGR valve wiring connector.
19 Unscrew the two bolts on the top of the valve and detach the metal EGR pipe flange from the base of the valve. Recover the gasket **(see illustration)**.
20 Unscrew the two nuts and two bolts securing the EGR valve to the intake manifold and lift off the engine cover bracket **(see illustration)**.

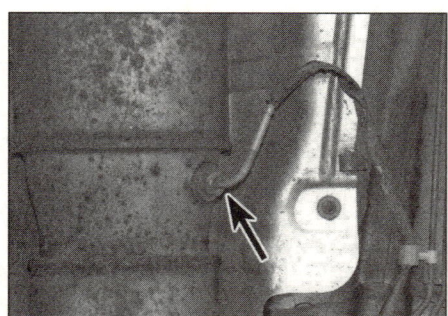

3.14b Rear exhaust gas temperature sensor

Emission control systems 4C•5

21 Refitting is the reverse of removal using new gaskets and tightening the retaining nuts and bolts to the specified torque.

4 Catalytic converter – general information and precautions

1 The catalytic converter is a reliable and simple device, which needs no maintenance in itself, but there are some facts of which an owner should be aware if the converter is to function properly for its full service life.

Petrol engines

a) DO NOT use leaded petrol/LRP in a car with a catalytic converter – the lead will coat the precious metals, reducing their converting efficiency, and may eventually destroy the converter.
b) Always keep the ignition and fuel systems well maintained in accordance with the manufacturer's schedule (see Chapter 1A).
c) If the engine develops a misfire, do not drive the car at all (or at least as little as possible) until the fault is cured.
d) DO NOT push- or tow-start the car – this will soak the catalytic converter in unburned fuel, causing it to overheat when the engine does start.
e) DO NOT switch the engine off at high engine speeds – ie, do not 'blip' the

3.19 Unscrew the two bolts, detach the metal EGR pipe flange and recover the gasket

throttle before switching off. Allow it to return to idle first.
f) DO NOT use fuel or engine oil additives – these may contain substances harmful to the catalytic converter.
g) DO NOT continue to use the car if the engine burns oil to the extent of leaving a visible trail of blue smoke.
h) Remember that the catalytic converter operates at very high temperatures. DO NOT, therefore, park the car in dry undergrowth, over long grass, or over piles of dead leaves, after a long run.
i) Remember that the catalytic converter is FRAGILE – do not strike it with tools during servicing work.

3.20 Unscrew the two nuts and two bolts securing the EGR valve to the intake manifold

j) In some cases a sulphurous smell (like that of rotten eggs) may be noticed from the exhaust. This is common to many catalytic converter-equipped cars and once the car has covered a few thousand miles the problem should disappear.
k) The catalytic converter, used on a well-maintained and well-driven car, should last for between 50 000 and 100 000 miles – if the converter is no longer effective it must be renewed.

Diesel engines

2 Refer to the information given in parts, f, g, h, i and k of the petrol engines information given above.

Notes

Chapter 5 Part A:
Starting and charging systems

Contents

	Section number
Alternator – removal and refitting	7
Alternator brushes and regulator – inspection and renewal	8
Alternator drivebelt – removal, refitting and tensioning	6
Battery – removal and refitting	4
Battery – testing and charging	3
Charging system – testing	5
Electrical fault finding – general information	2
General information and precautions	1
Glow plugs – removal, inspection and refitting	16
Ignition switch – removal and refitting	12
Oil level sensor – removal and refitting	14
Oil pressure warning light switch – removal and refitting	13
Pre/post-heating system – description and testing	15
Pre/post-heating system control unit – removal and refitting	17
Starter motor – removal and refitting	10
Starter motor – testing and overhaul	11
Starting system – testing	9

Degrees of difficulty

| **Easy,** suitable for novice with little experience | **Fairly easy,** suitable for beginner with some experience | **Fairly difficult,** suitable for competent DIY mechanic | **Difficult,** suitable for experienced DIY mechanic | **Very difficult,** suitable for expert DIY or professional |

Specifications

System type .... 12 volt, negative earth

Battery
Type .... Lead-acid, low-maintenance or 'maintenance-free' (sealed for life)
Battery capacity .... 60 to 85 amp-hour (depending on model)
Charge condition .... More than 12 volts

Alternator
Type:
  Petrol engines .... Bosch NC–14V 65-130A or Bosch E8–14V 75-140A
  Diesel engines .... Denso 14V 70 – 130A
Rated voltage 14V
Slip-ring diameter:
  Min. .... 15.4 mm
  New .... 14.4 mm
Minimum brush protrusion from holder .... 7.5 mm
Output current:
  Bosch NC:
    At 1800 rpm .... 65 amps
    At 6000 rpm .... 130 amps
  Bosch E8:
    At 1800 rpm .... 75 amps
    At 6000 rpm .... 140 amps
  Denso:
    At 1800 rpm .... 70 amps
    At 6000 rpm .... 130 amps

Starter motor
Type .... Bosch DW or Delco
Output:
  Petrol engines .... 1.4 to 1.8 kW
  Diesel engines .... 2.0 kW

5A•2 Starting and charging systems

Torque wrench settings	Nm	lbf ft
Alternator belt tensioner	45	33
Alternator mounting bolt:		
Petrol engines	20	15
Diesel engines	60	44
Engine mounting nut:		
Right-hand side	50	37
Rear	25	18
Glow plugs	10	7
Oil pressure switch:		
Petrol engines	18	13
Diesel engines	30	22
Starter motor:		
Petrol engines	45	33
Diesel engines	24	18

1 General information and precautions

General information

Because of their engine-related functions, the components of the starting and charging systems are covered separately from the body electrical devices such as the lights, instruments, etc (which are covered in Chapter 12). Refer to Part B of this Chapter for information on the ignition system.

The electrical system is of the 12 volt negative earth type. The battery fitted as original equipment is of low-maintenance or 'maintenance-free' (sealed for life) type. The battery is charged by the alternator, which is belt-driven from the crankshaft pulley. During the life of the car, the original battery may have been renewed with a standard type battery.

The starter motor is of the pre-engaged type, incorporating an integral solenoid. On starting, the solenoid moves the drive pinion into engagement with the flywheel/driveplate ring gear before the starter motor is energised. Once the engine has started, a one-way clutch prevents the motor armature being driven by the engine until the pinion disengages from the ring gear. Unlike some modern starter motors, it incorporates epicyclic reduction gears between the armature and the pinion.

Precautions

Further details of the various systems are given in the relevant Sections of this Chapter. While some repair procedures are given, the usual course of action is to renew the component concerned.

It is necessary to take extra care when working on the electrical system, to avoid damage to semi-conductor devices (diodes and transistors), and to avoid the risk of personal injury. In addition to the precautions given in *Safety first!* observe the following when working on the system:

• *Always remove rings, watches, etc, before working on the electrical system.* Even with the battery disconnected, capacitive discharge could occur if a component's live terminal is earthed through a metal object. This could cause a shock or nasty burn.

• *Do not reverse the battery connections.* Components such as the alternator, electronic control modules, or any other components having semi-conductor circuitry, could be irreparably damaged.

• If the engine is being started using jump leads and a slave battery, refer to *Jump starting*.

Caution: Never disconnect the battery terminals, the alternator, any electrical wiring, or any test instruments, when the engine is running.

• Do not allow the engine to turn the alternator when the alternator is not connected.

• Never 'test' for alternator output by 'flashing' the output lead to earth.

• Never use an ohmmeter of the type incorporating a hand-cranked generator for circuit or continuity testing.

• Always ensure that the battery negative lead is disconnected when working on the electrical system.

• Before using electric-arc welding equipment on the car, disconnect the battery, alternator, and components such as the fuel injection/ignition electronic control module, to protect them from the risk of damage.

2 Electrical fault finding – general information

Refer to Chapter 12.

3 Battery – testing and charging

Testing

Standard and low-maintenance battery

1 If the vehicle covers a small annual mileage, it is worthwhile checking the specific gravity of the electrolyte every three months, to determine the state of charge of the battery. Use a hydrometer to make the check, and compare the results with the following table. Note that the specific gravity readings assume an electrolyte temperature of 15°C; for every 10°C below 15°C, subtract 0.007. For every 10°C above 15°C, add 0.007. However, for convenience, the temperatures quoted in the following table are **ambient** (outdoor air) temperatures, above or below 25°C:

	Above 25°C	Below 25°C
Fully-charged	1.210 to 1.230	1.270 to 1.290
70% charged	1.170 to 1.190	1.230 to 1.250
Discharged	1.050 to 1.070	1.110 to 1.130

2 If the battery condition is suspect, first check the specific gravity of electrolyte in each cell. A variation of 0.040 or more between any cells indicates loss of electrolyte or deterioration of the internal plates.

3 If the specific gravity variation is 0.040 or more, the battery should be renewed. If the cell variation is satisfactory but the battery is discharged, it should be charged as described later in this Section.

Maintenance-free battery

4 In cases where a 'sealed for life' maintenance-free battery is fitted, topping-up and testing of the electrolyte in each cell is not possible. The condition of the battery can therefore only be tested using a battery condition indicator or a voltmeter.

5 A battery with a built-in charge condition indicator may be fitted. The indicator is located in the top of the battery casing, and indicates the condition of the battery from its colour. If the indicator shows green, then the battery is in a good state of charge. If the indicator turns darker, eventually to black, then the battery requires charging, as described later in this Section. If the indicator shows clear/yellow, then the electrolyte level in the battery is too low to allow further use, and the battery should be renewed. **Do not** attempt to charge, load or jump start a battery when the indicator shows clear/yellow.

All battery types

6 If testing the battery using a voltmeter, connect the voltmeter across the battery, and compare the result with those given in the Specifications under 'charge condition'. The test is only accurate if the battery has not been subjected to any kind of charge for the previous six hours, including charging by the

Starting and charging systems 5A•3

4.1 Removing the battery cover from the battery

4.2 Loosen the clamp nut and disconnect at the negative (earth) terminal first

4.3 Battery clamp retaining bolt

alternator. If this is not the case, switch on the headlights for 30 seconds, then wait four to five minutes after switching off the headlights before testing the battery. All other electrical circuits must be switched off, so check (for instance) that the doors and tailgate or boot lid are fully shut when making the test.

7 If the voltage reading is less than 12.2 volts, then the battery is discharged. A reading of 12.2 to 12.4 volts indicates a partially-discharged condition.

8 If the battery is to be charged, remove it from the vehicle (Section 4) and charge it as described in the following paragraphs.

Charging

Note: *The following is intended as a guide only. Always refer to the manufacturer's recommendations (often printed on a label attached to the battery) before charging a battery.*

Standard and low-maintenance battery

9 Charge the battery at a rate of 3.5 to 4 amps, and continue to charge the battery at this rate until no further rise in specific gravity is noted over a four hour period.

10 Alternatively, a trickle charger charging at the rate of 1.5 amps can safely be used overnight.

11 Specially rapid 'boost' charges, which are claimed to restore the power of the battery in 1 to 2 hours are not recommended, as they can cause serious damage to the battery plates through overheating.

12 While charging the battery, note that the temperature of the electrolyte should never exceed 38°C.

Maintenance-free battery

13 This battery type requires a longer period to fully recharge than the standard type, the time taken being dependent on the extent of discharge, but it can take anything up to three days.

14 A constant-voltage type charger is required to be set, where possible, to 13.9 to 14.9 volts with a charger current below 25 amps. Using this method, the battery should be usable within three hours, giving a voltage reading of 12.5 volts, but this is for a partially-discharged battery and, as mentioned, full-charging can take considerably longer.

15 Use of a normal trickle charger should not be detrimental to the battery, provided excessive gassing is not allowed to occur, and the battery is not allowed to become hot.

4 Battery – removal and refitting

Removal

1 The battery is located at the front left-hand side of the engine compartment. Unclip the cover from the battery **(see illustration)**.

2 Loosen the clamp nut and disconnect the lead at the negative (earth) terminal **(see illustration)**. Disconnect the lead at the positive terminal in the same way.

3 Unscrew the retaining bolt and remove the battery retaining clamp **(see illustration)** which secures the battery to the mounting bracket.

4 Lift the battery out of the engine compartment (take care not to tilt it excessively).

5 To remove the battery tray, undo the 3 retaining bolts and withdraw the battery tray **(see illustrations)**. As the tray is removed, depress the clips and slide up the fusible link junction box (where fitted).

Refitting

6 Refitting is a reversal of removal. Smear petroleum jelly on the terminals after reconnecting the leads, and always reconnect the positive lead first, and the negative lead last.

4.5a Undo the retaining bolts . . .

7 After reconnection, it will be necessary to reset the clock, and date information as described in the owners handbook.

8 It may also be necessary to reset the window 'pinch protection' function as follows:
1) *Shut the doors, start the car, and open the side window approximately 15 cm.*
2) *Close the window and hold the button in the closed position for at least 1 second after the window shuts.*
3) *Press the 'down' button and allow the window to open by itself.*
4) *Wait at least 1 second then close the window, holding the button until closing is confirmed by an audible signal.*

9 In some instances, it's possible that several diagnostic fault codes may be set as a result of the battery disconnection and reconnection. These codes can be ignored, and will not be regenerated once they have been deleted. As special diagnostic equipment is needed to delete these codes, entrust this task to a Saab dealer or suitably-equipped repairer.

5 Charging system – testing

Note: *Refer to the warnings given in 'Safety first!' and in Section 1 of this Chapter before starting work.*

1 If the ignition/no-charge warning light does not come on when the ignition is switched on, first check the alternator wiring connections for security. If satisfactory, check that the warning light bulb has not blown, and that the bulbholder

4.5b . . . and remove the battery tray

5A•4 Starting and charging systems

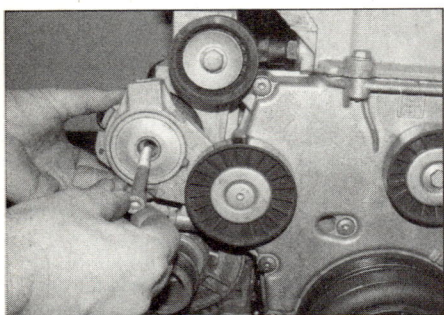

7.7 Removing the auxiliary belt tensioner . . .

7.8 . . . to access the upper alternator mounting bolt (arrowed)

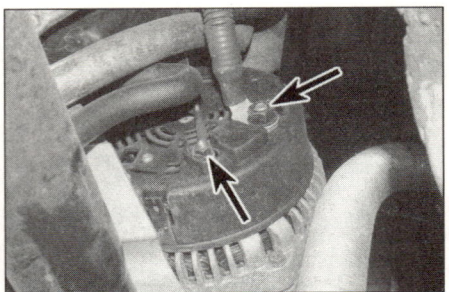

7.9 Unscrew the terminal nuts (arrowed) and disconnect the wiring from the rear of the alternator

is secure in its location in the instrument panel. If the light still fails to illuminate, check the continuity of the warning light feed wire from the alternator to the bulbholder. If all is satisfactory, the alternator is at fault, and should be taken to an auto-electrician for testing and repair, or else renewed.

2 If the ignition warning light comes on when the engine is running, stop the engine. Check that the drivebelt is intact and correctly tensioned (see Chapter 1A or 1B), and that the alternator connections are secure. If all is satisfactory, check the alternator brushes and slip-rings as described in Section 8. If the fault persists, the alternator should be taken to an auto-electrician for testing and repair, or else renewed.

3 If the alternator output is suspect even though the warning light functions correctly, the regulated voltage may be checked as follows.

4 Connect a voltmeter across the battery terminals, and start the engine.

5 Increase the engine speed until the voltmeter reading remains steady; the reading should be approximately 12 to 13 volts, and no more than 14 volts.

6 Switch on as many electrical accessories as possible (eg, the headlights, heated rear window and heater blower), and check that the alternator maintains the regulated voltage at around 13 to 14 volts.

7 If the regulated voltage is not as stated, the fault may be due to worn brushes, weak brush springs, a faulty voltage regulator, a faulty diode, a severed phase winding, or worn or damaged slip-rings. The brushes and slip-rings may be checked (see Section 8), but if the fault persists, the alternator should be taken to an auto-electrician for testing and repair, or else renewed.

6 Alternator drivebelt – removal, refitting and tensioning

Refer to the procedure given for the auxiliary drivebelt in Chapter 1A or 1B.

7 Alternator – removal and refitting

Removal

1 Open the bonnet and unclip the covers from top of the engine and battery, then disconnect the battery negative lead.

2 Apply the handbrake, then jack up the front of the car and support on stands (see *Jacking and vehicle support*). Remove the right-hand front wheel and engine undershield, where fitted.

3 Remove the right-hand front wing inner plastic moulding/wheel arch liner for access to the rear of the engine.

4 Remove the auxiliary drivebelt as described in Chapter 1A or 1B.

Petrol models

5 Remove the intake manifold as described in Chapter 4A, Section 18.

6 Remove the front exhaust pipe section (including catalytic converter) as described in Chapter 4A, Section 20.

7 Undo the retaining bolt and remove the auxiliary belt tensioner **(see illustration)**.

8 Unscrew and remove the alternator upper mounting bolt **(see illustration)**.

9 Note the position of the wires on the rear of the alternator, then unscrew the terminal nuts and disconnect the wires **(see illustration)**.

10 Unscrew the alternator lower mounting bolt **(see illustration)**.

11 Note the alternator will be a tight fit the mounting bracket, metal sleeves in the mounting bolt holes will need to be carefully moved outwards to release the alternator **(see illustrations)**.

12 Lift the alternator upwards from its position to remove from the engine compartment.

Diesel models

13 Remove the alternator upper mounting bolts **(see illustration)**.

7.10 Removing the alternator lower mounting bolt

7.11a Metal sleeve (arrowed) in the mounting bracket . . .

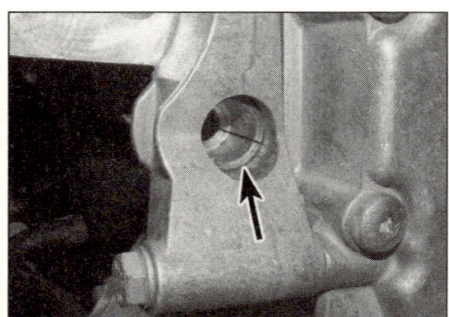

7.11b . . . this sleeve (arrowed) will need to be tapped outwards to release the alternator

7.13 Alternator upper mounting bolts – arrowed

Starting and charging systems 5A•5

14 Remove the suspension right-hand lower arm balljoint pinch-bolt, and use a lever to lower the arm and balljoint from the hub carrier (see Chapter 10). Use a block of wood to wedge the arm in the lowered position.
15 Tap the right-hand driveshaft from the support bearing, and push the driveshaft to one side.
16 Undo the nuts and disconnect the electrical connections from the rear of the alternator.
17 Undo the bolts, remove the alternator lower mounting bolt, and lower the alternator from the rear of the engine (see illustration).

Refitting

18 Refitting is a reversal of removal, however, clean the alternator mounting points, and coat them with petroleum jelly after fitting to ensure a good electrical connection to the engine. Ensure that the alternator mountings are securely tightened, and refit the components referring to the relevant Chapters.

8 Alternator brushes and regulator – inspection and renewal

Note: *The Bosch E8–14V 75–140A alternator, is shown in the illustrations, other alternators similar.*

1 Remove the alternator as described in Section 7.
2 Unscrew the large terminal nuts and the screw securing the cover to the rear of the alternator (see illustration).
3 Using a screwdriver, carefully lever off the rear cover, and remove it from the alternator.
4 Unscrew and remove the retaining screws, and remove the regulator/brush holder from the rear of the alternator (see illustration).
5 Measure the protrusion of each brush from its holder, using a steel rule or vernier calipers (see illustration). If less than 7.5 mm, a new regulator/brush assembly should be obtained.
6 If the brushes are in good condition, clean them and check that they move freely in their holders.
7 Clean the alternator slip-rings with a fuel-moistened cloth. Check for signs of scoring or burning on the surface of the slip-rings. It may

7.17 Alternator lower front mounting bolt – arrowed

be possible to have the slip-rings renovated by an electrical specialist.
8 Refit the regulator/brush holder assembly, and securely tighten the retaining screws.
9 Refit the cover, then insert and tighten the retaining screws and refit the large terminal nut.
10 Refit the alternator with reference to Section 7.

9 Starting system – testing

Note: *Refer to the precautions given in 'Safety first!' and in Section 1 of this Chapter before starting work.*

1 If the starter motor fails to operate when the ignition key is turned to the appropriate position, the following possible causes may apply:
 a) The battery is faulty.
 b) The electrical connections between the switch, solenoid, battery and starter motor are somewhere failing to pass the necessary current from the battery through the starter to earth.
 c) The solenoid is faulty.
 d) The starter motor is mechanically or electrically defective.

2 To check the battery, switch on the headlights. If they dim after a few seconds, this indicates that the battery is discharged – recharge (see Section 3) or renew the battery. If the headlights glow brightly, operate the starter on the ignition switch, and observe the lights. If

they dim, this indicates that current is reaching the starter motor – therefore, the fault must lie in the starter motor. If the lights continue to glow brightly (and no clicking sound can be heard from the starter motor solenoid), this indicates that there is a fault in the circuit or solenoid – see the following paragraphs. If the starter motor turns slowly when operated, but the battery is in good condition, then this indicates that either the starter motor is faulty, or that there is considerable resistance somewhere in the circuit.

3 If a fault in the circuit is suspected, disconnect the battery leads, the starter/solenoid wiring and the engine/transmission earth strap. Thoroughly clean the connections, and reconnect the leads and wiring, then use a voltmeter or test light to check that full battery voltage is available at the battery positive lead connection on the solenoid, and that the earth is sound.

4 If the battery and all connections are in good condition, check the circuit by disconnecting the wire from the solenoid terminal. Connect a voltmeter or test light between the wire end and a good earth (such as the battery negative terminal), and check that the wire is live when the ignition switch is turned to the 'start' position. If it is, then the circuit is sound – if not, the circuit wiring can be checked as described in Chapter 12.

5 The solenoid contacts can be checked by connecting a voltmeter or test light between the terminal on the starter side of the solenoid, and earth. When the ignition switch is turned to the 'start' position, there should be a reading or lighted bulb, as applicable. If there is no reading or lighted bulb, the solenoid or contacts are faulty and the solenoid should be renewed.

6 If the circuit and solenoid are proved sound, the fault must lie in the starter motor. Begin checking the starter motor by removing it (see Section 10), and checking the brushes (see Section 11). If the fault does not lie in the brushes, the motor windings must be faulty. In this event, it may be possible to have the starter motor overhauled by a specialist, but check on the availability and cost of spares before proceeding, as it may prove more economical to obtain a new or exchange motor.

8.2 Unscrew the nuts and screw (arrowed) securing the rear cover

8.4 Undo the regulator/brush holder screws – arrowed

8.5 Measuring the brush protrusion from the holder

5A•6 Starting and charging systems

10.3 Withdraw the upper starter motor mounting bolt from the top of the transmission bellhousing

10.5 Remove the cable-tie (arrowed) to release the wiring loom

10.6 Unscrew the starter motor lower mounting nut (arrowed)

10.7 Undo the nuts and release the wiring harness from the support bracket

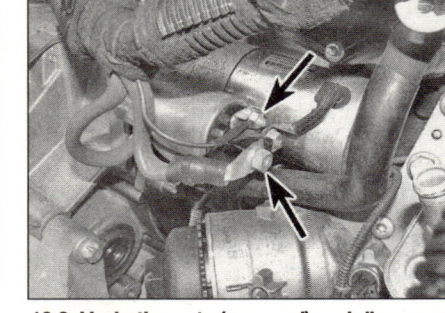

10.8 Undo the nuts (arrowed) and disconnect the starter solenoid wiring connectors

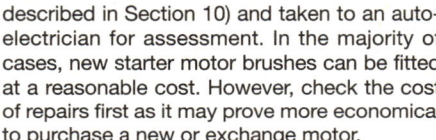

10.9 Unscrew the nut (arrowed) and disconnect the earth lead from the starter motor stud bolt

10 Starter motor – removal and refitting

Removal

1 The starter motor is located on the left-hand rear side of the engine, and is bolted to the engine endplate and transmission. First remove the cover from the battery and disconnect the negative lead.
2 Apply the handbrake, then jack up the front of the car and support on axle stands (see *Jacking and vehicle support*).

Petrol models

3 From inside the engine compartment, remove the starter motor upper mounting bolt **(see illustration)**.
4 Unscrew the nut(s) and disconnect the wiring terminal(s) from the starter/solenoid.
5 Cut and release the cable-tie/strap from around the solenoid to release the wiring loom **(see illustration)**.
6 From under the vehicle, unscrew the lower starter motor mounting nut, then lower the starter motor from the engine compartment **(see illustration)**.

Diesel models

7 Working above the engine, remove the starter motor upper mounting bolts, and remove the bracket from the coolant pipe and wiring harness **(see illustration)**.
8 Note their fitted positions, then undo the nuts and detach the electrical connections from the starter motor **(see illustration)**.
9 Undo the lower mounting nut and detach the earth cable from the starter motor lower mounting stud **(see illustration)**.
10 Remove the starter motor lower mounting stud by using two nuts locked together.
11 Manoeuvre the starter motor from position.

Refitting

12 Refitting is a reversal of removal. Tighten all wire connections securely.

11 Starter motor – testing and overhaul

Note: *At the time of writing, no individual starter motor components were available from Saab. An auto-electrical specialist should be able to supply and fit parts such as brushes.*

If the starter motor is thought to be defective, it should be removed from the vehicle (as described in Section 10) and taken to an auto-electrician for assessment. In the majority of cases, new starter motor brushes can be fitted at a reasonable cost. However, check the cost of repairs first as it may prove more economical to purchase a new or exchange motor.

12 Ignition switch – removal and refitting

Refer to the procedure given in Chapter 12, Section 4, for the removal and refitting procedure.

13 Oil pressure warning light switch – removal and refitting

Removal

Petrol models

1 The switch is screwed into the front of the cylinder block, adjacent to the oil filter. To gain access to the switch, remove the plastic cover from the top of the engine.
2 Disconnect the wiring connector then unscrew the switch (using a 27 mm ring spanner or socket) and recover the sealing washer. Be prepared for oil spillage. If the switch is to be left removed from the engine for any length of time, plug the switch aperture.

Diesel models

3 The switch is screwed into the oil filter housing at the rear of the engine **(see illustration)**.

13.3 Oil pressure warning light switch – arrowed

Starting and charging systems 5A•7

14.2 Slide off the retaining clip (arrowed) and free the oil level sensor wiring connector from the sump

14.3 Where fitted, undo the retaining bolts and remove the oil baffle plate

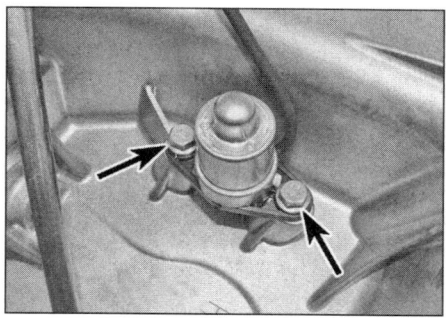

14.4 Undo the two bolts (arrowed) and remove the oil level sensor from the sump

4 Firmly apply the handbrake, and then jack up the front of the car and support it securely on axle stands (see *Jacking and vehicle support*).
5 Undo the bolts and remove the undershield (where fitted) from beneath the engine.
6 Disconnect the wiring connector then unscrew the switch and recover the sealing washer. Be prepared for oil spillage, and if the switch is to be left removed from the engine for any length of time, plug the switch aperture.

Refitting

7 Examine the sealing washer for signs of damage or deterioration and if necessary renew.
8 Refit the switch and washer, tightening it to the specified torque, and reconnect the wiring connector.
9 On diesel engine models, refit the engine undershield.
10 Lower the vehicle to the ground (where applicable) and then check the oil level. If necessary, top-up the engine oil as described in *Weekly checks*.

14 Oil level sensor – removal and refitting

Note: *Oil level sensors may not be fitted to all models, check around the sides of the sump to locate position of sensor, where fitted.*

Removal

1 The oil level sensor is located in the sump, remove the sump as described in Chapter 2A or 2B.
2 With the sump removed, slide off the retaining clip and free the sensor wiring connector from the sump (see illustration).
3 Where fitted, undo the retaining bolts and remove the oil baffle plate from inside the sump (see illustration).
4 Note the correct routing of the wiring then undo the retaining bolts and remove the sensor assembly from the sump (see illustration). Check the wiring connector seal for signs or damage and renew if necessary.

Refitting

5 Prior to refitting remove all traces of locking compound from the sensor retaining bolt and sump threads. Apply a drop of fresh locking compound to the bolt threads and lubricate the wiring connector seal with a smear of engine oil.
6 Fit the sensor, making sure the wiring is correctly routed, and securely tighten its retaining bolts. Ease the wiring connector through the sump, taking care not to damage its seal, and secure it in position with the retaining clip.
7 Ensure the sensor is correctly refitted then, where applicable, refit the oil baffle plate.
8 Refit the sump as described in Chapter 2A or 2B.

15 Pre/post-heating system – description and testing

Description

1 Each cylinder of the engine is fitted with a heater plug (commonly called a glow plug) screwed into it. The plugs are electrically-operated before and during start-up when the engine is cold. Electrical feed to the glow plugs is controlled via the pre/post-heating system control unit.
2 A warning light in the instrument panel tells the driver that pre/post-heating is taking place. When the light goes out, the engine is ready to be started. The voltage supply to the glow plugs continues for several seconds after the light goes out. If no attempt is made to start, the timer then cuts off the supply, in order to avoid draining the battery and overheating the glow plugs.
3 The glow plugs also provide a 'post-heating' function, whereby the glow plugs remain switched on after the engine has started. The length of time 'post-heating' takes place is also determined by the control unit, and is dependent on engine temperature.
4 The fuel filter is fitted with a heating element to prevent the fuel 'waxing' in extreme cold temperature conditions and to improve combustion. The heating element is an integral part of the fuel filter housing and is controlled by the pre/post-heating system control unit.

Testing

5 If the system malfunctions, testing is ultimately by substitution of known good units, but some preliminary checks may be made as follows.
6 Connect a voltmeter or 12 volt test lamp between the glow plug supply cable and earth (engine or vehicle metal). Make sure that the live connection is kept clear of the engine and bodywork.
7 Have an assistant switch on the ignition, and check that voltage is applied to the glow plugs. Note the time for which the warning light is lit, and the total time for which voltage is applied before the system cuts out. Switch off the ignition.
8 At an underbonnet temperature of 20°C, typical times noted should be approximately 3 seconds for warning light operation. Warning light time will increase with lower temperatures and decrease with higher temperatures.
9 If there is no supply at all, the control unit or associated wiring is at fault.
10 To locate a defective glow plug, disconnect the wiring connector from each plug.
11 Use a continuity tester, or a 12 volt test lamp connected to the battery positive terminal, to check for continuity between each glow plug terminal and earth. The resistance of a glow plug in good condition is very low (less than 1 ohm), so if the test lamp does not light or the continuity tester shows a high resistance, the glow plug is certainly defective.
12 If an ammeter is available, the current draw of each glow plug can be checked. After an initial surge of 15 to 20 amps, each plug should draw 12 amps. Any plug that draws much more or less than this is probably defective.
13 As a final check, the glow plugs can be removed and inspected as described in the following Section.

16 Glow plugs – removal, inspection and refitting

Caution: *If the pre/post-heating system has just been energised, or if the engine has been running, the glow plugs will be very hot.*

Removal

1 The glow plugs are located at the rear of the cylinder head above the intake manifold.

16.3 Unscrew the glow plugs and remove them from the cylinder head

17.1 Pre/post-heating control unit location

2 Remove the plastic cover by pulling it upwards off the mounting studs.
3 Pull the connectors from the glow plugs, then unscrew and remove them from the cylinder head **(see illustration)**.

Inspection

4 Inspect each glow plug for physical damage. Burnt or eroded glow plug tips can be caused by a bad injector spray pattern. Have the injectors checked if this type of damage is found.
5 If the glow plugs are in good physical condition, check them electrically using a 12 volt test lamp or continuity tester as described in the previous Section.
6 The glow plugs can be energised by applying 12 volts to them, to verify that they heat up evenly and in the required time. Observe the following precautions.

a) Support the glow plug by clamping it carefully in a vice or self-locking pliers. Remember it will become red-hot.
b) Make sure that the power supply or test lead incorporates a fuse or overload trip to protect against damage from a short-circuit.
c) After testing, allow the glow plug to cool for several minutes before attempting to handle it.

7 A glow plug in good condition will start to glow red at the tip after drawing current for 5 seconds or so. Any plug which takes much longer to start glowing, or which starts glowing in the middle instead of at the tip, is defective.

Refitting

8 Carefully refit the plugs and tighten to the specified torque. Do not overtighten, as this can damage the glow plug element. Push the electrical connectors firmly onto the glow plugs.
9 The remainder of refitting is a reversal of removal, checking the operation of the glow plugs on completion.

17 Pre/post-heating system control unit – removal and refitting

Note: *If the control unit is to be renewed, Saab's diagnostic equipment must be used to download and reset various stored values before the old unit is removed and after the new one is fitted. Entrust this task to a Saab dealer or suitably-equipped specialist.*
Note: *These electronic modules are very sensitive to static electricity. Before handling the unit, earth yourself by touching a bare metal part of the vehicle body.*

Removal

1 The control unit is located on the right-hand side of the engine compartment, on the inner wing panel in front of the power steering fluid reservoir **(see illustration)**.
2 Undo the retaining bolt and withdraw the control unit from the inner wing panel.
3 Disconnect the wiring plug from the control unit as it is removed.

Refitting

4 Refitting is a reversal of removal.

Chapter 5 Part B:
Ignition system – petrol engines

Contents

	Section number		Section number
General information	1	Ignition system – testing	2
Ignition discharge module – removal and refitting	3	Ignition timing – general information	6
Ignition HT coils – general information	4	Slotted rotor for crankshaft sensor – removal and refitting	5

Degrees of difficulty

Easy, suitable for novice with little experience	**Fairly easy,** suitable for beginner with some experience	**Fairly difficult,** suitable for competent DIY mechanic	**Difficult,** suitable for experienced DIY mechanic	**Very difficult,** suitable for expert DIY or professional

Specifications

System type .... Direct Ignition (DI) system incorporated in Trionic engine management system

Direct Ignition (DI) system
Ignition discharge module:
   Capacitor voltage .... 400 volts
   Ignition voltage (maximum) .... 40 000 volts
Ignition timing .... Pre-programmed in ECM

Firing order .... 1-3-4-2 (No 1 cylinder at timing chain end)

Torque wrench settings

	Nm	lbf ft
Crankshaft pulley bolt	175	129
Ignition discharge module	12	9
Spark plugs	28	21

5B•2 Ignition system – petrol engines

1.2 Separate coils (arrowed) – one for each cylinder

1.8a Direct Ignition cartridge

1 Transformer (12 volts/ 400 volts)
2 Capacitor
3 Ignition coil
4 Spark plug

1.8b Direct Ignition capacitor (arrowed) located in the cartridge

1 General information

1 All models have a Direct Ignition system, which is incorporated into the Saab Trionic engine management system. With this system, a single electronic control module (ECM) controls both the fuel injection and ignition functions. More information on the system components are given in Chapter 4A.
2 The Direct Ignition system uses a separate HT coil for each spark plug **(see illustration)**. The system's electronic control module monitors the engine by means of various sensors, in order to determine the most efficient ignition timing.
3 The components of the system are a crankshaft position/speed sensor, ignition discharge module with one coil per plug, diagnostic socket, ECM, pressure sensor in the intake manifold (to determine engine load), and a solenoid valve (to regulate the turbocharger operation).
4 During starting at a crankshaft speed in excess of 150 rpm, HT sparks are triggered in the cylinder pair with the pistons at TDC. Under difficult conditions, multi-sparking occurs during this period, to aid starting. The ECM determines in which cylinder combustion is taking place by monitoring the flow of current across the spark plug electrodes, and then uses this information to determine the firing.
5 When the engine starts, the ignition timing is always set to 10° BTDC, and will remain at this setting until the engine speed exceeds

3.2 Slacken and remove the four screws (arrowed) securing the ignition cartridge

825 rpm. The ECM will regulate the ignition timing at engine speeds above 825 rpm.
6 When the ignition is switched off and the engine stops, the main relay remains operational for a further 6 seconds. During this period, the Trionic control module earths all the trigger leads 210 times a second for 5 seconds in order to burn off impurities from the spark plug electrodes.
7 Because the system does not use any HT leads, radio suppression must be incorporated in the spark plugs, so resistor-type plugs must always be used.
8 The Direct Ignition system uses the capacitive discharge method of producing an HT spark. Approximately 400 volts is stored in a capacitor **(see illustrations)**, and at the time of ignition, this voltage is discharged through the primary circuit of the relevant coil. Approximately 40 000 volts is induced in the HT secondary coil, and this is discharged across the spark plug electrodes.
9 Should a fault occur in the system, a fault code is stored in the ECM. This code can only be accessed by a Saab dealer, using dedicated equipment.
10 Note that the starter motor must never be operated with the ignition cartridge disconnected from the spark plugs but still connected to the wiring loom. This can cause irreversible damage to the cartridge.
11 The engine management system controls engine pre-combustion via a knock sensor incorporated into the ignition system. Mounted onto the cylinder block, the sensor detects the high frequency vibrations caused when the engine starts to pre-ignite, or 'pink'. Under these conditions, the knock sensor sends an electrical signal to the ECM, which in turn retards the ignition advance setting in small steps until the 'pinking' ceases. With the Saab Trionic system, the spark plugs themselves are used as knock sensors, instead of employing a separate knock detector in the cylinder block. It achieves this by applying a small, direct current voltage across each spark plug. When two cylinders approach TDC, this voltage causes an ionisation current to flow across the terminals of the spark plug in the cylinder under combustion; a high current indicates that knock is occurring thus indicating which cylinder requires ignition retardation. Sequential control of the fuel injection is achieved in the same manner (see Chapter 4A).

2 Ignition system – testing

⚠ **Warning: Voltages produced by an electronic ignition system are considerably higher than those produced by conventional ignition systems. Extreme care must be taken when working on the system with the ignition switched on. Persons with surgically implanted cardiac pacemaker devices should keep well clear of the ignition circuits, components and test equipment. Refer to the precautions in Chapter 5A, Section 1, before starting work. Always switch off the ignition before disconnecting or connecting any component, and when using a multimeter to check resistances.**

1 If a fault appears in the engine management system, first check that all wiring is secure and in good condition. If necessary, individual components of the Direct Ignition system may be removed for visual investigation as described later in this Chapter. The coils are best checked by substituting a suspect one with a known good coil, and checking if the misfire is cured.
2 Due to the location of the spark plugs beneath the ignition discharge module, it is not possible to easily check the HT circuit for faults. Further testing should be carried out by a Saab dealer, who will have equipment to access fault codes stored in the system ECM.

3 Ignition discharge module – removal and refitting

Removal

1 Open the bonnet, unclip the cover from the top of the battery and disconnect the battery negative lead.
2 Unscrew the four screws securing the ignition cartridge to the top of the cylinder head **(see illustration)**.

Ignition system – petrol engines

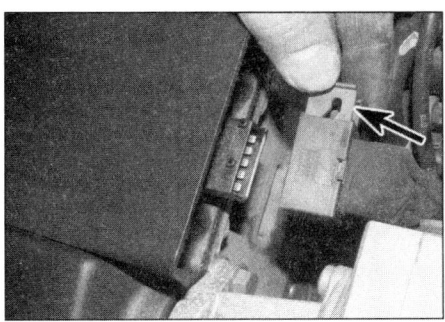

3.3 Release the retaining clip (arrowed) and disconnect the wiring connector

3.5 Lift the cartridge straight up to release it from the spark plugs

3.6a Unscrew the screws (three shown) . . .

3 Disconnect the wiring plug, located on the left-hand end of the ignition discharge module **(see illustration)**.

4 Where applicable, disconnect any wiring support clips or earth lead.

5 Lift the ignition cartridge, at the same time releasing it from the tops of the spark plugs **(see illustration)**.

⚠ **Warning: When the ignition discharge module is removed, it must be kept in the upright position. If the ignition discharge module has been turned upside down for a length of time, leave it in the fitted position for a couple of hours before starting.**

6 If necessary, the shroud may be removed from the bottom of the cartridge, by inverting it and removing the retaining screws. Separate the black (lower) shroud from the cartridge **(see illustrations)**.

7 The HT springs may be removed from the shroud by careful use of a screwdriver **(see illustration)**.

Refitting

8 Refitting is a reversal of removal, but tighten the retaining screws to the specified torque.

4 Ignition HT coils – general information

The four ignition coils are an integral part of the ignition discharge module upper assembly and can only be purchased from Saab as a complete unit.

If required, the ignition discharge module

3.6b . . . and separate the black lower shroud from the cartridge

can be removed from the vehicle as described in Section 3, then taken to your local Saab dealer or motor vehicle electrical specialist where they can check the ignition module.

⚠ **Warning: When the ignition discharge module is removed, it must be kept in the upright position. If the ignition discharge module has been turned upside down for a length of time, leave it in the fitted position for a couple of hours before starting.**

5 Slotted rotor for crankshaft sensor – removal and refitting

Removal

1 The slotted rotor is located on the flywheel/driveplate end of the crankshaft. Remove the crankshaft as described in Chapter 2C.

2 Using a Torx key, unscrew the four screws

3.7 Rubber sleeve and spring from inside lower shroud

securing the slotted rotor to the crankshaft, and then remove the rotor over the end of the crankshaft.

Refitting

3 Refitting is a reversal of removal. Note that the rotor can only be fitted in one position, since the bolt holes are unequally-spaced.

6 Ignition timing – general information

The ignition timing is pre-programmed into the system ECM, and cannot be adjusted or even checked with any accuracy. If the timing is thought to be incorrect, the car should be taken to a Saab dealer who will have the necessary equipment to extract any fault codes stored in the ECM. For further information see Chapter 4A.

Notes

Chapter 6
Clutch

Contents

	Section number		Section number
Clutch assembly – removal, inspection and refitting	3	Clutch pedal – removal and refitting	2
Clutch hydraulic system – bleeding	6	Clutch slave cylinder/release bearing – removal and refitting	4
Clutch master cylinder – removal and refitting	5	General description	1

Degrees of difficulty

Easy, suitable for novice with little experience | **Fairly easy,** suitable for beginner with some experience | **Fairly difficult,** suitable for competent DIY mechanic | **Difficult,** suitable for experienced DIY mechanic | **Very difficult,** suitable for expert DIY or professional

Specifications

System type .... Single dry-plate clutch with diaphragm spring, operated by master/slave cylinder hydraulic release system

Friction plate
Diameter:
  Petrol .... 228 mm
  Diesel .... 240 mm
Thickness:
  New .... 7.3 mm
  Minimum .... 5.5 mm

Hydraulic release mechanism
Slave cylinder stroke .... 8.0 mm
Master cylinder piston diameter .... 15.87 mm

Torque wrench settings
	Nm	lbf ft
Clutch pedal/master cylinder mounting bracket to bulkhead	24	18
Clutch pressure plate retaining bolts	30	22
Master cylinder securing nuts	20	15
Slave cylinder securing screws	10	7
Supply pipe to slave cylinder	22	16
Vacuum servo unit stud bolts*	20	15

* Use new nuts/bolts

1 General description

1 The hydraulic clutch system is of single dry-plate type, and consists of the following main components: the clutch pedal, master cylinder, release bearing/slave cylinder, friction plate, and pressure plate with its integral diaphragm spring and cover **(see illustration)**.

2 The friction plate is free to slide along the splines of the transmission input shaft. This is held in position between the flywheel and the pressure plate by the pressure exerted on the pressure plate by the diaphragm spring. Friction lining material is riveted to both sides of the friction plate. Spring cushioning between the friction linings and the hub absorbs transmission shocks, and helps to ensure a smooth take-up of power as the clutch is engaged.

1.1 Hydraulic clutch release system

6•2 Clutch

3 The diaphragm spring is mounted on pins, and is held in place in the cover by annular fulcrum rings.
4 Effort is transmitted from the clutch pedal to the master cylinder, mounted on the rear of the engine compartment bulkhead, via a pushrod. The master cylinder piston forces hydraulic fluid through a supply pipe to the slave cylinder, which is located inside the transmission casing, mounted concentrically over the transmission input shaft. The fluid forces the piston out of the slave cylinder, thus actuating the release bearing.
5 When the clutch pedal is depressed, the release bearing is forced to slide along the input shaft sleeve, to bear against the centre of the diaphragm spring, thus pushing the centre of the diaphragm spring inwards. The diaphragm spring acts against a circular fulcrum ring in the cover. When the centre of the spring is pushed in, the outside of the spring is pushed out, so allowing the pressure plate to move backwards away from the friction plate.
6 When the clutch pedal is released, the diaphragm spring forces the pressure plate into contact with the friction linings on the friction plate. This simultaneously pushes the friction plate forwards on its splines, forcing it against the flywheel. The friction plate is now firmly sandwiched between the pressure plate and the flywheel, and drive is taken up.
7 The fluid used in the hydraulic clutch system is the same as that used in the braking system; hence fluid is supplied to the master cylinder from a tapping on the brake fluid reservoir. The clutch hydraulic system must be sealed before work is carried out on any of its components and then, on completion, topped-up and bled to remove any air bubbles. Details of these procedures are given in Section 6 of this Chapter.

2 Clutch pedal – removal and refitting

Note: *The clutch pedal is part of the pedal bracket assembly and cannot be removed separately.*

Removal

1 Remove the facia panel as described in Chapter 11.
2 On right-hand drive models, from inside the engine bay, remove the cover from the top of the engine and the intake manifold.
3 On left-hand drive models, remove the battery, then undo the retaining bolts/nuts and remove the central electric unit and fuse holder from the left-hand side top strut mounting.
4 From inside the engine bay, undo the four retaining nuts from the pedal bracket assembly. **Note:** *Two of the nuts are the clutch master cylinder retaining nuts.*
5 From inside the vehicle, undo the retaining bolts and remove the knee shield from across the lower part of the steering column and bulkhead.
6 Disconnect the wiring connector from the pedal switch, then undo the retaining bolts securing the pedal bracket to the facia mounting crossmember.
7 Unhook the spring from the clutch pedal, remove the securing clip and withdraw the pivot pin.
8 Undo the lower steering column shaft joint securing bolt, and detach it from the splines on the steering rack. **Note:** *Do not prise open the joint to remove (see Chapter 10 for further information).*

⚠ **Warning:** *As the steering column is moved away from the bulkhead, take care that the upper and lower parts of the steering column do not separate, see Chapter 10.*

9 Undo the retaining bolts from the facia mounting crossmember, then withdraw the crossmember to allow enough room to withdraw the pedal bracket assembly from the footwell.

Refitting

10 Refitting is a reversal of removal procedure. Ensure that the pedal return spring is correctly fitted and all retaining bolts are tightened to the specified torque.

3 Clutch assembly – removal, inspection and refitting

⚠ **Warning:** *Dust created by clutch wear and deposited on the clutch components may contain asbestos, which is a health hazard. DO NOT blow it out with compressed air, nor inhale any of it. DO NOT use petrol or petroleum-based solvents to clean off the dust. Brake system cleaner or methylated spirit should be used to flush the dust into a suitable receptacle. After the clutch components are wiped clean with clean rags, dispose of the contaminated rags and cleaner in a sealed, marked container.*
Note: *Although some friction materials may no longer contain asbestos, it is safest to assume that they DO, and to take precautions accordingly*

Removal

1 Unless the complete engine/transmission

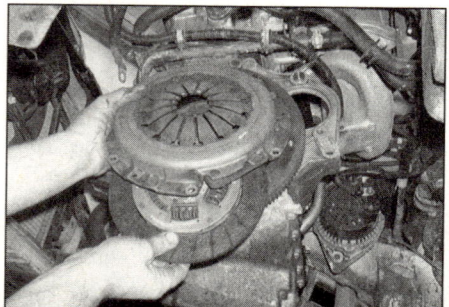

3.5 Lift off the pressure plate, then recover the friction plate, noting its orientation

is to be removed from the car and separated for major overhaul (see Chapter 2C), the clutch can be accessed by removing the transmission, as described in Chapter 7A.
2 Before disturbing any of the clutch components, mark the relationship between the pressure plate, friction plate and the flywheel.
3 To aid the removal of the pressure plate, the flywheel should ideally be locked in position by bolting a locking tool to one of the transmission mounting holes, and engaging it with the flywheel ring gear. If a universal flywheel locking tool is not available, the crankshaft (and hence the flywheel) can be held stationary using a wrench and socket on the crankshaft sprocket bolt. The help of an assistant will be required to complete this task.
4 Working diagonally across the pressure plate, progressively slacken the mounting bolts, half a turn at a time, until they can be removed by hand.
5 With all the bolts removed, lift off the clutch assembly. Be prepared to catch the friction plate as the cover assembly is lifted from the flywheel, and note which way round the friction plate is fitted **(see illustration)**.

Inspection

Note: *Due to the amount of work necessary to remove and refit clutch components, it is usually considered good practice to renew the clutch friction plate, pressure plate assembly and release bearing as a matched set, even if only one of these is actually worn enough to require renewal.*

6 When cleaning clutch components, observe the warning at the beginning of this Section regarding the hazards of handling the friction materials contained in clutch components; remove dust using a clean, dry cloth, and working in a well-ventilated atmosphere.
7 Check the friction plate facings for signs of wear, damage or oil contamination. If the friction material is cracked, burnt, scored or damaged, or if it is contaminated with oil or grease (shown by shiny black patches), the friction plate must be renewed.
8 If the friction material is still serviceable, check that the centre boss splines are unworn, that the torsion springs are in good condition and securely fastened, and that all the rivets are tightly fastened. If any wear or damage is found, the friction plate must be renewed.
9 If the friction material is fouled with oil, this must be due to an oil leak from the crankshaft left-hand oil seal, from the sump-to-cylinder block joint, or from the transmission input shaft; renew the seal or repair the joint, as appropriate, as described in Chapter 2A, 2B or 7A before installing the new friction plate.
10 Check the pressure plate assembly for obvious signs of wear or damage; shake it to check for loose rivets or worn or damaged fulcrum rings, and check that the drive straps securing the pressure plate to the cover do not show signs of overheating (such as a deep

yellow or blue discoloration). If the diaphragm spring is worn or damaged, or if its pressure is in any way suspect, the pressure plate assembly should be renewed.

11 Examine the machined bearing surfaces of the pressure plate and of the flywheel **(see illustration)**; they should be clean, completely flat and free from scratches or scoring. If either is discoloured from excessive heat or shows signs of cracks it should be renewed, although minor damage of this nature can sometimes be polished away using emery paper.

12 Check that the release bearing contact surface rotates smoothly and easily, with no sign of noise or roughness, and that the surface itself is smooth and unworn, with no signs of cracks, pitting or scoring. If there is any doubt about its condition, the bearing must be renewed; refer to Section 4 for guidance.

Refitting

Standard clutch

13 On reassembly, ensure that the bearing surfaces of the flywheel and pressure plate are completely clean, smooth and free from oil or grease. Use solvent to remove any protective grease from new components.

14 Offer up the friction plate so that its spring hub assembly faces away from the flywheel; observe any manufacturer's markings which show which way around the plate should be fitted **(see illustration)**.

15 Refit the pressure plate assembly to the flywheel, engaging it with its locating dowels; align the marks made on dismantling if the original pressure plate is being re-used. Fit the pressure plate bolts, hand-tightening them only at this stage, so that the friction plate can be rotated to aid alignment, if necessary.

16 The friction plate must now be centralised inside the pressure plate assembly, so that when the transmission is refitted, the input shaft will pass through the splines at the centre of the friction plate. This can be achieved by passing a large screwdriver or wrench extension bar through the friction plate and into the hole in the crankshaft; the friction plate can then be moved around until it is centred over the crankshaft hole. Alternatively, a universal clutch alignment tool can be used; these can be obtained from most car accessory shops. Ensure that the friction plate alignment is correct before proceeding any further.

17 When the friction plate is centralised, progressively tighten the pressure plate bolts in a diagonal sequence and to the specified torque setting.

18 Where applicable, remove the flywheel locking tool.

19 Apply a thin smear of high melting-point grease to the splines of the friction plate and the transmission input shaft.

20 Refit the transmission as described in Chapter 7A.

3.11 With the clutch removed, check the machined surface of the flywheel (arrowed)

Self Adjusting Clutch (SAC)

21 The clutch pressure plate is unusual, as there is a pre-adjustment mechanism to compensate for wear in the friction plate (this is termed by Saab as a self-adjusting clutch (SAC), which is slightly ambiguous as all hydraulic clutches are essentially self-adjusting). However, this mechanism must be reset before refitting the pressure plate. A new plate may be supplied preset, in which case this procedure can be ignored.

22 A large diameter bolt (M14 at least) long enough to pass through the pressure plate, a matching nut, and several large diameter washers, will be needed for this procedure. Mount the bolt head in the jaws of a sturdy bench vice, with one large washer fitted.

23 Offer the plate over the bolt, friction plate surface facing down, and locate it centrally over the bolt and washer – the washer should bear on the centre hub **(see illustration)**.

3.23 Mount a large bolt and washer in a vice, then fit the pressure plate over it

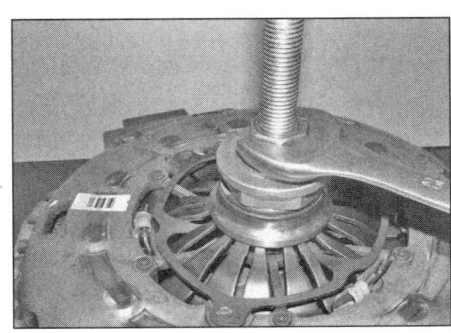

3.25a Tighten the nut until the spring adjuster is free to turn . . .

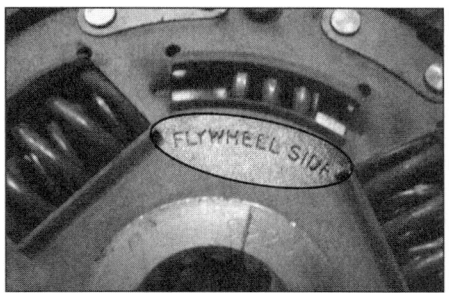

3.14 Place the friction plate against the flywheel; the stamped lettering FLYWHEEL SIDE should face towards the flywheel

24 Fit several further large washers over the bolt, so that they bear on the ends of the spring fingers, then add the nut and tighten by hand to locate the washers **(see illustration)**.

25 The purpose of the procedure is to turn the plate's internal adjuster disc so that the three small coil springs visible on the plate's outer surface are fully compressed. Tighten the nut just fitted until the adjuster disc is free to turn. Using a pair of thin-nosed, or circlip, pliers in one of the two windows in the top surface, open the jaws of the pliers to turn the adjuster disc anti-clockwise, so that the springs are fully compressed **(see illustrations)**.

26 Hold the pliers in this position, and then unscrew the centre nut. Once the nut is released, the adjuster disc will be gripped in position, and the pliers can be removed. Take the pressure plate from the vice, and it is ready to fit.

3.24 Fit large washers and a nut to the bolt and hand-tighten

3.25b . . . then open the jaws of suitable pliers to compress the springs

6•4 Clutch

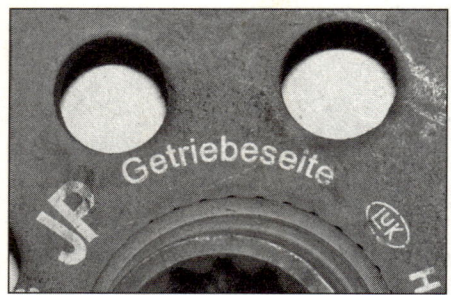

3.29 The lettering 'transmission side' or 'Getriebeseite' on the friction plate must face towards the transmission

3.30 Fit the pressure plate assembly over the friction plate

3.32 Centralise the friction plate using a clutch aligning tool or similar

27 On reassembly, ensure that the friction surfaces of the flywheel and pressure plate are completely clean, smooth, and free from oil or grease. Use solvent to remove any protective grease from new components.

28 Lightly grease the teeth of the friction plate hub with high melting-point grease. Do not apply too much; otherwise it may eventually contaminate the friction plate linings.

29 Locate the friction plate on the flywheel, making sure that the lettering 'transmission side' or 'Getriebeseite' points towards the transmission **(see illustration)**.

30 Refit the pressure plate assembly, aligning the marks made on dismantling (if the original pressure plate is re-used). Apply a little thread-locking compound then refit the pressure plate bolts, but tighten them only finger-tight so that the friction plate can still be moved **(see illustration)**.

31 The friction plate must now be centralised so that, when the transmission is refitted, its input shaft will pass through the splines at the centre of the friction plate.

32 Centralisation can be achieved by passing a screwdriver or other long bar through the friction plate and into the hole in the crankshaft. The friction plate can then be moved around until it is centred on the crankshaft hole. Alternatively, a clutch-aligning tool can be used to eliminate the guesswork; these can be obtained from most accessory shops **(see illustration)**.

33 When the friction plate is centralised, tighten the pressure plate bolts evenly and in a diagonal sequence to the specified torque setting.

34 Refit the transmission as described in Chapter 7A.

4 Clutch slave cylinder/ release bearing – removal and refitting

Note: *The clutch slave cylinder and thrust release bearing are integrated and can only be purchased as a complete assembly.*

Removal

1 Unless the complete engine/transmission unit is to be removed from the car and separated for major overhaul (see Chapter 2C), the clutch release cylinder can be reached by removing the transmission only, as described in Chapter 7A.

2 Wipe clean the outside of the slave cylinder then slacken the union nut and disconnect the hydraulic pipe. Wipe up any spilt fluid with a clean cloth.

3 Unscrew the three retaining bolts and slide the slave cylinder from the transmission input shaft **(see illustration)**. Where applicable, remove the sealing ring, which is fitted between the cylinder and transmission housing and discard it; a new one must be used on refitting. Whilst the cylinder is removed, take care not to allow any debris to enter the transmission unit.

4 The slave cylinder is a sealed unit and cannot be overhauled. If the cylinder seals have failed or the release bearing is noisy or rough in operation, then the complete unit must be renewed.

Refitting

5 Ensure the slave cylinder and transmission mating surfaces are clean and dry, then fit the new sealing ring to the transmission recess.

6 Lubricate the slave cylinder seal with a smear of transmission oil then carefully ease the cylinder along the input shaft and into position. Ensure the sealing ring is still correctly seated in its groove then refit the slave cylinder retaining bolts and tighten them to the specified torque.

7 Reconnect the hydraulic pipe to the slave cylinder, tightening its union nut to the specified torque.

8 Prime and bleed the slave cylinder with hydraulic fluid, as described in Section 6.

9 Refit the transmission unit as described in Chapter 7A.

5 Clutch master cylinder – removal and refitting

Removal

1 Remove the cover from the battery, then disconnect the battery negative cable and position it away from the terminal.

2 Referring to Chapter 11 for guidance, remove the sound insulating trim panel from underneath the facia, on the driver's side.

3 At the connection point between the master cylinder link rod and the clutch pedal, use a pair of long-nosed pliers to remove the clip from the spigot, and then pull off the link rod. Also release the clutch pedal return spring.

4 As a precaution, place a dustsheet under the clutch pedal in the footwell, to catch any hydraulic fluid spillage.

5 On right-hand drive models, from inside the engine bay, remove the cover from the top of the intake manifold.

6 On left-hand drive models, from inside the engine bay, undo the retaining bolts/nuts and remove the central electric unit and fuse holder from the left-hand side top strut mounting.

4.3 Slave cylinder

1 Release bearing   2 Hydraulic fluid pipe   3 Securing screws

Warning: *Observe the warnings given in Section 6, regarding the hazards of handling hydraulic fluid.*

7 From inside the engine bay, seal the flexible supply hose from the fluid reservoir, using a proprietary brake hose clamp between the fluid reservoir and the master cylinder.

8 Release the hose clip, and pull the supply hose off the master cylinder port. Be prepared for a small amount of hydraulic fluid loss; position a container or a wad of rags underneath the joint to catch any spillage.

9 Slide out the retaining clip and free the hydraulic delivery pipe from the front of the master cylinder **(see illustration)**. Plug the pipe end and master cylinder port to minimise fluid loss and prevent the entry of dirt. Where applicable, recover the sealing ring from the union and discard it; a new one must be used on refitting. Refit the retaining clip to the master cylinder groove, to prevent loss of the clip.

10 Remove the two nuts from the retaining bolts, and lift the master cylinder away from the bulkhead, guiding the link rod through the aperture. Recover the gasket and inspect it for damage; renew it if necessary.

Refitting

11 Refit the master cylinder by following the removal procedure in reverse. Noting the following points:
a) Make sure the delivery pipe to the master cylinder is secured correctly in position with the retaining clip.
b) Observe the specified torque wrench setting when tightening the master cylinder-to-pedal bracket nuts.
c) On completion, refer to Section 6 and bleed the hydraulic system.

6 Clutch hydraulic system – bleeding

5.9 Remove the nut securing the right-hand side of the clutch pedal/master cylinder bracket to the rear of the engine compartment bulkhead

1 Securing nut   2 Supply hose   3 Delivery pipe   4 Retaining clip

Warning: *Hydraulic fluid is poisonous; thoroughly wash off spills from bare skin without delay. Seek immediate medical advice if any fluid is swallowed or gets into the eyes. Certain types of hydraulic fluid are inflammable, and may ignite when brought into contact with hot components. When servicing any hydraulic system, it is safest to assume that the fluid IS inflammable, and to take precautions against the risk of fire as though it is petrol that is being handled. It is also hygroscopic (absorbs moisture from the air); excess moisture content lowers the fluid boiling point to an unacceptable level, resulting in a loss of hydraulic pressure. Old fluid may have suffered contamination, and should not be re-used. When topping-up or renewing the fluid, always use the recommended grade, and ensure that it comes from a freshly opened sealed container.*

General information

1 The correct operation of any hydraulic system is only possible after removing all air from the components and circuit; this is achieved by bleeding the system.

2 The manufacturer's stipulate that the system must be initially bled by the 'back-bleeding' method using Saab special bleeding equipment. This entails connecting a pressure bleeding unit containing fresh brake fluid to the release cylinder bleed screw, with a collecting vessel connected to the brake fluid master cylinder reservoir. The pressure bleeding unit is then switched on, the bleed screw is opened and hydraulic fluid is delivered under pressure, backwards, to be expelled from the reservoir into the collecting vessel. Final bleeding is then carried out in the conventional way.

3 In practice, this method would normally only be required if new hydraulic components have been fitted, or if the system has been completely drained of hydraulic fluid. If the system has only been disconnected to allow component removal and refitting procedures to be carried out, such as removal and refitting of the transmission (for example for clutch renewal) or engine removal and refitting, then it is quite likely that normal bleeding will be sufficient.

4 Our advice would therefore be as follows:
a) If the hydraulic system has only been partially disconnected, try bleeding by the conventional methods described in paragraphs 10 to 15, or 16 to 19.
b) If the hydraulic system has been completely drained and new components have been fitted, try bleeding by using the pressure bleeding method described in paragraphs 20 to 22.
c) If the above methods fail to produce a firm pedal on completion, it will be necessary to 'back-bleed' the system using Saab bleeding equipment, or suitable alternative equipment as described in paragraphs 23 to 28.

5 During the bleeding procedure, add only clean, unused hydraulic fluid of the recommended type; never re-use fluid that has already been bled from the system. Ensure that sufficient fluid is available before starting work.

6 If there is any possibility of incorrect fluid being already in the system, the hydraulic circuit must be flushed completely with uncontaminated, correct fluid.

7 If hydraulic fluid has been lost from the system, or air has entered because of a leak, ensure that the fault is cured before continuing further.

8 The bleed screw is located in the hose end fitting which is situated on the top of the transmission housing **(see illustration)**. On some models access to the bleed screw is limited and it may be necessary to jack up the front of the vehicle and support it on axle stands so that the screw can be reached from below, or remove the battery and battery box as described in Chapter 5A, so that the screw can be reached from above.

9 Check that all pipes and hoses are secure, unions tight and the bleed screw is closed. Clean any dirt from around the bleed screw.

6.8 Clutch hydraulic system bleed nipple (arrowed)

Bleeding procedure

Conventional method

10 Collect a clean glass jar, a suitable length of plastic or rubber tubing which is a tight fit over the bleed screw, and a ring spanner to fit the screw. The help of an assistant will also be required.

11 Unscrew the master cylinder fluid reservoir cap (the clutch shares the same fluid reservoir as the braking system), and top the master cylinder reservoir up to the upper (MAX) level line. Ensure that the fluid level is maintained at least above the lower level line in the reservoir throughout the procedure.

12 Remove the dust cap from the bleed screw. Fit the spanner and tube to the screw, place the other end of the tube in the jar, and pour in sufficient fluid to cover the end of the tube.

13 Have the assistant fully depress the clutch pedal several times to build-up pressure, and then maintain it on the final downstroke.

14 While pedal pressure is maintained, unscrew the bleed screw (approximately one turn) and allow the compressed fluid and air to flow into the jar. The assistant should maintain pedal pressure and should not release it until instructed to do so. When the flow stops, tighten the bleed screw again, have the assistant release the pedal slowly, and recheck the reservoir fluid level.

15 Repeat the steps given in paragraphs 13 and 14 until the fluid emerging from the bleed screw is free from air bubbles. If the master cylinder has been drained and refilled allow approximately five seconds between cycles for the master cylinder passages to refill.

Using a one-way valve kit

16 As their name implies, these kits consist of a length of tubing with a one-way valve fitted, to prevent expelled air and fluid being drawn back into the system; some kits include a translucent container, which can be positioned so that the air bubbles can be more easily seen flowing from the end of the tube.

17 The kit is connected to the bleed screw, which is then opened.

18 The user returns to the driver's seat, depresses the clutch pedal with a smooth, steady stroke, and slowly releases it; this is repeated until the expelled fluid is clear of air bubbles.

19 Note that these kits simplify work so much that it is easy to forget the clutch fluid reservoir level; ensure that this is maintained at least above the lower level line at all times.

Pressure-bleeding method

20 These kits are usually operated by the reservoir of pressurised air contained in the spare tyre. However, note that it will probably be necessary to reduce the pressure to a lower level than normal; refer to the instructions supplied with the kit.

21 By connecting a pressurised, fluid-filled container to the clutch fluid reservoir, bleeding can be carried out simply by opening the bleed screw and allowing the fluid to flow out until no more air bubbles can be seen in the expelled fluid.

22 This method has the advantage that the large reservoir of fluid provides an additional safeguard against air being drawn into the system during bleeding.

'Back-bleeding' method

23 The following procedure describes the bleeding method using Saab equipment. Alternative equipment is available and should be used in accordance with the maker's instructions.

24 Connect the pressure hose (88 19 096) to the bleed screw located in the hose end fitting situated on the top of the transmission housing (see illustration 6.8). Connect the other end of the hose to a suitable pressure-bleeding device set to operate at approximately 2.0 bars.

25 Attach the cap (30 05 451) to the master cylinder reservoir, and place the hose in a collecting vessel.

26 Switch on the pressure bleeding equipment, open the bleed screw, and allow fresh hydraulic fluid to flow from the pressure bleeding unit, through the system and out through the top of the reservoir and into the collecting vessel. When fluid free from air bubbles appears in the reservoir, close the bleed screw and switch off the bleeding equipment.

27 Disconnect the bleeding equipment from the bleed screw and reservoir.

28 Carry out a final conventional bleeding procedure as described in paragraphs 10 to 15, or 16 to 19.

All methods

29 When bleeding is complete, no more bubbles appear and correct pedal feel is restored, tighten the bleed screw securely (do not overtighten). Remove the tube and spanner, and wash off any spilt fluid. Refit the dust cap to the bleed screw.

30 Check the hydraulic fluid level in the master cylinder reservoir, and top-up if necessary (see Weekly checks).

31 Discard any hydraulic fluid that has been bled from the system; it will not be fit for re-use.

32 Check the operation of the clutch pedal. If the clutch is still not operating correctly, air must still be present in the system, and further bleeding is required. Failure to bleed satisfactorily after a reasonable repetition of the bleeding procedure may be due to worn master cylinder/release cylinder seals.

Priming the slave cylinder

33 Providing that the slave cylinder has not been removed from the transmission during servicing or repair, the procedure described in the preceding sub-section should cause all air to be expelled from the clutch hydraulic system. If however, a large amount of fluid has drained from the slave cylinder, allowing air to enter, or if a new slave cylinder has been fitted, the procedures described may not be sufficient to purge all the air from the slave cylinder. This is because the bleed nipple is positioned at the point where the hydraulic fluid enters the top of the slave cylinder – fluid is not forced through the slave cylinder during the bleeding process and the cylinder is not fully primed with hydraulic fluid. Consequently, some air may remain inside the slave cylinder housing.

34 To overcome this, the slave cylinder must be primed before the transmission is refitted to the transmission, as follows.

35 Take a 450 mm length of 8 mm diameter clear plastic hose and fit it to the slave cylinder bleed nipple.

36 Open the bleed nipple then press the release bearing along the input shaft sleeve towards the transmission, so that the piston is pushed fully into the slave cylinder. Catch any fluid ejected from the hose in a container.

37 Hold the hose vertically, and then fill it to a height of 350 mm (measured from the bleed nipple) with new brake fluid **(see illustration)**.

38 Connect a foot pump or bicycle pump to the end of the hose, ensuring a good seal. Gradually apply pressure to the hose using the pump, until the brake fluid flows into the slave cylinder. Allow the piston to be pushed out of the slave cylinder to the end of its travel, *but no further* – the resistance felt at the pump should increase when the piston reaches the end of its travel.

40 Press the release bearing back along the input shaft sleeve towards the transmission, so that the piston is pushed back fully into the slave cylinder. Allow the air bubbles now flowing through the brake fluid to escape from the end of the plastic hose.

41 Repeat the steps described in paragraphs 34 and 35 until no more air escapes from the slave cylinder.

42 Leave the piston fully retracted inside the slave cylinder, then disconnect and drain the plastic hose. Refit the transmission as described in Chapter 7A, without disturbing the slave cylinder. On completion, bleed the entire hydraulic system as described in the previous sub-sections.

6.37 Fill the hose to a height of 350 mm (measured from the bleed nipple) with new brake fluid

Chapter 7 Part A:
Manual transmission

Contents

	Section number		Section number
Gearchange linkage – adjustment	3	Speedometer drive – removal and refitting	7
Gearchange linkage – removal, inspection and refitting	4	Transmission – draining and refilling	2
General information	1	Transmission – removal and refitting	8
Oil seals – renewal	5	Transmission overhaul – general information	9
Reversing light switch – testing, removal and refitting	6		

Degrees of difficulty

Easy, suitable for novice with little experience	Fairly easy, suitable for beginner with some experience	Fairly difficult, suitable for competent DIY mechanic	Difficult, suitable for experienced DIY mechanic	Very difficult, suitable for expert DIY or professional

Specifications

General
Type .... Transversely mounted, front-wheel-drive layout, with integral transaxle differential/final drive. Five forward speeds, one reverse, all with synchromesh. Transmission code FM

Gear ratios (typical)
1st	3.38 : 1
2nd	1.76 : 1
3rd	1.12 : 1
4th	0.89 : 1
5th	0.70 : 1
Reverse	3.17 : 1
Final drive	3.61 : 1

Torque wrench settings
	Nm	lbf ft
Bellhousing-to-engine block bolts:		
M10	40	30
M12	70	52
Gear lever bracket-to-engine mounting bolts	8	6
Gear lever housing-to-floorpan bolts	8	6
Gear lever-to-selector rod bolt	22	16
Left-hand oil seal retaining housing	24	18
Oil level, filler and drain plugs	50	37
Reversing light switch	24	18
Selector rod pinch-bolt	22	16

1 General information

The manual transmission is mounted transversely in the engine bay, bolted directly to the engine. This layout has the advantage of providing the shortest possible drive path to the front wheels, as well as locating the transmission in the airflow through the engine bay, optimising cooling.

The unit is cased in aluminium alloy, and has oil filler, drain and level plugs. The case has two mating faces; one to the bellhousing, which is sealed with 'liquid gasket' compound, and one to the gearbox end cover, which sealed with a solid gasket. A 'labyrinth' vent at the top of the gearcase allows for air expansion, and permits gases produced by the lubricant to escape. The vent also houses a filter to keep out ingress of water and dirt.

Drive from the crankshaft is transmitted via the clutch to the gearbox input shaft, which is splined to accept the clutch friction plate. All six driving gears (pinions) are mounted on the input shaft; reverse, first and second speed pinions are journalled on sliding contact bearings, and the third, fourth and fifth speed pinions are carried on needle bearings.

The driven gears for all five forward speeds are mounted on the output shaft, again with third, fourth and fifth speed gears carried on needle bearings. Reverse gear is integral with the first/second speed synchromesh sleeve.

The pinions are in constant mesh with their corresponding driven gears, and are free to rotate independently of the gearbox shafts until a speed is selected. The difference in diameter and number of teeth between the pinions and gears provides the necessary shaft speed reduction and torque multiplication. Drive is then transmitted to the final drive gears/differential through the output shaft.

All gears are fitted with syncromeshes, including reverse. When a speed is selected, the movement of the floor-mounted gear lever is communicated to the gearbox by a selector rod. This in turn actuates a series of selector forks inside the gearbox, which are slotted onto the synchromesh sleeves. The sleeves, which are locked to the gearbox shafts, but can slide axially by means of splined hubs, press baulk rings into contact with the respective gear/pinion. The

7A•2 Manual transmission

2.4 Location of transmission plugs

1 Filler plug   2 Level plug   3 Drain plug

coned surfaces between the baulk rings and the pinion/gear act as a friction clutch, progressively matching the speed of the synchromesh sleeve (and hence the gearbox shaft) with that of the gear/pinion. The dog teeth on the outside of the baulk ring prevent the synchromesh sleeve ring from meshing with the gear/pinion until their speeds are exactly matched; this allows gearchanges to be carried out smoothly, and greatly reduces the noise and mechanical wear caused by rapid gearchanges.

When reverse gear is engaged, an idler gear is brought into mesh between the reverse pinion and the teeth on the outside of the first/second speed synchromesh sleeve. This arrangement introduces the necessary speed reduction, and also causes the output shaft to rotate in the opposite direction, allowing the vehicle to be driven in reverse.

2 Transmission – draining and refilling

General information

1 The gearbox is filled with the correct quantity and grade of oil at manufacture. The level must be checked regularly, and if necessary topped-up in accordance with the maintenance schedule (see Chapter 1A or 1B). However, there is no requirement to drain and renew the oil during the normal lifetime of the gearbox, unless repair or overhaul is carried out.

Draining

2 Take the car on a road test of sufficient length to warm the engine/transmission up to normal operating temperature; this will speed up the draining process, and any sludge and debris will be more likely to be drained out.
3 Park the car on level ground, switch off the ignition, and apply the handbrake firmly. For improved access, jack up the front of the car and support it securely on axle stands. **Note:** *The car must be lowered to the ground and parked on a level surface, to ensure accuracy when refilling and checking the oil level.* Undo the screws, and remove the engine undershield (where fitted).
4 Wipe clean the area around the filler plug, which is situated on the top surface of the transmission. Unscrew the plug from the casing, and recover the sealing washer **(see illustration)**.

2.5a Unscrew the drain plug from the transmission casing

2.5b Note that the drain plug contains a removable magnetic insert

5 Position a container with a capacity of at least 2.5 litres (ideally with a large funnel) under the drain plug **(see illustrations)**. The drain plug is located below the left-hand side driveshaft; use a wrench to unscrew the plug from the casing. Note that the drain plug contains an integral magnet, designed to catch the metal fragments produced as the transmission components wear. If the plug is clogged with a large amount of metal debris, this may be an early indication of component failure.
6 Allow all the oil to drain completely into the container. If the oil is still hot, take precautions against scalding. Clean both the filler and drain plugs thoroughly, paying particular attention to the threads. Discard the original sealing washers; they should be always renewed whenever they are disturbed.

Refilling

7 When the oil has drained out completely, clean the plug hole threads in the transmission casing. Fit a new sealing washer to the drain plug. Coat the thread with thread-locking compound, and tighten it into the transmission casing. If the car was raised for the draining operation, lower it to the ground.
8 When refilling the transmission, allow plenty of time for the oil level to settle completely before attempting to check it. Note that the car must be parked on a flat, level surface when checking the oil level. Use a funnel if necessary to maintain a gradual, constant flow and avoid spillage.
9 Refill the transmission with the specified grade and quantity of oil, then check the oil level as described in Chapter 1A or 1B. If a large quantity flows out when the level checking plug is removed, refit both the filler and level plugs, then drive the car for a short distance so that the new oil is distributed fully around the transmission components. Recheck the level again upon your return.
10 On completion, fit the filler and level plugs with new sealing washers. Coat their threads with thread-locking compound and tighten them securely. Refit the engine undershield (where applicable).

3 Gearchange linkage – adjustment

1 If the action of the gearchange linkage is stiff, slack or vague, the alignment between the gearchange linkage and the gearbox selector rod may be incorrect (also check the oil level and type is correct). The operations in the following paragraphs describe how to check and, if necessary, adjust the alignment.
2 Park the vehicle, apply the handbrake and switch off the ignition.
3 Locate the alignment hole at the top of the gearbox casing, adjacent to the part number plate **(see illustrations)**. Prise out the plug to expose the alignment hole. Select fourth gear, then take the locking tool (a screwdriver

Manual transmission 7A•3

with a shaft diameter of approximately 4 mm), and insert it into the alignment hole; this will lock the gearbox in fourth gear. **Note:** *Use a screwdriver; the handle will prevent the screwdriver from falling into the gearbox.*

4 Inside the car, remove the gear lever gaiter and mounting frame to expose the gearchange lever housing. Using a locking pin (screwdriver or drill bit) with a diameter of approximately 4 mm, insert it into the alignment hole in the side of the lever housing **(see illustration)**.

5 If the locking pin can be inserted without difficulty, then the gearchange linkage alignment is correct, and hence cannot be blamed for the poor gearchange quality; the best course of action now is to remove the gearchange linkage and inspect it for wear or damage – refer to Section 4 for details.

6 If the locking pin (screwdriver or drill bit) cannot be inserted into the alignment hole, then the gearchange linkage is incorrectly adjusted.

7 From the engine bay, at the point where the selector rod passes through the bulkhead, slacken the pinch-bolt adjacent to the rubber coupling to allow movement between the two halves of the selector rod **(see illustration)**.

8 Move the gearchange lever such that the locking pin (screwdriver shaft or drill bit) can be inserted into the alignment hole in the lever housing; ensure that the lever is still in the 4th gear position.

9 In the engine bay, tighten the pinch-bolt on the selector rod, observing the correct torque.

10 Remove the screwdriver from the gearbox alignment hole, and fit the plastic plug.

11 Remove the screwdriver from the gear lever housing alignment hole.

12 Refit the gear lever gaiter and mounting frame.

13 Before moving the vehicle, check that the gear lever can be moved from neutral to all six gear positions. **Note:** *Check the key can be removed while reverse is selected.*

14 Finally, road test the vehicle, and check that all gears can be obtained smoothly and precisely.

4 Gearchange linkage – removal, inspection and refitting

Gear lever

Housing removal

1 Park the vehicle, switch off the ignition, and apply the handbrake.

2 Referring to Chapter 11, remove the gear lever gaiter, centre console and side carpet trim panels.

3 Open the bonnet and undo the pinch-bolt clamp to the gear selector rod universal joint.

4 Slacken and remove the bolts that secure the gearchange lever housing to the floorpan.

5 Disconnect the wiring plug from the ignition switch, then lift the gear lever housing up and withdraw it from the vehicle. Unbolt the gear lever from the selector shaft **(see illustration)**.

3.3a Prise the plug from the alignment hole at the top of the transmission casing . . .

3.3b . . . then select fourth gear, and insert a screwdriver into the alignment hole; this will lock the transmission in fourth gear

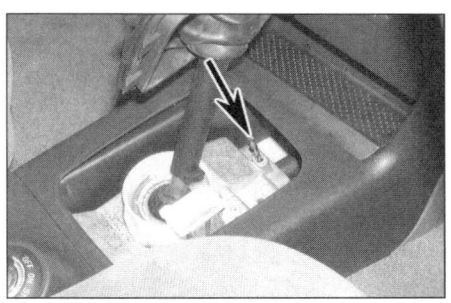

3.4 Inside the vehicle, insert a locking tool (drill bit) into the alignment hole in the side of the lever housing

3.7 Slackening the selector rod pinch-bolt

4.5 Gearchange lever and housing assembly

1. Gearchange lever
2. Gearchange lever-to-selector rod screw
3. Stop-plate
4. Locking plate
5. Selector rod
6. Screw and collar
7. Locking plate spring
8. Gearchange lever housing
9. Gear lever ball socket

7A•4 Manual transmission

4.6 Gearchange lever selector rod bushes (inset)
1 Gearchange lever   2 Sleeve   3 Bushes

5.4 Driveshaft intermediate shaft (arrowed)

Recover all bushes, washers and spacers, and remove the housing.

Inspection

6 It is possible to remove the gear lever from its housing, to allow the bearings to be inspected and renewed. It is most likely, however, that any slack found in the mechanism will be caused by worn bushes between the gear lever and the selector rod. Extract the bushes from the gear lever linkage **(see illustration)** and inspect them; if they appear worn or corroded, renew them.

Lever removal

7 To remove the gear lever from the housing **(see illustration 4.5)**, first withdraw the lockplate holder then unclip the locking plate spring.
8 Using a screwdriver, disengage the pawl, which is controlled by the ignition switch. Lift up the locking plate together with its plastic bracket and remove the stop-plate.
9 Set the gear lever to reverse, and then undo the screw securing the selector rod to the gear lever.
10 Remove the gear lever and ball socket by carefully pressing the three locking tabs on the socket using a screwdriver.

Refitting

11 Refit the gearchange lever and housing by reversing the removal sequence, noting the following:
a) Observe the correct torque for the gear lever-to-selector rod bolt and the gear lever housing-to-floorpan bolts.
b) Refit the wiring plug connector to the ignition switch.
c) On completion, check that the gear lever can be moved from neutral to all six gear positions. **Note:** Check the key can be removed while reverse is selected.
d) Finally, road test the vehicle, and check that all gears can be obtained smoothly and precisely.

Selector rod

Removal

12 Refer to the previous sub-section, and remove the gear lever and housing. Ensure that 4th gear is selected before removal. Remove the plug from the alignment hole in the top of the gearbox casing, and lock the gearbox in 4th gear using a suitable screwdriver, as described in Section 3.
13 From within the engine bay, at the point where the selector rod passes through the bulkhead, slacken the pinch-bolt collar to detach the selector rod from the gearbox.
14 From inside the cabin, carefully withdraw the selector rod through the bulkhead, taking care to avoid damaging the rubber grommet in the bulkhead.

Refitting

15 Lubricate the selector rod with silicone grease, and push it through the grommet in the bulkhead; do not tighten the pinch-bolt collar at the gearbox at this stage.
16 Refit the gear lever and housing as described earlier in this Section. Fit the bushes, and bolt the gear lever to the selector rod.
17 Lock the gear lever in 4th gear by inserting a screwdriver with a 4 mm shaft into the

5.5 Levering out the oil seal, using a block of wood to allow better leverage

alignment hole on the gear lever housing, with reference to Section 3.
18 Tighten the pinch-bolt collar on the selector rod at the gearbox, observing the specified torque.
19 Remove the screwdriver from the housing, and refit the gear lever gaiter.
20 Before moving the vehicle, check that the gear lever can be moved from neutral to all six gear positions. Finally, road test the vehicle, and check that all gears can be obtained smoothly and precisely.

5 Oil seals – renewal

Right-hand driveshaft oil seal

1 Park the vehicle on a level surface, apply the handbrake, and chock the rear wheels. Remove the wheel centre caps, and slacken the wheel bolts.
2 Apply the handbrake, then raise the front of the vehicle, rest it securely on axle stands and remove the roadwheels; refer to *Jacking and vehicle support* for guidance.
3 Refer to Section 2 and drain the transmission oil. Clean and refit the drain plug as described in Section 2.
4 Working from Chapter 8, remove the intermediate driveshaft and bearing assembly **(see illustration)**.
5 Using a suitable lever, prise the driveshaft oil seal out from the transmission housing **(see illustration)**, taking care not to damage the sealing surface. Discard the old seal.
6 Thoroughly clean the mating surfaces of the bearing housing and differential casing, take precautions to prevent debris entering the bearings of either assembly.
7 Lubricate the new oil seal with clean oil, and carefully refit it into the transmission housing, ensuring that it is seated squarely **(see illustration)**.

Manual transmission

8 Refer to Chapter 8 and refit the intermediate driveshaft and bearing assembly.
9 Refit the roadwheels, and lower the vehicle to the ground. Tighten the roadwheel bolts to the correct torque, and refit the wheel centre caps/trims.
10 Refer to Section 2 and refill the transmission with oil of the correct grade.

Left-hand driveshaft oil seal and O-ring

11 Park the vehicle on a level surface, apply the handbrake, and chock the rear wheels. Remove the wheel centre caps, and slacken the wheel bolts.
12 Apply the handbrake, then raise the front of the vehicle, rest it securely on axle stands and remove the roadwheels; refer to *Jacking and vehicle support* for guidance.
13 Refer to Section 2 and drain the transmission oil. Clean and refit the drain plug as described in Section 2.
14 Working from the relevant section of Chapter 8, disconnect the left-hand driveshaft from the transmission at the inboard universal joint.
15 Place a container beneath the driveshaft housing mating face, then slacken and withdraw the five retaining screws.
16 Withdraw the seal retaining housing from the transmission, then remove the O-ring seal from the housing (see illustration).
17 Note the fitted depth of the oil seal in its housing and the correct fitted position. Using a suitable lever, carefully prise the oil seal out from the housing, taking care not to damage the sealing surface.
18 Thoroughly clean the mating surfaces of the bearing housing and differential casing; take precautions to prevent debris entering the bearings of either assembly.
19 Lubricate the new oil seal with clean oil, and carefully refit it into the oil seal retaining housing, ensuring that it is seated squarely (see illustration 5.7).
20 Refit the O-ring seal to the seal retaining housing, then refit the housing to the transmission. Tighten the five retaining screws to the specified torque setting.
21 Refer to Chapter 8, and reconnect the left-hand driveshaft at the universal joint.
22 Refit the roadwheels, and lower the vehicle to the ground. Tighten the roadwheel bolts to the correct torque, and refit the wheel centre caps/trims.
23 Refer to Section 2 and refill the transmission with oil of the correct grade.

Input shaft oil seal

24 The oil seal is part of the clutch slave cylinder assembly and cannot be renewed separately; see Chapter 6, Section 4 (*Clutch slave cylinder/release bearing – removal and refitting*) for further information.

Selector rod oil seal

25 Clean off the area around the selector rod seal in the transmission, to prevent dirt entering the transmission.

5.7 Using a large socket to refit the oil seal, making sure it seats squarely

26 Ensure that 4th gear is selected, remove the plug from the alignment hole in the top of the gearbox casing, and lock the gearbox in 4th gear using a suitable 4 mm locking tool/screwdriver, as described in Section 3.
27 Slacken and remove the selector rod retaining bolt, then select 3rd gear to disengage the selector rod from the transmission.
28 Note the fitted position of the oil seal in its housing, then using a suitable lever carefully prise the oil seal out from the transmission, taking care not to damage the sealing surface.
29 Thoroughly clean the sealing surface and selector rod, check there are no burrs on the selector rod; take precautions to prevent debris entering the transmission.
30 Lubricate the new oil seal and selector rod with clean oil, and carefully refit the new seal into the transmission housing, ensuring that it is seated squarely.
31 Refit the selector rod and securely tighten the retaining bolt. Remove the locking tool/screwdriver from the housing, and check the gearchange linkage adjustment as described in Section 3.
32 Before moving the vehicle, check that the gear lever can be moved from neutral to all six gear positions. Check the transmission oil level. Finally, road test the vehicle, and check that all gears can be obtained smoothly and precisely.

6 Reversing light switch – testing, removal and refitting

Testing

1 Disconnect the battery negative cable, and position it away from the terminal.
2 Unplug the wiring harness from the reversing light switch at the connector. The switch is located on the rear of the transmission casing (see illustration).
3 Connect the probes of a continuity tester, or a multimeter set to the resistance function, across the terminals of the reversing light switch.
4 The switch contacts are normally open, so with any gear other than reverse selected; the tester/meter should indicate an open-circuit.

5.16 O-ring seal fitted to the driveshaft seal retaining housing

When reverse gear is then selected, the switch contacts should close, causing the tester/meter to indicate a short-circuit.
5 If the switch appears to be constantly open- or short-circuit, or is intermittent in its operation, it should be renewed.

Removal

6 If not already done, disconnect the battery negative cable, and position it away from the terminal.
7 Unplug the wiring harness from the reversing light switch at the connector.
8 Using a suitable spanner, unscrew the switch, recovering any washers that may be fitted; these must be refitted, to ensure that the correct clearance exists between the switch shaft and the reverse gear shaft.

Refitting

9 Refit the switch by reversing the removal procedure, reconnect the battery negative cable.

7 Speedometer drive – removal and refitting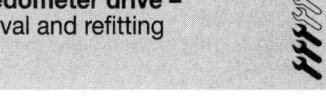

General information

1 Vehicles are fitted with an electronic transducer in place of the drivegear. This device measures the rotational speed of the transmission final drive, and converts the information into an electronic signal, which is then sent to the speedometer module in the instrument panel. The signal is also used as

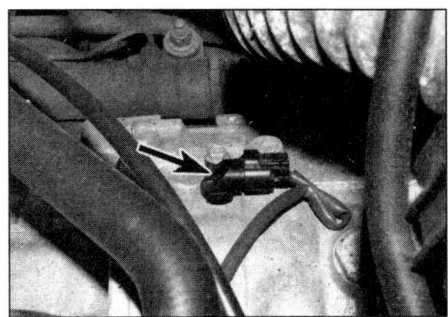

6.2 Reversing light switch location (arrowed)

7A•6 Manual transmission

8.6 Undo the battery tray bolts (arrowed)

8.17 Remove the lower flywheel cover plate (arrowed)

8.20 Remove the retaining bolts and nut (arrowed)

an input by the engine management system ECM (and where fitted, by the cruise control ECM, the trip computer and the traction control system ECM).

Removal

2 Locate the speed transducer, which is on the differential housing, at the rear of the transmission case.
3 Unplug the wiring harness from the transducer, at the connector.
4 Remove the transducer retaining screw, and unscrew the unit from the transmission casing.
5 Where applicable, recover and discard the O-ring seal.

Refitting

6 Refit the transducer by following the removal procedure in reverse. **Note:** *Where applicable, a new O-ring seal must be used on refitting.*

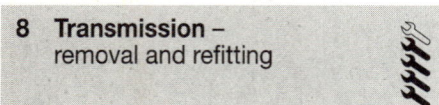

8 Transmission – removal and refitting

Note: *Refer to Chapter 2C for details on removal of the engine and transmission as a complete assembly.*

Removal

1 Park the vehicle on a level surface, apply the handbrake and chock the rear wheels. Remove the wheel centre caps, and slacken the wheel bolts.
2 Apply the handbrake, then raise the front of the vehicle, rest it securely on axle stands and remove the roadwheels; refer to *Jacking and vehicle support* for guidance.
3 Refer to Section 2 of this Chapter and drain the oil from the transmission. Refit and tighten the drain plug as described in Section 2.
4 Refer to Section 3, and set the gearchange linkage in a reference position, to ensure correct alignment of the linkage on refitting. Undo the retaining bolt and disconnect the gear linkage from the transmission.
5 Referring to Chapter 5A, remove the battery cover, disconnect both battery cables and remove the battery.
6 Unbolt the battery tray from the side of the engine bay **(see illustration)**.

7 Working from Chapter 6, seal off the clutch hydraulic system by fitting a clamp to the flexible section of the slave cylinder supply hose.
8 Release the securing clip and disconnect the connection for the fluid delivery at the top of the transmission. Refit the securing clip to the connector after it has been disconnected for safe-keeping. Plug both sides of the open fuel lines to minimise leakage and to prevent the ingress of foreign material.
9 Unplug the wiring connector from the reversing light switch at the transmission; refer to Section 6 of this Chapter for further information.
10 Slacken and remove the three upper transmission retaining bolts.
11 Unplug the wiring connector(s) from the oxygen sensor; refer to Chapter 4B, Section 2, for further information.
12 Slacken and remove the centre retaining nut from the rear engine mounting, and then slacken the three outer mounting bolts.
13 Position a lifting beam across the engine bay, locating the support legs securely in the sills at either side, in line with the strut top mountings. Hook the jib onto the engine lifting eyelet and raise it, so that the weight of the engine is taken off the transmission mounting. Most people won't have access to an engine lifting beam, but it may be possible to hire one. Alternatively, an engine hoist may be used to support the engine, but when using this method, bear in mind that if the vehicle is lowered on its axle stands to adjust the working height, for example, then the hoist will have to be lowered accordingly, to avoid straining the engine mountings.
14 Remove the subframe from under the engine with reference to Chapter 10.
15 Remove the three retaining bolts from the rear engine mounting bracket and withdraw it from the engine bay.
16 With reference to Chapter 8, remove the both driveshafts from the transmission.
17 Undo the retaining bolts and remove the lower cover plate from the flywheel **(see illustration)**. **Note:** *On HOT Aero models (B235R) also remove the bolts between the transmission and the engine oil sump.*
18 Undo the retaining bolt(s) and disconnect the earth cable(s) from the transmission housing.

19 Position a jack underneath the transmission, and raise it to take the weight of the unit. Check that nothing remains connected to the transmission before attempting to separate it from the engine.
20 Unscrew the bolts securing the left-hand engine/transmission mounting bracket to the bodywork and the centre nut from the mounting **(see illustration)**. Make sure the transmission is supported, taking care to avoid straining the other engine mountings as you do this. Withdraw the mounting from the inner wing panel and transmission.
21 Work around the circumference of the bellhousing, and remove the last retaining bolts from the bellhousing. Pull the transmission away from the engine, extracting the input shaft from the clutch friction plate – this task should only be attempted with the help of an assistant.

 Warning: *Maintain firm support on the transmission, to ensure that it remains steady on the jack head.*

22 When the input shaft is clear of the clutch friction plate, lower the transmission out of the engine bay using the jack.
23 At this point with the transmission removed, it would be a good opportunity to check and if required renew the clutch assembly, see Chapter 6 for further information

Refitting

24 Refit the transmission by reversing the removal procedure, noting the following points:
 a) Apply a smear of high melting-point grease to the transmission input shaft. Do not apply an excessive amount, as there is a possibility of the clutch friction plate being contaminated.
 b) Refit the subframe with reference to Chapter 10.
 c) Refit the engine/transmission mountings with reference to Chapter 2A or 2B.
 d) Observe the specified torque wrench settings (where applicable) when tightening all nuts and bolts after refitting.
 e) Bleed the clutch hydraulic system, referring to Chapter 6 for reference.
 f) On completion, if the transmission was drained, refill with the specified type and quantity of oil as described in Section 2.

9 Transmission overhaul – general information

The overhaul of a manual transmission is a complex (and often expensive) engineering task for the DIY home mechanic to undertake, which requires access to specialist equipment. It involves dismantling and reassembly of many small components, measuring clearances precisely, and if necessary adjusting them by the selection shims and spacers. Internal transmission components are also often difficult to obtain, and in many instances extremely expensive. Because of this, if the transmission develops a fault or becomes noisy, the best course of action is to have the unit overhauled by a specialist repairer, or to obtain an exchange reconditioned unit.

Nevertheless, it is not impossible for the more experienced mechanic to overhaul the transmission, if the special tools are available and the job is carried out in a deliberate step-by-step manner, to ensure that nothing is overlooked.

The tools necessary for an overhaul include internal and external circlip pliers, bearing pullers, a slide hammer, a set of pin punches, a dial test indicator (dial gauge), and possibly a hydraulic press. In addition, a large, sturdy workbench and a vice will be required.

During dismantling of the transmission, make careful notes of how each component is fitted, to make reassembly easier and accurate.

Before dismantling the transmission, it will help if you have some idea of where the problem lies. Certain problems can be closely related to specific areas in the transmission, which can make component examination and renewal easier. Refer to *Fault finding* at the end of this manual for more information.

Notes

Chapter 7 Part B:
Automatic transmission

Contents

	Section number
Fluid cooler – general information	7
General information	1
Oil seals – renewal	6
Selector cable – adjustment	3
Selector cable – removal and refitting	4
Selector lever assembly – removal and refitting	5
Transmission – removal and refitting	9
Transmission control system electrical components – removal and refitting	8
Transmission fluid – draining and refilling	2
Transmission overhaul – general information	10

Degrees of difficulty

Easy, suitable for novice with little experience	Fairly easy, suitable for beginner with some experience	Fairly difficult, suitable for competent DIY mechanic	Difficult, suitable for experienced DIY mechanic	Very difficult, suitable for expert DIY or professional

Specifications

General
Type .... Five-speed electronically controlled automatic with manual Sentronic change function. Transmission code FA57

Torque wrench settings

	Nm	lbf ft
Drain plug	40	30
Driveplate/lower bellhousing cover plate	7	5
Engine-to-transmission unit bolts	See Chapter 2A or 2B	
Fluid filler pipe retaining nut	22	16
Fluid temperature sensor	25	18
Fluid temperature sensor cover plate bolt	25	18
Input shaft speed sensor bolt	6	4
Gear selector position sensor:		
Switch-to-transmission nut/bolt	8	6
Lever to position sensor	25	18
Left-hand engine mounting	See Chapter 2A or 2B	
Oil cooler unions	27	20
Output shaft speed sensor bolt	6	4
Subframe mounting bolts	See Chapter 10	
Torque converter-to-driveplate bolts	30	22

7B•2 Automatic transmission

1 General information

1 The automatic transmission is an electronically-controlled five-speed unit, incorporating a lock-up function. It consists mainly of a planetary gear unit, a torque converter with lock-up clutch, a hydraulic control system and an electronic control system. The unit is controlled by the electronic control module (ECM) via four electrically-operated solenoid valves. The transmission unit has three driving modes: normal (economy), sport and winter modes.

2 The normal (economy) mode is the standard mode for driving in which the transmission shifts up at relatively low engine speeds to combine reasonable performance with economy. If the transmission unit is switched into sport mode, using the button on the selector lever, the transmission shifts up only at high engine speeds, giving improved acceleration and overtaking performance. When the transmission is in sport mode, the indicator light in the instrument panel is illuminated. If the transmission is switched into winter mode, using the button on the selector lever indicator panel, the transmission will select third gear as the vehicle pulls away from a standing start; this helps to maintain traction on very slippery surfaces.

3 The torque converter provides a fluid coupling between engine and transmission, which acts as an automatic clutch, and also provides a degree of torque multiplication when accelerating.

4 The epicyclic gear train provides one of the forward or reverse gear ratios, according to which of its component parts are held stationary or allowed to turn. The components of the gear train are held or released by brakes and clutches that are activated by the control unit. A fluid pump within the transmission provides the necessary hydraulic pressure to operate the brakes and clutches.

5 Driver control of the transmission is by a seven-position selector lever. The 'drive' D position, allows automatic changing throughout the range of all five gear ratios. An automatic kickdown facility shifts the

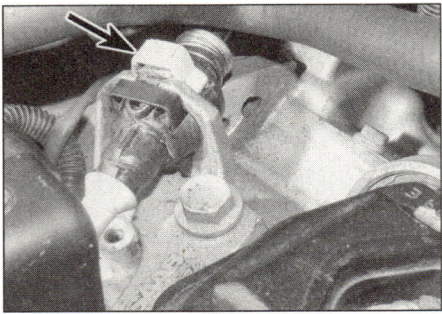

3.4 Remove the locking clip (arrowed) from the selector cable

transmission down a gear if the accelerator pedal is fully depressed.

6 Due to the complexity of the automatic transmission, any repair or overhaul work must be left to a Saab dealer with the necessary special equipment for fault diagnosis and repair. The contents of the following Sections are therefore confined to supplying general information, and any service information and instructions that can be used by the owner.

2 Transmission fluid – draining and refilling

Refer to the information given in Chapter 1A or 1B.

3 Selector cable – adjustment

1 Operate the selector lever throughout its entire range and check that the transmission engages the correct gear indicated on the selector lever position indicator.

2 Check the play in the selector lever while it's in position N and position D. If it is not the same, then adjustment is necessary, continue as follows.

3 Inside the vehicle, position the selector lever in the P (Park) position.

4 Working in the engine compartment, lift the adjustment retaining clip on the transmission end of the selector cable (see illustration).

5 Locate the lever on the transmission range switch, to which the selector cable is connected. Position the lever so that the transmission is set in the Park position.

6 With the handbrake in the off position, roll the car until the Park interlock engages.

7 With the aid of an assistant, hold the selector lever rearward in the park position to take up the free play.

8 Working in the engine compartment, press down the adjustment clip at the transmission end to lock the cable.

9 Check the selector lever as described in paragraphs 1 and 2, if necessary, repeat the adjustment procedure.

10 On completion, road test the vehicle to check the correct operation of the gearchange.

4 Selector cable – removal and refitting

Removal

1 Working in the engine compartment, to gain access to the transmission end of the selector cable, remove the battery and battery tray (see Chapter 5A).

2 With the gear selector in the Park position, locate the lever on the transmission range switch, to which the selector cable is connected. Remove the retaining nut and detach the lever from the range switch (see illustration).

3 Withdraw the locking clip and disengage the selector cable from the transmission casing (see illustrations).

4 Remove the selector lever assembly, as described in Section 5.

5 Work back along the cable, noting its correct routing, and free it from all the relevant retaining clips. Free the cable grommet from the bulkhead and remove it from the vehicle.

6 Examine the cable, looking for worn end fittings or a damaged outer casing, and for signs of fraying of the inner cable. Check the cable's operation; the inner cable should move smoothly and easily through the outer casing. Remember that a cable that appears serviceable when tested off the car may well be much heavier in operation when curved into its working position. Renew the cable if

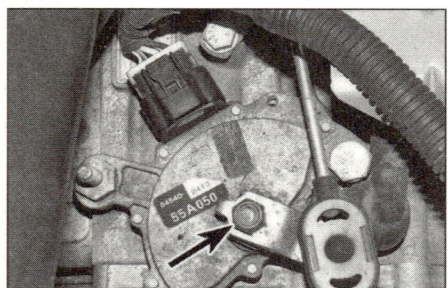

4.2 Remove the retaining nut (arrowed) and detach the selector lever from the position sensor

4.3a Withdraw the locking clip . . .

4.3b . . . and release the selector cable from the bracket

Automatic transmission 7B•3

5.2a Remove the locking clip . . .

5.2b . . . and the anti-rattle clip . . .

5.2c . . . then withdraw the pin from the selector

it shows any signs of excessive wear or any damage.

Refitting

7 Refitting is a reversal of removal, noting the following points.
8 Refit the selector lever assembly, as described in Section 5.
9 Ensure the cable is correctly routed and passes through the selector lever housing then located securely in the bulkhead.
10 Pass the transmission end of the cable through its mounting bracket and clip the outer cable securely in position. Connect the cable end to the transmission lever then secure it in position with the locking clip. Fit the lever to the transmission range switch, then fit the nut and tighten it securely.

5 Selector lever assembly – removal and refitting

Removal

1 Remove the centre console, and rear compartment air ducts, as described in Chapter 11.
2 Remove the locking clip and anti-rattle clip, the drive out the pin while removing the end of the cable from the ball **(see illustrations)**.
3 Slacken and remove the retaining bolts then lift the gear selector lever housing away from the floor pan.
4 Disconnect any wiring block connectors from the gear selector housing, release any cable-ties from the wiring loom **(see illustrations)**.
5 Using a screwdriver, withdraw the securing clip and release the selector cable from the housing **(see illustrations)**. Remove the gear selector housing from the vehicle.
6 Inspect the selector lever mechanism for signs of wear or damage.

Refitting

7 Refitting is a reversal of removal, noting the following points.
8 Refit the cable to the selector lever and housing, making sure all securing clips are correctly located.
9 Adjust the selector cable as described in Section 3.
10 On completion, refit the centre console, as described in Chapter 11, and refit all components removed to gain access to the transmission end of the cable.

6 Oil seals – renewal

Driveshaft oil seals

1 Refer to Chapter 7A.

Torque converter oil seal

2 Remove the transmission as described in Section 9.
3 Carefully slide the torque converter off the transmission shaft whilst being prepared for fluid spillage.
4 Note the correct fitted position of the seal in the oil pump housing then carefully lever the seal out of position taking care not to mark the housing or input shaft.
5 Remove all traces of dirt from the area around the oil seal aperture then press the new seal into position, ensuring its sealing lip is facing inwards.
6 Lubricate the seal with clean transmission fluid then carefully ease the torque converter into position.
7 Refit the transmission (see Section 9).

7 Fluid cooler – general information

The transmission fluid cooler is an integral part of the radiator assembly. Refer to Chapter 3 for removal and refitting details. If the cooler is damaged the complete radiator assembly must be renewed.

5.4a Disconnect the wiring connector from the gear selector . . .

5.4b . . . and the ignition switch

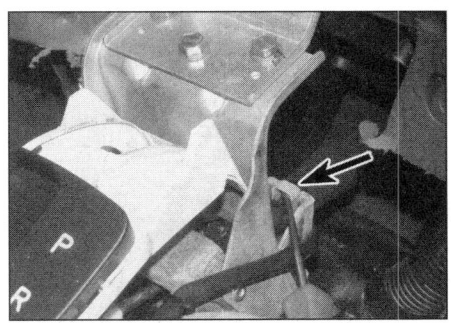

5.5a Using a screwdriver lever out the securing clip . . .

5.5b . . . and release the selector cable (arrowed) from the housing

8.4 Remove the securing nut (arrowed) to release the fluid dipstick tube

8.5 Remove the retaining nut (arrowed) and detach the selector lever from the position sensor

8.9 Automatic transmission control module (arrowed), next to the engine management control module

8 Transmission control system electrical components – removal and refitting

Gear selector position sensor

General information

1 As well as informing the transmission ECM which gear is currently selected, the gear selector position sensor also contains contacts which control the operation of the reversing lights relay, and the starter motor inhibitor relay.

Removal

2 Remove the battery from its mounting tray as described in Chapter 5A, then undo the retaining bolts and remove the battery tray.
3 Where necessary, release the power steering fluid hose from its mounting bracket and move it to one side.
4 Where applicable, undo the securing nut and release the transmission fluid dipstick tube from the side of the transmission position sensor (see illustration). Note: *Later models do not have a dipstick tube fitted.*
5 Select Park, then undo the retaining nut and disconnect the selector lever from the transmission position sensor (see illustration).
6 Slacken and remove the nuts/bolts that secure the gear selector position sensor to the transmission.
7 Unplug the position sensor wiring connector, then withdraw the position sensor from the transmission selector shaft and remove it from the engine compartment.

Refitting

8 Refitting is a reversal of removal. Tighten the switch securing nut/bolt to the specified torque and on completion, check the adjustment of the selector cable with reference to Section 3.

Electronic control module (ECM)

Removal

9 The ECM is located in the front passenger footwell, behind the glovebox (see illustration). Prior to removal, disconnect the battery negative terminal.
10 Prise out the retaining clips and remove the undercover from the passenger side of the facia. Remove the glovebox from the facia (see Chapter 11) to gain access to the ECM.
11 Release the retaining clip and disconnect the wiring connector from the ECM. Release the mounting bracket from the body and remove the ECM from the vehicle.

Refitting

12 Refitting is the reverse of removal, ensuring that the wiring is securely reconnected.

Input and output shaft speed sensors

Removal

13 The speed sensors are fitted to the top of the transmission unit. The input shaft speed sensor is the front of the two sensors and is nearest to the left-hand end of the transmission. The output shaft sensor is the rear of the two (see illustration).
14 To gain access to the sensors, remove the battery from its mounting plate as described in Chapter 5A. Access can be further improved by unclipping the coolant expansion tank from its mountings and positioning it clear.
15 Disconnect the wiring connector located on a mounting bracket at the left hand end of the cylinder head. Wipe clean the area around the relevant sensor.
16 Undo the retaining bolt and remove the sensor from the transmission. Remove the sealing ring from the sensor and discard it, a new one should be used on refitting.

Refitting

17 Fit the new sealing ring to the sensor groove and lubricate it with a smear of transmission fluid.
18 Ease the sensor into position then refit the retaining bolt and tighten it to the specified torque setting. Reconnect the wiring connector.
19 Refit the battery and clip the expansion tank (where necessary) back into position.

Fluid temperature sensor

Removal

20 The fluid temperature sensor is screwed into the base of the transmission unit, at the front. Before removing the sensor, disconnect the battery negative terminal.
21 Firmly apply the handbrake then jack up the front of the vehicle and support it on axle stands (see *Jacking and vehicle support*).
22 Trace the wiring back from the sensor, noting its correct routing. Disconnect the wiring connector and free the wiring from its retaining clips.
23 Undo the retaining bolts and remove the cover plate from the sensor (see illustration).

8.13 Automatic transmission input shaft speed sensor (A) and output shaft speed sensor (B) locations

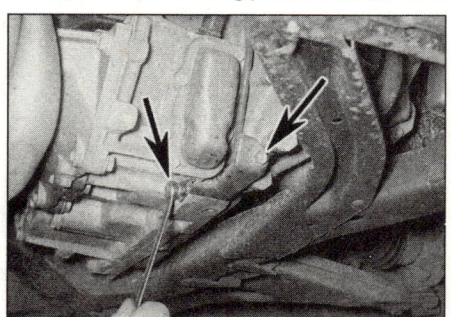

8.23 Undo the retaining bolts (arrowed) and remove the cover plate . . .

8.24 . . . to gain access to the fluid temperature sensor (arrowed)

Automatic transmission 7B•5

9.4a Disconnect the earth cable (arrowed) from the front of the transmission ...

9.4b ... and the earth cable (arrowed) from the end of the transmission

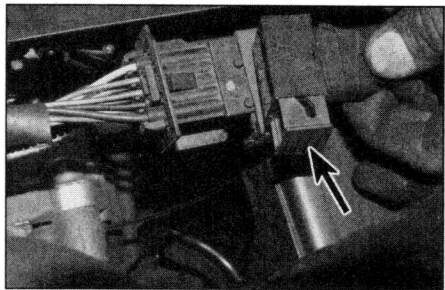

9.8 Release the securing clip (arrowed) and disconnect the wiring block connectors

24 Wipe clean the area around the sensor and have a suitable plug ready to minimise fluid loss as the sensor is removed (see illustration).
25 Unscrew the sensor and remove it from the transmission unit along with its sealing washer. Quickly plug the transmission aperture and wipe up any spilt fluid.

Refitting

26 Fit a new sealing washer to the sensor then remove the plug and quickly screw the sensor into the transmission unit. Tighten the sensor to the specified torque and wipe up any spilt fluid. Refit the cover plate and tighten its retaining bolts to the specified torque.
27 Ensure the wiring is correctly routed and retained by all the necessary clips then securely reconnect the wiring connector.
28 Lower the vehicle to the floor and reconnect the battery. Check the transmission fluid level as described in Chapter 1A or 1B.

9 Transmission – removal and refitting

Note 1: *Refer to Chapter 2C for details on removal of the engine and transmission as a complete assembly.*
Note 2: *New torque converter-to-driveplate bolts and fluid cooler union sealing rings will be required on refitting.*

Removal

1 Chock the rear wheels, apply the handbrake, and place the selector lever in the N (Neutral) position. Jack up the front of the vehicle, and securely support it on axle stands (see *Jacking and vehicle support*). Remove both front roadwheels then remove the retaining screws and fasteners and (where necessary) remove the undercover panels from beneath the engine/transmission unit.
2 Drain the transmission fluid as described in Chapter 1A or 1B, then refit the drain plug and tighten it to the specified torque.
3 Remove the battery from its mounting plate as described in Chapter 5A, then undo the retaining bolts and remove the battery tray.
4 Disconnect the battery earthing cable(s) from the transmission casing (see illustrations).

Release the cabling from the transmission fluid dipstick tube.
5 Withdraw the dipstick and its tube from the transmission casing and plug the open hole, to prevent contamination.
6 Disconnect the breather hose (where fitted) from the top of the transmission unit.
7 Disconnect the selector cable from the transmission as described in Sections 3 and 4.
8 Unplug the transmission control system wiring at the two connectors, located at the front of the battery tray (see illustration).
9 Trace the wiring back from the transmission switches and sensors, and disconnect the various connectors by lifting their retaining clips. Release the main wiring harness from any clips or ties securing it to the transmission unit.
10 Remove the air cleaner and intake ducting as described in Chapter 4A or 4B. Remove the cover panel from the top of the throttle body and remove the intercooler-to-throttle body ducting.
11 Position a lifting beam across the engine bay, locating the support legs securely in the sills at either side, in line with the strut top mountings. Hook the jib onto the engine lifting eyelet and raise it, so that the weight of the engine is taken off the transmission mounting. Most people won't have access to an engine lifting beam, but it may be possible to hire one. Alternatively, an engine hoist may be used to support the engine, but when using this method, bear in mind that if the vehicle is lowered on its axle stands to adjust the working height, for example, then the hoist

will have to be lowered accordingly, to avoid straining the engine mountings.
12 Unbolt and remove the exhaust system front pipe and catalytic converter (see Chapter 4A or 4B).
13 Slacken the unions and disconnect the transmission fluid cooler pipes from the front of the transmission casing. Recover the sealing washers.
14 Slacken and remove the three upper transmission retaining bolts.
15 Slacken and remove the centre retaining nut from the rear engine mounting, and then slacken the three outer mounting bolts.
16 Remove the subframe from under the engine with reference to Chapter 10.
17 Remove the three retaining bolts from the rear engine mounting bracket and withdraw it from the engine bay.
18 With reference to Chapter 8, remove the both driveshafts from the transmission.
19 Undo the retaining bolts and remove the lower cover plate from the flywheel. Using the crankshaft pulley to turn the engine, slacken and remove all the torque converter retaining bolts as they become accessible (see illustrations). Discard the retaining bolts; new ones must be used on refitting. Note: *As the transmission is removed, the torque converter must stay in the transmission bellhousing and not slide off the transmission shaft. A bracket can be made and bolted to the bellhousing to hold the torque converter in place.*
20 Position a jack underneath the transmission, and raise it to take the weight of the unit. Check that nothing remains connected

9.19a Undo the retaining bolts (arrowed) and remove the cover plate ...

9.19b ... then undo the torque converter bolts (one arrowed) – turn engine to access other bolts

9.21 Undo the bolts and nut (arrowed) to remove mounting

to the transmission before attempting to separate it from the engine.

21 Unscrew the bolts securing the left-hand engine/transmission mounting bracket to the bodywork and the centre nut from the mounting **(see illustration)**. Make sure the transmission is supported, taking care to avoid straining the other engine mountings as you do this. Withdraw the mounting from the inner wing panel and transmission.

22 Work around the circumference of the bellhousing, and remove the last retaining bolts from the bellhousing.

⚠ **Warning: Maintain firm support on the transmission, to ensure that it remains steady on the jack head.**

23 Make a final check that any components which would prevent the removal of the transmission from the car have been removed or disconnected. Ensure that components such as the gear selector cable are secured so that they cannot be damaged on removal.

24 Withdraw the transmission from the engine; keep the unit horizontal until the bellhousing is clear of the driveplate and its mounting dowels. Make sure the torque converter does not slide off the transmission shaft.

25 Slowly lower the transmission assembly from the engine compartment, making sure that it clears the components on the surrounding panels. Lower the assembly to the ground and remove it from the underside of the engine compartment.

Refitting

26 The transmission is refitted by a reversal of the removal procedure, bearing in mind the following points.
a) Prior to refitting, remove all traces of old locking compound from the torque converter threads by running a tap of the correct thread diameter and pitch down the holes. In the absence of a suitable tap, use one of the old bolts with slots cut in its threads.
b) Prior to refitting, ensure the engine/transmission locating dowels are correctly positioned and apply a smear of molybdenum disulphide grease to the torque converter locating pin and its centring bush in the crankshaft end.
c) Once the transmission and engine are correctly joined, refit the securing bolts, tightening them to the specified torque setting.
d) Fit the new torque converter-to-driveplate bolts and tighten them lightly only to start then go around and tighten them to the specified torque setting in a diagonal sequence.
e) Tighten all nuts and bolts to the specified torque (where given).
f) Renew the driveshaft oil seals (see Chapter 7A) and refit the driveshafts to the transmission as described in Chapter 8.
g) Fit new sealing rings to the fluid cooler hose unions and ensure both unions are securely retained by their clips.
h) When refitting the subframe, ensure that the spacer washers are fitted to the two rearmost bolts and observe the alignment markings made during removal. Do not tighten the subframe bolt to their final torque until the full weight of the engine and transmission assembly is resting upon it.
i) Ensure that all earthing cables are securely refitted.
j) On completion, refill the transmission with the specified type and quantity of fluid as described in Chapter 1A or 1B and adjust the selector cable as described in Section 3.

10 Transmission overhaul – general information

1 In the event of a fault occurring with the transmission, it is first necessary to determine whether it is of a mechanical or hydraulic nature, and to do this, special test equipment is required. It is therefore essential to have the work carried out by a Saab dealer if a transmission fault is suspected.

2 Do not remove the transmission from the car for possible repair before professional fault diagnosis has been carried out, since most tests require the transmission to be in the vehicle.

Chapter 8
Driveshafts

Contents

	Section number
Driveshaft gaiters – renewal	4
Driveshafts – inspection, joint renewal and cleaning	3
Driveshafts – removal and refitting	2
General information	1
Intermediate driveshaft and support bearing – removal, overhaul and refitting	5

Degrees of difficulty

Easy, suitable for novice with little experience	Fairly easy, suitable for beginner with some experience	Fairly difficult, suitable for competent DIY mechanic	Difficult, suitable for experienced DIY mechanic	Very difficult, suitable for expert DIY or professional

Specifications

General
Driveshaft type .... Steel shafts with outer constant velocity joints and inner tripode joints. Intermediate shaft from right-hand side of transmission to driveshaft

Lubrication (overhaul or repair only) .... Use only special grease supplied in sachets with gaiter/overhaul kits; joints are otherwise prepacked with grease and sealed

Joint grease quantity
Outer joint .... 120 g
Inner joint:
   Automatic transmission .... 200 g
   Manual transmission .... 185 g

Torque wrench settings

	Nm	lbf ft
Driveshaft/hub nut*	230	170
Front suspension lower balljoint clamp bolt	50	37
Intermediate driveshaft bracket-to-engine bolts	30	22
Intermediate driveshaft bracket-to-engine bolts:		
Petrol models	47	35
Diesel models	20	15
Wheel bolts	110	81

*Do not re-use

8•2 Driveshafts

2.2a Use a small chisel to free the metal dust cover . . .

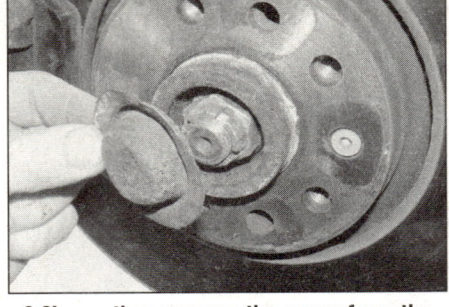

2.2b . . . then remove the cover from the hub flange

2.3a With an assistant depressing the footbrake pedal, loosen the hub nut . . .

2.3b . . . then unscrew it completely

2.4 Disconnect the sensor arm (arrowed) from the lower arm

1 General information

Power is transmitted from the transmission final drive to the roadwheels by the driveshafts. The outer joints on all models are of 'constant velocity' (CV) type, consisting of six balls running in axial grooves. The driveshaft outer joints incorporate stub axles, which are splined to the hubs located in the front suspension hub carriers. The inner 'universal' joints are designed to move in a smaller arc than the outer CV joints, and can also move axially to allow for movements of the front suspension. They are of tripod type consisting of a three-armed 'spider' with needle bearings and outer race splined to the driveshaft, and an outer housing with three corresponding cut-outs for the bearing races to slide in.

An intermediate shaft, with its own support bearing, is fitted between the transmission and right-hand driveshaft – a design which equalises driveshaft angles at all suspension positions, and reduces driveshaft flexing, improving directional stability under hard acceleration.

The universal and CV joints allow smooth transmission of drive to the wheels at all steering and suspension angles. The joints are protected by rubber gaiters that are packed with grease, to provide permanent lubrication. In the event of wear being detected, the joint can be renewed separately from the driveshaft. The joints do not require additional lubrication, unless they have been renovated or the rubber gaiters have been damaged, allowing the grease to become contaminated. Refer to Chapter 1A or 1B for guidance in checking the condition of the driveshaft gaiters.

2 Driveshafts – removal and refitting

Removal

1 Jack up the front of the vehicle and support it on axle stands (see *Jacking and vehicle support*). Remove the relevant roadwheel and, where applicable, the engine undershield.

2 Tap off the metal dust cover for access to the hub nut **(see illustrations)**. Note that the cover cannot be removed with the roadwheel in position, so it is not possible to loosen the hub nut before raising the front of the vehicle.

3 Temporarily refit two of the roadwheel bolts and tighten them to hold the brake disc onto the hub flange, then have an assistant depress the footbrake pedal, while the hub nut is being loosened. Unscrew and remove the hub nut **(see illustrations)**. Discard the nut, as a new one must be used on refitting.

4 Remove the inner splash cover from inside the wheel arch. If removing the right-hand driveshaft on models fitted with a headlamp position sensor, disconnect the sensor arm from the lower suspension arm **(see illustration)**, and if required, unbolt the sensor from its mounting bracket and position it to one side.

5 Unscrew the clamp bolt securing the front suspension lower balljoint to the hub carrier, then lever down the lower arm and disconnect the balljoint. Secure the lower arm in this position using a block of wood positioned between the arm and anti-roll bar.

6 If removing the left-hand driveshaft, carefully lever the inner joint from the transmission. Be prepared for some loss of oil, and take care not to force the inner joint apart.

7 If removing the right-hand driveshaft, use a soft-faced mallet to drive the driveshaft from the intermediate shaft. Note that the right-hand driveshaft inner joint splines incorporate a circlip, which engages a groove inside the splined end of the intermediate shaft.

8 Release the brake hydraulic hose and ABS cable from the front suspension strut.

9 Pull out the front suspension strut, then use the soft-faced mallet to drive the driveshaft out from the hub. Withdraw it from under the vehicle **(see illustrations)**. Take care not to

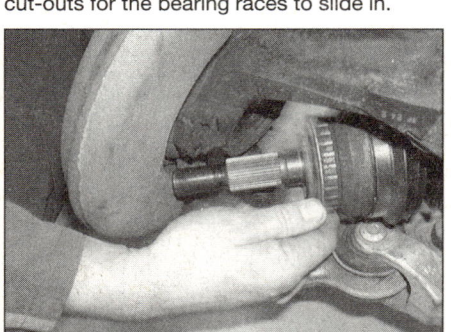

2.9a Removing the driveshaft from the splines in the hub

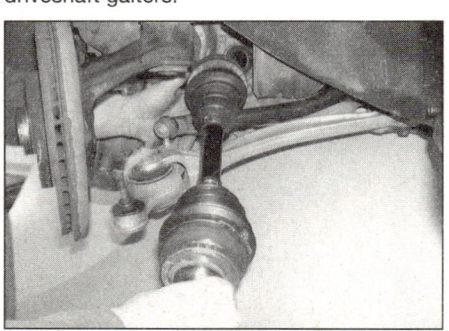

2.9b Withdrawing the driveshaft from the transmission

Driveshafts 8•3

2.11 Checking the circlip on the inner end of the driveshaft

damage the hub nut threads on the driveshaft. If the driveshaft is tight, a suitable three-legged puller may be used to force it out of the hub.

Refitting

10 Before refitting the left-hand driveshaft, check the oil seal in the transmission and if necessary renew it with reference to Chapter 7A or 7B. Lightly smear the oil seal with fresh transmission oil.
11 On both left- and right-hand driveshafts, check that the inner retaining circlip is in good condition and correctly located in the driveshaft groove **(see illustration)**.
12 Ensure that the splines at the outboard end of the driveshaft are clean, then pull out the strut and insert the driveshaft through the hub into engagement with the hub splines. Refit the new hub nut and hand-tighten it at this stage.
13 Lubricate the splines at the inner end of the driveshaft with transmission oil, then locate the inner end in the transmission sun gear (left-hand side) or intermediate shaft (right-hand side), pressing it fully in until the circlip is heard to snap into the groove.
14 Attach the brake hydraulic hose and ABS cable to the front suspension strut.
15 Relocate the front suspension lower balljoint to the hub carrier, make sure it is fully entered, then insert the clamp bolt and tighten to the specified torque.
Caution: Make sure that the balljoint is fully entered in the hub carrier.
16 Refit the headlamp position sensor and inner splash cover as applicable.
17 With two of the roadwheel bolts holding the brake disc in position, have an assistant depress the footbrake pedal, and then tighten the hub nut to the specified torque.
18 Tap the metal dust cover onto the hub flange.
19 Check and if necessary top-up the transmission oil/fluid level with reference to Chapter 1A or 1B.
20 Refit the undershield where applicable, then refit the roadwheel and lower the vehicle to the ground. Tighten the wheel bolts to the specified torque.

3 Driveshafts – inspection, joint renewal and cleaning

Inspection

1 If any of the checks described in Chapter 1A or 1B reveal apparent excessive wear or play, first remove the wheel cover and check that the hub nut (driveshaft outer nut) is tightened to the specified torque. Repeat this check on the hub nut on the other side.
2 To check for driveshaft wear, road test the vehicle, driving it slowly in a circle on full steering lock (carry out the test on both left and right lock), while listening for a metallic clicking or knocking sound coming from the front wheels. An assistant in the passenger seat can listen for the sound from the nearside joint. If such a sound is heard, this indicates wear in the outer joint.
3 If vibration proportional to roadspeed is felt through the car when accelerating or on over-run, there is a possibility of wear in the inner joints. For a more thorough check, remove and dismantle the driveshafts where possible as described in the following Sections. Refer to a Saab dealer for information on the availability of driveshaft components.
4 Continual noise from the area of the right-hand driveshaft, increasing with roadspeed, may indicate wear in the support bearing.

Outer joint renewal

5 Remove the driveshaft as described in Section 2, then thoroughly clean it and mount it in a vice. It is important that foreign matter, such as dust and dirt, is prevented from entering the joint.
6 Release the large clip securing the rubber gaiter to the outer joint housing **(see illustration)**, then similarly release the small clip securing the rubber gaiter to the driveshaft. Note the fitted position of the gaiter.
7 Slide the rubber gaiter along the driveshaft, away from the joint **(see illustration)**. Scoop out as much of the grease as possible from the joint and gaiter.
8 Using a dab of paint, mark the outer joint and driveshaft in relation to each other to ensure correct refitting.
9 Using circlip pliers at the inner end of the joint, open the circlip then slide the joint from the end of the driveshaft **(see illustrations)**. If it is tight, use a hammer and soft drift to tap the joint hub from the splines. Note that on later models, it may not be necessary to open the circlip, as it will release from the driveshaft as the joint is being tapped off.
10 With the joint removed, slide the rubber

3.6 Remove the clip . . .

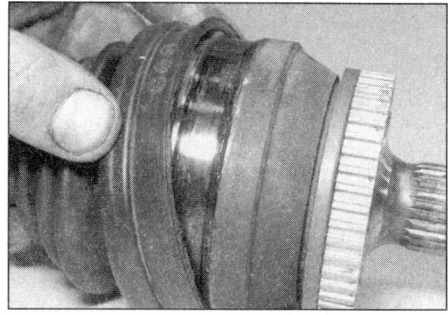

3.7 . . . release the rubber gaiter from the joint housing . . .

3.9a . . . then use circlip pliers to open the circlip . . .

3.9b . . . and slide the outer joint from the end of the driveshaft

3.10 Removing the outer rubber gaiter

3.11 The circlip is captive in the outer joint

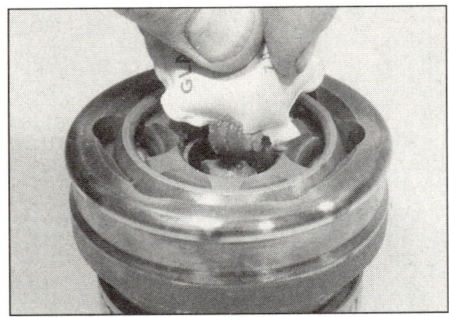

3.13 Pack the CV joint with grease from the service kit

3.22a Remove the circlip . . .

3.22b . . . then use a puller to remove the spider from the driveshaft splines

gaiter and small clip from the driveshaft **(see illustration)**. Check the rubber gaiter for cracks or slits, and renew it if necessary.

11 Thoroughly clean the splines of the driveshaft and outer joint, and also the rubber gaiter contact surfaces. If the joint has been contaminated with road grit or water, it must be dismantled and cleaned as described later in this Section. Check the condition of the circlip, which is captive in the outer joint, and renew it if necessary **(see illustration)**.

12 Locate the gaiter, together with small clip,

3.26 On the inner joint, make sure that the chamfer is located against the inner shoulder on the driveshaft

on the outer end of the driveshaft. Smear a little grease onto the driveshaft to facilitate this.

13 Pack the joint with the specified quantity of grease, working it well into the cavities of the housing **(see illustration)**.

14 Locate the outer joint onto the driveshaft splines in its previously-noted position, and press it on until the internal circlip engages with the groove.

15 Reposition the rubber gaiter onto the joint outer housing in its previously-noted position, and then refit the two clips. Tighten the clips securely.

16 Refit the driveshaft with reference to Section 2.

Inner joint renewal

17 Remove the driveshaft as described in Section 2, then thoroughly clean it and mount it in a vice. It is important that foreign matter, such as dust and dirt, is prevented from entering the joint.

3.28 Using a crimping tool to tighten the gaiter clips

18 Release the large clip securing the rubber gaiter to the inner joint housing, then similarly release the small clip securing the rubber gaiter to the driveshaft. Note the fitted position of the gaiter. Where the original factory gaiter is fitted, it will be necessary to bend up the metal plate to release it from the joint housing; however, it is not necessary to bend the plate down for the refitting procedure.

19 Slide the rubber gaiter along the driveshaft, away from the joint.

20 Scoop out as much of the grease as possible from the joint and gaiter.

21 Mark the driveshaft and inner joint housing in relation to each other using a centre-punch or dab of paint, then withdraw the housing from the tripod.

22 Mark the driveshaft and tripod in relation to each other using a centre-punch or dab of paint. Using circlip pliers, expand and remove the circlip from the end of the driveshaft, then use a puller to remove the tripod together with needle roller bearings **(see illustrations)**. Note that the chamfered edge of the tripod faces the centre of the driveshaft.

23 Slide the rubber gaiter and small clip from the driveshaft. Check the rubber gaiter for cracks or slits, and renew it if necessary.

24 Thoroughly clean the splines of the driveshaft and inner joint, and also the rubber gaiter contact surfaces. If the joint has been exposed to road grit or water, it should be thoroughly cleaned as described later in this Section. Check the condition of the circlip and renew it if necessary. Check that the three tripod bearings are free to rotate without resistance, and that they are not excessively worn.

25 Locate the gaiter, together with small clip, on the inner end of the driveshaft. Smear a little grease onto the driveshaft to facilitate this.

26 Locate the tripod on the driveshaft splines, chamfered edge first, making sure that the previously-made marks are aligned **(see illustration)**. Using a socket or metal tube, drive the tripod fully onto the driveshaft, then refit the circlip, making sure that it is correctly located in its groove.

27 Pack the tripod joint and inner joint housing with the specified quantity of grease, working it well into the bearings. Locate the inner joint housing onto the tripod in its previously-noted position.

28 Reposition the rubber gaiter onto the inner joint housing in its previously-noted position, then refit the two clips. Tighten the clips securely. If crimp-type clips are being fitted, use a crimping tool to tighten them **(see illustration)**.

29 Refit the driveshaft with reference to Section 2.

Joint cleaning

30 Where a joint has been contaminated with road grit or water through a damaged rubber gaiter, the joint should be completely dismantled and cleaned. Remove the joint as described previously in this Section.

5.12 Disconnect the sensor arm from the lower arm

5.18 Intermediate driveshaft support bearing bracket bolts

5.19 Removing the intermediate driveshaft from the transmission

31 To dismantle the outer joint, mount it vertically in a soft-jawed vice, then turn the splined hub and ball cage so that the balls can be removed individually. Remove the hub followed by the ball cage.
32 The inner joint is dismantled during removal, however, the tripod joint bearings should be washed in suitable solvent to remove all traces of grease.
33 Thoroughly clean the inner and outer joint housings, together with the ball-bearings, cages and hubs, removing all traces of grease and foreign matter.
34 To reassemble the outer joint, first insert the cage, followed by the splined hub. Manoeuvre the hub and carrier so that the balls can be inserted one at a time.

4 Driveshaft gaiters – renewal

1 Obtain a kit comprising new gaiters and retaining clips from a Saab dealer or motor factor.
2 Removal and refitting of the gaiters is described in Section 3.

5 Intermediate driveshaft and support bearing – removal, overhaul and refitting

Removal

1 Disconnect the battery negative lead.
2 Apply the handbrake, then jack up the front of the vehicle and support it on axle stands (see *Jacking and vehicle support*). Remove the right-hand front roadwheel.
3 Working under the right-hand wheel arch, undo the fasteners and remove the splash cover for access to the right-hand side of the engine.
4 In the engine compartment, remove the engine top cover.
5 Remove the clamp for the power steering servo pipe.
6 Support the right-hand side of the engine with a trolley jack and block of wood beneath the sump. Alternatively, wedge a block of wood between the subframe and engine sump.

7 Unbolt and remove the right-hand upper engine mounting bracket (refer to Chapter 2A or 2B if necessary).
8 Note the fitted routing of the auxiliary drivebelt, and mark it with an arrow to indicate its normal running direction.
9 Using a square-drive extension bar, turn the tensioner clockwise to release its tension, then slip the auxiliary drivebelt off of the crankshaft, alternator, air conditioning compressor and idler pulleys. Release the tensioner.
10 Using an 8.0 mm Allen key, unbolt the tensioner from the engine. Also, unscrew and remove the alternator upper mounting bolt.
11 Unclip the front brake hydraulic hose, and move the hose to one side. Also disconnect the ABS wiring.
12 On models fitted with a headlamp position sensor, disconnect the sensor arm to the lower suspension arm (see illustration), then (if required) unbolt the sensor from its mounting bracket and position it to one side.
13 Unscrew and remove the clamp bolt securing the front suspension lower balljoint to the hub carrier, noting which way round the bolt is fitted. Lever the lower arm downwards and disconnect the balljoint from the hub carrier, then hold the arm in this position with a block of wood between the arm and anti-roll bar.
14 Using a soft-faced mallet, tap the driveshaft inner joint off of the intermediate shaft and lower the driveshaft onto the subframe and lower arm. If the retaining circlip is tight, hold the joint firmly against the circlip before tapping it with the mallet. If necessary,

have an assistant pull out the strut while the driveshaft is being disconnected.
15 On the rear of the alternator, unscrew the nuts and disconnect the battery positive cable together with the warning light cable.
16 Unscrew the alternator lower mounting bolt and position the alternator to one side.
17 Position a container beneath the transmission to catch spilled oil/fluid when the intermediate shaft is removed.
18 Unscrew the bolts securing the support-bearing bracket to the rear of the cylinder block (see illustration).
19 Using a screwdriver, lever the bracket away from the dowels on the cylinder block, then withdraw the intermediate driveshaft from the splined sun gear in the transmission (see illustration).

Overhaul

20 With the intermediate shaft and bracket on the bench, remove the dust seal from the end of the shaft. The seal may have come away with the right-hand driveshaft (see illustration).
21 Using circlip pliers, extract the outer small circlip from the end of the intermediate shaft (see illustration).
22 The intermediate shaft must now be pressed out of the bearing. To do this, support the bracket in a vice, then press or drive out the shaft. If the shaft is being renewed, extract the inner small circlip from the shaft (see illustration).
23 Using circlip pliers, extract the large circlip securing the bearing in the bracket. The

5.20 Intermediate driveshaft dust seal

5.21 Intermediate shaft bearing small circlip (A) and large circlip (B)

5.22 Inner small circlip on the driveshaft

bearing must now be pressed or driven out of the bracket. Support the bracket in a vice to do this.

24 Support the bracket with its open end upwards, then locate the new bearing and press or drive it fully in using a metal tube on the outer race. Fit the large circlip to secure the bearing in the bracket.

25 With the intermediate driveshaft mounted in the vice, refit the small circlip to the driveshaft, then refit the bearing with bracket onto the driveshaft and press or drive on the bearing inner race until it contacts the circlip. Make sure that the bracket is fitted the correct way round, and press only on the inner race.

26 Fit the small circlip in the groove, making sure that the concave side faces the bearing.

27 Fit a new dust seal over the outer end of the intermediate shaft.

Refitting

28 Wipe clean the transmission oil seal then smear a little oil on the seal lips. It is recommended that the oil seal is always renewed, with reference to Chapter 7A or 7B, considering the amount of work necessary to renew it separately.

29 Insert the intermediate driveshaft into the transmission side gear, and engage the splines with each other.

30 Locate the bracket on the dowels, then refit the bolts and tighten to the specified torque.

31 Refer to Chapter 5A and check that the alternator adjuster sleeves in the mounting bracket are tapped out approximately 1.0 mm, then refit the alternator mounting bolts and tighten securely.

32 Reconnect the battery positive and warning light cables to the rear of the alternator and tighten securely.

33 Pull out the strut, then locate the driveshaft inner joint splines in the splined intermediate shaft. Press on the joint until the internal circlip engages with its groove at the end of the splines.

34 Remove the block of wood, and hold the suspension lower arm down while the balljoint is located in the hub carrier. Make sure the balljoint is fully entered in the hub carrier, then refit the clamp bolt with its head in the previously-noted position and tighten to the specified torque.

35 Refit the headlamp position sensor (where fitted) and tighten the mounting bolts.

36 Refit the brake hydraulic hose to the strut clips, and reconnect the ABS wiring.

37 Refit the alternator upper mounting bolt and tighten securely.

38 Refit the auxiliary drivebelt tensioner and tighten the bolts with the 8.0 mm Allen key.

39 Using the square drive, turn the tensioner clockwise then refit the auxiliary drivebelt on the pulleys. Make sure that it is routed correctly, and engaged with all of the pulley grooves, then release the tensioner.

40 Refit the right-hand upper engine mounting bracket and tighten the bolts to the specified torque (see Chapter 2A or 2B). Remove the support from the right-hand side of the engine.

41 Refit the clamp for the power steering servo pipe.

42 Top-up the transmission oil/fluid with reference to Chapter 1A or 1B.

43 Refit the engine top cover.

44 Refit the splash cover under the right-hand wheel arch.

45 Refit the roadwheel, then lower the vehicle to the ground.

46 Reconnect the battery negative lead.

Chapter 9
Braking system

Contents

	Section number
Anti-lock Braking System (ABS) – general information and fault finding	21
Anti-lock Braking System (ABS) components – removal and refitting	22
Brake pedal – removal and refitting	19
Electronic Stability Program (ESP) components – removal and refitting	23
Front brake caliper – removal, overhaul and refitting	6
Front brake disc – inspection, removal and refitting	8
Front brake pads – renewal	4
General information	1
Handbrake – adjustment	15
Handbrake cables – removal and refitting	16
Handbrake lever – removal and refitting	17
Handbrake 'on' warning light switch – removal, testing and refitting	18
Handbrake shoes – inspection, removal and refitting	10
Hydraulic pipes and hoses – renewal	3
Hydraulic system – bleeding	2
Master cylinder – removal, overhaul and refitting	11
Rear brake caliper – removal, overhaul and refitting	7
Rear brake disc – inspection, removal and refitting	9
Rear brake pads – renewal	5
Stop-light switch – removal, testing and refitting	20
Vacuum pump – removal and refitting	14
Vacuum servo unit – testing, removal and refitting	13
Vacuum servo unit non-return valve – removal, testing and refitting	12

Degrees of difficulty

Easy, suitable for novice with little experience | **Fairly easy,** suitable for beginner with some experience | **Fairly difficult,** suitable for competent DIY mechanic | **Difficult,** suitable for experienced DIY mechanic | **Very difficult,** suitable for expert DIY or professional

Specifications

General
Brake system type and layout:
- Footbrake .... Diagonally-split dual hydraulic circuits; front left/rear right and front right/rear left. Discs fitted front and rear, ventilated at the front. Single-piston, sliding calipers on the front, double-piston fixed calipers (early) or floating calipers (late) on the rear. Anti-lock Braking System (ABS) fitted as standard on all models. Vacuum servo assistance. Electronic Stability Program (ESP) option on some models
- Handbrake .... Lever and cable operation, acting on shoes in drums incorporated in rear discs

Front brakes
Discs:
- Type .... Ventilated
- Outside diameter .... 288.0 mm
- Thickness (new disc) .... 25.0 mm
- Minimum thickness after grinding .... 23.5 mm
- Minimum wear thickness .... 22.0 mm
- Maximum run-out .... 0.08 mm
- Maximum variation in disc thickness .... 0.015 mm

Calipers:
- Type .... Single-piston, floating
- Piston diameter .... 57.0 mm

Pads:
- Minimum friction material thickness .... 2.0 mm

Rear brakes
Discs:
  Type .... Solid
  Outside diameter .... 286.0 mm
  Thickness (new disc) .... 10.0 mm
  Minimum thickness after grinding .... 8.5 mm
  Minimum wear thickness .... 8.0 mm
  Maximum run-out .... 0.08 mm
  Maximum variation in disc thickness .... 0.015 mm
  Handbrake drum inner diameter .... 160.0 mm
  Handbrake drum maximum out-of-round ... 0.08 mm

Calipers:
  Type:
    Early .... Fixed, double-piston
    Late .... Floating, single-piston
  Piston diameter .... 38.0 mm

Pads:
  Minimum friction material thickness .... 2.0 mm

Handbrake:
  Shoe minimum friction material thickness . 1.0 mm

ABS components
Wheel sensors:
  Resistance .... 1600 ± 160 ohms at 20°C
  Clearance between sensor and tooth (not adjustable) ... 0.2 to 1.3 mm

Torque wrench settings

	Nm	lbf ft
ABS hydraulic unit mounting nut	20	15
ESP hydraulic unit	20	15
Front brake caliper:		
Guide bolts	28	21
Hose to caliper	40	30
Mounting bracket:		
Stage 1	140	103
Stage 2	Angle-tighten a further 45°	
Handbrake cable support bracket	8	6
Master cylinder	25	18
Master cylinder hydraulic lines	16	12
Rear fixed brake caliper:		
Caliper to backplate	80	59
Pipe union nut	16	12
Rear floating brake caliper:		
Guide bolts	28	21
Hose to caliper	43	32
Mounting bracket	80	59
Rear wheel hub to rear axle:		
Stage 1	50	37
Stage 2	Angle-tighten a further 30°	
Steering column-to-gear clamp bolt	25	18
Vacuum pump banjo bolt	24	18
Vacuum pump mounting bolt	24	18
Vacuum servo	25	18
Wheel bolts	110	81

1 General information

Braking is achieved by a dual-circuit hydraulic system, assisted by a vacuum servo unit. All models have discs fitted at the front and rear. The front discs are ventilated, to improve cooling and reduce brake fade.

The dual hydraulic circuits are diagonally-split; on LHD models, the primary circuit operates the front left and rear right brakes, and the secondary circuit operates the front right and rear left brakes. On RHD models, the circuits are opposite. This design ensures that at least 50% of the vehicle's braking capacity will be available should pressure be lost in one of the hydraulic circuits. Under these circumstances, the diagonal layout should prevent the vehicle from becoming unstable if the brakes are applied when only one circuit is operational.

The front brake calipers are of floating single-piston type. Each caliper has two brake pads, one inboard and one outboard of the disc. During braking, hydraulic pressure forces the piston along its cylinder, and presses the inboard brake pad against the disc. The caliper body reacts to this effort by sliding along its guide bolts, bringing the outboard pad into contact with the disc. In this manner, equal pressure is applied to each side of the disc by the brake pads. When the brake pedal is released, the hydraulic pressure drops and the piston seal retracts the piston from the brake pad.

The rear brake calipers on early models are of fixed double-piston type with two brake pads, one inboard and one outboard of the disc. Later models have a floating, single-piston caliper with two brake pads. The pistons in the early type operate independently of each other, although, the later type function as described for the front calipers.

The rear discs incorporate drums with internal brake shoes for operation of the handbrake. A single primary cable, together with two secondary cables from the handbrake lever, operate the lever on each rear brake expander. The handbrake is not self-adjusting, and must be adjusted regularly.

The brake vacuum servo unit uses engine intake manifold vacuum to boost the effort applied to the master cylinder by the brake pedal. In order to supply sufficient vacuum to the servo on automatic transmission and diesel models, the intake manifold vacuum is supplemented by an additional vacuum pump driven from the exhaust camshaft. The vacuum pump is mounted on the left-hand end of the cylinder head and driven by the camshaft. Manual transmission petrol models are fitted with an 'ejector' device to boost the vacuum to the vacuum servo. The device is fitted in the charge air pipe, and operates by speeding up the flow of air across a venturi, thus providing vacuum to the servo.

The anti-lock braking system (ABS), fitted as standard to all models, prevents wheel lock-up under heavy braking, and not only optimises stopping distances, but also improves steering control. By electronically monitoring the speed of each roadwheel in relation to the other wheels, the system can detect when a wheel is about to lock-up, before control is actually lost. The brake fluid pressure applied to that wheel's brake caliper is then decreased and restored ('modulated') several times a second until control is regained. The system components comprise four wheel speed sensors, a hydraulic unit with integral electronic control module (ECM), brake lines and a dashboard-mounted warning light. The four wheel sensors are mounted on the wheel hub carriers. Each wheel has a rotating toothed hub mounted on the driveshaft (front) or on the hub (rear). The wheel speed sensors are mounted in close proximity to these hubs. The teeth produce a voltage waveform whose frequency varies with the speed of the hubs. These waveforms are transmitted to the ECM, and used to calculate the rotational speed of each wheel. The ECM has a self-diagnostic facility, to inhibit the operation of the ABS if a fault is detected, lighting the dashboard-mounted warning light. The braking system will then revert to conventional, non-ABS operation. If the nature of the fault is not immediately obvious upon inspection, the vehicle *must* be taken to a Saab dealer, who will have the diagnostic equipment required to interrogate the ABS ECM electronically and pin-point the problem.

The traction control system (TCS) is available as an option on some models, and uses the basic ABS system, with an additional pump and valves fitted to the hydraulic actuator. If wheelspin is detected at a speed below 30 mph, one of the valves opens, to allow the pump to pressurise the relevant brake, until the spinning wheel slows to a rotational speed corresponding to the speed of the vehicle. This has the effect of transferring torque to the wheel with most traction. At the same time, the throttle plate is closed slightly, to reduce the torque from the engine.

The electronic stability program (ESP) system adds another function to the ABS system. Sensors measure the position of the steering wheel, the pressure in the brake master cylinder, the yaw velocity/rate, and the lateral acceleration. With this information, the system can compare the driver's intention with the vehicle's movement, and apply the appropriate corrective action.

2 Hydraulic system – bleeding

Warning: Hydraulic fluid is poisonous; wash off immediately and thoroughly in the case of skin contact, and seek immediate medical advice if any fluid is swallowed or gets into the eyes. Certain types of hydraulic fluid are inflammable, and may ignite when brought into contact with hot components; when servicing any hydraulic system, it is safest to assume that the fluid is inflammable, and to take precautions against the risk of fire as though it is petrol that is being handled. Hydraulic fluid is also an effective paint stripper, and will attack plastics; if any is spilt, it should be washed off immediately, using copious quantities of fresh water. Finally, it is hygroscopic (it absorbs moisture from the air) – old fluid may be contaminated and unfit for further use. When topping-up or renewing the fluid, always use the recommended type, and ensure that it comes from a freshly-opened sealed container.

General

1 The correct operation of any hydraulic system is only possible after removing all air from the components and circuit; this is achieved by bleeding the system.
2 During the bleeding procedure, add only clean, unused hydraulic fluid of the recommended type; never re-use fluid that has already been bled from the system. Ensure that sufficient fluid is available before starting work.
3 If there is any possibility of incorrect fluid being already in the system, the brake components and circuit must be flushed completely with uncontaminated, correct fluid, and new seals should be fitted to the various components.
4 If hydraulic fluid has been lost from the system, or air has entered because of a leak, ensure that the fault is cured before proceeding further.
5 Park the vehicle over an inspection pit or on car ramps. Alternatively, apply the handbrake then jack up the front and rear of the vehicle and support it on axle stands (see *Jacking and vehicle support*). For improved access with the vehicle jacked up, remove the roadwheels.
6 Check that all pipes and hoses are secure, unions tight and bleed screws closed. Clean any dirt from around the bleed screws.
7 Unscrew the master cylinder reservoir cap, and top the master cylinder reservoir up to the MAX level line; refit the cap loosely, and remember to maintain the fluid level at least above the MIN level line throughout the procedure, otherwise there is a risk of further air entering the system.
8 There is a number of one-man, do-it-yourself brake bleeding kits currently available from motor accessory shops. It is recommended that one of these kits is used whenever possible, as they greatly simplify the bleeding operation, and also reduce the risk of expelled air and fluid being drawn back into the system. If such a kit is not available, the basic (two-man) method must be used, which is described in detail below.
9 If a kit is to be used, prepare the vehicle as described previously, and follow the kit manufacturer's instructions, as the procedure may vary slightly according to the type being used; generally, they are as outlined below in the relevant sub-section.
10 Whichever method is used, the same sequence must be followed (paragraphs 11 and 12) to ensure the removal of all air from the system.

Bleeding sequence

11 If the system has been only partially disconnected, and suitable precautions were taken to minimise fluid loss, it should only be necessary to bleed that part of the system (ie, the primary or secondary circuit).
12 If the complete system is to be bled, then it should be done working in the following sequence:
 a) *Right-hand front brake.*
 b) *Left-hand rear brake.*
 c) *Left-hand front brake.*
 d) *Right-hand rear brake.*

Bleeding

Basic (two-man) method

13 Collect together a clean glass jar, a suitable length of plastic or rubber tubing, which is a tight fit over the bleed screw, and a ring spanner to fit the screw. The help of an assistant will also be required.
14 Remove the dust cap from the first bleed screw in the sequence **(see illustration)**. Fit the spanner and tube to the screw, place the other end of the tube in the jar, and pour in sufficient fluid to cover the end of the tube.

2.14 Dust cap on the caliper bleed screw

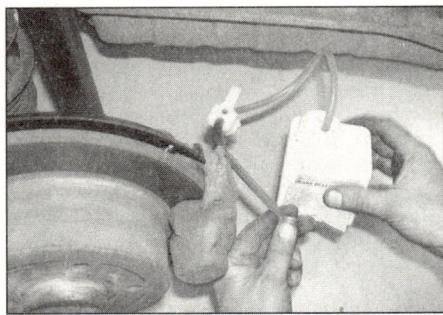

2.22 Using a one-way valve kit to bleed the rear brake circuit

15 Ensure that the master cylinder reservoir fluid level is maintained at least above the MIN level mark throughout the procedure.
16 Have the assistant fully depress and release the brake pedal several times to build-up initial pressure in the system.
17 Unscrew the bleed screw approximately half a turn then have the assistant slowly depress the brake pedal down to the floor and hold it there. Tighten the bleed screw and have the assistant slowly release the pedal to its rest position.
18 Repeat the procedure given in paragraph 17 until the fluid emerging from the bleed screw is free from air bubbles. After every two or three depressions of the pedal, check the level of fluid in the reservoir and top-up if necessary.
19 When no more air bubbles appear, securely tighten the bleed screw, remove the tube and spanner, and refit the dust cap. Do not overtighten the bleed screw.
20 Repeat the procedure on the remaining screws in the sequence until all air is removed from the system and the brake pedal feels firm again.

Using a one-way valve kit

21 As the name implies, these kits consist of a length of tubing with a one-way valve fitted, to prevent expelled air and fluid being drawn back into the system; some kits include a translucent container, which can be positioned so that the air bubbles can be more easily seen flowing from the end of the tube.
22 The kit is connected to the bleed screw, which is then opened **(see illustration)**. The user returns to the driver's seat, depresses the brake pedal with a smooth, steady stroke, and slowly releases it; this is repeated until the expelled fluid is clear of air bubbles.
23 Note that these kits simplify work so much that it is easy to forget the master cylinder reservoir fluid level; ensure that this is maintained at least above the MIN level line at all times.

Using a pressure-bleeding kit

24 These kits are usually operated by a reservoir of pressurised air contained in the spare tyre. However, note that it will probably be necessary to reduce the pressure to a lower level than normal; refer to the instructions supplied with the kit.
25 By connecting a pressurised, fluid-filled container to the master cylinder reservoir, bleeding can be carried out simply by opening each screw in turn (in the specified sequence), and allowing the fluid to flow out until no more air bubbles can be seen in the expelled fluid.
26 This method has the advantage that the large reservoir of fluid provides an additional safeguard against air being drawn into the system during bleeding.
27 Pressure-bleeding is particularly effective when bleeding 'difficult' systems, or when bleeding the complete system at the time of routine fluid renewal.

All methods

28 When bleeding is complete, and firm pedal feel is restored, wipe off any spilt fluid, securely tighten the bleed screws, and refit the dust caps.
29 Check the hydraulic fluid level in the master cylinder reservoir, and top-up if necessary (see *Weekly checks*).
30 Discard any hydraulic fluid that has been bled from the system; it will not be fit for re-use.
31 Check the feel of the brake pedal. If it feels at all spongy, air must still be present in the system, and further bleeding is required. Failure to bleed satisfactorily after a reasonable repetition of the bleeding procedure may be due to worn master cylinder seals.

3 Hydraulic pipes and hoses – renewal

1 If any pipe or hose is to be renewed, minimise fluid loss by first removing the master cylinder reservoir cap, then tightening it down onto a piece of polythene to obtain an airtight seal. The cap incorporates a level warning float, so hose clamps can be fitted to flexible hoses to isolate sections of the circuit; metal brake pipe unions can be plugged (if care is taken not to allow dirt into the system) or capped immediately they are disconnected. Place a wad of rag under any union that is to be disconnected, to catch any spilt fluid.
2 If a flexible hose is to be disconnected, unscrew the brake pipe union nut before removing the spring clip that secures the hose to its mounting bracket **(see illustrations)**. Where applicable, unscrew the banjo union bolt securing the hose to the caliper and recover the copper washers. When removing the front flexible hose, pull out the spring clip and disconnect it from the strut.
3 To unscrew union nuts, it is preferable to obtain a 'split' brake pipe spanner of the correct size; these are available from most motor accessory shops. Failing this, a close-fitting open-ended spanner will be required, though if the nuts are tight or corroded, their flats may be rounded-off if the spanner slips. In such a case, a self-locking wrench is often the only way to unscrew a stubborn union, but it follows that the pipe and the damaged nuts must be renewed on reassembly. Always clean a union and surrounding area before disconnecting it. If disconnecting a component with more than one union, make a careful note of the connections before disturbing any of them.
4 If a brake pipe is to be renewed, it can be obtained, cut to length and with the union nuts and end flares in place, from a dealer's parts shop. All that is then necessary is to bend it to shape, following the line of the original, before fitting it to the car. Alternatively, most motor accessory shops can make up brake pipes from kits, but this requires very careful measurement of the original, to ensure that the new part is of the correct length. The safest answer is usually to take the original to the shop as a pattern.
5 On refitting, do not overtighten the union nuts.
6 When refitting hoses to the calipers, always

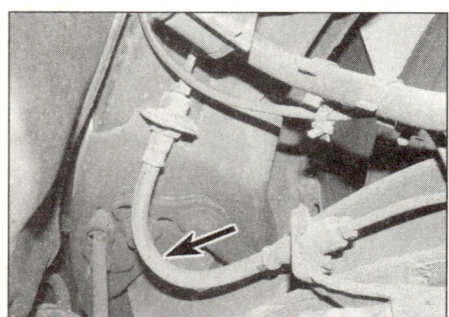

3.2a Rear brake flexible hose located between the underbody and trailing arm

3.2b Withdraw the spring clip from the mounting bracket

Braking system 9•5

4.2 Using slip-joint pliers to press the piston into the caliper

4.3a Lever out the retaining spring . . .

4.3b . . . and remove it from the caliper

4.4 Remove the dust caps . . .

4.5a . . . then unscrew the guide bolts . . .

4.5b . . . and lift the caliper and pads away from the mounting bracket

use new copper washers and tighten the banjo union bolts to the specified torque. Make sure that the hoses are positioned so that they will not touch surrounding bodywork or the roadwheels.

7 Ensure that the pipes and hoses are correctly routed, with no kinks, and that they are secured in the clips or brackets provided. After fitting, remove the polythene from the reservoir, and bleed the hydraulic system as described in Section 2. Wash off any spilt fluid, and check carefully for fluid leaks.

4 Front brake pads – renewal

Warning: *Renew BOTH sets of front brake pads at the same time – NEVER renew the pads on only one wheel, as uneven braking may result. Note that the dust created by wear of the pads may contain asbestos, which is a health hazard. Never blow it out with compressed air, and do not inhale any of it. Use brake cleaner or methylated spirit to clean brake components.*

1 Apply the handbrake, then jack up the front of the vehicle and support it on axle stands (see *Jacking and vehicle support*). Remove both front roadwheels.

2 Using slip-joint pliers, press the piston fully into the caliper **(see illustration)**. *Note: Provided that the master cylinder reservoir has not been overfilled with hydraulic fluid, there should be no spillage, but keep a careful watch on the fluid level while retracting the piston. If the fluid level rises above the MAX level line at any time, the surplus should be siphoned off or ejected via a plastic tube connected to the bleed screw.*

Caution: *Pushing back the piston causes a reverse-flow of brake fluid, which has been known to 'flip' the master cylinder rubber seals, resulting in a total loss of braking. To avoid this, clamp the caliper flexible hose and open the bleed screw – as the piston is pushed back, the fluid can be directed into a suitable container using a hose attached to the bleed screw. Close the screw just before the piston is pushed fully back, to ensure no air enters the system.*

3 Carefully lever off the retaining spring from the holes on the outer surface of the caliper, noting how the spring is located on the caliper mounting bracket **(see illustrations)**

4 Remove the dust caps from the inner ends of the guide bolts **(see illustration)**.

5 Using an Allen key, unscrew the guide bolts from the caliper, and lift the caliper and pads away from the mounting bracket **(see illustrations)**. Tie the caliper to the suspension strut using a suitable piece of wire. Do not allow the caliper to hang unsupported on the flexible brake hose.

6 Remove the inner and outer pads from the caliper, noting that the inner one is retained in the piston by a spring clip attached to the pad backing plate **(see illustrations)**. *Note: On some models, an acoustic wear warning device is fitted to the outer pad, consisting of a metal strip, which contacts the brake disc when the thickness of the friction material is less than 3.0 mm. This device causes a scraping noise that warns the driver that the pads are worn excessively.*

7 Brush the dirt and dust from the caliper, but take care not to inhale it. Carefully remove any rust from the edge of the brake disc.

4.6a Remove the outer pad from the caliper . . .

4.6b . . . then the inner pad, noting that it is retained in the piston by a spring clip

9•6 Braking system

4.11a Outer (A) and inner (B) front brake pads

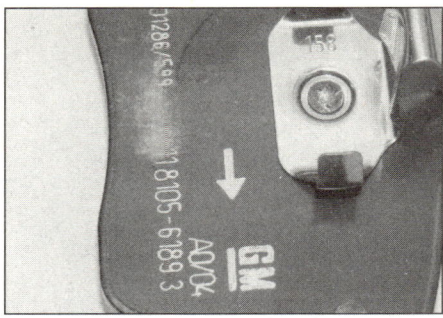

4.11b The pads must be fitted with the arrow pointing the normal, forward rotation of the brake disc

8 Measure the thickness of the friction material on each brake pad (excluding the backing plate). If either pad is worn at any point to the specified minimum thickness or less, all four pads must be renewed. The pads should also be renewed if any are contaminated with oil or grease; there is no satisfactory way of degreasing friction material. Trace and rectify the cause of contamination before reassembly.

9 If the brake pads are still serviceable, clean them using a clean, fine wire brush or similar, paying particular attention to the sides and back of the metal backing. Carefully clean the pad locations in the caliper body/mounting bracket.

10 Prior to fitting the pads, check that the guide bolts are a good fit in the caliper bushes. Brush the dust and dirt from the caliper and piston (see **Warning** at the beginning of this Section). Apply a little high melting-point copper brake grease to the areas on the pad backing plates which contact the caliper and piston. Inspect the dust seal around the piston for damage, and the piston for evidence of fluid leaks, corrosion or damage. If attention to any of these components is necessary, refer to Section 6.

11 Fit the inner pad to the caliper, ensuring that its clip is correctly located in the caliper piston. Make sure that the arrows on the pad point in the normal, forward direction of rotation of the brake disc **(see illustrations)**.

12 Fit the outer pad to the caliper mounting bracket, ensuring that its friction material is facing the brake disc. The acoustic wear indicators must face downwards.

13 Slide the caliper and inner pad into position over the outer pad, and locate it in the mounting bracket.

14 Insert the caliper guide bolts, and then tighten them to the specified torque setting.

15 Refit the guide bolt dust caps.

16 Refit the retaining spring to the caliper, ensuring that its ends are correctly located in the caliper holes.

17 Depress the brake pedal repeatedly, until normal pedal pressure is restored.

18 Repeat the above procedure on the remaining front brake caliper.

19 Refit the roadwheels, then lower the vehicle to the ground and tighten the roadwheel bolts to the specified torque setting.

20 Check the hydraulic fluid level as described in *Weekly checks*.

5 Rear brake pads – renewal

⚠ *Warning: Renew BOTH sets of rear brake pads at the same time – NEVER renew the pads on only one wheel, as uneven braking may result. Note that the dust created by wear of the pads may contain asbestos, which is a health hazard. Never blow it out with compressed air, and do not inhale any of it. Use brake cleaner or methylated spirit to clean brake components.*

1 Chock the front wheels, then jack up the rear of the vehicle and support on axle stands (see *Jacking and vehicle support*). Remove the rear roadwheels.

Fixed caliper

2 Note how the anti-squeal spring is located, then drive out the upper and lower pad retaining pins from the outside of the caliper using a punch **(see illustration)**.

3 Remove the anti-squeal spring **(see illustration)**.

4 Move the pads away from the disc slightly using a suitable lever or a pair of large adjustable pliers, and then withdraw the outer pad from the caliper using pliers or a special removal tool.

5 Withdraw the inner pad from the caliper **(see illustrations)**.

Floating caliper

6 Using slip-joint pliers, press the piston fully into the caliper **(see illustration)**. Note: *Provided that the master cylinder reservoir has*

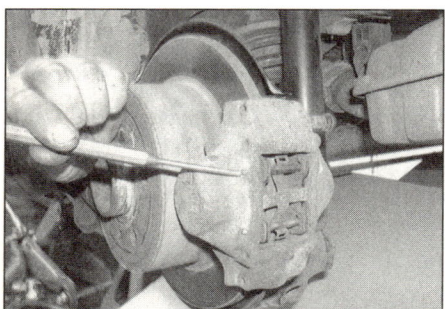

5.2 Using a punch to drive out the rear brake pad retaining pins

5.3 Removing the anti-squeal spring

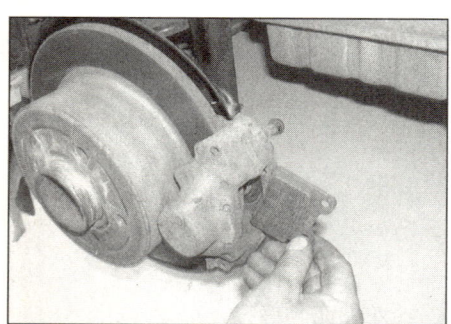

5.5a Removing the inner rear brake pad

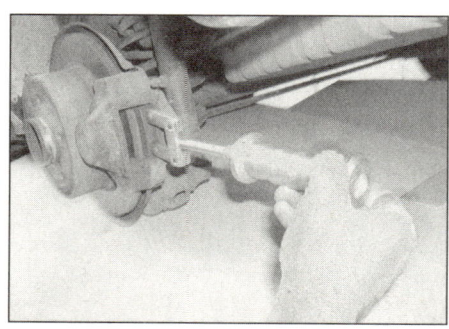

5.5b Using a removal tool to remove the inner rear brake pad

5.6 Using slip-joint pliers to press the piston fully into the caliper

Braking system 9•7

5.7 Use a screwdriver to lever off the retaining spring

5.8a Remove the dust caps...

5.8b ...then use an Allen key to unscrew the guide bolts...

5.8c ...and remove them from the caliper...

5.8d ...then lift the caliper and pads from the mounting bracket...

5.8e ...and suspend the caliper from the suspension coil spring

not been overfilled with hydraulic fluid, there should be no spillage, but keep a careful watch on the fluid level while retracting the piston. If the fluid level rises above the MAX level line at any time, the surplus should be siphoned off or ejected via a plastic tube connected to the bleed screw.

Caution: *Pushing back the piston causes a reverse-flow of brake fluid, which has been known to 'flip' the master cylinder rubber seals, resulting in a total loss of braking. To avoid this, clamp the caliper flexible hose and open the bleed screw – as the piston is pushed back, the fluid can be directed into a suitable container using a hose attached to the bleed screw. Close the screw just before the piston is pushed fully back, to ensure no air enters the system.*

7 Carefully lever off the retaining spring from the holes on the outer surface of the caliper, noting how the spring is located on the caliper mounting bracket **(see illustration)**.

8 Remove the dust caps, then use an Allen key to unscrew the guide bolts from the caliper, and lift the caliper and pads away from the mounting bracket. Tie the caliper to the suspension coil spring using a suitable piece of wire **(see illustrations)**. Do not allow the caliper to hang unsupported on the flexible brake hose.

9 Remove the outer and inner pads from the caliper, noting that the inner one is retained in the piston by a spring clip attached to the pad backing plate **(see illustrations)**.

All models

10 Brush the dirt and dust from the caliper, but take care not to inhale it. Carefully remove any rust from the edge of the brake disc.

11 Measure the thickness of the friction material on each brake pad (excluding the backing plate). If either pad is worn at any point to the specified minimum thickness or less, all four pads must be renewed. The pads should also be renewed if any are contaminated with oil or grease; there is no satisfactory way of degreasing friction material. Trace and rectify the cause of contamination before reassembly.

12 If the brake pads are still serviceable, clean them using a clean, fine wire brush or similar, paying particular attention to the sides and back of the metal backing. Carefully clean the pad locations in the caliper body/mounting bracket.

13 Prior to fitting the pads, clean and check the guide bolts/retaining pins are a good fit in the caliper. Brush the dust and dirt from the caliper and piston (see **Warning** at the beginning of this Section). Apply a little high melting-point copper brake grease to the areas on the pad backing plates that contact the caliper and piston **(see illustration)**.

5.9a Remove the outer pad...

5.9b ...and inner pad with location spring from the caliper

5.13 Apply a little high melting-point brake grease to the backs of the brake pads

9•8 Braking system

5.15 Correct position of the piston in the rear brake caliper (early models)

Inspect the dust seal around the piston(s) for damage, and the piston(s) for evidence of fluid leaks, corrosion or damage. If attention to any of these components is necessary, refer to Section 7.

14 If new brake pads are to be fitted, the caliper piston(s) must be pushed back into the cylinder(s) to make room for them. Either use a G-clamp or similar tool, or use suitable pieces of wood as levers. Provided that the master cylinder reservoir has not been overfilled with hydraulic fluid, there should be no spillage, but keep a careful watch on the fluid level while retracting the piston(s). If the fluid level rises above the MAX level line at any time, the surplus should be siphoned off or ejected via a plastic tube connected to the bleed screw.

⚠ **Warning: Do not siphon the fluid by mouth, as it is poisonous; use a syringe or an old antifreeze tester.**

Caution: Pushing back the piston causes a reverse-flow of brake fluid, which has been known to 'flip' the master cylinder rubber seals, resulting in a total loss of braking. To avoid this, clamp the caliper flexible hose and open the bleed screw – as the piston is pushed back, the fluid can be directed into a suitable container using a hose attached to the bleed screw. Close the screw just before the piston is pushed fully back, to ensure no air enters the system.

Fixed caliper

15 Where applicable, use a steel rule to check that the cutaway recess in the pistons are positioned correctly **(see illustration)**. The recesses must be at the bottom of the caliper. If necessary, carefully turn the pistons to their correct positions.

16 Locate the new pads in the caliper. Ensure that the friction material faces the disc, and check that the pads are free to move.

17 Locate the anti-squeal spring on the pads, then insert the pad retaining pins from the inside edge of the caliper, while depressing the spring. Tap the pins firmly into the caliper.

Floating caliper

18 Locate the inner and outer pads in the caliper, making sure that the inner pad location spring is fully entered in the piston.

19 Slide the caliper and pads over the disc and onto the mounting bracket.

20 Insert the caliper guide bolts, and then tighten them to the specified torque setting.

21 Refit the guide bolt dust caps.

22 Refit the retaining spring to the caliper, ensuring that its ends are correctly located in the caliper holes.

All models

23 Depress the brake pedal repeatedly until normal pedal pressure is restored.

24 Repeat the above procedure on the remaining rear brake caliper.

25 Refit the roadwheels, then lower the vehicle to the ground and tighten the roadwheel bolts to the specified torque setting.

26 Check the hydraulic fluid level as described in *Weekly checks*.

6 Front brake caliper – removal, overhaul and refitting

Removal

1 Apply the handbrake, then jack up the front of the vehicle and support it on axle stands (see *Jacking and vehicle support*). Remove the roadwheel.

2 Minimise fluid loss by first removing the master cylinder reservoir cap, then tightening it down onto a piece of polythene to obtain an airtight seal. Alternatively, use a brake hose clamp to clamp the flexible hose leading to the brake caliper.

3 Clean the area around the caliper brake hose union. Note the fitted angle of the hose (to ensure correct refitting), then unscrew and remove the union bolt and recover the copper sealing washer from each side of the hose union. Discard the washers; new ones must be used on refitting. Plug the hose end and caliper hole to minimise fluid loss and prevent the ingress of dirt into the hydraulic system.

4 Remove the brake pads as described in Section 4, then remove the caliper from the vehicle.

5 If necessary, unbolt the caliper mounting bracket from the hub carrier **(see illustrations)**.

Overhaul

Note: *Before dismantling the brake caliper check on the availability and cost of parts, as it may be more economical to renew the complete unit.*

6 With the caliper on the bench, clean away all external dirt and debris.

7 Withdraw the piston from the caliper body, and remove the dust seal. The piston can be withdrawn by hand or, if necessary, pushed out by applying compressed air to the brake hose union hole. Only low pressure should be required, such as from a foot pump.

8 Using a small screwdriver, carefully remove the piston seal from the caliper, taking care not to mark the bore.

9 Remove the guide bushes from the caliper body.

10 Thoroughly clean all components, using only methylated spirit or clean hydraulic fluid. Never use mineral-based solvents such as petrol or paraffin. Dry the components using compressed air or a clean, lint-free cloth. If available, use compressed air to blow clear the fluid passages.

11 Check all components, and renew any that are worn or damaged. If the piston and/or cylinder bore are scratched excessively, renew the complete caliper body. Similarly check the condition of the guide bushes and bolts; both bushes and bolts should be undamaged and a reasonably tight sliding fit. If there is any doubt about the condition of any component, renew it. Renew the caliper seals and dust covers as a matter of course; these are available as a repair kit together with assembly grease.

12 On reassembly, ensure that all components are absolutely clean.

13 Lubricate the new seal with the grease supplied, or dip it in clean hydraulic fluid. Locate the seal in the cylinder bore groove, using only the fingers to manipulate it into position.

14 Fill the inner cavity of the dust seal with the grease supplied, or dip it in clean hydraulic fluid, then locate it on the piston.

15 Locate the piston on the caliper, then carefully press it fully into the bore, twisting it from side-to-side to ensure it enters the internal seal correctly. At the same time, make sure that the inner end of the dust seal enters the groove on the caliper body, and the outer end enters the groove in the piston.

6.5a Unscrew the bolts . . .

6.5b . . . and remove the caliper mounting bracket from the hub carrier

16 Insert the guide bushes in the caliper body, using suitable grease to lubricate them.

Refitting

17 Locate the caliper mounting bracket on the hub carrier, then apply locking fluid to the threads of the mounting bolts, insert them, and tighten to the specified torque.
18 Refit the brake pads as described in Section 4, together with the caliper that at this stage will not have the hose attached.
19 Position a new copper sealing washer on each side of the hose union, and connect the brake hose to the caliper. Ensure that the hose is correctly positioned against the caliper body lug, then install the union bolt and tighten securely.
20 Remove the brake hose clamp or the polythene, where fitted, and bleed the hydraulic system as described in Section 2. Note that, providing the precautions described were taken to minimise brake fluid loss, it should only be necessary to bleed the relevant front brake.
21 Refit the roadwheel, then lower the vehicle to the ground and tighten the roadwheel bolts to the specified torque.

7 Rear brake caliper – removal, overhaul and refitting

Removal

1 Chock the front wheels, then jack up the rear of the vehicle and support on axle stands (see *Jacking and vehicle support*). Remove the roadwheel.
2 Minimise fluid loss by first removing the master cylinder reservoir cap, then tightening it down onto a piece of polythene to obtain an airtight seal. Alternatively, use a brake hose clamp on the flexible hose leading to the brake line on the rear axle (early models with fixed caliper) **(see illustration)** or to the floating caliper (late models).

Fixed caliper

3 Clean the area around the hydraulic line union nut, and then loosen the nut **(see illustration)**. Do not fully unscrew the nut at this stage.
4 Remove the brake pads as described in Section 5.
5 Unscrew and remove the mounting bolts securing the caliper to the backplate **(see illustration)**. Recover the cover plate from under the bolt heads.
6 Fully unscrew the union nut and disconnect the hydraulic line from the caliper, then withdraw the caliper from the disc **(see illustration)**. Tape over or plug the hydraulic line to prevent entry of dust and dirt.

Floating caliper

7 Clean the area around the brake hose on the caliper, then loosen the hose end fitting. The hose cannot be fully unscrewed from the caliper at this stage.

7.2 Brake hose clamp fitted to the flexible hose leading from the body to the brake line on the rear axle

8 At the other end of the brake hose, unscrew the union nut and disconnect the rigid brake line from the hose end fitting on the rear suspension trailing arm. Be prepared for some loss of brake fluid. Recover the clip, and withdraw the hose from the bracket. Tape over or plug the ends of the rigid line and hose to prevent entry of dust and dirt.
9 Remove the brake pads as described in Section 5, then remove the caliper from the vehicle. Fully unscrew the hose from the caliper.
10 If necessary, unbolt the caliper mounting bracket from the backplate.

Overhaul

Note: *Before dismantling the brake caliper check on the availability and cost of parts, as it may be more economical to renew the complete unit.*

11 With the caliper on the bench, clean away all external dirt and debris.
12 Withdraw the piston(s) from the caliper body, and remove the dust seal(s). The piston(s) can be withdrawn by hand, or if necessary pushed out by applying compressed air to the brake hose union hole. Only low pressure should be required, such as from a foot pump.

Caution: On the fixed caliper, keep each piston identified for position to ensure correct refitting.

13 Using a small screwdriver, carefully remove the piston seal(s) from the caliper, taking care not to mark the bore(s).
14 On the floating caliper, remove the guide bushes from the caliper body.

7.5 Removing the rear brake caliper mounting bolts

7.3 Unscrewing the hydraulic line union nut from the rear brake caliper

15 Thoroughly clean all components, using only methylated spirit or clean hydraulic fluid. Never use mineral-based solvents such as petrol or paraffin. Dry the components using compressed air or a clean, lint-free cloth. If available, use compressed air to blow clear the fluid passages.
16 Check all components, and renew any that are worn or damaged. If the piston(s) and/or cylinder bore(s) are scratched excessively, renew the complete caliper body. On the floating caliper, check the condition of the guide bushes and bolts; both bushes and bolts should be undamaged and a reasonably tight sliding fit. Renew the caliper seals and dust covers as a matter of course; these are available as a repair kit together with assembly grease.
17 On reassembly, ensure that all components are absolutely clean.
18 Lubricate the new seal(s) with the grease supplied, or dip them in clean hydraulic fluid, then locate them in the cylinder bore groove(s), using only the fingers to manipulate them into position.
19 Fill the inner cavities of the dust seals with the grease supplied, or dip them in clean hydraulic fluid, then locate them on the piston(s).
20 Locate the piston(s) on the caliper, then carefully press it fully into the caliper body, twisting it from side-to-side to ensure it enters the internal seal correctly. At the same time, make sure that the inner end of the dust seal(s) enters the groove on the caliper body, and the outer end enters the groove in the piston. On

7.6 Removing the rear brake caliper

9•10 Braking system

8.5 Checking the front brake disc run-out with a dial gauge

the fixed caliper, make sure that the piston cutaway recesses are positioned as described in Section 5.

Refitting

Fixed caliper

21 With both pistons refitted, locate the caliper over the disc and onto the backplate, then insert the hydraulic line and screw in the union nut. Do not fully-tighten the nut at this stage.
22 Apply a little locking fluid to the threads of the mounting bolts, then refit the cover plate and bolts, and tighten the bolts to the specified torque.
23 Refit the brake pads (see Section 5).
24 Fully tighten the hydraulic union nut.

Floating caliper

25 Locate the caliper mounting bracket on the backplate, then apply locking fluid to the threads of the mounting bolts, insert them, and tighten to the specified torque.
26 Screw the brake hose into the caliper and tighten it to the specified torque.
27 Refit the brake pads as described in Section 5, together with the caliper.
28 Locate the brake hose in the bracket making sure that it is not twisted. Refit the clip, then insert and tighten the rigid brake line union nut.

All models

29 Remove the polythene, where fitted, and bleed the hydraulic system as described in Section 2. Note that, providing the precautions described were taken to minimise brake fluid

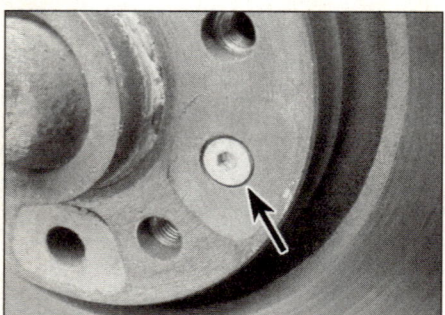

8.11a Front brake disc securing screw

8.7 Use a micrometer to check the disc thickness

loss, it should only be necessary to bleed the relevant rear brake.
30 Refit the roadwheel, then lower the vehicle to the ground and tighten the roadwheel bolts to the specified torque.

8 Front brake disc – inspection, removal and refitting

Inspection

1 Apply the handbrake, then jack up the front of the vehicle and support it on axle stands (see *Jacking and vehicle support*). Remove both front roadwheels.
2 For an accurate check and for access to each side of the disc, the brake caliper should be unbolted and suspended to one side as described later in this Section. Alternatively, just the brake pads can be removed as described in Section 5.
3 Check that the brake disc securing screw is tight, then fit spacers approximately 10.0 mm thick to each of the roadwheel bolts, and refit and tighten the bolts. This will hold the disc in its normal running position.
4 Rotate the brake disc, and examine it for deep scoring or grooving. Light scoring is normal, but if excessive, the disc should be removed and either renewed or machined (within the specified limits) by an engineering works. The minimum thickness is given in the Specifications at the beginning of this Chapter.
5 Using a dial gauge, or a flat metal block

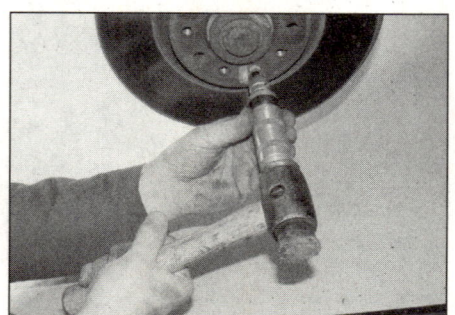

8.11b Using an impact driver to loosen the brake disc securing screw

and feeler blades, check that the disc run-out does not exceed the figure given in the Specifications **(see illustration)**.
6 If the disc run-out is excessive, remove the disc as described later, and check that the disc-to-hub surfaces are perfectly clean. Refit the disc and check the run-out again. If the run-out is still excessive, the disc should be renewed.
7 Using a micrometer check that the disc thickness is not less than that given in the Specifications **(see illustration)**. Take readings at several points around the disc.
8 Repeat the inspection on the other front brake disc.

Removal

9 Remove the roadwheel bolts and spacers used when checking the disc.
10 Remove the disc pads as described in Section 4, and tie the caliper to one side. Also remove the front brake caliper mounting bracket with reference to Section 6.
11 Remove the securing screw and withdraw the disc from the hub. If the screw is tight, use an impact driver to loosen it **(see illustrations)**.

Refitting

12 Refitting is a reversal of removal, but make sure that the mating faces of the disc and hub are perfectly clean, and apply a little locking fluid to the threads of the securing screw before tightening it. If a new disc is being fitted, remove the protective coating from the surface, using an appropriate solvent. Refit the disc pads as described in Section 4, then refit the roadwheel and lower the vehicle to the ground.

9 Rear brake disc – inspection, removal and refitting

Inspection

1 Chock the front wheels, then jack up the rear of the vehicle and support on axle stands (see *Jacking and vehicle support*). Remove both rear roadwheels.
2 For an accurate check and for access to each side of the disc, the brake caliper should

8.11c Removing the front brake disc

Braking system 9•11

9.13a Unscrew the bolts . . .

9.13b . . . and remove the caliper mounting bracket from the rear suspension trailing arm

9.14 Back off the handbrake shoe adjustment using a screwdriver through the access hole in the disc

be unbolted and suspended to one side as described later in this Section. Alternatively, just the brake pads can be removed as described in Section 5.

3 Check that the brake disc securing screw is tight, then fit spacers approximately 10.0 mm thick to each of the roadwheel bolts, and refit and tighten the bolts. This will hold the disc in its normal running position.

4 Rotate the brake disc, and examine it for deep scoring or grooving. Light scoring is normal, but if excessive, the disc should be removed and either renewed or machined (within the specified limits) by an engineering works. The minimum thickness is given in the Specifications at the beginning of this Chapter.

5 Using a dial gauge, or a flat metal block and feeler blades, check that the disc run-out does not exceed the figure given in the Specifications.

6 If the disc run-out is excessive, remove the disc as described later, and check that the disc-to-hub surfaces are perfectly clean. Refit the disc and check the run-out again. If the run-out is still excessive, the disc should be renewed.

7 Using a micrometer check that the disc thickness is not less than that given in the Specifications **(see illustration 8.7)**. Take readings at several points around the disc.

8 Repeat the inspection on the other rear brake disc.

Removal

9 Remove the roadwheel bolts and spacers used when checking the disc.
10 Remove the disc pads as described in Section 5.

Fixed caliper

11 Carefully release the rear brake hydraulic line from the clip on the rear axle, taking care not to bend the line excessively.
12 Unbolt and remove the rear brake caliper with reference to Section 7, and tie it to one side. A convenient place to secure the caliper on the left-hand side is to the exhaust system, using a long plastic cable-tie.

Floating caliper

13 With the caliper already removed in order to remove the disc pads, unscrew the bolts and remove the mounting bracket from the rear suspension trailing arm **(see illustrations)**.

All models

14 Using a screwdriver through the access hole, back off the handbrake shoe adjustment with reference to Section 16 **(see illustration)**.
15 Remove the securing screw and withdraw the disc from the hub **(see illustrations)**.

Refitting

16 Refitting is a reversal of removal, but make sure that the mating faces of the disc and hub are perfectly clean, and apply a little locking fluid to the threads of the securing screw before tightening it. If a new disc is being fitted, remove the protective coating from the surface, using an appropriate solvent. Adjust the handbrake as described in Section 15 and the handbrake cables as described in Section 16. Refit the roadwheel and lower the vehicle to the ground.

10 Handbrake shoes – inspection, removal and refitting

⚠️ **Warning:** *Renew BOTH sets of rear brake shoes at the same time. Note that the dust created by wear of the pads may contain asbestos, which is a health hazard. Never blow it out with compressed air, and do not inhale any of it. Use brake cleaner or methylated spirit to clean brake components.*

Inspection

1 The handbrake operates independently of the footbrake, using brake shoes inside drums integral with the discs.

2 A quick check of the handbrake shoe wear may be made without removing the rear brake disc. Chock the front wheels, then jack up the rear of the vehicle and support it on axle stands (see *Jacking and vehicle support*). Turn the brake disc so that the automatic adjuster is visible through the hole in the disc. If the adjuster has more than 10 threads visible, the shoes are worn excessively and should be renewed.

3 For a thorough check, remove the rear brake disc as described in Section 9, then check the minimum thickness of the friction material on each handbrake shoe. If any one of the shoes has worn below the specified limit, all four handbrake shoes must be renewed as a set.

Removal

4 With the rear brake disc removed, clean the dust and dirt from the brake shoes and backplate.

5 It is possible to remove and refit the shoes without removing the rear hub, although we found it much easier with the hub removed and the backplate on the bench, particularly for the reassembly procedure. Refer to Chapter 10 and remove the rear hub, and the backplate complete with handbrake shoes.

6 Unhook the cable return spring from the

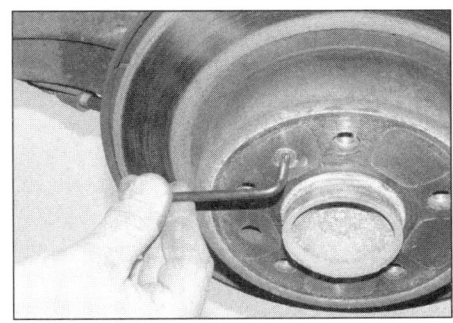

9.15a Remove the screw . . .

9.15b . . . and remove the rear brake disc

9•12 Braking system

10.6 Unhook and remove the cable return spring

10.7 Disconnecting the handbrake cable end fitting from the lever on the backplate

10.8a Handbrake shoes fitted to the rear brake backplate

10.8b Handbrake shoe adjuster (left-hand rear brake) . . .

10.8c . . . expander . . .

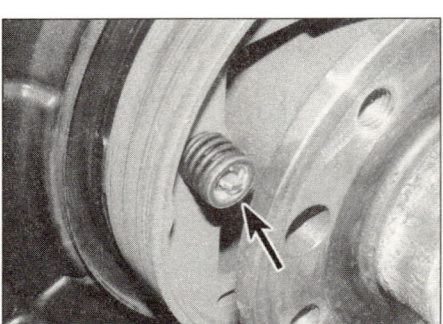

10.8d . . . and hold-down springs

hole in the backplate and from the cable end fitting **(see illustration)**.

7 Unhook the cable end fitting from the lever on the bottom of the backplate **(see illustration)**.

8 Note the fitted position of all components, and if necessary make a sketch of them **(see illustrations)**.

9 Remove the shoe hold-down cups, springs and pins by depressing the cups and turning them through 90° using a pair of pliers **(see illustration)**. If the hub is still fitted, insert a suitable tool through the hole in the hub flange.

10 Carefully lift the shoes directly from the backplate anchors and guide the expander lever through the rubber grommet **(see illustration)**.

11 Pull the shoes apart and remove the adjuster, followed by the upper return spring **(see illustrations)**.

12 Swivel the upper ends of the shoes inwards, and remove the expander from the bottom ends **(see illustrations)**.

13 Unhook the lower return spring from the shoes **(see illustration)**.

14 Dismantle the adjuster and expander components for cleaning **(see illustration)**.

15 If both handbrake assemblies are dismantled at the same time, take care not to mix them up.

10.9 Removing the handbrake shoe hold-down cups, springs and pins

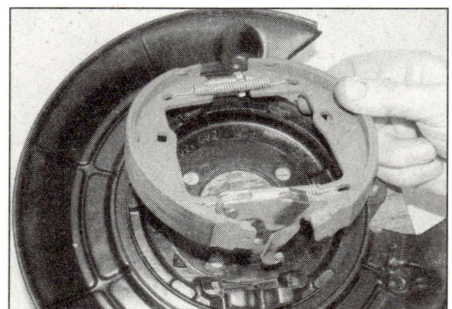

10.10 Lift the shoes directly from the backplate

10.11a Remove the adjuster . . .

10.11b . . . followed by the upper return spring

10.12a Swivel the upper ends of the shoes inwards . . .

16 Clean all components, then examine them for wear and damage. Renew worn or damaged components. Make sure that the expander and adjuster operate freely and are not seized – apply a spot of oil to the expander pivots, and apply a little high melting-point grease to the threads of the adjuster before reassembling it. Set the adjuster to its minimum length.

Refitting

17 Clean the backplate thoroughly, and apply a little copper grease to the shoe contact points (see illustration).
18 Assemble the shoes onto the backplate using a reversal of the removal procedure.
19 Refit the backplate and rear hub with reference to Chapter 10.
20 Hook the cable end fitting on the expander lever and locate the cable holder in the bracket.
21 Hook the cable return spring in the backplate hole and on the end fitting.
22 Refit the rear brake disc and caliper as described in Section 9.
23 Adjust the handbrake shoes as described in Section 15, then refit the roadwheels and lower the vehicle to the ground.

11 Master cylinder – removal, overhaul and refitting

Removal

1 Exhaust the vacuum present in the brake servo unit by repeatedly depressing the brake pedal.
2 On left-hand drive models, remove the main fusebox and holder, then disconnect the wiring from the anti-theft alarm switch. To provide more working room, unbolt and remove the bracket.
3 Where fitted, disconnect the wiring from the brake fluid warning switch in the reservoir.
4 Siphon out the fluid from the reservoir. Alternatively, open any convenient bleed screw in the system, and gently pump the brake pedal to expel the fluid through a plastic tube connected to the bleed screw (see Section 2).

 Warning: Do not siphon the fluid by mouth, as it is poisonous; use a syringe or an old poultry baster.

5 Place cloth rags beneath the master cylinder to catch spilt fluid.
6 On manual transmission models, disconnect the clutch hydraulic hose from the brake fluid reservoir.
7 Refit the filler cap on the reservoir, then carefully lever the reservoir from the rubber grommets in the top of the master cylinder using a wide-bladed screwdriver.
8 Note the position of the brake lines, then unscrew the union nuts and move the lines to one side so that they are just clear of the master cylinder. Do not bend the brake lines excessively. If available use a split spanner to

10.12b . . . and remove the expander

10.14 Dismantling the expander

unscrew the nuts, as they can be very tight. Tape over or plug the outlets of the brake lines and master cylinder.
9 Unscrew the mounting nuts and withdraw the master cylinder from the front of the vacuum servo (see illustration). Recover the seal. Wrap the master cylinder in cloth rags and remove it from the engine compartment. Take care not to spill fluid on the vehicle paintwork.

Overhaul

10 Before dismantling the master cylinder check on the availability and cost of parts, as it may be more economical to renew the complete unit.
11 Clean all dirt and debris from the exterior of the master cylinder.
12 Prise out the reservoir rubber seals from the top of the master cylinder (see illustration overleaf).

11.9 Master cylinder mounting nuts – arrowed

10.13 Unhook the lower return spring

10.17 Apply a little copper grease to the shoe contact points

13 Remove the cover and the lockpin from the fluid aperture to the secondary piston.
14 Using circlip pliers, extract the circlip from the mouth of the master cylinder while slightly depressing the piston against the spring tension.
15 Remove the primary and secondary pistons, together with their springs, from the master cylinder bore, noting their order of removal. If the pistons are tight, tap the cylinder on the work bench or on a block of wood to release them.
16 Thoroughly clean the master cylinder components with methylated spirit or clean brake fluid, and examine them for wear and damage. In particular, check the bore surfaces and rubber seals. The bore surface must not be pitted or scored, and the rubber seals must not be perished or worn. Clean the fluid entry ports of any rust or sediment.
17 If the cylinder bore is in good condition but the rubber seals are worn excessively, obtain new seals or complete new pistons and seals.
18 Lubricate the seals and bore surface with clean brake fluid. Insert the secondary piston assembly with the slot in line with the top of the cylinder, and then insert the lockpin and cover to hold the piston in place. Make sure that the seal lip is not damaged as it enters the cylinder.
19 Insert the primary piston assembly; again making sure that the seal lip is not damaged as it enters the cylinder.
20 Depress the primary piston, then fit the circlip in the groove in the cylinder mouth. Release the piston.
21 Dip the rubber seals in clean fluid and

locate them in the apertures on the top of the master cylinder.

Refitting

22 Ensure the mating surfaces are clean and dry then fit the new seal to the rear of the master cylinder.
23 Fit the master cylinder to the studs on the vacuum servo unit, ensuring that the servo unit pushrod enters the master cylinder piston centrally. Fit the retaining nuts and tighten them securely.
24 Remove the tape or plugs, and reconnect the brake lines to the master cylinder. Tighten the union nuts initially with the fingers to prevent cross-threading, then fully tighten them with a spanner.
25 Locate the fluid reservoir stubs in the rubber seals, and press firmly until it is fully entered.
26 On manual transmission models, reconnect the clutch hydraulic hose to the brake fluid reservoir.
27 Fill the fluid reservoir with fresh brake fluid up to the MAX level mark.
28 Reconnect the wiring to the brake fluid warning switch in the reservoir filler cap.
29 On left-hand drive models, reconnect the wiring to the anti-theft alarm switch. Refit the bracket, main fusebox and holder.
30 Bleed the hydraulic system as described in Section 2. Thoroughly check the operation of the braking system before using the vehicle on the road.

12 Vacuum servo unit non-return valve – removal, testing and refitting

Removal

1 The non-return valve is located in the hose leading from the vacuum servo unit to the intake manifold. It cannot be obtained separately from the hose.
2 Carefully ease the hose adapter from the rubber grommet on the front of the servo unit.
3 Unscrew the union nut and disconnect the hose from the intake manifold.
4 Release the hose from the support and remove from the engine compartment.

Testing

5 Examine the check valve and hose for signs of damage, and renew if necessary. The valve may be tested by blowing through the hose in both directions. Air should flow through the valve in one direction only – when blown through from the servo unit end. Renew the valve and hose complete if necessary.
6 Examine the sealing grommet in the vacuum servo unit for signs of damage or deterioration, and renew as necessary.

Refitting

7 Refitting is a reversal of removal, but tighten the union nut securely. On completion, start the engine and check the function of the brakes; also check that there are no air leaks.

13 Vacuum servo unit – testing, removal and refitting

Testing

1 To test the operation of the servo unit, with the engine off, depress the footbrake several times to dissipate the vacuum. Now start the engine, keeping the pedal firmly depressed. As the engine starts, there should be a noticeable 'give' in the brake pedal as the vacuum builds-up. Allow the engine to run for at least two minutes, and then switch it off. The brake pedal should now feel normal, but further applications should result in the pedal feeling firmer, the pedal stroke decreasing with each application.
2 If the servo does not operate as described, first inspect the servo unit check valve as described in Section 12.
3 If the servo unit still fails to operate satisfactorily, the fault lies within the unit itself. Repairs to the unit are not possible; if faulty, the servo unit must be renewed.

Right-hand drive models

Removal

4 Remove the master cylinder as described in Section 11.
5 Remove both windscreen wiper arms as described in Chapter 12. Remove the plastic cover from the engine compartment rear bulkhead area for access to the wiper linkage.
6 Ease the vacuum hose adapter from the rubber grommet in the front of the vacuum servo unit.
7 To provide more working room, remove the crankcase breather valve and hoses.
8 Working inside the vehicle, remove the facia lower trim panel from beneath the steering column.
9 Unhook the brake pedal return spring, then extract the spring clip and pull out the pivot pin securing the pushrod clevis to the brake pedal **(see illustrations)**.
10 On the bulkhead next to the wiper linkage,

11.12 Exploded view of the brake master cylinder

1 Fluid reservoir rubber seal
2 Cover
3 Lockpin
4 Fluid reservoir rubber seal
5 Master cylinder body
6 Secondary piston assembly
7 Primary piston assembly
8 Circlip

Braking system 9•15

unscrew the servo bracket mounting bolt and nuts. Withdraw the servo unit and upper mounting bracket from the bulkhead, and remove from the engine compartment.

11 Undo the nuts and remove the bracket from the rear of the servo unit.

Refitting

12 Fit the bracket to the rear of the servo unit, and tighten the nuts.

13 Locate the servo unit and mounting bracket on the bulkhead making sure that the upper bracket locates correctly on the lower bracket. Refit the mounting bolt and nuts, and tighten securely.

14 Inside the vehicle, connect the pushrod clevis on the pedal, then insert the pivot pin and secure with the spring clip. Reconnect the brake pedal return spring **(see illustration)**.

15 Refit the facia lower trim panel beneath the steering column.

16 Refit the crankcase breather valve and hoses.

17 Press the vacuum hose adapter in the rubber grommet in the front of the vacuum servo unit.

18 Refit the plastic cover to the rear bulkhead area, then refit the windscreen wiper arms with reference to Chapter 12.

19 Refit the master cylinder with reference to Section 11, and bleed the brake hydraulic system as described in Section 2.

Left-hand drive models

Removal

20 Remove the master cylinder as described in Section 11.

21 Clean the area around the master cylinder-to-ABS unit rear brake line, note its position, then unscrew the union nut and remove the line from the ABS unit. Tape over or plug the aperture and line ends to prevent entry of dust and dirt.

22 Ease the vacuum hose adapter from the rubber grommet in the front of the vacuum servo unit.

23 Unscrew the mounting nuts securing the servo unit to the bracket, then remove the clip from the pushrod and withdraw the servo unit from the vehicle.

Refitting

24 Locate the servo unit on the bracket and engage the brake pedal pushrod with the servo pushrod. Refit and tighten the mounting nuts.

25 Refit the clip to the pushrod, and then depress the brake pedal to lock the clip.

26 Press the vacuum hose adapter into the rubber grommet on the front of the servo unit.

27 Refit the rear brake line to the ABS unit in its previously-noted position, and then tighten the union nut.

28 Refit the brake master cylinder with reference to Section 11, and bleed the brake hydraulic system as described in Section 2.

13.9a Unhook the brake pedal return spring . . .

13.9c . . . and remove the pushrod pivot pin

14 Vacuum pump – removal and refitting

Mechanical vacuum pump

Removal

1 Unclip and remove the engine top cover.

2 Disconnect the vacuum hose from the pressure sensor located on the side of the turbocharger.

3 Undo the screw, and detach the bypass pipe from the turbocharger inlet pipe.

4 Disconnect the bypass valve from the charge air pipe.

5 Disconnect the wiring from the temperature sensor on the charge air pipe.

6 Loosen the clips securing the charge air pipe to the throttle body and turbocharger, then

14.7 Depress the red locking ring to release the vacuum hose

13.9b . . . extract the spring clip . . .

13.14 Fitted position of the brake pedal return spring

unscrew the mounting bolt from the bracket on the cylinder head, and withdraw the pipe from the engine compartment. Temporarily tape over or cover the turbocharger and throttle body apertures.

7 Disconnect the vacuum hose from the vacuum pump on the left-hand end of the cylinder head. To do this, press in the red locking ring while pulling the hose out **(see illustration)**.

8 Disconnect the wiring from the ignition discharge module on the cylinder head.

9 Place some cloth rags below the vacuum pump lubrication banjo, then unscrew and remove the banjo bolt. Recover the outer seal.

10 Unscrew the pump mounting bolts, including the bracket bolt, and then withdraw it from the cylinder head **(see illustration)**. Recover the inner lubrication seal and the main pump seal. Discard all seals as new ones must be used for refitting.

14.10 Mechanical brake vacuum pump mounting bolts

15.7 Handbrake cable adjustment nut on the handbrake lever

Refitting

11 Clean the contact surfaces of the pump and cylinder head. Position the new inner and main seals on the pump and retain with a little grease.
12 Position the pump drive dog so that it will engage with the slot in the end of the camshaft when refitted. Locate the pump on the cylinder head, and refit the mounting bolts, hand-tight at this stage. Wipe away any spilt oil from the cylinder head.
13 Refit the banjo bolt, together with a new O-ring seal, and tighten it to the specified torque.
14 Insert the mounting bolts, and first tighten the two in the cylinder head to the specified torque, then tighten the remaining bolt in the bracket to the specified torque.
15 Reconnect the wiring to the ignition discharge module, then reconnect the vacuum hose to the pump.
16 Refit the charge air pipe to the throttle body and turbocharger, and tighten the mounting bolt. If necessary, apply a little petroleum jelly to the throttle body O-ring to facilitate refitting it. Tighten the pipe securing clips.
17 Reconnect the wiring to the temperature sensor on the charge air pipe.
18 Reconnect the bypass valve to the charge air pipe, then reconnect the bypass pipe to the turbocharger inlet pipe and tighten the screw.
19 Reconnect the vacuum hose to the pressure sensor.
20 Refit the engine top cover.

Electrical vacuum pump

Removal

21 Apply the handbrake, then jack up the front of the vehicle and support it on axle stands (see *jacking and vehicle support*). Remove the left-hand front wheel.
22 Remove the wheel arch liner, and where applicable, the engine undershield
23 Disconnect the vacuum hose from the pump.
24 Disconnect the wiring from pump.
25 Unscrew the mounting nuts and bolts and withdraw the vacuum pump from the inner wing panel.

Refitting

26 Refitting is the reversal of the removal procedure.

15 Handbrake – adjustment

1 First chock the front wheels, then jack up the rear of the vehicle and support on axle stands (see *Jacking and vehicle support*). Remove both rear wheels. Fully release the handbrake lever.
2 Check that the cables are not pulling the expander levers on the rear backplates. If they are, loosen the cable adjusting nut as necessary with reference to paragraph 6.
3 Working on each side at a time, adjust the shoe positions as follows. Turn the rear disc/drum until the access hole is positioned over the upper adjuster serrations. Using a screwdriver through the hole, turn the adjuster serrations until the disc/drum is locked. Now back off the serrations until the disc/drum is just free to turn. Repeat the adjustment on the remaining disc/drum.
4 Refit the rear wheels and tighten the bolts.
5 Set the handbrake lever on the 1st notch.
6 Open the lid of the centre console, and remove the mat for access to the handbrake cable, adjusting nut.
7 Tighten the cable adjusting nut until slight resistance is felt when turning the rear wheels **(see illustration)**. Fully release the handbrake lever and check that the rear wheels turn freely, then set the lever on the 2nd or 3rd notch and check that the rear wheels are locked firmly. If necessary, make a final adjustment of the adjusting nut.
8 If only one rear wheel locks, one of the brake cables may be seized, and this must be attended to before finally adjusting the handbrake.
9 On completion, lower the vehicle to the ground.

16 Handbrake cables – removal and refitting

Removal

1 One primary and a double secondary cable are fitted. An equaliser is permanently attached to the front of the secondary inner cables, and the primary cable is attached to the centre of the equaliser. The secondary cables are supplied as one assembly. First, chock the front wheels then jack up the rear of the vehicle and support on axle stands (see *Jacking and vehicle support*).
2 Refer to Chapter 4A or 4B and separate the exhaust front and rear sections, then disconnect the rubber mounting from the left-hand side of the exhaust and lower the exhaust.
3 Unscrew the rear nuts from the heat shield on the underbody, then bend down the heat shield for access to the handbrake equaliser.
4 At the rear brake backplates, disconnect the handbrake cable return springs from the expander levers.
5 Unhook each cable end fitting from the expander levers.
6 Turn the primary cable end fitting through 90° and disconnect it from the equaliser.
7 Release the front ends of each cable from the supports.
8 Support the fuel tank with a trolley jack and large block of wood, then unscrew the fuel tank front support strap bolts. Pull down the straps to release the handbrake secondary cables.
9 Release the cables from the supports and withdraw from under the vehicle.

Refitting

10 Refitting is a reversal of removal, but adjust the handbrake as described in Section 15.

17 Handbrake lever – removal and refitting

Removal

1 Chock the front wheels, then jack up the rear of the vehicle and support on axle stands (see *Jacking and vehicle support*). Remove both rear wheels.
2 Working at each rear wheel brake, disconnect the left- and right-hand return springs from the holes in the backplates then unhook the cable fittings from the handbrake shoe operating levers.
3 Remove the centre console as described in Chapter 11, and lift up the gaiter.
4 Disconnect the wiring from the handbrake warning light switch, and release the wiring from the cable-ties.
5 Unscrew the nuts securing the handbrake assembly to the floor.
6 Raise the handbrake assembly directly from the floor, and carefully ease the equaliser up through the floor aperture. Tie a length of string to the equaliser so that it can be recovered for refitting.
7 Turn the primary cable end fitting through 90° and disconnect it from the equaliser. Withdraw the handbrake lever assembly from inside the vehicle.

Refitting

8 Refitting is a reversal of removal, but finally adjust the handbrake as described in Section 15. Tighten the handbrake lever mounting bolts securely.

18 Handbrake 'on' warning light switch – removal, testing and refitting

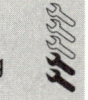

Removal

1 The handbrake 'on' warning light switch is mounted on the front of the handbrake lever mounting bracket **(see illustration)**. Refer to

Chapter 11 and remove the centre console.
2 Disconnect the wiring from the switch.
3 Undo the mounting screw and remove the switch.

Testing

4 Connect a multimeter or battery test probe to the wiring contact and switch body.
5 With the switch plunger at rest, there should be continuity and the multimeter should read no resistance, or the test light should light. With the plunger depressed, there should be infinity resistance or the test light should be extinguished.
6 Failure to operate correctly may indicate corroded contacts or ultimately a faulty switch. Check that there is a 12 volt supply to the wiring with the ignition switched on. Renew the switch if necessary.

Refitting

7 Refitting is a reversal of removal.

19 Brake pedal – removal and refitting

Removal

1 Move the driver's seat fully rearwards.

Right-hand drive models

2 Remove the brake vacuum servo unit as described in Section 13.
3 With the vacuum servo removed, unscrew the four nuts securing the brake pedal bracket to the bulkhead.
4 Working inside the vehicle, remove the facia panel complete, as described in Chapter 11.
5 Refer to Chapter 10 and detach the steering column from the steering gear pinion, taking care not to separate the splined/telescopic section. The front wheels must be pointing straight-ahead and the steering wheel should be taped in position as a precaution.
6 Disconnect the wiring from the pedal switches.
7 Unbolt the steering column assembly from the bulkhead and pedal bracket, and move it rearwards as far as possible without straining the wiring.
8 Lift the pedal bracket assembly from the bulkhead and remove from the vehicle. Recover the foam packing.

Left-hand drive models

9 Remove the battery from the front left-hand corner of the engine compartment (Chapter 5A).
10 Remove the ABS/TCS/ESP hydraulic unit as described in Section 22.
11 Unbolt and remove the main fusebox from the rear left-hand corner of the engine compartment after disconnecting the wiring.
12 Disconnect the engine wiring harness and remove the retaining box from the bulkhead partition behind the engine.
13 Unscrew the four nuts securing the brake pedal bracket to the bulkhead.

18.1 Handbrake 'on' warning light switch

14 Refer to Chapter 11 and remove the lower facia trim from the driver's side.
15 Remove the stepping motor located beneath the brake pedal.
16 Refer to Chapter 10 and detach the steering column from the steering gear pinion, taking care not to separate the splined/telescopic section. The front wheels must be pointing straight-ahead and the steering wheel should be taped in position as a precaution.
17 Unscrew the two bolts securing the pedal assembly to the steering column assembly.
18 Disconnect the wiring from the pedal switches.
19 Unhook the return spring from the pedal, then remove the circlip and pull out the clevis pin connecting the pedal to the pushrod.
20 Lift the pedal bracket assembly from the bulkhead and remove from the vehicle. Recover the foam packing.

Refitting

21 Refitting is a reversal of removal, but tighten all nuts and bolts to their correct specified torque where given.

20 Stop-light switch – removal, testing and refitting

Removal

1 The stop-light switch is mounted on top of the pedal bracket. An internal spring tensions the switch plunger so that the contacts are normally closed, however, when the brake pedal

20.3 Remove the stop-light switch from the bracket . . .

is released, the pedal return spring tension is greater than the switch spring, so the contacts are separated when the pedal is in its released position. When the brake pedal is depressed, the switch supplies a current of 12 volts to the central electronic control module, which then supplies the stop-lights with power. The control unit checks the three stop-light bulbs and if necessary displays a warning on the instrument panel. Where a trailer is being towed, current to the trailer stop-lights is supplied direct from the stop-light switch.
2 To remove the switch, first remove the lower trim panel from the facia with reference to Chapter 11.
3 Twist the switch anti-clockwise 90° and withdraw it from the mounting bracket (see illustration).
4 Disconnect the wiring from the switch (see illustration).

Testing

5 The switch is a single-pole device, and has normally-closed contacts. The operation of the switch can be tested using either a multimeter (switched to the ohmmeter function), or a continuity tester made up of a flashlight bulb, dry cell battery and two pieces of wire. Connect the meter/tester to the switch connector terminals with the switch in its rest position, and check that the meter reads zero resistance or the tester lights up.
6 Press the switch plunger down, and check that the meter reads infinity resistance (open-circuit) or the tester is extinguished.
7 If the switch does not behave as described, or is intermittent in its operation, then a new switch must be fitted; the unit is not serviceable.

Refitting

8 Refit the brake stop-light switch by reversing the removal procedure.

21 Anti-lock Braking System (ABS) – general information and fault finding

General information

1 The Anti-lock Braking System (ABS) is managed by an electronic control module

20.4 . . . and disconnect the wiring

(ECM), which has the capacity to monitor the status and condition of all the components in the system, including itself. If the ECM detects a fault it responds by shutting down the ABS and illuminating the dashboard-mounted ABS warning light. Under these circumstances, conventional non-ABS braking is maintained. Note also that the warning light will be illuminated if the power supply to the ABS ECM is disconnected (eg, if the supply fuse blows). On models manufactured from late 1998, when the ABS warning light is illuminated the standard brake warning light and central warning light are also illuminated.

2 If the ABS warning lights indicate a fault, it is very difficult to diagnose problems without the equipment and expertise to electronically 'interrogate' the ECM for fault codes. Therefore, this Section is limited firstly to a list of the basic checks that should be carried out, to establish the integrity of the system.

3 If the cause of the fault cannot be immediately identified using the checklist described, the *only* course of action open is to take the vehicle to a Saab dealer for examination. Dedicated test equipment is needed to interrogate the ABS ECM to determine the nature of the fault.

Basic fault finding checks

Brake fluid level

4 Check the brake fluid level (see *Weekly checks*). If the level is low, check the complete braking system for signs of leaks. Refer to Chapter 1A and 1B and carry out a check of the brake hoses and pipes throughout the vehicle. If no leaks are apparent, remove each road wheel in turn, and check for leaks at the brake caliper pistons.

Fuses and relays

5 The fuse for the ABS is located beneath a cover on the end of the instrument panel. Remove the cover and pull out the fuse. Visually check the fuse filament; if it is difficult to see whether or not it has blown, use a multimeter to check the continuity of the fuse. If any of the fuses are blown, determine the cause before fitting a new one – if necessary; have the vehicle inspected by a Saab dealer.

6 The ABS system relay is located beneath a cover on the left-hand side of the engine compartment. In general, relays are difficult to test conclusively without any electrical specification. However, the metal contacts inside a relay can usually be felt (and often heard) to open or close as it operates – if the relay in question does not behave in this way when the ignition switch is turned on, it may be faulty. It should be noted that this is not a conclusive test, and substitution with a known good relay *of the same type* is the only way to verify the component operation. If any of the relays is suspected of being faulty, it can be renewed by pulling it out of its socket – noting its orientation – and pushing in a new unit.

Electrical connections and earthing points

7 The engine bay is a hostile environment for electrical connections, and even the best seals can sometimes be penetrated. Water, chemicals and air will induce corrosion on the connector's contacts and prevent good continuity, sometimes intermittently. Disconnect the battery negative cable, and then check the security and condition of all connectors at the ABS hydraulic unit, situated on the left-hand side of the engine bay.

8 Unplug each connector, and examine the contacts inside. Clean any contacts that are found to be dirty or corroded. Avoid scraping the contacts clean with a blade, as this will accelerate corrosion later. Use a piece of lint-free cloth in conjunction with a proprietary cleaning solvent to produce a clean, shiny contact surface.

9 In addition, check the security and condition of the system electrical earthing point on the side of the hydraulic unit.

22 Anti-lock Braking System (ABS) components – removal and refitting

Note: *If the ABS system is faulty, have it checked by a Saab dealer before removing any component.*

Front wheel sensor

Removal

1 Apply the handbrake, then jack up the front of the vehicle and support it on axle stands (see *Jacking and vehicle support*). Remove the relevant roadwheel.

2 Disconnect the wiring plug in the engine compartment. For the front left-hand sensor, it is located next to the battery, and it is recommended that the battery and battery tray are removed (see Chapter 5A); also, if required, unclip the coolant expansion tank and position it to one side. For the right-hand sensor it is located behind the power steering fluid reservoir, and it will be necessary to release the locking tab on the wiring connector; if required, remove the power steering fluid reservoir and position it to one side.

3 Clean the area around the wheel sensor on the front hub carrier, then unscrew the mounting bolt and remove the sensor.

4 Prise the rubber grommet from the inner wing panel, and pull out the wiring.

5 Release the wiring from the retaining clips on the inner wing panel and brake hose.

Refitting

6 Refitting is a reversal of removal, but tighten the mounting bolt securely.

Rear wheel sensor

Removal

7 The rear wheel sensors are integral with the rear wheel hubs, so this section essentially describes the removal of the hub. First, chock the front wheels then jack up the rear of the vehicle and support on axle stands (see *Jacking and vehicle support*). Remove the relevant roadwheel.

8 Remove the rear brake disc as described in Section 9.

9 Where fitted, remove the protective cover from the bottom of the rear suspension trailing arm, and unbolt the handbrake cable support bracket.

10 Disconnect the wiring from the wheel sensor on the rear of the hub.

11 Unscrew the mounting nuts and withdraw the hub assembly from the rear axle. Leave the backplate, handbrake shoes and the spacer(s) hanging on the cable. **Note:** *Discard the hub nuts, as new ones must be used on refitting.* Recover the shims where fitted.

Refitting

12 Clean the mounting faces of the rear axle; backplate, spacer(s) and hub then mount the components in the correct order. Fit and progressively tighten the new nuts to the torque wrench setting and angle given in the Specifications.

13 Reconnect the wiring to the wheel sensor.

14 If removed, refit the handbrake cable support bracket and the protective cover to the bottom of the rear suspension trailing-arm.

15 Refit the rear brake disc (see Section 9) and adjust the handbrake shoes (see Section 15).

16 Refit the roadwheel, then lower the vehicle to the ground.

17 Depress the footbrake pedal firmly to set the rear brake pads in their normal position.

ABS/ESP/TCS hydraulic unit

Note: *The ABS electronic control module (ECM) is supplied as an integral part of the hydraulic unit and cannot be removed separately. After fitting a new unit, the ECM must be calibrated by a Saab dealer using the Saab Tech2 hand-held diagnostic instrument. It is recommended that the ESP system be switched off until the calibration has been carried out.*

Removal

18 Disconnect the battery negative lead.

19 Cut the plastic cable-ties holding the battery positive cable to the main fusebox, then unscrew the nuts and position the fusebox to one side without disconnecting the wiring. If necessary, suspend the fusebox using a piece of string.

20 Minimise fluid loss by first removing the master cylinder reservoir cap, then tightening it down onto a piece of polythene to obtain an airtight seal. Also, place cloth rags beneath the ABS unit to catch spilt fluid.

21 Disconnect the wiring plug from the electronic control module, cut the plastic cable-ties holding the cable and position the wiring connector plug to one side **(see illustration)**.

22 Identify each hydraulic brake pipe for its location on the hydraulic unit, then unscrew the union nuts and disconnect the pipes. Tape over or plug the apertures and pipe ends to prevent entry of dust and dirt.
23 Unscrew the mounting nuts and remove the ABS hydraulic unit from the engine compartment **(see illustration)**. Take care not to spill hydraulic fluid on the vehicle paintwork.

Refitting

24 Refitting is a reversal of removal, but tighten the unit mounting nuts and the hydraulic brake pipe union nuts to the specified torque, and finally bleed the hydraulic system as described in Section 2.

23 Electronic Stability Program (ESP) components – removal and refitting

Yaw rate (gyro) sensor

Removal

1 Remove the centre console as described in Chapter 11.
2 On manual transmission models, remove the gear lever housing with reference to Chapter 7A; on automatic transmission models, remove the selector lever housing with reference to Chapter 7B.
3 Note the fitted position of the sensor, and the forward direction of the arrow on the upper face, then undo the mounting screws.
4 Release the locking tab, then disconnect the wiring and remove the sensor.

Refitting

5 Refitting is a reversal of removal, but make sure that the arrow points to the front of the vehicle.

Steering wheel angle sensor

Note: *After fitting a new steering wheel angle sensor, the sensor must be calibrated by a Saab dealer using the Saab Tech2 hand-held diagnostic instrument. It is recommended that the ESP system be switched off until the calibration has been carried out.*

 Warning: Never fit a damaged steering wheel angle sensor, as the vehicle may react dangerously in the event of an emergency. Do not use excessive force when removing or refitting the sensor.

Removal

6 Remove the steering column assembly as described in Chapter 10.
7 The inner steering column consists of two splined sections, which are collapsible and will only fit together in one position. First, mark both inner column sections and the outer column housing in relation to each other.
8 Carefully pull the lower inner column, together with the bearing bracket and angle sensor, from the outer column.

22.21 Disconnect the wiring connector (arrowed) from the control unit

9 Undo the locking screw securing the bearing bracket to the bearing carrier, then use a screwdriver to depress the plastic retaining catch on the opposite side, and withdraw the bracket over the lower inner column.
10 Using circlip pliers, expand the circlip and remove it from the lower inner column/intermediate shaft, followed by the spring washer **(see illustration)**.
11 Remove the bearing carrier and the steering wheel angle sensor from the lower inner column/intermediate shaft.

Refitting

12 Locate the sensor on the lower inner column/intermediate shaft, and engage its groove with the raised tab **(see illustration)**. If a new sensor is being fitted, complete the label and attach it to the sensor.
13 Locate the bearing carrier onto the shaft, engaging the arms with the sensor leg.
14 Refit the spring washer and the circlip, making sure that the circlip fully enters the groove.
15 Locate the bracket onto the bearing carrier, making sure that the plastic retaining catch engages correctly, then insert and tighten the locking screw.
16 Align the marks made on both inner column sections with the marks made on the outer column housing, then engage the upper and lower inner columns with each other. Do not force the columns if they are not correctly aligned.

23.10 Steering wheel angle sensor components

1 Circlip
2 Spring washer
3 Bearing carrier
4 Steering wheel angle sensor

22.23 ABS hydraulic unit upper mounting bracket

17 Refit the steering column assembly with reference to Chapter 10.
18 Have the steering wheel angle sensor calibrated by a Saab dealer at the earliest opportunity.

Brake pressure sensor

Removal

19 The brake pressure sensor is located on the rear of the hydraulic unit, at the left-hand rear corner of the engine compartment. Have ready a means of plugging the sensor hole to prevent loss of brake fluid.
20 Disconnect the wiring from the sensor.
21 Using a 24.0 mm spanner, unscrew the sensor from the hydraulic unit. Plug the opening immediately, taking care not to allow dust and dirt to enter the circuit.

Refitting

22 Refitting is a reversal of removal, but tighten the sensor securely. Finally, bleed the hydraulic circuit with reference to Section 2; if minimal fluid was lost, it is only necessary to bleed the front left- and rear right-hand brakes.

ESP/TCS switch

Removal

23 The ESP/TCS on/off switch is located on the instrument panel. To remove it, carefully ease it out using a flat-bladed screwdriver.
24 Disconnect the wiring.

Refitting

25 Refitting is a reversal of removal.

23.12 Steering wheel angle sensor location raised tab (1) on the intermediate shaft

Notes

Chapter 10
Suspension and steering

Contents

	Section number
Front anti-roll bar – removal, overhaul and refitting	4
Front hub bearing – renewal	6
Front hub carrier – removal and refitting	5
Front lower arm – removal, overhaul and refitting	3
Front strut – removal, overhaul and refitting	2
Front subframe – removal, overhaul and refitting	7
General information	1
Power steering hydraulic system – draining, refilling and bleeding	18
Power steering pump – removal and refitting	19
Rear anti-roll bar – removal, overhaul and refitting	9
Rear hub assembly – removal and refitting	10
Rear lower transverse link – removal and refitting	13
Rear strut/shock absorber – removal, overhaul and refitting	8
Rear subframe – removal, overhaul and refitting	14
Rear trailing arm – removal, overhaul and refitting	11
Rear upper transverse link – removal and refitting	12
Steering column – removal and refitting	16
Steering gear assembly – removal and refitting	17
Steering rack rubber gaiter – renewal	20
Steering wheel – removal and refitting	15
Track rod end – removal and refitting	21
Wheel alignment and steering angles – general information	22

Degrees of difficulty

Easy, suitable for novice with little experience	Fairly easy, suitable for beginner with some experience	Fairly difficult, suitable for competent DIY mechanic	Difficult, suitable for experienced DIY mechanic	Very difficult, suitable for expert DIY or professional

Specifications

General
Front suspension type	Independent with MacPherson struts, hub carriers and anti-roll bar. Struts incorporate gas-filled shock absorbers and coil springs. Subframe with lower arms and balljoints
Rear suspension type	Independent with struts and anti-roll bar. The struts incorporate gas-filled shock absorbers and coil springs. Subframe with upper and lower transverse links to trailing arms
Steering type	Rack-and-pinion, hydraulic power assistance on all models

Wheel alignment
Front:
- Toe-in:
  - 15 in wheels: 2.0 ± 0.6 mm
  - 16 in wheels: 2.2 ± 0.6 mm
  - 17 in wheels: 2.2 ± 0.6 mm
- Camber:
  - 15 in wheels: -0.8° (at body height of 600 mm)
  - 16 in wheels: -0.9° (at body height of 610 mm)
  - 17 in wheels: -0.8° (at body height of 630 mm)
- Castor: 2.9° ± 0.5°
- Swivel pin inclination: 12.6° ± 0.5°

Rear:
- Toe-in:
  - 15 in wheels: 3.0 ± 1.4 mm
  - 16 in wheels: 3.2 ± 1.4 mm
  - 17 in wheels: 3.4 ± 1.4 mm
- Camber:
  - 15 in wheels: -0.9° (at body height of 590 mm)
  - 16 in wheels: -0.8° (at body height of 605 mm)
  - 17 in wheels: -0.8° (at body height of 620 mm)

Steering angle toe-out on turns:
- Outer wheel: 20.0°
- Inner wheel: 21.25° ± 0.5°

Roadwheels
Size:
- Standard: 6 x 15, 6.5 x 16 or 7 x 17
- Compact spare: 4.0 x 16

Tyres
Size .... 195/65R15, 205/65R15, 215/55R16, 225/45R17 & 235/45R17
Tyre pressures .... See end of *Weekly checks* on page 0•16

Power steering
Steering wheel turns, lock-to-lock .... 2.9 turns

Torque wrench settings

	Nm	lbf ft
Front suspension		
Anti-roll bar link	90	66
Anti-roll bar to subframe	25	18
Engine rear mounting to engine bracket	50	37
Engine rear mounting to subframe	25	18
Hub bearing and backplate to carrier:		
Stage 1	90	66
Stage 2	Angle-tighten 45°	
Hub (driveshaft) nut (new)	230	170
Lower arm rear mounting to lower arm	75	55
Lower arm mounting to subframe:		
Stage 1	120	89
Stage 2	Angle-tighten 90°	
Lower balljoint to hub carrier	49	36
Lower balljoint to lower arm:		
Stage 1	20	15
Stage 2	Angle-tighten 90°	
Shock absorber piston rod upper retaining nut	75	55
Strut to hub carrier:		
Stage 1	100	74
Stage 2	Angle-tighten 90°	
Strut top mounting bolts	30	22
Subframe mounting to underbody:		
Stage 1	100	74
Stage 2	Angle-tighten 45°	
Subframe rear crossmember support bracket	65	48
Rear suspension		
Anti-roll bar to crossmember	50	37
Hub assembly to trailing arm:		
Stage 1	50	37
Stage 2	Angle-tighten 30°	
Shock absorber/strut lower mounting bolt	190	140
Shock absorber/strut piston rod top mounting	20	15
Shock absorber/strut to body	55	41
Subframe:		
Stage 1	90	66
Stage 2	Angle-tighten 60°	
Trailing arm bracket to underbody:		
Stage 1	90	66
Stage 2	Angle-tighten 30°	
Trailing arm to mounting bracket:		
Stage 1	90	66
Stage 2	Angle-tighten 60°	
Upper and lower transverse links to trailing arm:		
Stage 1	90	66
Stage 2	Angle-tighten 60°	
Steering		
Power steering pump	25	18
Power steering pump delivery pipe support	30	22
Power steering pump delivery pipe union nut	30	22
Steering column	25	18
Steering column-to-pinion gear clamp bolt	30	22
Steering gear mounting bolts	95	70
Steering gear supply and return pipe union bolts	30	22
Steering wheel	38	28
Track rod end locknut	70	52
Track rod end to steering arm	35	26
Wheels		
Roadwheel bolts	110	81

Suspension and steering 10•3

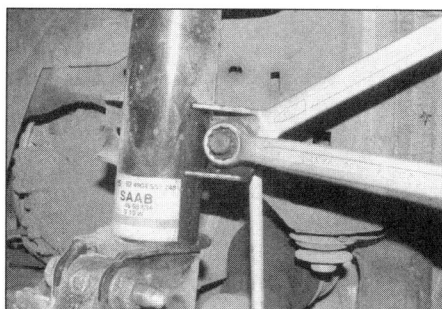

2.2a Unscrew the nut . . .

2.2b . . . and remove the anti-roll bar link from the suspension strut

2.5 Front suspension strut upper mounting bolts

1 General information

The front suspension is fully independent, with MacPherson struts and an anti-roll bar. The struts incorporate shock absorbers and gas-filled coil springs, and the hub carriers are bolted to the bottom of the struts. The hub carriers are located on the outer ends of the lower arms by renewable balljoints bolted onto the arms. The hub bearings can be renewed separately, although, on later models the hub and bearings are integral, and are bolted to the carriers separately. The lower arms and anti-roll bar are mounted on the front suspension subframe located beneath the engine compartment.

The rear suspension is fully independent, with trailing arms, struts, upper and lower transverse links and an anti-roll bar. The struts incorporate shock absorbers and coil springs, and the hubs are bolted to the trailing arms. The transverse links and anti-roll bar are mounted on the rear suspension subframe. The rear hubs have double-row bearings and are supplied as integral units that cannot be dismantled; they are attached to the trailing arms by studs and nuts. Each rear hub incorporates an internal ABS sensor to monitor the wheel speed.

Power-assisted steering is fitted to all models. The steering rack is essentially a hydraulic ram, which is actuated mechanically by a pinion gear, and hydraulically by pressurised hydraulic fluid, supplied by the power steering pump. The steering column transmits effort applied at the steering wheel to the pinion, and a control valve supplies hydraulic fluid to the steering rack ram. When the steering wheel is turned, the valve directs fluid to the appropriate side of the ram, assisting the movement of the rack. The power steering pump is mounted externally on the engine, and is driven by the auxiliary drivebelt.

The design and mounting position of the steering column are such that, in the event of a head-on collision, it will absorb impact by crumpling longitudinally, and will also be deflected away from the driver.

2 Front strut – removal, overhaul and refitting

Removal

1 Apply the handbrake, then jack up the front of the vehicle and support it on axle stands (see *Jacking and vehicle support*). Remove the roadwheel.
2 Unscrew the nut and remove the anti-roll bar link from the suspension strut. Hold the link spindle with one spanner while the nut is being loosened (see illustrations).
3 Note that the bolts securing the strut to the hub carrier are fitted with their heads facing forwards. Unscrew and remove the bolts, and move the holder for the ABS wheel sensor and brake hydraulic hose to one side. The bolts have small location splines on their shanks, and must not be turned within the hub carrier; hold the bolt head stationary and unscrew the nut from it.
4 Hold the strut inwards while the hub carrier is tilted outwards from it. Do not strain the brake flexible hydraulic hose.
5 Support the strut, and then unscrew the upper mounting bolts on the suspension tower in the rear corner of the engine compartment. Note that the mounting bolts also secure an upper cover. Withdraw the strut from under the front wing (see illustration).

Overhaul

⚠ **Warning:** Before attempting to dismantle the front suspension strut, the coil spring must be first held in compression, using a purpose-made tool. Universal coil spring compressors are available from motor factors or car accessory shops, and are essential for this operation. DO NOT attempt to dismantle the strut without such a tool, as damage and/or personal injury is likely.

Note: *A new top-mounting nut must be used on reassembly.*

6 Support the strut by clamping it in a soft-jawed vice.
7 Using the spring compressor, compress the coils of the spring just enough to relieve all pressure from the upper spring seat (see illustration).
8 The shock absorber piston rod must be held stationary while the top bearing retaining nut is unscrewed. To do this, use a ring spanner and Allen key (see illustrations). Discard the nut, as a new one must be fitted on reassembly.

2.7 Compressing the coil spring using the spring compressor tools

2.8a Hold the piston rod with an Allen key while loosening the top bearing retaining nut . . .

2.8b . . . then unscrew and remove the nut

10•4 Suspension and steering

2.9a Remove the top mounting . . .

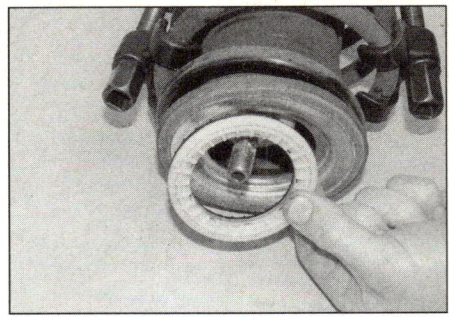
2.9b . . . race . . .

2.9c . . . upper spring seat and rubber gaiter . . .

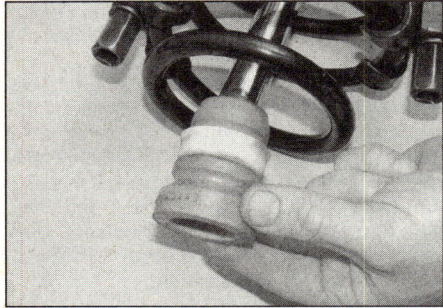
2.9d . . . followed by the bump stop . . .

2.9e . . . and coil spring

2.10 Front suspension strut with coil spring removed

9 Remove the top mounting, race, upper spring seat and rubber gaiter, followed by the bump stop and coil spring **(see illustrations)**.
10 Further dismantling of the strut is not possible; therefore if the shock absorber is faulty, the strut itself must be renewed **(see illustration)**.
11 Clean all the components and examine them for wear and damage. Check the upper mounting bearing for smooth operation by turning it by hand. Renew the components as necessary.
12 Locate the bottom end (small diameter) of the coil spring onto the strut; making sure its end abuts the location stop on the lower spring seat **(see illustration)**. **Note:** *If a new spring is being fitted, first compress the coils using the spring compressor.*
13 Fit the bump stop over the piston rod, followed by the rubber gaiter.
14 Fit the upper spring seat on top of the spring, followed by the bearing race, top mounting and a new retaining nut.
15 Tighten the nut to the specified torque while holding the piston rod stationary with the Allen key.
16 Carefully loosen the spring compressor while at the same time making sure that the bottom of the spring remains located correctly in the lower spring seat. Remove the compressor.

Refitting

17 Locate the strut under the front wing and lift it into position. Note that the small hole is used for locating the upper bearing in the strut tower. Insert the upper mounting bolts and tighten them to the specified torque.
18 Tilt the hub carrier inwards and engage it with the bottom of the strut. Insert the bolts from the front and refit the ABS wheel sensor/brake hose holder. Apply locking fluid to the threads of the bolts, then screw on the nuts and tighten them to the specified torque. Hold the bolt heads stationary while the nuts are tightened.
19 Refit the anti-roll bar link to the strut and tighten the nut to the specified torque.
20 Refit the roadwheel and lower the vehicle to the ground.

3 Front lower arm – removal, overhaul and refitting

Removal

1 Apply the handbrake, then jack up the front of the vehicle and support it on axle stands (see *Jacking and vehicle support*). Remove the roadwheel.
2 Unscrew and remove the bolts securing the lower arm rear mounting to the subframe.
3 Unscrew and remove the lower arm front mounting bolt, and pull the lower arm down from the subframe.
4 Unscrew and remove the clamp bolt securing the lower arm balljoint to the bottom of the hub carrier. If necessary, prise the clamp apart slightly using a screwdriver or lever. Withdraw the lower arm from the hub carrier.
5 Note the fitted position of the rear mounting on the lower arm, then unscrew the nut and remove the mounting **(see illustration)**.
6 Unscrew the bolts and remove the front suspension lower balljoint from the lower arm **(see illustration)**.

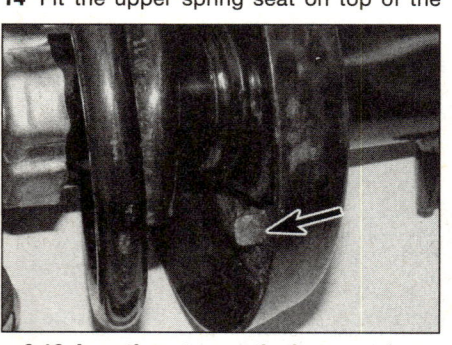
2.12 Location stop on the lower spring seat

3.5 Nut securing the rear mounting to the front suspension lower arm

Suspension and steering 10•5

Overhaul

7 Clean the components and examine them for wear and damage.
8 If the front mounting bush is worn excessively, press out the old bush and similarly press in the new bush. If a standard press is not available, use a long bolt together with tubing and washers to complete the task. Saab technicians use a tapered tool for the fitting procedure; the outer rubber is compressed to a diameter less than that of the bore in the lower arm.
9 Check the rear mounting for wear, and renew it if necessary.
10 Check the lower arm for damage and if necessary renew it.
11 Check the lower balljoint stub for good articulation. If it is dry or seized, renew it. Also, check that the balljoint rubber boot is not damaged.

Refitting

12 Fit the lower balljoint to the arm and tighten the bolts to the specified torque.
13 Locate the rear mounting on the lower arm so that its axis is in line with the arm (see illustration). Refit the nut and tighten to the specified torque.
14 Lift the lower arm into position and insert the lower balljoint stub into the bottom of the hub carrier. Make sure that the stub is fully entered so that the annular groove is opposite the clamp bolt hole. Insert the clamp bolt and tighten to the specified torque and angle.
15 Locate the inner end of the lower arm on the subframe and insert the front mounting bolt hand-tight at this stage.
16 Insert the rear mounting bolt hand-tight, then raise the outer end of the lower arm with a trolley jack until the weight of the front of the vehicle is on the front suspension, and fully-tighten the arm mounting bolts to their specified torque. If preferred, the bolts can be fully-tightened after lowering the vehicle to the ground.
17 Refit the roadwheel and lower the vehicle to the ground.
18 Have the front wheel alignment checked and if necessary adjusted at the earliest opportunity.

4 Front anti-roll bar – removal, overhaul and refitting

Removal

1 Apply the handbrake, then jack up the front of the vehicle and support it on axle stands (see *Jacking and vehicle support*). Remove both front roadwheels.
2 The engine assembly must be supported while the rear of the subframe is lowered. To do this, use a suitable hoist or engine support bar that straddles the engine compartment. Slightly lift the engine assembly so that its weight is supported.

3.6 Bolts retaining the suspension lower balljoint to the lower arm

3 At the rear of the engine, unscrew the nut securing the rear engine mounting to the engine bracket, then unbolt the mounting from the subframe and remove it.
4 Working under the vehicle, unbolt the crossmember from the rear of the subframe.
5 The exhaust front section must be lowered before lowering the subframe. To do this, refer to Chapter 4A or 4B and either remove the exhaust or separate it at the joint and release it from the rubber mountings.
6 Unscrew and remove the two bolts securing the steering gear to the subframe.
7 Support the subframe with a trolley jack, then unscrew and remove the centre mounting bolts and lower the rear of the subframe as far as possible for access to the front anti-roll bar mountings.
8 Note the fitted position of the side links on the anti-roll bar, then unscrew the nuts and detach them. If preferred, the side links may be detached from the strut.
9 Note the position of the two anti-roll bar mounting clamps, then unscrew the bolts and remove the clamps (see illustration).
10 Withdraw the anti-roll bar from one side of the vehicle, taking care not to damage the brake hoses and wiring.
11 Note the fitted position of the split clamp mounting rubbers, and then prise them from the anti-roll bar.

Overhaul

12 Check the anti-roll bar and mountings for signs of wear and damage. Also check the side links.
13 Check the split clamp mounting rubbers and renew them if necessary.

Refitting

14 Clean the anti-roll bar, then dip the split clamp mounting rubbers in soapy water and fit them with their splits facing rearwards.
15 Locate the anti-roll bar onto the subframe and refit the mounting clamps. Insert the mounting bolts and tighten them to the specified torque.
16 Refit the side links to the anti-roll bar (or strut if applicable) and tighten the nuts to the specified torque.
17 Raise the subframe and refit the centre mounting bolts. Tighten the bolts to the specified torque and angle. Remove the trolley jack.

3.13 Align the front suspension rear mounting bush before tightening the retaining nut (1)

18 Insert the steering gear mounting bolts and tighten them to the specified torque.
19 Refit the exhaust front section with reference to Chapter 4A or 4B.
20 Refit the crossmember to the rear of the subframe and tighten the mounting bolts to the specified torque.
21 Refit the rear engine mounting and tighten the bolts to the specified torques.
22 Remove the hoist or support bar.
23 Refit the roadwheels and lower the vehicle to the ground.

5 Front hub carrier – removal and refitting

Removal

1 Jack up the front of the vehicle and support it on axle stands (see *Jacking and vehicle support*). Remove the relevant roadwheel and, where applicable, the engine undershield.
2 Where applicable, tap off the metal dust cover for access to the hub nut. Note that the cover cannot be removed with the roadwheel in position, so it is not possible to loosen the hub nut before raising the front of the vehicle.
3 Temporarily refit two of the roadwheel bolts and tighten them to hold the brake disc onto the hub flange, then have an assistant depress the footbrake pedal, while the hub nut is being loosened. Unscrew and remove the hub nut. Discard the nut as a new one must be used on refitting.

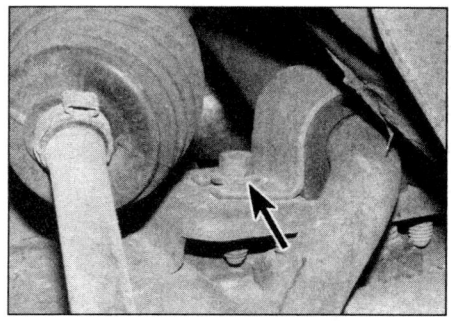

4.9 Front anti-roll bar mounting clamp bolt

10•6 Suspension and steering

5.4 Disconnect the sensor arm from the lower arm

5.5 Removing the front brake disc

5.6a Unscrew the bolt . . .

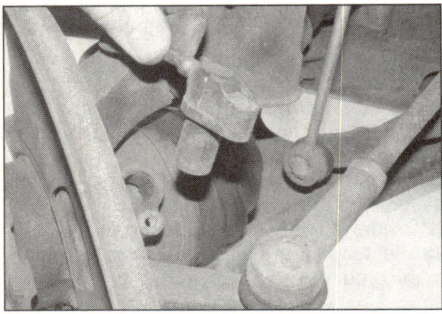

5.6b . . . and remove the ABS sensor from the hub carrier

5.8a Undo the screws . . .

5.8b . . . and remove the brake backplate

4 On models fitted with a headlamp position sensor, carefully unclip the sensor arm from the lower suspension arm and position it to one side **(see illustration)**.

5 Refer to Chapter 9 and remove the front brake disc **(see illustration)**. Suspend the caliper from the front coil spring with a piece of wire or cable-tie, without disconnecting the flexible hydraulic fluid hose.

6 Unscrew the bolt and remove the ABS sensor from the hub carrier **(see illustrations)**. Position it to one side.

7 Detach the steering track rod end from the hub carrier with reference to Section 21.

8 Undo the screws and remove the brake backplate from the hub carrier – access to the screws is gained through the holes in the hub flange **(see illustrations)**.

9 Note that the bolts securing the strut to the hub carrier are fitted with their heads facing forwards. Unscrew and remove the bolts, and move the holding plate for the ABS wheel sensor wiring and brake hydraulic hose to one side **(see illustration)**. The bolts have fine location splines on their shanks, and must not be turned within the hub carrier; hold the bolt head stationary and unscrew the nut from it. Lower the assembly so that the driveshaft is resting on the front subframe.

10 Unscrew and remove the clamp bolt securing the lower arm balljoint to the bottom of the hub carrier **(see illustration)**.

11 Push the splined section of the driveshaft out of the hub. If it is tight, temporarily refit the hub nut onto the threads and tap the end of the driveshaft using a soft-faced mallet to free it. Lift the hub carrier from the lower balljoint and withdraw from the vehicle **(see illustrations)**. If necessary, prise the clamp apart slightly using a screwdriver or lever.

12 If required, remove the hub bearing from the carrier as described in Section 6.

Refitting

13 Refit the hub bearing to the carrier with reference to Section 6.

14 Locate the hub onto the end of the driveshaft and engage the hub splines with the driveshaft splines. Draw the hub onto the

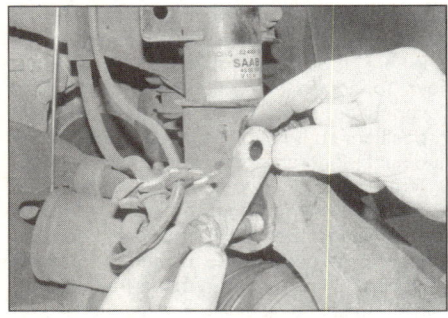

5.9 Removing the strut-to-hub carrier bolts together with the wiring/hose holding plate

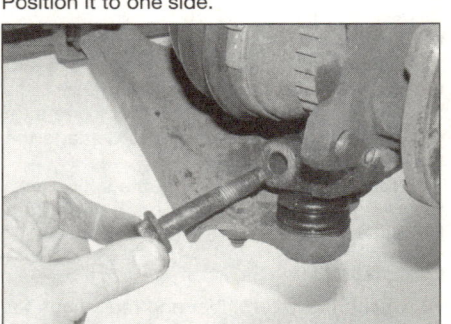

5.10 Removing the lower arm balljoint clamp bolt

5.11a Slide the driveshaft from the hub . . .

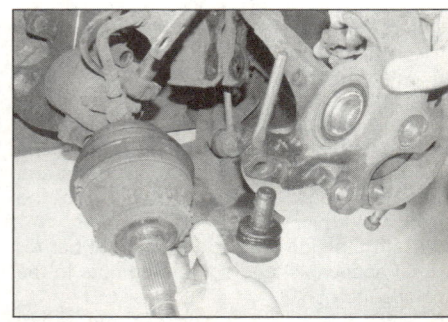

5.11b . . . and lift the hub carrier from the lower balljoint

Suspension and steering

driveshaft using the new hub centre nut, but do not fully-tighten the nut at this stage.

15 Locate the top of the hub carrier in the bottom of the strut, and insert the bolts with their heads facing forwards, together with the holder for the ABS wheel sensor and brake hydraulic hose. Apply locking fluid to the threads of the bolts, then screw on the nuts and tighten them to the specified torque. Hold the bolt heads stationary while the nuts are tightened.

16 Refit the brake backplate and tighten the retaining screws securely.

17 Lift the lower arm into position and insert the lower balljoint stub into the bottom of the hub carrier. Make sure that the stub is fully entered and the location cut-out is opposite the clamp bolt hole **(see illustration)**. Insert the clamp bolt and tighten to the specified torque and angle.

18 Refit the steering track rod end to the hub carrier and tighten the nut to the specified torque.

19 Refit the ABS sensor to the hub carrier and tighten the bolt securely.

20 Refit the front brake caliper and disc with reference to Chapter 9.

5.17 The location cut-out (arrowed) must align with the bolt hole

21 Refit the headlamp position sensor and inner splash cover as applicable.

22 With two of the roadwheel bolts holding the brake disc in position, have an assistant depress the footbrake pedal, and then tighten the hub nut to the specified torque.

23 Where fitted, tap the metal dust cover onto the hub flange.

24 Refit the undershield where applicable, then refit the roadwheel and lower the vehicle to the ground. Tighten the wheel bolts to the specified torque.

6 Front hub bearing – renewal

1 The hub and bearing assembly is bolted to the carrier separately **(see illustration)**. With the vehicle parked on a level surface, remove the wheel trim (and hub dust cap where applicable). Loosen the hub centre nut half a turn.

2 Apply the handbrake, then jack up the front of the vehicle and support it on axle stands (see *Jacking and vehicle support*). Remove the roadwheel.

3 Fully unscrew and remove the hub centre nut. Discard the nut, as a new one must be used on refitting.

4 Refer to Chapter 9 and remove the front brake disc. Suspend the caliper from the front coil spring with a piece of wire or cable-tie, without disconnecting the flexible hydraulic fluid hose.

5 Unscrew the bolt and remove the ABS sensor from the hub carrier. Position it to one side.

6 Detach the steering track rod end from the hub carrier with reference to Section 21.

7 Unscrew and remove the clamp bolt securing the lower arm balljoint to the bottom of the hub carrier. If necessary, prise the clamp apart slightly using a screwdriver or lever. Pull down the lower arm from the hub carrier.

8 Push the splined section of the driveshaft out of the hub. If it is tight, temporarily refit the hub nut onto the threads and tap the end of the driveshaft using a soft-faced mallet to free it, while supporting the hub carrier.

9 Unscrew the bolts and withdraw the hub bearing and backplate assembly from the carrier **(see illustration)**.

10 Clean the carrier, then locate the new hub bearing and backplate assembly on the carrier and tighten the mounting bolts to the specified torque.

11 Locate the hub and carrier onto the end of the driveshaft and engage the hub splines with those of the driveshaft. Draw the hub onto the driveshaft using the new hub centre nut, but do not fully-tighten the nut at this stage.

12 Lift the lower arm into position and insert the lower balljoint stub into the bottom of the

6.1 Front hub carrier components

1 Hub carrier
2 Hub and bearing assembly
3 Splined bolt securing the hub carrier to the front suspension strut

6.9 One of the bolts securing the hub bearing to the carrier

10•8 Suspension and steering

7.9 Reinforcement crossmember on the rear of the subframe

1 Bolts retaining the centre section and inner ends of the triangular plates
2 Bolts retaining the outer ends of the triangular plates and the rear of the subframe

7.10 Steering gear mounting bolts on the subframe

hub carrier. Make sure that the stub is fully entered so that the annular groove is opposite the clamp bolt hole. Insert the clamp bolt and tighten to the specified torque.
13 Refit the steering track rod end to the hub carrier and tighten the nut to the specified torque.
14 Refit the ABS sensor to the hub carrier and tighten the bolt securely.
15 Refit the front brake caliper and disc with reference to Chapter 9.
16 Refit the roadwheel and lower the vehicle to the ground.
17 Tighten the hub centre nut to the specified torque.

7 Front subframe – removal, overhaul and refitting

Removal

1 Apply the handbrake, then jack up the front of the vehicle and support it on axle stands (see *Jacking and vehicle support*). Remove both front wheels, and then remove the underbody splash covers.
2 Unbolt the engine rear mounting from the subframe with reference to Chapter 2A or 2B.
3 Support the weight of the engine and transmission with a hoist attached to the rear engine lifting eye.
4 Support the radiator and air conditioning condenser on the engine compartment front crossmember using cable-ties.
5 Disconnect the wiring connector for the oxygen sensors.
6 Where applicable, unbolt the oil cooler and allow it to hang from its hoses.
7 Unscrew the power steering fluid cooler mounting bolts and support the cooler with cable-ties.
8 Mark the position of the subframe on the underbody to ensure correct refitting. One way to do this is to spray paint around the subframe mountings using an aerosol; the outline of the mountings will be marked clearly on the underbody.
9 Unbolt the reinforcement crossmember from the rear of the subframe. Note that the outer bolts are also the subframe rear mounting bolts **(see illustration)**. **Note:** *The two outer triangles are separate from the centre section.*
10 Unscrew the steering gear mounting bolts from the subframe **(see illustration)**. To support the steering gear while the subframe is lowered, use cable-ties between the track rods and underbody.
11 Remove the exhaust front pipe section with reference to Chapter 4A or 4B.
12 Unbolt the front engine mounting/transmission torque arm from the subframe.
13 Unscrew and remove the clamp bolts securing the lower arm balljoints to the bottom of the hub carriers. If necessary, prise the clamps apart slightly using a screwdriver or lever. Pull down the lower arms from the hub carriers.
14 Unscrew the nuts and disconnect the anti-roll bar links from the front suspension struts. Hold the link stubs with one spanner while loosening the retaining nuts.
15 Where applicable, disconnect the wiring from the load angle sensor.
16 Unscrew the nuts retaining the air cleaner to the subframe.
17 Remove the air conditioning pipes from their mounting brackets. Also, detach the power steering pipe from the support clips.
18 Support the weight of the front suspension subframe on trolley jacks.
19 Unscrew the side and front mounting bolts and lower the subframe to the ground. Make sure that the radiator upper mountings remain located in the crossmember; the lower mounting stubs will be released from the rubber grommets in the subframe **(see illustrations)**. Note that the reinforcement crossmember mounting bolts have smaller washers and 20 mm heads when compared to the main subframe mounting bolts.

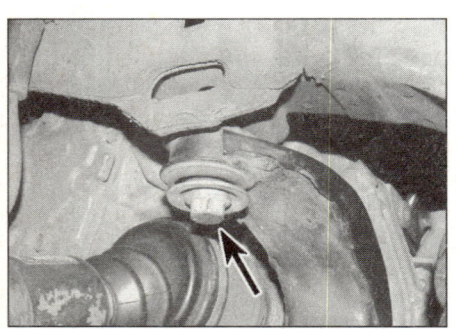

7.19a Subframe side mounting bolt

7.19b Subframe front mounting bolt

7.19c Radiator and air conditioning mounting stubs and rubber grommets

Suspension and steering

8.2 Rear shock absorber/strut mounting bolts

8.3 Rear shock absorber/strut lower mounting bolt

8.4 Removing the rear shock absorber/strut from the vehicle

Overhaul

20 Check the subframe and mounting bushes for wear and damage, and renew as necessary.

21 The mounting bushes can be renewed if necessary using a press or, alternatively, metal tubing, washers and a long bolt. Press in the new bushes using the same method.

Refitting

22 Refitting is a reversal of removal, but position the subframe as noted before removal, and tighten the mounting bolts to the specified torque.

8 Rear strut/shock absorber – removal, overhaul and refitting

Note: *Optional self-levelling rear suspension may be fitted for certain markets; at the time of writing, no information was available.*

Removal

1 Chock the front wheels then jack up the rear of the vehicle and support on axle stands (see *Jacking and vehicle support*). Remove the roadwheel.

2 The shock absorber/strut is mounted on the body with 4 bolts; unscrew and remove the two lower bolts and loosen the upper bolts two or three turns **(see illustration)**. The upper bolt holes are open-ended, however, with the lower bolts removed, the rear anti-roll bar will still exert some upward pressure.

3 Support the strut, then unscrew and remove the mounting bolt securing the rear shock absorber/strut to the trailing arm, and recover the washer **(see illustration)**. Discard both the bolt and washer as new ones must be used on refitting.

4 Withdraw the rear shock absorber/strut from the vehicle **(see illustration)**.

Overhaul

Warning: *Before attempting to dismantle the rear shock absorber/strut, the coil spring must be first held in compression, using a purpose-made tool. Universal coil spring compressors are available from motor factors or car accessory shops, and are essential for this operation. DO NOT attempt to dismantle the strut without such a tool, as damage and/or personal injury is likely.*

Note: *A new top mounting nut must be used on reassembly.*

8.7 Using a spring compressor tool, compress the coil sufficiently to relieve all pressure from the upper spring seat

5 Use a dab of paint to mark the rear coil spring for position. Note that the small diameter coils are at the bottom of the spring.

6 Support the strut by clamping it in a soft-jawed vice.

7 Using the spring compressor, compress the coils of the spring just enough to relieve **all** pressure from the upper spring seat **(see illustration)**.

8 The shock absorber piston rod must be held stationary while the top bearing retaining nut is unscrewed. To do this, use a ring spanner and Allen key **(see illustration)**. Discard the nut, as a new one must be fitted on reassembly.

9 Fully unscrew the nut and recover the upper domed washer and upper rubber bush **(see illustrations)**.

10 Lift off the upper bracket, then remove the upper spring seat, followed by the spacer, lower rubber bush, lower domed washer,

8.8 Using a ring spanner and Allen key to loosen the top bearing retaining nut

8.9a Unscrew and remove the nut . . .

8.9b . . . recover the upper domed washer . . .

8.9c . . . and remove the upper rubber bush

10•10 Suspension and steering

8.10a Lift off the upper bracket ...

8.10b ... and remove the upper spring seat ...

8.10c ... spacer ...

8.10d ... lower rubber bush ...

8.10e ... lower domed washer ...

8.10f ... buffer stop ...

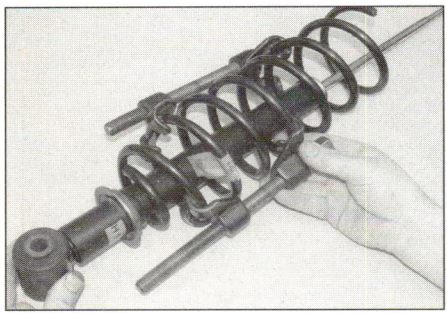

8.10g ... and coil spring ...

8.10h ... rear shock absorber/strut with coil spring components removed

9.2 Bolt securing the rear anti-roll bar link to the trailing arm

buffer stop and coil spring, noting their fitted locations **(see illustrations)**.
11 Clean all the components and examine them for wear and damage. With the shock absorber mounted in the vice, operate the piston rod over its full stroke several times and check for tight spots or seizing. The rod should move smoothly with constant resistance. Renew the components as necessary.
12 Refit the coil spring with its small diameter coils downwards, making sure that its lower end locates correctly on the lower spring seat.
13 Refit the buffer stop, followed by the washer, lower rubber bush and spacer.
14 Refit the upper spring seat to the upper bracket, then locate the assembly on the coil spring, making sure that the end of the coil locates in the special recess in the spring seat.
15 Screw on the new top mounting nut by hand as far as possible.
16 Hold the piston rod stationary (as for dismantling) and tighten the mounting nut to the specified torque.

Refitting

17 Locate the shock absorber/strut on the loose upper mounting bolts, then insert the lower mounting bolts loosely. Push the strut upwards, and then tighten the bolts to the specified torque.
18 Fit the new lower mounting bolt and washer on the trailing arm, and tighten to the specified torque.
19 Refit the roadwheel and lower the vehicle to the ground.

9 Rear anti-roll bar – removal, overhaul and refitting

Removal

1 Chock the front wheels then jack up the rear of the vehicle and support on axle stands (see *Jacking and vehicle support*). Remove both rear roadwheels.
2 Unscrew the bolts securing the anti-roll bar links to the trailing arms **(see illustration)**.
3 As applicable, release the ABS wiring from the clips on the rear anti-roll bar.
4 Unscrew the nuts and bolts from the clamps, and remove the anti-roll bar from the rear crossmember **(see illustration)**. The bolts will probably remain in the clamps.

Overhaul

5 Check the split mounting rubbers and side links mountings for wear and damage, and renew them as necessary.

Suspension and steering 10•11

9.4 Clamp bolt securing the anti-roll bar to the rear crossmember

10.2 Unbolt the support bracket from the trailing arm

10.4 Removing the rear hub assembly from the trailing arm and brake backplate

6 To renew the split mounting rubbers, first note their fitted position on the anti-roll bar. To remove them, mount the clamps in a vice and tap out the bolts, then unhook the clamp retaining plates from the slot in the intermediate plates. Prise the rubbers from the anti-roll bar. Clean the bar, then dip the split clamp mounting rubbers in soapy water and fit them in the previously-noted positions. Assemble the intermediate plates and hook on the retaining plates. Make sure that the split sides of the rubbers contact the intermediate plates.
7 To renew the side links, mount the anti-roll bar in a vice then press off the links. It may be possible to renew the link mountings, but check with your Saab dealer first. To remove the mountings, press them out using metal tubing and a vice. Press in the new mountings using the same method.

Refitting

8 Locate the anti-roll bar on the rear crossmember, insert the nuts and bolts and tighten to the specified torque.
9 Insert the bolts securing the anti-roll bar links to the trailing arms and tighten securely.
10 Clip the ABS wiring to the anti-roll bar as applicable.
11 Refit the roadwheels and lower the vehicle to the ground.

10 Rear hub assembly – removal and refitting

Note: The rear hub bearings cannot be renewed separately; if they are worn excessively, the hub assembly must be renewed.

Removal

1 Remove the rear brake disc as described in Chapter 9.
2 Where fitted, remove the protective cover from the bottom of the rear suspension trailing arm, and unbolt the handbrake cable, wiring and brake pipe support brackets **(see illustration)**.
3 Disconnect the wiring from the ABS sensor located on the rear of the hub assembly.
4 Unscrew the nuts securing the rear hub assembly to the trailing arm, noting the location of the bracket on one of the hub studs, then withdraw the hub assembly, leaving the brake backplate suspended by the handbrake cable **(see illustration)**. Recover the two shims located between the backplate and trailing arm. Discard the nuts, as new ones must be used on refitting.

Refitting

5 Clean the contact surfaces of the hub, backplate and trailing arm.
6 Locate the backplate on the hub studs, followed by the shims, then locate the assembly on the trailing arm and tighten the new nuts to the specified torque. Make sure the shims are positioned correctly between the backplate and trailing arm.
7 Reconnect the wiring to the ABS sensor.
8 Where applicable, refit the support brackets for the handbrake cable, wiring and brake pipe, then refit the protective cover to the bottom of the rear suspension lower arm.
9 Refit the rear brake disc with reference to Chapter 9.

11 Rear trailing arm – removal, overhaul and refitting

Removal

1 Remove the hub assembly as described in Section 10.
2 Unscrew and remove the lower mounting bolt securing the rear shock absorber/strut to the trailing arm, and recover the washer.

11.10 Nut securing the rubber damper to the front of the trailing arm

Discard both the bolt and washer as new ones must be used on refitting.
3 Unscrew the bolt and remove the lower transverse link from the trailing arm. Note that the bolt head faces forward.
4 Unbolt the handbrake cable support bracket from the trailing arm.
5 Unhook the handbrake cable return spring and remove the cable.
6 Unscrew the bolt and remove the anti-roll bar link from the trailing arm.
7 Unscrew the bolt and remove the upper transverse link from the trailing arm. Note that the bolt head faces forward.
8 Mark the trailing arm front mounting bracket in relation to the underbody, then unscrew and remove the bolts and withdraw from the vehicle.
9 At this stage, Saab technicians fit a small jig tool to hold the trailing arm in its normal position in relation to the mounting bracket. If this tool is not available, mark the two parts in relation to each other to ensure correct refitting. Unscrew the nut and bolt and remove the mounting bracket from the trailing arm. Note that the bolt head faces the outside of the arm.
10 Where fitted, unscrew the nut and remove the rubber damper from the front of the trailing arm **(see illustration)**.

Overhaul

11 Check the trailing arm for wear and damage, and renew if necessary.
12 The front mounting bush can be renewed if necessary using metal tubing and a vice to press it out. First, cut off the edges of the rubber bush with a hacksaw for ease of removal. The transverse link bushes can also be renewed in the same way.
13 Press in the new bush using the same method, but position it correctly **(see illustration)**. Note that the rubber bush outer sides will swell, and this is quite normal.

Refitting

14 Where fitted, refit the rubber damper to the front of the trailing arm and tighten the nut securely.
15 Locate the bracket on the front of the trailing arm and insert the bolt. Position the bracket and arm in their previously-noted

10•12 Suspension and steering

11.13 Rear suspension trailing arm bush renewal

position, and tighten the bolt to the specified torque and angle.
16 Lift the trailing arm and bracket onto the underbody and insert the mounting bolts. Position the bracket to align the previously-made marks, then insert the bolts and tighten them to the specified torque and angle.
17 Refit the upper transverse link and tighten the bolt to the specified torque.
18 Refit the anti-roll bar link and tighten the bolt securely.
19 Refit the handbrake cable and reconnect the return spring.
20 Refit the handbrake cable support bracket, and tighten the bolt securely.
21 Refit the lower transverse link and tighten the bolt to the specified torque.
22 Refit the rear shock absorber/strut to the trailing arm, and secure with a new lower mounting bolt and washer. Tighten the bolt to the specified torque.
23 Refit the hub assembly with reference to Section 10.
24 Have the rear wheel alignment checked and adjusted at the earliest opportunity.

12 Rear upper transverse link – removal and refitting

Removal
1 Chock the front wheels then jack up the rear of the vehicle and support on axle stands (see *Jacking and vehicle support*). Remove the roadwheel.
2 If removing the left-hand transverse link, unhook the exhaust system central and rear mounting rubbers and lower the exhaust onto axle stands. Make sure that the front flexible section is not unduly strained.
3 Unscrew the nut and bolt, and remove the lower transverse link from the trailing arm. Note that the bolt head faces forward. Discard the nut, as a new one must be used on refitting.
4 Unscrew the bolt and remove the upper transverse link from the trailing arm **(see illustration)**. Note that the bolt head faces forward. Discard the nut, as a new one must be used on refitting.

5 Unscrew the bolt and remove the anti-roll bar link from the trailing arm.
6 Support the rear suspension crossmember on a trolley jack, then unscrew and remove the crossmember-to-underbody bolts on the side being worked on. Loosen the crossmember mounting bolts on the opposite side. Lower the crossmember slightly.
7 Unscrew the bolt and remove the lower transverse link from the suspension crossmember. Note that the bolt head faces forward. Discard the nut, as a new one must be used on refitting.
8 Unscrew the bolt and remove the upper transverse link from the suspension crossmember. Note that the bolt head faces forward. Discard the nut, as a new one must be used on refitting.

Refitting
9 Refitting is a reversal of removal, but tighten all nuts and bolts to the specified torque where given. Note that the transverse link-to-crossmember mounting bolts and (new) nuts should initially be tightened by hand only, and then fully-tightened with the full weight of the vehicle on the rear suspension. Note that the bolts incorporate special sleeves to protect the fuel tank and fuel filler pipe in the event of a collision; **do not** use different types of bolt.
10 Have the rear wheel alignment checked and adjusted at the earliest opportunity.

13 Rear lower transverse link – removal and refitting

Removal
1 Chock the front wheels then jack up the rear of the vehicle and support on axle stands (see *Jacking and vehicle support*). Remove the roadwheel.
2 If removing the left-hand transverse link, unhook the exhaust system central and rear mounting rubbers and lower the exhaust onto axle stands. Make sure that the front flexible section is not unduly strained.
3 Unscrew the nut and bolt, and remove the lower transverse link from the trailing arm **(see illustration)**. Note that the bolt head faces forward. Discard the nut, as a new one must be used on refitting.
4 Unscrew the bolt and remove the upper transverse link from the trailing arm. Note that the bolt head faces forward. Discard the nut, as a new one must be used on refitting.
5 Unscrew the bolt and remove the anti-roll bar link from the trailing arm.
6 Support the rear suspension crossmember on a trolley jack, then unscrew and remove the crossmember-to-underbody bolts on the side being worked on. Loosen the crossmember mounting bolts on the opposite side. Lower the crossmember slightly.
7 Unscrew the bolt and remove the lower transverse link from the suspension

12.4 The bolt head for the upper transverse link must face forward

13.3 Lower transverse link mounting on the trailing arm

Suspension and steering 10•13

crossmember **(see illustration)**. Note that the bolt head faces forward. Discard the nut, as a new one must be used on refitting.

Refitting

8 Refitting is a reversal of removal, but tighten all nuts and bolts to the specified torque where given. Note that the transverse link-to-crossmember mounting bolts and (new) nuts should initially be tightened by hand only, and finally fully-tightened with the full weight of the vehicle on the rear suspension. Note that the bolts incorporate special sleeves to protect the fuel tank and fuel filler pipe in the event of a collision; **do not** use a different type of bolt.
9 Have the rear wheel alignment checked and adjusted at the earliest opportunity.

14 Rear subframe – removal, overhaul and refitting

Removal

1 Remove the rear suspension anti-roll bar as described in Section 9.
2 Remove the right-hand and left-hand rear suspension upper and lower transverse links as described in Sections 12 and 13, however, do not remove the subframe mounting bolts.
3 Support the subframe with a trolley jack and length of wood.
4 Unscrew and remove the subframe mounting bolts and washers **(see illustration)**.
5 Lower the subframe from the underbody and withdraw from beneath the vehicle.

Overhaul

6 Check the subframe and mounting bushes for wear and damage, and renew as necessary.
7 The mounting bushes can be renewed if necessary using a press or alternatively, metal tubing, washers and a long bolt. Press in the new bushes using the same method.

Refitting

8 Raise the subframe onto the underbody, and insert the mounting bolts hand-tight at this stage.
9 Refit the right-hand and left-hand rear suspension upper and lower transverse links with reference to Sections 12 and 13.

13.7 Lower transverse link mounting on the crossmember

10 Refit the rear suspension anti-roll bar with reference to Section 9.
11 Fully-tighten the subframe mounting bolts to the specified torque, and lower the vehicle to the ground.

15 Steering wheel – removal and refitting

Removal

1 Turn the ignition to the OFF position, leaving the key in the switch, with the steering lock released, turn the steering wheel 90° to the left.
2 At the lower part of the steering wheel, insert a small screwdriver through the hole in the rear of the steering wheel to release the securing clip. Turn the steering wheel through 180° and insert a small screwdriver through the hole in

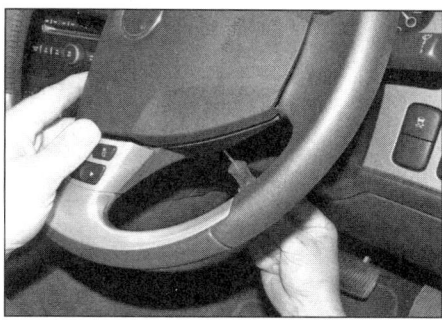

15.2a Insert the screwdriver . . .

15.3 Disconnect the airbag wiring connectors

15.4 Unscrew the steering wheel retaining nut

14.4 Rear suspension subframe mounting bolt

the rear of the steering wheel to release the second securing clip **(see illustrations)**.
3 With the two securing clips released, withdraw the airbag module from the steering wheel, and then disconnect the airbag wiring connectors as it is removed **(see illustration)**. **Caution: Observe the safety instructions given in Chapter 11.**
4 Turn the steering wheel back to the straight-ahead position. Mark the relationship between the steering wheel and steering column with a dab of paint, then unscrew the steering wheel retaining nut, and washer where fitted **(see illustration)**. **Caution: Do not use the steering lock to brace the column whilst the nut is being removed, as this may cause damage.**
5 Carefully ease the steering wheel from the column splines, and disconnect the wiring connector as the steering wheel is removed **(see illustrations)**. **Note:** *If the steering*

15.2b . . . and release the securing clips (arrowed)

15.5a Withdraw the steering wheel . . .

10•14 Suspension and steering

15.5b . . . and disconnect the wiring connector

wheel is a tight fit on the splines, temporarily leave the retaining nut and washer on the last few threads, to prevent any damage when it releases from the column splines.

Caution: Do not drive the steering wheel from the splines, as this may damage the collapsible inner column. Also take care not to damage the airbag contact spring unit located over the top of the column.

Refitting

6 First check that the front wheels are still pointing in the straight-ahead position.
7 Locate the steering wheel on the column splines, while connecting the wiring connector to the steering contact spring unit. Make sure the previously-made marks are correctly aligned.
8 Refit the retaining nut and washer (where applicable) and then tighten the nut to the specified torque.
9 Locate the driver's airbag module on the steering wheel, and reconnect the airbag wiring connectors. Secure the airbag unit to the steering wheel, by pressing it firmly until the securing clips are located.

10 Have the vehicle electronic control system checked for fault codes by a Saab dealer.

16 Steering column – removal and refitting

⚠ **Warning: Do not separate the steering intermediate shaft from the inner column during removal of the steering column.**

Removal

1 Remove the steering wheel as described in Section 15.
2 Release the steering wheel height adjustment lever.
3 Remove the steering column upper and lower shrouds. There are two screws facing upwards in the upper shroud, and one screw located beneath the lower shroud **(see illustrations)**.
4 Remove the lighting and wiper combination switches from the column and disconnect the wiring with reference to Chapter 12. Where applicable, unclip the wiring conduit from the steering column.
5 Disconnect the wiring then remove the airbag contact spring unit (see Chapter 11).
6 Mark the position of the holder for the contact spring unit and combination switches on the steering column, and then loosen the clamp screw. Using a screwdriver, release the airbag wiring socket from the holder, then withdraw the holder from the steering column. Also release the airbag wiring socket from the support **(see illustrations)**.

16.3a Undo the upper screws . . .

16.3b . . . and lower screw . . .

16.3c . . . then remove the shrouds

16.6a Use a felt-tip pen to mark the position of the holder on the steering column . . .

16.6b . . . then loosen the clamp screw . . .

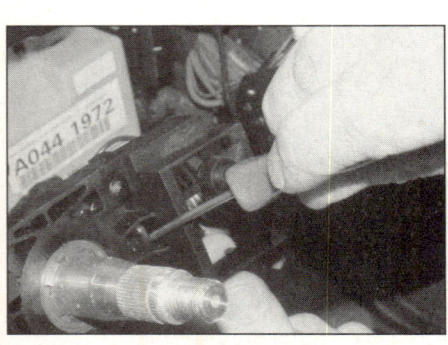

16.6c . . . and use a screwdriver to release the airbag socket . . .

16.6d . . . withdraw the contact spring holder . . .

16.6e . . . and release the airbag wiring socket from the support

Suspension and steering 10•15

16.7 Removing the knee protector

16.8a Unscrew the clamp bolt . . .

16.8b . . . and slide the universal joint from the steering gear pinion shaft

7 Remove the facia lower trim panel and air duct on the driver's side with reference to Chapter 11. Where applicable, remove the knee protector from the steering column **(see illustration)**.
8 At the bottom of the steering column, unscrew and remove the clamp bolt and slide the universal joint from the steering gear pinion shaft **(see illustrations)**. Mark the shaft and column if necessary to ensure correct refitting. Make sure that the column intermediate shaft remains together with the upper column for the period when the steering column is removed.
9 Unscrew the steering column lower mounting bolt. The bolt cannot be removed completely at this stage **(see illustration)**.
10 Release the relevant wiring from the plastic cable-ties, and move to one side.
11 Manoeuvre the rubber dust excluder gaiter over the steering wheel height adjustment lever, to allow the lever to be removed together with the steering column.
12 Unscrew and remove the upper mounting bolts **(see illustration)** and withdraw the steering column from inside the vehicle. The lower mounting bolt can now be removed from the column.

Refitting

13 Locate the lower mounting bolt in the steering column, then position the steering column onto the bulkhead and hand-tighten the bolt to hold the assembly. Insert the upper mounting bolts, and then fully-tighten all the bolts to the specified torque.
14 Engage the universal joint on the bottom of the column with the splines on the steering gear pinion shaft, making sure that the bolt hole is aligned with the cut-out in the shaft and the alignment marks are adjacent as previously-noted. Tighten the clamp bolt to the specified torque.
15 Reposition the rubber dust excluder gaiter over the steering wheel height adjustment lever, so that the lever protrudes through its hole in the gaiter.
16 Secure the relevant wiring with new plastic cable-ties. Secure the wiring conduit to the steering column.
17 Refit the facia lower trim panel and air duct on the driver's side with reference to Chapter 11. Refit the knee protector to the steering column.

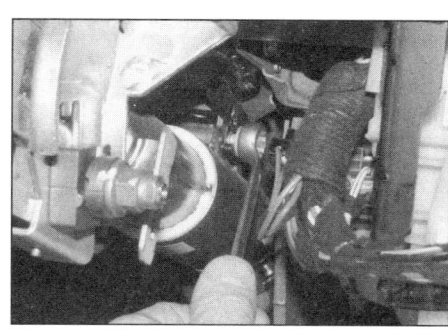

16.9 Unscrew the steering column lower mounting bolt (note it cannot be removed completely at this stage)

18 Refit the holder for the contact spring unit and combination switches with the groove uppermost, and tighten the bolts. Make sure that it is still held in its central position with the adhesive tape.
19 Reconnect the wiring for the airbag contact spring unit at the connector.
20 Refit the lighting and wiper combination switches and reconnect the wiring with reference to Chapter 12.
21 Refit the steering column upper and lower shrouds and tighten the screws.
22 Refit the steering wheel with reference to Section 15.

17 Steering gear assembly – removal and refitting

Removal

1 Apply the handbrake, then jack up the front of the vehicle and support it on axle stands (see *Jacking and vehicle support*). Remove both front roadwheels.
2 Drain the hydraulic fluid from the power steering system as described in Section 18, then return the steering to the straight-ahead position. The steering wheel must remain in its central position during the following procedure; use adhesive tape to secure it to the facia.
Caution: Damage will occur to the airbag contact spring unit if the steering wheel is not secured in its central position.

16.12 Steering column upper mounting bolts

3 Disconnect the battery negative lead.
4 At the bottom of the steering column, unscrew and remove the clamp bolt and slide the universal joint from the steering gear pinion shaft. Mark the shaft and column if necessary to ensure correct refitting. Make sure that the column intermediate shaft remains together with the upper column for the period when the steering gear is removed.
5 The engine assembly must be supported while the rear of the subframe is lowered. To do this, use a suitable hoist or engine support bar that straddles the engine compartment. Slightly lift the engine assembly so that its weight is supported. If a support bar is being used, it may be necessary to remove the cover from over the intake manifold.
6 At the rear of the engine, unscrew the nut securing the rear engine mounting to the engine bracket, then unbolt the mounting from the subframe and remove it.
7 If the track rod ends are to be removed from the steering gear, loosen the adjusting nuts securing the ends to the track rods a quarter of a turn at this stage.
8 Using a balljoint separator tool, disconnect the steering track rod ends from the steering arms on the hub carriers with reference to Section 21. If required, unscrew the track rod ends from the track rods, counting the exact number of turns necessary to remove them, to ensure correct refitting.
9 Working under the vehicle, unbolt the crossmember and support bracket from the rear of the subframe.
10 The exhaust front section must be lowered

10•16 Suspension and steering

before lowering the subframe. To do this, refer to Chapter 4A or 4B and either remove the exhaust or separate it at the joint and release it from the rubber mountings.
11 Support the subframe with a trolley jack, then unscrew and remove the centre mounting bolts and lower the rear of the subframe as far as possible.
12 Position a container beneath the steering gear to catch spilt fluid. Identify the supply and return hydraulic pipes for location, then unscrew the union nuts and carefully position the pipes to one side. Recover the O-ring seals and valve body dust cover. Tape over or plug the ends of the pipes and the steering gear apertures to prevent entry of dust and dirt. Where applicable, cut the plastic cable-ties securing the wiring to the pipes.
13 Unscrew and remove the two nuts and bolts securing the steering gear to the subframe. Note the position of the nut retaining the support bracket for the delivery pipe.
14 Withdraw the steering gear from one side of the vehicle, taking care not to damage the rubber gaiters.
15 Examine the mounting rubbers for wear and damage and renew them if necessary. If a new steering gear is to be fitted, transfer the internal pipes from the old unit and fit new O-ring seals. Tighten the union nuts securely. Check the bulkhead rubber gaiter and renew if necessary.

Refitting

16 Before refitting the steering gear make sure that its rack is in its central position, and that the front wheels are still pointing straight-ahead.
17 Locate the steering gear onto the subframe and connect the supply and return hydraulic pipes together with new O-ring seals. Do not fully-tighten the union bolts at this stage.
18 Insert the steering gear mounting bolts from under the subframe and screw on the nuts, but do not fully-tighten them at this stage. Make sure the delivery pipe support bracket is fitted as previously-noted.
19 Fully-tighten the supply and return hydraulic pipe union bolts to their specified torque. Hold the pipes against rotation while the bolts are tightened.
20 Fully-tighten the steering gear mounting bolts to the specified torque.
21 Secure the wiring to the hydraulic pipes with new plastic cable-ties.
22 Raise the subframe and refit the centre mounting bolts. Tighten the bolts to the specified torque and angle. Remove the trolley jack.
23 Refit the exhaust front section with reference to Chapter 4A or 4B.
24 Refit the crossmember and support bracket to the rear of the subframe and tighten the mounting bolts to the specified torque.
25 If removed, screw on the track rod ends to the track rods the exact number of turns previously-noted.

26 Refit the track rod ends to the steering arms on the hub carriers, then refit the nuts and tighten to the specified torque. With the track rod ends held in their central positions, tighten the locknuts securely.
27 Refit the rear engine mounting and tighten the bolts to the specified torques.
28 Remove the hoist or support bar, and where necessary refit the cover over the intake manifold.
29 Make sure that the steering wheel is still in its central position, then engage the universal joint on the bottom of the column with the splines on the steering gear pinion shaft, making sure that the bolt hole is aligned with the cut-out in the shaft and the alignment marks are adjacent as previously-noted. Tighten the clamp bolt to the specified torque. Remove the adhesive tape from the steering wheel.
30 Reconnect the battery negative lead.
31 Fill the power steering system with the specified hydraulic fluid and bleed the system with reference to Section 18.
32 Refit the front roadwheels and lower the vehicle to the ground.
33 Have the front wheel alignment checked at the earliest opportunity.

18 Power steering hydraulic system – draining, refilling and bleeding

Note: *The power steering hydraulic system must be bled if any part of the system has been disconnected.*

Draining

1 To drain the complete hydraulic system of fluid, position a container (having a capacity of at least one litre) beneath the power steering pump on the right-hand front of the engine. Unclip the reservoir from its mounting, then loosen the clip and disconnect the return hose from the pump. Allow the fluid to drain into the container from the return hose.
2 Secure the container in the engine bay, away from any moving components and direct sources of heat. Start the engine, and allow the hydraulic fluid to be pumped into the container. Turn the steering wheel lock-to-lock several times, to purge the fluid from the steering rack. When the flow of fluid ceases, turn off the engine immediately; **do not** allow the power steering pump to run dry for any length of time.
3 Reconnect the return hose and tighten the clip, then reposition the reservoir on its mounting.

Refilling

4 Remove the fluid reservoir filler cap, and top-up to the maximum level mark with fluid of the specified type and grade; refer to *Lubricants and fluids* for guidance.

Bleeding

5 Park the vehicle on a level surface and apply the handbrake.

6 With the engine stopped, slowly move the steering from lock-to-lock several times to purge any trapped air, then top-up the level in the fluid reservoir. Repeat this procedure until the fluid level in the reservoir does not drop any further.
7 Start the engine, then slowly move the steering from lock-to-lock several times to purge out any remaining air in the system. Repeat this procedure until bubbles cease to appear in the fluid reservoir.
8 If an abnormal noise is heard from the pump or fluid pipes when the steering is operated, this is an indication that there is still air in the system. Confirm this by turning the wheels to the straight-ahead position and switching off the engine. If the fluid level in the reservoir rises, then air is present in the system, and further bleeding will be necessary. Repeat the above procedure as necessary.
9 Once all traces of air have been purged from the power steering hydraulic system, stop the engine and allow the system to cool. Finally, check that the fluid level is up to the maximum mark on the reservoir, and top-up if necessary.

19 Power steering pump – removal and refitting

Removal

1 Drain the hydraulic fluid from the power steering system as described in Section 18, then return the steering to the straight-ahead position and refit the fluid reservoir.
2 At the right-hand front corner of the engine compartment, loosen the clips and disconnect the air intake hose and mass airflow meter. Place the hose and meter to one side.
3 Remove the auxiliary drivebelt as described in Chapter 1A or 1B.
4 Place a container beneath the power steering pump, then loosen the clip and disconnect the fluid reservoir-to-pump hose.
5 Unscrew the bolt securing the delivery pipe support to the pump, then unscrew the union nut and disconnect it from the pump. Access to the support bolt is gained through the hole in the pulley. Recover the O-ring seal.
6 Unscrew the bolts securing the power steering pump to the mounting bracket, and withdraw it from the engine. Wrap the pump in cloth rag to prevent fluid dropping onto the vehicle paintwork.

Refitting

7 Locate the pump on the engine, then insert the mounting bolts and tighten them to the specified torque.
8 Fit a new O-ring seal to the delivery pipe end fitting, and then locate it on the pump. Tighten the union nut and support bolt to the specified torque.
9 Reconnect the reservoir-to-pump hose and tighten the clip.

10 Refit the auxiliary drivebelt as described in Chapter 1A or 1B.
11 Refit the air intake hose and mass airflow meter.
12 Refill and bleed the power steering hydraulic system with reference to Section 18.

20 Steering rack rubber gaiter – renewal

1 Apply the handbrake, then jack up the front of the vehicle and support it on axle stands (see *Jacking and vehicle support*). Remove the relevant roadwheel.
2 Loosen the track rod end locknut on the track rod a quarter of a turn.
3 Using a balljoint separator tool, disconnect the steering track rod end from the steering arm on the hub carrier **(see illustration)**.
4 Unscrew the track rod end from the track rod, counting the exact number of turns necessary to remove it, to ensure correct refitting.
5 Note the position of the track rod end locknut, and then unscrew it from the track rod.
6 Wipe clean the track rod, and then loosen the rubber gaiter retaining clips on the rod and steering gear housing.
7 Release the gaiter from the housing groove and slide it from the track rod.
8 Wipe clean the steering gear housing and track rod, and lubricate the track rod inner balljoint with lithium grease. Smear a little grease on the track rod to assist sliding on the new gaiter.
9 Slide on the new gaiter and locate in the grooves. Fit and tighten the retaining clips. If new Saab clips are fitted, they must be tightened by crimping with a pair of pliers or pincers.
10 Screw on the track rod end locknut to its previously-noted position.
11 Screw on the track rod end by the number of turns previously-noted.
12 Locate the track rod end on the steering arm, and tighten the nut to the specified torque.
13 Tighten the track rod end locknut to the specified torque.
14 Refit the roadwheel and lower the vehicle to the ground.
15 Have the front wheel alignment checked at the earliest opportunity.

21 Track rod end – removal and refitting

Removal

1 Apply the handbrake, then jack up the front of the vehicle and support it on axle stands (see *Jacking and vehicle support*). Remove the relevant roadwheel.

2 Note that the track rod ends are 'handed', and curve slightly rearwards in relation to the track rods. They are marked LH and RH on top of the balljoint for identification.
3 Loosen the track rod end locknut on the track rod a quarter of a turn.
4 Using a balljoint separator tool, disconnect the steering track rod end from the steering arm on the hub carrier.
5 Unscrew the track rod end from the track rod, counting the exact number of turns necessary to remove it, to ensure correct refitting.

Refitting

6 Screw on the track rod end the exact number of turns noted on removal.
7 Locate the track rod end stub on the steering arm, then tighten the nut to the specified torque.
8 Tighten the track rod end locknut to the specified torque.
9 Refit the roadwheel and lower the vehicle to the ground.
10 Have the front wheel alignment checked at the earliest opportunity.

22 Wheel alignment and steering angles – general information

1 Accurate front wheel alignment is essential to provide positive steering, and to prevent excessive tyre wear. Before considering the steering/suspension geometry, check that the tyres are correctly inflated, that the wheels are not buckled, and that the steering linkage and suspension joints are in good order, without slackness or wear. Alignment of the front subframe is also critical to the front suspension geometry.
2 Wheel alignment consists of four factors **(see illustration)**:
Camber is the angle at which the front wheels are set from the vertical, when viewed from the front of the vehicle. 'Positive camber' is the amount (in degrees) that the wheels are tilted outward at the top of the vertical.
Castor is the angle between the steering axis and a vertical line, when viewed from each side of the car. 'Positive castor' is when the steering axis is inclined rearward at the top.
Steering axis inclination is the angle (when viewed from the front of the vehicle) between the vertical and an imaginary line drawn through the suspension strut upper mounting and the lower suspension arm balljoint.
Toe setting is the amount by which the distance between the front inside edges of the roadwheel rims (measured at hub height) differs from the diametrically opposite distance measured between the rear inside edges of the roadwheel rims.
3 Owing to the need for precision gauges to measure the small angles of the steering and suspension settings, the checking of camber,

20.3 Using a balljoint separator tool to release the track rod end balljoint

22.2 Wheel alignment and steering angles

castor and steering axis inclination must be carried out by a service station having the necessary equipment. The readings vary according to wheel size and body height as given in the Specifications; the heights are measured on the underbody, just inside of the roadwheels. Any deviation from the specified angle will be due to accident damage or gross wear in the suspension mountings.

4 Two methods are available to the home mechanic for checking the front wheel toe setting. One method is to use a gauge to measure the distance between the front and rear inside edges of the roadwheels. The other method is to use a scuff plate, in which each front wheel is rolled across a movable plate which records any deviation, or scuff, of the tyre from the straight-ahead position as it moves across the plate. Relatively inexpensive equipment of both types is available from accessory outlets.

5 If, after checking the toe setting using whichever method is preferable, it is found that adjustment is necessary, proceed as follows.

6 Turn the steering wheel onto full-left lock, and record the number of exposed threads on the right-hand track rod. Now turn the steering onto full-right lock, and record the number of threads on the left-hand track rod. If there are the same number of threads visible on both sides, then subsequent adjustment can be made equally on both sides. If there are more threads visible on one side than the other, it will be necessary to compensate for this during adjustment. After adjustment, there must be the same number of threads visible on each track rod. This is most important.

7 To alter the toe setting, slacken the locknuts on the track rods, and turn the track rods using self-locking pliers to achieve the desired setting. Only turn the track rods by a quarter of a turn each time, and then recheck the setting.

8 After adjustment, tighten the locknuts and check that the exposed thread on each track rod is the same. Reposition the steering gear rubber gaiters, to remove any twist caused by turning the track rods.

Rear wheel alignment

9 The rear wheel toe setting may also be checked and adjusted, but as this additionally requires alignment with the front wheels, it should be left to a service station having the necessary equipment.

Chapter 11
Bodywork and fittings

Contents

	Section number		Section number
Body exterior fittings – removal and refitting	23	General information	1
Bonnet lock – removal and refitting	11	Glovebox – removal and refitting	30
Bonnet release cable and lever – removal and refitting	10	Interior trim panels – removal and refitting	27
Bonnet, struts and hinges – removal and refitting	9	Maintenance – bodywork and underframe	2
Boot lid, support struts and hinges – removal and refitting	17	Maintenance – upholstery and carpets	3
Boot lid/tailgate lock components – removal and refitting	19	Major body damage – repair	5
Centre console – removal and refitting	28	Minor body damage – repair	4
Door handle and lock components – removal and refitting	14	Radiator grille panels – removal and refitting	8
Door inner trim panel – removal and refitting	13	Rear bumper – removal and refitting	7
Door window glass – removal and refitting	15	Seat belts – removal and refitting	26
Door window regulator – removal and refitting	16	Seats – removal and refitting	24
Doors – removal, refitting and adjustment	12	Sunroof assembly – removal and refitting	22
Driver's seat control module – removal and refitting	25	Supplementary Restraint System (SRS) components – removal and refitting	31
Exterior door mirror and glass – removal and refitting	20	Tailgate, support struts and hinges – removal and refitting	18
Facia assembly – removal and refitting	29	Windscreen, rear window and fixed windows – general information	21
Front bumper – removal and refitting	6		

Degrees of difficulty

Easy, suitable for novice with little experience	Fairly easy, suitable for beginner with some experience	Fairly difficult, suitable for competent DIY mechanic	Difficult, suitable for experienced DIY mechanic	Very difficult, suitable for expert DIY or professional

Specifications

Torque wrench settings	Nm	lbf ft
Front seats	24	18
Front seat belt:		
Reel	45	33
Stalk	33	24
Rear bumper	40	30
Rear seat belt	45	33
Rear seat belt guide (Estate models)	22	16
Rear seat hinge pin (Estate models)	24	18
Side airbag	7	5
Side impact sensor	5	4

11•2 Bodywork and fittings

1 General information

The vehicle's body is constructed from pressed-steel sections that are either spot-welded or seam-welded together. The overall rigidity of the body is increased by the use of stiffening beams built into the body panels, steel flanges in the window and door openings, and the application of adhesive in fixed glass joints.

The front subframe assembly provides mounting points for the engine/transmission unit, front suspension and steering gear. The front wings are bolted on, rather than welded on, allowing accident damage to be repaired easily.

The vehicle's underside is coated with underseal and an anti-corrosion compound. This treatment provides protection against the elements, and also serves as an effective sound insulation layer. The cabin, luggage area and engine compartment are also lined with bituminous felt and other sound-insulating materials, to provide further noise damping.

All models are fitted with electric windows at the front and rear. The window glass is raised and lowered by an electric motor, directly operating a window regulator.

Electrically-operated front seats are available as an option, with a control module located on the underside of the driver's seat. The module contains the memory for position and movement control, and a communication function for diagnosis. The system also memorises the position of the electrically-operated rear view mirrors. With reverse gear engaged, it is possible to tilt down the passenger door mirror towards the rear wheel; when reverse gear is disengaged; the system automatically repositions the mirrors.

Remote control central locking is fitted to all models, and operates the locks on all four doors, the boot lid/tailgate, and the fuel filler cap. The lock mechanisms are actuated by servo motor units, and the system is controlled by an electronic control module (ECM).

All models are fitted with a driver's airbag located in the centre of the steering wheel, side airbags and seat belt tensioners on driver's and passenger's sides. The passenger airbag is an optional extra. A knee shield made of foam plastic, sheet metal and aluminium is attached to the steering column. On the passenger side, the glovebox lid is reinforced with sheet metal to protect the passenger's knees.

The front seat belts incorporate automatic tensioners, which operate in the event of a front-end collision. The airbags form part of the Supplementary Restraint System (SRS), which is controlled by an electronic control module (ECM). Sensors, built into the ECM casing and the front of the engine bay, are triggered in the event of a front-end collision, and prompt the ECM to activate the airbag(s) and the seat belt tensioners.

2 Maintenance – bodywork and underframe

The general condition of a vehicle's bodywork is the one thing that significantly affects its value. Maintenance is easy, but needs to be regular. Neglect, particularly after minor damage, can lead quickly to further deterioration and costly repair bills. It is important also to keep watch on those parts of the vehicle not immediately visible, for instance the underside, inside all the wheel arches, and the lower part of the engine compartment.

The basic maintenance routine for the bodywork is washing – preferably with a lot of water, from a hose. This will remove all the loose solids that may have stuck to the vehicle. It is important to flush these off in such a way as to prevent grit from scratching the finish. The wheel arches and underframe need washing in the same way, to remove any accumulated mud, which will retain moisture and tend to encourage rust. Paradoxically enough, the best time to clean the underframe and wheel arches is in wet weather, when the mud is thoroughly wet and soft. In very wet weather, the underframe is usually cleaned of large accumulations automatically, and this is a good time for inspection.

Periodically, except on vehicles with a wax-based underbody protective coating, it is a good idea to have the whole of the underframe of the vehicle steam-cleaned, engine compartment included, so that a thorough inspection can be carried out to see what minor repairs and renovations are necessary. Steam-cleaning is available at many garages, and is necessary for the removal of the accumulation of oily grime, which sometimes is allowed to become thick in certain areas. If steam-cleaning facilities are not available, there are one or two excellent grease solvents available, which can be brush-applied; the dirt can then be simply hosed off. Note that these methods should not be used on vehicles with wax-based underbody protective coating, or the coating will be removed. Such vehicles should be inspected annually, preferably just prior to Winter, when the underbody should be washed down, and any damage to the wax coating repaired. Ideally, a completely fresh coat should be applied. It would also be worth considering the use of such wax-based protection for injection into door panels, sills, box sections, etc, as an additional safeguard against rust damage, where such protection is not provided by the vehicle manufacturer.

After washing paintwork, wipe off with a chamois leather to give an unspotted clear finish. A coat of clear protective wax polish will give added protection against chemical pollutants in the air. If the paintwork sheen has dulled or oxidised, use a cleaner/polisher combination to restore the brilliance of the shine. This requires a little effort, but such dulling is usually caused because regular washing has been neglected. Care needs to be taken with metallic paintwork, as special non-abrasive cleaner/polisher is required to avoid damage to the finish. Always check that the door and ventilator opening drain holes and pipes are completely clear, so that water can be drained out. Brightwork should be treated in the same way as paintwork. Windscreens and windows can be kept clear of the smeary film that often appears, by the use of proprietary glass cleaner. Never use any form of wax or other body or chromium polish on glass.

3 Maintenance – upholstery and carpets

Mats and carpets should be brushed or vacuum-cleaned regularly, to keep them free of grit. If they are badly stained, remove them from the vehicle for scrubbing or sponging, and make quite sure they are dry before refitting. Seats and interior trim panels can be kept clean by wiping with a damp cloth. If they do become stained (which can be more apparent on light-coloured upholstery), use a little liquid detergent and a soft nail brush to scour the grime out of the grain of the material. Do not forget to keep the headlining clean in the same way as the upholstery. When using liquid cleaners inside the vehicle, do not over-wet the surfaces being cleaned. Excessive damp could get into the seams and padded interior, causing stains, offensive odours or even rot. If the inside of the vehicle gets wet accidentally, it is worthwhile taking some trouble to dry it out properly, particularly where carpets are involved. *Do not leave oil or electric heaters inside the vehicle for this purpose.*

4 Minor body damage – repair

Minor scratches

If the scratch is very superficial, and does not penetrate to the metal of the bodywork, repair is very simple. Lightly rub the area of the scratch with a paintwork renovator, or a very fine cutting paste, to remove loose paint from the scratch, and to clear the surrounding bodywork of wax polish. Rinse the area with clean water.

Apply touch-up paint to the scratch using a fine paintbrush; continue to apply fine layers of paint until the surface of the paint in the scratch is level with the surrounding paintwork. Allow the new paint at least two weeks to harden, and then blend it into the surrounding paintwork by rubbing the scratch area with a paintwork renovator or a very fine cutting paste. Finally, apply wax polish.

Where the scratch has penetrated right through to the metal of the bodywork, causing the metal to rust, a different repair technique is required. Remove any loose rust from the bottom of the scratch with a penknife, and then apply rust-inhibiting paint, to prevent the formation of rust in the future. Using a rubber or nylon applicator, fill the scratch with bodystopper paste. If required, this paste can be mixed with cellulose thinners, to provide a very thin paste, which is ideal for filling narrow scratches. Before the stopper-paste in the scratch hardens, wrap a piece of smooth cotton rag around the top of a finger. Dip the finger in cellulose thinners, and quickly sweep it across the surface of the stopper-paste in the scratch; this will ensure that the surface of the stopper-paste is slightly hollowed. The scratch can now be painted over as described earlier in this Section.

Dents

When deep denting of the vehicle's bodywork has taken place, the first task is to pull the dent out, until the affected bodywork almost attains its original shape. There is little point in trying to restore the original shape completely, as the metal in the damaged area will have stretched on impact, and cannot be reshaped fully to its original contour. It is better to bring the level of the dent up to a point, which is about 3 mm below the level of the surrounding bodywork. In cases where the dent is very shallow anyway, it is not worth trying to pull it out at all. If the underside of the dent is accessible, it can be hammered out gently from behind, using a mallet with a wooden or plastic head. Whilst doing this, hold a suitable block of wood firmly against the outside of the panel, to absorb the impact from the hammer blows and thus prevent a large area of the bodywork from being 'belled-out'.

Should the dent be in a section of the bodywork that has a double skin, or some other factor making it inaccessible from behind, a different technique is called for. Drill several small holes through the metal inside the area – particularly in the deeper section. Then screw long self-tapping screws into the holes, just sufficiently for them to gain a good purchase in the metal. Now the dent can be pulled out by pulling on the protruding heads of the screws with a pair of pliers.

The next stage of the repair is the removal of the paint from the damaged area, and from an inch or so of the surrounding 'sound' bodywork. This is accomplished most easily by using a wire brush or abrasive pad on a power drill, although it can be done just as effectively by hand, using sheets of abrasive paper. To complete the preparation for filling, score the surface of the bare metal with a screwdriver or the tang of a file, or alternatively, drill small holes in the affected area. This will provide a really good 'key' for the filler paste.

To complete the repair, see the Section on filling and respraying.

Rust holes or gashes

Remove all paint from the affected area, and from an inch or so of the surrounding 'sound' bodywork, using an abrasive pad or a wire brush on a power drill. If these are not available, a few sheets of abrasive paper will do the job most effectively. With the paint removed, you will be able to judge the severity of the corrosion, and therefore decide whether to renew the whole panel (if this is possible) or to repair the affected area. New body panels are not as expensive as most people think, and it is often quicker and more satisfactory to fit a new panel than to attempt to repair large areas of corrosion.

Remove all fittings from the affected area, except those, which will act as a guide to the original shape of the damaged bodywork (e.g. headlamp shells etc). Then, using tin snips or a hacksaw blade, remove all loose metal and any other metal badly affected by corrosion. Hammer the edges of the hole inwards, in order to create a slight depression for the filler paste.

Wire-brush the affected area to remove the powdery rust from the surface of the remaining metal. Paint the affected area with rust-inhibiting paint; if the back of the rusted area is accessible, treat this also.

Before filling can take place, it will be necessary to block the hole in some way. This can be achieved by the use of aluminium or plastic mesh, or aluminium tape.

Aluminium or plastic mesh, or glass-fibre matting is probably the best material to use for a large hole. Cut a piece to the approximate size and shape of the hole to be filled, then position it in the hole so that its edges are below the level of the surrounding bodywork. It can be retained in position by several blobs of filler paste around its periphery.

Aluminium tape should be used for small or very narrow holes. Pull a piece off the roll, trim it to the approximate size and shape required, then pull off the backing paper (if used) and stick the tape over the hole; it can be overlapped if the thickness of one piece is insufficient. Burnish down the edges of the tape with the handle of a screwdriver or similar, to ensure that the tape is securely attached to the metal underneath.

Filling and re-spraying

Before using this Section, see the Sections on dent, deep scratch, rust holes and gash repairs.

Many types of body filler are available, but generally speaking, those proprietary kits that contain a tin of filler paste and a tube of resin hardener are best for this type of repair. A wide, flexible plastic or nylon applicator will be found invaluable for imparting a smooth and well-contoured finish to the surface of the filler.

Mix up a little filler on a clean piece of card or board – measure the hardener carefully (follow the maker's instructions on the pack), otherwise the filler will set too rapidly or too slowly. Using the applicator, apply the filler paste to the prepared area; draw the applicator across the surface of the filler to achieve the correct contour and to level the surface. As soon as a contour that approximates to the correct one is achieved, stop working the paste – if you carry on too long, the paste will become sticky and begin to 'pick-up' on the applicator. Continue to add thin layers of filler paste at 20-minute intervals, until the level of the filler is just proud of the surrounding bodywork.

Once the filler has hardened, the excess can be removed using a metal plane or file. From then on, progressively finer grades of abrasive paper should be used, starting with a 40-grade production paper, and finishing with a 400-grade wet-and-dry paper. Always wrap the abrasive paper around a flat rubber, cork, or wooden block – otherwise the surface of the filler will not be completely flat. During the smoothing of the filler surface, the wet-and-dry paper should be periodically rinsed in water. This will ensure that a very smooth finish is imparted to the filler at the final stage.

At this stage, the 'dent' should be surrounded by a ring of bare metal, which in turn should be encircled by the finely 'feathered' edge of the good paintwork. Rinse the repair area with clean water, until all of the dust produced by the rubbing-down operation has gone.

Spray the whole area with a light coat of primer – this will show up any imperfections in the surface of the filler. Repair these imperfections with fresh filler paste or body stopper, and once more smooth the surface with abrasive paper. If body stopper is used, it can be mixed with cellulose thinners, to form a really thin paste that is ideal for filling small holes. Repeat this spray-and-repair procedure until you are satisfied that the surface of the filler, and the feathered edge of the paintwork, are perfect. Clean the repair area with clean water, and allow to dry fully.

The repair area is now ready for final spraying. Paint spraying must be carried out in a warm, dry, windless and dust-free atmosphere. This condition can be created artificially if you have access to a large indoor working area, but if you are forced to work in the open, you will have to pick your day very carefully. If you are working indoors, dousing the floor in the work area with water will help to settle the dust, which would otherwise be in the atmosphere. If the repair area is confined to one body panel, mask off the surrounding panels; this will help to minimise the effects of a slight mis-match in paint colours. Bodywork fittings (e.g. chrome strips, door handles, etc) will also need to be masked off. Use genuine masking tape, and several thicknesses of newspaper, for the masking operations.

Before commencing to spray, agitate the aerosol can thoroughly, and then spray a test area (an old tin, or similar) until the technique is mastered. Cover the repair area with a thick coat of primer; the thickness should be built up

11•4 Bodywork and fittings

6.1 Removing the splash shields

6.2 Undo the upper securing screws

using several thin layers of paint, rather than one thick one. Using 400-grade wet-and-dry paper, rub down the surface of the primer until it is really smooth. While doing this, the work area should be thoroughly doused with water, and the wet-and-dry paper periodically rinsed in water. Allow to dry before spraying on more paint.

Spray on the topcoat, again building up the thickness by using several thin layers of paint. Start spraying at the top of the repair area, and then, using a side-to-side motion, work downwards until the whole repair area and about 2 inches of the surrounding original paintwork is covered. Remove all masking material 10 to 15 minutes after spraying on the final coat of paint.

Allow the new paint at least two weeks to harden, then, using a paintwork renovator or a very fine cutting paste, blend the edges of the paint into the existing paintwork. Finally, apply wax polish.

Plastic components

With the use of more and more plastic body components by the vehicle manufacturers (e.g. bumpers, spoilers, and in some cases major body panels), rectification of more serious damage to such items has become a matter of either entrusting repair work to a specialist in this field, or renewing complete components. Repair of such damage by the DIY owner is not really feasible, owing to the cost of the equipment and materials required for effecting such repairs. The basic technique involves making a groove along the line of the crack in the plastic, using a rotary burr in a power drill. The damaged part is then welded back together, using a hot air gun to heat up and fuse a plastic filler rod into the groove. Any excess plastic is then removed, and the area rubbed down to a smooth finish. It is important that a filler rod of the correct plastic is used, as body components can be made of a variety of different types (e.g. polycarbonate, ABS, polypropylene).

Damage of a less serious nature (abrasions, minor cracks etc) can be repaired by the DIY owner using a two-part epoxy filler repair. Once mixed in equal, this is used in similar fashion to the bodywork filler used on metal panels. The filler is usually cured in twenty to thirty minutes, ready for sanding and painting.

If the owner is renewing a complete component himself, or if he has repaired it with epoxy filler, he will be left with the problem of finding a suitable paint for finishing which is compatible with the type of plastic used. At one time, the use of a universal paint was not possible, owing to the complex range of plastics encountered in body component applications. Standard paints, generally speaking, will not bond to plastic or rubber satisfactorily, but suitable paints to match any plastic or rubber finish, can be obtained from dealers. However, it is now possible to obtain a plastic body parts finishing kit, which consists of a pre-primer treatment, a primer and coloured top coat. Full instructions are normally supplied with a kit, but basically, the method of use is to first apply the pre-primer to the component concerned, and allow it to dry for up to 30 minutes. Then the primer is applied, and left to dry for about an hour before finally applying the special-coloured topcoat. The result is a correctly coloured component, where the paint will flex with the plastic or rubber, a property that standard paint does not normally posses.

5 Major body damage – repair

Where serious damage has occurred, or large areas need renewal due to neglect, it means that complete new panels will need welding-in, and this is best left to professionals. If the damage is due to impact, it will also be necessary to check completely the alignment of the body shell, and this can only be carried out accurately by a dealer using special jigs. If the body is left misaligned, it is primarily dangerous, as the car will not handle properly, and secondly, uneven stresses will be imposed on the steering, suspension and possibly transmission, causing abnormal wear, or complete failure, particularly to such items as the tyres.

6 Front bumper – removal and refitting

Removal

1 Apply the handbrake, then jack up the front of the vehicle and support it on axle stands (see *Jacking and vehicle support*). Undo the screws and remove the splash shields from under the front of the vehicle **(see illustration)**.
2 With the bonnet open, remove the two outer retaining screws from the top of the bumper/grille cover **(see illustration)**.
3 Using a small punch, press the centre of the clip down and remove the two inner retaining clips from the top of the bumper/grille cover **(see illustrations)**.
4 Working beneath the wheel arches on each side; undo the screws securing the wheel arch liners to the front bumper **(see illustration)**.
5 Reach inside the bumper on the right-hand side, and disconnect the wiring connector for

6.3a Press in the centre pin . . .

6.3b . . . and remove the retaining clip

6.4 Screws securing the wheel arch liners to the front bumper

the front foglights and exterior temperature sensor on the front bumper (see illustration).
6 On models with headlight washer jets, reach inside the bumper on the left-hand side, and disconnect the washer pipe from the washer bottle. **Note:** *A blanking plug will be required to block the pipe on the washer bottle, to prevent all the water draining from the washer bottle.*
7 With the aid of an assistant, release the outer corners of the front bumper from the wings and wheel arch liners (see illustrations), then withdraw the bumper from the front of the vehicle.
8 If the bumper is being renewed, remove the grille, number plate, foglights, exterior temperature sensor, headlight washer jets and lower grille as applicable, and transfer them to the new bumper.

Refitting

9 With the aid of an assistant, locate the bumper onto the front of the vehicle; making sure that it is correctly positioned across the front of the vehicle.
10 Press the bumper into position, then attach the outer corners, making sure that they are located securely with the liners.
11 On models with headlight washer jets, reach inside the bumper on the left-hand side, and reconnect the washer pipe to the washer bottle.
12 Reach inside the bumper on the right-hand side, and reconnect the wiring connector to the front foglights and exterior temperature sensor on the front bumper.
13 With the bumper cover in position, refit and tighten the screws securing the wheel arch liners.
14 Refit and tighten the two screws securing the upper part of the bumper/grille to the crossmember.
15 Refit the two securing clips securing the upper part of the bumper/grille to the crossmember (see illustration). **Note:** *Press the centre pin out through the top of the clip for refitting and then press the pin down until it is flush with the securing clip to secure in place.*
16 Refit the splash shields to the bumper lower edge and subframe, and then lower the vehicle to the ground.

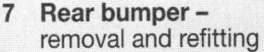

7 **Rear bumper –**
removal and refitting

Removal

1 With the boot lid/tailgate open, release the rubber weatherstrips and pull back the carpet at the rear of the luggage area, for access to the bumper mounting nuts.
2 On Estate models, lift out the cover trim and remove the corner storage compartment from inside the luggage compartment, under the rear light units (see illustrations).

6.5 Disconnect the wiring connector

6.7b ... and withdraw the bumper cover

3 With the carpet removed from inside the rear of the luggage compartment, remove the insulation pads and undo the bumper mounting nuts (see illustrations). **Note:** *Mounting nuts may only be fitted to the upper studs.*

7.2a On Estate models, remove the cover ...

7.3a Remove the insulating pads ...

6.7a Release the corners ...

6.15 Refit the clips with the centre pin in the upwards position

4 At the front ends of the bumper on each side of the vehicle, undo the two screws securing the bumper to the wheel arches (see illustration).
5 With the aid of an assistant, release the

7.2b ... and storage compartments

7.3b ... to access the mounting nuts (arrowed)

11•6 Bodywork and fittings

7.4 Screws securing the wheel arch liners to the rear bumper

7.5a Release the retaining clips . . .

7.5b . . . and unclip the bumper cover from under the rear lights

7.6 Disconnect the wiring for the Saab Parking Assistance (SPA) system

outer corners of the rear bumper from the wings and wheel arch liners **(see illustrations)**, then withdraw the bumper from the rear of the vehicle.

6 As the bumper is removed, where applicable, disconnect the wiring from the Saab Parking Assistance (SPA) system **(see illustration)**.

Refitting

7 Refitting is a reversal of removal, but tighten all nuts and bolts securely. Make sure the bumper engages correctly with the side brackets and below the rear light units.

8 Radiator grille panels – removal and refitting

Removal

1 Remove the front bumper as described in Section 6.
2 Working your way around the grille panels, release the securing clips on the inside of the bumper cover, and then remove the grille panels **(see illustrations)**.

Refitting

3 Locate the grille in the slotted holes in the bumper cover and press firmly into place.
4 Refit the front bumper with reference to Section 6.

9 Bonnet, struts and hinges – removal and refitting

Bonnet

Removal

1 Support the bonnet in its open position, then place some cloth rags or card between the rear edge of the bonnet and the windscreen valance.
2 Release the sound insulation, and disconnect the washer tube at the connection. Unclip and remove the tubing from the bonnet hinge.
3 Using a pencil, mark the position of the hinges on the bonnet.
4 With the help of an assistant, support both sides of the bonnet, then disconnect the gas-filled struts by prising out the special springs **(see illustration)**. Lower the struts onto the inner wings.
5 Unscrew the mounting nuts and carefully remove the bonnet from the hinges **(see illustration)**. Place it away from the vehicle in a safe position, taking care not to damage the paintwork. Note that it is only necessary to loosen the upper hinge bolts, since the bolt hole is open-ended.
6 If necessary, remove the weatherseal, sound insulation and washer jets from the old bonnet, and transfer them to the new unit.

Refitting

7 Refitting is a reversal of removal. When first closing the bonnet, lower it slowly and check that the striker is aligned with the lock. Also check that the bonnet is positioned centrally between the front wings. If necessary, loosen the bolts and reposition the bonnet on the hinges before fully closing the bonnet. Tighten the bolts on completion. Check that the front of the bonnet is level with the front wings, and if necessary screw the rubber stops located in

8.2a Release the retaining clips (arrowed) . . .

8.2b . . . and remove the grille from the bumper cover

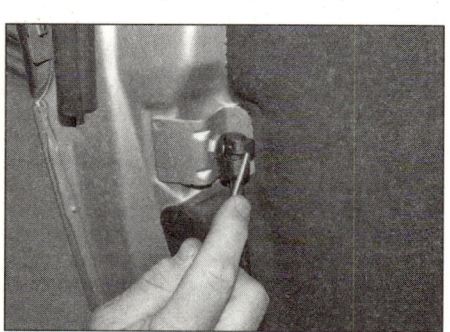

9.4 Release the securing clip

9.5 Bonnet hinge mounting nuts

Bodywork and fittings 11•7

9.10 Release the securing clip from the lower part of the strut

10.1 Undo the screw from the outer cable clamp...

10.2 ... and release the inner cable from the lock spring

the front corners of the engine compartment in or out – it may also be necessary to adjust the two strikers located on the underside of the bonnet. The rear height is adjusted by loosening the bolts securing the hinges to the body.

Struts

Removal

8 Open the bonnet. If removing just one strut, the remaining strut will hold the bonnet up, however if removing both struts an assistant will be required to hold the bonnet open. Alternatively, use a length of wood to prop the bonnet open.
9 Using a screwdriver, prise the spring clip from the top of the strut and disconnect the strut from the ball-pin **(see illustration 9.4)**.
10 Disconnect the bottom of the strut from the lower ball-pin by prising out the spring clip **(see illustration)**.

Refitting

11 Refitting is a reversal of removal.

Hinges

Removal

12 Remove the bonnet as described earlier in this Section.
13 Using a pencil, mark the position of the hinge on the body, then unscrew the bolts and remove the hinge.

Refitting

14 Refitting is a reversal of removal, but tighten the bolts securely and adjust the bonnet as described earlier.

10 Bonnet release cable and lever – removal and refitting

Removal

1 With the bonnet open, loosen the clamp screws on the crossmember **(see illustration)**, and release the main outer cable and intermediate outer cable.
2 Release the inner cable end stop adjustment screws from both lock spring eyes **(see illustration)**.

10.5 Bonnet release lever and cable

3 Remove the windscreen wiper arms (see Chapter 12), and remove the rubber seals from the spindles.
4 Pull off the weatherstrip located at the rear of the engine compartment, then undo the screws and remove the scuttle cover by lifting its front edge and pulling it from the rear retaining clips.
5 Inside the vehicle, remove the lower facia trim panel on the driver's side for access to the lever **(see illustration)**.
6 Remove the kickplate from the inner sill panel on the driver's side footwell, and fold back the carpet.
7 Depress the top and bottom of the bonnet lever holder, and release the bonnet lever by sliding it rearwards.
8 Pull the lever and cable into the passenger compartment and withdraw from the vehicle. As an aid to refitting, tie a length of string to the

11.2 Bonnet lock retaining bolts – undo from under panel

10.9 Adjustment grub screw (arrowed) for bonnet release cable

front end of the cable and leave it in position until the refitting procedure. To prevent the cable catching, wrap adhesive tape around its sharp edges.

Refitting

9 Refitting is a reversal of removal, but adjust the position of the end stops **(see illustration)** to provide approximately 1.0 mm clearance between the stop and return spring.
10 Close the bonnet and check that the cable operates the release springs correctly.

11 Bonnet lock – removal and refitting

Removal

1 With the bonnet open, release the inner cable end stop screws from both locks, pull out the cable until it is released from the lock spring eyes **(see illustration 10.2)**.
2 From underneath the front crossmember panel, unscrew the mounting bolts and remove the bonnet locks **(see illustration)**.

Refitting

3 Refitting is a reversal of removal, but adjust the position of the end stops to provide approximately 1.0 mm clearance between the stop and return spring **(see illustration 10.9)**. Lubricate the spring contacts with a little grease.

11•8 Bodywork and fittings

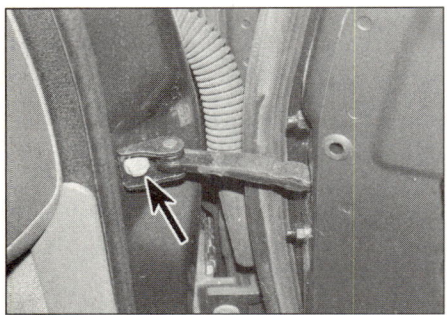

12.3 Front door check strap retaining bolt

12.5 Door hinge retaining nut/bolt

12.8 Front door striker on the B-pillar

12 Doors – removal, refitting and adjustment

Front

Removal

1 Before removing the door, check the gap between the door and surrounding bodywork with the door shut. Any adjustment to the hinges on the A-pillar can then be made with the door removed, as the adjustment may not be possible with the door fitted. Similarly, adjustment of the front edge of the door in relation to the front wing is best achieved with the door removed.

2 Open the door, then prise out the rubber grommet and disconnect the wiring located between the door and A-pillar.

3 Unbolt the check strap from the A-pillar (see illustration).

4 Mark the position of the door hinge plates on the A-pillar hinge brackets.

5 With the help of an assistant, unscrew first the lower mounting bolt then the upper bolt, and withdraw the door from the A-pillar hinge brackets (see illustration). Take care not to damage the paintwork.

Refitting and adjustment

6 Refitting is a reversal of removal. Check that the gap between the door and surrounding bodywork is equal when the door is shut, and where necessary remove the door to make the adjustment. Note that adjustment of the door front edge in relation to the front wing is possible with the door fitted, but only with the front wing removed. To adjust the vertical or horizontal position of the door, loosen the hinge bracket bolts on the A-pillar (there are 3 bolts per hinge); to adjust the position of the door front edge, loosen the nuts securing the door hinge plates to the hinge brackets. Tighten all nuts and bolts to their specified torque, where given.

7 If only minor adjustment is necessary, it is possible to remove the sleeves from the nuts securing the door hinge plates to the hinge brackets. With the door open, unscrew the nuts and remove the sleeves, then refit the nuts, adjust the door position as necessary and retighten the nuts.

8 Check that the door lock aligns correctly with the striker on the B-pillar as the door is closed, and if necessary adjust the striker by loosening the two screws (see illustration). Do not fully unscrew the screws, as the spacer plate will drop down inside the B-pillar.

Rear

Removal

9 Open the front door on the relevant side in order to access the rear door wiring harness rubber grommet in the B-pillar. Remove the rubber grommet and disconnect the wiring (see illustration).

10 Open the rear door and unbolt the check strap from the B-pillar (see illustration).

11 Mark the position of the door hinge plates on the B-pillar hinge brackets

12 With the help of an assistant, unscrew first the lower mounting bolt then the upper bolt, and withdraw the door from the B-pillar hinge brackets (see illustration). Take care not to damage the paintwork.

Refitting and adjustment

13 Refitting is a reversal of removal. Check that the gap between the door and surrounding bodywork is equal when the door is shut. To adjust the vertical or horizontal position of the door, loosen the hinge bracket bolts on the B-pillar (there are 2 upper and 3 lower bolts); to adjust the position of the door front edge, loosen the nuts securing the door hinge plates to the hinge brackets. Tighten all nuts and bolts to their specified torque, where given.

14 Check that the door lock aligns correctly with the striker on the C-pillar as the door is closed (see illustration), and if necessary adjust the striker by loosening the two screws. Do not fully unscrew the screws, as the spacer plate will drop down inside the C-pillar.

12.9 Disconnecting the rear door wiring at the B-pillar

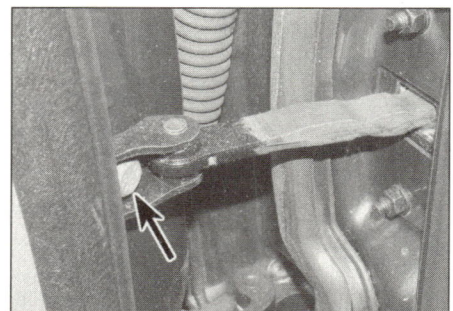

12.10 Rear door check strap mounting bolt on the B-pillar

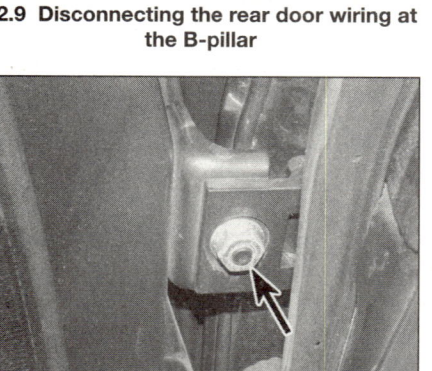

12.12 Rear door upper hinge plate nut/bolt

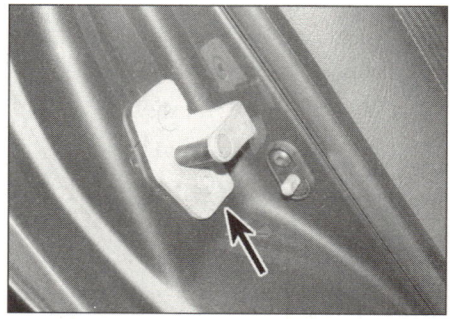

12.14 Rear door striker on the C-pillar

Bodywork and fittings 11•9

13.1 Remove the inner trim panel

13.3a Prise out the cover and undo the screw . . .

13.3b . . . then unclip the interior door handle

13.4a Prise off the plastic trim cover . . .

13.4b . . . and undo the retaining screws (arrowed)

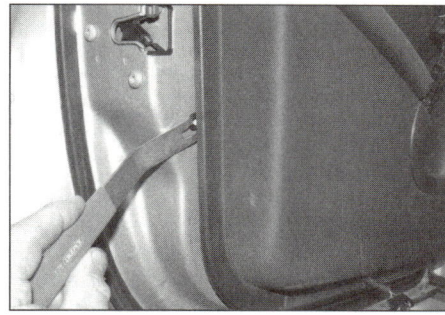

13.5 Carefully release the front door trim panel clips

13 Door inner trim panel – removal and refitting

Removal

1 Carefully prise the curved trim panel from the upper half of the door (around the window glass opening) using a wide-bladed screwdriver (see illustration). The clips may pull out of the metal frame, in which case they should be removed from the trim and pressed back into position.
2 On the front doors, disconnect the wiring plug for the exterior door mirror.
3 Prise out the plastic cover, undo the screw, then remove the interior door handle and unclip it from the operating rod (see illustrations).
4 Prise off the plastic cover, and then undo the screws from the door grip handle (see illustrations).
5 Using a trim tool (or wide-bladed screwdriver), carefully prise out the clips and release the trim panel from the door (see illustration). Take care not to damage the trim panel or break the clips by prising as near to the clip positions as possible.
6 Release the door courtesy light from the bottom of the trim panel, and disconnect the wiring connector (see illustration)
7 With the trim clips released, lift the trim panel upwards over the locking button (see illustration). Disconnect any wiring from the door switches (where applicable), as the trim is removed.

8 If necessary carefully remove the waterproof membrane from the door inner panel (see illustration).

Refitting

9 Refitting is a reversal of removal.

13.6 Disconnect the courtesy light connection

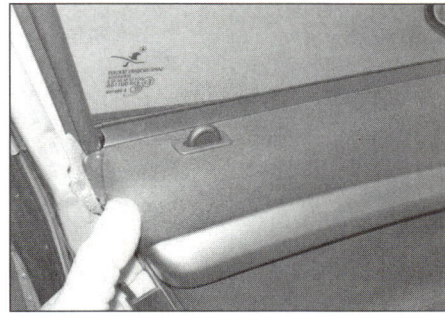

13.7a Lift the panel from over the door lock button . . .

13.7b . . . and disconnect the wiring from any switches on the trim panel

13.8 Cutting the waterproof membrane from the door inner panel

11•10 Bodywork and fittings

14 Door handle and lock components – removal and refitting

Interior door handle

1 Prise the plastic cover from the inner door handle, and then undo the screw and unclip the handle from the operating rod **(see illustrations 13.3a and 13.3b)**.
2 Refitting is a reversal of removal.

Front door lock

3 Open the window, then remove the door trim and waterproof membrane as described in Section 13.
4 Slightly loosen the door exterior mirror retaining screws to release the front of the exterior glass weatherstrip, then undo the screw from its rear end and withdraw the weatherstrip from the door.
5 Lower the window so that the lower glass channel is visible in the large inner door panel aperture. Using tape, support the glass in this position while the winder arms are disconnected from the lower channel.
6 Disconnect the window winder arms from the rollers in the glass lower channel by pulling out the clips, then using a wide-bladed screwdriver to prise out the arms. Insert the screwdriver near the ball, between the arm and channel, to prevent deforming the arm.
7 Carefully lift and tilt the rear of the glass, and withdraw it from the outside of the door frame. Position it in a safe place.

14.8a Drive out the rivet centre pin remains . . .

14.8b . . . then drill out the rivets . . .

14.8c . . . detach the cable . . .

14.8d . . . remove the bracket . . .

8 The window regulator cable support bracket must now be removed. To do this, drive out the rivet centre pin remains, then drill out the rivets, remove the bracket and release the cable, and unhook it from the lock **(see illustrations)**.

9 Undo the nut and bolt from the security guard plate, then undo the screws securing the bottom of the rear glass channel to the door, pull the channel forwards, and withdraw the guard plate **(see illustrations)**.

10 Undo the lock mounting screws from the

14.8e . . . and unhook the cable from the lock

14.9a Unscrew the retaining nuts and bolts . . .

14.9b . . . then remove the security guard plate

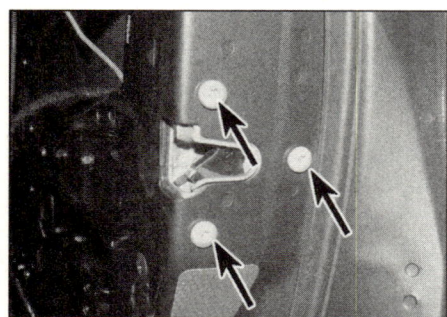
14.10a Undo the lock mounting screws . . .

14.10b . . . then disconnect the pullrods . . .

14.10c . . . and exterior door handle pushrod

Bodywork and fittings 11•11

14.11a Disconnect the wiring . . .

14.11b . . . and remove the front door lock

14.15 Removing the rear door lock mounting screws

rear edge of the door, then tilt the lock and disconnect the pullrods. At the same time, disconnect the exterior handle pushrod (see illustrations).

11 Disconnect the wiring and withdraw the front door lock from the door (see illustrations). Recover the lock seal.

12 Refitting is a reversal of removal, however, lightly grease the winder rollers and channel, and then refit the clips to the rollers. With the clips refitted, press the arm balls fully into the rollers until they are heard to engage.

13 Before refitting the door trim, make sure that the lock operates correctly. Use new rivets to secure the metal support bracket.

Rear door lock

14 Remove the door trim and waterproof membrane as described in Section 13.
15 Undo the lock mounting screws from the rear edge of the door (see illustration).
16 Release the locking knob and inner handle cables from their support clips (see illustrations).
17 Unhook the exterior handle locking rod from the lock, then withdraw the rear door lock through the aperture in the inner door panel (see illustration).
18 Disconnect the wiring from the lock (see illustration).
19 Unhook the locking knob operating cable. Unhook the interior door handle operating cable from the lock (see illustrations).
20 Refitting is a reversal of removal.

14.16a Release the clips . . .

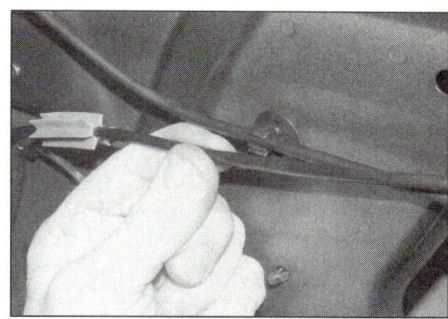

14.16b . . . and unclip the cables

Exterior door handle

21 Remove the door lock as described earlier in this Section.
22 Reach through the aperture in the door inner panel, unscrew the nut(s) and remove the security plate from the exterior door handle (see illustrations).

Front doors

23 Insert the ignition key in the door lock and turn it anti-clockwise. Tilt the rear of

14.17 Withdraw the rear door lock . . .

14.18 . . . and disconnect the wiring

14.19a Unhook the locking knob operating cable . . .

14.19b . . . and interior door handle operating cable

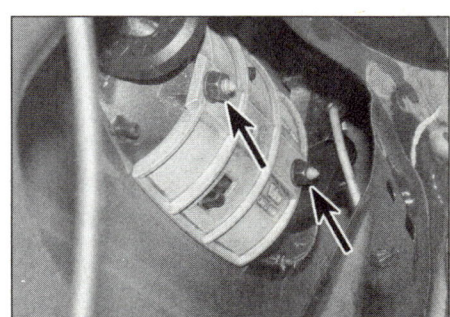

14.22a Unscrew the nuts (arrowed) . . .

11•12 Bodywork and fittings

14.22b ... and remove the security plate

14.24 Removing the exterior handle from the front door

14.25 Removing the exterior door handle from the rear door

14.28a Unhook the operating rod ...

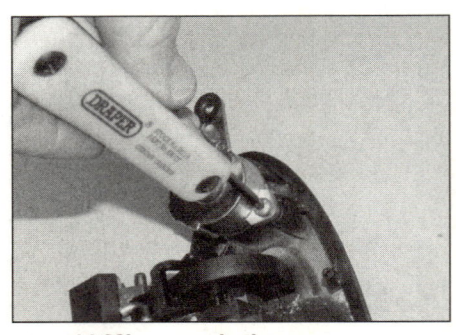

14.28b ... undo the screws ...

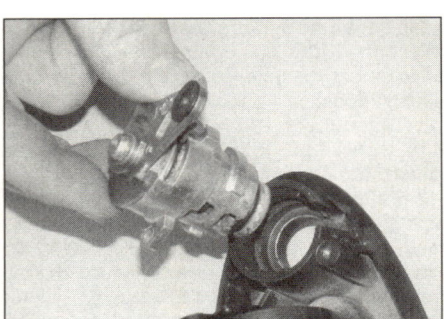

14.28c ... and remove the lock cylinder

the handle, so that the end of the operating pullrod locates in the lever groove, then pull up the handle and withdraw it as far as possible from the door. Take care not to damage the paintwork; if necessary tape some card to the door as a precaution.

24 Hold the handle away from the door, then undo the lock cylinder holder retaining screw. Ideally, use an angled screwdriver to do this. Rotate the lock cylinder holder clockwise (viewed from the rear of the handle) while pressing it through the handle. Unhook the lock cylinder lever from the operating rod, and withdraw the exterior door handle **(see illustration)**. Recover the gasket.

Rear doors
25 Withdraw the door handle from the door panel **(see illustration)**. Recover the gasket.

All doors
26 Refitting is a reversal of removal.

15.5 Removing the front door window glass

Front door lock cylinder
27 Remove the front door exterior door handle and lock cylinder holder as described earlier.
28 On some models, the cylinder is separate from the holder and is retained by screws, however on other models, the holder and cylinder are supplied as one unit. Where applicable, unhook the operating rod, undo the screws and remove the lock cylinder **(see illustrations)**.
29 Refitting is a reversal of removal.

15 Door window glass – removal and refitting

Front door
Removal
1 Open the window, then remove the door trim and waterproof membrane as described in Section 13.
2 Loosen slightly the door exterior mirror retaining screws to release the front of the exterior glass weatherstrip, then undo the screw from its rear end and withdraw the weatherstrip from the door.
3 Lower the window so that the lower glass channel is visible in the large inner door panel aperture. To do this, temporarily reconnect the switch to the winder motor, keeping hands and clothing clear of the winder while repositioning it, and disconnect the switch before continuing. Using tape, support the glass in this position while the winder arms are disconnected from the lower channel.
4 Disconnect the window winder arms from the rollers in the glass lower channel by pulling out the clips, then using a wide-bladed screwdriver to prise out the arms. Insert the screwdriver near the ball, between the arm and channel, to prevent deforming the arm.
5 Carefully lift and tilt the rear of the glass, and withdraw it from the outside of the door frame **(see illustration)**.
6 Remove the rollers from the channel.

Refitting
7 Refitting is a reversal of removal, however, lightly grease the winder rollers and channel, and then refit the clips to the rollers. With the clips refitted, press the arm balls fully into the rollers until they are heard to engage.

Rear door
Removal
8 Open the window, then remove the door trim and waterproof membrane as described in Section 13.
9 Carefully pull the weatherstrip from the outer edge of the window aperture **(see illustration)**.
10 Lower the window so that the lower glass channel is visible in the inner door panel aperture. To do this, temporarily reconnect the switch to the winder motor, keeping hands and clothing clear of the winder while repositioning it, and disconnect the switch before continuing. Using tape, support the glass in this position while the winder arm is disconnected from the lower channel.

Bodywork and fittings 11•13

15.9 Pull the weatherstrip from the outer edge of the window aperture

15.13a Undo the screw behind the seal . . .

15.13b . . . then carefully prise out the weatherstrip. Note the tape to protect the paintwork

15.14 Removing the window rear guide channel screws

15.15a Unscrew the mounting nuts . . .

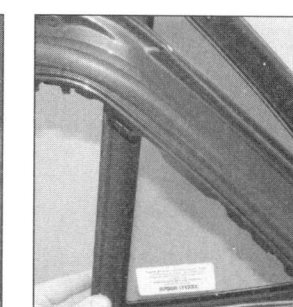

15.15b . . . and remove the fixed window from the rear door

11 Disconnect the window winder arm from the glass lower channel by removing the clip from the roller, then using a wide-bladed screwdriver to prise out the arm. Insert the screwdriver near the ball, between the arm and channel, to prevent the arm deforming.

12 Lower the glass to the bottom of the door.

13 Undo the screw securing the front of the glass weatherstrip to the door frame, then carefully prise out the weatherstrip. Use tape to protect the paintwork (see illustrations).

14 Unscrew and remove the window rear guide channel upper and lower screws (see illustration).

15 Unscrew the mounting nuts from the fixed window, then press the window forward and withdraw it upwards from the door (see illustrations). Take care not to damage the paintwork.

16 Lift up the door window glass and withdraw it from the outside of the door (see illustration).

Refitting

17 Refitting is a reversal of removal, however, lightly grease the winder roller and channel before inserting the window glass in the door. With the spring clip in position, press the ball of the winder arm into the clip until a 'double click' is heard to engage. On completion, check the operation of the window.

16 Door window regulator – removal and refitting

Front door

Removal

1 Open the window, then remove the door trim and waterproof membrane as described in Section 13.

2 Lower the window so that the lower glass channel is visible in the large aperture at the bottom of the inner door panel (see illustration). To do this, temporarily reconnect the switch to the winder motor, keeping the hands clear of the winder while repositioning it, and disconnect the switch before continuing. Using tape, support the glass in this position while the winder arms are disconnected from the lower channel.

3 Disconnect the window winder arms from the rollers in the glass lower channel by pulling out the clips, then using a wide-bladed screwdriver to prise the arms from the rollers. Insert the screwdriver near the ball, between the arm and channel, to prevent deforming the arm (see illustrations).

4 Drive out the remains of the rivet centre pins securing the window regulator to the door, then drill out the rivets (see illustrations).

5 Disconnect the window regulator wiring at the plug (see illustration).

15.16 Removing the window glass from the rear door

16.2 Lower the glass channel into the aperture . . .

16.3a . . . then pull out the retaining clips . . .

11•14 Bodywork and fittings

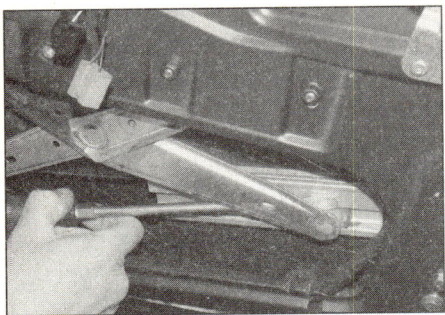
16.3b ... and prise the arms from the rollers

16.4a Drive out the remains of the rivet centre pins ...

16.4b ... then drill out the rivets

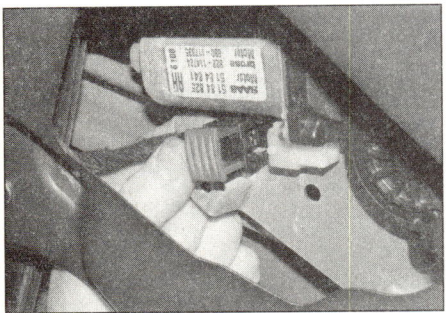
16.5 Disconnecting the window regulator wiring

16.6 Undo the mounting nuts ...

16.7 ... and withdraw the regulator through the door inner panel aperture

6 Mark the regulator guide rail nut positions on the inner door panel, then unscrew and remove them together with the regulator mounting nuts **(see illustration)**.
7 Withdraw the regulator through the large hole in the door inner panel **(see illustration)**.

Refitting and adjustment

8 Refitting is a reversal of removal, but use new rivets to secure the regulator. Lightly grease the winder rollers and channel before inserting the glass in the door. With the clips refitted, press the arm balls fully into the rollers until they are heard to engage.
9 Check that the window glass is aligned with the door frame when closed, and if necessary adjust it as follows. Position the glass half open, then loosen the guide rail screws and push the glass firmly to the rear so that its rear edge is fully engaged with the rear channel. With the glass held in this position, fully tighten the screws.

Rear door

Removal

10 Open the window, then remove the door trim and waterproof membrane as described in Section 13.
11 Lower the window so that the lower glass channel is visible in the inner door panel aperture. To do this, temporarily reconnect the switch to the winder motor, keeping the hands clear of the winder while repositioning it, and disconnect the switch before continuing. Using tape, support the glass in this position while the winder arm is disconnected from the lower channel **(see illustrations)**.
12 Disconnect the window winder arm from the glass lower channel by removing the clip from the roller, then using a wide-bladed screwdriver to prise out the arm. Insert the screwdriver near the ball, between the arm and channel, to prevent the arm deforming **(see illustrations)**.
13 Lower the glass to the bottom of the door.
14 Disconnect the window regulator wiring at the plug.
15 Drive out the remains of the rivet centre

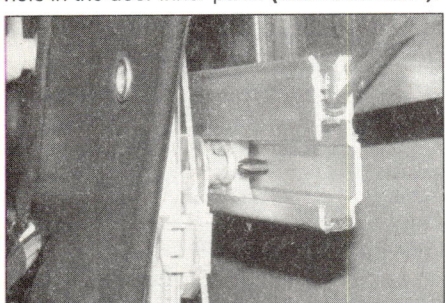
16.11a Lower the window glass channel into the door aperture ...

16.11b ... then use tape to support the glass

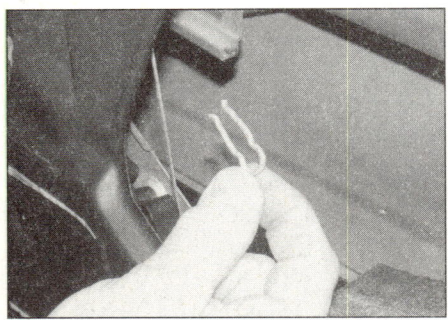
16.12a Remove the clip from the roller ...

16.12b ... then prise out the arm using a screwdriver

Bodywork and fittings 11•15

pins securing the window regulator to the door, then drill out the rivets **(see illustrations)**.

16 Lower the regulator and withdraw the upper part through the hole in the inner door panel **(see illustration)**. *Note: The motor and regulator cannot be separated.*

Refitting

17 Refitting is a reversal of removal, but use new rivets to secure the regulator **(see illustration)**. Lightly grease the winder roller and channel before inserting the window glass in the door. With the spring clip in position, press the ball of the winder arm into the roller until a 'double click' is heard to engage. On completion, check the operation of the window. No adjustment is possible for the rear window glass.

17 Boot lid, support struts and hinges – removal and refitting

Boot lid

Removal

1 Open the boot lid, then reach into the rear left-hand corner of the luggage compartment and open the hatch for access to the boot lid wiring harness connector. Disconnect the plug from the connector.
2 Prise out the wiring grommet from the body and release it from the hinge. Pull the wiring up from the luggage compartment.
3 With the help of an assistant, support the boot lid open, then prise out the clips and disconnect the support strut upper ends from the hinges.
4 Using a pencil, mark the outline of the hinges on the boot lid **(see illustration)**.
5 Unscrew and remove the lower nuts securing the hinges to the boot lid, then loosen the upper bolts and carefully lift the boot lid from the hinges. The upper bolt holes in the hinges are open-ended.

Refitting and adjustment

6 With the upper bolts loosely fitted, lower the boot lid onto them and refit the lower bolts. Tighten the bolts securely.
7 When first closing the boot lid, lower it slowly and check that the striker is aligned with the lock – if not, loosen the bolt(s), reposition the striker, then tighten the bolt(s) **(see illustration)**. *Note: It may be necessary to remove the rear trim panel to access the striker plate securing bolts.* Check that the boot lid is positioned central in its body aperture. Forward and backward adjustment is made by loosening the nuts and repositioning the boot lid on the hinges. Height adjustment of the front of the boot lid is made by repositioning the front end of the hinges on the body. Height adjustment of the rear of the boot lid (when it is closed) is made by turning the two rubber buffers in or out. Height adjustment of the **entire** boot lid is made by loosening the bolts securing the hinges to the body. Tighten all nuts and bolts.
8 Reconnect the support strut upper ends to the hinges and refit the clips.
9 Insert the wiring into the luggage compartment, and refit the wiring grommet. Attach the grommet to the hinge.
10 Reconnect the wiring plug and close the hatch.

Support struts

Removal

11 Support the boot lid in its open position, and note the fitted positions of the support struts. The piston end of the strut faces downwards **(see illustrations)**.
12 Prise out the clips and disconnect the support strut upper and lower ends from the hinges **(see illustration 9.4)**. Withdraw the strut from the vehicle.

Refitting

13 Refitting is a reversal of removal.

16.15a Drive out the rivet centre pins . . .

16.15b . . . then drill out the rivets

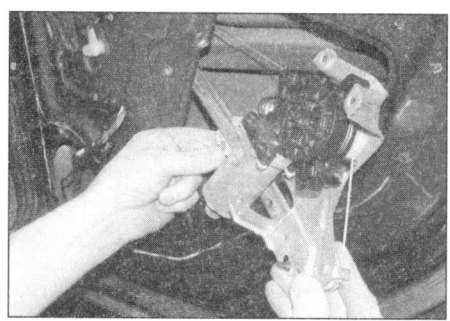
16.16 Removing the window regulator through the door aperture

16.17 Secure the window regulator with new rivets

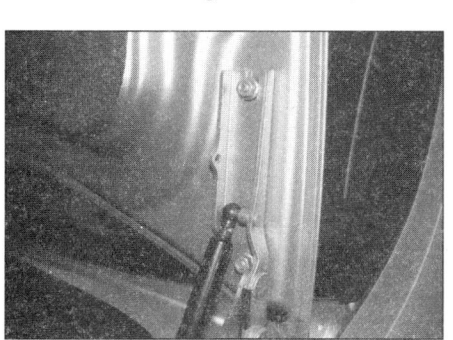
17.4 Boot lid hinge and mounting nuts

17.7 Remove trim panel to access boot lid striker (arrowed)

17.11a Boot lid support strut lower mounting . . .

11•16 Bodywork and fittings

Hinges

Removal

14 Remove the boot lid as described earlier in this Section.
15 Prise out the clip and disconnect the support strut lower end from the hinge. Place the strut to one side.
16 Using a pencil, mark the outline of the hinge on the body, then unscrew the bolts and remove the hinge.

Refitting

17 Refitting is a reversal of removal, but tighten the bolts securely and adjust the boot lid as described earlier.

18 Tailgate, support struts and hinges – removal and refitting

Tailgate

Removal

1 With the tailgate open, place some cloth rags or card between the tailgate and the bodywork to prevent any damage.
2 Undo the retaining screws and remove the covers/seals from the tailgate hinges (see illustration), then prise apart and remove the wiring duct.
3 Carefully prise out the covers then undo the screws and remove the upper trim mouldings from around the rear window aperture inside the tailgate.

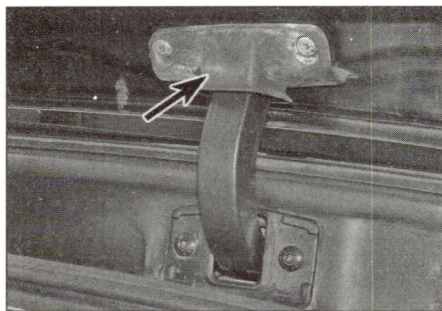

18.2 Remove the tailgate hinge covers/seals – one side shown

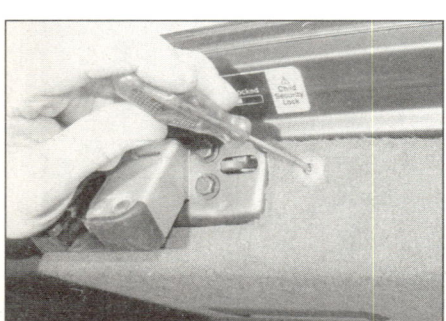

18.5a Depress the centre pins . . .

17.11b . . . and upper mounting

4 Undo the retaining screws and remove the inner handgrip from the lower edge of the tailgate panel (see illustration).
5 Release the fasteners from the lower edge of the trim panel by depressing their centre pins, then pull down the top of the panel to release it from the upper clips, and pull it to the rear to release the guide pin at the handgrip (see illustrations).
6 Note the fitted location of the wiring harness, and then disconnect it and release it from the support clips. Also disconnect the rear washer tube. Carefully extract the wiring from the tailgate at the hinges. Note: *If it is required to remove the tailgate complete with all the wiring, the D-pillar trim must be removed and the rear headlining lowered for access to the wiring connectors and earth cables.*
7 Using a pencil, mark the outline of the hinges on the tailgate.
8 With the help of an assistant, support the

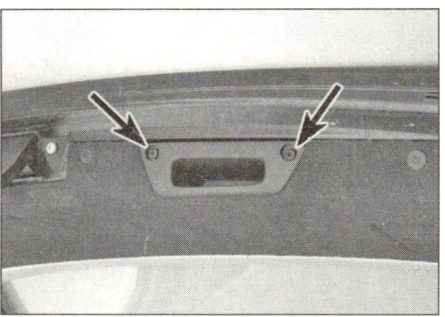

18.4 Inner hand grip trim retaining screws (arrowed)

18.5b . . . and remove the fasteners . . .

weight of the tailgate, then unscrew the bolts and withdraw the tailgate from the hinges.

Refitting

9 Locate the tailgate on the hinges and insert the bolts. With the tailgate aligned with the previously-made marks, tighten the mounting bolts securely. When first closing the tailgate, lower it slowly and check that the striker is aligned with the lock – if not, loosen the bolt, reposition the striker, and then tighten the bolt. Check that the tailgate is positioned centrally in its body aperture. Forward, backward and sideway adjustment is made by loosening the bolts and repositioning the boot lid on the hinges. Upward and downward adjustment is made by loosening the bolts securing the hinges to the body, however, it will be necessary to remove the D-pillar trim and lower the rear headlining. Check that the two rubber support pads located above the rear tail light positions, are adjusted so that the tailgate is supported adequately when closed.

Support struts

Removal

10 Remove the D-pillar trim, the rear headlining trim, and the two mouldings between the C- and D-pillars. Extract the clips from the headlining, and also remove the cargo safety net holders. Carefully bend down the rear of the headlining for access to the strut mountings.
11 Support the tailgate in its open position, and note the fitted position of the support struts. Unbolt the metal yokes from over the front mountings of the struts on the roof panel crossmember.
12 Prise out the clips and disconnect the support strut upper and lower ends from the hinge and body. Withdraw the strut from the vehicle.

Refitting

13 Refitting is a reversal of removal, but lubricate the strut ball sockets with grease before refitting them.

Hinges

Removal

14 Remove the tailgate complete with wiring as described earlier in this Section.
15 Prise out the clips and disconnect the rear ends of the support struts from the hinges.

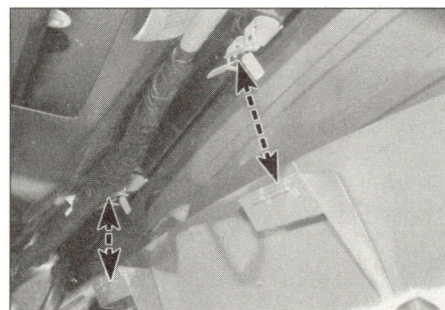

18.5c . . . then release the trim panel from the upper retaining clips

Bodywork and fittings 11•17

19.1a Remove the handgrip . . .

19.1b . . . then depress their centres . . .

19.1c . . . and remove the fastenings . . .

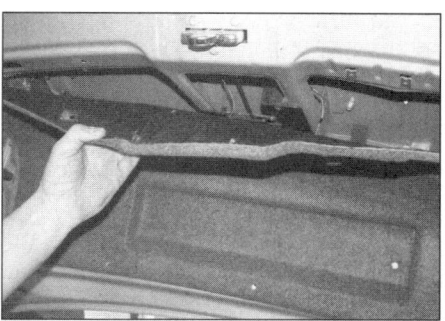

19.1d . . . and prise the trim from the boot lid

19.2 Boot lid lock mounting bolts

19.4 Removing the boot lid lock

16 Working through the hole in the roof rear crossmember, unscrew and remove the hinge inner mounting bolts.
17 Mark the positions of the tailgate rubber buffers, then unbolt and remove them.
18 Pull down the rubber weatherstrip from the upper half of the tailgate body aperture, and remove the side and upper cover plates.
19 Unscrew the mounting bolts and withdraw the hinges from the roof rear crossmember.

Refitting

20 Refitting is a reversal of removal, but lubricate the strut ball sockets with grease before refitting them. Adjust the tailgate as described earlier in this Section.

19 Boot lid/tailgate lock components – removal and refitting

Boot lid lock

Removal

1 With the boot lid open, undo the screws and remove the handgrip, then release the fastenings and carefully prise away the trim panel, using a wide-bladed screwdriver positioned next to each retaining clip **(see illustrations)**.
2 Unscrew and remove the lock mounting bolts located on the boot lid lower edge **(see illustration)**.
3 Working through the hole on the boot lid inner panel, disconnect the lock operating rod from the lock motor. To do this, press the plastic retainer to one side.

4 Remove the boot lid lock together with the operating rod **(see illustration)**.

Refitting

5 Refitting is a reversal of removal but tighten the mounting bolts securely.

Tailgate lock

Removal

6 With the tailgate open, carefully prise off the surround from the inner door handle.
7 Undo the screws from the lower edge of the trim panel, then pull down the top of the panel to release it from the upper clips, and pull it to the rear to release the guide pin at the handgrip. **Do not** pull down the rear of the panel before releasing the top, as the guide pin will be broken.
8 Inside the tailgate, note the location of the operating rods on the lock, then press the plastic retainers to one side and disconnect them **(see illustration)**.
9 Disconnect the wiring plug, then unscrew the mounting bolts and withdraw the lock **(see illustrations)**.

19.8 Disconnecting the operating rods

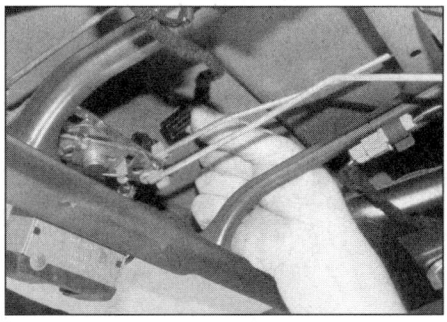

19.9a Disconnect the wiring . . .

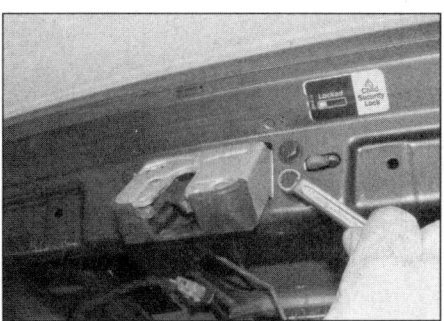

19.9b . . . then unscrew the mounting bolts . . .

11•18 Bodywork and fittings

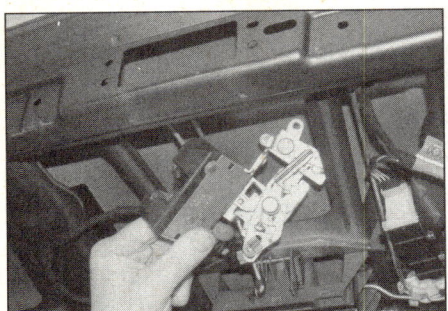

19.9c ... and withdraw the tailgate lock

19.12a Remove the cover ...

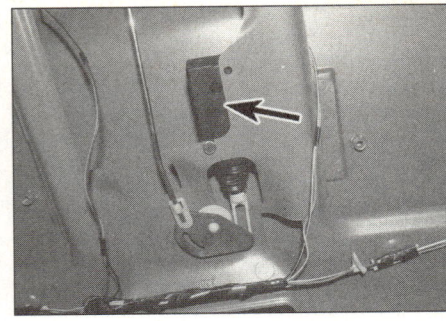

19.12b ... for access to the boot lid lock motor

Refitting

10 Refitting is a reversal of removal.

Boot lid lock motor

Removal

11 With the boot lid open, undo the screws and remove the handgrip, then release the fasteners and carefully prise away the trim panel, using a wide-bladed screwdriver positioned next to each retaining clip.

12 Remove the lock motor cover, then, working through the hole on the boot lid inner panel, disconnect the lock operating rod from the lock motor **(see illustrations)**. To do this, press the plastic retainer to one side.

13 Disconnect the private lock operating rod driver from the motor by pressing out the centre pin, using a hooked instrument. Allow the driver to hang loose on the private lock operating rod.

14 Unscrew the mounting bolts, withdraw the motor, and disconnect the wiring plug.

Refitting

15 Refitting is a reversal of removal.

Tailgate lock motor

Removal

16 With the tailgate open, carefully prise off the surround from the inner door handle.

17 Undo the screws from the lower edge of the trim panel, then pull down the top of the panel to release it from the upper clips, and pull it to the rear to release the guide pin at the handgrip. **Do not** pull down the rear of the panel before releasing the top, as the guide pin will be broken.

18 Working through the hole on the tailgate inner panel, disconnect the wiring plug from the lock motor **(see illustration)**.

19 Unscrew the mounting bolts, then disconnect the private lock operating rod driver from the motor by pressing out the centre pin, using a hooked instrument. Allow the driver to hang loose on the private lock operating rod. Carefully lower and tilt the motor, and withdraw it from the tailgate. Take care not to damage the pin on the driver **(see illustrations)**.

Refitting

20 Refitting is a reversal of removal.

Tailgate lock cylinder

Removal

21 With the tailgate open, carefully prise off the surround from the inner door handle.

22 Undo the screws from the lower edge of the trim panel, then pull down the top of the panel to release it from the upper clips, and pull it to the rear to release the guide pin at the handgrip. **Do not** pull down the rear of the panel before releasing the top, as the guide pin will be broken.

23 Disconnect the lock operating rod from the lever on the lock cylinder. To do this, press the plastic clip to one side **(see illustration)**.

24 Disconnect the wiring, unscrew the mounting nuts, and withdraw the lock cylinder from the tailgate **(see illustrations)**. Check the seal and if necessary obtain a new one.

Refitting

25 Refitting is a reversal of removal, but tighten all nuts and bolts securely.

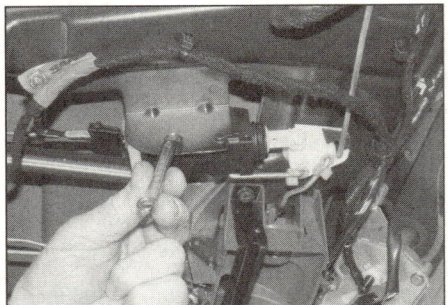

19.18 Disconnect the wiring ...

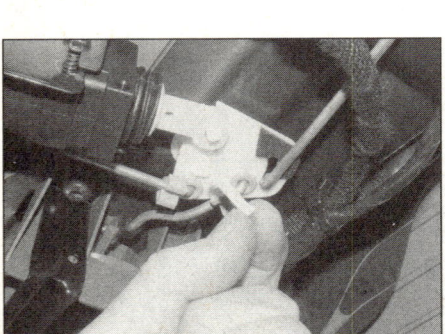

19.19a ... unscrew the mounting bolts ...

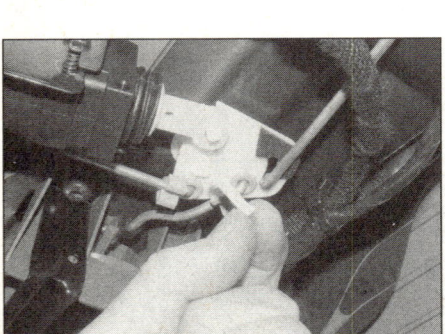

19.19b ... remove the centre pin ...

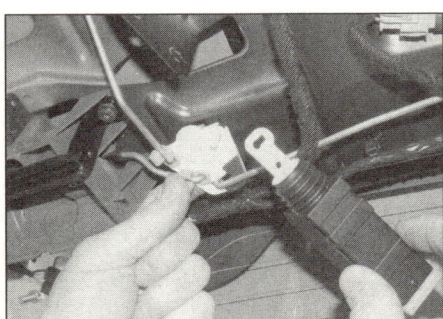

19.19c ... and withdraw the tailgate lock motor

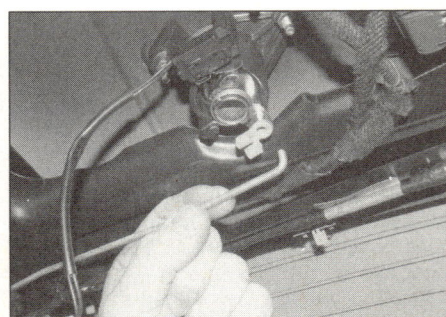

19.23 Disconnecting the lock operating rod from the lever on the lock cylinder

Bodywork and fittings 11•19

19.24a Disconnect the wiring...

19.24b ...unscrew the mounting nuts...

19.24c ...and withdraw the lock cylinder from the tailgate

19.34a Disconnect the manual operating rod...

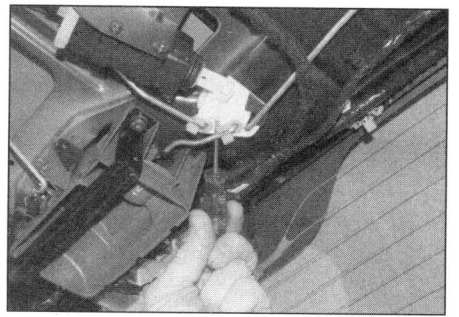
19.34b ...and central locking operating rod

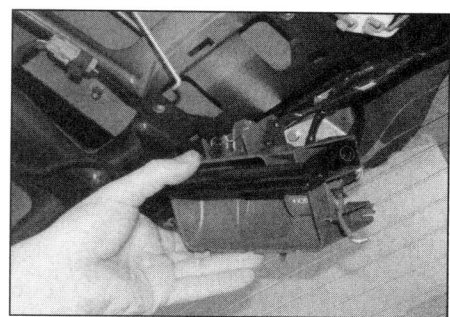
19.35 Removing the inner door handle from the tailgate

Boot lid handle

Removal

26 Remove the number plate.
27 With the boot lid open, undo the screws and remove the handgrip, then carefully prise away the trim panel, using a wide-bladed screwdriver positioned next to each retaining clip.
28 Undo the four nuts and remove the decor panel.
29 Remove the left-hand rear light unit by unscrewing the nuts and depressing the clips (refer to Chapter 12, Section 7).
30 Unscrew the mounting bolts, withdraw the handle, and disconnect the wiring.

Refitting

31 Refitting is a reversal of removal.

Tailgate inner handle

Removal

32 With the tailgate open, undo the screws and remove the inner handgrip. Also carefully prise off the surround from the inner door handle.
33 Undo the screws from the lower edge of the trim panel, then pull down the top of the panel to release it from the upper clips, and pull it to the rear to release the guide pin at the handgrip.
34 Disconnect the two operating rods (see illustrations).
35 Undo the mounting screws and withdraw the inner handle from the tailgate (see illustration).

Refitting

36 Refitting is a reversal of removal.

Tailgate outer handle

Removal

37 With the tailgate open, undo the screws and remove the inner handgrip.
38 Undo the screws from the lower edge of the trim panel, then pull down the top of the panel to release it from the upper clips, and pull it to the rear to release the guide pin at the handgrip.
39 Remove the left-hand rear tailgate light cluster as described in Chapter 12, Section 7.
40 Undo the retaining nuts and bolts, release the clips, and withdraw the outer handle from the tailgate, then disconnect the wiring.

Refitting

41 Refitting is a reversal of removal.

20.1a Prise off the window surround...

20 Exterior door mirror and glass – removal and refitting

Mirror

Removal

1 Carefully prise off the window surround from the inside the door, then disconnect the switch wiring (see illustrations).
2 Remove the foam seal and disconnect the wiring from the exterior door mirror (see illustrations).
3 Support the exterior door mirror, and then unscrew the mounting bolts. Note that the front bolt is located on the front edge of the door (see illustration).
4 Unhook the mirror and remove it from the

20.1b ...and disconnect the switch wiring

11•20 Bodywork and fittings

20.2a Remove the foam seal . . .

20.2b . . . and disconnect the mirror wiring

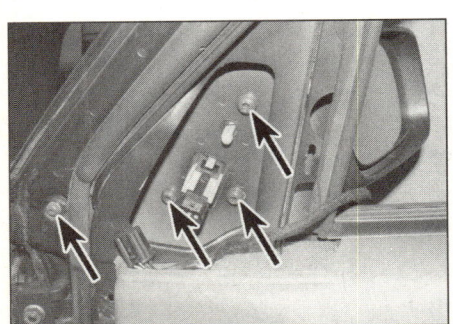

20.3 Unscrew the mounting bolts . . .

20.4 . . . and remove the exterior door mirror

outside of the door **(see illustration)**. Check the sealing gasket and renew it if necessary.

Refitting

5 Refitting is a reversal of removal, but tighten the mounting bolts progressively.

Glass

Removal

6 Swivel the exterior door mirror fully forwards, then angle out the inner edge of the mirror glass. Hold a piece of cloth over the glass to prevent it falling out.
7 Carefully insert a small screwdriver behind the glass, and release the retaining spring **(see illustration)**.
8 Withdraw the glass and disconnect the heater wiring **(see illustration)**.

Refitting

9 Make sure the spring clips are correctly located on the rear of the mirror.

20.7 Release the retaining spring with a screwdriver . . .

10 Reconnect the heater wiring.
11 Locate the glass on the motor, and use a wad of cloth to press it on until it is fully engaged.
12 Swivel the mirror rearwards, and check that it operates correctly.

21 Windscreen, rear window and fixed windows – general information

Windscreen and rear window

1 The windscreen and rear window glass are bonded in position with a special adhesive. Renewal of such fixed glass is a complex, messy and time-consuming task, which is beyond the scope of the home mechanic; without the benefit of extensive practise, it is difficult to attain a secure, waterproof fit. Furthermore, the task carries a high risk of

20.8 . . . withdraw the mirror and disconnect the wiring

accidental breakage – this applies especially to the laminated glass windscreen. In view of this, owners are strongly advised to entrust work of this nature to a Saab dealer, or one of the many specialist windscreen fitters.

Fixed rear side window

2 On Estate models, the fixed rear side window is bonded in position the same as the windscreen and rear window. Refer to paragraph 1.

22 Sunroof assembly – removal and refitting

1 Due to the complexity of the tilt/slide sunroof mechanism, considerable expertise is required to repair, renew or adjust the sunroof components successfully. Removal of the sunroof first requires that the headlining be removed, which is a tedious, time-consuming operation. Therefore, this Section is limited to removal of the glass hatch and drive motor, and it is recommended that any other work related to the sunroof is referred to a Saab dealer.

Glass hatch

Removal

2 Open the sunroof then undo the screws from the front cover strip.
3 Close the sunroof and tilt the rear edge. Pull the rear edge of the cover strip rearwards to release the clips, then pull out the strip taking care not to damage the paintwork.
4 Carefully pull the side cover strips from the retaining clips.
5 Raise the rear of the hatch, undo the two retaining bolts and lift out the glass hatch.

Refitting

6 Refitting is a reversal of removal, but adjust the glass hatch so that it is level with the surrounding roof panel. The front edge of the hatch can be slightly lower than the roof panel.

Drive motor assembly

Note: *If the drive motor is faulty, it is possible to operate the sunroof using a screwdriver. Slide off the cover from the overhead switch panel, and turn the motor shaft with the screwdriver. Turn the shaft anti-clockwise to close the sunroof.*

Removal

7 Open the sunroof then undo the screws from the front cover strip.
8 Close the sunroof and tilt the rear edge. Pull the rear edge of the cover strip rearwards to release the clips, and then pull out the strip taking care not to damage the paintwork.
9 Carefully pull the side cover strips from the retaining clips.
10 Close the sunroof and check that the wires' slide mountings are centred between the two marks on the slide rail. **Note:** *The*

Bodywork and fittings 11•21

sunroof must be closed when fitting a new motor, as it is supplied in the closed position.
11 Undo the screws and remove the sun visors; disconnect the wiring for the mirror light.
12 Prise out the lens from the interior light with a screwdriver, then undo the screws and remove the roof console.
13 Undo the screws and remove the rear view mirror.
14 Carefully bend down the front of the headlining and unscrew the drive motor mounting bolts. Take care not do damage the headlining. Withdraw the motor and disconnect the wiring.

Refitting
15 Refitting is a reversal of removal. Move the motor backwards and forwards as required to ensure the gears engage correctly before inserting the mounting bolts.

23 Body exterior fittings – removal and refitting

Door protective mouldings

Removal
1 Use a screwdriver to prise away the rear edge of the moulding – protect the paintwork with adhesive tape.
2 Pull the moulding and retaining clips from the sockets in the door panel, and slide it rearwards from the front mounting hole. If the clips come away from the moulding, or the sockets come out of the door panel, refit them in their correct positions.

Refitting
3 Refitting is a reversal of removal. Where fitted, leave the protective tape on the front of the moulding as this will allow it to slide forwards in the front mounting hole.

Sill scuff plate

Removal
4 Undo the screw securing the front of the scuff plate to the front wheel arch liner.
5 Unscrew the nut securing the front of the scuff plate to the front wing.

24.2 Removing the front seat rear mounting bolts

6 Prise out the rubber strip from the top of the scuff plate.
7 Unscrew the nut securing the scuff plate to the rear wheel arch liner.
8 Undo the screws and nuts securing the scuff plate to the sill.
9 Pull out the rear wheel arch liner, and withdraw the scuff plate.

Refitting
10 Refitting is a reversal of removal.

Wheel arch liners

Removal
11 Raise the front or rear of the vehicle (as applicable) and support it on axle stands (see *Jacking and vehicle support*). Remove the roadwheel.
12 Undo the plastic retaining nuts/bolts securing the liner to the body or wing.
13 Press the liner away from the outer edge of the wing, and withdraw it from the wheel housing.

Refitting
14 Refitting is a reversal of removal.

24 Seats – removal and refitting

Front seat

1 Adjust the seat fully forwards. On models with an electrically-operated front seat,

24.4 Removing the front seat front mounting bolts

if the seat motor is seized or inoperative, raise the seat as high as possible using the spring-loaded lever, and remove the upper seat cowl, then remove the front bolt. Undo the Torx screws, grasp the shaft and pull out the bevel gear. The gear can now be dismantled and a suitable tool attached to it with Jubilee clips to manually move the front seat.
2 Unscrew and remove the seat rear mounting bolts **(see illustration)**.
3 Adjust the seat fully rearwards.
4 Unscrew and remove the seat front mounting bolts **(see illustration)**.
5 Lift the front of the seat and disconnect the multipin wiring plug from under the seat base – also release the cable-tie and clip **(see illustrations)**.
6 Lift the seat from inside the vehicle, and, if necessary, release the seat belt from it (refer to Section 26).
7 Refitting is a reversal of removal, but tighten the mounting bolts to the specified torque. The inner bolt should be tightened first both at the front and rear.

Rear seat cushion

8 Fold the rear seat cushion forwards.
9 Release the plastic clip from the hinge **(see illustration)**.
10 Where applicable, disconnect the multipin plug from the underside of the seat cushion.
11 Withdraw the cushion from the vehicle **(see illustration)**.
12 Refitting is a reversal of removal.

24.5a Disconnect the multi-pin wiring plug . . .

24.5b . . . and release the cable-tie and clip

24.9 Removing the plastic clip from the hinge . . .

11•22 Bodywork and fittings

24.11 ... and remove the rear seat cushion

24.15a Release the catch retainer plate ...

24.15b ... and then withdraw the seat from the pivot (arrowed)

Rear seat backrest

40% section

13 On Saloon and Estate models, fold the rear seat cushion forwards and the backrest downwards, then fasten the seat belts in their holders on the C-pillars.
14 Fold the backrest slightly forwards and unhook the upholstery hooks at the seatbelt mounting.
15 Reach behind the seat pivot and release the retaining plate (If necessary use a small screwdriver to prise out the pivot retainer plate), then lift the backrest and withdraw it from the inner pivot pin **(see illustrations)**. Lift the backrest from inside the vehicle.
16 Refitting is a reversal of removal. Press down on the backrest until the catch locks. Make sure that the centre seat belt is located in front of the backrest.

60% section

17 Remove the 40% section rear seat backrest as described earlier.
18 On Saloon models, release the lock by pressing with a finger, and then pull the backrest from the anchor pins. Lift the backrest from inside the vehicle.
19 On Estate models, unscrew the bolt from the centre seat belt lower mounting, and unscrew the hinge pin from the centre support. Unhook the upholstery clip, and then lift the backrest from the left-hand side mounting. Slide the backrest towards the door to release the centre pin lug from the support, and withdraw the backrest from inside the vehicle **(see illustrations)**.
20 Refitting is a reversal of removal. Press down on the backrest until the catch locks. On Saloon models, make sure that the centre seat belt is located in front of the backrest.

25 Driver's seat control module – removal and refitting

Note: *The control module is only fitted to models with an electrically-operated seat.*

Removal

1 The front seat control module is located on the underside of the driver's seat. It contains the memory for position and movement control, and a communication function for diagnosis. The system also memorises the position of the electrically-operated rear view mirrors.
2 Remove the front seat as described in Section 24.
3 Disconnect the wiring from the module.
4 Undo the retaining screws and withdraw the module from the seat. Note that one of the module body bolt holes is open-ended and it is only necessary to loosen the bolt in this position, and slide the module from it.

Refitting

5 Refitting is a reversal of removal.

26 Seat belts – removal and refitting

⚠️ *Warning: If the vehicle has been involved in an accident, which causes the seat belt pretensioner to be activated, the complete seat*

24.19a Unscrew the bolt from the centre seat belt lower mounting ...

24.19b ... unscrew the hinge pin from the centre support ...

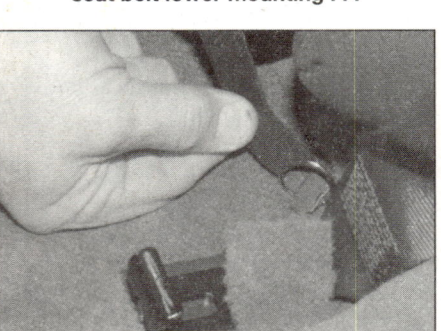

24.19c ... unhook the upholstery clip ...

24.19d ... release the outer left-hand side mounting ...

24.19e ... and release the centre pin lug from the support

Bodywork and fittings 11•23

26.1a Where fitted, undo the screws . . .

26.1b . . . and remove the plastic side cover

26.2a Depress the catch with a screwdriver . . .

26.2b . . . and release the seat belt

26.3a Remove the trim from the B-pillar . . .

26.3b . . . and pull through the seat belt

belt, together with pretensioner, must be renewed.

Front belt and tensioner

1 Adjust the seat as far forward as possible. Make sure that the ignition is switched off and if necessary remove the plastic side trim cover **(see illustrations)**.

2 Release the seat belt from the front seat by pressing in the catch with a small screwdriver **(see illustrations)**.

3 Pull back the weather seal from the B-pillar, then using a wide-bladed screwdriver, carefully lever the trim from the B-pillar and lift it from the air duct. Pull the seat belt through the trim **(see illustrations)**.

4 Disconnect the wiring for the belt pretensioner **(see illustration)**.

5 Unscrew the two nuts/bolts and single screw, and withdraw the front seat inertia reel and belt tensioner **(see illustration)**.

6 To remove the stalk from the inner side of the front seat, first remove the seat (see Section 24), then disconnect the reminder warning light wiring on the underside of the seat and cut the plastic cable-tie. Unscrew the bolt and remove the stalk.

7 Refitting is a reversal of removal, but tighten the mounting bolts to the specified torque. Check that the belt is fitted correctly to the front seat by pulling it directly upwards; the catch must be visible on the outside of the mounting. Saab recommend that the airbag system is checked for fault codes after fitting the front seat belt inertia reel and belt tensioner.

Rear outer belt

Saloon models

8 Fold the seat cushion forwards, then unscrew the nut securing the lower end of the seat belt to the floor **(see illustration)**.

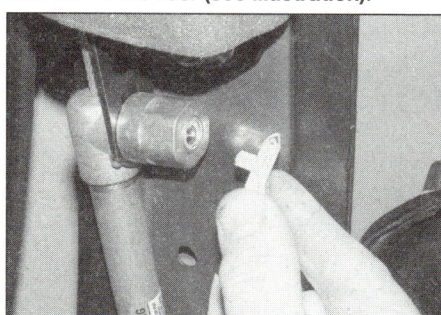

26.4 Disconnecting the belt pretensioner wiring

26.8 Seat belt mounting securing nut (arrowed)

9 Remove the securing clip and remove the speaker grille from the parcel shelf **(see illustration)**.

10 Pull back the weatherseal from the C-pillar, and then remove the trim panel from the pillar by carefully prising it away with a wide-bladed

26.5 Front seat belt inertia reel and belt tensioner mounting bolts

26.9 Remove the speaker grille

11•24 Bodywork and fittings

26.10 Unclip the trim panel from the C-pillar

26.11a Rear seat belt inertia reel mounting bolts

Estate models

13 Remove the rear parcel shelf, and also remove the storage box (where fitted), from the luggage compartment (see illustration).
14 Remove the scuff plate from the tailgate opening.
15 Remove the headlining rear trim, then prise away the D-pillar trim using a wide-bladed screwdriver.
16 Prise out the covers, then undo the screws and prise away the parcel shelf support (see illustrations).
17 Fold up the rear seat cushion, and fold down the backrest.
18 Lift the door weatherstrip and pull out the top of the side bolster, then unhook the bottom and withdraw (see illustrations).
19 Undo the screws and pull the trim from the backrest, then disconnect the wiring for the CD player, where fitted.
20 Starting at the top, pull away the trim from the C-pillar, noting the locating pin at the bottom rear (see illustration).
21 Unscrew the nut and remove the lower end of the belt from the floor.
22 Remove the guide from the C-pillar trim, then feed the belt tongue and belt through the guide.
23 Remove the insulating pad and guide, then unbolt and remove the seat belt reel (see illustrations).
24 To remove the stalk, unscrew the retaining nut/bolt and withdraw it from the rear floor panel (see illustration).
25 Refitting is a reversal of removal, but

26.11b Seat belt stalk securing nut (arrowed)

26.13 Rear luggage compartment storage box removal

screwdriver to release the retaining clips (see illustration). Draw the seat belt through the hole in the panel.
11 Unscrew the mounting nuts and remove the seat belt reel from the C-pillar. To remove the stalk, unscrew the mounting nut and remove it from the floor (see illustrations).
12 Refitting is a reversal of removal, but tighten the mounting nuts and bolts to the specified torque.

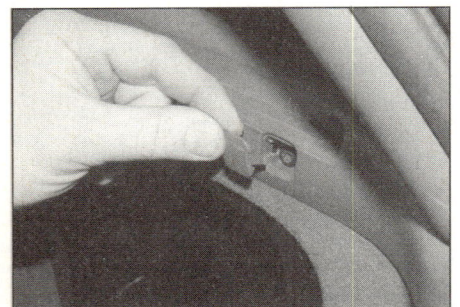

26.16a Prise out the covers . . .

26.16b . . . undo the screws . . .

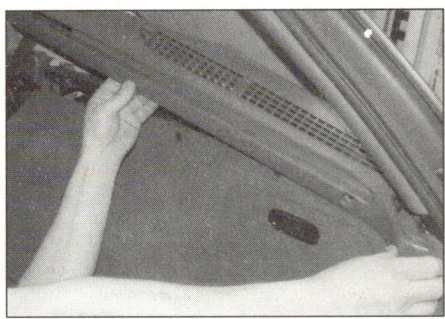

26.16c . . . and remove the parcel shelf support

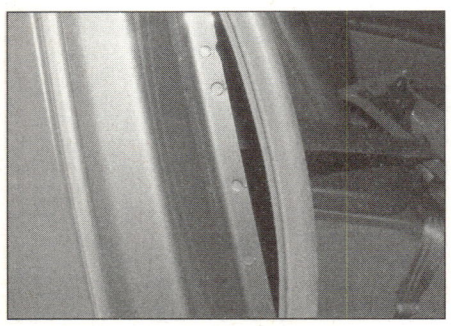

26.18a Lift the door weatherstrip . . .

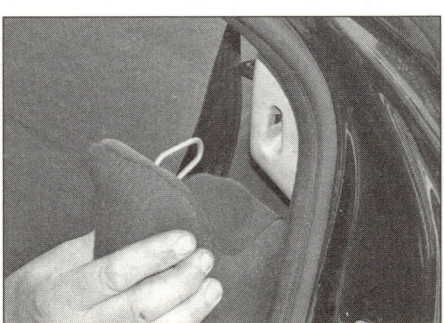

26.18b . . . then unhook the side bolster

26.20 Removing the trim from the C-pillar

Bodywork and fittings 11•25

26.23a Removing the insulation pad

26.23b Rear seat belt reel and anchor mounting bolts

26.24 Rear seat belt stalks

26.26 Remove the rear headrests

26.27a Release the retaining clips . . .

26.27b . . . and remove the rear shelf panel

tighten the mounting nuts/bolts to the specified torque. Make sure that the rubber weatherstrip is located correctly over the D-pillar trim, headlining and scuff plate.

Rear centre belt

Saloon models

26 Fold down the rear seat backrests, undo the securing screws and remove the head restraints from the rear parcel shelf **(see illustration)**.
27 Remove the securing clips along the front edge of the rear parcel shelf and remove both speaker grilles and parcel shelf trim from the vehicle **(see illustrations)**. Unclip the centre belt as the trim is removed.
28 Unscrew the mounting nut and remove the centre belt from the floor **(see illustration)**.
29 Unscrew the mounting nut and remove the seat belt reel from the rear parcel shelf crossmember **(see illustration)**.
30 To remove the stalk, unscrew the mounting nut and remove it from the floor **(see illustration 26.11b)**.
31 Refitting is a reversal of removal but tighten the mounting nuts to the specified torque. Make sure the belt is located over the front of the backrest.

Estate models

32 Fold the rear seat cushions forwards, and secure the rear seat belts in their holders.
33 Fold the 40% backrest slightly forwards and remove the trim retaining clip.
34 Using a screwdriver, release the lower catch and lift out the backrest.
35 Unscrew the centre belt lower mounting,

remove the centre pivot hinge pin, however, do not remove the retaining bolts.
36 Unclip the trim from the 60% backrest. With the backrest upright, release it from the left-hand side bracket. Now move it towards the door and release the centre pivot pin. Withdraw the backrest.
37 Undo the screw and unclip the cover from the catch.
38 Unclip the plate from the backrest, remove the trim from the groove and withdraw the plate. Take care not the break the corner.
39 Undo the screws and remove the belt plate from the rear of the backrest.
40 Remove the guide from the backrest and belt.
41 Cut the foam as necessary, undo the screws and remove the guide. Release the guide from the belt.
42 Unbolt and remove the inertia reel together with the seat belt.

26.28 Centre belt anchorage securing nut (arrowed)

43 To remove the stalk, unscrew the retaining nut/bolt and withdraw it from the rear floor panel.
44 Refitting is a reversal of removal, but tighten the mounting nuts/bolts to the specified torque.

27 Interior trim panels – removal and refitting

A-pillar trim panels

Note: *Special absorbent material is fitted between the headlining and roof panel to protect the driver and passenger's heads in the event of a collision, take care not to disturb this material.*

1 Open the relevant front door, and pull the rubber weatherseal from the door aperture at the A-pillar.

26.29 Centre seat belt inertia reel mounting nut (arrowed)

11•26 Bodywork and fittings

2 Working from the headlining down, grasp the trim panel firmly and progressively ease it away from the pillar, allowing the press-studs beneath to disengage one at a time.
3 Release the upper clips from the trim panel; however, **do not** remove the clip and strap from the pillar as this forms part of the energy absorption system fitted to the headlining (see note).
4 Refitting is a reversal of removal.

B-pillar trim panels

5 Move the front seat fully forwards, then carefully pull off the B-pillar trim panel and lift it out of the air duct.
6 Using an angled screwdriver, press in the catch and release the seat belt mounting from the front seat.
7 Remove the belt guide and pull the belt through the B-pillar trim panel. Withdraw the trim panel.
8 Refitting is a reversal of removal.

C-pillar trim panels

Saloon models

9 Fold down the rear seat backrest, then undo the screw and remove the head restraint **(see illustration 26.13)**.
10 Release the retaining clip and remove the radio speaker grille from the parcel shelf **(see illustration 26.9)**.
11 Carefully pull the trim panel from the C-pillar, then unbolt the seat belt and feed it through the panel **(see illustration 26.26)**.
12 Refitting is a reversal of removal.

Estate models

13 Remove the rear roof cross panel from the rear of the headlining. This is necessary to provide sufficient clearance for the D-pillar trim.
14 Carefully pull the D-pillar trim panel forwards and release it from the retaining clips.
15 Undo the screws and remove the parcel shelf support from under the rear side window.
16 Starting at the top, pull away the C-pillar trim panel, noting the location pin at the rear lower edge.
17 Fold the rear seat cushion forwards, then unscrew the lower seat belt mounting nut.
18 Remove the guide from the C-pillar and pull the belt through the trim.
19 Refitting is a reversal of removal.

Luggage area side trim panel

Saloon models

20 Where applicable, remove the CD changer on the left-hand side of the luggage compartment and the protective net from the right-hand side.
21 Lift up the floor panel and unclip the scuff plate from the rear valance.
22 Fold down the rear seat backrest, then undo the screws and unclip the floor panel at the front.
23 Undo the screw and unclip the radio speaker grille from the parcel shelf.
24 Unscrew the plastic nuts and withdraw the side trim panel.
25 Refitting is a reversal of removal.

Estate models

26 Remove the storage compartment from the luggage compartment.
27 Prise off the covers and undo the screws, then unclip the scuff plate from the rear valance.
28 Remove the rear roof cross panel from the rear of the headlining. This is necessary to provide sufficient clearance for the D-pillar trim.
29 Carefully pull the D-pillar trim panel forwards and release it from the retaining clips.
30 Undo the screws and remove the parcel shelf support from under the rear side window.
31 Pull out the top of the side bolster, then unhook the bottom and withdraw.
32 Undo the screws from the top of the side trim panel, then, where necessary, carefully pull out the panel and disconnect the wiring from the CD player. Withdraw the panel.
33 Refitting is a reversal of removal. When refitting the side trim panel, insert the rearmost retaining screw first.

Lower facia panel

Driver's side

34 Undo the screws and remove the lower facia trim panel together with the air duct on the driver's side **(see illustrations)**.
35 Undo the screws and remove the diagnostic socket and data link wiring **(see illustrations**.
36 Remove the footwell light from the lower facia trim panel, or disconnect the wiring **(see illustration)**.
37 Refitting is a reversal of removal.

Headlining

Note: *Special absorbent material is fitted between the headlining and roof panel to protect the driver and passenger's heads in the event of a collision, take care not to disturb this material.*

38 Undo the screws and remove the sun visors. Where applicable, disconnect the wiring from the mirror light.
39 Carefully prise out the interior light lens from the roof console.
40 Undo the screws and remove the roof

27.34a Undo the screws . . .

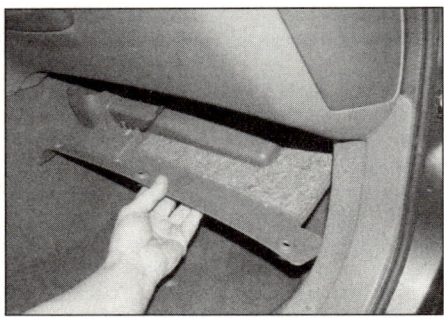

27.34b . . . and remove the lower facia trim panel with air duct

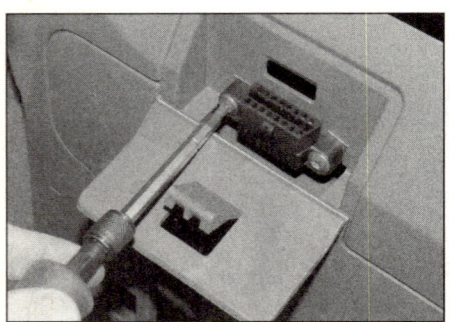

27.35a Undo the screws . . .

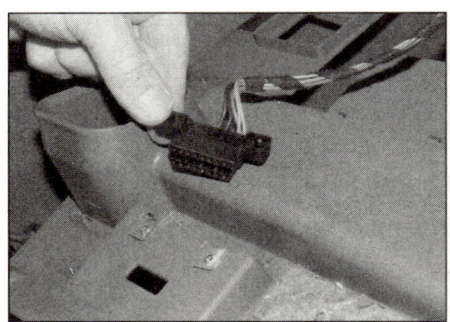

27.35b . . . and remove the diagnostic socket and data link wiring

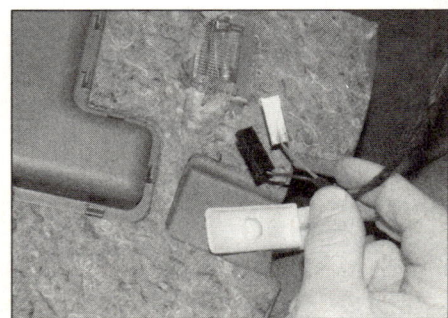

27.36 Disconnecting the wiring from the footwell light

Bodywork and fittings 11•27

console. Where fitted, it will be necessary to disconnect the wiring from the interior temperature sensor and microphone.
41 Undo the screws and remove the rear view mirror (see illustration).
42 Remove the A-pillar trim panels as described earlier in this Section.
43 Undo the screws and remove the handgrips located over the door apertures.
44 On models with a sunroof, remove the three clips from the rear of the sunroof aperture.
45 Remove the B-pillar trim panel on the passenger's side as described earlier in this Section.

Saloon models

46 Unclip the top of each C-pillar trim.
47 Unclip the high-level brake light cover and disconnect the wiring. Pull the wiring clear of the console.
48 Release the rear of the headlining by twisting the two clips through 90°.
49 Adjust the front seats as low and as far rearwards as possible, and fold down the backrests to provide as much working room as possible.
50 Carefully pull out the headlining from the driver and passenger's door sealing mouldings.
51 On models with a sunroof, release the headlining from the hooks near the sunroof.
52 Note that some wiring is taped to the top of the headlining. Disconnect the wiring in the roof console aperture, and where applicable disconnect the alarm wiring.
53 Adjust the steering wheel fully forwards. On manual transmission models, select reverse. On automatic transmission models, select first.
54 With the help of an assistant, carefully lift the headlining through the passenger door aperture. Take care not to crack the headlining.
Caution: Check that the energy-absorbent pads on the top of the headlining are still intact. If any are damaged, the complete headlining must be renewed.

Estate models

55 Release the clips securing the headlining rear crossmember to the roof.
56 Disconnect the wiring from the glass breakage sensor and luggage compartment light.

27.41 Rear view mirror retaining screws

57 Carefully pull away the trim panels from the D-pillars, and then remove the trim panels from between the C- and D-pillars.
58 Release the clips securing the top of the C-pillar trim panels.
59 Remove the cargo safety net mountings, prise off the covers and undo the clips.
60 Release the rear of the headlining by twisting the two clips through 90°.
61 Carefully pull out the headlining from the driver and passenger's door sealing mouldings.
62 On models with a sunroof, release the headlining from the hooks near the sunroof.
63 Note that some wiring is taped to the top of the headlining. Disconnect the wiring in the roof console aperture, and where applicable disconnect the alarm wiring.
64 With the help of an assistant, carefully lift the headlining through the tailgate aperture. Take care not to crack the headlining.

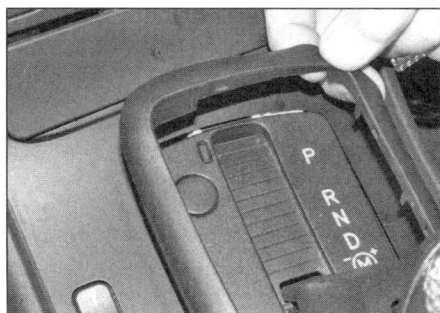

28.1 Removing the selector lever surround (automatic transmission models)

Caution: Check that the energy-absorbent pads on the top of the headlining are still intact. If any are damaged, the complete headlining must be renewed.

All models

65 If a new headlining is being fitted, transfer the wiring from the old one and secure with new tape.
66 Refitting is a reversal of removal.

28 Centre console – removal and refitting

Removal

1 On manual transmission models, prise the gear lever gaiter from the centre console. On automatic transmission models, use a screwdriver to prise up the selector lever surround (see illustration).
2 Where an ashtray is fitted, open it and detach the outer trim panel with the ashtray (see illustration).
3 Using a screwdriver, prise back the retaining tabs and prise the ashtray/oddments box from the centre console (see illustrations). Use tape to protect the walnut veneer.
4 Undo the screws and remove the gear lever/selector cover. Identify the wiring locations then disconnect the plugs – there are plugs for the central locking and cigarette lighter (see illustrations). Also disconnect the wiring from the switch seat heating and seat ventilation, where fitted.

28.2 Removing the outer trim panel from the ashtray

28.3a Prise back the retaining tabs (one at each side) . . .

28.3b . . . and remove the ashtray box from the centre console

28.4a Undo the screws (arrowed) . . .

11•28 Bodywork and fittings

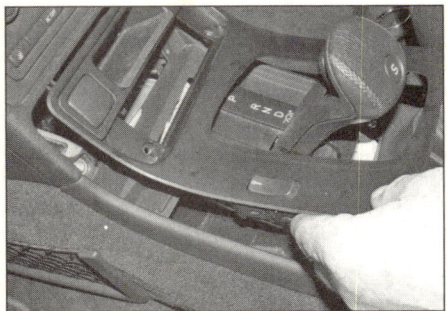

28.4b ... remove the gear/selector cover ...

28.4c ... then disconnect the wiring from the central locking switch ...

28.4d ... and cigarette lighter

28.5a Undo the retaining screw ...

28.5b ... lift the rear end part of the console ...

28.5c ... and disconnect the wiring

5 Open the armrest lid and undo the upper retaining screw. Then lift the rear end trim and remove it from the rear of the console, disconnect the wiring connector(s) as it is removed (see illustrations).
6 Select reverse (manual transmission) or P (automatic transmission). Remove the ignition key.
7 Twist the theft protection antenna unit bayonet fitting from the ignition switch and disconnect the wiring (see illustrations). Insert the ignition key and select Neutral.

8 Prise out the electric window switch panel and disconnect the wiring. If necessary, access may be gained by first prising out the small panel behind the switch (see illustrations).
9 Undo the screws and remove the upper surround panel from the centre console, at

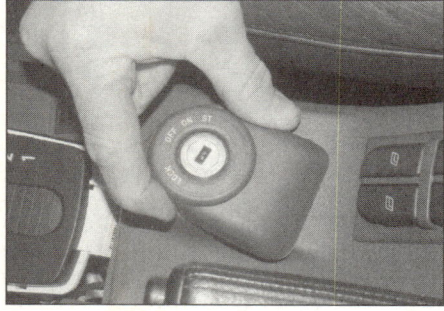

28.7a Remove the theft protection antenna unit ...

28.7b ... and disconnect the wiring

28.8a Prise out the small panel ...

28.8b ... then push out the electric window switch panel ...

28.8c ... and disconnect the wiring

28.9a Undo the retaining screws (arrowed) ...

28.9b ... and rear screws (arrowed) ...

28.9c ... noting the location of the spring for the storage compartment lid ...

28.9d ... then remove the upper surround panel from the centre console

28.10a Remove the fasteners ...

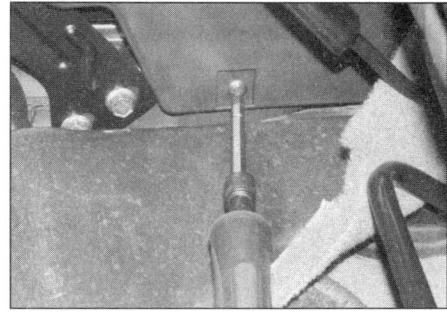

28.10b ... undo the side screws ...

28.10c ... and rear screws (arrowed) ...

the same time pulling off the handbrake lever gaiter **(see illustrations)**.

10 Remove the fasteners and fold back the carpet, then undo the console front and rear mounting screws **(see illustrations)**.

11 Withdraw the centre console from inside the vehicle **(see illustration)**.

Refitting

12 Refitting is a reversal of removal.

29 Facia assembly – removal and refitting

⚠️ **Warning:** Observe the safety precautions given in Section 31 when working on or near the airbags.

Removal

1 Disconnect the battery negative lead.

2 Carefully prise out the speaker grilles from each side of the facia **(see illustration)**. They are secured with clips.

3 Undo the screws and lift out the speakers. Disconnect the wiring **(see illustrations)**.

4 Carefully remove the cover from the

28.11 ... then remove the centre console

centre top of the facia by initially pushing it forwards, then lifting it. Remove the anti-theft warning LED, then disconnect the wiring from the solar sensor and push it down through the hole in the facia, noting its routing **(see illustrations)**.

29.2 Prise out the speaker grilles ...

29.3a ... then undo the screws, lift out the speaker ...

29.3b ... and disconnect the wiring

29.4a Remove the centre cover from the facia ...

11•30 Bodywork and fittings

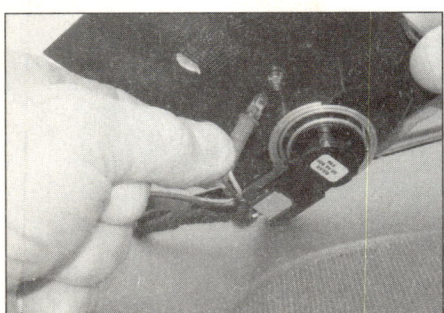

29.4b ... remove the anti-theft warning LED ...

29.4c ... and disconnect the solar sensor wiring

29.16a Undo the screws (arrowed) ...

29.16b ... and remove the steering column gaiter

lower facia trim panel, or disconnect the wiring.
10 On manual transmission models, prise the gear lever gaiter from the centre console. On automatic transmission models, use a screw-driver to prise up the selector lever surround.
11 Using a screwdriver prise out the ashtray and holder, or oddments tray as applicable. Undo the screws located behind the aperture.
12 Disconnect the wiring from the central locking switch.
13 Raise the gear lever cover and disconnect the wiring for the seat heater and cigarette lighter.
14 Remove the instrument panel and surround as described in Chapter 12.
15 Unbolt the fusebox from the bulkhead.
16 Undo the screws and remove the steering column gaiter (**see illustrations**).
17 Undo the screws and remove the air ducts on the driver and passenger's sides (**see illustrations**).
18 On models with a passenger airbag, disconnect the airbag wiring, then undo the screw and remove the airbag retaining strap. Also release the wiring loom from the Velcro strap near the airbag (**see illustration**).
19 Remove the scuff plates from the door sills on each side (**see illustration**).
20 Remove the fasteners, then pull back the carpet from the front footwells, then unscrew the nuts and remove the plates for the lower facia mountings (**see illustrations**).
21 Remove the rear end part of the console by lifting it, and disconnect the wiring.

5 Remove the glovebox as described in Section 30 and lift out the air duct.
6 Remove the steering wheel as described in Chapter 10.
7 Undo the screws and remove the lower facia trim panel together with the air duct on the driver's side.
8 Undo the screws from the diagnostic socket, and also disconnect the wiring.
9 Remove the footwell light from the

29.17a Undo the screws ...

29.17b ... and remove the air ducts on both sides

29.18 Velcro strap retaining the wiring near the passenger airbag

29.19 Removing the door sill scuff plates

29.20a Remove the fasteners ...

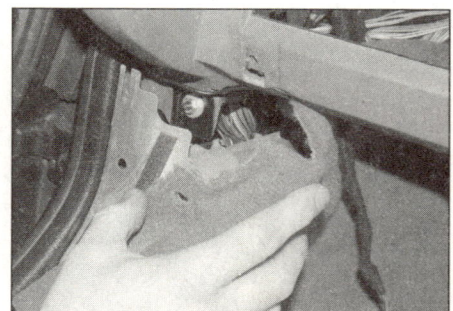

29.20b ... pull back the carpet ...

Bodywork and fittings 11•31

29.20c ... undo the nuts (arrowed) ...

29.20d ... and remove the plates for the lower facia mountings

29.26a Unscrew the nuts ...

29.26b ... and remove the locating pin bracket from the front of the centre console

29.27 Facia upper central mounting nut – it is only necessary to loosen this nut

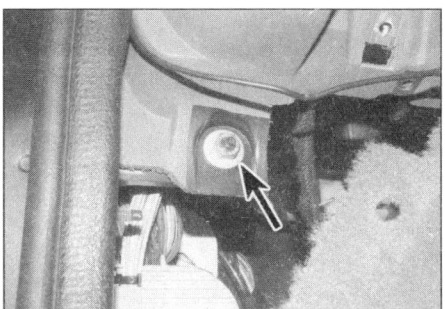

29.28a Unscrew the facia lower outer nuts ...

22 Select reverse (manual transmission) or P (automatic transmission). Remove the ignition key.
23 Twist the theft protection antenna unit bayonet fitting from the ignition switch and disconnect the wiring. Insert the ignition key and select Neutral.
24 Prise out the electric window switch and disconnect the wiring.
25 Undo the screws and remove the upper surround panel from the centre console.
26 Mark its fitted position, then unbolt and remove the metal bracket and locating pin from the front of the centre console (see illustrations).
27 Unscrew the centre nut and outer bolts from the front edge of the facia panel (see illustration). Note that it is only necessary to loosen the centre nut as its hole is slotted, however, the outer bolts must be removed.

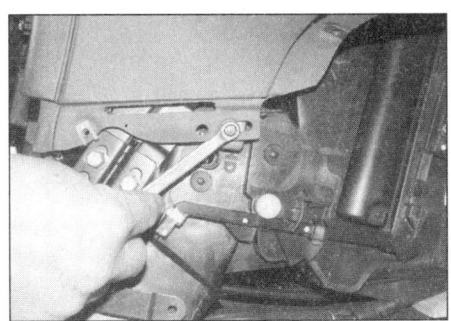

29.28b ... and the central nuts securing the facia to the heater

28 Unscrew the facia lower outer mounting nuts, and the central nuts securing the facia to the heater (see illustrations).
29 With the help of an assistant, carefully lift the facia assembly from the bulkhead and withdraw it through one of the front door apertures (see illustration).
30 Where fitted, unscrew the nuts and remove the passenger airbag from the facia panel.

Refitting

31 Refitting is a reversal of removal, but refer to Section 31 for details of refitting the airbags.

30 Glovebox – removal and refitting

Removal

1 Remove the carpet cover from the heater/

29.29 Removing the facia assembly from inside the car

ventilation unit beneath the glovebox (see illustration).
2 Undo the screws and remove the lower facia trim panel, then remove the footwell light or disconnect the wiring from it (see illustrations).

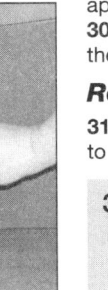

30.1 Removing the carpet cover from the heater/ventilation unit beneath the glovebox

30.2a Undo the screws ...

11•32 Bodywork and fittings

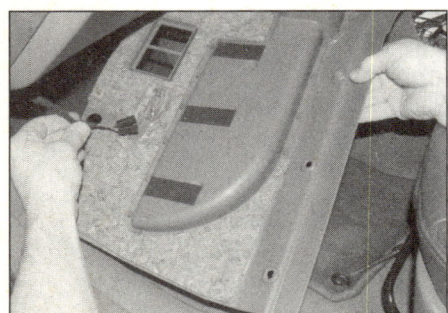

30.2b ... remove the lower facia trim panel, and disconnect the footwell light wiring

30.3a Undo the lower screws ...

30.3b ... and upper screws ...

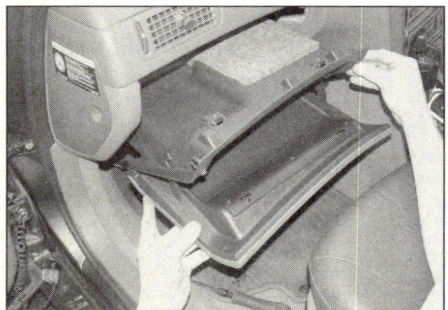

30.3c ... then withdraw the glovebox ...

30.3d ... disconnect the wiring from the illumination light ...

30.4 ... and release the air conditioning cold air hose from the glovebox

3 Unscrew the three mounting screws underneath and three screws inside the glovebox, then withdraw the glovebox sufficiently to disconnect the wiring from the illumination light **(see illustrations)**.

4 On models with air conditioning, release the cold air hose from the glovebox **(see illustration)**.

5 Withdraw the glovebox from the facia.

Refitting

6 Refitting is a reversal of removal.

31 Supplementary Restraint System (SRS) components – removal and refitting

General information

The operation of the SRS is managed by an electronic control module (ECM). When the vehicle's ignition switch is turned on, the ECM performs self-test checks of the system's components; if a fault is detected, the ECM records it in memory as a fault. Following this, the ECM illuminates the instrument panel-mounted SRS warning light. If this should occur, the vehicle should be taken to a Saab dealer for examination. Dedicated test equipment is needed to interrogate the SRS ECM, firstly to determine the nature and incidence of the fault, and secondly to clear the stored fault, thus preventing the fault from being displayed by the warning light once the fault has been rectified.

The SRS ECM incorporates an electro-mechanical safety sensor of magnetic reed type, a microprocessor, three back-up power sources, a voltage converter and an accelerometer. After deployment of either the driver or passenger's airbag, a permanent fault code is generated in the ECM, which cannot be cleared, requiring the renewal of the ECM.

Caution: The SRS ECM must be renewed after deployment of either the driver's or passenger's airbag. However, it may be re-used a total of three times after deployment of the side airbags and/or seat belt tensioners.

The ECM's wiring connector incorporates short-circuiting jumpers, which are activated when the connector is unplugged. The circuits concerned are the electric detonators for the front airbags and side airbags, and also the circuit for the airbag warning lamp. This ensures the airbags cannot be deployed with the ECM connector unplugged.

For safety reasons, owners are strongly advised against attempting to diagnose problems with the SRS using standard workshop equipment. The information in this Section is therefore limited to those components in the SRS which must occasionally be removed to gain access to other components on the vehicle.

 Warning: A number of additional precautions must be observed when working on vehicles with airbags/SRS:

- *Always switch the ignition off and remove the ignition key before working on the SRS system components. Although not a manufacturer's requirement, the battery may also be disconnected as a further precaution.*
- **Do not** *attempt to splice into any of the electric cables in the SRS wiring harness.*
- *Avoid hammering or causing any harsh vibration at the front of the vehicle, particularly in the engine bay, as this may trigger the crash sensors and activate the SRS.*
- *Do not use ohmmeters or any other device capable of supplying current on any of the SRS components, as this may cause accidental detonation.*
- *Airbags (and seat belt tensioners) are classed as pyrotechnical (explosive) devices, and must be stored and handled according to the relevant laws in the country concerned. In general, do not leave these components disconnected from their electrical wiring any longer than is absolutely necessary; in this state they are unstable, and the risk of accidental detonation is introduced. Rest a disconnected airbag with the metal bracket facing downwards, away from flammable materials – never leave it unattended.*
- *The seat belt tensioners must not be exposed to temperatures in excess of 100°C.*

Driver's airbag

Removal

1 Turn the ignition to the OFF position, leaving the key in the switch, with the steering lock released, turn the steering wheel 90° to the left.

Bodywork and fittings 11•33

31.2a Insert a screwdriver into the rear of the steering wheel . . .

31.2b . . . and release the retaining spring clips (arrowed)

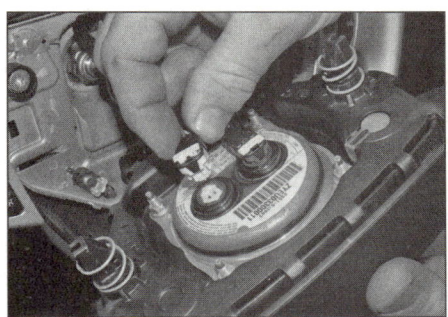

31.3 Disconnect the wiring from the airbag unit

2 At the lower part of the steering wheel, insert a small screwdriver through the hole in the rear of the steering wheel to release the securing clip. Turn the steering wheel through 180° and insert a small screwdriver through the hole in the rear of the steering wheel to release the second securing clip **(see illustrations)**.
3 With the two securing clips released, carefully withdraw the airbag module from the steering wheel, and then disconnect the airbag wiring connectors as it is removed **(see illustration)**.
4 Rest the airbag in a safe place with the metal bracket facing downwards.

Refitting

5 Locate the airbag over the steering wheel and reconnect the wiring, making sure that it is securely connected onto the terminal.
6 Lower the airbag into the steering wheel, and press firmly, making sure the retaining clips are located securely.
7 Switch on the ignition and check that the SRS warning light goes out. If the warning light does not go out, the control unit probably has a fault code stored in it and it will be necessary to have a Saab dealer check the system.

Passenger's airbag

Removal

8 Ensure the ignition is switched off, then remove the facia as described in Section 29.
9 Disconnect the wiring from the passenger airbag module **(see illustration)**.
10 Undo the retaining nuts and remove the passenger's airbag from the facia **(see illustration)**.
11 Rest the airbag in a safe place with the metal bracket facing downwards (ie, airbag facing upwards).

Refitting

12 Position the airbag in the facia and tighten the nuts securely.
13 Refit the facia with reference to Section 29.
14 Switch on the ignition and check that the SRS warning light goes out. If the warning light does not go out, the control unit probably has a fault code stored in it and it will be necessary to have a Saab dealer check the system.

Side airbag

Note: *This work involves removing the rear fabric from the seat, and may be considered a job for an upholsterer rather than the home mechanic.*

Removal

15 Ensure the ignition is switched off.
16 Remove the front seat as described in Section 24.
17 Release the seat backrest upholstery from the bottom of the seat and remove the retaining strip.
18 Release the staples and remove the cardboard.
19 Remove the retaining strips and fold out the upholstery.
20 Disconnect the wiring from the side airbag, then unscrew the retaining nuts and withdraw the unit.

Refitting

21 Locate the side airbag on the front seat and tighten the nuts to the specified torque.
22 Refit the upholstery and cardboard and secure with new staples.
23 Refit the front seat with reference to Section 24.

Airbag contact spring unit

Removal

24 Ensure the ignition is switched off.
25 Remove the steering wheel as described in Chapter 10.
26 Remove the steering column upper and lower shrouds. There are two screws facing upwards in the upper shroud, and one screw located beneath the lower shroud.
27 Remove the steering column switches as described in Chapter 12.
28 Note the contact spring unit is secured to the central position by a locking peg when the wiring connector is disconnected **(see illustration)**.
29 Working under the steering column, disconnect the wiring for the contact spring unit at the connector, and release the wiring from any retaining clips **(see illustrations)**.
30 Note its fitted position, then undo the screws and remove the airbag contact spring unit from the steering column holder **(see illustration)**.

Refitting

31 Locate the unit onto the steering column then insert and tighten the retaining bolts.

31.9 Disconnect the passenger airbag wiring . . .

31.10 . . . then undo the retaining nuts

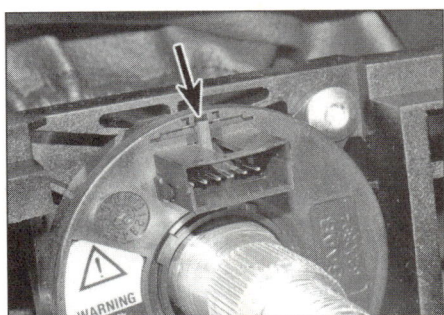

31.28 Contact spring unit locking peg (arrowed)

11•34 Bodywork and fittings

31.29a Cut the cable-tie . . .

31.29b . . . and disconnect the wiring

31.30 Undo the contact spring unit retaining screws (arrowed)

31.37a Undo the two mounting bolts (arrowed) . . .

31.37b . . . and remove the side impact sensor from inside the door

31.40 SRS airbag electronic control unit

32 Plug in the wiring connector and locate the loom in the retaining clips. Make sure the wiring is not twisted.
33 Refit the steering column switches with reference to Chapter 12.
34 Refit the steering column shrouds, then refit the steering wheel with reference to Chapter 10.
35 Switch on the ignition and check that the SRS warning light goes out. If the warning light does not go out, the control module probably has a fault code stored in it and it will be necessary to have a Saab dealer check the system.

Side impact sensor

Removal

36 The side impact sensor is located inside the door, behind the loudspeaker. First, remove the door inner trim panel and waterproof membrane as described in Section 13.
37 Undo the retaining bolts, withdraw the sensor from inside the door, and disconnect the wiring (see illustrations).

Refitting

38 Refitting is a reversal of removal, but tighten the retaining screws to the specified torque. The sensor wiring connector must face downwards.

Electronic control module (ECM)

Note: *If a new ECM is fitted, it must be programmed by a Saab dealer using a special diagnostic tool.*

Removal

39 Ensure the ignition is switched off.
40 Remove the centre console as described in Section 28. The electronic control module is located centrally on the floor panel beneath the centre console (see illustration).
41 Disconnect the wiring from the control unit.
42 Note its fitted position, and then undo the mounting bolts and withdraw the control unit from inside the vehicle.

Refitting

43 Refitting is a reversal of removal, but tighten the mounting bolts securely. **Do not** connect the wiring before tightening the mounting bolts. Make sure that the arrow on the ECM points to the **rear** of the vehicle; this is important, as otherwise the airbag system will not function.

Chapter 12
Body electrical system

Contents

	Section number
Aerial amplifier and filter – removal and refitting	21
Anti-theft alarm system components – general information, removal and refitting	25
Audio amplifier – removal and refitting	19
CD changer – removal and refitting	20
Cigarette lighter – removal and refitting	11
DICE control module – general information, removal and refitting	23
Electrical fault finding – general information	2
Exterior light bulbs – renewal	6
Exterior light units – removal and refitting	7
Fuses and relays – general information	3
General information and precautions	1
Headlight beam adjustment – general information	8
Heated and ventilated seat components – general information, removal and refitting	22
Horn – removal and refitting	12
Instrument panel and electronic unit – removal and refitting	9
Interior light bulbs – renewal	5
Loudspeakers – removal and refitting	18
Parking aid components – general information, removal and refitting	24
Radio/CD player – removal and refitting	17
Rain sensor – removal and refitting	14
Saab Information Display (SID) module – general information, removal and refitting	10
Switches and controls – removal and refitting	4
Windscreen and tailgate wiper arms – removal and refitting	13
Windscreen and tailgate wiper motor and linkage – removal and refitting	15
Windscreen, tailgate and headlight washer system – removal and refitting	16

Degrees of difficulty

Easy, suitable for novice with little experience | **Fairly easy,** suitable for beginner with some experience | **Fairly difficult,** suitable for competent DIY mechanic | **Difficult,** suitable for experienced DIY mechanic | **Very difficult,** suitable for expert DIY or professional

Specifications

System type	12 volt negative earth
Bulb ratings	**Watts**
Front and rear direction indicators	24
Front foglights	55
Headlights – main and dipped:	
Halogen	55
Xenon	37
High-level stop-light:	
Estate (LED)	4
Saloon	5
Illumination for switches and front ashtray	1.2 or 2.0
Interior dome light, courtesy light, luggage compartment light, glove compartment light	10
Number plate lights	5
Reading light (rear)	4
Rear foglight, reversing light	21
Seat belt warning, reading light (front), overhead console	5
Sidelights	5
Side repeater light	5 (or 2.2 for certain markets)
Stop/tail lights	21/5

Torque wrench setting	Nm	lbf ft
Windscreen wiper motor and linkage	8	6

12•2 Body electrical system

1.3a Xenon load sensor fitted to the front suspension lower arm . . .

1.3b . . . and rear suspension lower arm

1.4 Diagnostic socket located beneath the driver's side of the facia

1 General information and precautions

Warning: Before carrying out any work on the electrical system, read through the precautions given in 'Safety First!' at the beginning of this manual and Chapter 5A.

Warning: When working on xenon headlights, always switch off the ignition and turn the key to its LOCK position. Never connect voltage to the xenon headlight without its protective cover being fitted. Never attempt to repair the wiring of xenon headlights; faulty wiring must be renewed in its entirety. It is recommended that protective gloves and glasses are worn.

The electrical system is of 12 volt negative earth type and comprises a 12 volt battery, an alternator with integral voltage regulator, a starter motor and related electrical accessories, components and wiring.

All models are fitted with an anti-theft alarm and immobiliser system including door sensors, a boot lid/tailgate sensor, a bonnet sensor and a glass breakage sensor. The system is controlled by a central electronic control module, which operates the warning horn on getting a signal from one of the sensors. A tilt angle sensor (fluid filled) is also fitted to some models to monitor any attempt to jack up the vehicle while the alarm is enabled. Both the glass and tilt sensors can be disabled individually if required, leaving just the main alarm functional. The system antenna is incorporated in the ignition switch, and the transponder for the immobiliser is located in the ignition key fob.

Some models are equipped with xenon dipped headlights that are designed to last the life of the vehicle. To ensure these headlights do not dazzle oncoming traffic, an automatic levelling system is fitted incorporating load sensors on the front and rear suspension arms **(see illustrations)**.

This Chapter covers repair and service procedures for the various electrical components not associated with the engine. Information on the battery, alternator and starter motor can be found in Chapter 5A. Many of the electrical circuits are linked to control units, which can be tested for faults using a purpose-made diagnostic instrument connected to the socket located beneath the driver's side of the facia **(see illustration)**.

It should be noted that prior to disconnecting wiring from any components in the electrical system, the battery negative terminal should first be disconnected, to prevent the possibility of electrical short circuits and/or fires. Note also that the alarm must be disabled before disconnecting the battery.

2 Electrical fault finding – general information

Note: *Refer to the precautions given in 'Safety first!' and in Section 1 of this Chapter before starting work. The following tests relate to testing of the main electrical circuits, and should not be used to test delicate electronic circuits (such as engine management systems, anti-lock braking systems, etc), particularly where an electronic control module (ECM) is used.*

General

A typical electrical circuit consists of an electrical component, any switches, relays, motors, fuses, fusible links or circuit breakers related to that component, and the wiring and connectors which link the component to both the battery and the body. To help pin-point a problem in an electrical circuit, wiring diagrams are included at the end of this Chapter.

Before attempting to diagnose an electrical fault, first study the appropriate wiring diagram, to obtain a complete understanding of the components included in the particular circuit concerned. The possible sources of a fault can be narrowed down by noting if other components related to the circuit are operating properly. If several components or circuits fail at one time, the problem is likely to be related to a shared fuse or earth connection.

Electrical problems usually stem from simple causes, such as loose or corroded connections, a faulty earth connection, a blown fuse, a melted fusible link, or a faulty relay (refer to Section 3 for details of testing relays). Visually inspect the condition of all fuses, wires and connections in a problem circuit before testing the components. Use the wiring diagrams to determine which terminal connections will need to be checked in order to pin-point the trouble spot.

The basic tools required for electrical fault finding include a circuit tester or voltmeter (a 12 volt bulb with a set of test leads can also be used for certain tests), an ohmmeter (to measure resistance and check for continuity), a battery and set of test leads, and a jumper wire (preferably with a circuit breaker or fuse incorporated), which can be used to bypass suspect wires or electrical components. Before attempting to locate a problem with test instruments, use the wiring diagram to determine where to make the connections.

To find the source of an intermittent wiring fault (usually due to a poor or dirty connection, or damaged wiring insulation), a 'wiggle' test can be performed on the wiring. This involves wiggling the wiring by hand to see if the fault occurs as the wiring is moved. It should be possible to narrow down the source of the fault to a particular section of wiring. This method of testing can be used in conjunction with any of the tests described in the following sub-Sections.

Apart from problems due to poor connections, two basic types of fault can occur in an electrical circuit – open-circuit or short-circuit.

Open circuit faults are caused by a break somewhere in the circuit, which prevents current from flowing. An open circuit fault will prevent a component from working, but will not cause the relevant circuit fuse to blow.

Short circuit faults are caused by a 'short' somewhere in the circuit, which allows the current flowing in the circuit to 'escape' along an alternative route, usually to earth. Short circuit faults are normally caused by a breakdown in wiring insulation, which allows a feed wire to touch either another wire, or an earthed component such as the bodyshell. A short circuit fault will normally cause the relevant circuit fuse to blow.

Finding an open-circuit

To check for an open circuit, connect one lead of a circuit tester or the negative lead

Body electrical system 12•3

3.2a Fusebox located on the right-hand end of the facia . . .

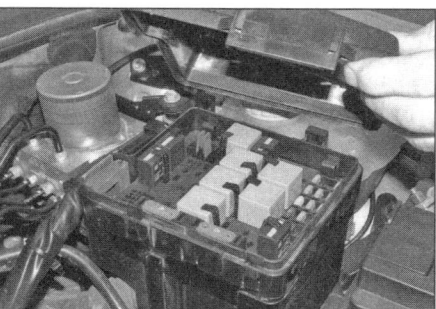

3.2b . . . and in the engine compartment

3.2c High amp fusible links on the side of the battery tray

of a voltmeter either to the battery negative terminal or to a known good earth.

Connect the other lead to a connector in the circuit being tested, preferably nearest to the battery or fuse.

Switch on the circuit, bearing in mind that some circuits are live only when the ignition switch is moved to a particular position.

If voltage is present (indicated either by the tester bulb lighting or a voltmeter reading, as applicable), this means that the section of the circuit between the relevant connector and the switch is problem-free.

Continue to check the remainder of the circuit in the same fashion.

When a point is reached at which no voltage is present, the problem must lie between that point and the previous test point with voltage. Most problems can be traced to a broken, corroded or loose connection.

Finding a short-circuit

To check for a short circuit, first disconnect the load(s) from the circuit (loads are the components which draw current from a circuit, such as bulbs, motors, heating elements, etc).

Remove the relevant fuse from the circuit, and connect a circuit tester or voltmeter to the fuse connections.

Switch on the circuit, bearing in mind that some circuits are live only when the ignition switch is moved to a particular position.

If voltage is present (indicated either by the tester bulb lighting or a voltmeter reading, as applicable), this means that there is a short circuit.

If no voltage is present during this test, but the fuse still blows with the load(s) reconnected, this indicates an internal fault in the load(s).

Finding an earth fault

The battery negative terminal is connected to 'earth' – the metal of the engine/transmission unit and the vehicle body – and many systems are wired so that they only receive a positive feed, the current returning via the metal of the car body. This means that the component mounting and the body form part of that circuit. Loose or corroded mountings can therefore cause a range of electrical faults, ranging from total failure of a circuit, to a puzzling partial failure. In particular, lights may shine dimly (especially when another circuit sharing the same earth point is in operation), motors (eg, wiper motors or the radiator cooling fan motor) may run slowly, and the operation of one circuit may have an apparently unrelated effect on another. Note that on many vehicles, earth straps are used between certain components, such as the engine/transmission and the body, usually where there is no metal-to-metal contact between components, due to flexible rubber mountings, etc.

To check whether a component is properly earthed, disconnect the battery and connect one lead of an ohmmeter to a known good earth point. Connect the other lead to the wire or earth connection being tested. The resistance reading should be zero; if not, check the connection as follows.

If an earth connection is thought to be faulty, dismantle the connection, and clean back to bare metal both the bodyshell and the wire terminal or the component earth connection mating surface. Be careful to remove all traces of dirt and corrosion, and then use a knife to trim away any paint, so that a clean metal-to-metal joint is made. On reassembly, tighten the joint fasteners securely; if a wire terminal is being refitted, use serrated washers between the terminal and the bodyshell, to ensure a clean and secure connection. When the connection is remade, prevent the onset of corrosion in the future by applying a coat of petroleum jelly or silicone-based grease, or by spraying on (at regular intervals) a proprietary ignition sealer or a water dispersant lubricant.

3.4a Use the plastic tool provided . . .

3 Fuses and relays – general information

Fuses

1 Fuses are designed to break an electrical circuit when a predetermined current limit is reached, in order to protect the components and wiring which could be damaged by excessive current flow. Any excessive current flow will be due to a fault in the circuit, usually a short-circuit (see Section 2).

2 The fuses are located either in the fusebox located on the right-hand end of the facia, or in the fusebox located in the left-hand rear of the engine compartment (see illustrations). High amp fusible links are also located next to the battery on the left-hand front corner of the engine compartment.

3 Access to the facia fusebox is gained by opening the driver's door and releasing the plastic cover. The engine compartment fusebox is opened by opening the bonnet and lifting the plastic cover.

4 To remove a fuse, use the plastic tool provided in the fusebox to pull the fuse from its socket (see illustration).

5 Inspect the fuse from the side, through the transparent plastic body – a blown fuse can be recognised by its melted or broken wire.

6 Spare fuses are provided in the blank terminal positions in the fusebox.

7 Before renewing a blown fuse, trace and rectify the cause, and always use a fuse of the

3.4b . . . to remove a fuse from the fusebox

12•4 Body electrical system

3.8a Undo the screw . . .

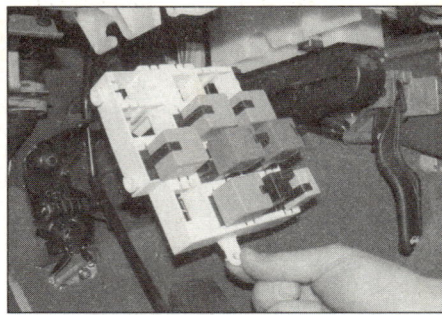

3.8b . . . and lower the relay holder from its housing

correct rating (refer to the wiring diagrams at the end of this Chapter).
Caution: Never substitute a fuse of a higher rating, or make temporary repairs using wire or metal foil; more serious damage, or even a fire, could result.

Relays

8 Relays are remote electrically-operated switches used in certain circuits. The relays are located under the right-hand side of the facia, or on the left-hand side of the engine compartment. Access to the facia-mounted relays is gained by undoing the screw and lowering the relay holder (**see illustrations**).
9 If a component controlled by a relay becomes inoperative and the relay is suspect, listen to the relay as the circuit is operated. If the relay is functioning, it should be possible to hear it click as it is energised. If the relay proves satisfactory, the fault lies with the components or wiring of the system. If the relay is not being energised, then either the relay is not receiving a switching voltage, or the relay itself is faulty. Do not overlook the relay socket terminals when tracing faults. Testing is by the substitution of a known good unit, but be careful; some relays are identical in appearance and in operation, but perform different functions.
10 To renew a relay first ensure that the ignition switch is off. The relay can then simply be pulled out from the socket and the new relay pressed in.

4 Switches and controls – removal and refitting

Ignition switch cylinder

Removal

1 Remove the ignition key antenna unit from around the switch cylinder by turning it slightly clockwise and lifting it up.
2 Turn the ignition key to the OFF position, but leave it inserted.
3 Bend a length of welding rod at right angles and insert it through the rear hole in the switch housing so that the locking catch is released. The lock cylinder can now be withdrawn directly from the housing. Refer to the cylinder removal included in *Ignition switch and lock* removal below for the location to insert the rod.

Refitting

4 Refitting is a reversal of removal.

Ignition switch and lock

Removal

5 The ignition switch and lock is incorporated in the gearchange assembly between the front seats. Remove the centre console as described in Chapter 11; the ignition switch is incorporated in the gearchange housing.
6 To remove the manual transmission gearchange housing, select 4th gear then loosen the clamp at the universal joint. Unscrew the bolts securing the housing to the floor, then lift the housing and disconnect the wiring. Also remove the heater air duct.
7 To remove the automatic transmission selector housing, remove the air duct, disconnect the upper wiring, then extract the circlip and drive out the cable ball-pin while disconnecting the cable end fitting. Unscrew the bolts securing the housing to the floor, then lift the housing and disconnect the wiring and release the cable-ties. Pull out the clip

4.7a Remove the air duct . . .

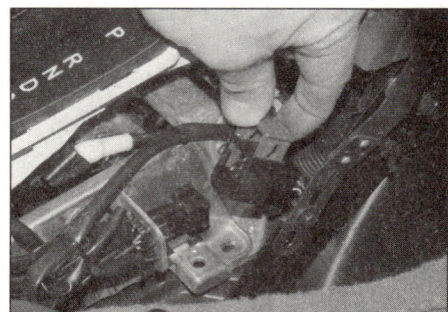

4.7b . . . disconnect the wiring connector . . .

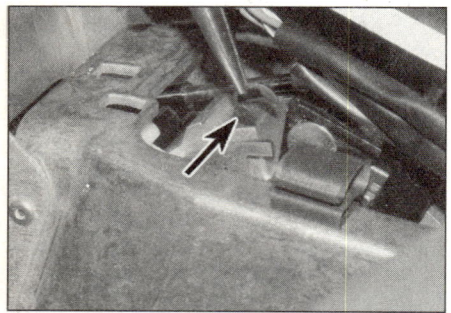

4.7c . . . then extract the circlip . . .

4.7d . . . and remove the cable ball-pin . . .

4.7e . . . ball-pin shown removed . . .

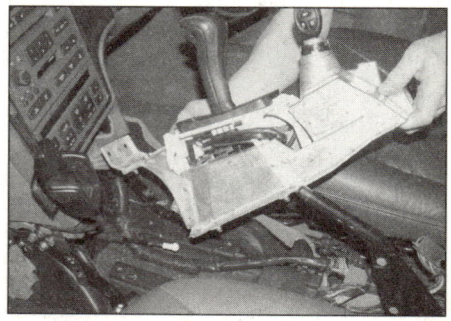

4.7f . . . lift the housing . . .

Body electrical system 12•5

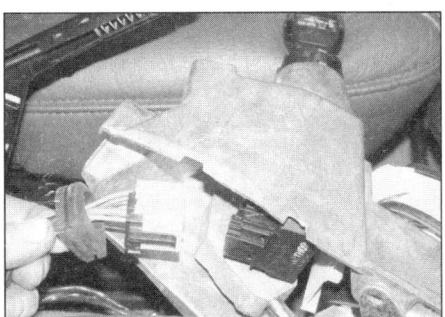

4.7g ... disconnect the lower wiring ...

4.7h ... and detach the selector cable from the housing

4.8a Depress the catch ...

and lift the selector cable from the housing **(see illustrations)**.

8 Remove the ignition switch cylinder as described earlier in this Section, then undo the screws and remove the switch from the housing. Note the location of the spacer **(see illustrations)**.

Refitting

9 Refitting is a reversal of removal.

Steering column switch

Removal

10 Adjust the steering wheel to its lowest and most rearward position, then lock it. To make access easier, remove the steering wheel as described in Chapter 10.

11 Remove the steering column upper and lower shrouds. There are two screws facing upwards in the upper shroud, and one screw located beneath the lower shroud.

4.8b ... remove the ignition switch cylinder ...

12 Release the retaining clips and slide out the combination switch, then disconnect the wiring **(see illustrations)**.

Refitting

13 Refitting is a reversal of removal.

4.8c ... undo the screws (arrowed) ...

Electric window control switch

Removal

14 Using a screwdriver, carefully prise up the front of the switch from the centre console.

4.8d ... and remove the ignition switch ...

4.8e ... and then the spacer

4.12a Remove the indicator/lighting combination switch ...

4.12b ... and disconnect the wiring

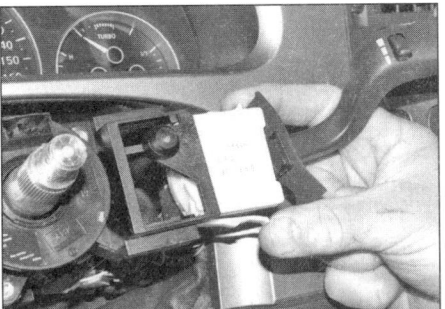

4.12c Remove the wiper/washer combination switch ...

4.12d ... and disconnect the wiring

12•6 Body electrical system

4.15 Disconnecting the wiring from the electric window control switch

15 Disconnect the wiring **(see illustration)**.

Refitting

16 Refitting is a reversal of removal.

Headlight height switch

Removal

17 Using a screwdriver, carefully prise the switch from the facia panel. If it is tight, remove the lighting switch (see paragraph 23) and press the switch out from behind.
18 Disconnect the wiring.

Refitting

19 Refitting is a reversal of removal.

Interior lighting control switch

Removal

20 Using a screwdriver, carefully prise the switch from the centre console rear section. Access to the lighting switches on the

4.24 ... and disconnect the wiring

4.36 Courtesy light switch retaining screw

4.20 Removing the map reading light switch

headlining console is gained after removing the lens and cover **(see illustration)**.
21 Disconnect the wiring.

Refitting

22 Refitting is a reversal of removal.

Lighting and rear foglight switch/instrument illumination rheostat

Removal

23 Remove the lid from the main fusebox on the end of the facia. Insert a finger through the fusebox opening and press out the lighting switch from behind **(see illustration)**.
24 Disconnect the wiring **(see illustration)**.

Refitting

25 Refitting is a reversal of removal.

Stop-light switch

Removal

26 To remove the switch, first remove the

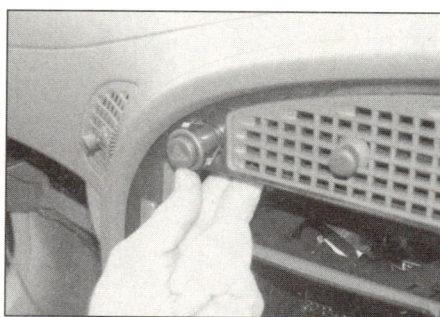

4.30 Removing the hazard warning light switch

4.39 Removing the TCS switch (early models)

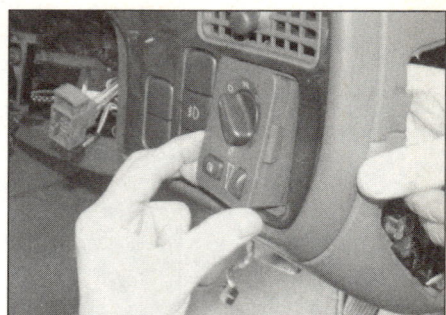

4.23 Press out the lighting switch from behind . . .

lower trim panel from the facia with reference to Chapter 11.
27 Twist the switch anti-clockwise 90° and withdraw it from the mounting bracket.
28 Disconnect the wiring from the switch.

Refitting

29 Refitting is a reversal of removal.

Hazard warning light switch

Removal

30 The switch is held in position by two tensioned plastic tabs which have both fitting and removal ramps. Carefully prise the switch from the facia using a screwdriver, or alternatively press out the switch from behind after removing the SID module or radio/CD player, depending on model **(see illustration)**.
31 Disconnect the wiring.

Refitting

32 Refitting is a reversal of removal.

Electric door mirror switch

Removal

33 Carefully prise the switch from the triangular cover on the front door.
34 Disconnect the wiring.

Refitting

35 Refitting is a reversal of removal.

Courtesy light switch

Removal

36 Open the door then undo the screw securing the courtesy light switch to the B- or C-pillar **(see illustration)**.
37 Remove the switch and disconnect the wiring. Tape the wire to the pillar to prevent it dropping inside.

Refitting

38 Refitting is a reversal of removal.

TCS switch

Removal

39 Using a screwdriver, carefully prise out the switch from the facia. On earlier models, remove the radio/CD player unit and press out the switch from behind **(see illustration)**. On later models, remove the lighting switch (see paragraph 23) and press the switch out from behind.

Body electrical system 12•7

4.42 Removing the front foglight switch

5.2 Undo the screws . . .

40 Disconnect the wiring.

Refitting

41 Refitting is a reversal of removal.

Front foglight switch

Removal

42 Carefully prise out the switch from the facia, or alternatively remove the lighting switch and press out the switch from behind (see illustration).
43 Disconnect the wiring.

Refitting

44 Refitting is a reversal of removal.

5 Interior light bulbs – renewal

Instrument panel

1 Remove the instrument panel as described in Section 9.
2 Undo and remove the 8 screws securing the back panel to the module (see illustration). Note: *Four of the screws are short and four are long, so record their positions.*
3 Release the 2 side clips and withdraw the back panel (see illustration).

4 Disconnect the wiring plugs and remove the printed circuit boards (see illustrations).
5 Twist the relevant bulbholder and remove it from the instrument panel; the bulbholder positions are marked on the printed circuit board (see illustrations).
6 Fit the new bulb using a reversal of the removal procedure.

Rear interior lights

Passenger compartment

7 Using a screwdriver, carefully prise down the interior light lens (see illustration). Note that the glass breakage sensor is located in the light cover.

5.3 . . . release the clips, and withdraw the back panel

5.4a Disconnect the wiring plugs . . .

5.4b . . . and remove the printed circuit boards

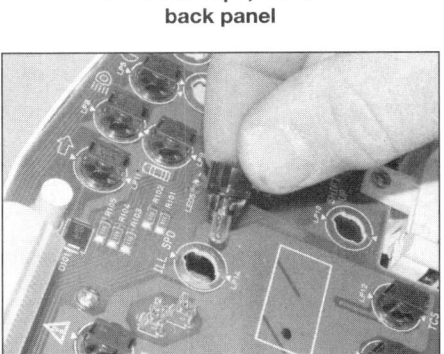

5.5a Removing a bulb/bulbholder from the printed circuit board

5.5b The bulb positions are marked on the printed circuit

5.7 Prise down the interior light lens . . .

12•8 Body electrical system

5.8 ... then depress and twist the side bulbs, or release the central festoon-type bulb from its terminals

5.10 Removing the luggage compartment interior light lens ...

5.11 ... and bulb

5.16 Prise out the interior light lens ...

5.17 ... and remove the festoon-type bulb from the terminals

8 To remove the side bulbs, depress and twist them; to remove the centre festoon-type bulb, release it from the terminals **(see illustration)**.
9 Fit the new bulb using a reversal of the removal procedure.

Estate luggage compartment

10 Using a screwdriver, carefully prise out the interior light lens **(see illustration)**.
11 Remove the festoon-type bulb from the terminals **(see illustration)**.

12 Fit the new bulb using a reversal of the removal procedure.

Saloon luggage compartment

13 Using a screwdriver carefully prise the interior light lens from the trim panel.
14 Remove the festoon-type bulb from the terminals.
15 Fit the new bulb using a reversal of the removal procedure.

Tailgate loading light

16 Using a screwdriver, carefully prise the interior light/lens from the trim panel **(see illustration)**.
17 Remove the festoon-type bulb from the terminals **(see illustration)**.
18 Fit the new bulb using a reversal of the removal procedure.

Glovebox illumination

19 With the glovebox open, use a screwdriver to prise out the lens/light unit.
20 Remove the festoon-type bulb from the terminals.
21 Fit the new bulb using a reversal of the removal procedure.

Front interior/map reading lights

22 Prise off the lens using a small screwdriver, and remove the festoon-type bulb from the terminals **(see illustrations)**.
23 Undo the cover retaining screw. Where applicable, remove the microphone and temperature sensor from the cover **(see illustrations)**.
24 To remove the spotlight bulb, turn the

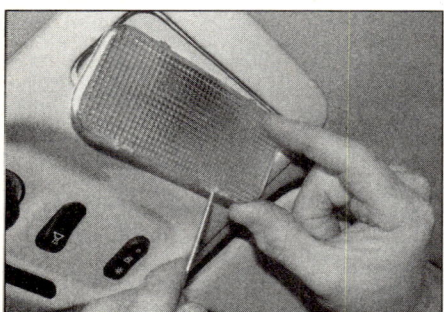

5.22a Prise off the lens ...

5.22b ... and remove the festoon-type bulb

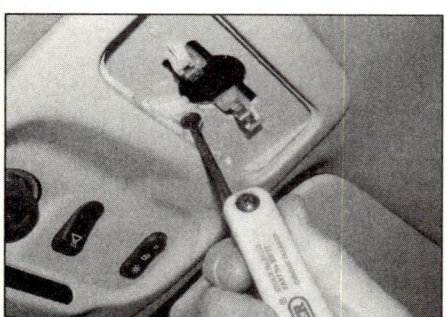

5.23a Undo the retaining screw ...

5.23b ... lower the cover ...

5.23c ... and remove the microphone (1) and temperature sensor (2)

Body electrical system 12•9

5.24a Turn the spotlight reflector anti-clockwise from the housing . . .

5.24b . . . and pull out the wedge-type bulb

5.24c Use washer tubing to remove. . .

5.24d . . . the wedge-type illumination bulbs

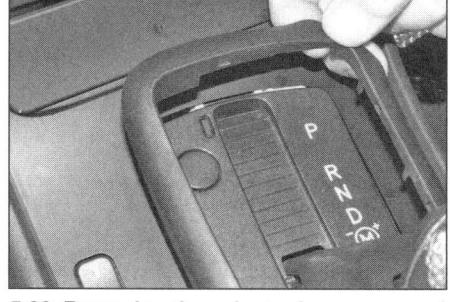

5.26 Removing the selector lever surround (automatic transmission models)

5.27 Removing the outer trim panel from the ashtray

spotlight reflector anti-clockwise and pull out the wedge-type bulb. To remove the illumination bulbs, use a length of washer tubing to grip the wedge-type bulbs **(see illustrations)**.

25 Fit the new bulb using a reversal of the removal procedure.

Cigarette lighter

26 On manual transmission models, prise the gear lever gaiter from the centre console. On automatic transmission models, use a screwdriver to prise up the selector lever surround **(see illustration)**.

27 Open the ashtray and remove the outer trim panel together with the ashtray **(see illustration)**.

28 Using a screwdriver, prise back the retaining tabs and prise the ashtray/oddments box from the centre console **(see illustrations)**. Use tape to protect the walnut veneer.

29 Undo the screws and remove the gear lever/selector cover. Identify the wiring locations then disconnect the plugs – there are plugs for the seat heating, seat ventilation and cigarette lighter. Also disconnect the wiring from the central locking switch **(see illustrations)**.

30 With the cover removed, disconnect the bulb wiring from the rear of the cigarette lighter, then remove the bulbholder and extract the bulb.

31 Fit the new bulb using a reversal of the removal procedure.

Window switch illumination

32 Remove the electric window control switch as described in Section 4.

33 Using a screwdriver, twist the bulbholder anti-clockwise to remove it.

34 Fit the new bulb using a reversal of the removal procedure.

5.28a Prise back the retaining tabs . . .

5.28b . . . and remove the ashtray box from the centre console

Automatic transmission selector illumination

35 Remove the position indicator panel,

5.29a Undo the retaining screws . . .

5.29b . . . and remove the gear lever/selector cover

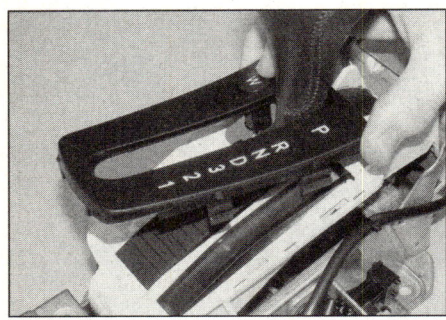
5.35a Remove the position indicator panel . . .

5.35b . . . followed by the green strip . . .

5.35c . . . and slider . . .

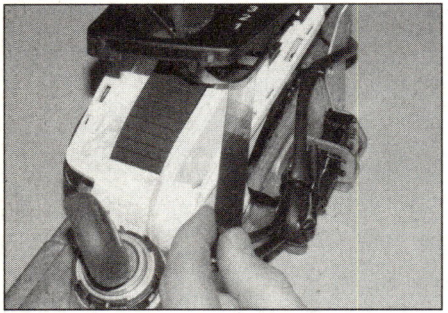
5.36a . . . remove the graded strip . . .

5.36b . . . and use a suitable rubber tube to extract the bulb

5.39 Removing the bulbholder from the Saab Information Display (SID) module

followed by the green strip and slider **(see illustrations)**.
36 Remove the graded strip, then use a suitable rubber tube to extract the illumination bulb **(see illustrations)**.
37 Fit the new bulb using a reversal of the removal procedure.

Saab Information Display module illumination

38 Remove the SID module (see Section 10).
39 Using a screwdriver, twist the bulbholder anti-clockwise and remove it from the module **(see illustration)**. There are 6 bulbholders in all, and Saab recommend that all are renewed at the same time as they all have an identical life expectancy.
40 Fit the new bulb using a reversal of the removal procedure.

Lighting switch illumination

41 Remove the lighting switch (see Section 4).

42 Twist the bulbholder from the rear of the switch **(see illustration)**.
43 Fit the new bulb using a reversal of the removal procedure.

Hazard switch illumination

44 Remove the hazard switch as described in Section 4.
45 Twist the bulbholder from the side of the switch **(see illustration)**.
46 Fit the new bulb using a reversal of the removal procedure.

Climate control module illumination

47 Remove the climate control module as described in Chapter 3, Section 9.
48 Using a screwdriver, twist the bulbholder from the rear of the module **(see illustration)**.
49 Fit the new bulb using a reversal of the removal procedure.

6 Exterior light bulbs – renewal

1 Whenever a bulb is renewed, note the following points:
a) Switch off all exterior lights and the ignition.
b) Remember that if the light has just been in use, the bulb may be extremely hot.
c) Always check the bulb contacts and holder, ensuring that there is clean metal-to-metal contact.
d) Always ensure that the new bulb is of the correct rating and that it is completely clean before fitting it.
e) Do not touch the glass of halogen-type bulbs (headlights, front foglights) with the fingers, as this may lead to premature failure of the new bulb; if the glass

5.42 Removing the bulbholder from the rear of the lighting switch

5.45 Removing the bulbholder from the side of the hazard switch

5.48 Removing the bulbholder from the rear of the climate control module

Body electrical system 12•11

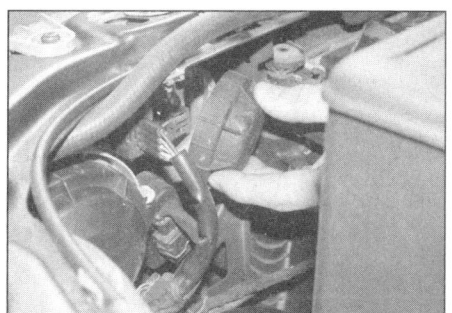
6.2 Unscrew the plastic cover...

6.3 ...disconnect the wiring...

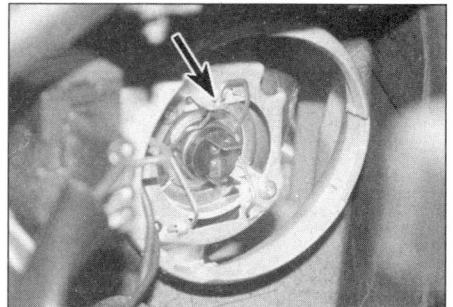
6.4a ...release the spring clip...

is accidentally touched, clean it with methylated spirit.

Halogen headlight

2 With the bonnet open, remove the cover from the rear of the headlight **(see illustration)**. Access to the left-hand headlight can be improved by unclipping the cover from the battery. Depending on model, access to the right-hand headlight can be improved by moving the air intake hose to one side.

3 Disconnect the wiring from the main beam bulb **(see illustration)**.

4 Release the spring clip and remove the bulb **(see illustrations)**.

5 Fit the new bulb using a reversal of the removal procedure, but make sure that the bulb location lugs engage correctly in the rear of the headlight. On later models, the plastic cover must be refitted with the tab facing upwards.

Xenon headlight

⚠ *Warning: It is recommended that protective gloves and safety glasses be worn when renewing xenon headlamp bulbs. The bulbs contain mercury and are highly pressurised. Do not switch on the headlamps with the bulb removed – high voltages (23 000 volts minimum) are present which could cause personal injury.*

Dipped beam

6 Remove the headlight as described in Section 7.

7 Remove the cover from the rear of the headlight **(see illustration)**.

8 Release the securing clips and withdraw the xenon light bulb unit slightly, then disconnect the wiring connector **(see illustrations)**.

9 Withdraw the bulb and xenon light bulb unit from the headlamp **(see illustration)**.

10 Fit the new bulb unit using a reversal of the removal procedure.

Main beam

11 With the bonnet open, unclip the round rubber cover from the rear of the headlight **(see illustration)**. Access to the left-hand headlight can be improved by unclipping the cover from the battery. Depending on model, access to the right-hand headlight can be

6.4b ...and remove the bulb

improved by moving the air intake hose to one side.

12 Disconnect the wiring from the bulb **(see illustration)**.

13 Release the spring clips and pull the bulb

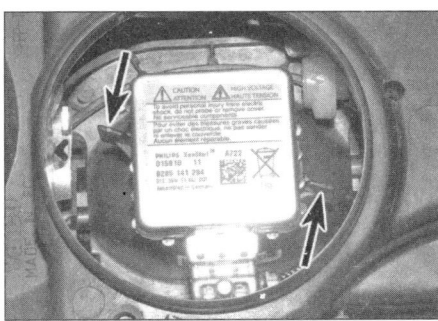
6.8a ...release the clips in the direction of the arrows...

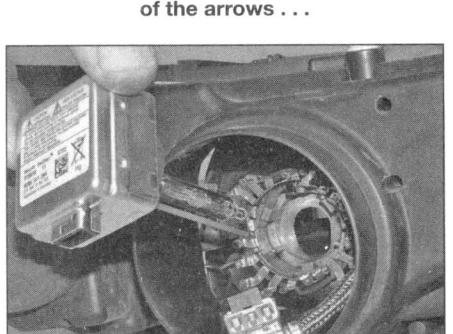
6.9 ...and withdraw the xenon light bulb unit

6.7 Remove the rubber cover...

from the bulbholder **(see illustrations)**. Use a tissue or clean cloth to prevent touching the bulb.

14 Fit the new bulb using a reversal of the removal procedure, but make sure that the

6.8b ...then disconnect the wiring...

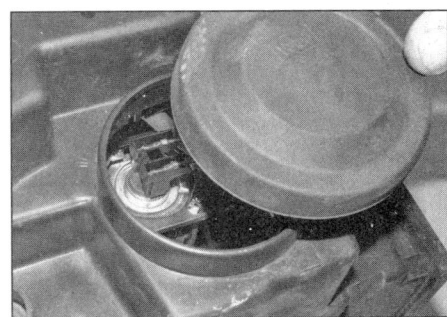
6.11 Unclip the rubber cover...

12•12 Body electrical system

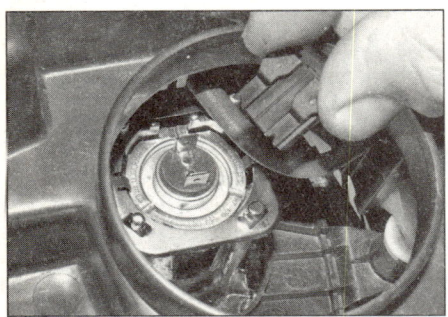
6.12 ... disconnect the wiring ...

6.13a ... release the spring clips (arrowed) ...

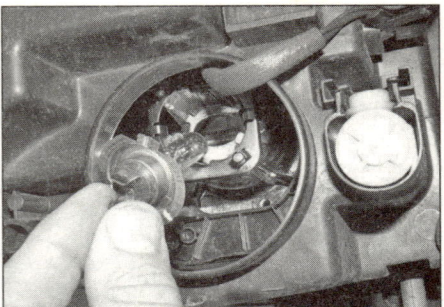
6.13b ... and remove the bulb

6.16a Pull the front sidelight bulbholder from the headlight ...

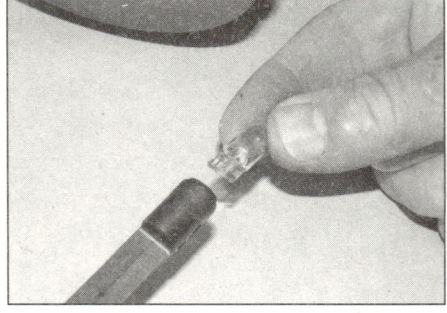
6.16b ... and pull out the wedge-type bulb

6.19 Unclip the rubber cover ...

bulb location lugs engage correctly in the rear of the headlight. The plastic cover must be refitted with the UP arrow facing upwards.

Sidelight

15 With the bonnet open, locate the plastic peg at the lower rear of the headlight unit. Access to the left-hand headlight can be improved by unclipping the cover from the battery. Depending on model, access to the right-hand headlight can be improved by moving the air intake hose to one side.

16 Pull the bulbholder from the headlight unit, and then pull the wedge-type bulb from the bulbholder (see illustrations).

17 Fit the new bulb using a reversal of the removal procedure.

Direction indicator

18 Remove the front headlight unit as described in Section 7 of this Chapter.
19 Remove the cover from the rear of the headlight (see illustration).
20 Release the retaining clips and pull the bulbholder from the light unit (see illustrations).
21 Fit the new bulb using a reversal of the removal procedure.

Side repeater lights

22 Carefully press the light forwards against the tension of the plastic clip, and then release the rear of the light from the front wing (see illustration).

6.20a ... release the retaining clips (arrowed) ...

6.20b ... and remove the bulb and holder

6.22 Press the side repeater light forwards ...

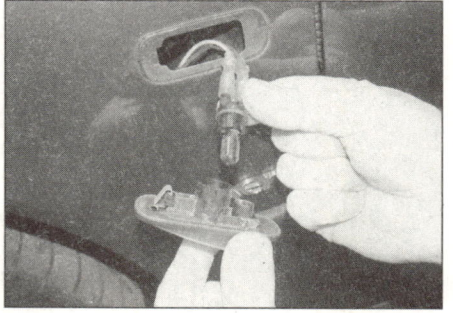
6.23a ... remove the bulbholder ...

6.23b ... then pull out the wedge-type bulb

Body electrical system 12•13

6.26 Unclip the trim panel

6.27a Squeeze together the locking tabs and remove the bulbholder ...

6.27b ... or on the boot lid twist the bulbholder to remove

23 Twist the bulbholder and remove the lens unit, then pull out the wedge-type bulb **(see illustrations)**. Do not allow the wiring to drop into the space behind the wing.

24 Fit the new bulb using a reversal of the removal procedure.

Rear light light unit

Saloon models

25 The rear light assembly consists of light units in the rear body and also in the boot lid.

26 To access the body light unit, open the boot lid and unclip the plastic trim from the rear of the light unit **(see illustration)**. To access the boot lid light unit, release the trim by removing the grab handle and relevant fasteners (depress the fastener centres).

27 Squeeze together the locking tabs and remove the bulbholder from the light unit **(see illustrations)**. In the boot lid, twist the bulbholder from the rear of the light unit.

28 Depress and twist the relevant bulb and remove it from the bulbholder **(see illustration)**.

29 Fit the new bulb using a reversal of the removal procedure. Before refitting the fasteners, pull out their centres.

Estate models

30 The rear light assembly consists of light units in the rear body and also in the tailgate.

31 To access the body light unit bulb, remove the rear light unit as described in Section 7. To access the tailgate light unit bulb, open the tailgate then turn the fastener a quarter turn anti-clockwise and remove the cover **(see illustration)**.

32 Release the retaining clips, and remove the bulbholder from the light unit.

33 Depress and twist the bulb and remove it from the bulbholder **(see illustrations)**.

34 Fit the new bulb using a reversal of the removal procedure.

Front foglight

35 Apply the handbrake, then jack up the front of the vehicle and support it on axle stands (see *Jacking and vehicle support*).

36 Reach up behind the foglight and disconnect the wiring connector, twist the bulbholder anti-clockwise to remove it **(see illustrations)**.

6.28 Depress and twist the bulb to remove

37 Pull the bulb from the bulbholder. **Note:** *The bulb may be part of the bulbholder, check with your local Saab dealer.*

38 Fit the new bulb using a reversal of the removal procedure.

6.33a Remove the bulbholder, then depress and twist the bulb to remove it

6.36a Disconnect the wiring connector ...

6.31 To access the tailgate light unit bulb, open the access flap

Number plate light

39 Using a small screwdriver carefully unclip the lens from the number plate light **(see illustrations)**. Recover the seal, and check it for damage.

6.33b Removing a body rear light unit bulb

6.36b ... then twist and remove the bulbholder

12•14 Body electrical system

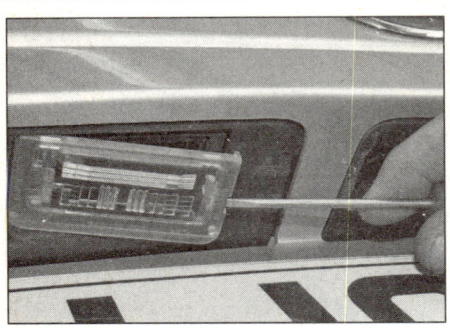
6.39a Using a small screwdriver . . .

6.39b . . . unclip the light unit lens

6.40 Pull out the festoon-type bulb

6.42a Release the securing clips . . .

6.42b . . . and remove the plastic trim cover

6.43 Pull out the wedge-type bulb

40 Pull out the festoon-type bulb from the bulbholder **(see illustration)**.
41 Fit the new bulb using a reversal of the removal procedure.

High-level stop-light
Saloon models
42 Remove the cover panel from the rear of the headlining by carefully pressing in the two clips on each side **(see illustrations)**.
43 Pull out the relevant wedge-type bulb from the bulbholder **(see illustration)**.
44 Fit the new bulb using a reversal of the removal procedure. Make sure the cover panel is fully entered in the clips.

Estate models
45 With the tailgate open, prise off the covers, then undo the screws and remove the rear window side and upper trim covers **(see illustrations)**.
46 Disconnect the wiring from the high-level stop-light, then unscrew the nuts and withdraw the light unit from the tailgate **(see illustrations)**.
47 Undo the screws and separate the printed

6.45a Remove the rear window side trim covers . . .

6.45b . . . and upper trim cover

6.46a Disconnect the wiring . . .

6.46b . . . then unscrew the nuts . . .

6.46c . . . and withdraw the light unit from the tailgate

Body electrical system 12•15

circuit board together with the LEDs **(see illustrations)**. Take care not to damage the guide pins.

48 Fit the new printed circuit board using a reversal of the removal procedure.

7 Exterior light units – removal and refitting

Headlight

 Warning: On models with xenon headlights, the ignition switch must be off and in its LOCK position.

1 Remove the front bumper as described in Chapter 11.
2 Undo the upper and lower headlight mounting bolts **(see illustrations)**.
3 Withdraw the headlight unit forwards, releasing it from the mounting brackets **(see illustration)**.
4 Disconnect the wiring plug as the headlight unit is withdrawn from the vehicle **(see illustration)**.
5 Refitting is a reversal of removal, but have the headlight beam alignment checked and adjusted as soon as possible.

Direction indicator light

6 The front indicator unit is part of the headlight unit, remove the headlight unit as described in paragraphs 1 to

6.47a Undo the screws . . .

6.47b . . . and separate the printed circuit board and LEDs

Side repeater light

7 See procedure for side repeater lights in Section 6 (exterior light bulbs) of this Chapter.

Rear light units

Saloon models

8 The rear light units consist of lights in the rear body and also in the boot lid.
9 To remove the body light unit, open the boot lid and pull back the carpet flap in the luggage compartment.
10 To remove the boot lid light unit, release the trim by removing the grab handle and relevant fasteners (depress the fastener centres).
11 Remove the bulbholders from the rear light units as described in Section 6 (exterior light bulbs) of this Chapter.

12 Unscrew the nuts and withdraw the rear light unit from the vehicle **(see illustrations)**.
13 On the boot lid light unit, remove the rubber grommet from the edge of the boot lid to access the outer retaining nut **(see illustrations)**.
14 Refitting is a reversal of removal, but firmly tighten the nuts.

Estate models

15 The rear light units consist of light units in the rear body and also in the tailgate.
16 To remove the body light unit open the tailgate and then undo the retaining screws on the inside edge of the rear light unit. Pull the light unit out to the rear of the car, to release it from the inner retaining clip at its front edge. Disconnect the wiring connector as the light is withdrawn **(see illustrations)**.

7.2a Unscrew the headlight upper . . .

7.2b . . . and lower mounting bolts

7.3 Withdraw the headlight . . .

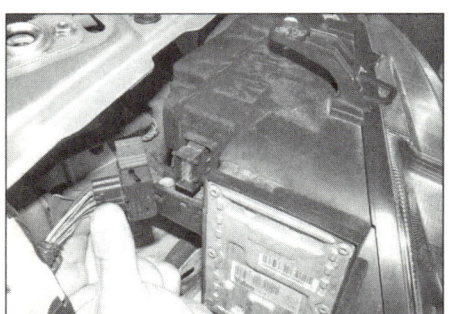

7.4 . . . and disconnect the wiring connector

7.12a Undo the rear light unit mounting nuts (arrowed) . . .

7.12b . . . and withdraw the light unit

12•16 Body electrical system

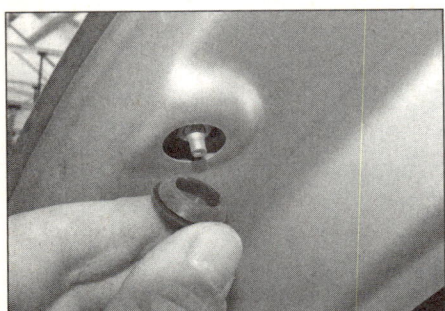

7.13a Remove the rubber grommet . . .

7.13b . . . and undo the light unit mounting nuts (arrowed) . . .

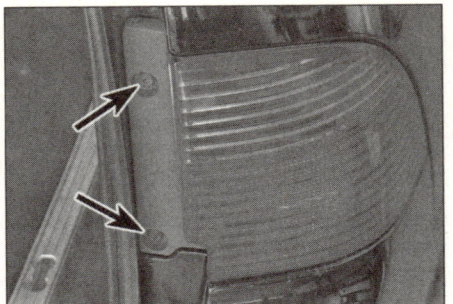

7.16a Undo the retaining screws . . .

7.16b . . . and withdraw the light unit to the rear to release it from the retaining clip (arrowed)

7.16c Disconnect the wiring connector

17 To remove the tailgate light unit, remove the rear cover panel and unclip the bulbholder from the rear of the light unit. Then remove the rubber grommet from the edge of the tailgate to access the outer securing nut, undo the retaining nuts and withdraw the light unit from the tailgate (see illustrations).

18 Refitting is a reversal of removal. Before refitting the body light unit, remove the fastener from the body and refit it to the light unit. Check the tailgate light unit seal before refitting it.

Front foglight

19 Apply the handbrake, then jack up the front of the vehicle and support it on axle stands (see *Jacking and vehicle support*).

20 Reach up behind the foglight and twist the bulbholder anti-clockwise to remove it. If necessary, the bulbholder can be disconnected from the wiring.

21 Undo the retaining screws, and then withdraw the foglight from the rear of the bumper (see illustrations).

22 Refitting is a reversal of removal. To adjust the foglight, park the vehicle 10 metres from a wall and mark the wall with a cross at the same height as the centre of the lens. Make a further mark 10 to 20 cm below the cross, then adjust the foglight beam onto this mark by turning the adjuster knob at the inside of the light unit (see illustration).

Number plate light

23 To remove the light unit, release the trim by removing the grab handle and relevant fasteners from the boot lid/tailgate.

24 Undo the retaining nuts from the inside of the boot lid/tailgate and remove the number plate light.

25 Disconnect the wiring as the light unit is removed.

26 Refitting is a reversal of removal.

High-level stop-light

Saloon models

27 Remove the cover panel from the rear of

7.17a Unclip the bulbholder . . .

7.17b . . . and undo the light retaining nuts (arrowed)

7.21a Undo the retaining screws (arrowed) . . .

7.21b . . . and remove the foglight from the bumper cover

7.22 Foglight adjusting screw (arrowed)

Body electrical system 12•17

7.28a Undo the two retaining screws ...

7.28b ... and remove the light unit from the roof panel

7.35 Undo the screws (arrowed) to remove the xenon headlight control module

the headlining by carefully pressing in the two clips on each side (see illustrations 6.42a and 6.42b).

28 Undo the bulbholder retaining screws then unplug the wiring and withdraw the light unit from the roof panel (see illustrations).

29 Refitting is a reversal of removal.

Estate models

30 With the tailgate open, prise off the covers, then undo the screws and remove the rear window trim covers.

31 Unscrew the nuts, withdraw the high-level stop-light and disconnect the wiring as described in Section 6, paragraph 46.

32 Undo the screws and separate the printed circuit board together with the LEDs. Take care not to damage the guide pins (see illustrations 6.47a and 6.47b).

33 Refitting is a reversal of removal.

Xenon headlight control module

Warning: Observe the safety precautions for models with xenon headlights, given earlier in this Chapter. Also, note that the module is sensitive to static electricity; earth yourself regularly during the module removal and refitting procedure.

Note: *If the module is renewed, it must be programmed by a dealer using specialist equipment.*

34 Remove the headlight as described earlier in this Section.

35 Undo the six screws and withdraw the module from the headlight (see illustration).

36 Disconnect the wiring and remove the module.

37 Check the condition of the module seal and renew it if necessary.

38 Refitting is a reversal of removal.

8 Headlight beam adjustment – general information

1 Accurate adjustment of the headlight beam is only possible using optical beam-setting equipment, and this work should therefore be carried out by a Saab dealer or suitably-equipped workshop. In an emergency, it is possible to adjust the headlights by turning the knobs located on the rear of the headlight.

2 Some models have a headlight beam adjustment control, which allows the aim of the headlights to be adjusted to compensate for variation in the vehicle's payload. The aim is altered by means of facia-mounted switch, which controls electric adjuster motors located in the rear of the headlight assemblies. The switch should be positioned as follows, according to the load being carried in the vehicle:

Vehicle load	Switch position
Up to 3 occupants (no more than one in the rear seat), no luggage	0
Up to 3 occupants in rear seats, up to 30 kg in luggage	1
Up to 3 occupants in rear seats, up to 80 kg in luggage	2
Up to 5 occupants, luggage area full	3
Up to 5 occupants, luggage area full, towing caravan/trailer	3

3 Models with xenon headlights have an automatic levelling system. If a fault occurs in this system, a warning light will show up on the instrument panel, and the headlights will be angled down to avoid dazzling oncoming traffic. If this happens, the driving speed must be adjusted accordingly to allow for decreased visibility.

4 To make a temporary adjustment of the headlights, position the vehicle on a level surface 10 metres from a wall. The tyres must all be at the correct pressure, the fuel tank half full, and a person must be sitting in the driver's seat. Turn on the ignition, and where applicable check that the manual headlight setting is at 0. Measure the distance from the ground to the cross in the centre of the headlight, then deduct 5.0 cm for models with halogen lights and 7.5 cm for models with xenon lights. Draw a mark on the wall at this height, and then adjust the headlight beam centre point onto this mark by turning the adjustment knobs on the rear of the headlight unit (see illustrations).

9 Instrument panel and electronic unit – removal and refitting

Instrument panel

Removal

1 Adjust the steering wheel to its lowest and most rearward position, then lock it.

2 Remove the steering column upper and

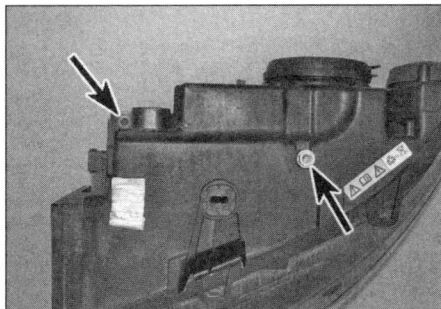

8.4a Manual headlight adjustment screws

8.4b Altering the vertical adjustment screw ...

8.4c ... and the horizontal adjustment screw

12•18 Body electrical system

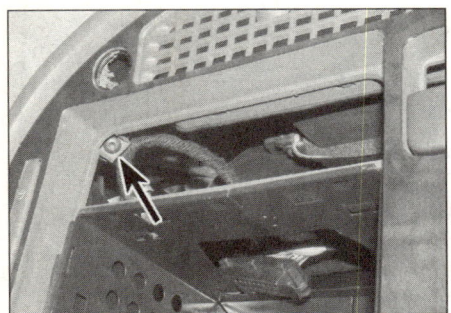

9.10a The retaining screws are located inside the apertures

9.10b Removing the instrument surround panel

9.10c Screws retaining the cup holder to the instrument surround panel

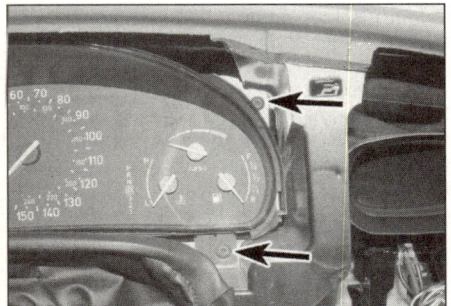

9.11a Undo the mounting screws on each side . . .

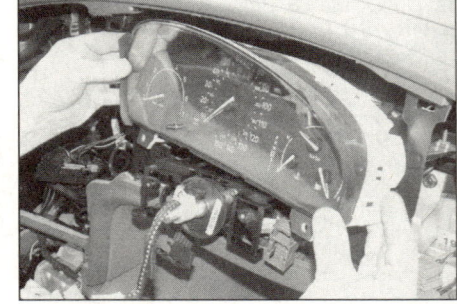

9.11b . . . withdraw the instrument panel from the facia . . .

9.11c . . . and disconnect the wiring

lower shrouds. There are two screws facing upwards in the upper shroud, and one screw located beneath the lower shroud.

3 Depress the retaining clips and withdraw the direction indicator and windscreen wiper combination switches, then disconnect the wiring.

4 Remove the radio/CD player and mounting box as described in Section 17.

5 Where applicable, remove the Saab Information Display (SID) unit (depending on models), as described in Section 10.

6 Remove the air conditioning/heating ventilation unit as described in Chapter 3. Do not remove the seat heating unit.

7 Remove the facia switches located on the inner side of the steering column.

8 Remove the lid from the main fusebox on the end of the facia. Insert a finger through the fusebox opening and press out the lighting switches from behind. Disconnect the black, green and orange wiring connectors, noting their location.

9 Carefully prise out the button blanks from the facia.

10 Undo the screws and remove the instrument surround panel – there are 6 screws and 4 clips located inside the various apertures. With the surround removed, if necessary the cup holder may be removed after undoing the retaining screws **(see illustrations)**.

11 Undo the instrument panel mounting screws, then withdraw the unit and unplug the wiring connectors. Withdraw the unit from the bulkhead **(see illustrations)**.

Refitting

12 Refitting is a reversal of removal.

Electronic unit

Removal

13 Remove the instrument panel as described.

14 Undo and remove the 8 screws securing the back panel to the module. Note that there are four screws, which are short, and four that are long, so record their positions.

15 Release the 2 side clips and withdraw the back panel.

16 Disconnect the wiring plugs and remove the printed circuit boards, then undo the screws and withdraw the electronic unit **(see illustrations)**.

Refitting

17 Refitting is a reversal of removal.

10 Saab Information Display (SID) module – general information, removal and refitting

Note: *If a new SID module is fitted, it must be programmed by a Saab dealer using the special Saab Tech2 diagnostic tool.*

General information

1 The Saab Information Display (SID) module provides the driver with information, and also controls the display lighting and trip computer. The module also displays service reminders. It uses the following components:
 a) Outside temperature sensor.
 b) Steering wheel horn and audio controls.
 c) Coolant level sensor.
 d) Washer fluid level sensor.
 e) Headlight filament sensor.
 f) Display lighting rheostat.
 g) Interior light sensor for automatic control of the display illumination.

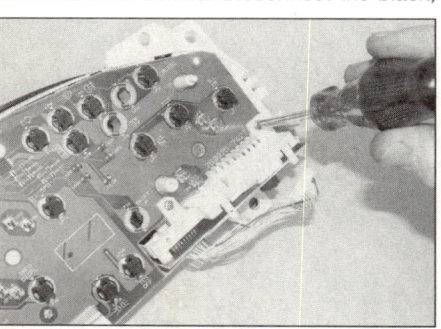

9.16a Undo the screws . . .

9.16b . . . and remove the electronic unit

Body electrical system 12•19

10.3a Reach through the radio/CD player aperture and push out the SID unit

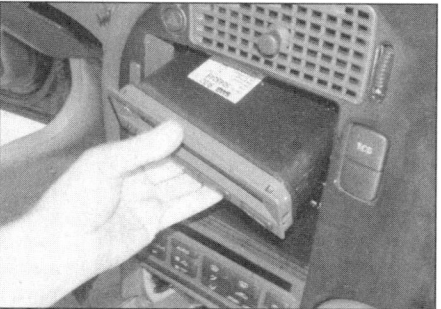

10.3b Remove the SID unit . . .

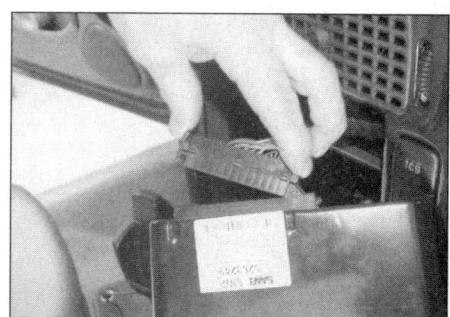

10.4 . . . and disconnect the wiring

Removal

Note: *This procedure is for models with the SID module fitted above the radio/CD player.*

2 First remove the radio/CD player as described in Section 17.
3 Reach in behind the SID module and push it out of the facia panel **(see illustrations)**.
4 Disconnect the wiring and remove the module **(see illustration)**.

Refitting

5 Refitting is a reversal of removal.

11 Cigarette lighter – removal and refitting

Removal

1 There are two cigarette lighters, one above the ashtray and the other on the rear of the centre console.

Front cigarette lighter

2 To remove the front cigarette lighter on manual transmission models, prise the gear lever gaiter from the centre console. On automatic transmission models, use a screwdriver to prise up the selector lever surround.
3 Using a screwdriver, release the retaining clips and remove the ashtray and holder, or oddments tray (as applicable), with reference to Chapter 11, Section 28.
4 Undo the screws and remove the gear lever cover. Identify the wiring locations then disconnect the plugs from the switches and cigarette lighter **(see illustration)**.
5 Remove the lighter element, then release the cigarette lighter socket and illumination ring from the cover.

Rear cigarette lighter

6 Remove the rear end part of the centre console, with reference to Chapter 11, Section 28.
7 Remove the lighter element, then release the cigarette lighter socket and illumination ring **(see illustration)**.

Refitting

8 Refitting is a reversal of removal.

12 Horn – removal and refitting

Removal

1 Remove the front bumper cover as described in Chapter 11.
2 Disconnect the wiring from the horn **(see illustration)**.
3 Note that the horns are each marked to indicate their tone – the high tone horn is marked with an H, and the low tone horn with an L.
4 Unscrew the bracket mounting nut and withdraw the horn assembly **(see illustration)**.

Refitting

5 Refitting is a reversal of removal. When

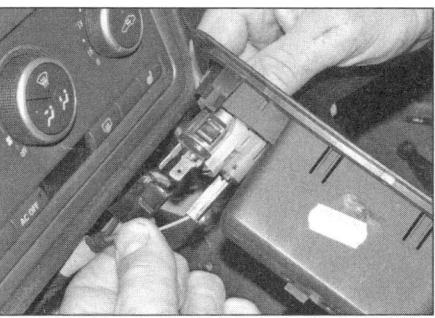

11.4 Disconnect the front cigarette lighter wiring connectors

12.2 Horn wiring plug

fitted, the horn must be angled downwards and outwards by 15° to 20°.

13 Windscreen and tailgate wiper arms – removal and refitting

Windscreen wiper arm

1 Make sure that the windscreen wipers are at their rest positions. Use a piece of tape to mark the position on the windscreen.
2 Where fitted, prise up the cover from the windscreen wiper arm securing nut.
3 Unscrew the nut securing the wiper arm to the spindle **(see illustration)**.
4 Ease the arm from the spindle by carefully rocking it side-to-side. If it is tight, use a small puller to remove it **(see illustration)**.
5 Refitting is a reversal of removal.

11.7 Disconnect the rear cigarette lighter wiring connectors

12.4 Two horns positioned behind the front grille

12•20 Body electrical system

13.3 Unscrew the nut . . .

13.4 . . . then use a small puller to remove the wiper arm from the spindle

13.8 Unscrew the nut . . .

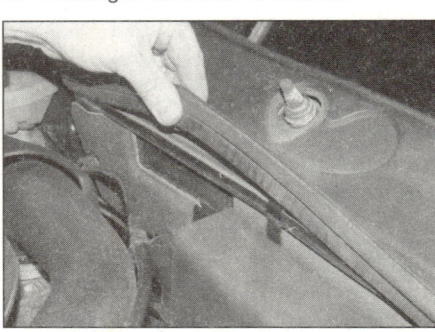

13.9 . . . and ease the arm from the shaft

Tailgate wiper arm

6 Make sure that the tailgate wiper is at its rest position. Use a piece of tape to mark the position on the windscreen.
7 Lift up the cover at the base of the tailgate wiper arm.
8 Unscrew the nut securing the wiper arm to the shaft (see illustration).
9 Ease the arm from the shaft by carefully rocking it side-to-side (see illustration). If it is tight, use a small puller to remove it.
10 Refitting is a reversal of removal.

14 Rain sensor – removal and refitting

Removal

1 The rain sensor is located centrally, at the top of the windscreen, just in front of the rear view mirror.
2 Saab technicians use a special removal tool to remove the cover from the rain sensor; however, a suitable plastic or wooden lever may be used. To spread the force and prevent the windscreen from cracking, place a thin piece of wood on the windscreen to lever against. Carefully lever off the cover by pressing the sides individually towards the headlining.
3 Carefully press the sensor towards the windscreen, then bend out the retaining clamps and withdraw the sensor from the bracket. Take care not to scratch or damage the windscreen.
4 Disconnect the wiring and withdraw the sensor.

Refitting

5 Thoroughly clean the windscreen surface before refitting the sensor. Check that the sensor retaining clamps are in good condition; if not, renew them.
6 Refitting is a reversal of removal.

15 Windscreen and tailgate wiper motor and linkage – removal and refitting

Windscreen wiper motor

Removal

1 Remove the wiper arms as described in Section 13.
2 Remove the rubber seals from the spindles (see illustration).
3 Pull off the rubber weatherstrip from the front of the scuttle area (see illustration).
4 Remove the fasteners, and then withdraw the windscreen scuttle cover from the spindles, noting the location of the catches beneath the windscreen (see illustrations).

15.2 Removing the rubber seals from the spindles

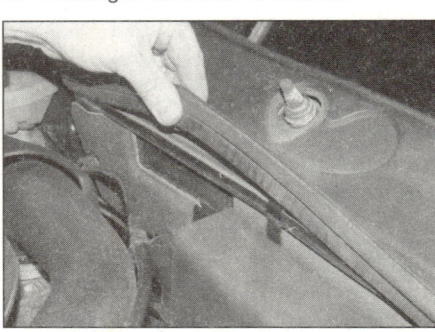

15.3 Pulling off the rubber weatherstrip

15.4a Unscrew the centre pins . . .

15.4b . . . remove the fasteners . . .

15.4c . . . and withdraw the scuttle cover

Body electrical system 12•21

15.5a Remove the plastic cover . . .

15.5b . . . and disconnect the wiring from the wiper motor

15.6 Removing the wiper motor and linkage

15.7 Wiper motor-to-frame mounting bolts

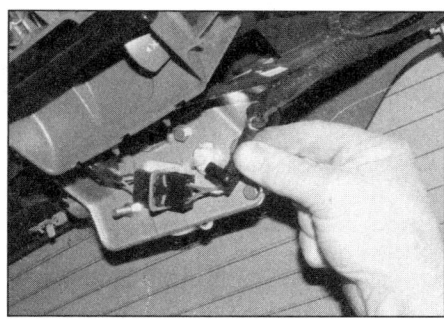
15.13a Disconnect the washer hose . . .

15.13b . . . and wiring from the tailgate wiper motor

5 Remove the plastic cover, and then disconnect the wiring from the wiper motor **(see illustrations)**.
6 Unscrew the mounting bolts and lift the wiper motor and linkage from the bulkhead **(see illustration)**.
7 If necessary, the wiper motor may be unbolted from the frame after disconnecting the link arm and removing it from the driveshaft **(see illustration)**. Note that it may be necessary to turn the crank arm slightly in order to access one of the mounting bolts.

Refitting

8 Refitting is a reversal of removal, but tighten the mounting bolts to the specified torque.

Tailgate wiper motor

Removal

9 Remove the wiper arm as described in Section 13.

10 With the tailgate open, prise off the covers, then undo the screws and remove the rear window trim covers.
11 Undo the screws and remove the inner handgrip from the tailgate trim panel.
12 Undo the screws from the lower edge of the trim panel, then pull down the top of the panel to release it from the upper clips, and pull it to the rear to release the guide pin at the handgrip.
13 Disconnect the washer hose and wiring from the tailgate wiper motor **(see illustrations)**.
14 Undo the mounting bracket screws, and withdraw the wiper motor assembly from the tailgate, while guiding the spindle housing through the rubber grommet **(see illustrations)**.
15 Unbolt the mounting bracket from the wiper motor.

Refitting

16 Refitting is a reversal of removal.

16 Windscreen, tailgate and headlight washer system – removal and refitting

Removal

1 The washer fluid reservoir and pump are located beneath the front left-hand wing **(see illustration)**. For access to them, remove the wheel arch liner. For additional working room, remove the front bumper.
2 To remove the pump, position a container beneath the reservoir, then disconnect the pump wiring and washer tubes and allow the fluid to drain **(see illustration)**. Pull the pump out of the reservoir then remove the rubber bush.

15.14a Undo the mounting bracket bolts (Saloon model) . . .

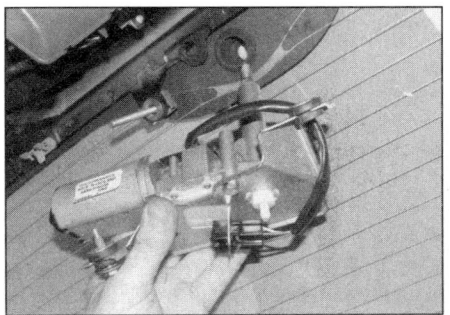
15.14b . . . and withdraw the wiper motor assembly from the tailgate

15.14c Mounting bracket retaining nuts (Estate model)

12•22 Body electrical system

16.1 Washer fluid reservoir and pump (front bumper removed)

16.2 Washer pump wiring connector

16.3 Washer fluid reservoir rear mounting bolt

16.5a Carefully unclip the washer jet trim cover . . .

16.5b . . . disconnect the washer pipe . . .

tabs and withdraw the jets from the bonnet.

5 To remove the headlight washer jets, first remove the front bumper cover as described in Chapter 11. Pull out the washer jet and unclip the cover from the jet. Then, working on the inside of the bumper, disconnect the washer fluid pipe, remove the securing clip and remove the washer jet assembly from the bumper cover **(see illustration)**.

Refitting

6 Refitting is a reversal of removal.

17 Radio/CD player – removal and refitting

16.5c . . . release the securing clip . . .

3 To remove the reservoir, disconnect the wiring connectors and washer fluid pipe from the washer pump. Remove the filler cap from the top of the filler neck, then unscrew the mounting bolts and remove the reservoir down and out from the front wing

17.1a Using strong sticky tape to remove plastic caps

16.5d . . . and unclip the washer jet assembly from the bumper cover

panel **(see illustration)**. If necessary (where fitted), remove the fluid level sensor from the reservoir.
4 To remove the windscreen washer jets, release the insulation from the bonnet, disconnect the tubes then depress the locking

17.1b Undo the four radio/CD player retaining screws

Caution: All models are fitted with a radio/CD player programmed for the specific vehicle it is fitted to, and no radio code is supplied or required. If a unit is removed from one vehicle and fitted to another vehicle, it must be reprogrammed by a Saab dealer using the special Tech2 equipment. Note also that the equipment must be used to 'divorce' the unit from the original vehicle before it is removed.

Removal

1 For models with radio/CD players retained by screws, first carefully remove the blanking caps (new blanking caps may be required for refitting). Undo the four retaining screws, two at each side **(see illustrations)**.
2 For models with radio/CD players retained by DIN fixings, two DIN removal tools will be required to release the retaining clips. The tools are available from car accessory shops, and are inserted into the holes on each side of the unit until they are felt to engage with the retaining strips **(see illustration)**.
3 With the clips/screws released, carefully withdraw the unit from the facia. Note the wiring and aerial sockets, which engage with the plugs, attached to the mounting box **(see illustrations)**.
4 Where applicable (depending on model), the radio mounting box can be removed from the facia by bending up the retaining tabs, withdrawing it, then disconnecting the wiring and aerial plugs.

Body electrical system 12•23

17.2 Using two DIN removal tools to release the radio/CD player retaining clips

17.3a Withdraw the audio unit from the facia panel ...

17.3b ... and disconnect the wiring connectors and the aerial cable socket

Refitting

5 Refitting is a reversal of removal. Press the radio/CD unit firmly into the mounting box until the retaining strips engage.

18 Loudspeakers – removal and refitting

Facia-mounted speakers

Removal

1 Using a screwdriver carefully prise out the grille from the relevant speaker (see illustration).
2 Using a Torx key, undo the screws securing the speaker in the facia, and carefully lift it out.
3 Disconnect the wiring and tape it to the facia to prevent it dropping down inside (see illustration).

Refitting

4 Refitting is a reversal of removal.

Door-mounted speaker

Removal

5 Remove the door inner trim panel as described in Chapter 11.
6 Undo the mounting screws, then withdraw the speaker and disconnect the wiring (see illustrations).

Refitting

7 Refitting is a reversal of removal.

Parcel shelf speaker

Removal

8 Lower the rear seat backrest then unclip the speaker grille.
9 Undo the screws and lift out the speaker, then disconnect the wiring.

Refitting

10 Refitting is a reversal of removal.

Luggage compartment speaker

Removal

11 Lower the rear seat backrest, then remove the right-hand side bolster from between the right-hand door and backrest by pulling out the top and lifting it from the lower mounting. Also remove the trim panel.
12 Remove the right-hand storage compartment from the floor.
13 Remove the tailgate opening scuff plate by prising out the covers and undoing the screws. The plate is retained with clips as well.
14 Remove the headlining rear trim panel and disconnect the lighting wiring.
15 Remove the trim from the right-hand D-pillar, then undo the screws and remove the right-hand shelf support.
16 Undo the screws and remove the luggage compartment right-hand trim panel.
17 Unscrew the mounting bolts and withdraw the bass speaker, then disconnect the wiring.

Refitting

18 Refitting is a reversal of removal.

18.1 Prise out the grille ...

18.6a Undo the mounting screws ...

19 Audio amplifier – removal and refitting

Note: Although similar in appearance, the amplifiers for Saloon and Estate models are different due to the different cabin areas inside each vehicle.

Removal

1 With the passenger's door open, remove the inner sill trim panel.
2 Remove the facia lower trim panel from under the glovebox.
3 Fold back the carpet and unscrew the audio amplifier lower mounting nuts. Loosen only the upper mounting nut.
4 Lift out the amplifier and disconnect the wiring plug.

18.3 ... remove the speaker, and disconnect the wiring

18.6b ... remove the speaker, and disconnect the wiring

12•24 Body electrical system

Refitting

5 Refitting is a reversal of removal.

20 CD changer – removal and refitting

Caution: As with the radio/CD player, the CD changer is programmed for the specific vehicle it is fitted to, and no radio code is supplied or required. If a unit is removed from one vehicle and fitted to another vehicle, it must be reprogrammed by a Saab dealer using the special Tech2 equipment. Note also that the equipment must be used to 'divorce' the unit from the original vehicle before it is removed.

Removal

1 Where fitted, the CD changer is located in the luggage compartment. Undo the mounting screws – there are two at the front and two at the rear.
2 Move the CD changer to one side and disconnect the wiring. Withdraw the unit from the luggage compartment.
3 If the CD changer is to be stored in a horizontal position, change the end setting so that the pointer points to the H mark. Note that four red transport screws are fitted to new units.

Refitting

4 Refitting is a reversal of removal.

21 Aerial amplifier and filter – removal and refitting

1 On Saloon models, the separate AM aerial loop is integrated into the top of the rear window, and the FM aerial is integral with the rear or side window heater element. The aerial signal is amplified by an amplifier located on the right-hand C-pillar, and an aerial filter located on the left-hand C-pillar.
2 One of two systems is fitted to Estate models. The first system uses an AM/FM aerial integrated into the rear right-hand side window and an adjacent amplifier and filter located on the D-pillar. In addition, the second system uses an FM aerial integrated into the rear left-hand side window and an adjacent amplifier and filter located on the D-pillar. The second system has a diversity function whereby the aerial with the best signal reception is used by the radio receiver.

Aerial amplifier (Saloon models)

Removal

3 Remove the trim panel from the right-hand C-pillar as described in Chapter 11.
4 Note the location of the wiring to the amplifier, and then disconnect it.
5 Disconnect the aerial from the amplifier; however, take care not to damage the internal contacts.
6 Unscrew the retaining nuts and withdraw the amplifier from inside the car.

Refitting

7 Refitting is a reversal of removal.

Aerial filter (Saloon models)

Removal

8 Remove the trim panel from the left-hand C-pillar as described in Chapter 11.
9 Disconnect the single wire leading to the filter at the connector.
10 Undo the nut securing the filter lead to the body, and withdraw the filter from inside the car.

Refitting

11 Refitting is a reversal of removal.

Aerial amplifier and filter (Estate models)

Removal

12 Refer to Chapter 11 and remove the D-pillar trim, the rear headlining trim, and the two mouldings between the C- and D-pillars. Extract the clips from the headlining, and also remove the cargo safety net holders. Carefully bend down the rear of the headlining for access to the amplifier.
13 Note the location of the wiring to the amplifier and filter, and then disconnect it.
14 Disconnect the aerial from the amplifier; however, take care not to damage the internal contacts.
15 Unscrew the retaining nuts and withdraw the amplifier and filter from inside the car.

Refitting

16 Refitting is a reversal of removal.

22 Heated and ventilated seat components – general information, removal and refitting

General information

1 Certain models are fitted with thermostatically-regulated heated front and rear seats. Individual control switches are provided for each seat, which allow the heating

23.6a Undo the screws . . .

element temperature to be set to one of three levels, or switched off completely. Two heating element pads are fitted to each seat – one in the backrest, and one in the seat cushion.
2 Seat cooling is also available for the front seats on certain models, with individual control switches for each seat providing three fan speeds together with an off position. The fans extract the warm air from the seat fabric in contact with the body.

Removal and refitting

3 Access to the heating elements can only be gained by removing the upholstery from the seat – this is an operation which should be entrusted to a Saab dealer.
4 To remove the cooling fan, first remove the front seat as described in Chapter 11. Where a programmable control module is fitted to the driver's seat, remove this as described in Chapter 11 for access to the cooling fan. Unscrew the fan motor retaining nuts, disconnect the wiring and release the wiring from the cable-ties. Refitting is a reversal of removal.

23 DICE control module – general information, removal and refitting

General information

1 The Dash Integrated Central Electronics (DICE) system is a central control system for the vehicle main electrical circuits. The control module communicates with the various systems via the vehicle wiring harness and the instrument bus (I-bus). DICE is able to diagnose faults within the circuits and generate trouble codes, which can then be read to determine the faulty component or circuit. The main functions controlled by DICE is as follows:
a) Exterior lighting.
b) Interior lighting.
c) Rheostat control.
d) Acoustic warning for ignition and parking lights.
e) Intermittent wiper operation between 2 and 15 seconds.
f) Headlight washer system operation.
g) Electrically-heated rear window and door mirrors.
h) Radiator cooling fan.
i) Air conditioning.

2 The DICE control module is programmable according to the country of origin. With the lighting system, this affects how main and dipped beam lighting functions, and whether daylight driving lights are necessary. The module is located next to the fusebox on the driver's side of the facia.

Removal

3 Disconnect the battery negative lead.
4 Remove the lower facia panel from the driver's side.
5 Undo the screw and lower the relay holder

Body electrical system 12•25

from the housing for improved access to the DICE control module.
6 Undo the screws and withdraw the module from the housing **(see illustrations)**.
7 Disconnect the wiring from the control module.

Refitting
8 Refitting is a reversal of removal. If a new module is being fitted, it must be programmed specifically for the car by a Saab dealer.

24 Parking aid components – general information, removal and refitting

General information
1 The Saab Parking Assistance (SPA) system is available as an option for all models. Four ultrasound sensors located in the rear bumper measure the distance to the closest object behind the car, and inform the driver using acoustic signals on the facia SID display unit. The nearer the object, the more frequent the acoustic signals. The text PARK ASSIST appears on the display unit when reverse gear is selected, and the signal tone changes to continuous when an object is closer than 12 inches (30 cm).
2 On Saloon models, the SPA control module is located behind the rear backrest, beneath the side trim on the left-hand side. On Estate models, it is located beneath the floor in the luggage compartment.

Control module
Saloon models
3 With the left-hand rear door open, fold the 60% rear seat cushion and backrest forwards.
4 Pull back the door weatherseal for access to the rear side trim. Release the upper clip and carefully bend out the side trim.
5 Remove the sound insulation cushion.
6 Loosen the control module retaining screws, then lift the module and withdraw the screws through the slotted holes.
7 Disconnect the wiring and remove the module from inside the vehicle.
8 Refitting is a reversal of removal. Make sure that the grey plug is fitted to the grey socket, and the black plug to the black socket. Where fitted, the washers must be located in front of the mounting plate.

Estate models
9 Lift the rear seat cushions and fold the backrest forwards.
10 Unclip the front floor of the luggage compartment for access to the front of the lower trim. Remove the lower trim from the clips and lift it up.
11 Disconnect the wiring.
12 Unscrew the mounting nuts and withdraw the module from inside the vehicle.
13 Refitting is a reversal of removal. Make sure that the grey plug is fitted to the grey socket, and the black plug to the black socket.

23.6b . . . and withdraw the module from the housing

Where fitted, the washers must be located in front of the mounting plate.

Range/distance sensor
Saloon models
14 Working on each side, carefully prise out the rear bumper corner protection strips where they abut the centre strip. Saab technicians use a special tool to do this, however, careful use of a screwdriver is possible.
15 Prise out the centre strip from the bumper for access to the four distance sensors.
16 Release the plastic clips and remove the sensors from the retainers, then disconnect the wiring.
17 Depress the large and small fasteners and remove the retainers from the centre strip.
18 Refitting is a reversal of removal. Press the retainers firmly into the centre strip so that the fasteners engage.

Estate models
19 The distance sensors are fitted to the rear bumper upper centre panel, which can be removed separately to the main part of the rear bumper.
20 Working on each side, carefully prise off the rear bumper corner protection strips.
21 With the tailgate open, undo the rear bumper upper centre panel mounting screws.
22 Release the bottom of the centre panel from the retaining clips, then lift the panel to free the tabs from the screws. Press in the corners of the panel and withdraw it directly rearwards.
23 Release the plastic clips and remove the sensors from the retainers, then disconnect the wiring.

25.8 Glass breakage sensor located in the rear passenger interior light

24 Depress the large and small fasteners and remove the retainers from the centre strip.
25 Refitting is a reversal of removal. Press the retainers firmly into the centre strip so that the fasteners engage.

25 Anti-theft alarm system components – general information, removal and refitting

General information
1 The Saab anti-theft alarm system is referred to as TWICE (Theft Warning Integrated Central Electronics). The TWICE electronic control module operates the following systems:
 a) Lamp check including parking and brake lights.
 b) Seat belt warning including passenger seat occupation sensor.
 c) Electrically-heated rear seat.
 d) Electrically-powered passenger seat.
 e) Central locking.
 f) Electric opening of the boot lid.
 g) Theft protection immobilisation.
 h) Anti-theft alarm including glass breakage and angle sensors.

Electronic control module
Caution: If a new electronic control module is to be fitted, it must be reprogrammed by a Saab dealer using the special Tech2 equipment. All transponders and remote controls must be renewed, and all new ignition keys must be programmed at the same time.

Removal
2 Remove the left-hand front seat as described in Chapter 11.
3 Fold back the carpet and if necessary remove the moulding for access to the control module on the floor panel.
4 Disconnect the wiring multiplug from the control module.
5 Unscrew the plastic nuts and remove the module from inside the car.

Refitting
6 Refitting is a reversal of removal. If a new module is being fitted, it must be programmed specifically for the car by a Saab dealer.

Glass breakage sensor
Note: *On Estate models there are two glass breakage sensors, a central one over the rear passenger area, and a rear one in the luggage compartment interior light. The rear sensor is integral with the light unit and cannot be renewed separately.*

Removal
7 Carefully prise off the lens from the rear interior light, then use a screwdriver to release the light retainers and withdraw the unit from the headlining.
8 Disconnect the wiring and remove the glass breakage sensor from the lens cover **(see illustration)**.

25.29 Remote control receiver location

Refitting

9 Refitting is a reversal of removal, however, note that there are two types of sensor, one for models with fabric seat covers and the other for models with leather seats.

Warning LED on top of facia

Removal

10 The LED is fitted to a plate; slide the plate forwards and remove it.
11 Press the LED from the plate, then disconnect the wiring and remove the diode. The LED terminal legs are fragile; so take care not to break them.

Refitting

12 Refitting is a reversal of removal.

Bonnet switch

Removal

13 With the bonnet open, slide the bonnet switch up from its location on the fusebox in the left-hand rear of the engine compartment.
14 Disconnect the wiring.

Refitting

15 Refitting is a reversal of removal.

Luggage compartment switch

Note: *On Estate models, the switch is integral with the tailgate lock and cannot be renewed separately.*

Removal

16 Remove the boot lid lock as described in Chapter 11.
17 With the lock on the bench, prise off the grip washers and remove the switch from the lock.

Refitting

18 Refitting is a reversal of removal.

Alarm horn/siren

Removal

19 Apply the handbrake, then jack up the front of the vehicle and support it on axle stands (see *Jacking and vehicle support*). Remove the left-hand front roadwheel.
20 Working beneath the front left-hand wheel arch, remove the front section of the wheel arch liner for access to the alarm horn.
21 Disconnect the wiring from the horn.
22 Undo the retaining nut and bolt and withdraw the alarm horn from under the front wing.

Refitting

23 Refitting is a reversal of removal.

Tilt angle sensor

Removal

24 Refer to Chapter 11 and remove the inner sill trim from the front and rear of the B-pillar.
25 Remove the right-hand front seat (Chapter 11) then release the lower B-pillar clips and unclip the carpet. Fold the carpet to one side for access to the tilt sensor.
26 Disconnect the wiring then unscrew the retaining nuts and withdraw the tilt sensor from inside the car.

Refitting

27 Refitting is a reversal of removal. After fitting the tilt sensor, check the system by activating the alarm and checking that the diode glows for about 10 seconds, then flashes. Wait for 15 seconds then deactivate the alarm. Ideally, the system should be checked for trouble codes by a Saab dealer.

Remote control receiver

Removal

28 Raise the armrest on the centre console, then use a screwdriver to release the front edge of the console rear panel until the clip is released. Lift the rear panel up and tilt it outwards, then disconnect the switch wiring.
29 Where fitted, remove the clip from the console sidewall. Remove the control receiver and disconnect the wiring **(see illustration)**.

Refitting

30 Refitting is a reversal of removal. Where necessary, use additional tape to secure the wiring to the console, and also use an extra clip.

Saab 9-5 wiring diagrams

Diagram 1

Key to symbols

Bulb
Flashing bulb
Switch
Multiple contact switch (ganged)
Fuse/fusible link
Resistor
Variable resistor
Connecting wires
Wire colour (Black with brown tracer) — Bk/Bn

Item no.
Single speed pump/motor
Gauge/meter
Earth point & location
Diode
Light emitting diode (LED)
Solenoid actuator
Heating element
Wire splice or soldered joint

Dashed outline denotes part of a larger item, containing in this case an electronic or solid state device.
e.g. 30 - standard DIN terminal designation (battery positive), pin no. 2.

Key to circuits

Diagram 1	Information for wiring diagrams.
Diagram 2	Starting, charging, engine cooling fan & horn.
Diagram 3	Side, tail, number plate, stop & reversing lights.
Diagram 4	Halogen & xenon headlights.
Diagram 5	Foglights, direction indicators & hazard warning lights.
Diagram 6	Instrument cluster, cigarette lighter & electric sunroof.
Diagram 7	Heated seats, heated rear window, electric mirrors & compressor clutch.
Diagram 8	Central locking & electric windows.
Diagram 9	Interior lighting & audio system.
Diagram 10	Headlight levelling, front & rear wash/wipe, headlight washer.

Earth locations

E1	On slam panel behind LH headlight
E2	In luggage compartment under LH tail light
E3	On centre console between front seats
E4	On engine
E5	On cross member under LH front seat
E6	On cross member under RH front seat
E7	On gearbox
E8	LH inner wing behind battery
E9	On slam panel behind RH headlight
E10	Behind LH kick panel at bottom LH end of dashboard
E11	On LH 'A' pillar at LH end of dashboard
E12	Behind centre of dashboard
E13	Behind centre of dashboard
E14	On RH 'A' pillar at RH end of dashboard
E15	Behind centre of dashboard
E16	On parcel shelf by RH rear speaker
E17	In roof above LH 'D' pillar
E18	On RH inner wing by filler cap opening

Typical engine compartment fuses

Fuse	Rating	Circuit protected
F1	40A	LH & RH engine cooling fan
F2	40A	ESP
F3	30A	ESP
F4	7.5A	Load angle sensor
F5	15A	Auxiliary heater
F6	10A	Alarm, A/C compressor
F7	15A	Headlight flasher, main beam relay
F8	-	-
F9	20A	Headlight washer pump
F10	15A	LH main beam
F11	15A	LH dipped beam
F12	15A	RH main beam
F13	15A	RH dipped beam
F14	30A	RH radiator fan, high speed
F15	15A	Fog lights
F16	30A	Rear window wiper, headlight washer motor
F17	15A	Horn

Typical passenger compartment fuses

Fuse	Rating	Circuit protected
FA	30A	Trailer lighting
FB	10A	Traction control
FC	7.5A	Electric door mirrors, DICE, manual headlight adjustment
F1	15A	Stop light switch
F2	15A	Reversing lights
F3	10A	LH sidelight
F4	10A	RH sidelight
F5	7.5A	DICE/TWICE
F6	30A	Electric windows RH - pre-installed trailer wiring
F6B	10A	Stop lights - pre-installed trailer wiring
F7	10A	Fuel injection
F8	15A	Luggage compartment lighting, luggage compartment lock, door lighting, circulation pump, parking assistance, SID
F9	15A	Audio system, CD changer, diagnostic socket
F10	15A	Heated rear seat, sunroof, central locking
F11	30A	Electrically adjusted passenger's seat
F12	7.5A	Traction control
F13	20A	Amplifier
F14	30A	Engine management
F15	20A	Fuel pump, pre-heating oxygen sensor
F16	20A	DICE, direction indicators
F16B	7.5A	Road toll provision, OnStar
F17	20A	Engine management, instrument cluster, DICE/TWICE
F18	40A	Heated rear window and mirrors
F19	10A	Provision for mobile phone, OnStar
F20	15A	Automatic climate control, interior lighting, rear foglights
F21	10A	Radio, automatic dimming mirror, navigation, automatic headlight levelling, cruise control
F22	40A	Blower motor
F23	15A	Central locking, telephone, door mirrors with memory
F24	20A	Light switch
F25	30A	Electrically adjusted driver's seat
F26	7.5A	Parking assistance, memory seats, sunroof, door mirrors with memory, climate control
F27	10A	Engine management, instrument cluster, SID, DICE
F28	7.5A	Airbag
F29	10A	ESP
F30	7.5A	Starter motor
F31	7.5A	Cruise control, water valve, front fog lights, rain sensor, DICE
F32	-	Spare
F33	7.5A	Direction indicator switch
F34	30A	Cigarette lighter
F35	15A	Daytime driving lights
F36	30A	Electric window LH
F37	30A	Windscreen wipers
F38	30A	Heated seats
F39	20A	Petrol limp home solenoid (auto. trans.)
	30A	Diesel fuel filter heating element

H47127

12•28 Wiring diagrams

Diagram 2

Wire colours
- Bu Blue
- Vt Violet
- Og Orange
- Pk Pink
- Gy Grey
- Gn Green
- Rd Red
- Ye Yellow
- Bn Brown
- Wh White
- Bk Black

Key to items
1. Battery
2. Starter motor
3. Alternator
4. Ignition switch
5. Maxi-fusebox
6. Engine fusebox
7. Passenger fusebox
8. Transmission range switch
9. Starter relay
10. Low speed relay
11. LH fan high speed relay
12. DICE control unit
13. Air conditioning pressure sensor
14. LH engine cooling fan
15. RH engine cooling fan
16. RH fan high speed relay
17. SID control unit
18. Horn
19. Horn relay
20. Horn switch
21. Steering wheel clock spring
22. Remote audio controls
23. Engine management control unit
24. Coolant temperature sensor

H47128

Wiring diagrams 12•29

Diagram 3

Wire colours
- Bu Blue
- Vt Violet
- Og Orange
- Pk Pink
- Gy Grey
- Gn Green
- Rd Red
- Ye Yellow
- Bn Brown
- Wh White
- Bk Black

Key to items
1. Battery
4. Ignition switch
5. Maxi-fusebox
7. Passenger fusebox
8. Transmission range switch
12. DICE control unit
25. Stop light switch
26. TWICE control unit
27. LH rear light unit
   a = stop light
   b = tail light
28. RH rear light unit
   a = stop light
   b = tail light
29. High level brake light
30. Reversing light switch
31. LH Boot/tailgate lid light unit
   a = reversing light
32. RH Boot/tailgate lid light unit
   a = reversing light
33. Number plate light
34. LH headlight unit
   a = sidelight
35. RH headlight unit
   a = sidelight
36. Combined lighting switch
   a = light switch
   c = switch illumination

H47129

Typical stop lights

Typical reversing lights

Typical side, tail & number plate lights

* 4 door models
** 5 door models

12•32 Wiring diagrams

Diagram 6

Wire colours
- Bu Blue
- Vt Violet
- Og Orange
- Pk Pink
- Gy Grey
- Gn Green
- Rd Red
- Ye Yellow
- Bn Brown
- Wh White
- Bk Black

Key to items
1. Battery
4. Ignition switch
5. Maxi-fusebox
7. Passenger fusebox
36. Combined lighting switch
 a = light switch
50. Ignition relay
56. Low brake fluid switch
57. Handbrake switch
58. Fuel gauge sender unit
59. Oil pressure switch
60. Instrument cluster

H47132

Typical instrument cluster

Typical cigarette lighter

Typical electric sunroof

Wiring diagrams 12•33

Diagram 7

Wire colours
- Bu Blue
- Vt Violet
- Og Orange
- Pk Pink
- Gy Grey
- Gn Green
- Rd Red
- Ye Yellow
- Bn Brown
- Wh White
- Bk Black

Key to items
1. Battery
4. Ignition switch
5. Maxi-fusebox
7. Passenger fusebox
12. DICE control unit
38. Compressor clutch relay
50. Ignition relay
65. Engine management control unit
66. Engine management main relay
67. LH front heated seat cushion
68. RH front heated seat cushion
69. LH heated seat backrest
70. RH heated seat backrest
71. Heated rear window
72. Heated rear window relay
73. Antenna module
74. Noise suppressing filter
75. Fuel filler cap release switch
76. Fuel filler cap release solenoid
77. Fuel filler cap release relay
78. Electric mirror switch
79. Driver's door mirror assembly
80. Passenger's door mirror assembly
81. Air conditioning control panel
82. Compressor clutch

H47133

Typical heated seats

Typical heated rear window

Electric mirrors

Fuel compressor clutch

12•34 Wiring diagrams

Wire colours
- **Bu** Blue
- **Vt** Violet
- **Og** Orange
- **Pk** Pink
- **Gy** Grey
- **Gn** Green
- **Rd** Red
- **Ye** Yellow
- **Bn** Brown
- **Wh** White
- **Bk** Black

Key to items
1. Battery
4. Ignition switch
5. Maxi-fusebox
7. Passenger fusebox
26. TWICE control unit
50. Ignition relay
83. Electric window switch control unit
84. Driver's window motor
85. Passenger's window motor
86. LH rear window motor
87. RH rear window motor
88. LH rear window switch
89. RH rear window switch
90. Central locking remote control receiver
91. Boot lock motor (4 door)
92. Tailgate lock motor (5 door)
93. Luggage compartment light switch
94. Tailgate lock microswitch (5 door)
95. Fuel filler flap solenoid
96. Boot/tailgate release switch
97. Central locking master switch
98. Driver's lock assembly
99. Passenger's lock assembly
100. LH rear lock motor
101. RH rear lock motor

Diagram 8

H47134

Typical electric windows

Typical central locking

Wiring diagrams 12•35

Diagram 9

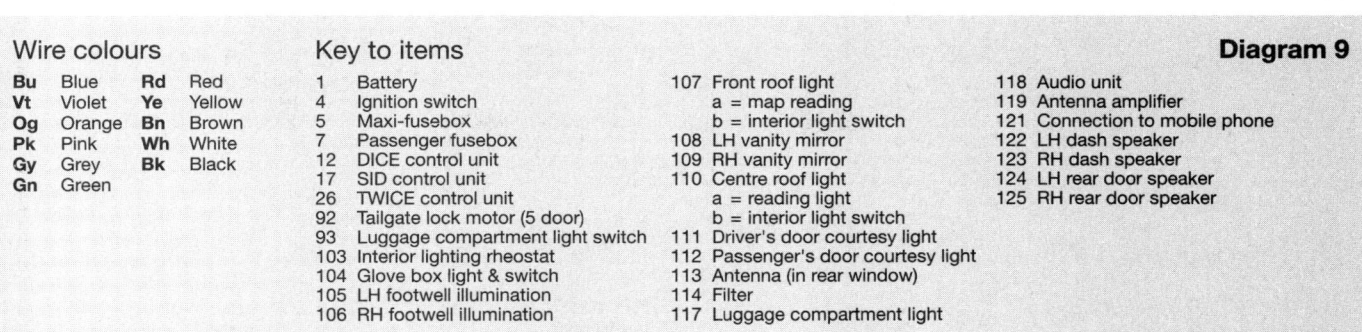

Wire colours
- Bu Blue
- Vt Violet
- Og Orange
- Pk Pink
- Gy Grey
- Gn Green
- Rd Red
- Ye Yellow
- Bn Brown
- Wh White
- Bk Black

Key to items
1. Battery
4. Ignition switch
5. Maxi-fusebox
7. Passenger fusebox
12. DICE control unit
17. SID control unit
26. TWICE control unit
92. Tailgate lock motor (5 door)
93. Luggage compartment light switch
103. Interior lighting rheostat
104. Glove box light & switch
105. LH footwell illumination
106. RH footwell illumination
107. Front roof light
   a = map reading
   b = interior light switch
108. LH vanity mirror
109. RH vanity mirror
110. Centre roof light
   a = reading light
   b = interior light switch
111. Driver's door courtesy light
112. Passenger's door courtesy light
113. Antenna (in rear window)
114. Filter
117. Luggage compartment light
118. Audio unit
119. Antenna amplifier
121. Connection to mobile phone
122. LH dash speaker
123. RH dash speaker
124. LH rear door speaker
125. RH rear door speaker

H47135

Typical interior lighting

Typical audio system

Reference

Dimensions and weights . . . . **REF•1**	Disconnecting the battery . . . . **REF•9**
Fuel economy. . . . . **REF•2**	Radio/cassette unit anti-theft system – precautions . **REF•9**
Conversion factors. . . . . **REF•6**	Tools and working facilities . . . . **REF•10**
Buying spare parts . . . . **REF•7**	MOT test checks . . . . **REF•12**
Vehicle identification. . . . . **REF•7**	Fault finding . . . . **REF•16**
General repair procedures . . . . **REF•8**	Index. . . . . **REF•24**
Jacking and vehicle support . . . . **REF•9**	

Dimensions and weights

Note: *All figures are approximate, and vary according to model. Refer to manufacturer's data for exact figures.*

Dimensions

Overall length (including bumpers):	
Saloon.	4836 mm
Estate	4841 mm
Overall width (including wing mirrors)	2042 mm
Overall height:	
Saloon.	1454 mm
Estate	1465 mm
Wheelbase	2703 mm
Track width (depending on wheel size):	
Front	1522 mm
Rear	1528 mm
Ground clearance (typical)	116 mm
Turning circle diameter:	
Wall to wall	11.9 m
Kerb to kerb	11.3 m
Luggage compartment length:	
Saloon:	
Rear seat upright	1092 mm
Rear seat folded down	1714 mm
Estate:	
Rear seat upright	1087 mm
Rear seat folded down	1732 mm

Weights

Gross Vehicle Weight (GVW):	
Saloon.	2070 to 2150 kg
Estate	2140 to 2220 kg
Kerb weight:	
Saloon.	1525 to 1700 kg
Estate	1590 to 1775 kg
Maximum axle load:	
Saloon:	
Front axle	1175 kg
Rear axle.	1050 kg
Estate:	
Front axle	1175 kg
Rear axle.	1125 kg
Maximum roof rack load	100 kg
Maximum luggage compartment load	80 kg
Maximum roof and luggage compartment weight combined:	
Saloon.	120 kg
Estate	120 kg
Maximum towing weight:	
Un-braked trailer.	750 kg
Braked trailer	1800 kg
Maximum load on ball hitch	50 to 75 kg

Fuel economy

Although depreciation is still the biggest part of the cost of motoring for most car owners, the cost of fuel is more immediately noticeable. These pages give some tips on how to get the best fuel economy.

Working it out

Manufacturer's figures

Car manufacturers are required by law to provide fuel consumption information on all new vehicles sold. These 'official' figures are obtained by simulating various driving conditions on a rolling road or a test track. Real life conditions are different, so the fuel consumption actually achieved may not bear much resemblance to the quoted figures.

How to calculate it

Many cars now have trip computers which will

display fuel consumption, both instantaneous and average. Refer to the owner's handbook for details of how to use these.

To calculate consumption yourself (and maybe to check that the trip computer is accurate), proceed as follows.

1. Fill up with fuel and note the mileage, or zero the trip recorder.
2. Drive as usual until you need to fill up again.
3. Note the amount of fuel required to refill the tank, and the mileage covered since the previous fill-up.
4. Divide the mileage by the amount of fuel used to obtain the consumption figure.

For example:

Mileage at first fill-up (a) = 27,903
Mileage at second fill-up (b) = 28,346
Mileage covered (b - a) = 443
Fuel required at second fill-up = 48.6 litres

The half-completed changeover to metric units in the UK means that we buy our fuel in litres, measure distances in miles and talk about fuel consumption in miles per gallon. There are two ways round this: the first is to convert the litres to gallons before doing the calculation (by dividing by 4.546, or see Table 1). So in the example:

48.6 litres ÷ 4.546 = 10.69 gallons
443 miles ÷ 10.69 gallons = 41.4 mpg

The second way is to calculate the consumption in miles per litre, then multiply that figure by 4.546 (or see Table 2).

So in the example, fuel consumption is:

443 miles ÷ 48.6 litres = 9.1 mpl
9.1 mpl x 4.546 = 41.4 mpg

The rest of Europe expresses fuel consumption in litres of fuel required to travel 100 km (l/100 km). For interest, the conversions are given in Table 3. In practice it doesn't matter what units you use, provided you know what your normal consumption is and can spot if it's getting better or worse.

Table 1: conversion of litres to Imperial gallons

litres	1	2	3	4	5	10	20	30	40	50	60	70
gallons	0.22	0.44	0.66	0.88	1.10	2.24	4.49	6.73	8.98	11.22	13.47	15.71

Table 2: conversion of miles per litre to miles per gallon

miles per litre	5	6	7	8	9	10	11	12	13	14
miles per gallon	23	27	32	36	41	46	50	55	59	64

Table 3: conversion of litres per 100 km to miles per gallon

litres per 100 km	4	4.5	5	5.5	6	6.5	7	8	9	10
miles per gallon	71	63	56	51	47	43	40	35	31	28

Fuel economy

Maintenance

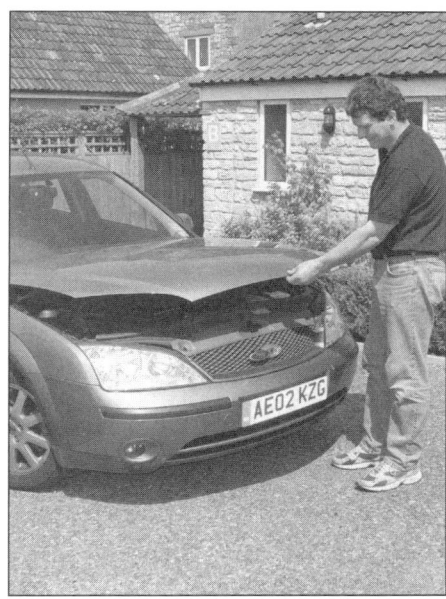

A well-maintained car uses less fuel and creates less pollution. In particular:

Filters
Change air and fuel filters at the specified intervals.

Oil
Use a good quality oil of the lowest viscosity specified by the vehicle manufacturer (see *Lubricants and fluids*). Check the level often and be careful not to overfill.

Spark plugs
When applicable, renew at the specified intervals.

Tyres
Check tyre pressures regularly. Under-inflated tyres have an increased rolling resistance. It is generally safe to use the higher pressures specified for full load conditions even when not fully laden, but keep an eye on the centre band of tread for signs of wear due to over-inflation.

When buying new tyres, consider the 'fuel saving' models which most manufacturers include in their ranges.

Driving style

Acceleration
Acceleration uses more fuel than driving at a steady speed. The best technique with modern cars is to accelerate reasonably briskly to the desired speed, changing up through the gears as soon as possible without making the engine labour.

Air conditioning
Air conditioning absorbs quite a bit of energy from the engine – typically 3 kW (4 hp) or so. The effect on fuel consumption is at its worst in slow traffic. Switch it off when not required.

Anticipation
Drive smoothly and try to read the traffic flow so as to avoid unnecessary acceleration and braking.

Automatic transmission
When accelerating in an automatic, avoid depressing the throttle so far as to make the transmission hold onto lower gears at higher speeds. Don't use the 'Sport' setting, if applicable.

When stationary with the engine running, select 'N' or 'P'. When moving, keep your left foot away from the brake.

Braking
Braking converts the car's energy of motion into heat – essentially, it is wasted. Obviously some braking is always going to be necessary, but with good anticipation it is surprising how much can be avoided, especially on routes that you know well.

Carshare
Consider sharing lifts to work or to the shops. Even once a week will make a difference.

REF•4 Fuel economy

Electrical loads
Electricity is 'fuel' too; the alternator which charges the battery does so by converting some of the engine's energy of motion into electrical energy. The more electrical accessories are in use, the greater the load on the alternator. Switch off big consumers like the heated rear window when not required.

Freewheeling
Freewheeling (coasting) in neutral with the engine switched off is dangerous. The effort required to operate power-assisted brakes and steering increases when the engine is not running, with a potential lack of control in emergency situations.

In any case, modern fuel injection systems automatically cut off the engine's fuel supply on the overrun (moving and in gear, but with the accelerator pedal released).

Gadgets
Bolt-on devices claiming to save fuel have been around for nearly as long as the motor car itself. Those which worked were rapidly adopted as standard equipment by the vehicle manufacturers. Others worked only in certain situations, or saved fuel only at the expense of unacceptable effects on performance, driveability or the life of engine components.

The most effective fuel saving gadget is the driver's right foot.

Journey planning
Combine (eg) a trip to the supermarket with a visit to the recycling centre and the DIY store, rather than making separate journeys.

When possible choose a travelling time outside rush hours.

Load
The more heavily a car is laden, the greater the energy required to accelerate it to a given speed. Remove heavy items which you don't need to carry.

One load which is often overlooked is the contents of the fuel tank. A tankful of fuel (55 litres / 12 gallons) weighs 45 kg (100 lb) or so. Just half filling it may be worthwhile.

Lost?
At the risk of stating the obvious, if you're going somewhere new, have details of the route to hand. There's not much point in achieving record mpg if you also go miles out of your way.

Parking
If possible, carry out any reversing or turning manoeuvres when you arrive at a parking space so that you can drive straight out when you leave. Manoeuvering when the engine is cold uses a lot more fuel.

Driving around looking for free on-street parking may cost more in fuel than buying a car park ticket.

Premium fuel
Most major oil companies (and some supermarkets) have premium grades of fuel which are several pence a litre dearer than the standard grades. Reports vary, but the consensus seems to be that if these fuels improve economy at all, they do not do so by enough to justify their extra cost.

Roof rack
When loading a roof rack, try to produce a wedge shape with the narrow end at the front. Any cover should be securely fastened – if it flaps it's creating turbulence and absorbing energy.

Remove roof racks and boxes when not in use – they increase air resistance and can create a surprising amount of noise.

Fuel economy REF•5

Short journeys
The engine is at its least efficient, and wear is highest, during the first few miles after a cold start. Consider walking, cycling or using public transport.

Speed
The engine is at its most efficient when running at a steady speed and load at the rpm where it develops maximum torque. (You can find this figure in the car's handbook.) For most cars this corresponds to between 55 and 65 mph in top gear.

Above the optimum cruising speed, fuel consumption starts to rise quite sharply. A car travelling at 80 mph will typically be using 30% more fuel than at 60 mph.

Supermarket fuel
It may be cheap but is it any good? In the UK all supermarket fuel must meet the relevant British Standard. The major oil companies will say that their branded fuels have better additive packages which may stop carbon and other deposits building up. A reasonable compromise might be to use one tank of branded fuel to three or four from the supermarket.

Switch off when stationary
Switch off the engine if you look like being stationary for more than 30 seconds or so. This is good for the environment as well as for your pocket. Be aware though that frequent restarts are hard on the battery and the starter motor.

Windows
Driving with the windows open increases air turbulence around the vehicle. Closing the windows promotes smooth airflow and

reduced resistance. The faster you go, the more significant this is.

And finally . . .
Driving techniques associated with good fuel economy tend to involve moderate acceleration and low top speeds. Be considerate to the needs of other road users who may need to make brisker progress; even if you do not agree with them this is not an excuse to be obstructive.

Safety must always take precedence over economy, whether it is a question of accelerating hard to complete an overtaking manoeuvre, killing your speed when confronted with a potential hazard or switching the lights on when it starts to get dark.

REF•6 Conversion factors

Length (distance)
Inches (in)	x 25.4	= Millimetres (mm)	x 0.0394	= Inches (in)
Feet (ft)	x 0.305	= Metres (m)	x 3.281	= Feet (ft)
Miles	x 1.609	= Kilometres (km)	x 0.621	= Miles

Volume (capacity)
Cubic inches (cu in; in^3)	x 16.387	= Cubic centimetres (cc; cm^3)	x 0.061	= Cubic inches (cu in; in^3)
Imperial pints (Imp pt)	x 0.568	= Litres (l)	x 1.76	= Imperial pints (Imp pt)
Imperial quarts (Imp qt)	x 1.137	= Litres (l)	x 0.88	= Imperial quarts (Imp qt)
Imperial quarts (Imp qt)	x 1.201	= US quarts (US qt)	x 0.833	= Imperial quarts (Imp qt)
US quarts (US qt)	x 0.946	= Litres (l)	x 1.057	= US quarts (US qt)
Imperial gallons (Imp gal)	x 4.546	= Litres (l)	x 0.22	= Imperial gallons (Imp gal)
Imperial gallons (Imp gal)	x 1.201	= US gallons (US gal)	x 0.833	= Imperial gallons (Imp gal)
US gallons (US gal)	x 3.785	= Litres (l)	x 0.264	= US gallons (US gal)

Mass (weight)
Ounces (oz)	x 28.35	= Grams (g)	x 0.035	= Ounces (oz)
Pounds (lb)	x 0.454	= Kilograms (kg)	x 2.205	= Pounds (lb)

Force
Ounces-force (ozf; oz)	x 0.278	= Newtons (N)	x 3.6	= Ounces-force (ozf; oz)
Pounds-force (lbf; lb)	x 4.448	= Newtons (N)	x 0.225	= Pounds-force (lbf; lb)
Newtons (N)	x 0.1	= Kilograms-force (kgf; kg)	x 9.81	= Newtons (N)

Pressure
Pounds-force per square inch (psi; lbf/in^2; lb/in^2)	x 0.070	= Kilograms-force per square centimetre (kgf/cm^2; kg/cm^2)	x 14.223	= Pounds-force per square inch (psi; lbf/in^2; lb/in^2)
Pounds-force per square inch (psi; lbf/in^2; lb/in^2)	x 0.068	= Atmospheres (atm)	x 14.696	= Pounds-force per square inch (psi; lbf/in^2; lb/in^2)
Pounds-force per square inch (psi; lbf/in^2; lb/in^2)	x 0.069	= Bars	x 14.5	= Pounds-force per square inch (psi; lbf/in^2; lb/in^2)
Pounds-force per square inch (psi; lbf/in^2; lb/in^2)	x 6.895	= Kilopascals (kPa)	x 0.145	= Pounds-force per square inch (psi; lbf/in^2; lb/in^2)
Kilopascals (kPa)	x 0.01	= Kilograms-force per square centimetre (kgf/cm^2; kg/cm^2)	x 98.1	= Kilopascals (kPa)
Millibar (mbar)	x 100	= Pascals (Pa)	x 0.01	= Millibar (mbar)
Millibar (mbar)	x 0.0145	= Pounds-force per square inch (psi; lbf/in^2; lb/in^2)	x 68.947	= Millibar (mbar)
Millibar (mbar)	x 0.75	= Millimetres of mercury (mmHg)	x 1.333	= Millibar (mbar)
Millibar (mbar)	x 0.401	= Inches of water (inH$_2$O)	x 2.491	= Millibar (mbar)
Millimetres of mercury (mmHg)	x 0.535	= Inches of water (inH$_2$O)	x 1.868	= Millimetres of mercury (mmHg)
Inches of water (inH$_2$O)	x 0.036	= Pounds-force per square inch (psi; lbf/in^2; lb/in^2)	x 27.68	= Inches of water (inH$_2$O)

Torque (moment of force)
Pounds-force inches (lbf in; lb in)	x 1.152	= Kilograms-force centimetre (kgf cm; kg cm)	x 0.868	= Pounds-force inches (lbf in; lb in)
Pounds-force inches (lbf in; lb in)	x 0.113	= Newton metres (Nm)	x 8.85	= Pounds-force inches (lbf in; lb in)
Pounds-force inches (lbf in; lb in)	x 0.083	= Pounds-force feet (lbf ft; lb ft)	x 12	= Pounds-force inches (lbf in; lb in)
Pounds-force feet (lbf ft; lb ft)	x 0.138	= Kilograms-force metres (kgf m; kg m)	x 7.233	= Pounds-force feet (lbf ft; lb ft)
Pounds-force feet (lbf ft; lb ft)	x 1.356	= Newton metres (Nm)	x 0.738	= Pounds-force feet (lbf ft; lb ft)
Newton metres (Nm)	x 0.102	= Kilograms-force metres (kgf m; kg m)	x 9.804	= Newton metres (Nm)

Power
Horsepower (hp)	x 745.7	= Watts (W)	x 0.0013	= Horsepower (hp)

Velocity (speed)
Miles per hour (miles/hr; mph)	x 1.609	= Kilometres per hour (km/hr; kph)	x 0.621	= Miles per hour (miles/hr; mph)

Fuel consumption*
Miles per gallon, Imperial (mpg)	x 0.354	= Kilometres per litre (km/l)	x 2.825	= Miles per gallon, Imperial (mpg)
Miles per gallon, US (mpg)	x 0.425	= Kilometres per litre (km/l)	x 2.352	= Miles per gallon, US (mpg)

Temperature
Degrees Fahrenheit = (°C x 1.8) + 32   Degrees Celsius (Degrees Centigrade; °C) = (°F - 32) x 0.56

*It is common practice to convert from miles per gallon (mpg) to litres/100 kilometres (l/100km), where mpg x l/100 km = 282

Buying spare parts REF•7

Spare parts are available from many sources, including maker's appointed garages, accessory shops, and motor factors. To be sure of obtaining the correct parts, it will sometimes be necessary to quote the vehicle identification number. If possible, it can also be useful to take the old parts along for positive identification. Items such as starter motors and alternators may be available under a service exchange scheme – any parts returned should be clean.

Our advice regarding spare parts is as follows.

Officially appointed garages

This is the best source of parts which are peculiar to your car, and which are not otherwise generally available (eg, badges, interior trim, certain body panels, etc). It is also the only place at which you should buy parts if the car is still under warranty.

Accessory shops

These are very good places to buy materials and components needed for the maintenance of your car (oil, air and fuel filters, light bulbs, drivebelts, greases, brake pads, touch-up paint, etc). Components of this nature sold by a reputable shop are usually of the same standard as those used by the car manufacturer.

Besides components, these shops also sell tools and general accessories, usually have convenient opening hours, charge lower prices, and can often be found close to home. Some accessory shops have parts counters where components needed for almost any repair job can be purchased or ordered.

Motor factors

Good factors will stock all the more important components which wear out comparatively quickly, and can sometimes supply individual components needed for the overhaul of a larger assembly (eg, brake seals and hydraulic parts, bearing shells, pistons, valves). They may also handle work such as cylinder block reboring, crankshaft regrinding, etc.

Engine reconditioners

These specialise in engine overhaul and can also supply components. It is recommended that the establishment is a member of the Federation of Engine Re-Manufacturers, or a similar society.

Tyre and exhaust specialists

These outlets may be independent, or members of a local or national chain. They frequently offer competitive prices when compared with a main dealer or local garage, but it will pay to obtain several quotes before making a decision. When researching prices, also ask what extras may be added – for instance fitting a new valve, balancing the wheel and tyre disposal all both commonly charged on top of the price of a new tyre.

Other sources

Beware of parts or materials obtained from market stalls, car boot sales, on-line auctions or similar outlets. Such items are not invariably sub-standard, but there is little chance of compensation if they do prove unsatisfactory. In the case of safety-critical components such as brake pads, there is the risk not only of financial loss, but also of an accident causing injury or death.

Second-hand components or assemblies obtained from a car breaker can be a good buy in some circumstances, but this sort of purchase is best made by the experienced DIY mechanic.

Vehicle identification

Modifications are a continuing and unpublicised process in vehicle manufacture, quite apart from major model changes. Spare parts manuals and lists are compiled upon a numerical basis, the individual vehicle identification numbers being essential to correct identification of the component required.

When ordering spare parts, always give as much information as possible. Quote the car model; year of manufacture, body and engine numbers as appropriate.

The *Vehicle Identification Number (VIN)* or *chassis number* appears in several places on the vehicle:
a) On a label, which is attached to the lower part of the passenger door B-pillar **(see illustration)**.
b) Stamped on the bulkhead at the rear of the engine compartment **(see illustration)**.
c) On the left-hand side of the facia, so that it can be seen through the bottom left-hand corner of the windscreen **(see illustration)**.

The *Engine number* is stamped on the front left-hand side of the cylinder block.

The *Transmission number* is printed on a plate, attached to the front/top of the transmission casing.

The *Tyre pressures and colour code label* is attached to the front facing edge on the passenger door B-pillar **(see illustration)**.

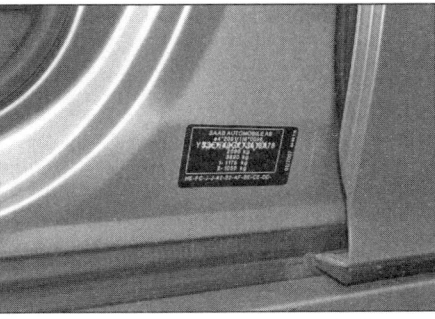

VIN label which is attached to the lower part of the passenger door B-pillar

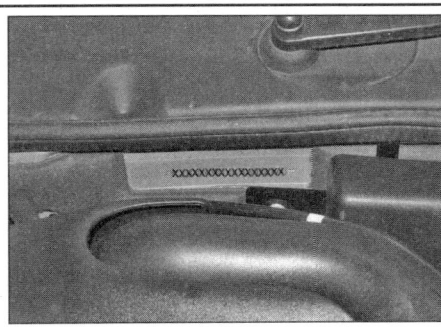

VIN stamped on the bulkhead at the rear of the engine compartment

VIN stamped on the left-hand side of the facia, so that it can be seen through the bottom left-hand corner of the windscreen.

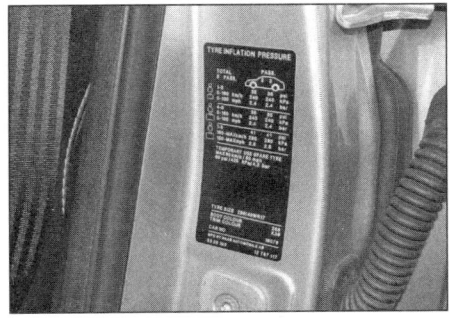

The tyre pressures and colour code label is attached to the front facing edge on the passenger door B-pillar

General repair procedures

Whenever servicing, repair or overhaul work is carried out on the car or its components, observe the following procedures and instructions. This will assist in carrying out the operation efficiently and to a professional standard of workmanship.

Joint mating faces and gaskets

When separating components at their mating faces, never insert screwdrivers or similar implements into the joint between the faces in order to prise them apart. This can cause severe damage which results in oil leaks, coolant leaks, etc upon reassembly. Separation is usually achieved by tapping along the joint with a soft-faced hammer in order to break the seal. However, note that this method may not be suitable where dowels are used for component location.

Where a gasket is used between the mating faces of two components, a new one must be fitted on reassembly; fit it dry unless otherwise stated in the repair procedure. Make sure that the mating faces are clean and dry, with all traces of old gasket removed. When cleaning a joint face, use a tool which is unlikely to score or damage the face, and remove any burrs or nicks with an oilstone or fine file.

Make sure that tapped holes are cleaned with a pipe cleaner, and keep them free of jointing compound, if this is being used, unless specifically instructed otherwise.

Ensure that all orifices, channels or pipes are clear, and blow through them, preferably using compressed air.

Oil seals

Oil seals can be removed by levering them out with a wide flat-bladed screwdriver or similar implement. Alternatively, a number of self-tapping screws may be screwed into the seal, and these used as a purchase for pliers or some similar device in order to pull the seal free.

Whenever an oil seal is removed from its working location, either individually or as part of an assembly, it should be renewed.

The very fine sealing lip of the seal is easily damaged, and will not seal if the surface it contacts is not completely clean and free from scratches, nicks or grooves. If the original sealing surface of the component cannot be restored, and the manufacturer has not made provision for slight relocation of the seal relative to the sealing surface, the component should be renewed.

Protect the lips of the seal from any surface which may damage them in the course of fitting. Use tape or a conical sleeve where possible. Where indicated, lubricate the seal lips with oil before fitting and, on dual-lipped seals, fill the space between the lips with grease.

Unless otherwise stated, oil seals must be fitted with their sealing lips toward the lubricant to be sealed.

Use a tubular drift or block of wood of the appropriate size to install the seal and, if the seal housing is shouldered, drive the seal down to the shoulder. If the seal housing is unshouldered, the seal should be fitted with its face flush with the housing top face (unless otherwise instructed).

Screw threads and fastenings

Seized nuts, bolts and screws are quite a common occurrence where corrosion has set in, and the use of penetrating oil or releasing fluid will often overcome this problem if the offending item is soaked for a while before attempting to release it. The use of an impact driver may also provide a means of releasing such stubborn fastening devices, when used in conjunction with the appropriate screwdriver bit or socket. If none of these methods works, it may be necessary to resort to the careful application of heat, or the use of a hacksaw or nut splitter device. Before resorting to extreme methods, check that you are not dealing with a left-hand thread!

Studs are usually removed by locking two nuts together on the threaded part, and then using a spanner on the lower nut to unscrew the stud. Studs or bolts which have broken off below the surface of the component in which they are mounted can sometimes be removed using a stud extractor.

Always ensure that a blind tapped hole is completely free from oil, grease, water or other fluid before installing the bolt or stud. Failure to do this could cause the housing to crack due to the hydraulic action of the bolt or stud as it is screwed in.

For some screw fastenings, notably cylinder head bolts or nuts, torque wrench settings are no longer specified for the latter stages of tightening, "angle-tightening" being called up instead. Typically, a fairly low torque wrench setting will be applied to the bolts/nuts in the correct sequence, followed by one or more stages of tightening through specified angles.

When checking or retightening a nut or bolt to a specified torque setting, slacken the nut or bolt by a quarter of a turn, and then retighten to the specified setting. However, this should not be attempted where angular tightening has been used.

Locknuts, locktabs and washers

Any fastening which will rotate against a component or housing during tightening should always have a washer between it and the relevant component or housing.

Spring or split washers should always be renewed when they are used to lock a critical component such as a big-end bearing retaining bolt or nut. Locktabs which are folded over to retain a nut or bolt should always be renewed.

Self-locking nuts can be re-used in non-critical areas, providing resistance can be felt when the locking portion passes over the bolt or stud thread. However, it should be noted that self-locking stiffnuts tend to lose their effectiveness after long periods of use, and should then be renewed as a matter of course.

Split pins must always be replaced with new ones of the correct size for the hole.

When thread-locking compound is found on the threads of a fastener which is to be re-used, it should be cleaned off with a wire brush and solvent, and fresh compound applied on reassembly.

Special tools

Some repair procedures in this manual entail the use of special tools such as a press, two or three-legged pullers, spring compressors, etc. Wherever possible, suitable readily-available alternatives to the manufacturer's special tools are described, and are shown in use. In some instances, where no alternative is possible, it has been necessary to resort to the use of a manufacturer's tool, and this has been done for reasons of safety as well as the efficient completion of the repair operation. Unless you are highly-skilled and have a thorough understanding of the procedures described, never attempt to bypass the use of any special tool when the procedure described specifies its use. Not only is there a very great risk of personal injury, but expensive damage could be caused to the components involved.

Environmental considerations

When disposing of used engine oil, brake fluid, antifreeze, etc, give due consideration to any detrimental environmental effects. Do not, for instance, pour any of the above liquids down drains into the general sewage system, or onto the ground to soak away. Many local council refuse tips provide a facility for waste oil disposal, as do some garages. You can find your nearest disposal point by calling the Environment Agency on 08708 506 506 or by visiting www.oilbankline.org.uk.

Note: *It is illegal and anti-social to dump oil down the drain. To find the location of your local oil recycling bank, call 08708 506 506 or visit www.oilbankline.org.uk.*

Jacking and vehicle support

The jack supplied with the vehicle tool kit should only be used for changing the roadwheels – see *Wheel changing* at the front of this manual. When carrying out any other kind of work, raise the vehicle using a hydraulic trolley jack, and always supplement the jack with axle stands positioned under the vehicle jacking points.

When using a trolley jack or axle stands, always position the jack head or axle stand head under, or adjacent to one of the relevant jacking points **(see illustration)**. Both front wheels can be raised by positioning the jack head beneath the front of the suspension subframe. Both rear wheels can be raised with the jack head adjacent to the rear towing eye, or beneath the towbar where fitted.

Do **not** attempt to jack the vehicle under the rear axle, floorpan, engine sump, transmission sump, or any of the suspension components.

The jack supplied with the vehicle locates in the jacking points on the underside of the sills – see *Wheel changing* at the front of this manual. Ensure that the jack head is correctly engaged before attempting to raise the vehicle.

Never work under, around, or near a raised vehicle, unless it is adequately supported in at least two places.

Jacking points for a trolley jack

Disconnecting the battery

Note: *If a non-standard radio/CD unit is installed, note the security code before disconnecting the battery.*

 Warning: Never disconnect the battery while the engine is running.

The battery is located on the front left-hand side of the engine compartment **(see illustrations)**.

Lift off the battery heat protection cover/box, then slacken the battery negative (-) terminal and lift it from the battery post. Always disconnect the negative terminal first.

Similarly slacken the battery positive (+) terminal and lift it from the battery post.

When reconnecting the battery terminals, always connect the negative terminal last.

Smear petroleum jelly on the terminals after reconnecting the leads.

After reconnection, it will be necessary to reset the clock and date information as described in the owner's handbook.

It may also be necessary to reset the window 'pinch protection' function as follows:
1) Shut the doors, start the car, and open the side window approximately 15 cm.
2) Close the window and hold the button in the closed position for at least 1 second after the window shuts.
3) Press the 'down' button and allow the window to open by itself.
4) Wait at least 1 second then close the window, holding the button until closing is confirmed by an audible signal.

In some instances, it's possible that several diagnostic fault codes may be set as a result of the battery disconnection and reconnection. These codes can be ignored, and will not be regenerated once they have been deleted. As special diagnostic equipment is needed to delete these codes, entrust this task to a Saab dealer or suitably-equipped repairer.

The battery is located on the front left-hand side of the engine compartment

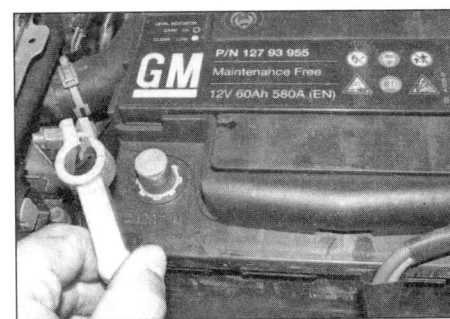

Always disconnect the negative lead first

Radio/cassette unit anti-theft system – precautions

The radio/cassette unit fitted as standard equipment, has an electronic security lock which is unique to the car in which the unit is fitted. When the audio system is switched on, a check is made to ensure that the vehicle and audio unit codes match each other. If they do, the unit is fully switched on, however, if they do not, the display will indicate that the unit is locked and it will be impossible to switch it on.

If a non-standard radio/cassette unit is fitted, it may be equipped with a built-in security code to deter thieves. If the power source to the unit is cut, the anti-theft system will activate. Even if the power source is immediately reconnected, the radio/cassette unit will not function until the correct security code has been entered. Therefore if you do not know the correct security code for the unit, **do not** disconnect the battery negative lead, or remove the radio/cassette unit from the vehicle.

If the security code is lost or forgotten, seek the advice of your Saab dealer. On presentation of proof of ownership, a Saab dealer will be able to provide you with a new security code.

REF•10 Tools and working facilities

Introduction

A selection of good tools is a fundamental requirement for anyone contemplating the maintenance and repair of a motor vehicle. For the owner who does not possess any, their purchase will prove a considerable expense, offsetting some of the savings made by doing-it-yourself. However, provided that the tools purchased meet the relevant national safety standards and are of good quality, they will last for many years and prove an extremely worthwhile investment.

To help the average owner to decide which tools are needed to carry out the various tasks detailed in this manual, we have compiled three lists of tools under the following headings: *Maintenance and minor repair*, *Repair and overhaul*, and *Special*. Newcomers to practical mechanics should start off with the *Maintenance and minor repair* tool kit, and confine themselves to the simpler jobs around the vehicle. Then, as confidence and experience grow, more difficult tasks can be undertaken, with extra tools being purchased as, and when, they are needed. In this way, a *Maintenance and minor repair* tool kit can be built up into a *Repair and overhaul* tool kit over a considerable period of time, without any major cash outlays. The experienced do-it-yourselfer will have a tool kit good enough for most repair and overhaul procedures, and will add tools from the *Special* category when it is felt that the expense is justified by the amount of use to which these tools will be put.

Maintenance and minor repair tool kit

The tools given in this list should be considered as a minimum requirement if routine maintenance, servicing and minor repair operations are to be undertaken. We recommend the purchase of combination spanners (ring one end, open-ended the other); although more expensive than open-ended ones, they do give the advantages of both types of spanner.

- [ ] *Combination spanners:*
  Metric - 8 to 19 mm inclusive
- [ ] *Adjustable spanner - 35 mm jaw (approx.)*
- [ ] *Spark plug spanner (with rubber insert) - petrol models*
- [ ] *Spark plug gap adjustment tool - petrol models*
- [ ] *Set of feeler gauges*
- [ ] *Brake bleed nipple spanner*
- [ ] *Screwdrivers:*
  Flat blade - 100 mm long x 6 mm dia
  Cross blade - 100 mm long x 6 mm dia
  Torx - various sizes (not all vehicles)
- [ ] *Combination pliers*
- [ ] *Hacksaw (junior)*
- [ ] *Tyre pump*
- [ ] *Tyre pressure gauge*
- [ ] *Oil can*
- [ ] *Oil filter removal tool (if applicable)*
- [ ] *Fine emery cloth*
- [ ] *Wire brush (small)*
- [ ] *Funnel (medium size)*
- [ ] *Sump drain plug key (not all vehicles)*

Repair and overhaul tool kit

These tools are virtually essential for anyone undertaking any major repairs to a motor vehicle, and are additional to those given in the *Maintenance and minor repair* list. Included in this list is a comprehensive set of sockets. Although these are expensive, they will be found invaluable as they are so versatile - particularly if various drives are included in the set. We recommend the half-inch square-drive type, as this can be used with most proprietary torque wrenches.

The tools in this list will sometimes need to be supplemented by tools from the *Special* list:

- [ ] *Sockets to cover range in previous list (including Torx sockets)*
- [ ] *Reversible ratchet drive (for use with sockets)*
- [ ] *Extension piece, 250 mm (for use with sockets)*
- [ ] *Universal joint (for use with sockets)*
- [ ] *Flexible handle or sliding T "breaker bar" (for use with sockets)*
- [ ] *Torque wrench (for use with sockets)*
- [ ] *Self-locking grips*
- [ ] *Ball pein hammer*
- [ ] *Soft-faced mallet (plastic or rubber)*
- [ ] *Screwdrivers:*
  Flat blade - long & sturdy, short (chubby), and narrow (electrician's) types
  Cross blade – long & sturdy, and short (chubby) types
- [ ] *Pliers:*
  Long-nosed
  Side cutters (electrician's)
  Circlip (internal and external)
- [ ] *Cold chisel - 25 mm*
- [ ] *Scriber*
- [ ] *Scraper*
- [ ] *Centre-punch*
- [ ] *Pin punch*
- [ ] *Hacksaw*
- [ ] *Brake hose clamp*
- [ ] *Brake/clutch bleeding kit*
- [ ] *Selection of twist drills*
- [ ] *Steel rule/straight-edge*
- [ ] *Allen keys (inc. splined/Torx type)*
- [ ] *Selection of files*
- [ ] *Wire brush*
- [ ] *Axle stands*
- [ ] *Jack (strong trolley or hydraulic type)*
- [ ] *Light with extension lead*
- [ ] *Universal electrical multi-meter*

Brake bleeding kit

Sockets and reversible ratchet drive

Hose clamp

Angular-tightening gauge

Torx key, socket and bit

Tools and working facilities

Special tools

The tools in this list are those which are not used regularly, are expensive to buy, or which need to be used in accordance with their manufacturers' instructions. Unless relatively difficult mechanical jobs are undertaken frequently, it will not be economic to buy many of these tools. Where this is the case, you could consider clubbing together with friends (or joining a motorists' club) to make a joint purchase, or borrowing the tools against a deposit from a local garage or tool hire specialist.

The following list contains only those tools and instruments freely available to the public, and not those special tools produced by the vehicle manufacturer specifically for its dealer network. You will find occasional references to these manufacturers' special tools in the text of this manual. Generally, an alternative method of doing the job without the vehicle manufacturers' special tool is given. However, sometimes there is no alternative to using them. Where this is the case and the relevant tool cannot be bought or borrowed, you will have to entrust the work to a dealer.

- ☐ *Angular-tightening gauge*
- ☐ *Valve spring compressor*
- ☐ *Valve grinding tool*
- ☐ *Piston ring compressor*
- ☐ *Piston ring removal/installation tool*
- ☐ *Cylinder bore hone*
- ☐ *Balljoint separator*
- ☐ *Coil spring compressors (where applicable)*
- ☐ *Two/three-legged hub and bearing puller*
- ☐ *Impact screwdriver*
- ☐ *Micrometer and/or vernier calipers*
- ☐ *Dial gauge*
- ☐ *Tachometer*
- ☐ *Fault code reader*
- ☐ *Cylinder compression gauge*
- ☐ *Hand-operated vacuum pump and gauge*
- ☐ *Clutch plate alignment set*
- ☐ *Brake shoe steady spring cup removal tool*
- ☐ *Bush and bearing removal/installation set*
- ☐ *Stud extractors*
- ☐ *Tap and die set*
- ☐ *Lifting tackle*

Buying tools

Reputable motor accessory shops and superstores often offer excellent quality tools at discount prices, so it pays to shop around.

Remember, you don't have to buy the most expensive items on the shelf, but it is always advisable to steer clear of the very cheap tools. Beware of 'bargains' offered on market stalls, on-line or at car boot sales. There are plenty of good tools around at reasonable prices, but always aim to purchase items which meet the relevant national safety standards. If in doubt, ask the proprietor or manager of the shop for advice before making a purchase.

Care and maintenance of tools

Having purchased a reasonable tool kit, it is necessary to keep the tools in a clean and serviceable condition. After use, always wipe off any dirt, grease and metal particles using a clean, dry cloth, before putting the tools away. Never leave them lying around after they have been used. A simple tool rack on the garage or workshop wall for items such as screwdrivers and pliers is a good idea. Store all normal spanners and sockets in a metal box. Any measuring instruments, gauges, meters, etc, must be carefully stored where they cannot be damaged or become rusty.

Take a little care when tools are used. Hammer heads inevitably become marked, and screwdrivers lose the keen edge on their blades from time to time. A little timely attention with emery cloth or a file will soon restore items like this to a good finish.

Working facilities

Not to be forgotten when discussing tools is the workshop itself. If anything more than routine maintenance is to be carried out, a suitable working area becomes essential.

It is appreciated that many an owner-mechanic is forced by circumstances to remove an engine or similar item without the benefit of a garage or workshop. Having done this, any repairs should always be done under the cover of a roof.

Wherever possible, any dismantling should be done on a clean, flat workbench or table at a suitable working height.

Any workbench needs a vice; one with a jaw opening of 100 mm is suitable for most jobs. As mentioned previously, some clean dry storage space is also required for tools, as well as for any lubricants, cleaning fluids, touch-up paints etc, which become necessary.

Another item which may be required, and which has a much more general usage, is an electric drill with a chuck capacity of at least 8 mm. This, together with a good range of twist drills, is virtually essential for fitting accessories.

Last, but not least, always keep a supply of old newspapers and clean, lint-free rags available, and try to keep any working area as clean as possible.

Micrometers

Dial test indicator ("dial gauge")

Oil filter removal tool (strap wrench type)

Compression tester

Fault code reader

REF•12 MOT test checks

This is a guide to getting your vehicle through the MOT test. Obviously it will not be possible to examine the vehicle to the same standard as the professional MOT tester. However, working through the following checks will enable you to identify any problem areas before submitting the vehicle for the test.

It has only been possible to summarise the test requirements here, based on the regulations in force at the time of printing. Test standards are becoming increasingly stringent, although there are some exemptions for older vehicles.

An assistant will be needed to help carry out some of these checks.

The checks have been sub-divided into four categories, as follows:

1 Checks carried out **FROM THE DRIVER'S SEAT**

2 Checks carried out **WITH THE VEHICLE ON THE GROUND**

3 Checks carried out **WITH THE VEHICLE RAISED AND THE WHEELS FREE TO TURN**

4 Checks carried out on **YOUR VEHICLE'S EXHAUST EMISSION SYSTEM**

---

1 Checks carried out **FROM THE DRIVER'S SEAT**

Handbrake

☐ Test the operation of the handbrake. Excessive travel (too many clicks) indicates incorrect brake or cable adjustment.
☐ Check that the handbrake cannot be released by tapping the lever sideways. Check the security of the lever mountings.

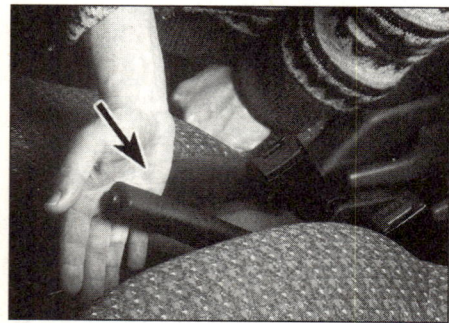

Footbrake

☐ Depress the brake pedal and check that it does not creep down to the floor, indicating a master cylinder fault. Release the pedal, wait a few seconds, then depress it again. If the pedal travels nearly to the floor before firm resistance is felt, brake adjustment or repair is necessary. If the pedal feels spongy, there is air in the hydraulic system which must be removed by bleeding.

☐ Check that the brake pedal is secure and in good condition. Check also for signs of fluid leaks on the pedal, floor or carpets, which would indicate failed seals in the brake master cylinder.
☐ Check the servo unit (when applicable) by operating the brake pedal several times, then keeping the pedal depressed and starting the engine. As the engine starts, the pedal will move down slightly. If not, the vacuum hose or the servo itself may be faulty.

Steering wheel and column

☐ Examine the steering wheel for fractures or looseness of the hub, spokes or rim.
☐ Move the steering wheel from side to side and then up and down. Check that the steering wheel is not loose on the column, indicating wear or a loose retaining nut. Continue moving the steering wheel as before, but also turn it slightly from left to right.
☐ Check that the steering wheel is not loose on the column, and that there is no abnormal

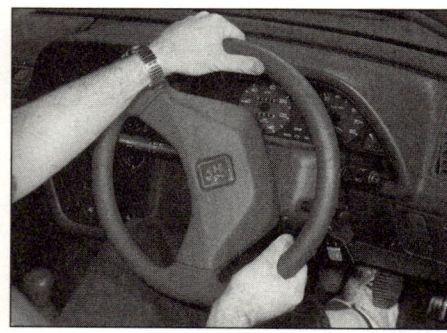

movement of the steering wheel, indicating wear in the column support bearings or couplings.

Windscreen, mirrors and sunvisor

☐ The windscreen must be free of cracks or other significant damage within the driver's field of view. (Small stone chips are acceptable.) Rear view mirrors must be secure, intact, and capable of being adjusted.

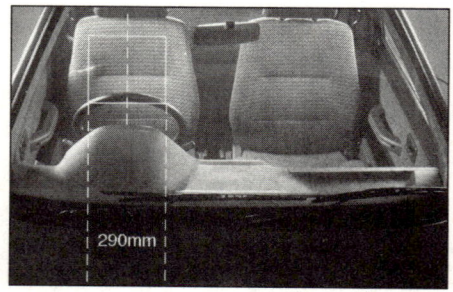

☐ The driver's sunvisor must be capable of being stored in the "up" position.

MOT test checks REF•13

Seat belts and seats

Note: *The following checks are applicable to all seat belts, front and rear.*

☐ Examine the webbing of all the belts (including rear belts if fitted) for cuts, serious fraying or deterioration. Fasten and unfasten each belt to check the buckles. If applicable, check the retracting mechanism. Check the security of all seat belt mountings accessible from inside the vehicle.

☐ Seat belts with pre-tensioners, once activated, have a "flag" or similar showing on the seat belt stalk. This, in itself, is not a reason for test failure.

☐ The front seats themselves must be securely attached and the backrests must lock in the upright position.

Doors

☐ Both front doors must be able to be opened and closed from outside and inside, and must latch securely when closed.

2 Checks carried out WITH THE VEHICLE ON THE GROUND

Vehicle identification

☐ Number plates must be in good condition, secure and legible, with letters and numbers correctly spaced – spacing at (A) should be at least twice that at (B).

☐ The VIN plate and/or homologation plate must be legible.

Electrical equipment

☐ Switch on the ignition and check the operation of the horn.

☐ Check the windscreen washers and wipers, examining the wiper blades; renew damaged or perished blades. Also check the operation of the stop-lights.

☐ Check the operation of the sidelights and number plate lights. The lenses and reflectors must be secure, clean and undamaged.

☐ Check the operation and alignment of the headlights. The headlight reflectors must not be tarnished and the lenses must be undamaged.

☐ Switch on the ignition and check the operation of the direction indicators (including the instrument panel tell-tale) and the hazard warning lights. Operation of the sidelights and stop-lights must not affect the indicators - if it does, the cause is usually a bad earth at the rear light cluster.

☐ Check the operation of the rear foglight(s), including the warning light on the instrument panel or in the switch.

☐ The ABS warning light must illuminate in accordance with the manufacturers' design. For most vehicles, the ABS warning light should illuminate when the ignition is switched on, and (if the system is operating properly) extinguish after a few seconds. Refer to the owner's handbook.

Footbrake

☐ Examine the master cylinder, brake pipes and servo unit for leaks, loose mountings, corrosion or other damage.

☐ The fluid reservoir must be secure and the fluid level must be between the upper (**A**) and lower (**B**) markings.

☐ Inspect both front brake flexible hoses for cracks or deterioration of the rubber. Turn the steering from lock to lock, and ensure that the hoses do not contact the wheel, tyre, or any part of the steering or suspension mechanism. With the brake pedal firmly depressed, check the hoses for bulges or leaks under pressure.

Steering and suspension

☐ Have your assistant turn the steering wheel from side to side slightly, up to the point where the steering gear just begins to transmit this movement to the roadwheels. Check for excessive free play between the steering wheel and the steering gear, indicating wear or insecurity of the steering column joints, the column-to-steering gear coupling, or the steering gear itself.

☐ Have your assistant turn the steering wheel more vigorously in each direction, so that the roadwheels just begin to turn. As this is done, examine all the steering joints, linkages, fittings and attachments. Renew any component that shows signs of wear or damage. On vehicles with power steering, check the security and condition of the steering pump, drivebelt and hoses.

☐ Check that the vehicle is standing level, and at approximately the correct ride height.

Shock absorbers

☐ Depress each corner of the vehicle in turn, then release it. The vehicle should rise and then settle in its normal position. If the vehicle continues to rise and fall, the shock absorber is defective. A shock absorber which has seized will also cause the vehicle to fail.

REF•14 MOT test checks

Exhaust system

☐ Start the engine. With your assistant holding a rag over the tailpipe, check the entire system for leaks. Repair or renew leaking sections.

3 Checks carried out WITH THE VEHICLE RAISED AND THE WHEELS FREE TO TURN

Jack up the front and rear of the vehicle, and securely support it on axle stands. Position the stands clear of the suspension assemblies. Ensure that the wheels are clear of the ground and that the steering can be turned from lock to lock.

Steering mechanism

☐ Have your assistant turn the steering from lock to lock. Check that the steering turns smoothly, and that no part of the steering mechanism, including a wheel or tyre, fouls any brake hose or pipe or any part of the body structure.

☐ Examine the steering rack rubber gaiters for damage or insecurity of the retaining clips. If power steering is fitted, check for signs of damage or leakage of the fluid hoses, pipes or connections. Also check for excessive stiffness or binding of the steering, a missing split pin or locking device, or severe corrosion of the body structure within 30 cm of any steering component attachment point.

Front and rear suspension and wheel bearings

☐ Starting at the front right-hand side, grasp the roadwheel at the 3 o'clock and 9 o'clock positions and rock gently but firmly. Check for free play or insecurity at the wheel bearings, suspension balljoints, or suspension mountings, pivots and attachments.

☐ Now grasp the wheel at the 12 o'clock and 6 o'clock positions and repeat the previous inspection. Spin the wheel, and check for roughness or tightness of the front wheel bearing.

☐ If excess free play is suspected at a component pivot point, this can be confirmed by using a large screwdriver or similar tool and levering between the mounting and the component attachment. This will confirm whether the wear is in the pivot bush, its retaining bolt, or in the mounting itself (the bolt holes can often become elongated).

☐ Carry out all the above checks at the other front wheel, and then at both rear wheels.

Springs and shock absorbers

☐ Examine the suspension struts (when applicable) for serious fluid leakage, corrosion, or damage to the casing. Also check the security of the mounting points.

☐ If coil springs are fitted, check that the spring ends locate in their seats, and that the spring is not corroded, cracked or broken.

☐ If leaf springs are fitted, check that all leaves are intact, that the axle is securely attached to each spring, and that there is no deterioration of the spring eye mountings, bushes, and shackles.

☐ The same general checks apply to vehicles fitted with other suspension types, such as torsion bars, hydraulic displacer units, etc. Ensure that all mountings and attachments are secure, that there are no signs of excessive wear, corrosion or damage, and (on hydraulic types) that there are no fluid leaks or damaged pipes.

☐ Inspect the shock absorbers for signs of serious fluid leakage. Check for wear of the mounting bushes or attachments, or damage to the body of the unit.

Driveshafts (fwd vehicles only)

☐ Rotate each front wheel in turn and inspect the constant velocity joint gaiters for splits or damage. Also check that each driveshaft is straight and undamaged.

Braking system

☐ If possible without dismantling, check brake pad wear and disc condition. Ensure that the friction lining material has not worn excessively, (A) and that the discs are not fractured, pitted, scored or badly worn (B).

☐ Examine all the rigid brake pipes underneath the vehicle, and the flexible hose(s) at the rear. Look for corrosion, chafing or insecurity of the pipes, and for signs of bulging under pressure, chafing, splits or deterioration of the flexible hoses.

☐ Look for signs of fluid leaks at the brake calipers or on the brake backplates. Repair or renew leaking components.

☐ Slowly spin each wheel, while your assistant depresses and releases the footbrake. Ensure that each brake is operating and does not bind when the pedal is released.

MOT test checks

☐ Examine the handbrake mechanism, checking for frayed or broken cables, excessive corrosion, or wear or insecurity of the linkage. Check that the mechanism works on each relevant wheel, and releases fully, without binding.

☐ It is not possible to test brake efficiency without special equipment, but a road test can be carried out later to check that the vehicle pulls up in a straight line.

Fuel and exhaust systems

☐ Inspect the fuel tank (including the filler cap), fuel pipes, hoses and unions. All components must be secure and free from leaks.

☐ Examine the exhaust system over its entire length, checking for any damaged, broken or missing mountings, security of the retaining clamps and rust or corrosion.

Wheels and tyres

☐ Examine the sidewalls and tread area of each tyre in turn. Check for cuts, tears, lumps, bulges, separation of the tread, and exposure of the ply or cord due to wear or damage. Check that the tyre bead is correctly seated on the wheel rim, that the valve is sound and properly seated, and that the wheel is not distorted or damaged.

☐ Check that the tyres are of the correct size for the vehicle, that they are of the same size

and type on each axle, and that the pressures are correct.

☐ Check the tyre tread depth. The legal minimum at the time of writing is 1.6 mm over at least three-quarters of the tread width. Abnormal tread wear may indicate incorrect front wheel alignment.

Body corrosion

☐ Check the condition of the entire vehicle structure for signs of corrosion in load-bearing areas. (These include chassis box sections, side sills, cross-members, pillars, and all suspension, steering, braking system and seat belt mountings and anchorages.) Any corrosion which has seriously reduced the thickness of a load-bearing area is likely to cause the vehicle to fail. In this case professional repairs are likely to be needed.

☐ Damage or corrosion which causes sharp or otherwise dangerous edges to be exposed will also cause the vehicle to fail.

4 Checks carried out on YOUR VEHICLE'S EXHAUST EMISSION SYSTEM

Petrol models

☐ The engine should be warmed up, and running well (ignition system in good order, air filter element clean, etc).

☐ Before testing, run the engine at around 2500 rpm for 20 seconds. Let the engine drop to idle, and watch for smoke from the exhaust. If the idle speed is too high, or if dense blue or black smoke emerges for more than 5 seconds, the vehicle will fail. Typically, blue smoke signifies oil burning (engine wear); black smoke means unburnt fuel (dirty air cleaner element, or other fuel system fault).

☐ An exhaust gas analyser for measuring carbon monoxide (CO) and hydrocarbons (HC) is now needed. If one cannot be hired or borrowed, have a local garage perform the check.

CO emissions (mixture)

☐ The MOT tester has access to the CO limits for all vehicles. The CO level is measured at idle speed, and at 'fast idle' (2500 to 3000 rpm). The following limits are given as a general guide:
At idle speed – Less than 0.5% CO
At 'fast idle' – Less than 0.3% CO
Lambda reading – 0.97 to 1.03

☐ If the CO level is too high, this may point to poor maintenance, a fuel injection system problem, faulty lambda (oxygen) sensor or catalytic converter. Try an injector cleaning treatment, and check the vehicle's ECU for fault codes.

HC emissions

☐ The MOT tester has access to HC limits for all vehicles. The HC level is measured at 'fast idle' (2500 to 3000 rpm). The following limits are given as a general guide:
At 'fast idle' – Less then 200 ppm

☐ Excessive HC emissions are typically caused by oil being burnt (worn engine), or by a blocked crankcase ventilation system ('breather'). If the engine oil is old and thin, an oil change may help. If the engine is running badly, check the vehicle's ECU for fault codes.

Diesel models

☐ The only emission test for diesel engines is measuring exhaust smoke density, using a calibrated smoke meter. The test involves accelerating the engine at least 3 times to its maximum unloaded speed.

Note: *On engines with a timing belt, it is VITAL that the belt is in good condition before the test is carried out.*

☐ With the engine warmed up, it is first purged by running at around 2500 rpm for 20 seconds. A governor check is then carried out, by slowly accelerating the engine to its maximum speed. After this, the smoke meter is connected, and the engine is accelerated quickly to maximum speed three times. If the smoke density is less than the limits given below, the vehicle will pass:
Non-turbo vehicles: 2.5m-1
Turbocharged vehicles: 3.0m-1

☐ If excess smoke is produced, try fitting a new air cleaner element, or using an injector cleaning treatment. If the engine is running badly, where applicable, check the vehicle's ECU for fault codes. Also check the vehicle's EGR system, where applicable. At high mileages, the injectors may require professional attention.

Fault finding

Engine
- [ ] Engine fails to rotate when attempting to start
- [ ] Starter motor turns engine slowly
- [ ] Engine rotates, but will not start
- [ ] Engine difficult to start when cold
- [ ] Engine difficult to start when hot
- [ ] Starter motor noisy or excessively-rough in engagement
- [ ] Engine starts, but stops immediately
- [ ] Engine idles erratically
- [ ] Engine misfires at idle speed
- [ ] Engine misfires throughout the driving speed range
- [ ] Engine stalls
- [ ] Engine hesitates on acceleration
- [ ] Engine lacks power
- [ ] Engine backfires
- [ ] Oil pressure warning light illuminated with engine running
- [ ] Engine runs-on after switching off
- [ ] Engine noises

Cooling system
- [ ] Overheating
- [ ] Overcooling
- [ ] External coolant leakage
- [ ] Internal coolant leakage
- [ ] Corrosion

Fuel and exhaust systems
- [ ] Excessive fuel consumption
- [ ] Fuel leakage and/or fuel odour
- [ ] Excessive noise or fumes from exhaust system

Clutch
- [ ] Pedal travels to floor – no pressure or very little resistance
- [ ] Clutch fails to disengage (unable to select gears)
- [ ] Clutch slips (engine speed increases, with no increase in vehicle speed)
- [ ] Judder as clutch is engaged
- [ ] Noise when depressing or releasing clutch pedal

Manual transmission
- [ ] Gear lever rattles
- [ ] Difficulty engaging gears
- [ ] Jumps out of gear
- [ ] Vibration
- [ ] Noisy in neutral with engine running
- [ ] Noisy in one particular gear
- [ ] Lubricant leaks

Automatic transmission
- [ ] Fluid leakage
- [ ] Transmission fluid brown, or has burned smell
- [ ] General gear selection problems
- [ ] Transmission will not downshift (kickdown) with accelerator pedal fully depressed
- [ ] Engine will not start in any gear, or starts in gears other than Park or Neutral
- [ ] Transmission slips, shifts roughly, is noisy, or has no drive in forward or reverse gears

Driveshafts
- [ ] Clicking or knocking noise on turns (at slow speed on full-lock)
- [ ] Vibration when accelerating or decelerating

Braking system
- [ ] Vehicle pulls to one side under braking
- [ ] Noise (grinding or high-pitched squeal) when brakes applied
- [ ] Brake pedal feels spongy when depressed
- [ ] Excessive brake pedal travel
- [ ] Excessive brake pedal effort required to stop vehicle
- [ ] Judder felt through brake pedal or steering wheel when braking
- [ ] Brakes binding
- [ ] Rear wheels locking under normal braking

Suspension and steering systems
- [ ] Vehicle pulls to one side
- [ ] Wheel wobble and vibration
- [ ] Excessive pitching and/or rolling around corners, or during braking
- [ ] Wandering or general instability
- [ ] Excessively-stiff steering
- [ ] Excessive play in steering
- [ ] Lack of power assistance
- [ ] Tyre wear excessive

Electrical system
- [ ] Battery will not hold a charge for more than a few days
- [ ] Ignition/no-charge warning light remains illuminated with engine running
- [ ] Ignition/no-charge warning light fails to come on
- [ ] Lights inoperative
- [ ] Instrument readings inaccurate or erratic
- [ ] Horn inoperative, or unsatisfactory in operation
- [ ] Windscreen/tailgate wipers inoperative, or unsatisfactory in operation
- [ ] Windscreen/tailgate washers inoperative, or unsatisfactory in operation
- [ ] Electric windows inoperative, or unsatisfactory in operation
- [ ] Central locking system inoperative, or unsatisfactory in operation

Introduction

The vehicle owner who does his or her own maintenance according to the recommended service schedules should not have to use this section of the manual very often. Modern component reliability is such that, provided those items subject to wear or deterioration are inspected or renewed at the specified intervals, sudden failure is comparatively rare. Faults do not usually just happen as a result of sudden failure, but develop over a period of time. Major mechanical failures in particular are usually preceded by characteristic symptoms over hundreds or even thousands of miles. Those components, which do occasionally fail without warning, are often small and easily carried in the vehicle.

With any fault-finding, the first step is to decide where to begin investigations. Sometimes this is obvious, but on other occasions, a little detective work will be necessary. The owner who makes half a dozen haphazard adjustments or replacements may be successful in curing a fault (or its symptoms), but will be none the wiser if the fault recurs, and ultimately may have spent more time and money than was necessary. A calm and logical approach will be found to be more satisfactory in the long run. Always take into account any warning signs or abnormalities that may have been noticed in the period preceding the fault – power loss, high or low gauge readings, unusual smells, etc – and remember that failure of components such as fuses or spark plugs may only be pointers to some underlying fault.

The pages which follow provide an easy-reference guide to the more common problems which may occur during the operation of the vehicle. These problems and their possible causes are grouped under headings denoting various components or systems, such as Engine, Cooling system, etc. The general

Fault finding REF•17

Chapter which deals with the problem is also shown in brackets; refer to the relevant part of that Chapter for system-specific information. Whatever the fault, certain basic principles apply. These are as follows:

Verify the fault. This is simply a matter of being sure that you know what the symptoms are before starting work. This is particularly important if you are investigating a fault for someone else, who may not have described it very accurately.

Don't overlook the obvious. For example, if the vehicle won't start, is there fuel in the tank? (Don't take anyone else's word on this particular point, and don't trust the fuel gauge either!) If an electrical fault is indicated, look for loose or broken wires before digging out the test gear.

Cure the disease, not the symptom. Substituting a flat battery with a fully charged one will get you off the hard shoulder, but if the underlying cause is not attended to, the new battery will go the same way. Similarly, changing oil-fouled spark plugs for a new set will get you moving again, but remember that the reason for the fouling (if it wasn't simply an incorrect grade of plug) will have to be established and corrected.

Don't take anything for granted. Particularly, don't forget that a 'new' component may itself be defective (especially if it's been rattling around in the boot for months), and don't leave components out of a fault diagnosis sequence just because they are new or recently fitted. When you do finally diagnose a difficult fault, you'll probably realise that all the evidence was there from the start.

Diesel fault diagnosis

The majority of starting problems on small diesel engines are electrical in origin. The mechanic who is familiar with petrol engines but less so with diesel may be inclined to view the diesel's injectors and pump in the same light as the spark plugs and distributor, but this is generally a mistake.

When investigating complaints of difficult starting for someone else, make sure that the correct starting procedure is understood and is being followed. Some drivers are unaware of the significance of the preheating warning light – many modern engines are sufficiently forgiving for this not to matter in mild weather, but with the onset of winter, problems begin.

As a rule of thumb, if the engine is difficult to start but runs well when it has finally got going, the problem is electrical (battery, starter motor or preheating system). If poor performance is combined with difficult starting, the problem is likely to be in the fuel system. The low-pressure (supply) side of the fuel system should be checked before suspecting the injectors and high-pressure pump. The most common fuel supply problem is air getting into the system, and any pipe from the fuel tank forwards must be scrutinised if air leakage is suspected. Normally the pump is the last item to suspect, since unless it has been tampered with, there is no reason for it to be at fault.

Engine

Engine fails to rotate when attempting to start
- [ ] Battery terminal connections loose or corroded (*Weekly checks*).
- [ ] Battery discharged or faulty (Chapter 5A).
- [ ] Broken, loose or disconnected wiring in the starting circuit (Chapter 5A).
- [ ] Defective starter solenoid or switch (Chapter 5A).
- [ ] Defective starter motor (Chapter 5A).
- [ ] Starter pinion or flywheel/driveplate ring gear teeth loose or broken (Chapters 2A or 5A).
- [ ] Engine earth cable broken or disconnected (Chapter 2A).

Starter motor turns engine slowly
- [ ] Partially-discharged battery (recharge, use jump leads, or push start) (Chapter 5A).
- [ ] Battery terminals loose or corroded (*Weekly checks*).
- [ ] Battery earth to body defective (Chapter 5A).
- [ ] Engine earth strap loose (Chapter 2A).
- [ ] Starter motor (or solenoid) wiring loose (Chapter 5A).
- [ ] Starter motor internal fault (Chapter 5A).

Engine rotates, but will not start
- [ ] Fuel tank empty.
- [ ] Battery discharged (engine rotates slowly) (Chapter 5A).
- [ ] Battery terminal connections loose or corroded (*Weekly checks*).
- [ ] Ignition components damp or damaged – petrol models (Chapters 1A and 5B).
- [ ] Broken, loose or disconnected wiring in the ignition circuit – petrol models (Chapters 1A and 5B).
- [ ] Worn, faulty or incorrectly-gapped spark plugs – petrol models (Chapter 1A).
- [ ] Preheating system faulty – diesel models (Chapter 5A).
- [ ] Fuel injection system faulty – petrol models (Chapter 4A).
- [ ] Air in fuel system – diesel models (Chapter 4B).
- [ ] Major mechanical failure (e.g. camshaft drive) (Chapter 2).

Engine difficult to start when cold
- [ ] Battery discharged (Chapter 5A).
- [ ] Battery terminal connections loose or corroded (*Weekly checks*).
- [ ] Worn, faulty or incorrectly-gapped spark plugs – petrol models (Chapter 1A).
- [ ] Preheating system faulty – diesel models (Chapter 5A).
- [ ] Fuel injection system faulty – petrol models (Chapter 4A).
- [ ] Other ignition system fault – petrol models (Chapters 1A and 5B).
- [ ] Low cylinder compressions (Chapter 2A or 2B).

Engine difficult to start when hot
- [ ] Air filter element dirty or clogged (Chapter 1A or 1B).
- [ ] Fuel injection system fault – petrol models (Chapter 4A).
- [ ] Low cylinder compressions (Chapter 2A or 2B).

Starter motor noisy or excessively rough in engagement
- [ ] Starter pinion or flywheel/driveplate ring gear teeth loose or broken (Chapters 2 or 5A).
- [ ] Starter motor mounting bolts loose or missing (Chapter 5A).
- [ ] Starter motor internal components worn or damaged (Chapter 5A).

Engine starts, but stops immediately
- [ ] Loose or faulty electrical connections in the ignition circuit – petrol models (Chapters 1A and 5B).
- [ ] Vacuum leak at the throttle body or intake manifold – petrol models (Chapter 4A).
- [ ] Blocked injector/fuel injection system fault – petrol models (Chapter 4A).

Engine idles erratically
- [ ] Air filter element clogged (Chapter 1A or 1B).
- [ ] Vacuum leak at the throttle body, intake manifold or associated hoses – petrol models (Chapter 4A).
- [ ] Worn, faulty or incorrectly-gapped spark plugs – petrol models (Chapter 1A).
- [ ] Uneven or low cylinder compressions (Chapters 2).
- [ ] Camshaft lobes worn (Chapter 2A or 2B).
- [ ] Timing chain incorrectly fitted (Chapter 2A).
- [ ] Timing belt incorrectly fitted (Chapter 2B).
- [ ] Blocked injector/fuel injection system fault – petrol models (Chapter 4A).
- [ ] Faulty injector(s) – diesel models (Chapter 4B).

REF•18 Fault finding

Engine (continued)

Engine misfires at idle speed
☐ Worn, faulty or incorrectly-gapped spark plugs – petrol models (Chapter 1A).
☐ Vacuum leak at the throttle body, intake manifold or associated hoses – petrol models (Chapter 4A).
☐ Blocked injector/fuel injection system fault – petrol models (Chapter 4A).
☐ Faulty injector(s) – diesel models (Chapter 4B).
☐ Uneven or low cylinder compressions (Chapter 2A or 2B).
☐ Disconnected, leaking, or perished crankcase ventilation hoses (Chapter 4C).

Engine misfires throughout the driving speed range
☐ Fuel filter choked (Chapter 1A or 1B).
☐ Fuel pump faulty, or delivery pressure low – petrol models (Chapter 4A).
☐ Fuel tank vent blocked, or fuel pipes restricted (Chapter 4A or 4B).
☐ Vacuum leak at the throttle body, intake manifold or associated hoses – petrol models (Chapter 4A).
☐ Worn, faulty or incorrectly-gapped spark plugs – petrol models (Chapter 1A).
☐ Faulty injector(s) – diesel models (Chapter 4B).
☐ Faulty ignition coil – petrol models (Chapter 5B).
☐ Uneven or low cylinder compressions (Chapter 2).
☐ Blocked injector/fuel injection system fault – petrol models (Chapter 4A).

Engine stalls
☐ Vacuum leak at the throttle body, intake manifold or associated hoses – petrol models (Chapter 4A).
☐ Fuel filter choked (Chapter 1A or 1B).
☐ Fuel pump faulty, or delivery pressure low – petrol models (Chapter 4A).
☐ Fuel tank vent blocked, or fuel pipes restricted (Chapter 4A or 4B).
☐ Blocked injector/fuel injection system fault – petrol models (Chapter 4A).
☐ Faulty injector(s) – diesel models (Chapter 4B).

Engine hesitates on acceleration
☐ Worn, faulty or incorrectly-gapped spark plugs – petrol models (Chapter 1A).
☐ Vacuum leak at the throttle body, intake manifold or associated hoses – petrol models (Chapter 4A).
☐ Blocked injector/fuel injection system fault – petrol models (Chapter 4A).
☐ Faulty injector(s) – diesel models (Chapter 4B).

Engine lacks power
☐ Timing chain/belt incorrectly fitted or tensioned (Chapter 2).
☐ Fuel filter choked (Chapter 1A or 1B).
☐ Fuel pump faulty, or delivery pressure low – petrol models (Chapter 4A).
☐ Uneven or low cylinder compressions (Chapter 2).
☐ Worn, faulty or incorrectly-gapped spark plugs – petrol models (Chapter 1A).
☐ Vacuum leak at the throttle body, intake manifold or associated hoses – petrol models (Chapter 4A).
☐ Blocked injector/fuel injection system fault – petrol models (Chapter 4A).
☐ Faulty injector(s) – diesel models (Chapter 4B).
☐ Brakes binding (Chapters 1A, 1B and 9).
☐ Clutch slipping (Chapter 6).

Engine backfires
☐ Timing chain/belt incorrectly fitted or tensioned (Chapter 2).
☐ Vacuum leak at the throttle body, intake manifold or associated hoses – petrol models (Chapter 4A).
☐ Blocked injector/fuel injection system fault – petrol models (Chapter 4A).

Oil pressure warning light illuminated with engine running
☐ Low oil level, or incorrect oil grade (*Weekly checks*).
☐ Faulty oil pressure sensor (Chapter 2 or 5A).
☐ Worn engine bearings and/or oil pump (Chapter 2A, 2B or 2C).
☐ Excessively high engine operating temperature (Chapter 3).
☐ Oil pressure relief valve defective (Chapter 2A, 2B or 2C).
☐ Oil pick-up strainer clogged (Chapter 2A, 2B or 2C).

Note: *Low oil pressure in a high-mileage engine at tick-over is not necessarily a cause for concern. Sudden pressure loss at speed is far more significant. In any event, check the gauge or warning light sender before condemning the engine.*

Engine runs-on after switching off
☐ Excessive carbon build-up in engine (Chapter 2C).
☐ High engine operating temperature (Chapter 3).
☐ Fuel injection system faulty – petrol models (Chapter 4A).

Engine noises

Pre-ignition (pinking) or knocking during acceleration or under load
☐ Ignition timing incorrect/ignition system fault – petrol models (Chapters 1A and 5B).
☐ Incorrect grade of spark plug – petrol models (Chapter 1A).
☐ Incorrect grade of fuel (Chapter 4A or 4B).
☐ Vacuum leak at the throttle body, intake manifold or associated hoses – petrol models (Chapter 4A).
☐ Excessive carbon build-up in engine (Chapter 2C).
☐ Blocked injector/fuel injection system fault – petrol models (Chapter 4A).

Whistling or wheezing noises
☐ Leaking intake manifold or throttle body gasket – petrol models (Chapter 4A).
☐ Leaking exhaust manifold gasket or pipe-to-manifold joint (Chapter 4A or 4B).
☐ Leaking vacuum hose (Chapters 4A, 4B, 5 and 9).
☐ Blowing cylinder head gasket (Chapter 2).

Tapping or rattling noises
☐ Worn valve timing gear or camshaft (Chapter 2C).
☐ Ancillary component fault (coolant pump, alternator, etc) (Chapters 3, 5A, etc).

Knocking or thumping noises
☐ Worn big-end bearings (regular heavy knocking, perhaps less under load) (Chapter 2C).
☐ Worn main bearings (rumbling and knocking, perhaps worsening under load) (Chapter 2C).
☐ Piston slap (most noticeable when cold) (Chapter 2C).
☐ Ancillary component fault (Coolant pump, alternator, etc) (Chapters 3, 5A, etc).

Fault finding REF•19

Cooling system

Overheating
- [ ] Auxiliary drivebelt broken – or, where applicable, incorrectly adjusted (Chapter 1).
- [ ] Insufficient coolant in system (*Weekly checks*).
- [ ] Thermostat faulty (Chapter 3).
- [ ] Radiator core blocked, or grille restricted (Chapter 3).
- [ ] Electric cooling fan or thermostatic switch faulty (Chapter 3).
- [ ] Pressure cap faulty (Chapter 3).
- [ ] Ignition timing incorrect, or ignition system fault (Chapters 1 and 5B).
- [ ] Inaccurate temperature gauge sender unit (Chapter 3).
- [ ] Airlock in cooling system (Chapter 1).

Overcooling
- [ ] Thermostat faulty (Chapter 3).
- [ ] Inaccurate temperature gauge sender unit (Chapter 3).

External coolant leakage
- [ ] Deteriorated or damaged hoses or hose clips (Chapter 1).
- [ ] Radiator core or heater matrix leaking (Chapter 3).
- [ ] Pressure cap faulty (Chapter 3).
- [ ] Water pump internal seal leaking (Chapter 3).
- [ ] Water pump-to-block O-ring or housing gasket leaking (Chapter 3).
- [ ] Boiling due to overheating (Chapter 3).
- [ ] Core plug leaking (Chapter 2).

Internal coolant leakage
- [ ] Leaking cylinder head gasket (Chapter 2).
- [ ] Cracked cylinder head or cylinder block (Chapter 2).

Corrosion
- [ ] Infrequent draining and flushing (Chapter 1).
- [ ] Incorrect coolant mixture or inappropriate coolant type (*Weekly checks*).

Fuel and exhaust systems

Excessive fuel consumption
- [ ] Air filter element dirty or clogged (Chapter 1A or 1B).
- [ ] Fuel injection system faulty – petrol models (Chapter 4A).
- [ ] Faulty injector(s) – diesel models (Chapter 4B).
- [ ] Ignition timing incorrect/ignition system faulty – petrol models (Chapters 1A and 5B).
- [ ] Brakes binding (Chapter 9).
- [ ] Tyres under-inflated (*Weekly checks*).

Fuel leakage and/or fuel odour
- [ ] Damaged or corroded fuel tank, pipes or connections (Chapters 4A or 4B).

Excessive noise or fumes from exhaust system
- [ ] Leaking exhaust system or manifold joints (Chapters 1 and 4).
- [ ] Leaking, corroded or damaged silencers or pipe (Chapters 1 and 4).
- [ ] Broken mountings causing body or suspension contact (Chapter 4A).

Clutch

Pedal travels to floor – no pressure or very little resistance
- [ ] Air in hydraulic system/faulty master or slave cylinder (Chapter 6).
- [ ] Faulty hydraulic release system (Chapter 6).
- [ ] Broken clutch release bearing (Chapter 6).
- [ ] Broken diaphragm spring in clutch pressure plate (Chapter 6).

Clutch fails to disengage (unable to select gears)
- [ ] Air in hydraulic system/faulty master or slave cylinder (Chapter 6).
- [ ] Faulty hydraulic release system (Chapter 6).
- [ ] Clutch disc sticking on gearbox input shaft splines (Chapter 6).
- [ ] Clutch disc sticking to flywheel or pressure plate (Chapter 6).
- [ ] Faulty pressure plate assembly (Chapter 6).
- [ ] Clutch release mechanism worn or incorrectly assembled (Chapter 6).

Clutch slips (engine speed increases, with no increase in vehicle speed)
- [ ] Faulty hydraulic release system (Chapter 6).
- [ ] Clutch disc linings excessively worn (Chapter 6).
- [ ] Clutch disc linings contaminated with oil or grease (Chapter 6).
- [ ] Faulty pressure plate or weak diaphragm spring (Chapter 6).

Judder as clutch is engaged
- [ ] Clutch disc linings contaminated with oil or grease (Chapter 6).
- [ ] Clutch disc linings excessively worn (Chapter 6).
- [ ] Faulty or distorted pressure plate or diaphragm spring (Chapter 6).
- [ ] Worn or loose engine or gearbox mountings (Chapter 2A or 2B).
- [ ] Clutch disc hub or gearbox input shaft splines worn (Chapter 6).

Noise when depressing or releasing clutch pedal
- [ ] Worn clutch release bearing (Chapter 6).
- [ ] Worn or dry clutch pedal bushes (Chapter 6).
- [ ] Faulty pressure plate assembly (Chapter 6).
- [ ] Pressure plate diaphragm spring broken (Chapter 6).
- [ ] Broken clutch disc cushioning springs (Chapter 6).

REF•20 Fault finding

Manual transmission

Gear lever rattles
☐ Fit a modified O-ring around the base of the gear lever ball socket (Chapter 7A, Section 4).

Difficulty engaging gears
☐ Clutch fault (Chapter 6).
☐ Worn or damaged gear linkage (Chapter 7A).
☐ Incorrectly-adjusted gear linkage (Chapter 7A).
☐ Worn synchroniser units (Chapter 7A).*

Jumps out of gear
☐ Worn or damaged gear linkage (Chapter 7A).
☐ Incorrectly-adjusted gear linkage (Chapter 7A).
☐ Worn synchroniser units (Chapter 7A).*
☐ Worn selector forks (Chapter 7A).*

Vibration
☐ Lack of oil (Chapter 1).
☐ Worn bearings (Chapter 7A).*

Noisy in neutral with engine running
☐ Input shaft bearings worn (noise apparent with clutch pedal released, but not when depressed) (Chapter 7A).*
☐ Clutch release bearing worn (noise apparent with clutch pedal depressed, possibly less when released) (Chapter 6).

Noisy in one particular gear
☐ Worn, damaged or chipped gear teeth (Chapter 7A).*

Lubricant leaks
☐ Leaking oil seal (Chapter 7A).
☐ Leaking housing joint (Chapter 7A).*
☐ Leaking input shaft oil seal (Chapter 7A).*

*Although the corrective action necessary to remedy the symptoms described is beyond the scope of this manual, the above information should be helpful in isolating the cause of the condition, so that the owner can communicate clearly with a professional mechanic.

Automatic transmission

Note: *Due to the complexity of the automatic transmission, it is difficult for the home mechanic to properly diagnose and service this unit. For problems other than the following, the vehicle should be taken to a dealer service department or automatic transmission specialist.*

Fluid leakage
☐ Automatic transmission fluid is usually deep red in colour. Fluid leaks should not be confused with engine oil, which can easily be blown onto the transmission by air flow.
☐ To determine the source of a leak, first remove all built-up dirt and grime from the transmission housing and surrounding areas, using a degreasing agent or by steam-cleaning. Drive the vehicle at low speed, so that air flow will not blow the leak far from its source. Raise and support the vehicle, and determine where the leak is coming from. The following are common areas of leakage.
a) *Fluid pan (transmission 'sump').*
b) *Dipstick tube (Chapter 1).*
c) *Transmission-to-fluid cooler fluid pipes/unions (Chapter 7B).*

Transmission fluid brown, or has burned smell
☐ Transmission fluid level low, or fluid in need of renewal (Chapter 1).

General gear selection problems
☐ The most likely cause of gear selection problems is a faulty or poorly-adjusted gear selector mechanism. The following are common problems associated with a faulty selector mechanism.
a) *Engine starting in gears other than Park or Neutral.*
b) *Indicator on gear selector lever pointing to a gear other than the one actually being used.*
c) *Vehicle moves when in Park or Neutral.*
d) *Poor gear shift quality, or erratic gear changes.*
Refer any problems to a Saab dealer, or an automatic transmission specialist.

Transmission will not downshift (kickdown) with accelerator pedal fully depressed
☐ Low transmission fluid level (Chapter 1).
☐ Incorrect selector cable adjustment (Chapter 7B).

Engine will not start in any gear, or starts in gears other than Park or Neutral
☐ Incorrect starter inhibitor switch adjustment – where applicable (Chapter 7B).
☐ Incorrect selector cable adjustment (Chapter 7B).

Transmission slips, shifts roughly, is noisy, or has no drive in forward or reverse gears
☐ There are many probable causes for the above problems, but the home mechanic should be concerned with only one possibility – incorrect transmission fluid level. Before taking the vehicle to a dealer or transmission specialist, check the fluid level and condition of the fluid as described in Chapter 1. Correct the fluid level as necessary, or change the fluid and filter if needed. If the problem persists, professional help will be necessary.

Fault finding REF•21

Driveshafts

Clicking or knocking noise on turns (at slow speed on full-lock)
☐ Lack of constant velocity joint lubricant, possibly due to damaged gaiter (Chapter 8).
☐ Worn outer constant velocity joint (Chapter 8).

Vibration when accelerating or decelerating
☐ Worn inner constant velocity joint (Chapter 8).
☐ Damaged or distorted driveshaft (Chapter 8).
☐ Worn intermediate bearing – where applicable (Chapter 8).

Braking system

Note: *Before assuming that a brake problem exists, make sure that the tyres are in good condition and correctly inflated, that the front wheel alignment is correct, and that the vehicle is not loaded with weight in an unequal manner. Apart from checking the condition of all pipe and hose connections, any faults occurring on the anti-lock braking system should be referred to a Saab dealer for diagnosis.*

Vehicle pulls to one side under braking
☐ Worn, defective, damaged or contaminated front or rear brake pads on one side (Chapters 1 and 9).
☐ Seized or partially-seized front or rear brake caliper piston (Chapter 9).
☐ A mixture of brake pad lining materials fitted between sides (Chapter 9).
☐ Brake caliper mounting bolts loose (Chapter 9).
☐ Worn or damaged steering or suspension components (Chapters 1 and 10).

Noise (grinding or high-pitched squeal) when brakes applied
☐ Brake pad friction lining material worn down to metal backing (Chapters 1 and 9).
☐ Excessive corrosion of brake disc – may be apparent after the vehicle has been standing for some time (Chapters 1 and 9).
☐ Foreign object (stone chipping, etc) trapped between brake disc and shield (Chapters 1A, 1B and 9).

Brake pedal feels spongy when depressed
☐ Air in hydraulic system (Chapter 9).
☐ Deteriorated flexible rubber brake hoses (Chapters 1 and 9).
☐ Master cylinder mountings loose (Chapter 9).
☐ Faulty master cylinder (Chapter 9).

Excessive brake pedal travel
☐ Faulty master cylinder (Chapter 9).

☐ Air in hydraulic system (Chapter 9).
☐ Faulty vacuum servo unit (Chapter 9).
☐ Faulty vacuum pump – diesel models (Chapter 9).

Excessive brake pedal effort required to stop vehicle
☐ Air in hydraulic system (Chapter 9).
☐ Brake fluid requires renewal (Chapter 1).
☐ Faulty vacuum servo unit (Chapter 9).
☐ Faulty vacuum pump – diesel models (Chapter 9).
☐ Disconnected, damaged or insecure brake servo vacuum hose (Chapters 1 and 9).
☐ Primary or secondary hydraulic circuit failure (Chapter 9).
☐ Seized brake caliper piston(s) (Chapter 9).
☐ Brake pads incorrectly fitted (Chapter 9).
☐ Incorrect grade of brake pads fitted (Chapter 9).
☐ Brake pads contaminated (Chapter 9).

Judder felt through brake pedal or steering wheel when braking
☐ Excessive run-out or distortion of brake disc(s) (Chapter 9).
☐ Brake pad linings worn (Chapters 1 and 9).
☐ Brake caliper mounting bolts loose (Chapter 9).
☐ Wear in suspension or steering components or mountings (Chapters 1 and 10).

Brakes binding
☐ Seized brake caliper piston(s) (Chapter 9).
☐ Incorrectly-adjusted handbrake mechanism (Chapter 9).
☐ Faulty master cylinder (Chapter 9).

Rear wheels locking under normal braking
☐ Seized brake caliper piston(s) (Chapter 9).
☐ Faulty brake pressure regulator (Chapter 9).

REF•22 Fault finding

Suspension and steering

Note: *Before diagnosing suspension or steering faults, be sure that the trouble is not due to incorrect tyre pressures, mixtures of tyre types, or binding brakes.*

Vehicle pulls to one side
- [ ] Defective tyre (*Weekly checks*).
- [ ] Excessive wear in suspension or steering components (Chapters 1 and 10).
- [ ] Incorrect front wheel alignment (Chapter 10).
- [ ] Accident damage to steering or suspension components (Chapters 1 and 10).

Wheel wobble and vibration
- [ ] Front roadwheels out of balance (vibration felt mainly through the steering wheel) (*Weekly checks*).
- [ ] Rear roadwheels out of balance (vibration felt throughout the vehicle) (*Weekly checks*).
- [ ] Roadwheels damaged or distorted (*Weekly checks*).
- [ ] Faulty or damaged tyre (*Weekly checks*).
- [ ] Worn steering or suspension joints, bushes or components (Chapters 1 and 10).
- [ ] Wheel bolts loose.

Excessive pitching and/or rolling around corners, or during braking
- [ ] Defective shock absorbers (Chapters 1 and 10).
- [ ] Broken or weak coil spring and/or suspension component (Chapters 1 and 10).
- [ ] Worn or damaged anti-roll bar or mountings (Chapter 10).

Wandering or general instability
- [ ] Incorrect front wheel alignment (Chapter 10).
- [ ] Worn steering or suspension joints, bushes or components (Chapters 1 and 10).
- [ ] Roadwheels out of balance (*Weekly checks*).
- [ ] Faulty or damaged tyre (*Weekly checks*).
- [ ] Wheel bolts loose.
- [ ] Defective shock absorbers (Chapters 1 and 10).

Excessively-stiff steering
- [ ] Lack of steering gear lubricant (Chapter 10).
- [ ] Seized track rod end balljoint or suspension balljoint (Chapters 1 and 10).
- [ ] Broken or incorrectly adjusted auxiliary drivebelt (Chapter 1).
- [ ] Incorrect front wheel alignment (Chapter 10).
- [ ] Steering rack or column bent or damaged (Chapter 10).

Excessive play in steering
- [ ] Worn steering column universal joint(s) (Chapter 10).
- [ ] Worn steering track rod end balljoints (Chapters 1 and 10).
- [ ] Worn rack-and-pinion steering gear (Chapter 10).
- [ ] Worn steering or suspension joints, bushes or components (Chapters 1 and 10).

Lack of power assistance
- [ ] Broken or incorrectly-adjusted auxiliary drivebelt (Chapter 1).
- [ ] Incorrect power steering fluid level (*Weekly checks*).
- [ ] Restriction in power steering fluid hoses (Chapter 1).
- [ ] Faulty power steering pump (Chapter 10).
- [ ] Faulty steering gear (Chapter 10).

Tyre wear excessive

Tyres worn on inside or outside edges
- [ ] Tyres under-inflated (wear on both edges) (*Weekly checks*).
- [ ] Incorrect camber or castor angles (wear on one edge only) (Chapter 10).
- [ ] Worn steering or suspension joints, bushes or components (Chapters 1 and 10).
- [ ] Excessively-hard cornering.
- [ ] Accident damage.

Tyre treads exhibit feathered edges
- [ ] Incorrect toe setting (Chapter 10).

Tyres worn in centre of tread
- [ ] Tyres over-inflated (*Weekly checks*).

Tyres worn on inside and outside edges
- [ ] Tyres under-inflated (*Weekly checks*).
- [ ] Worn shock absorbers (Chapters 1 and 10).

Tyres worn unevenly
- [ ] Tyres out of balance (*Weekly checks*).
- [ ] Excessive wheel or tyre run-out (*Weekly checks*).
- [ ] Worn shock absorbers (Chapters 1 and 10).
- [ ] Faulty tyre (*Weekly checks*).

Electrical system

Note: *For problems associated with the starting system, refer to the faults listed under 'Engine' earlier in this Section.*

Battery will not hold a charge for more than a few days
- [ ] Battery defective internally (Chapter 5A).
- [ ] Battery electrolyte level low – where applicable (Chapter 5A).
- [ ] Battery terminal connections loose or corroded (*Weekly checks*).
- [ ] Auxiliary drivebelt worn (Chapter 1).
- [ ] Alternator not charging at correct output (Chapter 5A).
- [ ] Alternator or voltage regulator faulty (Chapter 5A).
- [ ] Short-circuit causing continual battery drain (Chapters 5A and 12).

Ignition/no-charge warning light remains illuminated with engine running
- [ ] Auxiliary drivebelt broken or worn (Chapter 1).
- [ ] Internal fault in alternator or voltage regulator (Chapter 5A).
- [ ] Broken, disconnected, or loose wiring in charging circuit (Chapter 5A).

Ignition/no-charge warning light fails to come on
- [ ] Warning light bulb blown (Chapter 12).
- [ ] Broken, disconnected, or loose wiring in warning light circuit (Chapter 12).
- [ ] Alternator faulty (Chapter 5A).

Fault finding REF•23

Electrical system (continued)

Lights inoperative
- [ ] Bulb blown (Chapter 12).
- [ ] Corrosion of bulb or bulbholder contacts (Chapter 12).
- [ ] Blown fuse (Chapter 12).
- [ ] Faulty relay (Chapter 12).
- [ ] Broken, loose, or disconnected wiring (Chapter 12).
- [ ] Faulty switch (Chapter 12).

Instrument readings inaccurate or erratic

Fuel or temperature gauges give no reading
- [ ] Faulty gauge sender unit (Chapters 3 and 4).
- [ ] Wiring open-circuit (Chapter 12).
- [ ] Faulty gauge (Chapter 12).

Fuel or temperature gauges give continuous maximum reading
- [ ] Faulty gauge sender unit (Chapters 3 and 4).
- [ ] Wiring short-circuit (Chapter 12).
- [ ] Faulty gauge (Chapter 12).

Horn inoperative, or unsatisfactory in operation

Horn operates all the time
- [ ] Horn contacts permanently bridged or horn push stuck down (Chapter 12).

Horn fails to operate
- [ ] Blown fuse (Chapter 12).
- [ ] Cable or cable connections loose, broken or disconnected (Chapter 12).
- [ ] Faulty horn (Chapter 12).

Horn emits intermittent or unsatisfactory sound
- [ ] Cable connections loose (Chapter 12).
- [ ] Horn mountings loose (Chapter 12).
- [ ] Faulty horn (Chapter 12).

Windscreen/tailgate wipers inoperative, or unsatisfactory in operation

Wipers fail to operate, or operate very slowly
- [ ] Wiper blades stuck to screen, or linkage seized or binding (*Weekly checks* and Chapter 12).
- [ ] Blown fuse (Chapter 12).
- [ ] Cable or cable connections loose, broken or disconnected (Chapter 12).
- [ ] Faulty relay (Chapter 12).
- [ ] Faulty wiper motor (Chapter 12).

Wiper blades sweep over too large or too small an area of the glass
- [ ] Wiper arms incorrectly positioned on spindles (Chapter 12).
- [ ] Excessive wear of wiper linkage (Chapter 12).
- [ ] Wiper motor or linkage mountings loose or insecure (Chapter 12).

Wiper blades fail to clean the glass effectively
- [ ] Wiper blade rubbers worn or perished (*Weekly checks*).
- [ ] Wiper arm tension springs broken, or arm pivots seized (Chapter 12).
- [ ] Insufficient windscreen washer additive to adequately remove road film (*Weekly checks*).

Windscreen/tailgate washers inoperative, or unsatisfactory in operation

One or more washer jets inoperative
- [ ] Blocked washer jet.
- [ ] Disconnected, kinked or restricted fluid hose (Chapter 12).
- [ ] Insufficient fluid in washer reservoir (*Weekly checks*).

Washer pump fails to operate
- [ ] Broken or disconnected wiring or connections (Chapter 12).
- [ ] Blown fuse (Chapter 12).
- [ ] Faulty washer switch (Chapter 12).
- [ ] Faulty washer pump (Chapter 12).

Washer pump runs for some time before fluid is emitted from jets
- [ ] Faulty one-way valve in fluid supply hose (Chapter 12).

Electric windows inoperative, or unsatisfactory in operation

Window glass will only move in one direction
- [ ] Faulty switch (Chapter 12).
- [ ] Faulty motor (Chapter 11).

Window glass slow to move
- [ ] Regulator seized or damaged, or in need of lubrication (Chapter 11).
- [ ] Door internal components or trim fouling regulator (Chapter 11).
- [ ] Faulty motor (Chapter 11).

Window glass fails to move
- [ ] Blown fuse (Chapter 12).
- [ ] Regulator seized or jammed (Chapter 12)
- [ ] Faulty relay (Chapter 12).
- [ ] Broken or disconnected wiring or connections (Chapter 12).
- [ ] Faulty motor (Chapter 11).

Central locking system inoperative, or unsatisfactory in operation

Complete system failure
- [ ] Blown fuse (Chapter 12).
- [ ] Faulty relay (Chapter 12).
- [ ] Broken or disconnected wiring or connections (Chapter 12).
- [ ] Faulty motor (Chapter 11).

Latch locks but will not unlock, or unlocks but will not lock
- [ ] Faulty switch (Chapter 12).
- [ ] Broken or disconnected latch operating rods or levers (Chapter 11).
- [ ] Faulty relay (Chapter 12).
- [ ] Faulty motor (Chapter 11).

One solenoid/motor fails to operate
- [ ] Broken or disconnected wiring or connections (Chapter 12).
- [ ] Faulty motor (Chapter 11).
- [ ] Broken, binding or disconnected lock operating rods or levers (Chapter 11).
- [ ] Fault in door lock (Chapter 11).

Index

*Note: References throughout this index are in the form "**Chapter number**" • "**Page number**". So, for example, 2C•15 refers to page 15 of Chapter 2C.*

A

A-pillar trim panels – 11•25
ABS/ESP/TCS hydraulic unit – 9•18
Accelerator
  cable – 4A•3
  pedal – 4A•4
Accessory shops – REF•7
Acknowledgements – 0•4
Aerial
  amplifier – 12•24
  filter – 12•24
Air blending stepping motor – 3•11
Air conditioning – 3•8, 3•11, 3•12
  drain hoses – 1A•11, 1B•12
  refrigerant leaks – 1A•7, 1B•8
Air distribution stepping motor – 3•11
Air filter – 1A•13, 1B•13, 4A•3, 4B•4
Air pressure/temperature sensor – 4B•5
Airbags – 0•5, 1A•8, 1B•9, 11•32
Airflow
  meter – 4B•4
  sensor – 4A•9
Alarm system components – 12•25
Alternator – 5A•4
  brushes and regulator – 5A•5
Amplifier
  aerial – 12•24
  audio – 12•23
Antifreeze – 0•11, 0•16, 1A•10, 1A•14, 1B•10, 1B•16
Anti-lock Braking System (ABS) – 9•17, 9•18
Anti-roll bar – 10•5, 10•10
Anti-theft alarm system – 12•25, REF•9
Asbestos – 0•5
Audio amplifier – 12•23
Automatic transmission – 7B•1 et seq
  fault finding – REF•20
  fluid – 0•16, 1A•10, 1A•17, 1B•10, 1B•14
  fluid cooler – 7B•3
  fluid leaks – 1A•7, 1B•8
  fluid temperature sensor – 7B•4
  selector illumination – 12•9
Auxiliary drivebelt – 1A•11, 1A•15, 1B•12, 1B•14

B

B-pillar trim panels – 11•26
Balance shafts – 2C•14
Battery – 0•5, 0•14, 5A•2, 5A•3, REF•9
Big-end bearings – 2C•19, 2C•22
Bleeding
  brakes – 9•3
  clutch – 6•5
  fuel system – 4B•4
  power steering – 10•16
Blower motor – 3•8
  control unit – 3•11
Body corrosion – REF•15
Body electrical system – 12•1 et seq
Bodywork and fittings – 11•1 et seq
Bonnet – 11•6
  lock – 11•7
  release cable and lever – 11•7
  switch alarm system – 12•26
Boost
  bypass valve – 4A•13
  control valve – 4A•13
  pressure/temperature sensor – 4A•8
Boot lid – 11•15
  handle – 11•19
  lock – 11•17
  lock motor – 11•18
Braking system – 1A•9, 1B•10, 9•1 et seq, REF•12, REF•13, REF•14
  fault finding – REF•21
  fault finding (ABS) – 9•18
  fluid – 0•12, 0•16, 1A•17, 1B•16
  fluid leaks – 1A•7, 1B•8
  pads – 1A•11, 1B•11, 9•5, 9•6
Bulbs – 12•7, 12•10
Bumpers – 11•4, 11•5
Burning – 0•5
Buying spare parts – REF•7

C

C-pillar trim panels – 11•26
Cables
  accelerator – 4A•3
  bonnet release – 11•7
  handbrake – 9•16
  selector – 7B•2
Calipers – 9•8, 9•9
Cam followers – 2A•5, 2B•12
Camshafts – 2A•5, 2B•9, 2B•10, 2B•12
  oil seal – 2B•9
  sensor – 4B•5
  sprocket – 2B•7
Carpets – 11•2
Catalytic converter – 4A•18, 4B•13, 4C•4, 4C•5
CD player – 12•22
  anti-theft system – REF•9
  changer – 12•24
Centre console – 11•27
Charcoal canister – 4C•2
Charge air (boost)
  bypass valve – 4A•13
  control valve – 4A•13
  pressure/temperature sensor – 4A•8
Charging – 5A•3
Check Engine indicator lamp – 4A•5
Cigarette lighter – 12•19
  bulb – 12•9
Climate control systems – 3•7, 3•8
  control module – 3•10
  illumination – 12•10
Clutch – 6•1 et seq
  fault finding – REF•19
  fluid – 0•12, 0•16
  fluid leaks – 1A•7, 1B•8

Index REF•25

Note: *References throughout this index are in the form "**Chapter number**" • "**Page number**". So, for example, 2C•15 refers to page 15 of Chapter 2C.*

Coils – 5B•3
Compression test – 2A•3, 2B•3
Compressor – 3•13
Condenser – 3•12
Connecting rods – 2C•15, 2C•17, 2C•22
Console – 11•27
Control unit
    alarm system – 12•25
    automatic transmission – 7B•4
    blower motor – 3•11
    climate control – 3•10, 12•10
    cruise control – 4A•4
    DICE – 12•24
    engine management system – 4A•8
    fuel system – 4A•8, 4B•6
    instrument panel – 12•18
    parking aid – 12•25
    pre/post-heating system – 5A•8
    seats – 11•22
    SRS – 11•34
    xenon headlight – 12•17
Conversion factors – REF•6
Coolant – 0•11, 0•16, 1A•10, 1A•13, 1B•10, 1B•15
    pump – 3•6
    temperature sensor – 3•5, 4A•9, 4B•5
Cooling, heating and ventilation systems – 3•1 *et seq*
    fault finding – REF•19
    leaks – 1A•6, 1B•7
Courtesy light
    bulbs – 12•7
    switch – 12•6
Crankcase – 2C•16
    emissions control – 4C•1, 4C•3, 4C•4
Crankshaft – 2C•16, 2C•19, 2C•21
    oil seals – 2A•13, 2B•17
    position sensor – 4A•9
    pulley – 2B•5
    sensor – 4B•5, 5B•3
    sprocket – 2B•7
Cruise control system – 4A•4
Crushing – 0•5
Cylinder block – 2C•16
Cylinder head – 2A•6, 2B•13, 2C•7, 2C•8, 2C•9
    cover – 2A•4

D

Dents – 11•3
Depressurising fuel supply system – 4A•5
DICE control module – 12•24
Diesel engine in-car repair procedures – 2B•1 *et seq*
    fault finding – REF•17
Diesel injection equipment – 0•5, 4B•3
Dimensions – REF•1
Dipped beam – 12•11
Direction indicators – 12•12, 12•15
Discharge module (ignition) – 5B•2
Disconnecting the battery – REF•9
Discs – 9•10
Distance sensor parking aid – 12•25
Doors – 11•8, REF•13
    handle and lock components – 11•10
    inner trim panel – 11•9
    mirror – 11•19
    mirror switch – 12•6
    protective mouldings – 11•21
    window – 11•12
    window regulator – 11•13
Drivebelt – 1A•11, 1A•15, 1B•12, 1B•14
Driveplate – 2A•13, 2B•18
Driveshafts – 8•1 *et seq*, REF•14
    fault finding – REF•21
    gaiters – 1A•10, 1B•11, 8•5
    joints – 1A•10, 1B•11
    oil seals – 7A•4, 7A•5
Drivetrain – 1A•9, 1B•10

E

Earth fault – 12•3
Earthing points (ABS) – 9•18
EGR valve – 4C•4
Electric shock – 0•5
Electrical systems – 0•15, 1A•9, 1B•10, REF•13
    connections (ABS) – 9•18
    fault finding – 12•2, REF•22, REF•23
Electronic control module (ECM)
    alarm system – 12•25
    automatic transmission – 7B•4
    cruise control system – 4A•4
    engine management system – 4A•8
    fuel system – 4A•8, 4B•6
    instrument panel – 12•18
    SRS – 11•34
Electronic Stability Program (ESP) – 9•19
    hydraulic unit – 9•18
Emissions control systems – 4C•1 *et seq*, REF•15
Engine fault finding – REF•17, REF•18
Engine management system – 4A•5, 4A•7, 4A•8
Engine oil – 0•11, 0•16, 1A•6, 1B•6
    leaks – 1A•7, 1B•7
Engine reconditioners – REF•7
Engine removal and general overhaul procedures – 2C•1 *et seq*
ESP/TCS switch – 9•19
Evaporative emissions control – 4C•1, 4C•2
Exhaust emissions control – 4C•2, 4C•4
Exhaust gas
    recirculation system – 4C•2, 4C•4
    temperature sensors – 4C•4
Exhaust manifold – 4A•17, 4B•11
Exhaust specialists – REF•7
Exhaust system – 1A•10, 1B•11, 4A•17, 4B•12, REF•14, REF•15

F

Facia assembly – 11•29
Fan – 3•4

Index

Note: References throughout this index are in the form "**Chapter number**" • "**Page number**". So, for example, 2C•15 refers to page 15 of Chapter 2C.

Fault finding – REF•16 et seq
   ABS – 9•18
   automatic transmission – REF•20
   braking system – REF•21
   clutch – REF•19
   cooling system – REF•19
   diesel engine – REF•17
   driveshafts – REF•21
   electrical system – 12•2, REF•22, REF•23
   engine – REF•17, REF•18
   fuel and exhaust systems – REF•19
   ignition system – 5B•2
   manual transmission – REF•20
   suspension and steering systems – REF•22
Filling – 11•3
Filter
   air – 1A•13, 1B•13, 4A•3, 4B•4
   fuel – 1A•14, 1B•12
   oil – 1A•6, 1B•6, 2B•17
   particulate – 4B•13, 4C•4
   pollen – 1A•11
Fire – 0•5
Fluids – 0•16
   leaks – 1A•6, 1B•7
Flywheel – 2A•13, 2B•18
Foglight – 12•13, 12•16
   switch – 12•6, 12•7
Followers – 2A•5, 2B•12
Fuel and exhaust systems – diesel engines – 4B•1 et seq
Fuel and exhaust systems – petrol engines – 4A•1 et seq
   fault finding – REF•19
Fuel economy – REF•2 et seq
Fuel filter – 1A•14, 1B•12
Fuel gauge sender unit – 4A•7, 4B•4
Fuel injectors – 4A•11, 4B•7
   electrical components – 4B•4
Fuel pressure
   regulator – 4A•11, 4B•5
   sensor – 4B•5
Fuel pump – 4A•6, 4B•4, 4B•6
   relay – 4A•7
   sprocket – 2B•8
Fuel rail – 4A•11, 4B•7
Fuel system – REF•15
   leaks – 1A•7, 1B•7
Fuel tank – 4A•7, 4B•4
Fume or gas intoxication – 0•5
Fuses – 12•3
   fault finding (ABS) – 9•18

G

Gaiters
   driveshaft – 1A•10, 1B•11, 8•5
   steering rack – 10•17
Garages – REF•7
Gashes – 11•3
Gear lever – 7A•3
Gear selector position sensor – 7B•4

Gearchange linkage – 7A•2, 7A•3
General repair procedures – REF•8
Glass breakage sensor (alarm system) – 12•25
Glovebox – 11•31
   illumination – 12•8
Glow plugs – 5A•7
Grille panels – 11•6

H

Halogen headlight – 12•11
Handbrake – 1A•8, 1B•9, 9•16, REF•12
   cables – 9•16
   'on' warning light switch – 9•16
   shoes – 9•11
Handles
   boot lid – 11•19
   doors – 11•10
   tailgate – 11•19
Hazard warning light switch – 12•6
   illumination – 12•10
Headlight – 12•11, 12•15
   beam adjustment – 12•17
   control module – 12•17
   height switch – 12•6
   washer system – 12•21
Headlining – 11•26
Heat shield(s) – 4B•13, 4A•18
Heated and ventilated seat – 12•24
Heater unit – 3•9
   blower motor – 3•8
   blower motor control unit – 3•11
   matrix – 3•9
High-level stop-light – 12•14, 12•16
High-pressure diesel injection system – 4B•3
   fuel pump – 4B•6
   fuel pump sprocket – 2B•8
Hinges
   bonnet – 11•7
   boot lid – 11•16
   lubrication – 1A•11, 1B•11
   tailgate – 11•16
Horn – 12•19
   alarm system – 12•26
Hoses – 1A•11, 1B•12, 3•2, 9•4
   leaks – 1A•6, 1B•7
HT coils – 5B•3
Hub bearing – 10•7, 10•11
Hub carrier – 10•5
Hydrofluoric acid – 0•5

I

Identifying leaks – 0•9
Idler pulley – 2B•9
Ignition switch and lock – 12•4
Ignition system – petrol engines – 5B•1 et seq
   fault finding – 5B•2
Impact sensor – 11•34
Indicators – 12•12, 12•15

Index REF•27

*Note: References throughout this index are in the form "**Chapter number**" • "**Page number**". So, for example, 2C•15 refers to page 15 of Chapter 2C.*

Injectors – 4A•11, 4B•7
   electrical components – 4B•4
Input shaft
   oil seal – 7A•5
   speed sensor – 7B•4
Instrument panel – 1A•9, 1B•10, 12•17
   bulbs – 12•7
   illumination rheostat – 12•6
Intake manifold – 4A•16, 4B•9
   changeover flap actuator drive – 4B•10
Intercooler – 4A•16
Interior lights – 12•8
   switch – 12•6
Interior temperature sensor – 3•11
Introduction – 0•4

J

Jacking and vehicle support – REF•9
Jump starting – 0•7

L

Leakdown test – 2B•3
Leaks – 0•9, 1A•6, 1B•7
Light units – 12•15
   bulbs – 12•7, 12•10
Lighting switch – 12•6
   illumination – 12•10
Limp-home solenoid – 4A•13
Locks
   bonnet – 11•7
   boot lid – 11•17, 11•18
   doors – 11•10
   ignition – 12•4
   lubrication – 1A•11, 1B•11
   tailgate – 11•17, 11•18
Loudspeakers – 12•23
Lower arm – 10•4
Lower facia panel – 11•26
Lower transverse link – 10•12
Lubricants and fluids – 0•16
Luggage compartment
   bulb – 12•8
   side trim panel – 11•26
   switch (alarm system) – 12•26

M

Main beam – 12•11
Main bearings – 2C•19
Manifold absolute pressure sensor – 4A•8
Manifolds
   exhaust – 4A•17, 4B•11
   intake – 4A•16, 4B•9
Manual transmission – 7A•1 *et seq*
   fault finding – REF•20
   oil – 0•16, 1A•12, 1B•14, 7A•2
Map reading lights – 12•8
Mass airflow sensor – 4A•9

Master cylinder
   brake – 9•13
   clutch – 6•4
Matrix – 3•9
Mirror – 11•19, REF•12
   switch – 12•6
Mixed air sensor – 3•11
MOT test checks – REF•12 *et seq*
Motor factors – REF•7
Mountings – 2A•14
Multifunction control switch (cruise control system) – 4A•4

N

Number plate light – 12•13, 12•16

O

Oil
   engine – 0•11, 0•16, 1A•6, 1B•6
   manual gearbox – 0•16, 1A•12, 1B•14, 7A•2
Oil cooler/adapter – 2A•12
Oil filter – 1A•6, 1B•6
   housing – 2B•17
Oil leaks – 1A•7, 1B•7
Oil level sensor – 5A•7
Oil pressure warning light switch – 2A•12, 5A•6
Oil pump – 2A•10, 2B•16
Oil seals
   camshaft – 2B•9
   crankshaft – 2A•13, 2B•17
   driveshaft – 7A•4, 7A•5
   input shaft – 7A•5
   selector rod – 7A•5
   torque converter – 7B•3
Open-circuit – 12•2
Output shaft speed sensor – 7B•4
Oxygen sensors – 4C•3

P

Pads – 1A•11, 1B•11, 9•5, 9•6
Parking aid components – 12•25
Particulate filter – 4B•13
   pressure sensor – 4C•4
Parts – REF•7
Passenger compartment bulb – 12•7
Pedals
   accelerator – 4A•4
   brake – 9•17
   clutch – 6•2
   switches (cruise control system) – 4A•4
Petrol engine in-car repair procedures – 2A•1 *et seq*
Pipes – 9•4
Piston rings – 2C•20
Pistons – 2C•15, 2C•17, 2C•22
Plastic components – 11•4
Poisonous or irritant substances – 0•5
Pollen filter – 1A•11, 1B•11

Index

Note: *References throughout this index are in the form* **"Chapter number" • "Page number"**. *So, for example, 2C•15 refers to page 15 of Chapter 2C.*

Power steering fluid – 0•16,– 1A•9,– 1B•9
    bleeding – 10•16
    leaks – 1A•7, 1B•8
Power steering pump – 10•16
Pre/post-heating system – 5A•7
    control unit – 5A•8
Priming and bleeding fuel system – 4B•4
Puncture repair – 0•8
Purge valve – 4C•2

R

Radiator – 1A•14, 1B•15, 3•3
    grille panels – 11•6
Radio/CD player – 12•22
    anti-theft system – REF•9
Rain sensor – 12•20
Range/distance sensor (parking aid) – 12•25
Rear light unit – 12•13, 12•15
Rear window – 11•20
Receiver/drier – 3•14
Refrigerant leaks – 1A•7, 1B•8
Regulator
    alternator – 5A•5
    window – 11•13
Relays – 12•4
    fault finding (ABS) – 9•18
    fuel pump – 4A•7
Release bearing – 6•4
Remote control receiver (alarm system) – 12•26
Repair procedures – REF•8
Re-spraying – 11•3
Reversing light switch – 7A•5
Road test – 1A•9, 1B•10
Roadside Repairs – 0•6 *et seq*
Routine maintenance – bodywork and underframe – 11•2
Routine maintenance – upholstery and carpets – 11•2
Routine maintenance and servicing – diesel models – 1B•1 *et seq*
Routine maintenance and servicing – petrol engines – 1A•1 *et seq*
Rust holes – 11•3

S

Saab 9-5 manual – 0•4
Saab Information Display (SID) module – 12•18
    illumination – 12•10
Safety first! – 0•5
Scalding – 0•5
Scratches – 11•2
Screen washer fluid – 0•12
Scuff plate – 11•21
Seat belts – 1A•8, 1B•9, 11•22
Seats – 11•21
    control module – 11•22
    heating – 12•24
    ventilation – 12•24

Selector
    cable – 7B•2
    illumination – 12•9
    lever – 7B•3
    position sensor – 7B•4
    rod – 7A•4
    rod oil seal – 7A•5
Service indicator resetting – 1A•6, 1B•7
Servo unit – 9•14
Shock absorber – 1A•8, 1B•9, 10•9, REF•13, REF•14
Shoes – 9•11
Short-circuit – 12•3
Shut-off control valve – 4C•3
Side repeater lights – 12•12, 12•15
Side window – 11•20
Sidelight – 12•12
Sill scuff plate – 11•21
Siren (alarm system) – 12•26
Slave cylinder/release bearing clutch – 6•4
    priming – 6•6
Solar sensor – 3•10
Spare parts – REF•7
Spark plugs – 1A•12
Speed sensors – 7B•4
Speedometer drive – 7A•5
Springs – REF•14
Sprockets
    camshafts – 2B•7
    crankshaft – 2B•7
    high-pressure fuel pump – 2B•8
    timing chain – 2C•11
Starting and charging systems – 5A•1 *et seq*
Start-up after overhaul – 2C•22
Steering – 1A•8, 1A•9, 1B•8, 1B•10, REF•13, REF•14
    angles – 10•17
    column – 10•14, REF•12
    column switch – 12•5
    gear – 10•15
    rack gaiters – 10•17
    wheel – 10•13, REF•12
    wheel angle sensor – 9•19
Stop-light – 12•14, 12•16
    switch – 9•17, 12•6
Struts
    bonnet – 11•7
    boot lid – 11•15
    suspension – 10•3, 10•9
    tailgate – 11•16
Subframe – 10•8, 10•13
Sump – 2A•9, 2B•15
Sunroof – 11•20
Supplementary Restraint System (SRS) – 11•32
Suspension and steering – 1A•8, 1A•9, 1B•8, 1B•10, 10•1 *et seq*, REF•13, REF•14
    fault finding – REF•22

Index REF•29

*Note: References throughout this index are in the form "**Chapter number**" • "**Page number**". So, for example, 2C•15 refers to page 15 of Chapter 2C.*

Switches and controls – 12•4
   bonnet alarm system – 12•26
   cruise control system – 4A•4
   ESP – 9•19
   handbrake 'on' warning light – 9•16
   hazard lights – 12•10
   light – 12•10
   luggage compartment (alarm system) – 12•26
   oil pressure warning light – 2A•12, 5A•6
   pedals – 4A•4
   reversing light – 7A•5
   stop-light – 9•17
   TCS – 9•19
   windows – 12•9

T

Tailgate – 11•16
   handle – 11•19
   loading light bulb – 12•8
   lock – 11•17
   lock motor – 11•18
   washer system – 12•21
   wiper arm – 12•20
   wiper motor – 12•21
Tappets – 2A•5, 2B•12
TCS
   hydraulic unit – 9•18
   switch – 9•19,– 12•6
Temperature sensor – 3•5, 3•11, 4A•8, 4A•9, 4C•4, 4B•5, 7B•4
Tensioner – 2B•8, 2C•14
Thermostat
   coolant – 3•4
   oil – 2A•12
Throttle body – 4A•10, 4B•5
Tilt angle sensor (alarm system) – 12•26
Timing
   ignition – 5B•3
   valves – 2B•5
Timing belt – 2B•6, 2B•7
Timing chain – 2C•11
   guides and tensioner – 2C•14
   cover – 2C•9
Tools and working facilities – REF•10 *et seq*
Top dead centre (TDC) for No 1 piston – 2A•3, 2B•3
Torque converter oil seal – 7B•3
Towbar – 1A•8, 1B•9
Towing – 0•9
Track rod end – 10•17
Trailing arm – 10•11
Transverse link – 10•12
Trim panels – 11•9, 11•21, 11•25
Turbocharger – 4A•14, 4B•10, 4B•11
   wastegate solenoid – 4B•6
Tyres – REF•15
   condition and pressure – 0•13
   pressures – 0•16
   specialists – REF•7

U

Underbonnet check points – 0•10
Underframe – 11•2
Unleaded petrol – 4A•4
Upholstery – 11•2
Upper transverse link – 10•12

V

Vacuum hoses leaks – 1A•7, 1B•8
Vacuum pump – 9•15
Vacuum servo unit – 9•14
Valves – 2C•8, 2C•9
   timing – 2B•5
Vehicle identification – REF•7, REF•13
Vehicle support – REF•9
Vibration damper – 2B•5

W

Washer system – 12•21
Wastegate solenoid – 4B•6
Water pump – 3•6
Weekly Checks – 0•10 *et seq*
Weights – REF•1
Wheels – REF•15
   alignment – 10•17
   bearings – 10•7, 10•11, REF•14
   changing – 0•8
   sensor (ABS) – 9•18
Wheel arch liners – 11•21
Windows
   doors – 11•12
   rear – 11•20
   regulator – 11•13
   side – 11•20
   switch – 12•5
   switch illumination – 12•9
Windscreen – 11•20, REF•12
   washer system – 12•21
   wiper arm – 12•19
   wiper motor – 12•20
Wipers
   arms – 12•19
   blades – 0•14
   motor – 12•20
Wiring diagrams – 12•27 *et seq*
Working facilities – REF•11

X

Xenon headlight – 12•11
   control module – 12•17

Y

Yaw rate (gyro) sensor – 9•19

Haynes Manuals – The Complete UK Car List

Title	Book No.
ALFA ROMEO Alfasud/Sprint (74 - 88) up to F *	0292
Alfa Romeo Alfetta (73 - 87) up to E *	0531
AUDI 80, 90 & Coupe Petrol (79 - Nov 88) up to F	0605
Audi 80, 90 & Coupe Petrol (Oct 86 - 90) D to H	1491
Audi 100 & 200 Petrol (Oct 82 - 90) up to H	0907
Audi 100 & A6 Petrol & Diesel (May 91 - May 97) H to P	3504
Audi A3 Petrol & Diesel (96 - May 03) P to 03	4253
Audi A4 Petrol & Diesel (95 - 00) M to X	3575
Audi A4 Petrol & Diesel (01 - 04) X to 54	4609
AUSTIN A35 & A40 (56 - 67) up to F *	0118
Austin/MG/Rover Maestro 1.3 & 1.6 Petrol (83 - 95) up to M	0922
Austin/MG Metro (80 - May 90) up to G	0718
Austin/Rover Montego 1.3 & 1.6 Petrol (84 - 94) A to L	1066
Austin/MG/Rover Montego 2.0 Petrol (84 - 95) A to M	1067
Mini (59 - 69) up to H *	0527
Mini (69 - 01) up to X	0646
Austin/Rover 2.0 litre Diesel Engine (86 - 93) C to L	1857
Austin Healey 100/6 & 3000 (56 - 68) up to G *	0049
BEDFORD CF Petrol (69 - 87) up to E	0163
Bedford/Vauxhall Rascal & Suzuki Supercarry (86 - Oct 94) C to M	3015
BMW 316, 320 & 320i (4-cyl) (75 - Feb 83) up to Y *	0276
BMW 320, 320i, 323i & 325i (6-cyl) (Oct 77 - Sept 87) up to E	0815
BMW 3- & 5-Series Petrol (81 - 91) up to J	1948
BMW 3-Series Petrol (Apr 91 - 99) H to V	3210
BMW 3-Series Petrol (Sept 98 - 03) S to 53	4067
BMW 520i & 525e (Oct 81 - June 88) up to E	1560
BMW 525, 528 & 528i (73 - Sept 81) up to X *	0632
BMW 5-Series 6-cyl Petrol (April 96 - Aug 03) N to 03	4151
BMW 1500, 1502, 1600, 1602, 2000 & 2002 (59 - 77) up to S *	0240
CHRYSLER PT Cruiser Petrol (00 - 03) W to 53	4058
CITROËN 2CV, Ami & Dyane (67 - 90) up to H	0196
Citroën AX Petrol & Diesel (87 - 97) D to P	3014
Citroën Berlingo & Peugeot Partner Petrol & Diesel (96 - 05) P to 55	4281
Citroën BX Petrol (83 - 94) A to L	0908
Citroën C15 Van Petrol & Diesel (89 - Oct 98) F to S	3509
Citroën C3 Petrol & Diesel (02 - 05) 51 to 05	4197
Citroën C5 Petrol & Diesel (01-08) Y to 08	4745
Citroën CX Petrol (75 - 88) up to F	0528
Citroën Saxo Petrol & Diesel (96 - 04) N to 54	3506
Citroën Visa Petrol (79 - 88) up to F	0620
Citroën Xantia Petrol & Diesel (93 - 01) K to Y	3082
Citroën XM Petrol & Diesel (89 - 00) G to X	3451
Citroën Xsara Petrol & Diesel (97 - Sept 00) R to W	3751
Citroën Xsara Picasso Petrol & Diesel (00 - 02) W to 52	3944
Citroën Xsara Picasso (03-08)	4784
Citroën ZX Diesel (91 - 98) J to S	1922
Citroën ZX Petrol (91 - 98) H to S	1881
Citroën 1.7 & 1.9 litre Diesel Engine (84 - 96) A to N	1379
FIAT 126 (73 - 87) up to E *	0305
Fiat 500 (57 - 73) up to M *	0090
Fiat Bravo & Brava Petrol (95 - 00) N to W	3572
Fiat Cinquecento (93 - 98) K to R	3501
Fiat Panda (81 - 95) up to M	0793
Fiat Punto Petrol & Diesel (94 - Oct 99) L to V	3251
Fiat Punto Petrol (Oct 99 - July 03) V to 03	4066
Fiat Punto Petrol (03-07) 03 to 07	4746
Fiat Regata Petrol (84 - 88) A to F	1167
Fiat Tipo Petrol (88 - 91) E to J	1625
Fiat Uno Petrol (83 - 95) up to M	0923
Fiat X1/9 (74 - 89) up to G *	0273
FORD Anglia (59 - 68) up to G *	0001
Ford Capri II (& III) 1.6 & 2.0 (74 - 87) up to E *	0283
Ford Capri II (& III) 2.8 & 3.0 V6 (74 - 87) up to E	1309
Ford Cortina Mk I & Corsair 1500 ('62 - '66) up to D*	0214
Ford Cortina Mk III 1300 & 1600 (70 - 76) up to P *	0070
Ford Escort Mk I 1100 & 1300 (68 - 74) up to N *	0171
Ford Escort Mk I Mexico, RS 1600 & RS 2000 (70 - 74) up to N *	0139
Ford Escort Mk II Mexico, RS 1800 & RS 2000 (75 - 80) up to W *	0735
Ford Escort (75 - Aug 80) up to V *	0280
Ford Escort Petrol (Sept 80 - Sept 90) up to H	0686
Ford Escort & Orion Petrol (Sept 90 - 00) H to X	1737
Ford Escort & Orion Diesel (Sept 90 - 00) H to X	4081
Ford Fiesta (76 - Aug 83) up to Y	0334
Ford Fiesta Petrol (Aug 83 - Feb 89) A to F	1030
Ford Fiesta Petrol (Feb 89 - Oct 95) F to N	1595
Ford Fiesta Petrol & Diesel (Oct 95 - Mar 02) N to 02	3397
Ford Fiesta Petrol & Diesel (Apr 02 - 07) 02 to 57	4170
Ford Focus Petrol & Diesel (98 - 01) S to Y	3759
Ford Focus Petrol & Diesel (Oct 01 - 05) 51 to 05	4167
Ford Galaxy Petrol & Diesel (95 - Aug 00) M to W	3984
Ford Granada Petrol (Sept 77 - Feb 85) up to B *	0481
Ford Granada & Scorpio Petrol (Mar 85 - 94) B to M	1245
Ford Ka (96 - 02) P to 52	3570
Ford Mondeo Petrol (93 - Sept 00) K to X	1923
Ford Mondeo Petrol & Diesel (Oct 00 - Jul 03) X to 03	3990
Ford Mondeo Petrol & Diesel (July 03 - 07) 03 to 56	4619
Ford Mondeo Diesel (93 - 96) L to N	3465
Ford Orion Petrol (83 - Sept 90) up to H	1009
Ford Sierra 4-cyl Petrol (82 - 93) up to K	0903
Ford Sierra V6 Petrol (82 - 91) up to J	0904
Ford Transit Petrol (Mk 2) (78 - Jan 86) up to C	0719
Ford Transit Petrol (Mk 3) (Feb 86 - 89) C to G	1468
Ford Transit Diesel (Feb 86 - 99) C to T	3019
Ford Transit Diesel (00-06)	4775
Ford 1.6 & 1.8 litre Diesel Engine (84 - 96) A to N	1172
Ford 2.1, 2.3 & 2.5 litre Diesel Engine (77 - 90) up to H	1606
FREIGHT ROVER Sherpa Petrol (74 - 87) up to E	0463
HILLMAN Avenger (70 - 82) up to Y	0037
Hillman Imp (63 - 76) up to R *	0022
HONDA Civic (Feb 84 - Oct 87) A to E	1226
Honda Civic (Nov 91 - 96) J to N	3199
Honda Civic Petrol (Mar 95 - 00) M to X	4050
Honda Civic Petrol & Diesel (01 - 05) X to 55	4611
Honda CR-V Petrol & Diesel (01-06)	4747
Honda Jazz (01 - Feb 08) 51 - 57	4735
HYUNDAI Pony (85 - 94) C to N	3398
JAGUAR E Type (61 - 72) up to L *	0140
Jaguar MkI & II, 240 & 340 (55 - 69) up to H *	0098
Jaguar XJ6, XJ & Sovereign; Daimler Sovereign (68 - Oct 86) up to D	0242
Jaguar XJ6 & Sovereign (Oct 86 - Sept 94) D to M	3261
Jaguar XJ12, XJS & Sovereign; Daimler Double Six (72 - 88) up to F	0478
JEEP Cherokee Petrol (93 - 96) K to N	1943
LADA 1200, 1300, 1500 & 1600 (74 - 91) up to J	0413
Lada Samara (87 - 91) D to J	1610
LAND ROVER 90, 110 & Defender Diesel (83 - 07) up to 56	3017
Land Rover Discovery Petrol & Diesel (89 - 98) G to S	3016
Land Rover Discovery Diesel (Nov 98 - Jul 04) S to 04	4606
Land Rover Freelander Petrol & Diesel (97 - Sept 03) R to 53	3929
Land Rover Freelander Petrol & Diesel (Oct 03 - Oct 06) 53 to 56	4623
Land Rover Series IIA & III Diesel (58 - 85) up to C	0529
Land Rover Series II, IIA & III 4-cyl Petrol (58 - 85) up to C	0314
MAZDA 323 (Mar 81 - Oct 89) up to G	1608
Mazda 323 (Oct 89 - 98) G to R	3455
Mazda 626 (May 83 - Sept 87) up to E	0929
Mazda B1600, B1800 & B2000 Pick-up Petrol (72 - 88) up to F	0267
Mazda RX-7 (79 - 85) up to C *	0460
MERCEDES-BENZ 190, 190E & 190D Petrol & Diesel (83 - 93) A to L	3450
Mercedes-Benz 200D, 240D, 240TD, 300D & 300TD 123 Series Diesel (Oct 76 - 85)	1114
Mercedes-Benz 250 & 280 (68 - 72) up to L *	0346
Mercedes-Benz 250 & 280 123 Series Petrol (Oct 76 - 84) up to B *	0677
Mercedes-Benz 124 Series Petrol & Diesel (85 - Aug 93) C to K	3253
Mercedes-Benz A-Class Petrol & Diesel (98-04) S to 54	4748
Mercedes-Benz C-Class Petrol & Diesel (93 - Aug 00) L to W	3511
Mercedes-Benz C-Class (00-06)	4780
MGA (55 - 62) *	0475
MGB (62 - 80) up to W	0111
MG Midget & Austin-Healey Sprite (58 - 80) up to W *	0265
MINI Petrol (July 01 - 05) Y to 05	4273
MITSUBISHI Shogun & L200 Pick-Ups Petrol (83 - 94) up to M	1944
MORRIS Ital 1.3 (80 - 84) up to B	0705
Morris Minor 1000 (56 - 71) up to K	0024
NISSAN Almera Petrol (95 - Feb 00) N to V	4053
Nissan Almera & Tino Petrol (Feb 00 - 07) V to 56	4612
Nissan Bluebird (May 84 - Mar 86) A to C	1223
Nissan Bluebird Petrol (Mar 86 - 90) C to H	1473
Nissan Cherry (Sept 82 - 86) up to D	1031
Nissan Micra (83 - Jan 93) up to K	0931
Nissan Micra (93 - 02) K to 52	3254
Nissan Micra Petrol (03-07) 52 to 57	4734
Nissan Primera Petrol (90 - Aug 99) H to T	1851
Nissan Stanza (82 - 86) up to D	0824
Nissan Sunny Petrol (May 82 - Oct 86) up to D	0895
Nissan Sunny Petrol (Oct 86 - Mar 91) D to H	1378
Nissan Sunny Petrol (Apr 91 - 95) H to N	3219
OPEL Ascona & Manta (B Series) (Sept 75 - 88) up to F *	0316
Opel Ascona Petrol (81 - 88)	3215
Opel Astra Petrol (Oct 91 - Feb 98)	3156
Opel Corsa Petrol (83 - Mar 93)	3160
Opel Corsa Petrol (Mar 93 - 97)	3159
Opel Kadett Petrol (Nov 79 - Oct 84) up to B	0634
Opel Kadett Petrol (Oct 84 - Oct 91)	3196
Opel Omega & Senator Petrol (Nov 86 - 94)	3157
Opel Rekord Petrol (Feb 78 - Oct 86) up to D	0543
Opel Vectra Petrol (Oct 88 - Oct 95)	3158
PEUGEOT 106 Petrol & Diesel (91 - 04) J to 53	1882
Peugeot 205 Petrol (83 - 97) A to P	0932
Peugeot 206 Petrol & Diesel (98 - 01) S to X	3757
Peugeot 206 Petrol & Diesel (02 - 06) 51 to 06	4613
Peugeot 306 Petrol & Diesel (93 - 02) K to 02	3073
Peugeot 307 Petrol & Diesel (01 - 04) Y to 54	4147
Peugeot 309 Petrol (86 - 93) C to K	1266
Peugeot 405 Petrol (88 - 97) E to P	1559
Peugeot 405 Diesel (88 - 97) E to P	3198
Peugeot 406 Petrol & Diesel (96 - Mar 99) N to T	3394
Peugeot 406 Petrol & Diesel (Mar 99 - 02) T to 52	3982

* Classic reprint

Title	Book No.
Peugeot 505 Petrol (79 - 89) up to G	0762
Peugeot 1.7/1.8 & 1.9 litre Diesel Engine (82 - 96) up to N	0950
Peugeot 2.0, 2.1, 2.3 & 2.5 litre Diesel Engines (74 - 90) up to H	1607
PORSCHE 911 (65 - 85) up to C	0264
Porsche 924 & 924 Turbo (76 - 85) up to C	0397
PROTON (89 - 97) F to P	3255
RANGE ROVER V8 Petrol (70 - Oct 92) up to K	0606
RELIANT Robin & Kitten (73 - 83) up to A *	0436
RENAULT 4 (61 - 86) up to D *	0072
Renault 5 Petrol (Feb 85 - 96) B to N	1219
Renault 9 & 11 Petrol (82 - 89) up to F	0822
Renault 18 Petrol (79 - 86) up to D	0598
Renault 19 Petrol (89 - 96) F to N	1646
Renault 19 Diesel (89 - 96) F to N	1946
Renault 21 Petrol (86 - 94) C to M	1397
Renault 25 Petrol & Diesel (84 - 92) B to K	1228
Renault Clio Petrol (91 - May 98) H to R	1853
Renault Clio Diesel (91 - June 96) H to N	3031
Renault Clio Petrol & Diesel (May 98 - May 01) R to Y	3906
Renault Clio Petrol & Diesel (June '01 - '05) Y to 55	4168
Renault Espace Petrol & Diesel (85 - 96) C to N	3197
Renault Laguna Petrol & Diesel (94 - 00) L to W	3252
Renault Laguna Petrol & Diesel (Feb 01 - Feb 05) X to 54	4283
Renault Mégane & Scénic Petrol & Diesel (96 - 99) N to T	3395
Renault Mégane & Scénic Petrol & Diesel (Apr 99 - 02) T to 52	3916
Renault Megane Petrol & Diesel (Oct 02 - 05) 52 to 55	4284
Renault Scenic Petrol & Diesel (Sept 03 - 06) 53 to 06	4297
ROVER 213 & 216 (84 - 89) A to G	1116
Rover 214 & 414 Petrol (89 - 96) G to N	1689
Rover 216 & 416 Petrol (89 - 96) G to N	1830
Rover 211, 214, 216, 218 & 220 Petrol & Diesel (Dec 95 - 99) N to V	3399
Rover 25 & MG ZR Petrol & Diesel (Oct 99 - 04) V to 54	4145
Rover 414, 416 & 420 Petrol & Diesel (May 95 - 98) M to R	3453
Rover 45 / MG ZS Petrol & Diesel (99 - 05) V to 55	4384
Rover 618, 620 & 623 Petrol (93 - 97) K to P	3257
Rover 75 / MG ZT Petrol & Diesel (99 - 06) S to 06	4292
Rover 820, 825 & 827 Petrol (86 - 95) D to N	1380
Rover 3500 (76 - 87) up to E *	0365
Rover Metro, 111 & 114 Petrol (May 90 - 98) G to S	1711
SAAB 95 & 96 (66 - 76) up to R *	0198
Saab 90, 99 & 900 (79 - Oct 93) up to L	0765
Saab 900 (Oct 93 - 98) L to R	3512
Saab 9000 (4-cyl) (85 - 98) C to S	1686
Saab 9-3 Petrol & Diesel (98 - Aug 02) R to 02	4614
Saab 9-3 Petrol & Diesel (02-07) 52 to 57	4749
Saab 9-5 4-cyl Petrol (97 - 04) R to 54	4156
SEAT Ibiza & Cordoba Petrol & Diesel (Oct 93 - Oct 99) L to V	3571
Seat Ibiza & Malaga Petrol (85 - 92) B to K	1609
SKODA Estelle (77 - 89) up to G	0604
Skoda Fabia Petrol & Diesel (00 - 06) W to 06	4376
Skoda Favorit (89 - 96) F to N	1801
Skoda Felicia Petrol & Diesel (95 - 01) M to X	3505
Skoda Octavia Petrol & Diesel (98 - Apr 04) R to 04	4285
SUBARU 1600 & 1800 (Nov 79 - 90) up to H *	0995

Title	Book No.
SUNBEAM Alpine, Rapier & H120 (67 - 74) up to N *	0051
SUZUKI SJ Series, Samurai & Vitara (4-cyl) Petrol (82 - 97) up to P	1942
Suzuki Supercarry & Bedford/Vauxhall Rascal (86 - Oct 94) C to M	3015
TALBOT Alpine, Solara, Minx & Rapier (75 - 86) up to D	0337
Talbot Horizon Petrol (78 - 86) up to D	0473
Talbot Samba (82 - 86) up to D	0823
TOYOTA Avensis Petrol (98 - Jan 03) R to 52	4264
Toyota Carina E Petrol (May 92 - 97) J to P	3256
Toyota Corolla (80 - 85) up to C	0683
Toyota Corolla (Sept 83 - Sept 87) A to E	1024
Toyota Corolla (Sept 87 - Aug 92) E to K	1683
Toyota Corolla Petrol (Aug 92 - 97) K to P	3259
Toyota Corolla Petrol (July 97 - Feb 02) P to 51	4286
Toyota Hi-Ace & Hi-Lux Petrol (69 - Oct 83) up to A	0304
Toyota RAV4 Petrol & Diesel (94-06) L to 55	4750
Toyota Yaris Petrol (99 - 05) T to 05	4265
TRIUMPH GT6 & Vitesse (62 - 74) up to N *	0112
Triumph Herald (59 - 71) up to K *	0010
Triumph Spitfire (62 - 81) up to X	0113
Triumph Stag (70 - 78) up to T *	0441
Triumph TR2, TR3, TR3A, TR4 & TR4A (52 - 67) up to F *	0028
Triumph TR5 & 6 (67 - 75) up to P *	0031
Triumph TR7 (75 - 82) up to Y *	0322
VAUXHALL Astra Petrol (80 - Oct 84) up to B	0635
Vauxhall Astra & Belmont Petrol (Oct 84 - Oct 91) B to J	1136
Vauxhall Astra Petrol (Oct 91 - Feb 98) J to R	1832
Vauxhall/Opel Astra & Zafira Petrol (Feb 98 - Apr 04) R to 04	3758
Vauxhall/Opel Astra & Zafira Diesel (Feb 98 - Apr 04) R to 04	3797
Vauxhall/Opel Astra Petrol (04 - 08)	4732
Vauxhall/Opel Astra Diesel (04 - 08)	4733
Vauxhall/Opel Calibra (90 - 98) G to S	3502
Vauxhall Carlton Petrol (Oct 78 - Oct 86) up to D	0480
Vauxhall Carlton & Senator Petrol (Nov 86 - 94) D to L	1469
Vauxhall Cavalier Petrol (81 - Oct 88) up to F	0812
Vauxhall Cavalier Petrol (Oct 88 - 95) F to N	1570
Vauxhall Chevette (75 - 84) up to B	0285
Vauxhall/Opel Corsa Diesel (Mar 93 - Oct 00) K to X	4087
Vauxhall Corsa Petrol (Mar 93 - 97) K to R	1985
Vauxhall/Opel Corsa Petrol (Apr 97 - Oct 00) P to X	3921
Vauxhall/Opel Corsa Petrol & Diesel (Oct 00 - Sept 03) X to 53	4079
Vauxhall/Opel Corsa Petrol & Diesel (Oct 03 - Aug 06) 53 to 06	4617
Vauxhall/Opel Frontera Petrol & Diesel (91 - Sept 98) J to S	3454
Vauxhall Nova Petrol (83 - 93) up to K	0909
Vauxhall/Opel Omega Petrol (94 - 99) L to T	3510
Vauxhall/Opel Vectra Petrol & Diesel (95 - Feb 99) N to S	3396
Vauxhall/Opel Vectra Petrol & Diesel (Mar 99 - May 02) T to 02	3930
Vauxhall/Opel Vectra Petrol & Diesel (June 02 - Sept 05) 02 to 55	4618
Vauxhall/Opel 1.5, 1.6 & 1.7 litre Diesel Engine (82 - 96) up to N	1222
VW 411 & 412 (68 - 75) up to P *	0091
VW Beetle 1200 (54 - 77) up to S	0036
VW Beetle 1300 & 1500 (65 - 75) up to P	0039

Title	Book No.
VW 1302 & 1302S (70 - 72) up to L *	0110
VW Beetle 1303, 1303S & GT (72 - 75) up to P	0159
VW Beetle Petrol & Diesel (Apr 99 - 07) T to 57	3798
VW Golf & Jetta Mk 1 Petrol 1.1 & 1.3 (74 - 84) up to A	0716
VW Golf, Jetta & Scirocco Mk 1 Petrol 1.5, 1.6 & 1.8 (74 - 84) up to A	0726
VW Golf & Jetta Mk 1 Diesel (78 - 84) up to A	0451
VW Golf & Jetta Mk 2 Petrol (Mar 84 - Feb 92) A to J	1081
VW Golf & Vento Petrol & Diesel (Feb 92 - Mar 98) J to R	3097
VW Golf & Bora Petrol & Diesel (April 98 - 00) R to X	3727
VW Golf & Bora 4-cyl Petrol & Diesel (01 - 03) X to 53	4169
VW Golf & Jetta Petrol & Diesel (04 - 07) 53 to 07	4610
VW LT Petrol Vans & Light Trucks (76 - 87) up to E	0637
VW Passat & Santana Petrol (Sept 81 - May 88) up to E	0814
VW Passat 4-cyl Petrol & Diesel (May 88 - 96) E to P	3498
VW Passat 4-cyl Petrol & Diesel (Dec 96 - Nov 00) P to X	3917
VW Passat Petrol & Diesel (Dec 00 - May 05) X to 05	4279
VW Polo & Derby (76 - Jan 82) up to X	0335
VW Polo (82 - Oct 90) up to H	0813
VW Polo Petrol (Nov 90 - Aug 94) H to L	3245
VW Polo Hatchback Petrol & Diesel (94 - 99) M to S	3500
VW Polo Hatchback Petrol (00 - Jan 02) V to 51	4150
VW Polo Petrol & Diesel (02 - May 05) 51 to 05	4608
VW Scirocco (82 - 90) up to H *	1224
VW Transporter 1600 (68 - 79) up to V	0082
VW Transporter 1700, 1800 & 2000 (72 - 79) up to V *	0226
VW Transporter (air-cooled) Petrol (79 - 82) up to Y *	0638
VW Transporter (water-cooled) Petrol (82 - 90) up to H	3452
VW Type 3 (63 - 73) up to M *	0084
VOLVO 120 & 130 Series (& P1800) (61 - 73) up to M *	0203
Volvo 142, 144 & 145 (66 - 74) up to N *	0129
Volvo 240 Series Petrol (74 - 93) up to K	0270
Volvo 262, 264 & 260/265 (75 - 85) up to C *	0400
Volvo 340, 343, 345 & 360 (76 - 91) up to J	0715
Volvo 440, 460 & 480 Petrol (87 - 97) D to P	1691
Volvo 740 & 760 Petrol (82 - 91) up to J	1258
Volvo 850 Petrol (92 - 96) J to P	3260
Volvo 940 petrol (90 - 98) H to R	3249
Volvo S40 & V40 Petrol (96 - Mar 04) N to 04	3569
Volvo S40 & V50 Petrol & Diesel (Mar 04 - Jun 07) 04 to 07	4731
Volvo S60 Petrol & Diesel (01-08)	4793
Volvo S70, V70 & C70 Petrol (96 - 99) P to V	3573
Volvo V70 / S80 Petrol & Diesel (98 - 05) S to 55	4263
DIY MANUAL SERIES	
The Haynes Air Conditioning Manual	4192
The Haynes Car Electrical Systems Manual	4251
The Haynes Manual on Bodywork	4198
The Haynes Manual on Brakes	4178
The Haynes Manual on Carburettors	4177
The Haynes Manual on Diesel Engines	4174
The Haynes Manual on Engine Management	4199
The Haynes Manual on Fault Codes	4175
The Haynes Manual on Practical Electrical Systems	4267
The Haynes Manual on Small Engines	4250
The Haynes Manual on Welding	4176

* Classic reprint

All the products featured on this page are available through most motor accessory shops, cycle shops and book stores. Our policy of continuous updating and development means that titles are being constantly added to the range. For up-to-date information on our complete list of titles, please telephone: (UK) +44 1963 442030 • (USA) +1 805 498 6703 • (Sweden) +46 18 124016 • (Australia) +61 3 9763 8100

Preserving Our Motoring Heritage

> The Model J Duesenberg Derham Tourster. Only eight of these magnificent cars were ever built – this is the only example to be found outside the United States of America

Almost every car you've ever loved, loathed or desired is gathered under one roof at the Haynes Motor Museum. Over 300 immaculately presented cars and motorbikes represent every aspect of our motoring heritage, from elegant reminders of bygone days, such as the superb Model J Duesenberg to curiosities like the bug-eyed BMW Isetta. There are also many old friends and flames. Perhaps you remember the 1959 Ford Popular that you did your courting in? The magnificent 'Red Collection' is a spectacle of classic sports cars including AC, Alfa Romeo, Austin Healey, Ferrari, Lamborghini, Maserati, MG, Riley, Porsche and Triumph.

A Perfect Day Out

Each and every vehicle at the Haynes Motor Museum has played its part in the history and culture of Motoring. Today, they make a wonderful spectacle and a great day out for all the family. Bring the kids, bring Mum and Dad, but above all bring your camera to capture those golden memories for ever. You will also find an impressive array of motoring memorabilia, a comfortable 70 seat video cinema and one of the most extensive transport book shops in Britain. The Pit Stop Cafe serves everything from a cup of tea to wholesome, home-made meals or, if you prefer, you can enjoy the large picnic area nestled in the beautiful rural surroundings of Somerset.

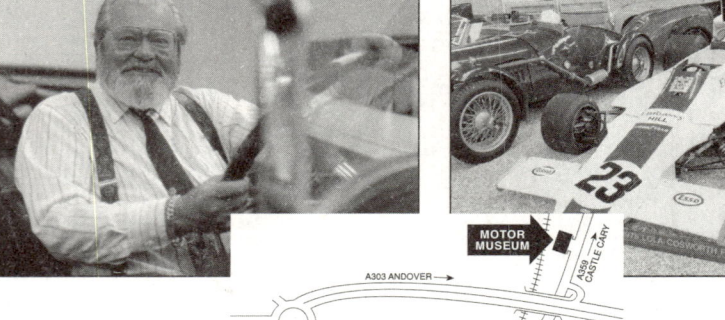

> John Haynes O.B.E., Founder and Chairman of the museum at the wheel of a Haynes Light 12.

> Graham Hill's Lola Cosworth Formula 1 car next to a 1934 Riley Sports.

The Museum is situated on the A359 Yeovil to Frome road at Sparkford, just off the A303 in Somerset. It is about 40 miles south of Bristol, and 25 minutes drive from the M5 intersection at Taunton.
Open 9.30am - 5.30pm (10.00am - 4.00pm Winter) 7 days a week, *except Christmas Day, Boxing Day and New Years Day*
Special rates available for schools, coach parties and outings Charitable Trust No. 292048